The Palgrave Handbook of Theatre and Race

Tiziana Morosetti • Osita Okagbue
Editors

The Palgrave Handbook of Theatre and Race

Editors
Tiziana Morosetti
Department of Theatre and Performance
Goldsmiths, University of London
London, UK

Osita Okagbue
Department of Theatre and Performance
Goldsmiths, University of London
London, UK

ISBN 978-3-030-43956-9   ISBN 978-3-030-43957-6   (eBook)
https://doi.org/10.1007/978-3-030-43957-6

© The Editor(s) (if applicable) and The Author(s) 2021
This work is subject to copyright. All rights are solely and exclusively licensed by the Publisher, whether the whole or part of the material is concerned, specifically the rights of translation, reprinting, reuse of illustrations, recitation, broadcasting, reproduction on microfilms or in any other physical way, and transmission or information storage and retrieval, electronic adaptation, computer software, or by similar or dissimilar methodology now known or hereafter developed.
The use of general descriptive names, registered names, trademarks, service marks, etc. in this publication does not imply, even in the absence of a specific statement, that such names are exempt from the relevant protective laws and regulations and therefore free for general use.
The publisher, the authors and the editors are safe to assume that the advice and information in this book are believed to be true and accurate at the date of publication. Neither the publisher nor the authors or the editors give a warranty, expressed or implied, with respect to the material contained herein or for any errors or omissions that may have been made. The publisher remains neutral with regard to jurisdictional claims in published maps and institutional affiliations.

Cover illustration: Roy JAMES Shakespeare/Getty Images

This Palgrave Macmillan imprint is published by the registered company Springer Nature Switzerland AG.
The registered company address is: Gewerbestrasse 11, 6330 Cham, Switzerland

Acknowledgements

When Palgrave approached us to compile the Handbook, it was a challenge and an honour, and we are indebted to an intelligent, sensitive and also rather patient publisher for allowing us to adjust our table of contents now and again. The volume has tried to identify emerging scholarship as well as established views on the topic, and the search for the widest range of topic possible has not always been easy but, we hope, productive. We have had to do without some promising contributors for reasons that tell a story of an academia increasingly strangled by bureaucratic concerns and idealised research products, as it would appear some universities have policies to discourage collaborative publications to promote individual work, such as monographs, that are felt to be more 'valuable' in REF (or other excellence frames) terms. Collaboration and a collective effort seemed, on the other hand, to be in this case not only advisable but entirely necessary, and our heartfelt gratitude goes to the contributors to this volume, who have worked relentlessly on their chapters, ploughing at times untrodden territory.

We would like to use this opportunity to acknowledge our dear colleague and friend, Dr Victor Ukaegbu, who had agreed to contribute to this book, but who unfortunately died before he could write his chapter. In preparing the book, we had the unstinting support of our two families. Tiziana warmly thanks her husband Luke and their daughter Noemi for their patience and encouragement. Osita's wife, Amaka, and his children, Solum, Chichi and Nedonna, were always around to encourage him, as they have always done.

CONTENTS

1 Introduction   1
Tiziana Morosetti and Osita Okagbue

Part I Race and Racism in Contemporary Theatre   19

2 The American Theatrical Canon and the Struggle for Racial Equality in British Theatre   21
Jami Rogers

3 Racialisation and Contemporary German Theatre   39
Priscilla Layne and Lizzie Stewart

4 'Dangerous Dialogues': Questioning Constructions of Race in South Pacific Theatre   61
David O'Donnell and Shailesh Lal

5 Staging the Ambiguities of Race: Polymorphous Indigenous Dramaturgies in Canada   81
Marc Maufort

6 Representing the Roma Experience on the Contemporary Romanian Stage: The Intersectional Lenses of Giuvlipen's Anti-racist and Feminist Theatre Works   101
Diana Benea

viii CONTENTS

Part II   War, Conflict and the Nation   121

7   **Race as Category in Nazi German Theatre**   123
    Anselm Heinrich

8   **Māori Theatre in Not-Quite-Post-Colonial Aotearoa New Zealand**   141
    Sharon Mazer

9   **Racial Nationalism and the Serbian Theatre: From *Radovan III* to DAH**   159
    Dennis Barnett

10 **The Palestinians in Israeli Theatre**   177
    Dan Urian

11 **Faces of a Long Unspoken Collective Trauma: Theatrical Representations of Friendship, Love, Betrayal, and Pain in the Landscape of War in Contemporary Turkey**   195
    Deniz Başar

12 **Staging Race in White South African Afrikaans Theatre**   219
    David Peimer

Part III   Blackness and the African Diaspora   237

13 **In the Prison of Their Skins: Performing Race in Caribbean Theatre**   239
    Osita Okagbue

14 **Black Women in Post-revolutionary Cuban Theatre**   255
    Lilianne Lugo Herrera

15 **Black Performances and Black Artists Performing in Contemporary Brazil**   273
    Victor Hugo Leite de Aquino Soares and Roberta K. Matsumoto

16 **Lackface: Blackface Masking in Contemporary US Theatre**   291
    Kevin Byrne

17 **Fighting Racism on the Contemporary Francophone Stage**   307
    Annette Bühler-Dietrich

CONTENTS   ix

18   'Though we are written into the landscape you don't see us'
(Testament, 2018). Black Faces in White Spaces: Whiteness as
Terror and the Terror of Un-belonging in *Black Men Walking*   327
Michael Pearce

Part IV   Constructions of Whiteness and the 'Other'   349

19   'A Wretched Caricature…Unworthy of America': Charles
Mathews's Representation of the Yankee   351
Jim Davis

20   The Language of Blackness: Representations of Africans
and African-Americans on the British Stage After
Uncle Tom's Cabin   369
Tiziana Morosetti

21   Susan Glaspell's *Trifles* and *Inheritors*: White Settler Hunger,
Debt and the Blackhawk Purchase Lands   391
Selena Couture

22   Beyond the Peyote Dance: The Raramuri Tribe and 'Mexico'
Representations in Antonin Artaud's Work   407
Luciana da Costa Dias

23   Representing and Re-presenting Others in Yorùbá
Performance   425
Ṣọlá Adéyẹmí

24   *Pigs and Dogs* and *The Bogus Woman*: Racialised Performance
in Anglo-British Women Playwrights   443
Serena Guarracino

25   Race, Occidentalism/Orientalism and Sino-centrism in
Contemporary Chinese Theatre   465
Mary Mazzilli

Index   487

Notes on Contributors

Ṣọlá Adéyẹmí is a Research Fellow at the Interweaving Performance Cultures International Research Centre in Berlin, Germany. He also lectures at Goldsmiths, University of London. His research focuses on world theatres and performance studies, particularly the writings of Nigerian playwright Fémi Òsófisan. He is the author of *Vision of Change in African Drama: Fémi Òsófisan's Dialectical Reading of History and Politics* (2019). His other books include *Portraits for an Eagle: Essays in Honour of Femi Osofisan* (ed., 2006) and *Femi Osofisan, Post-Negritude Tradition and 50 Years of Nigerian Literary Drama* (ed., 2018). Adéyẹmí is also the editor of a volume of short stories from Nigeria, *Goddess of the Storm and Other Stories* (2000).

Dennis Barnett is Associate Professor of Theatre Arts at Coe College. With an interest in works in translation, he has edited two collections of essays about theatre in Eastern Europe, *Theatre and Performance in Eastern Europe: The Changing Scene* (with Arthur Skelton, 2017) and *Dah Theatre: A Sourcebook* (2018). He leads courses in acting, directing and theatre history.

Deniz Başar is a theatre researcher, award-winning playwright (in Turkish and English), translator and a puppet maker (shadow puppets and muppets). She is working on her PhD in Humanities programme of Concordia University. She holds an MA degree from Boğaziçi University's Atatürk Institute for Modern Turkish History and graduated in 2014 with her MA thesis titled 'Performative Publicness: Alternative Theater in Turkey After 2000s'. Her article 'Modes of Pleasure: Contemporary Feminist Erotic Puppet Theatre; from Istanbul, with Love' has appeared in *Women and Puppetry: Critical and Historical Investigations* (2019).

Diana Benea is Assistant Professor in the English Department at the University of Bucharest, Romania, where she teaches courses in twentieth- and twenty-first-century American literature, contemporary American drama and methodologies in cultural studies. She was a Fulbright Senior Scholar grantee at the City University of New York, The Graduate Center (2017–2018), with a

NOTES ON CONTRIBUTORS

postdoctoral research project on the ethical and political stakes of contemporary community-based theatre in the U.S. She is completing a book manuscript on this topic.

Annette Bühler-Dietrich teaches in the German Department at University of Stuttgart. Her interest is in comparative literature, migration and globalisation. She holds a PhD from the University of Virginia and she is the author of *Auf dem Weg zum Theater* (2003). She is the Membership Secretary of the African Theatre Association.

Kevin Byrne is a scholar of black performance, musical theatre and popular culture, all of which are present in his book, *Minstrel Traditions: Mediated Blackface in the Jazz Age* (2020). He also serves on the editorial board of *The Journal of American Drama and Theatre*.

Selena Couture is an Assistant Professor at the University of Alberta, in Edmonton/Treaty 6 territory and Métis Regio No. 4. Her research engages with Indigenous performance, place, languages and historiography with a parallel inquiry into performative constructions of whiteness. Publications include *Against the Current and into the Light: Performing History and Land in Coast Salish Territories and Vancouver's Stanley Park* (2020) and *On This Patch of Grass: City Parks and Occupied Lands* (2018). Overlapping concerns of her research are land politics and the effects of transnational resource extraction, as well as site-based performance strategies that both refuse extraction and protect biotas.

Luciana da Costa Dias is core founder of the Performing Arts Graduate Program at the Federal University of Ouro Preto (PPGAC/UFOP), in Brazil, working at UFOP as Associate Professor of Aesthetic and Theatre Theory since 2011. She is also a founder member of the Brazilian research group 'APORIA: Studies in Philosophy and Performance' since 2014 and a core convener of Performance Philosophy network. Her research activities are focused on a hermeneutic-phenomenological approach to art and modernity. She is particularly interested in the crisis of modernity (as a metaphysical crisis and its possible overcoming through art) through the works of Nietzsche and Artaud, as well as in a transversal perspective on art/performance— as an immediacy of presence—and how this might affect theatre and performance studies.

Jim Davis is Professor of Theatre Studies at the University of Warwick. His major research interest is in nineteenth-century British theatre and his most recent books are *Plays from Dickens Vol. II* (2017), *Comic Acting and Portraiture in Late-Georgian and Regency England* (2015) and *Theatre & Entertainment* (Palgrave Macmillan, 2016). He is also joint-author of *Reflecting the Audience: London Theatre-Going 1840–1880* (2001).

Victor Hugo Leite de Aquino Soares (vhafro) is an actor and a performer, graduated in Theatre Interpretation from the Universidade de Brasília (UnB), Brazil, 2017. During his BA, he carried out a research fellowship (Cnpq) on 'Afroaesthetics and Education: Blackness and Images in Invention', under the guidance of Roberta K. Matsumoto in partnership with the Laboratory *Imagens e (m) cena* of UnB. He is studying for a Master's Programme (CAPES—research fellowship) in the Postgraduate Program in Performing Arts (PPG-CEN) at UnB, developing research on formation, aesthetics, acting and representation of black people in the performing arts.

Serena Guarracino is Associate Professor of English Literature at the Università dell'Aquila. Her research interests encompass theatre in English, theatre translation and postcolonial fiction, with a methodological preference for gender, performance and cultural studies. She has authored two monographs on Italian opera in the English-speaking world and a series of articles on the role of the postcolonial writer in the public arena, featuring as case studies J.M. Coetzee, Caryl Phillips and Chimamanda Ngozi Adichie. Her more recent study is *La traduzione messa in scena: Due rappresentazioni di Caryl Churchill in Italia* (2017).

Anselm Heinrich is Professor of Theatre Studies at University of Glasgow, and the College International Dean in the College of Arts. After studying English, history and pedagogy in Münster, he did his PhD at the University of Hull and subsequently worked first as a teaching assistant in Modern Languages at the University of Hull, then as a research associate at Lancaster University before moving to Glasgow in 2006. He is the author of *Theatre in Europe Under German Occupation* (2017); his other books include *Theater in der Region: Westfalen und Yorkshire 1918 bis 1945* (2012) and *Entertainment, Propaganda, Education: Regional Theatre in Germany and Britain Between 1918 and 1945* (2007).

Shailesh Lal works in the Faculty of Arts, Law and Education at the University of South Pacific at Suva, Fiji.

Priscilla Layne is Associate Professor of German at The University of North Carolina at Chapel Hill. Her interdisciplinary approach to twentieth- and twenty-first-century German literature and culture focuses in particular on questions of race and gender. In addition to her publications on Turkish-German culture, the dialectic of blackness and whiteness, hip-hop and (post) subculture studies, she is the author of *White Rebels in Black: German Appropriation of Black Popular Culture* (2018). She is the co-editor along with Melissa Etzler of *Rebellion and Revolution: Defiance in German Language, History and Art* (2010) and has translated into English works by Feridun Zaimoglu and Nurkan Erpulat.

Lilianne Lugo Herrera is UGrow Fellow in Digital Humanities in the UM Libraries. She is a PhD candidate in Literary, Cultural and Linguistic Studies (Modern Languages and Literatures Department). She holds a BFA in Theatre Studies from the University of Arts (ISA), in Havana, Cuba. She is interested in theatre and performance studies, media studies and women and gender studies.

xiv   NOTES ON CONTRIBUTORS

Roberta K. Matsumoto is Professor at the Department of Performing Arts, the Postgraduate Programme in Art and the Graduate Programme in Performing Arts at the Universidade de Brasília (UnB)—Brazil. She has received her doctorate degree in Film Anthropology from Université Paris X, Nanterre (1998), with research on capoeira and Afro-Brazilian issues. Her postdoctoral research was completed at Université Paris 8, Vincennes-Saint-Denis (2011–2012), focusing on the relations, influences and exchanges between the performing and audiovisual arts. She coordinates the Laboratory *Imagens e(m) cena* and the research group of the same name, in which she supervises students, from undergraduates to doctoral candidates, that work on research that problematises the boundaries between theatre, video, cinema, dance, performance and installation.

Marc Maufort is Professor of Anglophone Literatures at the Université Libre de Bruxelles (ULB), Belgium. He is an editor of *Recherche littéraire/Literary Research*, the bilingual state of art journal of the International Comparative Literature Association (ICLA). He has written and (co-)edited several books on Eugene O'Neill as well as postcolonial and multi-ethnic drama. He is the co-editor of *New Territories. Theatre, Drama, and Performance in Post-Apartheid South Africa* (with Greg Homann, 2015) and *Forays into Contemporary South African Theatre* (with Jessica Maufort, 2019).

Sharon Mazer is Professor of Theatre and Performance Studies in Te Ara Poutama, the Faculty of Māori and Indigenous Development at Auckland University of Technology. Perhaps best known for *Professional Wrestling: Sport and Spectacle* (1998; 2020), her research focuses on diverse aspects of theatre and performance in Aotearoa New Zealand. She is the author of *I Have Loved Me a Man: The Life and Times of Mika* (2018) and editor of *The Intricate Art of Actually Caring … and Other New Zealand Plays* (2018).

Mary Mazzilli is a Lecturer in the Department of Literature, Film and Theatre Studies at University of Essex. Prior to that, she worked at Goldsmiths, University of London, in the Theatre and Performance Department (2015–2016) and in 2012–2014 was a postdoctoral fellow at Nanyang Technological University, Singapore. She has written the monograph *Gao Xingjian's Post-Exile Plays: Transnationalism and Postdramatic Theatre* (2015).

Tiziana Morosetti is an Associate Lecturer with the Department of Theatre and Performance, Goldsmiths, University of London; she also teaches African Literature at the African Studies Centre, Oxford. She is the editor of *Staging the Other in Nineteenth-Century British Drama* (2015) and *Africa on the Contemporary London Stage* (Palgrave Macmillan 2018). She is the co-founder and deputy director of the journal *Quaderni del '900*, and the General Secretary of the African Theatre Association (AfTA).

David O'Donnell is Professor of Theatre at Victoria University of Wellington. He has worked in New Zealand theatre as a director, actor and dramaturg for

40 years; his most recent production was the Wellington Summer Shakespeare *Hamlet* (2019) which featured a female Hamlet and explored gender and power relationships in the play. He has published widely on New Zealand and Pacific theatre; with Marc Maufort, he co-edited the book *Performing Aotearoa* (2007), while with Lisa Warrington he wrote *Floating Islanders: Pasifika Theatre in Aotearoa* (2017). He has been editor of the Playmarket New Zealand Play Series since 2010; he is also on editorial boards for the peer-reviewed journals *Australian Drama Studies* and *Performance, Religion, and Spirituality* and the *Dramaturgies (Texts, Cultures and Performances) Series* of Peter Lang, Brussels. He has also been a member of the Summer Shakespeare Trust Board since 1999. His research projects include articles and book chapters on New Zealand and Pacific theatre and developing collaborative theatre projects with science-based themes.

Osita Okagbue is Professor of Theatre and Performance at Goldsmiths, University of London. Professor Okagbue's published works include *African Theatres and Performances* (2007), *CultureandIdentityin African and Caribbean Theatre* (2009), *African Theatre:Diasporas* (2009) co-edited with Christine Matzke, and *Performative Inter-Actions in African Theatre 1, 2 & 3* (2013) with Dr Kene Igweonu; he has also recently co-authored, with Professor Samuel Kasule, *East African Theatres and Performances* (2020).

Michael Pearce trained at the Jacques Lecoq School in Paris and worked as an actor/deviser, director and facilitator in southern Africa, Europe and the UK, before completing his PhD in 2013 at Exeter University, where he is Senior Lecturer. His research examines black British theatre in relation to the cultural and political spaces of Africa, the Caribbean and the USA, on which he has published the monograph *Black British Drama: A Transnational Story* (2017). He has published essays about contemporary Black British theatre and conducted filmed interviews with leading theatre practitioners for the National Theatre's Black Plays Archive website. He has also written a ten-part documentary about the history of black performance on the British stage and screen for BBC Radio 4 (2015). Pearce is a member of the AHRC Peer Review College.

David Peimer is Professor of Theatre and Performance Studies at Edge Hill University. He has worked for the University of the Witwatersrand (Johannesburg) and New York University (Global Division) and was a Fulbright Scholar at Columbia University. He has published widely, including his last play in *Armed Response: Plays from South Africa* (2009). Peimer has staged work for the Soros Open Society, Goethe Institute, Anglo American, South African National Arts Council, EU Parliament Culture Department, New York University, Columbia University, Amnesty International, Prague Quadrennial, Havel Foundation and others. He is working on an international project, Babel Re-Played, with the Dürrenmatt Centre, Neuchâtel, Switzerland. He is an associate researcher/director with the Pinter Centre, Goldsmiths.

Jami Rogers trained at the London Academy of Music and Dramatic Art (LAMDA) and holds an MA and a PhD from the Shakespeare Institute, the University of Birmingham. While at the University of Warwick working on the AHRC-funded Multicultural Shakespeare project, she created the British Black and Asian Performance Database, which documents ethnic minority performances of Shakespeare since 1930. The BBAS Performance Database also tracks casting policy and was featured on the front page of *The Stage* with the database's findings of discrimination within the entertainment industry. Prior to obtaining her doctorate, Rogers spent ten years working for PBS, the American public service broadcast television network, first at its headquarters in Washington, D.C., and then for eight years at WGBH/Boston working on *Masterpiece Theatre* and *Mystery!*, where awards included a Primetime Emmy from the Academy of Arts and Television Sciences. She has taught at the Universities of Warwick, Birmingham and Wolverhampton and the British American Drama Academy. She works regularly with David Thacker on Shakespeare and American drama at the Octagon Theatre, Bolton. She is on the board of the Act for Change Project and The Diversity School.

Lizzie Stewart is Lecturer in Modern Languages, Culture and Society at King's College London. She studied German and Russian as an undergraduate at the University of Edinburgh. This was followed by an MSc in European Theatre (awarded 2010), and a PhD (awarded 2015), both of which were AHRC-funded and taken at the University of Edinburgh. She taught German language, literature and culture from 2011 to 2014 at Edinburgh, and in 2014–2015 was a research fellow in Assessment Practices there. She held positions as Teaching Fellow in German at the University of St Andrews (2015–2016), and as Teaching Associate in Modern German Studies at University of Cambridge (2016–17). She was awarded a Leverhulme Fellowship in 2017, before being appointed at King's in 2017.

Dan Urian is Emeritus Professor at the Theatre Department, Tel Aviv University, and the Department of Theatre Studies, Western Galilee College. His research concerns sociology of the theatre, Israeli theatre, drama in education and television drama. His published books include *The Arab in Israeli Drama and Theatre* (1997), *The Judaic Nature of Israeli Theatre* (2000), *Television Drama* (Mofet—Ministry of Education, 2004, in Hebrew) and *Theatre and Society* (The Open University, 2008, in Hebrew). He is also editor of *Palestinians and Israelis in the Theatre* (a special issue of *Contemporary Theatre Review*, 1995) and co-editor, with Maria Shevtsova, of *The Sociology of Theatre* (2002).

CHAPTER 1

Introduction

Tiziana Morosetti and Osita Okagbue

1 PREMISE

As we write, issues of racism and race have again come to public attention in the most tragic way. The killing of George Floyd (1973–2020) on 25 May, and that of Rayshard Brooks (1993–2020) less than three weeks later, on 12 June, by police forces in the United States have sparked global outrage, re-igniting protests and requests of equality and justice for black[1] communities and individuals around the world. The appalling details of these murders, as well as a lack of distraction because of lockdowns following the emergency of COVID-19, have contributed, according to some commentators, to the unprecedented support of white people for the Black Lives Matter movement and to what seems a turning point in the long history of protest against the oppression suffered by black people worldwide. Looking around us in the United Kingdom, where we live, we see the toppling of the statue of the slave trader Edward Colston in Bristol (United Kingdom) on 7 June and the announcement of Oriel College, Oxford, that they are now ready to remove their statue of Cecil Rhodes[2] as welcome early developments in the aftermath of these killings.[3] It is essential that institutions first acknowledge the legacy of slavery, exploitation and colonialism surrounding and undermining black communities around the world, and it is paramount that young adults approaching higher education should feel safe and welcome independently of their skin colour.

T. Morosetti (✉) • O. Okagbue
Department of Theatre and Performance, Goldsmiths, University of London, London, UK
e-mail: t.morosetti@gold.ac.uk; o.okagbue@gold.ac.uk

© The Author(s), under exclusive license to Springer Nature
Switzerland AG 2021
T. Morosetti, O. Okagbue (eds.), *The Palgrave Handbook of Theatre and Race*, https://doi.org/10.1007/978-3-030-43957-6_1

Yet, deeper, structural change is desperately needed, and while it is doubtful what the controversial Commission on Race and Ethnic Disparities set up by British Prime Minister, Boris Johnson, may ultimately achieve,[4] plans for police reform in various parts of the United States should more substantially address at least police brutality, which, however, is only an aspect of the problem, if one of the most odious and shocking.[5] The more subterraneous, subtle and wide-spread under-representation, stigma, and stereotype attached to black communities and individuals have a long and complex history, and it is now more important than ever that the call for action of Black Lives Matter does not become 'an empty slogan' (Harker 2020), prompting instead long-term reflection too. Politics and tactics matter, in our view, as much as street protest, and we agree with Barak Obama as he observes that 'aspirations have to be translated into specific laws and institutional practices' (2020), which require, once protests have subsided, patience, study and a meticulousness directed at 'tailoring reforms for each community'. A scenario in which *specific* research and education become key to change itself speaks, of course, to not only the fragmentation and inconsistency of police forces in the United States (which, as is well known, are the most decentralised in the world), but also to the extreme disparity and ghettoisation of American black communities in each and every state of the United States. But specificity, research and complexity should be key words to a fuller understanding of what it means to be black, of black history *in its integrity*, also on the other side of the Atlantic. As David Olusoga has written in the concluding remarks of his *Black and British: A Forgotten History*,

> [t]he history symbolized by the *Empire Windrush* has become a part of the British History [...]. The *Empire Windrush* herself has entered the folklore and the vocabulary of the nation. [...] There is, however, a potential paradox in all this. The *Windrush* story has the capacity to obscure another deeper history. Those involved in black British history talk of the dangers of the [...] misconception that black history began with the coming of that one ship. Yet this idea in turn perpetuates the notion that black British history is exclusively a history of black settlement in Britain, rather than a global story of Britain's interaction with Africans on three continents. (2016, 523–524)

The celebration of iconic moments in history, as well as the removal of statues and symbols, and the renewed intention of institutions to refresh approaches to diversity and (eventually) education curricula are important and necessary steps towards equality, but should not exhaust themselves as facile ways to merely navigate a difficult transition.

Finally, it is essential that any debate around race and racism, especially if involving the history of black communities, should not reiterate imperialist or, at best, simplistic attitudes. If it is with a heavy heart that we finalise this introduction in light of the events in America, it is also with the hope that the collection of essays here presented may inspire a reflection serving a global approach that includes, but should not be limited to, the United States and Britain. Much has been written in these past weeks on the relation between racism in America and in the United Kingdom, with (not always appropriate) comparison between police forces, marginalisation of communities and issues of representation between the two countries. While these subjects cannot be debated enough, with some chapters (Chaps. 2, 16, 19, 20 and 21) in this volume examining theatre and race between the United States and Britain, this must not come to the exclusion of other contexts around the world, or with the assumption that these should somehow conform to 'standards' or comply with agendas that respond to the specific history of racism in the North. An article such as that appeared on 11 June on the South African *Mail & Guardian*, 'Black Lives Matter? Which Black Lives?' (Haupt 2020), may come in this respect as unsurprising. Citing the killing of Collins Khosa, a 40-year old black man, in the Alexandra township of Johannesburg by (black) police agents of the South African National Defence Force (SANDF) on 10 April this year, the author ascribes the 'disparity in responses to violence experienced by black people locally when compared to the uptake of social-media responses to events in the US' to 'US cultural and media imperialism' (Haupt 2020).[7] While several other factors are mentioned to account for the different responses, and while this should not detract us from the relevance and immense merits of the Black Lives Matter movement—as indeed, they are using what we may define as a hyper-visible position to spark long-needed global debate—the very suggestion of a hierarchy of 'importance' of black communities even in anti-racist discourses is troubling and deserves further scrutiny.

Where do theatre and the performing arts stand in all this? In the chapters included in this collection we have identified areas that exemplify the relation between theatre and race, ways in which the stage may have enhanced or challenged racial bias, histories of representation of diversity, articulations of black identities, as well as contexts in which, because of conflict and war, racism may have overlapped or been obliterated by nationalist discourses apparently unrelated to but profoundly grounded in ethnic divisions. That the events of the last month should be too recent to have been included in the scholarly reflection of this volume is in many ways a pity, and the briefness of this premise cannot do any justice (as nothing can) to the tragic loss of human life not only in the mentioned cases of Floyd, Brooks and Khosa, but also of the many others that this introduction could not discuss. At the same time, we hope the contribution we offer to the debate may encourage or enhance discussion of neglected nuances and communities, and provide a fuller picture of the dynamics of contrast, integration, representation and cohabiting.

2   On Race and Racism: Background Remarks and Literature

In his essay 'An Idiom of Race: A Critique of Presentism' (2000), Michael Banton quotes Julian Huxley and A. C. Haddon who, in their 1935 study *We Europeans: A Survey of 'Racial' Problems*, suggest strongly that 'the term race as applied to human groups should be dropped from the vocabulary of science because it had lost any sharpness of meaning' (quoted in Banton 2000/2009, 62). Also in 2000, then US president, Bill Clinton, in accepting the final draft of the Human Genome Project report, re-cited the 99.9 per cent mantra of the leading genomics researchers that 'race does not exist in our genes—we are all the same' (quoted by Sandra Soo-Jin Lee in Karim Murji and John Solomos eds. 2015, 26). What these two instances point to is the fact that race has always been and remains a problematic, unreliable and contested term to use as a marker of difference between human groups.

The unreliability of race as a marker is further demonstrated by the fact that even among Europeans, the very 'race' who invented the term race, its usage was confused and still is confusing. But this was more so 'during the high point of imperialism in the late nineteenth and early twentieth centuries' when 'racialised notions of national identity were pertinent outside the colonial context' and 'imperialist ideologues had developed a racial notion of national identity to refer to other European nations as well as colonial peoples' (Back and Solomos 2000/2009, 15). The problem with race is that, as David Smith points out:

> From the beginning, the idea of race was bound up with ideas of racial difference and superiority and inferiority. Considering only Europe, it is possible to find a conception of race and racial distinction in the writings of the ancient Greeks, for whom non-Greeks were generically 'barbarians' ... and usually regarded as by definition inferior to Greeks. (Smith in Hindpal Singh Bhui, 2008, 10)

Thus, it is not the term 'race' per se or the idea that human beings and social groups are different from each other that is the problem, but rather it is the hierarchical value of superior and inferior, civilised and primitive, developed and underdeveloped and so on that came to be attached to the comparative differentiation between black, white and yellow that is the issue. Race as we know it today, according to Michel Wieviorka (2002), 'is a later European invention, associated with the beginnings of maritime empire-building in the fifteenth century'; however, Wieviorka acknowledges that prior to this time, there existed what could be regarded as 'proto-racist'[8] conceptions of race and difference in classical Greece but that the current understanding of the term emerged from the seventeenth century, 'in European accounts of the African and native American peoples whose lands they invaded' (2002, 460). This bears out Robert Miles who, in offering what can best be described as a neo-Marxist iteration of race, asserts that '"races" are created within the context of political and social regulation' (Back and Solomos 2000/2009, 8). For Miles, race is 'an ideological effect, a mask that hides real economic relationships' (Back and Solomos 2000/2009, 7); thus the value of race is really not in its reality, but rather in its objective status as both an analytical tool and a basis for human behaviours and actions (Miles 1982, 42). Using the fact of migration in Britain and Europe as context, Miles argues that race is merely a political/

ideological construct, and that within the colonial contexts of Africa and the Caribbean, perceived biological differences between Africans, native Americans and the 'supposed European norm were noted, described, treated as signs or causes of inferiority, and explained mainly in terms of differences in the natural environment, especially climatic differences' (42). What emerges strongly from Miles's study and needs to be taken note of in any discussions on race is that while the term many not be real, it was and still remains an underlying basis on which certain human actions and behaviours—whether individual or at the level of policy—are enacted. Secondly, we note, as many of the theatre contexts and plays looked at in this book demonstrate, that the impact of these behaviours and actions are also real for the perpetrators and recipients of those actions and behaviours, in which case, race without being real seems/remains real for people. There is no doubt that colonialism and imperialism in the attempt to develop the often racist ideologies and practices, which it needed in order to justify and sustain itself, made a major contribution to the construction of the images of the European 'other', images which still circulate and are effective today. This perhaps illustrates the fact that despite its hoped-for demise, race remains a potent factor in human relationships in various contexts around the globe; in fact, all efforts within and by scholarship and research have not as yet managed to kill race off, with the result that it still features in thinking and actions in many contexts in which humans meet, coexist and interact with one another around the world.

Thus the incontrovertible fact is that what race meant then was unclear, as it was, and today still sometimes is, confused with ideas of nation. More recently, the term 'ethnicity' further complicates the issue of race as a term or marker because it raises the question of whether race in fact can be an 'ontologically valid concept'; Back and Solomos in the introduction to their collection certainly do not think so (2000/2009, 20). But our view is that this question needs to be asked so that the ontogenetic fallacy on which the idea of race was based—that is, selecting, fixing and making 'natural' certain biological features/qualities of social groups and using these to construct difference—and the racisms which it has sometimes given rise to historically can be exposed. Our introduction therefore proceeds, as will subsequent chapters in this book, on the basis that race is neither ontologically valid as a concept, nor is it useful or reliable in differentiating between peoples or social groups. But while we are not calling for its complete removal from the vocabularies of scholarship as Huxley and Haddon had done in 1935, we would advise that extreme caution be exercised in its deployment by anyone to ensure that the inherent problems associated with the term be always foregrounded whenever and in whatever context it is used.

The last two decades have seen a surge in studies on race and the theatre, with 11 volumes published between 2003 and 2014 only.[9] So, why a *Handbook of Theatre and Race* then? First and utmost, the answer must be found in that permanence of racial thinking and racism in our contemporary world already hinted at above, against which, come 2020, our societies still struggle to fully embrace diversity and equality as clearly shown by recent events in the United States and the reverberations around the world. We would, as made clear previously, certainly align our position to that of Critical Race theory, according to which 'race and races are products of social thought and relations. Not objective, inherent, or fixed, they correspond to no biological or genetic reality; rather, races are categories that society invents, manipulates, or retires when convenient' (Delgado 2017, 7). However, while agreeing that race is a social and political construct, that there is no truth to it, we also recognise that race had and still continues to have a material impact on the lives of very many people; sometimes positively, but negatively more of the time. So, in spite of scholars, such as Sir Huxley and Prof Haddon advising that race as a term should be excised from the 'vocabulary of science', that it should not feature in any study or understanding of society and human relations because of its loss of 'sharpness of meaning', or President Clinton's reiteration of the conclusions of leading genomicists that there is no race in our genes, that 'we are all the same'; race unfortunately still persists in theory and in practice, affecting thinking and relations between peoples. It is this continued pervasive presence of race in human affairs that engenders continued interest in it, for there is still the possibility that newer and perhaps changed understandings of race can be beneficial to humanity in the long term.

Thus, while publishing yet another study on this topic may seem an unnecessary effort to ultimately confirm the very existence of these invented categories, we feel the urgency to highlight ways in which racialised thinking and political systems may reiterate the exclusion of certain groups or inform societies at particular moments of their history. If biological racism may be a thing of the past (Fredrickson 2015, 4), it is our belief, and on evidence of current events, that racism is still endemic to many contemporary instances; this is even more so in the ongoing confrontation between an increasingly narrowed, isolationist and fragmented Western world against the perceived 'threat' of an unwelcome 'other'—be this Eastern European workers, Muslim communities worldwide or the thousands of refugees from Africa and elsewhere regularly dying while attempting to cross the Mediterranean into 'fortress' Europe, or the selective brutality of law enforcement agents against black people in America. As Fredrickson again writes, 'racism does not require the full and explicit support of the state and the law. Nor does it require an ideology centred on the concept of biological inequality. Discrimination by institutions and individuals against those perceived as racially different can long persist and even flourish under the illusion of nonracism' (4). Theatre can play an essential role in enhancing or challenging perceptions and constructions of 'race' both in contexts where racism can be an invisible but powerful undercurrent, and, indeed, in societies where institutional racism is visibly present, and Part II of this volume in particular wishes to acknowledge this central difference by highlighting how discourses on the nation and national belonging can be functional to institutional exclusion and discrimination. As Harvey Young in his own *Theatre and Race* (2013) stresses, theatre retains an important societal role in commenting on, conveying and challenging socio-political and cultural assumptions, and it therefore constitutes a privileged point of observation to consider issues of inclusion/exclusion in relation to race, gender and class. Theatre, as an art form that deals mainly in human physicality and is thus a barometre for capturing and measuring human behaviours and interaction, has always been well placed to enact, interrogate and often times aspires to manage or alter for the better these varieties of human conduct. Some of the performances and theatre forms from different contexts included in this book do this, from the representation of whiteness and the 'other' explored in Part IV of this collection, through the enactment of race and its socio-political and cultural impacts on life and relationships in the postslavery and postcolonial societies, which is the theme of Part III, to the manner in which, to use Maufort's words in his chapter (chap. 5), indigenous dramaturgies 'challenge and deconstruct notions of race by de-essentialising both Indigeneity and whiteness' while negating the racial purity that came about as the result of a long history of creolisation that has taken place in the Americas.

However, studies on race and the theatre have been largely focused on the trans-Atlantic context, with discussion of US-UK relations and related articulations of blackness, and/or on specific periods such as the Renaissance—with, unsurprisingly, great attention to Shakespeare[10]—or the immediate contemporaneity. If Roberta Uno's *The Color of Theatre* (2005) 'is an effort to create the primary perspective of a discourse and resource on race and performance emanating from artistic practice' (5), this is done with a dedicated focus on the twenty-first century that only partly allows for a global or historical perspective. Young's *Theatre and Race,* while being centred on 'how race is performed and how western theatrical practice has historically engaged with the topic' (2013, 2) over the centuries, also retains a heavy focus on the North American context, with extended examination of performances from the United States. The same author's *Embodying Black Experience* (2010) is equally concerned with the American scene, as is Daphne Brooks's *Bodies in Dissent* (2006), which examines black trans-Atlantic activists, actors and singers moving between the United States and the United Kingdom from the mid-nineteenth century to the early twentieth century. While studies such as Shannon Steen's *Racial Geometries* (2010), which examines 'performances that intertwine black and Asian racial signifiers' (5), or, more recently, Faedra Chatard Carpenter's *Coloring Whiteness* (2014) provide a widened scope on (and original points of entries in) intersections between theatre and race, a prevalent interest in the North American scene is still firmly in place. There are, of course, ample reasons why this should be the case; nonetheless this clearly creates an imbalance, in that the example of the United States, already overwhelmingly present in debates about racism in the United Kingdom and elsewhere, risks being assumed as the *typical* or primarily relevant context to be taken into account also when it comes to examining race on stage. This overshadows literary productions from other continents that, while overlapping at times with American history, may have little to nothing to do with constructions of race in the

United States. Building on these studies, the *Palgrave Handbook of Theatre and Race* brings together productions in English from diverse geographical areas, as well as performances in languages other than English, in the wish to offer a more diversified overview of the interaction between theatre and race in the modern and contemporary world. We have therefore deliberately limited contributions focusing on the United States not to repeat, but complement the excellent studies mentioned so far, while including chapters on other areas of the Americas, as well as on theatre from the South Pacific, Eastern and Central Europe, China, Africa, the Caribbean and the Middle East.[11]

We share with Steen the sense that 'race is not a domestic, internally derived national formation, but is shaped by international dynamics as well, and shapes those dynamic in return' (2010, 5), and that binary systems revolving around white/non-white, and/or American/foreign juxtapositions (6) should be further challenged and complicated. To do so, alongside addressing the imbalance of a long-term focus on the United States, the other two directions we have taken in putting together this collection are, first. A more nuanced approach to 'colour' generally by not making this necessarily our central scope (not even in title) but acknowledging, rather, the larger implications of perceived 'racial' or ethnic difference. While we acknowledge that colour has undoubtedly become a main and most defining feature of 'difference' in the history of racial thinking and racism, we have strived to include contributions that examine how 'race' has been articulated in terms (such as national belonging, ethnic difference or cultural distinctions) that do not primarily entail a difference in complexion. This means that even contributions, such as those in the last two sections of the collection, that mostly deal with representations of 'blackness' and 'whiteness' on stage, do so by not establishing or encouraging facile binaries between the two—which are, rather, put in scope and questioned—and examine 'colour' as only one factor that may account for difference or even discrimination.

Secondly, as discussions of 'colour' are to an extent somewhat inescapable in the light of the stress that has been put on this from the mid-nineteenth century to the present time, we have opted for including, alongside explorations of 'blackness' on stage, a further consideration of 'whiteness' and its construction in confrontation with non-white cultures, which we discuss, within the general context of representations of the 'other', especially in Part IV. This is not, to be clear, to suggest all societies, groups or indeed 'races' are or have been, after all, racialised or equally targeted by racism over time. This is, rather, to acknowledge ways in which whiteness itself has been defined, as well as the important differentiations on stage between similarly white (but not necessarily, socially and economically, equivalent) groups or cultures. As Lorimer (1978) has affirmed in his *Colour, Class and the Victorians*, '[t]he question "does a black man equal a white man?" had little meaning in an age [the nineteenth century] when few thought all white men deserved equality' (15).

While the present age may not as effectively distinguish between white 'races',[12] we find it important to stress that other factors (class, gender, sexuality) may well (as Brexit has perhaps demonstrated) affect perceptions of equally white-but-not-so-equal groups—so that, if whiteness remains undeniably conducive of mostly privileged backgrounds, its definition and perception deserve further scrutiny. In fact, some of the plays and indigenous performances from Africa and the Caribbean examined in this volume show how whiteness can be constructed often not as the prevalently dominant and privileged 'other' that it is in the Western literature or theatre (or when and where the West held sway), but rather as a disempowered, dismembered and silenced husk. This is particularly the case in Okagbue's chapter about the Caribbean in which the three plays discussed show whiteness paradoxically as powerful yet marginalised, bumbling and occasionally voiceless and hollow, and Adeyemi's on indigenous African (Yorùbá) theatre in which the white characters are presented as blundering and comically strange beings from elsewhere. It is interesting to note that these constructions of whiteness as comical and floundering 'other', especially in indigenous African(-derived) contexts and theatre, completely challenge the imperial and colonial superiority-inferiority gradation of white and black 'races'. In fact, these constructions of otherness illustrate two things; first, that as humans, we are each other's 'other'; and, second, that every 'other' is a packaged strangeness to another. All chapters tend to make a distinction between racial thinking and racism. We would agree with Fredrickson that while 'race' may just describe a group with coherent characteristics, '[i]t is when differences that might otherwise be considered ethnocultural are regarded as innate, indelible, and unchangeable that a racist attitude or ideology can be said to exist' (2015, 5). On the other hand, we also share with Young the sense that '[d]espite the historical baggage of race, the concept is not unredeemably negative. Although divisive [...] it can be used to rally a sense of cultural pride that is not necessarily dependent upon the denigration of others' (2013, 7). This is indeed at the core of Part III, in which blackness is described as conveying, alongside other things, a sense of belonging and cultural specificity, such as to challenge systematic oppression of black communities around the world.

3   Sections and Chapters

The contributions in this volume have been divided into four parts with different focuses, and, within these, chapters have been arranged in loose chronological order. These parts intend to dialogue with one another and have been conceived as porous and not absolute; given that chapters examine several overlapping areas, their subdivision merely reflects common themes and has been devised as a guideline for the reader rather than to suggest rigid interpretations. While Part I, 'Race and Racism in Contemporary Theatre', privileges the contemporaneity, this does not imply that others in the volume may not discuss recent or even ongoing performance; this is very patently the case, for example, with Annette Bühler-Dietrich's 'Fighting Racism on the Contemporary Francophone Stage', which, however, has been included under Part III, 'Blackness and the African Diaspora', as this chapter specifically addresses

African and black theatre—a subject for which we very much wanted a separate section. If blackness is variously discussed (Chaps. 20, 21 and 24) in Part IV, 'Constructions of Whiteness and the 'Other', this is through a different angle, that of the portrayal, representation and often stereotyping of other cultures, rather than a stress on their *active* creativity. Part II, 'War, Conflict and the Nation', groups chapters that offer insights into the history of specific regions of the world and their theatre, with a focus on territorial conflict, nation-building and/or the expression of racism in explicit war scenarios. This is not to assume, again, that other chapters in the collection (such as Maufort's on Canada) may not equally share the sense of nations that are still in progress, wanting much in terms of justice, balance and equality. In a wider perspective, in fact, tension, conflict and violence unfortunately and unmistakably emerge from all the chapters in this volume. In summarising sections and chapters, then, we have also taken the liberty to highlight common themes and possible connections to keep the dialogue going between contributors and areas of investigation.

Jami Rogers's piece 'The American Theatrical Canon and the Struggle for Racial Equality in British Theatre', on inclusive casting practices, opens *PART I, 'Race and Racism in Contemporary Theatre'*, as it sets the tone of the discussion by questioning ideas of Americanness and Britishness in theatre, and examining influences between the two sides of the Atlantic that problematise the relevance of American culture in European debates around racism. It is thus a good starting point for a section that investigates how theatrical practices or individual playwrights have challenged racism in a variety of contexts, from North America to the South Pacific to continental and Eastern Europe, in the last 50 years. Other relevant sub-themes include issues that are specific to these contexts, such as the (re)construction of national identities and racialisation processes in the aftermath of the Second World War in Stewart and Layne's 'Racialisation and Contemporary German Theatre'; colonialism/imperialism in O'Donnell and Lal's contribution on '"Dangerous Dialogues": Questioning Constructions of Race in South Pacific Theatre'; indigeneity and performance in Marc Maufort's 'Staging the Ambiguities of Race: Polymorphous Indigenous Dramaturgies in Canada'; and the demise of the Eastern Bloc and the persecution of the Roma people in Benea's 'Representing the Roma Experience on the Contemporary Romanian Stage'.

These chapters speak to others in different sections of the volume. Maufort's discussion of Canadian First Nations playwriting, the work of Tomson Highway in particular, to question binary oppositions in the construction of Indigenous and white identities; and O'Donnell's and Lal's analysis of how the work of playwrights Larry Thomas (Indigenous Fijian and European) and Victor Rodger (Indigenous Samoan and European) challenge racist narratives of European import in the South Pacific can both be complemented by that of Mazer on New Zealand Maori. On the other hand, Stewart and Layne's chapter, which surveys changes in debates around race from the Second World War to the present day, examining the work of racialised theatre makers on the

1 INTRODUCTION   11

contemporary German stage, is in dialogue with Heinrich's chapter on theatre practices in Nazi Germany. Benea's chapter on the work of the Roma theatre company Giuvlipen in contemporary Romania, which addresses questions of identity, representation and discrimination, is a good introduction, together with Barnett's chapter on contemporary Serbian performance, to theatre dynamics in post-communist Eastern Europe. On American theatre, Rogers's chapter may itself be accompanied by Byrne's discussion of blackface masking in contemporary American performance and Couture's analysis of Susan Glaspell's work.

PART II, 'War, Conflict and the Nation', gathers chapters that are mainly, as mentioned, dedicated to the relation between racialist thinking and the construction of the nation in scenarios of war or conflict around the world. The section opens with Anselm Heinrich's chapter on Nazi Germany, which examines productions of Shakespeare's *Merchant of Venice* during the Third Reich, as well as the work of Richard Euringer and Eberhard Wolfgang, in contrast with the Jewish *Kulturbund* theatres in Berlin. Sharon Mazer's 'Māori Theatre in Not-Quite-Post-Colonial Aotearoa New Zealand' examines, on its part, the relation between Maori theatrical practices and issues of national identity, with a focus on two plays from the 1990s by Hone Kouka, *Nga Tangata Toa* ('The Warrior People') and *Waiora: Te Ūka-ipō*—'The Homeland'. Dennis Barnett's 'Racial Nationalism and the Serbian Theatre: From *Radovan III* to DAH' explores theatre in former Yugoslavia with a survey of theatrical practices during and after Tito, and a focus on performance in twenty-first-century Serbia. This chapter also proposes a reading of 'racial nationalism' that clarifies intersections between national stances and racialist thinking in the Balkans. Dan Urian's 'The Palestinian in Israeli Theatre' and Deniz Başar's 'Faces of a Long Unspoken Collective Trauma' both deal with Middle Eastern theatre, exploring the conflict between Israelis and Palestinians on the one side,[13] and the Kurdish-Turkish war on the other. Urian examines the fluctuating images of the Palestinian in mainstream Israeli theatre, with a focus on the last two decades, which follow the Second Intifada (2000–2004); Başar, on her part, investigates alternative theatres in Turkish and Kurdish in contemporary Istanbul that have strived to promote different understandings of Kurdish people and culture and peaceful cohabitation. Both chapters demonstrate how theatre makers do in fact actively work to overcome division, and how the theatre stage, both mainstream and in the fringe, can provide a space for more constructive conversations. The conflictual contexts examined by Urian and Başar are not necessarily *explicitly* about race, but build on racialist assumptions that rather provide a dangerous undercurrent to political thought; these assumptions further highlight the imprecision and consequent blurring of the boundaries between notions of race and nation pointed out earlier in the introduction. Last but not least, David Peimer's 'Staging Race in White South African Afrikaans Theatre' investigates theatrical representations of race during and after Apartheid, examining in particular the work of the female white Afrikaner playwright, Reza de Wet.[14] Issues of race representation and the construction of 'whiteness' and 'blackness' in contemporary South African theatre are both addressed by this chapter, which complements the reading of Bühler-Dietrich and Adeyemi on, respectively, Francophone and West African theatre.

PART III, 'Blackness and the African Diaspora', centres, as per its title, on questions of race and identity in the theatre of black artists in the diaspora; while this section is well complemented by the chapters of Couture and Morosetti on representations of blackness between the United States and Britain in the nineteenth century, as well as by the contributions of Peimer and Adeyemi on African theatre, we have decided to group together discussions of contemporary diasporic black artists in acknowledgement of their common challenges and aspirations—albeit the significantly different contexts in which they live. This part opens with Okagbue's chapter, 'In the Prison of their Skins: Performing Race in Caribbean Theatre', which contextualises discourses of race in the 'New World' arguing that, while the category of 'race' has itself been disqualified by contemporary scientific thinking, race and racism remain a long-lasting issue and presence in diasporic contexts, where racialist thinking still affects people of colour specifically, both psychologically and materially. Examining three playwrights in particular, Derek Walcott from St. Lucia, Dennis Scott and Trevor Rhone from Jamaica, Okagbue reveals the continued presence and influence of race as a marker of difference as well as a measure of social positioning in postslavery and postcolonial Caribbean society. Focused on central and southern American theatre are also two chapters, Lilianne Lugo Herrera's 'Black Women in Post-Revolutionary Cuban Theatre', and Victor Hugo Leite and Roberta Matsumoto's 'Black Performances and Black Artists Performing in Contemporary Brazil'. Herrera's chapter examines articulations of female blackness by juxtaposing theatre strategies from the 1960s and from the twenty-first century, while discussing the work of Maité Vera, José Milián, Eugenio Hernández Espinosa, Rogelio Orizondo, Georgina Herrera and Fátima Patterson. Matsumoto and Leite, on the other hand, examine the black theatre scene in Brazil from Abdias Nascimento's *Teatro Experimental Negro* to the contemporary work of theatre companies *Bando de Teatro Olodum* (Bahia) and *AMOK Teatro* (Rio de Janeiro). Both chapters highlight the permanence of racism as an influential undercurrent in Cuban and Brazilian societies that is interpreted in the light of, respectively, the Cuban revolution and Brazil's claim to a 'racial democracy'. As they both deal with constructions of the nation, these chapters furthermore add to contributions on this topic in Part II. Kevin Byrne's 'Lackface: Blackface Masking in Contemporary US Performance' takes the book back to the United States to explore contemporary theatre works that incorporate the tropes of the minstrel show and the blackface mask; these tropes are questioned through an analysis of Branden Jacobs-Jenkins's and Young Jean Lee's plays, as well as the musicals *The Scottsboro Boys* and *Shuffle Along*. This chapter would therefore intersect quite well with Morosetti's chapter on representations of blackness on the Victorian stage that capitalise on the blackface minstrelsy tradition, as well as with Davis's contribution on the

'Yankee' impersonation of Charles Mathews in Georgian Britain. Annette Bühler-Dietrich's 'Fighting Racism on the Contemporary Francophone Stage' examines plays by Koffi Kwahulé (Ivory Coast) and Dieudonné Niangouna (Congo) that deal specifically with (black) boxing and the persona of Muhammad Ali. The chapter also examines one additional playwright, the Nigerian British Mojisola Adebayo, to further contextualise the interest for and in Ali's career and achievements, while exploring articulations of blackness on the contemporary African (and diasporic) stage. The final chapter of this section, Michael Pearce's '"Though we are written into the landscape you don't see us" (Testament, 2018). Black Faces in White Spaces: Whiteness as Terror and the Terror of Un-belonging in *Black Men Walking*', explores constructions of whiteness in contemporary Black British writing and it thus complements well contributions such as Davis's on Victorian British theatre, Couture's on Susan Glaspell and Adeyemi on Yoruba masquerade theatre that similarly discuss notions of whiteness. By focusing specifically on Testament's play *Black Men Walking*, Pearce's chapter examines ways in which black-authored dramas in Britain challenge white authority by providing a representation of whiteness as terror, and can thus also be read in connection to Rogers's and Guarracino's chapters on the contemporary British theatrical scene.

PART IV, 'Constructions of Whiteness and the "Other"', specifically focuses on representations of non-white cultures in European theatre (Britain and France), and, on the contrary, of whiteness in contexts like Nigeria and China. The title of the section hints at an ambivalence in discussions of whiteness; while this is made the target of revision, reinterpretation and subversion in Yoruba culture (Adeyemi) and in contemporary Chinese work (Mazzilli), it is also at once the target and the origin of theatrical interpretation in Mathews's impersonation of the 'Yankee' (Davis), Artaud's writing on Mexico (da Costa Dias) and Glaspell's understandings of American expansionism (Couture). Morosetti's chapter and Guarracino's deal, at the other end of the spectrum, with (white) European representations of non-white cultures, but in doing so, the chapters also highlight intersections with class and gender that complicate readings of race on the British stage.

Jim Davis's '"A Wretched Caricature…Unworthy of America": Charles Mathews's Representation of the Yankee' discusses Mathews's less-known impersonations of white Americans in his series *At Home* (1818–1834), and related notions of nationality and race in Georgian Britain. Morosetti's chapter 'The Language of Blackness: Representations of Africans and African-Americans on the British Stage after *Uncle Tom's Cabin*' also examines the linguistic strategies adopted in the representation of the black character on the Victorian stage, exploring the legacy of the 'minstrelised' stereotype promoted by black-face minstrelsy and later by theatrical adaptations of Harriet Beecher Stowe's novel. Selena Couture's 'Susan Glaspell's *Trifles* and *Inheritors*: White Settler Hunger, Debt and the Black Hawk Purchase Lands' discusses the construction of settler colonial whiteness as reflected in early twentieth-century American theatre, specifically in Glaspell's canonical work *Trifles* (1916), which Couture re-reads in relation to issues of precariousness and 'hunger' in American expansionism. These three chapters deal in many ways with constructions of the nation and are therefore in dialogue with contributions in Part II. Luciana da Costa Dias's 'Beyond the Peyote Dance: The Raramuri Tribe and "Mexico" Representations in Antonin Artaud's Work' examines, on the other hand, ways in which primitivism and the work of the great French artist intersect, focusing on the impact of Artaud's Mexican experience on his writings. While the focus is on the reception of Mexico, the discussion of Raramuri culture makes this chapter a good reading in connection with those on Central America in Part III. Sola Adeyemi's 'Representing and Re-presenting Others in Yorùbá Performance', which deals with a specific Nigerian culture and can therefore be read together with chapters on Africa in Parts II and III, examines representations of whiteness and the colonial encounter in the Egungun masquerade of Imesi-Ile, which subverts (Western) images of whiteness as automatically associated with superiority, 'seriousness', efficiency and power. The final two chapters, Serena Guarracino's 'Pigs and Dogs and Bogus Women: Racialized Performance in Anglo-British Women Playwrights' and Mary Mazzilli's 'Race, Occidentalism/Orientalism and Sino-centrism in Contemporary Chinese Theatre' deal, respectively, with the reception of racially marked characters in the work of Caryl Churchill, Sarah Kane, Shelagh Delaney and Kay Adshead, and—in reversed perspective—with notions of Chinese Occidentalism and the reception of Western culture in Wang Chong's *Revolutionary Model Play 2.0*. If Mazzilli explores how Sino-centrism disguises under a deconstructed racial fluidity, and examines ways in which white Western culture enters the Chinese through translations and adaptations of the Western canon, Guarracino discusses the intersection between white textual authorship and the performing black body.

In all the contributions included in this volume, the body of the performer as a signifier of overlapping racial identities and national and political constructions emerges clearly, theatre becoming a symbolic as well as a physical *locus* of the intersection of communities and culture, and for conversations about identity, heritage, resistance and struggle, and future perspectives especially at moments of change and of conflict. It is our hope that, while many areas and topics could be added to those we present in this collection, the chapters of this volume will further shed light on the complex, long-lasting and often very practical issues of race and racism, clarifying the dynamics of a category that, although seriously questioned and ultimately dismissed in theory, still in practice affects so significantly communities and individuals around the world.

Notes

1. The terms 'black' and 'white' will be capitalised in this volume only when they indicate groups (e.g. Black Germans, Black British).
2. The statue has been at the centre of controversy since the Rhodes Must Fall campaign started their activity in Cape Town (2015) and Oxford (2016) amongst other locations.

3. Steps in this direction have been taken by University College London, which has renamed three facilities formerly entitled to eugenicists Francis Galton and Karl Pearson (see https://www.theguardian.com/education/2020/jun/19/ucl-renames-three-facilities-that-honoured-prominent-eugenicists), and by the curator of the parliament's collection of art at Westminster, Melissa Hamnet, who has declared an intention to revise appropriateness and strategies behind the display of some items, and to commission new work portraying BAME and female MPs (see https://www.theguardian.com/uk-news/2020/jun/19/houses-of-parliament-art-has-a-lot-of-racist-history-says-its-curator). We use BAME (Black Asian and Minority Ethnic) as the acronym is used explicitly in the article from the *Guardian* mentioned above; it is important, however, to point to the growing problematisation of this definition, which is being rejected by several groups as fundamentally reductive and incorrect.

4. See https://www.independent.co.uk/news/uk/politics/black-lives-matter-uk-government-review-white-working-class-boris-johnson-a9566581.html, and https://www.theguardian.com/world/2020/jun/14/johnson-criticised-over-victimisation-comment-as-he-sets-up-racism-inquiry.

5. It is worth noting, though, that plans from Democrats, Republicans and the White House differ significantly in approach; for comparison of work-in-progress intentions see https://www.bbc.co.uk/news/world-us-canada-53083560.

6. On the *Empire Windrush* and the history of the West Indian community in Britain post-1948 see also Onyekachi Wambu (ed.), *Empire Windrush: Fifty Years of Writing about Black Britain* (London: Gollancz, 1998) and Paul Arnott, *Windrush: A Ship Through Time* (Stroud: The History Press, 2019).

7. See also https://freewestmedia.com/2020/06/04/death-of-collins-khosa-elicits-no-protests/.

8. For more on the term 'proto-racism', see Benjamin Isaac's *The Invention of Racism in Classical Antiquity*, New Jersey: Princeton University Press, 2006.

9. *Constructions of Race in Southern Theatre: From Federalism to the Federal Theatre Project* (Southeastern Theatre Conference and the University of Alabama Press, c2003), Roberta Uno's (ed.) *The Color of Theater: Race, Culture and Contemporary Performance* (Bloomsbury, 2005), Daphne Brooks's *Bodies in Dissent: Spectacular Performances of Race and Freedom, 1850–1910* (Duke University Press, 2006), Harvey Young's *Embodying Black Experience* (University of Michigan Press, 2010) and *Theatre and Race* (Palgrave Macmillan, 2013), Shannon Steen's *Racial Geometries of the Black Atlantic, Asian Pacific and American Theatre* (Palgrave Macmillan, 2010), Angela Chia-yi Pao's *No Safe Spaces: Re-casting Race, Ethnicity, and Nationality in American Theatre* (University of Michigan Press, c2010), Frieda Ekotto's *Race and Sex across the French Atlantic: the Color of Black in Literary, Philosophical, and Theater Discourse* (Lexington Books, 2011), Anne Crémieux, Xavier Lemoine, and Jean-Paul Rocchi's (eds.) *Understanding Blackness through Performance: Contemporary Arts and the Representation of Identity* (Palgrave Macmillan, 2013), Faedra Chatard Carpenter's *Coloring Whiteness: Acts of Critique in Black Performance* (University of Michigan Press, 2014) and Warren Hoffman's *The Great White Way: Race and the Broadway Musical* (Rutgers University Press, 2014). See also Helen Gilbert's *Sightlines: Race, Gender, and Nation in Contemporary Australian Theatre* (University of Michigan Press, 1998).

10. See Ayanna Thompson's (ed.) *Colorblind Shakespeare: New Perspectives on Race and Performance* (Routledge, 2006) and *Passing Strange: Shakespeare, Race, and Contemporary America* (Oxford University Press, 2011), Lara Bovilsky's *Barbarous Play: Race on the English Renaissance Stage* (University of Minnesota Press, c2008), Scott L. Newstok's (ed.) *Weyward Macbeth: Intersections of Race and Performance* (Palgrave Macmillan, 2010), and Delia Jarrett-Macauley's *Shakespeare, Race and Performance: The Diverse Bard* (Routledge, 2016).

11. Areas such as Japanese theatre, Native American performance in the United States, theatre in the Indian sub-continent or Southern Europe are not included in the volume; this is not, clearly, because they are not relevant to the subject but due to reasons all related to the long and at times difficult gestation of this volume. We deeply regret that seeking contributions on these areas did not ultimately bear results.

12. For an extensive discussion of Victorian perceptions of white races and scientific racism see Richard McMahon's *The Races of Europe: Construction of National Identities in the Social Sciences, 1839–1939* (London: Palgrave Macmillan, 2016).

13. We have tried to contact Palestinian companies and academics in the hope to have a chapter by a Palestinian voice on the subject, but this was not in the end possible, to our great regret.

14. One contribution that was due on black writing in contemporary South African theatre could not in the end be included.

References

Back, Les, and John Solomos. 2000/2009. *Theories of Race and Racism: A Reader.* London-New York: Routledge.

Banton, Michael. 2000/2009. An Idiom of Race: A Critique of Presentism. In *Theories of Race and Racism: A Reader*, ed. Les Back and John Solomos, 51–63. London and New York: Routledge.

Delgado, Richard. 2017. In *Critical Race Theory: An Introduction*, ed. Jean Stefancic. New York University Press.

Fredrickson, George M. 2015. *Racism: A Short Introduction.* Princeton University Press.

Harker, Joseph. 2020. "Black Lives Matter" Risks Becoming an Empty Slogan. It's Not Enough to Defeat Racism. *The Guardian*, 11 June. https://www.theguardian.com/commentisfree/2020/jun/11/black-lives-matter-racism-bristol-colston. Accessed 18 June 2020.

Haupt, Adam. 2020. Black Lives Matter? Which Black Lives?. *Mail & Guardian*, 11 June. https://mg.co.za/opinion/2020-06-11-black-lives-matter-which-black-lives/. Accessed 29 June 2020.

Lee, Sandra Soo-Jin. 2015. Race and the Science of Difference in the Age of Genomics. In *Theories of Race and Ethnicity: Contemporary Debates and Perspectives*, ed. Karin Murji and John Solomos, 26–39. Cambridge: Cambridge University Press.

Lorimer, Douglass. 1978. *Colour, Class and the Victorians: English Attitudes to the Negro in the Mid-Nineteenth Century.* Leicester University Press.

Miles, Robert. 1982. *Racism and Migrant Labour: A Critical Text.* London: Routledge and Kegan Paul.

Obama, Barak. 2020. How to Make this Moment the Turning Point for Real Change. *Medium.* https://medium.com/@BarackObama/how-to-make-this-moment-the-turning-point-for-real-change-9fa209806067. Accessed 19 June 2020.

Olusoga, David. 2016. *Black and British: A Forgotten History.* London: Macmillan.

Smith, David. 2008. Key Concepts and Theories about "Race". In *Race and Criminal Justice,* ed. Hindpal Singh Bhui, 9–29. London: Sage Publications.

Steen, Shannon. 2010. *Racial Geometries of the Black Atlantic, Asian Pacific and American Theatre.* Palgrave Macmillan.

Uno, Roberta. 2005. *The Color of Theater: Race, Culture and Contemporary Performance.* Bloomsbury.

Wieviorka, Michel. 2002. The Development of Racism in Europe. In *A Companion to Racial and Ethnic Studies,* eds. D.T. Goldberg and John Solomos. Oxford: Blackwell.

Young, Harvey. 2013. *Theatre and Race.* Basingstoke: Palgrave Macmillan.

PART I

Race and Racism in Contemporary Theatre

CHAPTER 2

The American Theatrical Canon and the Struggle for Racial Equality in British Theatre

Jami Rogers

1 Introduction

A revival of Tennessee Williams' *Cat on a Hot Tin Roof* opened on Broadway in 2008, directed by Debbie Allen. According to the American Theater Wing, this was the fifth time the play was produced on Broadway and—crucially for this chapter—the first time it had been staged with an all-African-American cast. It transferred to London's West End in 2009 and was substantially re-cast using major black British actors—including Adrian Lester as Brick—while retaining at its core a significant African-American presence in its two leads (James Earl Jones and Phylicia Rashad), director and producer (Stephen Byrd). Although American drama has been a staple on the British stage, the London transfer of Allen's *Cat on a Hot Tin Roof* was—like its American counterpart—the first time the play had been staged with an all-black cast in Britain.

For both the British and American runs, Allen moved the action of the play forward from its original 1955 setting. She explained her choice in the London programme: 'There were no black people in 1955 playing in the Super Bowl, or the Sugar Bowl, or anybody's bowl. Lynchings still happened. Civil rights was burning across America. Moving the play forward doesn't affect anything beyond allowing us to take a fresh look.' Allen's production of *Cat on a Hot Tin Roof* was not simply adjusting the time frame of Williams' play to accommodate the realities of the African-American experience in the United States,

J. Rogers (✉)
University of Warwick, Coventry, UK

© The Author(s), under exclusive license to Springer Nature
Switzerland AG 2021
T. Morosetti, O. Okagbue (eds.), *The Palgrave Handbook of Theatre and Race*, https://doi.org/10.1007/978-3-030-43957-6_2

the production was also challenging the *status quo* along with deeply ingrained notions of ownership of American drama.

The American canon of modern classic plays—including Williams, Arthur Miller and Eugene O'Neill—largely remains the province of white performers on both sides of the Atlantic. Although there have been productions with diverse casting—an all-black *Guys and Dolls* on Broadway in 1976 with Robert Guillaume playing Nathan Detroit and Joseph Marcell playing Willy Loman in *Death of a Salesman* in 2001 at the Leicester Haymarket in English regional theatre, for example—Allen's *Cat* was the first production in recent memory to have made inroads into the colour barrier that remains stubbornly intact in both Britain and America.

The subtext that runs through the British arts press's engagement with *Cat*'s London transfer highlights these ingrained prejudices that form the basis of a western drama colour bar. Lucy Powell's feature in *The Times* on Allen's production highlights the ways in which people of colour continue to be marginalised. Powell injects herself into the narrative as a way of challenging the statements of director and cast throughout the feature. For example, granted access to Allen, Jones, Rashad and Lester, Powell first reports Debbie Allen's response to a question about the race of the actors—'totally incidental'—but then responds to Allen in her own voice: 'Really? Can the fact that the cast is black be totally incidental to the production? "What are you saying child," [Allen] asks, and suddenly, I forget.' Powell then doubles down on her line of questioning—at least as recounted in *The Times*—and challenges the production's ethos on the basis of America's racial history by mentioning Emmett Till, segregation and Big Daddy. With this line of questioning Powell posits a question that implies the ethnicity of the actors disqualifies them from playing Tennessee Williams, again on historical grounds:

> And surely Big Daddy made a white man's fortune, his cotton-plantation millions emanating from the back of black men's labour? 'Anybody who says that,' a beautifully beaming James Earl Jones interjects, in an inimitable basso profundo, 'is betraying their ignorance. Black families also made money, a lot of it, from black labour. That is not the play's problem, I'm afraid to say, it's yours.' He smiles gently. (*The Times*, 18 November 2009)

The author's—or the paper's—agenda was further displayed in the piece's attitude to the RADA-trained, Olivier-award winning classical actor Adrian Lester: 'Every interview I've ever done,' [Lester] says, burning with indignation, 'whether its *Hamlet* or *Henry V*, it's the same thing. "What's the idea? If you're playing the part, what does it mean?" You're asking us to justify changes that need no justification.'

The choice to describe Lester as 'burning with indignation' is a not-so-subtle attempt at disregarding the actor's argument by painting him as irrational or the stereotypical angry black man. This exchange segues into yet another of Powell's exterior monologues, challenging every black actor in the room: 'But hang on. *Hamlet* is not a realistic play. Isn't it important to ask? Williams was describing the wider deterioration of the "old South," including its race relations, at a very particular moment in time, through the story of the white Pollitt family' (*The Times*, 18 November 2009). Powell's juxtaposition of *Hamlet* with a description of 'the white Pollitt family' is an unwitting acknowledgement that, while decades of inclusion in Shakespeare for ethnic minority performers has been normalised, Allen's staging of *Cat* was de-stabilising the *status quo* that privileges white performers in American classics. Powell was instinctively reinforcing ingrained ideas of what it means to be black in Britain, as portrayed in the live and recorded arts.

In an industry fuelled by stereotypes, what recurs 'with depressing frequency' for black actors, as actor and playwright Nathaniel Martello-White puts it, are roles that reinforce negative stereotypes, such as drug dealers (*The Independent*, 24 October 2012). The actor Danny Lee Wynter also recalls that the casting breakdown for his first audition after he left LAMDA called for 'a volatile black council estate kid' (*The Guardian*, 7 July 2014). Bolstering the anecdotal evidence of Martello-White, Wynter and performers such as Lenny Henry and David Oyelowo is a 2016 British Film Institute study, which found evidence of stereotyping in the genres of films that black British actors are likely to be cast, including crime (BFI press release, 6 October 2016). A study commissioned by Equity's Race Equality Committee that monitored diversity on broadcast television during the calendar year 2018 also shows that in the eight years since Martello-White's comment, little has changed within the industry. The Equity study found multiple forms of discrimination within scripted television: ongoing stereotyping of African-Caribbeans as criminals and servants, while south Asians and Middle Easterners were frequently portrayed as terrorists; the almost total exclusion of east Asians from scripted television; and that only 8% of leading roles in scripted programming had been played by actors from African-Caribbean, south Asian, east Asian or Middle Eastern heritage (see Rogers 2020).

This confining of black and Asian talent within certain 'types' of roles—and, crucially, plays—also means the exclusion of minority performers within a wider context also frequently occurs. At an Act For Change Project event at the National Theatre (NT) in June 2015, actor Kobna Holdbrook-Smith observed in his on-stage forum with the NT's artistic director, Rufus Norris,

> Sometimes there are people that are resistant to this idea of casting diversely, casting blindly, working in a new way and recruiting in a new way. Why are we listening to them? We've had conversations in private, I've had conversations with other [Artistic Directors] who have said there are some directors who just won't see anybody—doing a Chekov, for example—who doesn't look northern European. (2 June 2015)

The end result of these documented examples is that non-white actors have been largely shut out of influential segments of the industry. As Adrian Lester noted prior to playing Brick in *Cat on a Hot Tin Roof*, '[Tennessee] Williams was one of those writers who hadn't been on my radar as an actor because the perception was that his work wasn't ever going to apply to me' (*Metro*, 26 November 2009). This chapter provides a broad overview of the practice of integrated casting in twenty-first-century Britain, within the microcosm of the casting of the American dramatic canon. It begins with the mechanisms of inclusion and exclusion before investigating the ways in which American drama has become more diverse since 2013. It is worth noting at the outset that although black British inclusion in the American canon has increased, the same cannot be said of south Asian or east Asian performers.

2   'MECHANISMS OF INCLUSION AND EXCLUSION'

Adrian Lester's impression that the plays of Tennessee Williams—and by extension other plays in the twentieth-century-American canon—were not open to him speaks volumes to the perceptions about ownership of that work in the wider British culture. A vast body of drama by white male authors has dominated western theatrical tradition since its inception. The stories that are told—and re-told with frequency—have persistently examined the experiences of white men, from Shakespeare through to the early twenty-first century. Buried at the heart of this undeniable fact is the cultural perception that the experiences of women and minorities are less appealing than those of men to the decision makers (almost predominantly white men) at the helm of the majority of British theatres. As Glenda Jackson observed in 2016 on the BBC Radio Four programme *Woman's Hour*, 'creative writers don't find women interesting. And I just find that utterly bewildering … it is astonishing that we are still deemed to be uninteresting' (16 December 2016). As great as the inequality is between men and women in contemporary theatre, compared to the ways in which ethnic minorities are viewed by the dominant white culture, however, being deemed 'uninteresting' is positively benign.

What emerged in the eighteenth century as a by-product of slavery were, as David Olusoga notes, 'stereotypes of Africans as disloyal, untrustworthy and innately immoral' (2016: 105). Along with these labels, people of African descent were also systematically dehumanised as part of a cultural project that sought the repression of the enslaved race. These stereotypes have devolved in the post-Victorian era into persistent images of people of colour as intellectually inferior, violent and, as Paul Gilroy observes, regarded through a prism of fear of 'the hidden threat of excessive fertility' (2002: 65). The historical memory of slavery—and the dubious labels of inferiority placed on enslaved Africans—has lingered in contemporary attitudes in Britain towards their descendants. These persistent stereotypes are repeated through a casting bias that has black actors auditioning for peripheral parts in film and television as drug dealers or pimps. That the writer Anthony Horowitz claimed the actor Idris Elba was 'too street' to be considered to play James Bond helps to underscore deeply ingrained prejudices against black men in twenty-first-century Britain (Horowitz later apologised for his comment) (*The Guardian*, 31 August 2015).

What makes these stereotypes difficult to dislodge is that contemporary attitudes towards non-white immigrants and their descendants are also bound up in an exclusionary vision of nationhood. Paul Gilroy notes that Britain's sense of self relies heavily on 'conceptions of national belonging and homogeneity which not only blur the distinction between "race" and nation', the latter of which is 'represented in terms which are simultaneously biological and cultural' (2002: 44). Enoch Powell was arguably the founder of Britain's contemporary obsession with immigration—and its wish to return to the mythological days in which it was claimed that no 'foreigner' was on British soil. Powell's use of warlike imagery—'swamped' (which was mimicked by Thatcher 20 years later), 'occupied', 'invasion'—made clear, in violent terminology, that immigrants were diluting the nation's sense of self.

As Paul Gilroy observes, 'Powell drew attention to the difference between the merely formal membership of the national community provided by its laws'—for which read the Nationality Acts—'and the more substantive membership of the national community which derives from the historic ties of language, custom and "race"' (2002: 46–47). Powell's framework for his populist ideas was couched in terms of the country's traditions—largely white, Anglo-Saxon, Protestant—that lay at the foundations of the British (or, more accurately, English) psyche, including cricket, the monarchy and an Empire that once ruled not just Britannia's waves but over peoples of various ethnicities who were conquered and, thus, inevitably deemed 'inferior' by the act of being ruled. As James Hampshire notes, 'British nationhood could not, [Powell] believed, incorporate a substantial non-white presence' (2018: 373). Immigration and nationality legislation reinforced ideas of nationhood in an attempt to place a check on the non-white immigration that occurred in the immediate post-Second World War era.

Paul Gilroy views societal discourses regarding non-white immigration as a 'new racism' that remains 'primarily concerned with mechanisms of inclusion and exclusion' (2002: 45). The mechanics of exclusion can be observed in Adrian Lester's initial belief that Tennessee Williams was not a playwright whose work he had expected to be open to him as an actor. For performers of colour striving to gain recognition—and jobs—in mainstream theatre the struggle to be considered equal occurs in three distinct stages: exclusion, defiance and partial inclusion. The exclusion of performers from minority backgrounds from the majority of roles has often been under the terms that actor Frank Cousins has described. As he recalled, 'Mainstream parts were never considered appropriate for ethnic actors, and if one put oneself forward you were told you were too black, the accent wasn't right or you were just "not suitable"' (King-Dorset 2014: 159). This phase in the development of integrated casting can be viewed as an initial stage in the trajectory in people of colour's gradual admittance into mainstream British theatre: exclusion.

With mainstream theatre practising exclusionary tactics, the reaction by minority British artists has been to create their own work. In what can be viewed as a second phase in their quest for parity within professional theatre, black and Asian artists founded their own theatre companies. While operating on a far from equal basis with their white counterparts, companies like Negro Theatre Workshop in the 1950s and Temba, Tara Arts and Tamasha in the 1970s, followed by Talawa in the 1980s were able to carve out their own space in the margins (see Chambers 2011; Igweonu 2015; Hingorani 2006). They each told stories rooted in their communities—stories that mainstream white theatres were slow to produce, let alone commission—so that their experiences were reflected back to them in the theatrical art form. The third stage is one of partial acceptance as the work of performers of colour is gradually incorporated into mainstream theatre. This progression can take the form of a company being invited to show their work in one of the country's leading theatre buildings, as with Tara Arts' *The Little Clay Cart*, which played at the National Theatre in the Cottesloe in 1991. What these three stages means for the American drama canon in Britain has been almost total exclusion until the twenty-first century, followed by acts of defiance such as Debbie Allen's production of *Cat on a Hot Tin Roof*. The final stage—where British theatre has been since 2013, before the pandemic shut the theatres—occurs when actors of colour are being cast more frequently in the traditionally white roles within the American canon.

These three stages are executed within the microcosm of each dramatic genre in terms of casting practices. The trajectory towards full inclusion follows these patterns that begin with the exclusion of minority performers from the plays at the pinnacle of British theatre from Shakespeare to Restoration comedy through to those authors that have shaped the modern canon, including American playwrights such as Miller, Williams and O'Neill. The American dramatic canon has been particularly difficult to break into for performers of colour, but since 2013—as we will see—there has been extraordinary progress in the diversity of British productions of American plays.

3   Breaking the Stereotypes

In analysing the casting of non-white performers in British stagings of American drama, a sample of 171 productions was assembled. Using a time frame from 2010 to 2018, directly after Debbie Allen's groundbreaking *Cat on a Hot Tin Roof*, the survey includes West End, off-West End, 'fringe' and regional theatres. The sample concentrates on straight drama for comparative purposes—with the exception of *Guys and Dolls* because of the importance of Talawa's 2017 production with an all-black cast. The full sample includes plays by 64 authors ranging from popular works by Williams, Miller and O'Neill to August Wilson, Lynn Nottage, David Henry Hwang and Bruce Norris as well as emergent American dramatic writers. In categorising the casting practices that are embedded in the sample, three broad categories are used to describe the inclusion (or exclusion) of minority ethnic performers: traditional casting, non-traditional casting and productions with no actors of colour involved. The latter category is self-explanatory but for clarity, 'traditional casting' here refers to roles that specify the ethnicity of the character—primarily African-American—while 'non-traditional' casting refers to parts that have been traditionally played by a white actor. The characters of Tituba in Arthur Miller's *The Crucible* or Troy Maxson in August Wilson's *Fences* are examples of traditional casting while Adrian Lester as Brick in Tennessee Williams' *Cat on a Hot Tin Roof* is an example of non-traditional casting, as defined for purposes of this chapter.

Taking the year 2010 as the starting point for this analysis, there were 24 major productions of American plays produced that year. These productions included revivals of such staples as *The Crucible, Death of a Salesman* and *The Glass Menagerie* alongside a revival of John Guare's *Six Degrees of Separation* and productions of plays by African-American playwrights Lorraine Hansberry, August Wilson and Lynn Nottage. The sample shows a clear split between casts that included performers of colour and those from which they were excluded. Only 1 production used non-traditional casting, while 14 productions—an overwhelming majority of the 2010 sample—cast only white actors; the remaining 8 cast people of colour in racially specific roles.

All-white casts dominated the American drama output of British theatre in 2010; when black British men and women were cast, the scripts specified their characters' ethnicity. In the year after the all-black *Cat on a Hot Tin Roof*, numerous examples of these parts could be found on the British stage in various portraits of America. This included roles such as the servant Tituba in Arthur Miller's *The Crucible* as well as Paul in John Guare's *Six Degrees of Separation*, in which the character impersonates the son of the African-American film star Sidney Poitier. Bruce Norris' *Clybourne Park*—which has been hailed as a 'sequel' to Hansberry's *A Raisin in the Sun*—also calls for two black performers to double as a couple in 1959 and their modern-day equivalent in 2009. In his play about American and British involvement in Afghanistan after 9/11, J. T. Rogers' *Blood and Gifts* included characters that were Pakistani or Afghan, for which British south Asian actors were cast. In all of these plays, the characters' ethnicity was on display either as servant (Tituba), to establish white characters' racist behaviour (*Six Degrees, Clybourne Park*) or to portray the local population of the Afghanistan and Pakistan as British and American power attempted to crush Al Qaeda (*Blood and Gifts*).

The other layer of complexity within these apparent opportunities for performers of colour is that arguably none of the minority characters in these plays are the central characters and the leading roles remain universally the white men: John Procter in *The Crucible*, Karl/Steve in *Clybourne Park* and James Warnock in *Blood and Gifts*. Even Guare's *Six Degrees* centres around the effect of Paul on the central white couple (who were billed as the leads for the Old Vic's 2010 production). As with the increasing presence in other genres—for example, in British Shakespearean theatre—a glass ceiling for performers of colour continues to prevent their breaking through into leading roles. It is the casting manifestation of Paul Gilroy's assertion that the 'locally-born descendants' of non-white immigrants were playing the 'role of the perpetual outsider' (2002: xxxiii–xxxiv).

Where actors of colour were not marginalised into playing—at best—secondary characters was within minority-led productions of plays by African-American playwrights. This is significant because these productions are the equivalent of the middle phase in the struggle for equality that occurs when artists of colour create their own opportunities. Michael Buffong, Indhu Rubasingham and David Lan directed Lorraine Hansberry's *A Raisin in the Sun*, Lynn Nottage's *Ruined* and August Wilson's *Joe Turner's Come and Gone*, respectively. Collectively these plays centre on the African-American—or, in the case of *Ruined*, the African—experience and their central characters are either African-American or African. This is a crucial difference between the roles that were written specifically as 'black' in dramas like *Six Degrees of Separation* and *Clybourne Park*, for example. Rather than being secondary—or even peripheral—characters, this set of plays—*Raisin*, *Ruined* and *Joe Turner's*—provided opportunities for black British actors to appear at the heart of these stories. The rarity of these opportunities can be illustrated in the fact that only 4 out of the 24 major productions of American drama staged in 2010—*Raisin*, *Ruined*, *Joe Turner's* and Debbie Allen's *Cat*—had actors from African-Caribbean heritage playing leading roles in productions of the American dramatic canon, as most casting practices have kept performers of colour excluded from its most prestigious roles.

This marginalisation of performers of colour in the American dramas staged in Britain in the twenty-first century is symptomatic of the way these professionals are treated within the industry as a whole. Rarely are artists of black or Asian heritage given the opportunity to play leading roles in the much-lauded pieces of the western dramatic canon, be it Willy Loman or Hamlet. That only eight performers of colour have played Hamlet—arguably the pinnacle of an actor's career—in professional productions of the play in Britain since 1930 says volumes about access to the classical canon. The lack of access to Hamlet is in direct contrast with the fact that performers of colour are more likely to play the best friend of the title character (Horatio), Laertes or Ophelia in productions of *Hamlet* than they are to play Hamlet (Rogers 2016). While the figures from the British Black and Asian Shakespeare Performance Database show increased participation for practitioners of colour, there are still structural inequalities that prevent them from playing the most important roles in the traditionally white canon, the very roles by which their white peers are judged. If systemic prejudice is apparent within classical theatre, the American drama genre in Britain remains far more exclusionary than their Shakespearean counterparts for performers of colour. In order to discuss some of the changes that have occurred since 2013, it will be useful to highlight previous attempts at inclusion that have taken place intermittently during previous decades.

One influential non-traditional casting in an American drama in Britain was that of Josette Simon as Maggie in Arthur Miller's *After the Fall*, directed by Michael Blakemore at the National Theatre in 1990. Miller's biographer, Christopher Bigsby, recounts that Blakemore went to Connecticut to meet with the playwright to propose that Maggie—a character based on Marilyn

Monroe—be played by Simon: 'The idea at once appealed to Miller' (Bigsby 2011: 395). Miller's views on integrated casting had evolved from having once refused a request from George C. Scott to have Willy Loman's neighbour in *Death of a Salesman* played by a black actor because, as Bigsby recounts, it 'made no sense, given the social reality of the period in which the work was set. On the other hand, he had seen the same play with an all-black cast and it had worked well.... He had come to feel that any ethnic casting was acceptable provided that it served the play' (Bigsby 2011: 395). The reviews of Blakemore's *After the Fall* were largely favourable, but Josette Simon was inevitably referred to as a 'black actress', starkly highlighting Britain's casual racism. Perhaps more remarkably, the inference that Simon was cast solely because she was black—not because of her talent—is amply illustrated by Charles Osborne's review: 'In an attempt to distance the character from Monroe, this production casts a black actress in the role' (*Daily Telegraph*, 22 June 1990).

Despite the clear boundaries that had been broken, Josette Simon's casting would remain an anomaly in British theatre's reproductions of America until the twenty-first century. There is no discernible reason why the casting of Simon—and of other black actors in the early 1980s and 1990s, cast in plays as varied as Norman Beaton in Pinter's *The Caretaker*, Clive Rowe in Rodgers and Hammerstein's *Carousel* and Paterson Joseph in George Farquhar's *The Recruiting Officer*—failed to materialise into a more inclusive theatre landscape in Britain. One factor was likely the mainstream theatre critics who are periodically vociferous in their criticism or support of the practice of what they frequently term 'colourblind' casting, their point of view seemingly dictated by the political leaning of their respective publications. These have ranged from kneejerk dismissiveness—as with Quentin Letts' review of the National Theatre's internationally popular adaptation of Michael Morpurgo's *War Horse* ('I'm afraid I was also irritated by the colour-blind casting. The Devon of 1914 is rendered a multicultural affair. Oh, spare us' [*Daily Mail*, 19 October 2007]) to reasoned argument.

These periodic 'debates' about integrated casting in the press have also created a false impression that equality for minority ethnic artists has been achieved. Although Nicholas Hytner—who had directed Josette Simon as Isabella in Shakespeare's *Measure for Measure*—opined in 1990, 'Actors like Josette Simon playing such parts are succeeding in making multiracial casting a non-issue', his optimism was premature (*New Statesman and Society*, 15 June 1990). In the intervening decades since Simon played Maggie in Miller's *After the Fall*, there have been few productions of the classic American drama canon that have engaged a performer of colour to play a traditionally white leading role.

More recent progress in the second decade of the twenty-first century, however, can potentially be measured through press reaction to a rapidly changing landscape in the arts. One example was Dominic Cavendish's review of Sarah Frankcom's 2016 production of Tennessee Williams' *A Streetcar Named Desire* at the Royal Exchange Theatre, Manchester, when the renewed backlash against diverse casting hit the American drama canon. Frankcom cast Sharon Duncan-Brewster as Stella Kowalski in the production, opposite the white actress Maxine Peake's Blanche DuBois. With reference to Duncan-Brewster's race—'black actress'—Cavendish noted that in Frankcom's production Stella and Blanche 'are evidently not "related"'. Go figure' (*Daily Telegraph*, 14 September 2016). This not-so-veiled objection to diverse casting is one example among many of the arts press's gatekeeping of traditionally white preserves in theatre.

Any advances in representation within the live and recorded arts—and the American drama canon—since 2010 should be viewed as part of the wider cultural context that has foregrounded issues of inequality. Much of Britain was revelling in its multicultural heritage in 2012 when the Summer Olympics were held in London. British multiculturalism was embedded at the heart of London's bid to host the Olympic games and Tony Blair referenced it when the bid was successful: 'London is an open, multi-racial, multi-religious, multi-cultural city and rather proud of it. People of all races and nationalities mix in with each other and mix in with each other well' (*The Guardian*, 6 July 2005). Most importantly, the fact that the Cultural Olympiad—an arts festival that was embedded in the London 2012 bid—reflected that same multiculturalism in many theatre productions staged under its umbrella. This included the Royal Shakespeare Company's revivals of *Julius Caesar* and *Much Ado about Nothing*, which featured, respectively, all-black and all-south Asian casts. Performers of colour playing the leading roles of the traditionally white classical canon in major venues was an exception that shone a spotlight in systemic inequalities within the industry.

A second catalyst for greater representation undoubtedly came when the actor Danny Lee Wynter noticed a trailer for the upcoming ITV drama season contained only white actors. That spurred him on to found the influential charity The Act For Change Project in 2014 (full disclosure: I am one of its Committee members), which has been one of the leading advocates for better representation within the live and recorded arts in Britain. The voices of Lenny Henry and David Oyelowo—among others—have also been heard in an ongoing campaign to improve representation both in front of the camera and behind it. In the wake of this collective activism, representation across the industry slowly began to change, including within the American drama canon.

Since 2010, Manchester's Royal Exchange Theatre has led the way in integrating the American drama canon in Britain, through both its own productions and its collaborations with Talawa Theatre Company. The theatre's artistic director, Sarah Frankcom, began with little-noticed castings in a production of Arthur Miller's *A View From the Bridge* in 2011, before the industry's recent diversity conversations began in earnest. In a play about immigration—in a country that has an often-troubled relationship with immigrants—Frankcom hired three performers of colour—Abas Eljanabi as Mr Lipari and Qas Hamid and Mohammad Aljarrah—to play 'submarines' and longshoremen; all three made their professional theatre debuts in the production. These are not central roles in Miller's play, but they are pivotal because at its core *A View From the Bridge* is about immigrants coming to the New World for a better life and the unwelcome reception that America gives them. In Miller's play, Mr. Lipari shelters the two unnamed 'submarines' which Eddie Carbone uses as cover to oust his wife's cousins, who had themselves arrived in New York illegally.

The contemporary parallels of Frankcom's non-traditional castings for *A View From the Bridge* were abundantly clear, particularly as the cast's own descriptions of their characters are 'immigrants' and 'refugees' (Royal Exchange, 'Journey': 2011). After the May 2010 general election, David Cameron's Conservative party—with a manifesto that included stricter immigration controls—was in coalition government with Nick Clegg's Liberal Democrats. The combination of the initiation of then-Home Secretary Theresa May's 'hostile environment' policy and the burgeoning rise of the far-right anti-immigration party UKIP created an atmosphere in which British citizens—let alone foreign immigrants—were demonised, as Qas Hamid's experiences prior to rehearsals illustrate: 'Even though I'm not a refugee—I was born and bred in Rochdale, which is just outside Manchester—because of the political stuff about refugees and the influx, I still get pulled into that because, I believe, of the colour of my skin' (Royal Exchange, 'Journey': 2011).

Frankcom's casting was not only making a political point about the discourse of the immigration debates since 2010. She allowed her actors the chance to breathe and express the roles through their own lived experiences. All three performers of colour had been involved in a community group—the World Wide Workshop—that supports refugees who have come to the United Kingdom through its creative activities, which Frankcom incorporated into *A View From the Bridge*. As Mohammad Aljarrah noted, '[Frankcom] gave us room … to talk in our own language, to discuss things in our own language' which he felt culminated in 'an extra touch for the play as a whole' (Royal Exchange, 'Journey'). Frankcom did not transport the play to Manchester in 2011—it was clearly still New York's waterfront with its, in Libby Purves' description, 'minimal set' by James Cotterill that 'suggests all we need: grinding, clanging dock sounds echo round a fire-escape, a family table and a leaking hydrant' (*The Times*, 25 May 2011). Yet, as Aljarrah noted, *A View From the Bridge* could easily have become hidebound in tradition because 'Arthur Miller when he wrote it, he said these "submarines," they are from Sicily, so he limited in a way many directors' (Royal Exchange, 'Journey': 2011). By not adhering visibly to Miller's Italian characters and instead using actors of Middle Eastern heritage, Frankcom's non-traditional casting meant that although the play was still set in New York, the production reflected the nation and time in which it was being played.

Within the sample compiled for this chapter, there were 69 major productions of American drama between 2010 and 2013. Out of those, 42 had no performers of colour while 24 plays were of plays that required at least 1 ethnic minority actor for a character whose ethnicity was specified as non-white. In terms of non-traditional casting in American drama, only 3 productions out of the 69 over that 4-year period used some kind of non-traditional casting: Frankcom's *A View from the Bridge*, David Mamet's *House of Games* at the Almeida Theatre, London and Talawa's co-production with the Royal Exchange of Arthur Miller's *All My Sons* with an all-black cast. That two of these three early forays into the non-traditional casting of American drama were staged at Frankcom's Exchange illustrates the regional theatre's importance to the development of diverse casting within this sub-genre of dramatic literature.

The Royal Exchange facilitated ownership of the American drama canon by artists of colour through its co-production with Talawa of Arthur Miller's *All My Sons* in 2013. Talawa Theatre Company was established in 1986 in order to provide opportunities for black actors they would not ordinarily have been allowed to play in mainstream theatre. One of the company's earliest productions was Oscar Wilde's *The Importance of Being Earnest* with a diverse cast that included Oscar James, Mona Hammond and Ben Thomas and a production of *Antony and Cleopatra* that starred Jeffery Kissoon and Doña Croll. Thirty years later, Talawa's then-newly appointed artistic director, Michael Buffong, continued the work of Talawa's founding mothers and provided a group of black actors the opportunity to work on Arthur Miller's *All My Sons*. Buffong had already directed an acclaimed production of Lorraine Hansberry's rarely revived *A Raisin in the Sun* at the Royal Exchange in 2010—with Ray Fearon, Jenny Jules and the African-American actress Starletta DuPois—when Sarah Frankcom asked if he would like to direct *All My Sons* for Talawa at the Royal Exchange. It was the first production of the play to be staged in Britain with an all-black cast.

Talawa's 2013 production of *All My Sons* was a watershed moment in the history of integrated casting of American drama in Britain. While Debbie Allen's production of *Cat on a Hot Tin Roof* was an American import, Buffong's revival of Miller's play was a home-grown affair. What is important about the Talawa *All My Sons* was that it showed unequivocally that by appearing in American stories, black British actors did not have to be pigeonholed solely into dramas depicting the African-American experience or as characters that were peripheral to the main white characters, such as *Clybourne Park* or *Six Degrees of Separation*. As Buffong puts it, 'Black culture is so intertwined with everything in British society and culture, it's not just about "black" issues now. It used to be "This is who we are, this is where we come from." Now, we are integral to society and the theatre landscape but we haven't disappeared in it' (Bourke, creativetourist.com, 6 September 2013). In staging *All My Sons*, Buffong and his performers, including Don Warrington and Doña Croll as Joe and Kate Keller, showed that they were indeed integral to the theatre landscape, claiming this American classic set in post-World War II Ohio as their own.

One of the results of the language of war becoming a primary part of the anti-immigration discourse—as Paul Gilroy points out—is a demonising <u>and</u> dehumanising of people of colour, arguably to the point that it robs them of their humanity in the eyes of the dominant white culture. Alfred Hickling cited

Buffong's programme note in his review of *All My Sons* to observe 'there is no justification for presenting the play with an all-black cast other than "to tell the story"' (*The Guardian*, 3 October 2013). That Hickling sought a justification for casting choices speaks volumes about the ownership of these American plays in Britain; the reviewer's comments were the product of embedded cultural ideas of exclusion of minorities from particular stories. The limited scope of the black stories told on the British stage is also lurking within Buffong's comments in the programme. The section is a duologue between Buffong and Don Warrington, touching on the universal themes of the play. As Warrington says, 'Everyone has family. We all come from somewhere. We all feel a loyalty to somewhere, and we all want to look after them to the best of our abilities. It doesn't matter who we are.' Yet Buffong goes on to note that he had been asked what the 'relevance' of putting on *All My Sons* with an all-black cast was: 'Someone said, "Is there going to be a racism angle?", as if being black onstage means you only exist in a "racism prism" and you couldn't possibly do a play about greed and social responsibility and corruption."' What the production allowed was for British actors of African-Caribbean backgrounds to be able to show their humanity in ways that were the equal of their white counterparts within Miller's complex family drama.

Since Talawa's 2013 production of *All My Sons* there has been a marked increase in the number of non-traditional castings in the American drama canon across the British theatrical landscape. Also notable is the growth in the number of substantial or leading roles cast using people of colour, including Dr. Gibbs in *Our Town* (Rhashan Stone, Almeida Theatre, 2014), Tom in *The Glass Menagerie* (Danny Lee Wynter at the Nuffield Southampton, 2015) and Stella Kowalski in *A Streetcar Named Desire* (Sharon Duncan-Brewster, Royal Exchange, 2016). Michael Buffong and Talawa provided another groundbreaking opportunity to performers of colour in 2017 when they staged the first all-black production of *Guys and Dolls* at the Royal Exchange, shifting the action to Harlem in the late 1930s with Ray Fearon as Nathan Detroit and Ashley Zhangazha as Sky Masterson. In a move that shows how her practice in integrated casting has evolved, Sarah Frankcom staged Arthur Miller's *Death of a Salesman* with Don Warrington as Willy Loman, Ashley Zhangazha and Buom Tihngang as Biff and Happy with white actress Maureen Beattie as Linda Loman. A multiracial family in an American play on the twenty-first-century British stage speaks volumes about the progress towards inclusivity and representation since Debbie Allen's *Cat on a Hot Tin Roof* debuted in London in 2010 as a casting anomaly.

4   'It's One of the Best Parts I've Played'

In November 2018 the Chichester Festival Theatre's revival of the Tony Kushner and Jeanine Tesori musical *Caroline, Or Change* made its way to London's West End. Set in the Jim Crow American South, the production's star was Sharon D. Clarke, playing the African-American maid of a Jewish family in 1960s. Clarke is a Londoner, but like a significant number of her Black British peers she has a theatrical CV that contains a significant number of American drama credits. Although Clarke feels the industry has become more diverse in the recent past, she also notes that 'ninety-five per cent of my work is American. I don't have a problem with that, it's treated me very well in my career, but I am a British Londoner, and I think that we have our own stories to tell' (Curtis, *Evening Standard*, 14 November 2018). Clarke's comment was made around the time of the West End début of Natasha Gordon's 2018 play for the National Theatre, *Nine Night*. Along with the transfer of Arinzé Kene's *Misty*, *Nine Night* exposed the lack of Black British writing in the commercial theatre of London's West End. British theatre's obsession with American drama—perhaps particularly with African-American drama—poses questions about whether the genre has been used as a theatrical displacement to staging Black British writing.

There has been a clear cultural preference of staging plays by white authors, rather than produce plays about the black experience that go beyond stereotypes. One of the aspects of American drama that appeals to Ashley Zhangazha is the canon's propensity to illustrate political points through the prism of a family drama: 'Certainly the ones I've been in are rooted around a family, rooted around family dynamics and the breakdown and the power struggles within family groups' (Zhangazha 2018). Within the American drama canon, there is also a poetic quality that Theo Ogundipe found in doing Eugene O'Neill's *Desire Under the Elms* at the Crucible Theatre, Sheffield in 2017. 'He's such a creative writer,' Ogundipe reflected, 'the way he's connecting sounds and syllables to emphasise what is being said and meant. Breaking down his text is like breaking down Shakespeare's text' (Ogundipe 2018). Zhangazha also referenced Shakespeare in discussion of his American drama work, finding that the plays have an epic style as well as being rooted in family dynamics. American playwrights 'wrote big, big plays and they wrote in a classical style' with roles that have 'a real character arc' and situations 'that force you to confront things about your lives and consider things about the people in your lives' (Zhangazha 2018).

These epic situations are simply not available in the peripheral characters specified as African-American in the canon, the parts—until recently—that Black British actors have been confined to, such as Tituba in *The Crucible* or even a pivotal character such as Tom Robinson in Harper Lee's *To Kill A Mockingbird*. Only when performers of colour are placed at the centre of the story—as Zhangazha was by Sarah Frankcom in *Death of a Salesman* as Biff Loman—are they able to function in equality with their white peers. Part of the push towards greater diversity and representation in the industry has been about breaking stereotypes, which recent innovations in the casting of American drama productions have begun to illuminate.

The effect on the audience when performers of colour are playing major roles is obviously similar to that of their white peers, if audiences look beyond stereotypes and preconceptions. While appearing in August Wilson's *Fences*,

Zhangazha recalls, 'everywhere we went on the tour, it was getting this amazing response from people going "Troy is my dad" "What's happening to Corey is what's happening to me, I didn't feel I had a voice, I wasn't able to speak out to my dad, I felt oppressed by my dad." With Rose, who Tanya Moodie played, so many women recognised themselves in that character' (Zhangazha 2018).

The humanity and understanding that Zhangazha brought to Arthur Miller's character Biff in *Death of a Salesman* was vibrantly articulated as the actor discussed his work.

> At the beginning of the play, he's 34. He had so much promise and hope in his youth and something happened at that time that shattered his world. I think he's a lost man at the beginning of the play. I mean, it's not the only reason why things didn't work out, there were things within himself, but that situation that he saw his father in with a woman in a hotel, coupled with this kind of hot air that Willy passes on to Biff, this idea about being well-liked and it wasn't enough about hard work and more about if you're confident and you're in great shape, your life will be fine. He has a line, "I'm mixed up very bad" and he says he's lost—I think those are the two key things about him at the beginning of the play. But in the great journey he goes on, he probably is the only character at the end of the play who truly knows who he is. (Zhangazha 2018)

For Zhangazha, playing in American drama was 'incredibly rewarding' and Biff Loman is 'one of the best parts I've played' (Zhangazha 2018). Unlike Adrian Lester's initial perception of the American drama canon as work that 'wasn't ever going to apply to me' (*Metro*, 26 November 2009), the emerging generation of young Black British actors like Zhangazha have been given the opportunity to explore its major roles in theatre in the twenty-first century.

While Black British actors have begun to make their mark on the American drama canon in Britain, it is still rare to see a south Asian or east Asian performer in plays by American authors. Of the 176 productions in my sample, only 8 were by playwrights from backgrounds other than white or African-American. One of those eight was a production of David Henry Hwang's *Yellow Face*, which starred and was co-produced by Kevin Shen in 2013. The play is a semi-autobiographical trip through the minefield of American racial politics, centring on three episodes from the life of the lead character, an Asian-American playwright known by his initials DHH: Jonathan Pryce's controversial appearance as an Asian character in the musical *Miss Saigon*, DHH's mistakenly casting of a white actor to play an Asian part and DHH's father's involvement in a campaign finance scandal that resulted in xenophobic anti-Chinese hysteria.

Yellow Face had its British debut largely because Shen, as a performer from an under-represented group, was following in the footsteps of innumerable performers of colour in creating his own opportunities in British theatre. As Shen recounts, one of the catalysts that led to staging Hwang's play was an incident when as he was 'walking down the street and I saw a poster of a show at one of the big theatres in London, which had an Asian character in it and the poster just looked like it was a white girl in yellow face. So I went to the box office and said, "Is that a white woman playing an Asian part?"' (Shen 2018). The answer was affirmative and led to Shen pursuing and being granted the rights for *Yellow Face*.

After many rejections from a number of theatres that said it was 'too American' or 'too esoteric' or 'no one's going to come to see this Asian play' (Shen 2018), it was mounted at the newly opened Park Theatre in the Finsbury Park area of north London. The serendipity of *The Orphan of Zhao* controversy erupting at the Royal Shakespeare Company also undoubtedly played a part in raising awareness about the lack of east Asian representation on the British stage (see Thorpe 2014). The protests from the east Asian community that a Chinese classic was being performed by a predominantly white cast was a pivotal moment for British east Asians, but any breakthrough in American drama has yet to materialise.

5   Conclusions

While there has obviously been progress in terms of opening up the American drama canon for Black British actors, east Asian and south Asian performers have remained excluded in productions of the plays of Miller, Williams and O'Neill. This is not just limited to the American drama canon and, as Shen points out, 'Even off the back of *Yellow Face*, the West End run of Lucy Kirkwood's *Chimerica* and the Royal Shakespeare Company, I go in [to audition] for almost no non-race specific roles' (Shen 2018). While black actors are clearly being considered—albeit not universally—to play parts traditionally played by white actors, east Asian performers are still seen as more of a 'risk'. As Shen observes, 'We fall very low on the racial hierarchy and it's easier to tick the diversity box when there's higher visibility. From a casting perspective, there's more familiarity because you see more black actors' in both television and on stage (Shen 2018).

For east Asian actors, the universality of the family situations in the classic American drama canon currently remains out of reach, even as their African-Caribbean counterparts continued to be included in 2019. The Young Vic production of *Death of a Salesman*, which starred the African-American Wendell Pierce alongside Sharon D. Clarke, had an African-Caribbean family at its centre was arguably the most prominent example of this trend. With the coronavirus pandemic wreaking havoc on the industry, it remains to be seen whether British theatre will continue to advance towards greater equality for its performers from minority backgrounds. As seen by members of the industry, the danger is that white decision makers will rely on white stars within a resurgent white canon out of perceived box office necessity. The leaders of the community wrote an open letter to Culture Secretary Oliver Dowden in May 2020, stressing the danger to the sector that has 'seen an explosion of world-leading

Black, Asian and ethnically diverse artists transforming major UK theatrical organisations…. We are a great British success story, and will be essential to the arts returning at full strength and playing its part in our nation's recovery.' Whether the call has been heeded and American drama and other genres continue on the road to full integration will only be known long after this volume has been published.

References

Bigsby, Christopher. 2011. *Arthur Miller, 1962–2005.* London: Weidenfeld & Nicholson.

Chambers, Colin. 2011. *Black and Asian Theatre in Britain: A History.* London and New York: Routledge.

Gilroy, Paul. 2002. *There Ain't No Black in the Union Jack.* Reprint. Abingdon: Routledge Classics.

Hampshire, James. 2018. The Measure of a Nation. *The Political Quarterly,* Vol. 89, no. 3 (July–September).

Hingorani, Dominic. 2006. Tara Arts and Tamasha: Producing Asian Performance— Two Approaches. In *Alternatives within the Mainstream: British Black and Asian Theatres,* ed. Dimple Godiwala. Newcastle: Cambridge Scholars Press.

Igweonu, Kene. 2015. Talawa. In *British Theatre Companies, 1980–1994,* ed. Graham Saunders. London: Bloomsbury.

King-Dorset, Rodreguez. 2014. *Black British Theatre Pioneers: Yvonne Brewster and the First Generation of Actors, Playwrights and Other Practitioners.* Jefferson, NC: McFarland & Company.

Ogundipe, Theo. 2018. Interview with Author. 17 November.

Olusoga, David. 2016. *Black and British: A Forgotten History.* London: Macmillan.

Rogers, Jami, ed. 2016. *British Black and Asian Shakespeare Performance Database.* bbashakespeare.warwick.ac.uk.

———. 2020. *Diversity in Broadcast Peak Scripted Television, 2018.* London: Equity.

Royal Exchange Theatre, Manchester. 2011. Journey to the *Bridge.* 24 May. https://youtu.be/fwe_eO1ZQeU.

Shen, Kevin. 2018. Interview with Author. 15 October.

Thorpe, Ashley. 2014. Casting Matters: Colour Trouble in the RSC's *The Orphan of Zhao.* Contemporary Theatre Review, Vol. 24, No. 4.

Zhangazha, Ashley. 2018. Interview with Author. 19 October.

CHAPTER 3

Racialisation and Contemporary German Theatre

Priscilla Layne and Lizzie Stewart

1 Introduction

In the mid-to-late twentieth century, plays and directing practices in both East and West Germany became known internationally as some of the most politically and aesthetically radical work on the contemporary stage. Much of the impulse for that radicalism came from the desire to break with the social, political, intellectual and artistic legacies of the recent National Socialist past—a thoroughly racialised regime. Curiously, at the same time, the very word 'race' and the narratives, bodies and artistic practices of racialised citizens and residents of both East and West Germany tended to be absent from the countries' stages.[1] And when racial marginalisation was addressed by white German directors, they commonly employed white actors in what Katrin Sieg (2002) terms *ethnic drag*. Such directorial decisions were often accompanied by theoretical and aesthetic justifications, but nevertheless masked racist operations in German theatre at the institutional level. Following activist engagement with primarily anglophone discourses on race, and changes to state funding policies, the period following unification and particularly the first two decades of the twenty-first century have been marked, in contrast, by high-profile debate around

P. Layne
University of North Carolina at Chapel Hill, Chapel Hill, NC, USA
e-mail: playne@email.unc.edu

L. Stewart (✉)
King's College London, London, UK
e-mail: elizabeth.stewart@kcl.ac.uk

© The Author(s), under exclusive license to Springer Nature
Switzerland AG 2021
T. Morosetti, O. Okagbue (eds.), *The Palgrave Handbook of Theatre and Race*, https://doi.org/10.1007/978-3-030-43957-6_3

questions of race and casting in Germany, the use of blackface, and access to the material resources and cultural capital of the German theatrical establishment. This chapter therefore asks what happens if we explore recent German theatrical history and its legacies for contemporary theatrical production by placing questions of race, representation and racialised structures at the centre rather than the margin of our perspective.

While this chapter focuses on the post-unification period, and more space will be dedicated to the rapid developments from 2000 on, we begin with a briefer overview of post-war engagements with race and theatre in West Germany as a means of setting the scene for the interventions that follow. The relationship to race in the theatre of East Germany has been the subject of less research to date, and so we are unfortunately able to go into less detail there. It is important to note though that discourses of Soviet international solidarity and brotherhood shaped the history of migration to the German Democratic Republic (GDR) in very different ways to that of the Federal Republic of Germany (FRG) both in terms of the countries with which labour recruitment arrangements were made (these included Poland, Tanzania, Vietnam, Mozambique), and the politics of asylum and immigration (Göktürk et al. 2007, 67–69). Ideological differences, combined with the different ways in which this influenced the demographics of the GDR, also led to differences in the construction of race there. As Loren Kruger explains, the GDR state claimed 'to *see through race* to the socialist brotherhood beneath the skin' (2004, 290; emphasis in original). One example of how race entered the theatrical landscape in the GDR was through performances of African American plays, which were popular due to their focus on the experience of minorities in the USA who suffered from capitalist exploitation and racism, which was thought to be a by-product thereof (cf. Haas 2011). It was common practice in such productions for white actors to perform Black roles in blackface. At the same time, the construction of West Germany as the sole inheritor of the fascist past and thus the only part of the divided Germany with a need to undergo *Vergangenheitsbewältigung* (coming to terms with the past) led to the GDR's own omissions when it came to racialisation within its own borders. This took the form of 'de facto segregation of people described officially as 'migrants' from the local population and long-standing (if long-repressed) popular hostility to *Ausländer* [foreigners]' (Kruger 2004, 291). It is perhaps not surprising then that today it is both in the regions and the theatres of the former West that we primarily see the engagement with racialised representations and structures which this chapter intends to outline and explore.

The ambivalent legacy of *Verfremdung*, which is commonly translated as 'alienation' but more accurately as 'estrangement' (cf. Silbermann et al. 2015, 4–5), will provide the through thread for this exploration. *Verfremdung*, as an anti-naturalistic practice emanating from the influential work of Bertolt Brecht, has been a valuable tool for many theatre practitioners in the Federal Republic of Germany and beyond who are interested in exposing race as construct. In the German context, however, its prevalence has arguably also worked against the casting of actors of Colour where racialised characters are included on stage; a move that also reflects white German directors' failure to imagine or attempt to appeal to a non-white audience. As will be seen, the term is also invoked in, for example, discussions and defences of blackface in work by white directors and playwrights in Germany both in the 1980s (Sieg 2002, 1–13) and the 2000s (Sieg 2015). This shows significant differences in the understanding of race and representation in the German mainstream theatre than in theatres like the Ballhaus Naunynstraße, a theatre which opened in 2008 and which has intentionally made space for actors, directors and dramaturgs of Colour. Notably, the Ballhaus is not a state theatre (although it has received state funding) and therefore belongs to the *freie Szene* in which experimentation has been more prevalent since the 1960s.[2] However, the impact of this intervention means that such work is now also finding more space within the state-subsidised theatre scene as well, with the Maxim Gorki under the directorship of Shermin Langhoff in Berlin, serving as a prime example here. The chapter will also draw attention to the ways in which theatre practitioners of Colour work to disrupt, call attention to or work beyond the dominant performance legacies of Brecht and his artistic heirs. While Nurkan Erpulat and Jens Hillje's *Verrücktes Blut* (*Crazy Blood*) use the *Verfremdungseffekt* to draw attention not only to legacies of racial thought in the German Enlightenment but also to structural exclusion within the theatrical sphere, contemporary playwrights such as Olivia Wenzel turn to Afrofuturist performance techniques to reimagine modes of representation on the contemporary German stage and the worlds in which such stages might exist.

2   DEFINING TERMS: (NOT) TALKING ABOUT RACE IN THE AFTERMATH OF THE RACIAL STATE

Discussing race and racialisation in the German context, in the theatre as in other spheres, can be difficult simply on a linguistic level. Writing under the headline 'Suddenly, it's OK to be German and to talk about race' in the British newspaper *The Guardian* in September 2019, Mithu Sanyal explains the issue with the most direct translation of the term race into German, 'Rasse':

> When I was growing up there was no racism in Germany. In the 1980s every child learned at school that race was a construct that fascists had used to justify segregating and killing people. So if race didn't exist, it naturally followed that racism didn't exist either. If you wanted to talk about it people looked at you as if you were the Nazi.

The vocabulary to have the conversation is often missing, the very word 'Rasse' having been expunged as part of the denazification process in a manner which also seemed to expunge a consideration of the ways in which racialisation might continue or develop differently outwith a Nationalist Socialist ideology. This can create some odd distortions. As Sanyal notes, the

English-language term 'PoC' or 'People of Colour' is currently being adopted untranslated today to talk about racialised individuals, an Anglicism that seems to signal (whether as virtue or criticism) the discourse on race as an imported one from the Anglophone sphere.[3] Alternatively where German-language equivalents that avoid the re-use of national socialist language are sought, these can function to uncouple the individual's experience from the structural dimension of racism: thus Reni Eddo-Lodge's 2017 successful debut book on race, *Why I'm No Longer Talking to White People About Race* becomes, in German translation, *Warum ich nicht länger mit Weißen über Hautfarbe spreche* (Why I'm no longer talking to White People about Skin Colour; 2019), somewhat neutralising the political thrust of the original-language title. Similarly, in the theatrical sphere, Katrin Sieg suggests that an 'absence of language about or memory of racial masquerade in Germany points to the insufficient integration of past experiences into a postwar national consensus' (Sieg 2002, 8). In the immediate post-war period, we see, for example, cases of structural and staff continuity with the theatre practice of the racialised state of the Third Reich rather than a break with this. Theatres were included in West Germany's plan for reconstructing the country, but 'theatre in West Germany in the 1950s and 1960s was not in good shape' (Barnett 2005, 13–14). Gustaf Gründgens, the renowned stage actor, who had worked as an artistic director in Nazi Germany, and on whose career Klaus Mann's novel *Mephisto* (1936) is based, became the Vice President of Der Deutsche Bühnenverein, the leading German theatrical body of the day, in 1947. In this role, he 'set out a conservative agenda [...] to stage "productions which were true to the text"' (ibid). This resulted in what theatre critic Günther Rühle deemed a decade 'cleansed of politics, suffused with poetry' (Rühle, as cited in Barnett 2005, 15): theatre as escapism rather than space of engagement with the recent past, and the racial politics of that time in particular.

Indeed, what Sieg terms 'the detachment of a critique of fascism from a critique of race' became predominant in the social and political post-war German sphere (2002, 64). Perhaps counterintuitively, this detachment was also present even in the theatrical work of many of those who had fled National Socialism and who were now, along with their plays and theatrical practices, making their way back to the German-speaking lands. Bertolt Brecht, whose development of the *V-effekt* has been influential in many theatrical deconstructions of racialisation both in and beyond the German-speaking sphere, is a key example here.

A *Verfremdungseffekt* is a theatrical technique designed to 'make strange' the familiar and accepted, producing a new way of looking which is intended to disrupt common sense understandings of the relations structuring society and thus enable political critique or even intervention. While a powerful tool when subsequently turned to by later practitioners beyond Germany to address the role of racialisation in structuring societies (cf. Gaines 2017, 35), interestingly this was not the use which Brecht himself predominantly put it to, either following the National Socialist seizure of power in 1933, which led to his exile, or on his own return to the German context, specifically East Germany in 1947. A play such as *Furcht und Elend des Dritten Reiches* (*Fear and Misery of the Third Reich*, 1938)—or to give it its American title, which further stresses the role of race in National Socialist thought *The Private Life of the Master Race*—for example, might feature the character of a Jewish wife. However, the use of *V-effekte* there functions primarily to reveal National Socialist rule as characterised by the exploitation and oppression of the German working class (as opposed to as the realisation of that class's interest), rather than to expose and critique the physiological ways of viewing and marking Jewishness which were used to justify the targeting of a particular racialised group.

This is not to say that Brecht was unaware of anti-Semitism or of other forms of racialisation. Indeed Brecht did actively engage in racial discrimination in some of his early writings as a teenager (see Parker 2014, 152–53). John Fuegi thus brands Brecht quite simply a racist, although the picture painted in Parker is arguably rather of an individual from the centre of a racist environment in a process of unlearning these values in more or less successful ways at different points in his life and work. This part of his intellectual and political development may also be indebted to his personal circle. His wife, the Austrian actress Helene Weigel, and several of his close intellectual and artistic collaborators such as Walter Benjamin and Kurt Weill, for example, were Jewish and forced to flee persecution under the National Socialists. In a note to *Fear and Misery*, Brecht sets out his understanding of the dynamic of anti-Semitism in his own words:

> people find the persecution of the Jews, for instance, so exasperating, because it seems such an 'unnecessary' excess. They regard it as something extraneous, irrelevant to the business at hand. In their view pogroms are not essential to the conquest of markets and raw materials, and accordingly can be dispensed with. / They fail to understand that barbarism in Germany is a consequence of class conflicts, and so they cannot grasp the Fascist principle which demands that class conflicts be converted into race conflicts. (Brecht 2001a, 324; also quoted in Cronan 2017, 62)

On a theoretical level, his work at this time locates fascism as an extension of capitalism and engages with it on those terms. This conversion of class to race conflict is one which Brecht responds to by taking the focus of his artistic interventions in the theatre back to class, viewing this as the key thread to pull in unravelling the whole dynamic. Following Brecht's logic, in theory this should also unravel racialisation.

In some of Brecht's work we can see attempts to make this function. One interesting example is his play *Die Rundköpfe und die Spitzköpfe* (*The Round Heads and Pointed Heads*) written together with Margarete Steffin, Emil Burri, Elisabeth Hauptmann and Hanns Eisler between 1931 and 1938.[4] In this piece, set in the fictional country of Yahoo, economic problems have led to social unrest and dissatisfaction with the ruling class: a revolution led by the peasant workers looms. To redirect this dissatisfaction the Viceroy and Privy Councillor use physiological differences in head-shape present within the population of Yahoo to create a scapegoat population: a group who can be blamed, and punished, for the country's problems. 'The man's discovered that Yahoo has two / Quite separate races, living side by side, [...] / One race has rounded heads, the others pointed, / And each has a corresponding soul' (Brecht 2001b, 13). Following this 'discovery', or invention of a racial difference, those with the pointed heads are then dubbed the 'Ziks' and become the object of persecution by those with the rounded heads, dubbed the 'Zaks'. As Tod Cronan highlights, the instrumentalisation of physiological difference in the interests of a ruling class which Brecht and his collaborators saw at work in the Third Reich is made strange and thus newly available for criticism via abstraction into a parable setting, and, in the 1936 Copenhagen production, via the use of exaggerated prosthetics creating the titular head shapes (Cronan 2017, 64). The aim was 'to alienate an empathetically-oriented—that is, historical, emotional, and nonbiological—category like race' but also 'to redirect attention to what is obscured by it, class' (Cronan 2017, 66). While this redirection of attention has been subject to much criticism, Cronan argues that engagement with this play also reveals that 'Brecht formulated the notion of *Verfremdung*—his core aesthetic technique—in light of this analysis of race' (ibid). This connection between the practice of *Verfremdung* and an analysis of race was continued in Brecht's role in the casting of African American actors in whiteface in American productions of both *The Private Life of the Master Race* in 1945 and *The Duchess of Malfi* in 1946 (cf. Calico 2008, 83). In the case of *The Private Life*, Joy Calico explains that the African American actor, Maurice Ellis, was made-up as follows:

> sparingly and deliberately, so that his natural skin Colour was equally apparent, and he wore that makeup alongside other (white) actors who were similarly conspicuously made up. In other words, Ellis's narrator was decidedly not passing [...] Whiteface calls even more attention to the presence of the original Colour underneath [...] and to the racism that necessitated its concealment in the first place. (2008, 85)

Here we see an early, and rare, example of *Verfremdung* actively used to challenge practices of viewing and employment within the theatre industry, where such cross-casting was considered a radical move—and we might say therefore also valuable to Brecht's own reputation—in a still segregated America. As Joy Calico's work on Brecht's period in American Exile highlights, while Brecht engaged little with the local Black population during his time in LA, he did see potential for both his *Verfremdungseffekt* and his plays to be useful tools for African American theatre practitioners, as well as for those practitioners to further reveal relations between race and class.[5]

While attention to racial discrimination within the class politics of a diverse population has a significant if not always fully worked-through role to play in

Brecht's political and theatrical development, when it comes to the representation of figures and spaces which form part of the European colonial imagination of the world beyond European and American borders Brecht's engagement with race becomes somewhat different. Katrin Sieg, for example, suggests that more imperial 'racial presumptions haunted Brecht's writing in ways he might not have understood himself', analysing his famous 1936 essay '*Verfremdung* effects in Chinese Acting' (Sieg 2002, 16). There she argues, we see traces of Orientalism in the inscrutability attributed to the Chinese actor and the ways in which 'the Chinese performer is linked with conjuring, magic, primitivism, and nature. In contrast, the Western critical spectator is associated with science and knowledge.' She continues: 'The Brechtian spectator is thus firmly ensconced in the orientalist dichotomy of domination that empowers the Western subject with its colonial and racist underpinnings' (2008, 61). We also see slippage here between the Chinese actor, Mei Lan-fang, who Brecht saw perform on a visit to Moscow, as master of estrangement (artistic technique) and the Chinese actor as embodiment of otherness which makes his performance strange to Brecht. In this 1936 essay Brecht thus stated: 'When you see the Chinese acting it is at first very hard to discount the feeling of strangeness that they present in us as *Europeans*' (Brecht 2015, 181). This slippage is also evident in the use of race in relation to estrangement within earlier plays such as *Im Dickicht der Städte* (*In the Jungle of Cities*, 1921– 24) where the character of Kragler, a German figure, is described as black-skinned and 'African' in order to signal this soldier's role as violent disruptor of the society he returns to after fighting in WWI. This is a slippage which might also raise questions about the engagement of African American actors in the US productions discussed above. Here we might say racialised difference *serves Verfremdung*, rather than *Verfremdung* serving to unpack or explode racialisation.

A certain ambivalence in this regard can be traced throughout Brecht's dramaturgical engagement with China, an engagement Antony Tatlow explores in detail. On the one hand this forms part of a lengthy study of Chinese dramatists and philosophers on Brecht's part. On the other, in many instances where Chinese characters and settings are made use of, this is simply '"Chinese" exotica' (Tatlow 1977, 256). In plays such as *Im Dickicht der Städte* (*In the Jungle of Cities*, written between 1921 and 1924), Chinese characters are 'simply a means of making strange human behaviour' (Tatlow 1977, 260), while the setting of *Die Maßnahme* (translated as both *The Measures Taken* and *The Decision*, 1930), in China, despite links between Brecht's own circle and the Chinese communist party, mainly functions to create an 'alienating, parabolic action' (261). In Brecht's probably best-known 'Chinese' play, *Der gute Mensch von Sezuan* (*The Good Person of Szechwan*, 1938–41) Chiann Karen Tsui argues that:

> Brecht appears to wrestle with keeping Chinese elements at bay, yet still within arm's reach, effectively formulating a dialectic between maintaining Chinese specificity and diminishing it. His journal entry illustrates how much Brecht gave

> thought to establishing a balanced stage setting for *Der gute Mensch* that was neither authentically nor stereotypically Chinese; that is, to creating a plausibly real yet still imaginary China. (2015, 355)

Thus, Brecht's engagement with the 'other', in the post-war period, following his exile in the USA, shows continuities with how avant-garde artists in the interwar period, including Brecht, embraced foreign cultures. Chinese culture and China were useful for him, as far as he could employ them as signifiers to tell a story about Germans, but he was not actually interested in conveying anything true about China nor was he interested in creating authentic representation of Chinese people or Chinese culture. In Tatlow's words, 'it [China] offered a convenient, because remote and suggestive, source of images and symbols' (1977, 6).

3   THE 1960s–1980s: RACE AND *VERFREMDUNG* AFTER BRECHT

This kind of distanced interest in 'the other' would be challenged, however, as in the late 1950s onwards, guest workers and contract labourers would travel to both Germanies, raising issues of cultural difference for white Germans. In 1961, when the Berlin Wall was erected around West Berlin and along East Germany's border to the West, the wall cut off East German labourers who had previously commuted to the West and seasonal labourers who had previously come from countries such as Poland. This exacerbated an already struggling labour market due to the loss of potential male labourers who had perished during the war, but also because Germans were increasingly moving out of blue-collar jobs and into white-collar ones. Thus, the country was faced with the challenge of finding manual labourers who could help fuel an economy reignited by the Marshall Plan, aid given to Germany by the USA in 1947. In the 1960s, West Germany began inviting contract workers from Southern Europe to work in Germany for a brief period of time. In contrast to post-war labour migration to France and the UK from former colonies, workers arriving to West Germany under such labour recruitment agreements usually did not already speak any German. They tended to be segregated from Germans either because they were housed nearby the factories where they were employed or because Germans did not want to rent to them. The majority of these guest workers would go to West Germany, where, simultaneously, a challenge to the status quo of the theatre was brewing and would come by way of young artists who were both influenced by pre-war artists whose practices had been interrupted by the Third Reich, such as Brecht, but also culturally more oriented towards Anglo-American counterculture and sympathetic to the postcolonial struggles of so-called Third World countries like in Vietnam. One such artist was Rainer Werner Fassbinder who, in the 1960s, found an opportunity to experiment with a new kind of theatre that would then become a spring board to his career as a film director.

3 RACIALISATION AND CONTEMPORARY GERMAN THEATRE   47

Fassbinder's history in the theatre begins with the *action-theatre* in Munich, which began first as an *action-cinema* ran by Horst Söhnlein and Ursula Strätz who took over the conservative National-Kino (national-cinema) in 1967. Söhnlein and Strätz quickly realised the cinema would be too expensive to fund and therefore decided to convert the space into a theatre, performing experimental pieces which had become a trend among *Kellertheater* (basement theatres) and other theatres operating independently of state theatres. When Söhnlein was hospitalised for injuries that incurred during an accident, Strätz hired Wilhelm Rabenhauer (Peer Raben) to be the director. Raben jumped at the opportunity and chose to stage a performance of Brecht's *Antigone*—which at the time was being performed throughout Europe by *The Living Theatre* (on the Living Theatre see Boswell 2013). Raben decided not to stick to the text but rather depended on actors' recollections of the text. This is how Fassbinder became involved. Marite Greisil, an actress whom Fassbinder had met at the Fridl-Leonhard acting school, introduced Raben to the Action-Theater. She had a role in Raben's production of *Antigone*, which she invited Fassbinder to view. Fassbinder was fascinated by the production and returned several more times 'and was asked to stand in for one of the actors...who had accidentally injured himself' (Barnett 2005, 32). This would be Fassbinder's opportunity to gain more influence in the theatre, first by becoming a full member of the group, then persuading them to stop hiring hippies and instead engage serious actors and finally directing plays. Barnett explains, '[t]he development into a more Fassbinder-dominated theatre was marked by a small production that only featured members sympathetic to Fassbinder', which was *Hands Up, Heiliger Johannes* in 1967 (ibid, 37).

One of the plays Fassbinder would write and direct at the Action-Theatre was *Katzelmacher*, a dramatisation of how the young inhabitants of a Munich suburb react when a Greek guest worker moves into their neighbourhood. As would become a trademark of Fassbinder's films, the play addresses an important sociohistorical phenomenon that was key to the landscape of post-war Germany: the arrival of guest workers from the 1950s through the 1970s from Southern and Southeastern European countries like Greece, Italy, Spain, Portugal, Turkey and Yugoslavia. West Germany established its first guest worker agreement with Greece in 1960. In the initial years, German politicians celebrated the arrival of these workers because they were meant to help the economy. And as implied in the name 'guest worker', Germans expected they would eventually return to their home countries. But tensions arose from the German side over a variety of issues, among them German prejudice against Southern Europeans which is reflected in the 1961 essay 'The Integration of the Southern Labor Force and its Specific Adaptation Problems' (Maturi 2007). Germans viewed Southerners as lazy, hot-tempered, overly sensual and dirty. And as is frequently the case when it comes to racism, a lot of German anxieties revolved around the fear that guest workers would not only take jobs from German men, but also win over German women.

One sees this tension in the play; everyone believes that Elizabeth, the white German woman who is earning money from renting the Greek guest worker Jorgos a room, charging him for meals and paying him less than Germans, is just sex-crazed and sleeping with him. The group constantly gossips about her bad moral character. Helga says Jorgos has 'come over here to Elisabeth's. I always said she was man-crazy' (Fassbinder 1985, 79). German men, like Paul, become resentful and defensive: 'Because we're not good enough I guess' (ibid). In the end, now that the group's dynamic has been disturbed by this foreign presence, it can only be made whole again through collective expulsion through violence (the men beat up Jorgos) and collective prosperity through economic exploitation—everyone can agree that Elizabeth's idea of exploiting guest workers to keep more money in Germany is a good idea. In addition to the xenophobia, one also senses tensions left over from the post-war period, resentment towards German refugees who fled from the East. 'There are so many bums around here, refugees left over, and all sorts of others' (ibid).

The 'dedication to antiracism' we see in plays such as Fassbinder's can be considered 'a rare endeavour that sets them apart from the overall neglect, marginalization, and subsumption of "race" in diverse antifascist discourses' in both Germanies (Sieg 2002, 157). At the same time though, to some extent we see not only a reworking of Brechtian theatrical technique here, but also of his treatment of the 'Chinese other' as projection screen, this time, as Sieg puts it, 'the other as a blank screen, onto which a German community projects its fears and desires' (2002, 25).[6] The theatrical techniques at work here, including that of Brechtian *Verfremdung*, function to 'ventriloquize this ostensibly speechless, subaltern subject in order to further their political agendas' but are not 'primarily oriented toward changing interracial relations' (ibid), and, with characters like Jorgos being played by Fassbinder himself in the subsequent film version, certainly do not do so within the theatre or related creative industries. When discussing Fassbinder's thematisation of racism and discrimination, it is also important to acknowledge his problematic history of depicting Black men in films like *Whity* (1971) and *The Marriage of Maria Braun* (1979). In film scholarship, Fassbinder is often criticised for directing an objectifying and exploitative gaze towards the Black men in his films, a practice that was undoubtedly influenced by his personal relationship with several of his Black actors, including Black German actor Günter Kaufmann and Moroccan actor El Hedi ben Salem.[7]

So what was the relationship of the 'real Jorgos' to the theatre? Today the assumption on the part of the German theatrical establishment is often that lack of representation of Germans with a background of migration within the theatrical sphere is to do with the lack of theatrical culture in countries of origin such as Turkey and Greece. However, linguistically and socially alienated from German culture, many new arrivals to West Germany under the aegis of labour migration were in need for entertainment and some connection to home, and theatre was one such outlet.[8] According to Sven Sappelt, 'only a few of the performances were based on a dramatic text that was intended to be discussed as a literary text' (2000, 276). This is something migrant theatre would share with postdramatic theatre, a dominant theatrical form in Germany which emerged around the same time, and it is a characteristic that lives on in contemporary performances that take place in the *freie Szene* as opposed to in traditional, state theatre venues. As Sappelt states, some of these foreign-language theatre groups disbanded once their audience became integrated in German culture circles and more frequently attended German-language theatre. But one community which has had a constant presence in German theatre are Turkish Germans; once the largest group of guest workers and currently the largest ethnic minority in Germany.

The Turkish German theatre scene was supported by the long theatre tradition in Turkey, a tradition that was very much engaged with Western European trends, Brechtian theatre in particular. As Ela Gezen writes, Turkish Brecht enthusiasts participated in the student theatre festival in Erlangen from 1954 on and in the Brecht-Dialogues in East Berlin from the 1960s on (2018, 1–8). In the 1970s and 1980s, the worsening political situation in Turkey also meant that a number of significant leftist theatre professionals also made their way to Germany. But despite this lengthy exchange and Turkish Germans' decades' long presence in the country, Turkish German actors and directors did not necessarily have an easy time finding a place within the traditional German theatre system. In his study of Turkish German theatre, Erol Boran quotes Yüksel Pazarkaya in conversation, to reject the claim that Turkish theatre groups consciously separated themselves from German theatre. Pazarkaya states this makes no sense, considering that Turkish theatre has been based on Western European theatre since the nineteenth century (Boran 2004, 76). Recent studies by Misha Hadar (2019) and Lizzie Stewart (2013, 14) which address the policy, funding and production circumstances of individual productions from the 1980s highlight such separations as primarily originating from demands on the part of German policy and institutions for repetition of traditional Turkish plays rather than the further development of the more syncretic and experimental work many of the practitioners in question wanted to engage in.

According to Sappelt, German theatres themselves blamed language for the exclusion of so-called migrants from traditional theatre. He writes, 'Traditional theatre has argued that an adequate mastery of the stage language [German] is necessary, but even adequate language skills may not be enough to include non-European actors and actresses in ensembles as they are usually oriented towards a classical repertoire' (2000, 276–77). But besides language, what Sappelt is not *overtly* saying is that non-European actors, meaning those who are of African, Asian or visibly of Middle Eastern origin, may be excluded if their physical appearance is deemed unsuitable for 'classical' German roles. Curiously though this can also be the case even when moving away from classical roles into more experimental work, which increasingly became dominant in the most lauded of Germany's theatres in the 1970s, 1980s, 1990s, and 2000s. In Brechtian and post-Brechtian acting, the role of the actor is not to fool the audience into believing they are the character being played but rather to point to the disjunction between actor and character as part of the performance. While racially 'unmarked' parts in this period were seldom played by non-white actors, the dominant move away from naturalism meant that even where a playwright did write in a racialised character, this part would tend not be given to an actor of Colour. As Sieg highlights, the logic behind this draws again on Brechtian *Verfremdung*, arguing that a '"naturalistic," mimetic style of representation [...] always reproduces the operations of racial ideology, whereas cross-racial masquerade contests or even transforms social relations organized around race' (2002, 5). Similarly in an East German context Kruger notes the production of several plays by South African playwright Athol Fugard in the GDR which 'represent not only a critical engagement with solidarity, by way of anti-apartheid theatre and the South African liberation movements, but also with what looks like its antithesis: the erasure, in widely differing portrayals of Black South Africans by mostly white GDR actors, of the racialized subject of and in the officially anti-racist state.' Kruger gores on to argue that 'This equivocation between solidarity and erasure distinguishes East German practices of racial impersonation from the more ostentatiously theatrical practice in West Germany, which, especially in the last two decades, has included racial masquerade in its repertoire of ironic deconstructions of naturalistic norms' (Kruger 2004, 292). The unlooked for result, however, of this pose of political engagement as taken on within the realities of the German ensemble system is that actors of Colour are doubly excluded—both from unmarked roles and from those where the character to be played is a person of Colour.

This situation has been prevalent enough to make its way into stage directions in more contemporary plays influenced by Brechtian and postdramatic practices. A prominent case in point is Dea Loher's *Unschuld* (Innocence) which premiered in 2003 and was published in 2004. This play has two Black characters and the prevalence of the use of blackface make-up in Germany for such characters leads the playwright to include the following explicit direction on casting:

> If Elisio and Fadoul are cast with Black actors, they should be chosen because they're excellent actors, not for reasons of a dubious authenticity. No 'Schwarz-Malerei' (naturalistic black make-up), I recommend instead to emphasize the artificiality of theatrical means through the use of masks and the like. (as cited in Sieg 2015, 120)

As will be seen below the failure to follow that direction in the 2011 Deutsches Theatre production in favour of what the production team considered a Brechtian use of blackface would play a key role in the 'blackfacing debates' in Germany in the 2010s. As Sharon Dodua Otoo highlights, however even on a textual level, a white ensemble is assumed as in the character list and stage directions the other characters are 'all white by virtue of the fact their whiteness is uncommented' (2012, 55: see also 58–59). Otoo positions this as typical rather than exceptional in terms of German theatre (57), and this can also be seen beyond the high-profile *Innocence* case. Roland Schimmelpfennig's *Der goldene Drache* (2009), translated as *The Golden Dragon* (2011), for example, is a case in point. The play sets the invisibility and exploitation of Chinese immigrants with illegal status in Germany at the heart of everyday life there, and through the use of playful role-switching, cross-casting and parable, exposes the role of racialisation in the creation of convenient others on whom Germans can act out violence born of sexual and economic frustration. Here the character profiles are carefully constructed to allow an estranged portrayal of Asian characters by white actors. The character list thus does not structure itself by listing the 17 characters within the play, but rather divides these between the required 5 actors who will show their distance to the role by moving between 3 and 4 characters of different gender, age and ethnicity:

A YOUNG MAN (The grandfather, Asian Man, The Waitress, The Cricket)
A WOMAN OVER SIXTY (The granddaughter, Asian Woman, The Ant, The Shopkeeper).
A YOUNG WOMAN (The man with the Striped Shirt, Asian Man with Toothache, The Barbie-Fucker). (Schimmelpfennig 2011, 19)

While this allows a certain circumvention and plays with stereotype to political effect typical of *Verfremdung*, in each case the only ethnic ascription marked is Asian, signalling this as deviation from the assumed white norm of the other characters and by extension the actors' bodies. In contrast to the other attributes, when it comes to race and ethnicity, the assumption seems to be that the cross-casting will only work in one direction. Actors of Colour can thus find themselves in a triple bind: not white enough to play an unmarked German character (whether in the post-Brechtian style or not); not understood to be acting rather than playing themselves when given naturalistic roles; and not considered able to estrange the portrayal of a person of Colour when such a role does come up. Thus, inevitably the preference for whiteness and Germany's understanding of itself as white is what often excludes People of Colour from the theatre, whether or not they are fluent in German. And because of Germany and the European Union's long-standing belief that Turkey is *not* part of Europe, Turkish German actors may be just as affected by these prejudices as Black German actors, which we will discuss more below.

4   POST-UNIFICATION: THEATRE AND RACE IN 'POSTMIGRANT GERMANY'

Turkish German theatre underwent a major transformation in the early 2000s, and with it the space for discussions of race in German theatre. The mid-2000s saw the emergence of 'postmigrant theatre' a label coined by curator and artistic director Shermin Langhoff, for theatre which 'explicitly deals with the diversified plural society of the city' (Langhoff 2012). Thus, while the white German hegemony may continue to debate whether or not Germany is a country of immigration and whether or not immigrants have integrated, post-migrant theatre starts from an acknowledgment that the German nation is *already* a society shaped by migration and needs to move 'beyond belonging' (the title of a 2006 festival Langhoff curated) along ethnic and racialised lines. Although the term emerged in early festivals which Langhoff curated with support from the HAU theatre, postmigrant theatre really began to draw attention when it gained its own home at the Ballhaus Naunynstraße theatre in 2008, a space from which it developed successes like Nurkan Erpulat and Jens Hillje's *Verrücktes Blut* (Crazy Blood, 2010). Based loosely on the French film *La Journée de la Jupe* (The Day of the Skirt, 2008) directed by Jean-Paul Lilienfeld, *Crazy Blood* moves Germans with a migration background away from the margins and into the centre.

In this play, a literature teacher in a German school must get a class of rowdy teens through a lesson about Schiller. When one student accidentally drops a gun out of his backpack, the teacher, Sonja, initially seizes the gun for safety reasons, but then decides to use it to force her students to finally behave. At gunpoint, Sonja forces her students to recite lines from Schiller's plays *Die Räuber* (*The Robbers*, 1782) and *Kabale und Liebe* (*Love and Intrigue*, 1784). She hopes to teach them that they should turn away from the cultures of their parents' homeland and embrace German culture, which she associates with Enlightenment, democracy and tolerance. However, the students reveal that it is actually the teacher who is in need of an education about tolerance and that the arbitrary split between East and West is actually meaningless. At the play's conclusion, when its characters break out of their roles and become actors again, a Kurdish character breaks the fourth wall and turns to the audience, explaining that he doesn't want the play to the end because then he will go back to being typecast and forced to play a drug dealer or murderer because of his dark hair and eyes (Erpulat et al., 2012). Here Brechtian *Verfremdung* is used not only to dismantle the racialised gaze but also to critique the material conditions of theatrical production, turning Brecht's interventionist thinking onto the theatre industry itself.[9]

Crazy Blood received such positive reviews from critics and theatregoers alike that it became a stepping stone for Langhoff to move from the Ballhaus Naunynstraße Theatre to the state-subsidised Gorki Theatre in 2013. There, Langhoff continued with the programme of postmigrant theatre, expanding it to include directors and actors from abroad, such as the Israeli director Yael Ronen and several actors from Syria, Afghanistan and Palestine who make up the Exil Ensemble. Some of the plays, like Necat Öziri's *Get Deutsch or Die Tryin'* (English in original title, 2017), continue with an established formula of postmigrant theatre, using humour, irony and *Verfremdung* to tell the stories of the first generation of guest workers and how their migration has affected their children and grandchildren. However, other plays have incorporated new stories, like *The Situation* (English in original title, 2015) which addresses the Israel-Palestine conflict or *Winterreise* (Winter Journey, 2017), a road trip through Germany with a group of refugees who take a bus tour with a naïve,

3 RACIALISATION AND CONTEMPORARY GERMAN THEATRE 53

German liberal as their guide; both are directed by Ronen. Despite the Gorki's ability to address issues of race and discrimination, incorporate languages other than German in its plays and use English and Arabic surtitles to be more inclusive of non-German speaking audiences, the plays have been criticised for being too accommodating towards a white German audience, as to not make the subject matter too uncomfortable, even when discussing racism. In contrast, Black German theatre has been very upfront about not only speaking candidly about racism, but also creating theatre for a *Black* audience. This is something Öziri himself highlights and reflects on in a blogpost for German theatre website, *Nachtkritik*, from 2017 (here in our translation):

> I, Necati Öziri, move within a white system of thought, I operate along the predetermined power axes of our society, a system which privileges me with respect to other groups, which are disadvantaged more severely by racism, and simultaneously disadvantages me as a Person of Colour with respect to White people. Every day this causes me damage and simultaneously it profits me day in and day out.

As Öziri highlights there are both strong points of connection between the experiences of Turkish-origin artists in Germany and those from the Black German community, and at the same time points where the experiences of racialisation both on and offstage diverge significantly.

Much like Turkish Germans, Black Germans have faced similar challenges to working in theatre due to the ways in which they are racialised. One of the difficult things about writing a history of Black German theatre is knowing where to begin. Black Germans have acted on the stage at least since the early twentieth century, but we have little documentation of their performances, similar to how Black actors have been erased from German film history, if not for more recent attempts to recover their stories (on race and representation in Weimar cinema see Nagl 2009). One could begin with Olumide Popoola's *Also by Mail* (English in original title, 2013), which Jamele Watkins highlights as technically the first play published by a Black German (Watkins 2016b, 141). However, it is not the first play ever written by a Black German, since Cameroonian Alexandre Kum'a Ndumbe III wrote the plays *Ach, Kamerun! Unsere alte deutsche Kolonie. Ein Dokumentarstück* (O Cameroon! Our old German colony: A documentary play), *Kafra-Biatanga-Tragödie-Afrikas: ein Stück in elf Szenen* (Africa's Kafra-Biatange Tragody: a Play in Eleven Scenes) *Lumuba II* and *Das Fest der Liebe—Die Chance der Jugend* (The Festival of Love—The Opportunity of the Youth) in the 1970s. However Ndumbe's plays were never published in Germany. And neither Ndume's or Popoola's plays were performed, though there have been staged readings of Popoola's play (Watkins 2016b, 141). Thus, typically a history of Black German theatre begins in the 2000s, although there are anecdotes of Black German actors acting on stage prior to the 2000s, such as Günter Kaufmann, a close collaborator of Fassbinder's for a time, who played a small role in Völker Schlöndorff's *Baal* and Theodor Wonja Michael who was born in Germany in 1927 and who, in his memoir *German and also Black*, recalled finally being offered the role of Othello when he re-entered the acting profession after retirement in 1987 (Theodor 2017, 198–99). Loren Kruger also includes analysis of an 'underground performance [...] by two Germans of Colour in June 1986' in the GDR of *Sizwe Bansi is Dead*, by South African playwright Atholl Fugard (Kruger 2004, 318).

Jamele Watkins has written the first comprehensive account of Black German theatre in her 2016 dissertation, 'The Drama of Race: Contemporary Afro-German Theatre.'[10] In 'The Drama of Race' Watkins not only situates Black German theatre vis a vis older theoretical frameworks for performance from Brecht's *Verfremdung* effect to Augusto Boal's 'theatre of the oppressed' (itself influenced by Brecht's work) but she also engages in close analysis of several plays in order to trace a genealogy of Black German theatre. Watkins starts with plays involving non-professional actors who have been encouraged to use theatre as a form of empowerment like *real life: Deutschland* (English in original title, 2008) and ends with a fantastical work such as Olivia Wenzel's *Mais in Deutschland* (Corn in Germany) performed at the Ballhaus Naunynstraße in 2015, after Wagner Carvalho became artistic director and began to draw on his own networks to engage many more Black German artists.

Black Germans' increasing engagement with theatre could possibly be linked to the more public presence they achieved in 2011 with the creation of Bündnis Bühnenwatch (Alliance Stage Watch), which was founded to tackle the problem of blackface on German stages. Beginning with a performance of Herb Gardner's *Ich bin nicht Rappaport* (I Am not Rappaport) at the Schlosspark Theatre in Berlin during the 2011/2012 season, a series of incidents involving blackface in German theatres sparked outrage among Black German activists.[11] Bühnenwatch published a statement on their website, declaring '[i]t is our intention, to prevent any future racist depictions of blackface and racist discrimination against actors of Colour.'

Writing from the standpoint of 2018, Black German artist Simone Dede Ayivi—author of performances such as *Der kleine Bruder des Ruderers* (The Rower's Little Brother, at the Ballhaus 2012), *First Black Woman in Space* (English in original title, at the Sophiensälen in 2015) and *Queens* (English in original title, at the Sophiensälen in 2018)—reflects that while representation had improved, there was still a discrepancy between the number of Black Germans in state theatre ensembles and those active in the independent scene (2018, 74–83). There have been a few instances of state-funded theatres in Germany featuring performances that include Black German actors or Black German directors, for example, Michael Klammer's performance as Karl in Antú Romero Nunes' production of Schiller's *The Robbers* at the Staatstheatre in Stuttgart in 2013 and Anta Helena Recke's so-called *Schwarzkopie* (Black copy) of Josef Bierbichler's *Mittelreich* (Middle Kingdom) at the Munich Kammerspiele in 2017.[12] However, as Ayivi insists, most state theatre ensembles limit the number of Black actors to one at most. In contrast to state theatres, most Black German theatre takes place in spaces that are more informal, more precarious and experimental.

Currently, the German theatre most closely associated with Black German theatre is the Ballhaus. When Langhoff left for the Maxim Gorki state theatre in 2013 and Wagner Carvalho took over artistic direction, Black Germans' presence at the Ballhaus became much more visible as Carvalho oversaw productions like 'We are Tomorrow' (English title in original, 2015) and 'Republik Repair' (Repair Republic, 2017), both of which interrogated Germany's colonial past and its racist present from a Black German perspective presented by Black directors and actors. What stands out about the more recent plays directed and performed by Black Germans is the element of fantasy and futurism they entail, although sci-fi references are also present in earlier productions by Neco Çelik and Nurkan Erpulat. While it would be possible to create solely realistic representations that focus on the problem of racism in Germany, artists like Wenzel and Ayivi have experimented with Afrofuturist productions that may still confront racism but either do so in a fantastical absurdist manner, such as Ayivi's *Krieg der Hörnchen* (*War of the Squirrels*, 2013), or they employ sci-fi narratives or focus more on how they would like the future to be, such as Wenzel's collaborative performance *We are the Universe* (English title in original, 2015, written and performed with Hieu Huang, Banafshe Hourmazdi and Rahel Jankowski) or Ayivi's *First Black Woman in Space* (2015). What both the old and new productions have in common is a diasporic approach that draws on Black thought, history and culture from beyond Germany's borders, from Label Noir's use of Black Feminist thought in *Heimat bittersüsse Heimat* (*Home bittersweet Home*, 2010), to Popoola's setting of her play in Nigeria and Wenzel and Ayivi's references to African American jazz musician Sun Ra.[13] While Brechtian *Verfremdung* in its classic form created distantiation by situating action in a distant past or imagined version of a distant country, here it is the uncolonised future which is used to intervene in present representational forms, suggesting that Black German artists in the theatre will not allow themselves to be constricted by classical German forms or state institutions.

5   Conclusion

Writing in 2005, David Barnett describes 'the German theatre system' as 'the envy of the Western world'. He continues: 'Its virtues are twofold: it is exceptionally well funded and it is decentralized. The public money that flows into it, provided by national and regional taxation, has one central function—it makes drama and theatre virtually independent of the market' (2005, 12). Because of these unique characteristics, the audience and the actors are 'exposed to a more diverse range of dramaturgies and acting styles' (ibid). As we have seen 'diverse' here is used to signal variation in style, tradition and training rather than diversity in the backgrounds of individuals included whether as cultural producers or consumers. This is the sense of diversity increasingly used in public institutions in Germany as well as the Anglophone sphere; however, its slippage with concepts of 'diverse' offering reveal the commercial rather than rights-based origin of this particular phrasing. Despite the reputation of German theatre for aesthetic experimentation and political engagement a sustained focus on race and racialisation within German society or even German theatre has often been 'secondary' even to politically engaged and anti-fascist theatre-makers in the FRG: 'only a few treat it as the central object of analysis and intervention' (Sieg 2002, 259). Brechtian *Verfremdung*, a key technique developed in the context of what Brecht saw as the race-class nexus at the heart of National Socialism, has emerged in many contexts as one of the most successful ways of addressing racialisation in theatre and beyond: and Watkins compellingly stresses its uses in recent Black German theatre (see Watkins 2016, passim). However, we also see the paradoxical effect its usage can have on propagating structures of exclusion and racialised ways of viewing within the theatre in Germany.

This is not to suggest 'a monolithic story of German racism', however, which would equate the racism of the National Socialist state simply and ahistorically with that present in other spheres of German life at the time, or in previous and future incarnations of that state (cf. Watkins 2016a, 4). Neither should this position the German relationship to race as existing in a temporal lag to the Anglo-American discourse: if race is a construct that nonetheless alters lived realities, it is important to view it with regard to the localised and historicised ways in which it is constructed. While Anglo-American thought on race has had its effect on the German context, in Germany developments take their own direction. The albeit limited investment in artists of Colour from 2010 onwards in Germany and shifts in policy around the opening of the state-subsidised institutions are aspects which the Anglophone sphere could now look to emulate, for example. While in this chapter we have centred race in a manner rarely done when giving a brief history of post-war German theatre, we therefore close with a quotation from a practitioner who does this in his theatrical work. Shifting the perspective to include a focus on race and racialised theatre practitioners 'is not only about giving injured parties a space for empowerment, but rather precisely about the fact that as a society we need these perspectives; the whole society—and not just "the Others"—depends on such a space' (Öziri 2017, our translation).

NOTES

1. The term 'racialisation' acknowledges the fact that race is not a real, biological category; however, racialised groups are constructed in a society to fulfil certain ends. As Fatima El-Tayeb writes about the situation in Europe, 'though racializations always pretend to name natural, unchanging, obvious facts, they are always ambiguous, shifting and unstable...Racialized populations are thus externalized from contemporary Europe, and as a result, their long-standing presence within the continent is absent from most historical accounts' (El-Tayeb 2011: xiii; xxi).

2. On the position of the Ballhaus Naunynstraße in the German theatrical landscape and particularly the role of funding here see Nobrega 2011. For a brief historical overview of the relationship between theatre and migration in Germany see Sharifi 2017.
3. Ulrich Khoun, one of the directors at heart of the blackfacing scandal in 2012, having learnt the term still notes, 'I find it a bit problematic because I do think it [the term] won't be understood by everyone straight away. [...] I didn't understand it straight away either. Then I just learnt it' (our translation of Khoun, as cited in Voss 2014, 94). In *Wie Rassismus aus Wörtern spricht* (How Racism Speaks out of Words), Jasmin Dean describes People of Colour in the German context 'as a political concept which functions without reference to culture and "ethnic" belonging [...] a "People of Colour" politics is well-placed to fill a discursive gap into which many of those who felt themselves to belong neither to Black organisations nor to migrant communities had fallen up til now' (our translation of Dean 2015, 606).
4. Plays which bear Brecht's name as playwright tend to be the results of more complex processes of collaboration than the traditional European model of the author as lone genius and, today, as lone copyright holder, tend to allow for.
5. Between 1941 and 1942 he actively supported African American theatre practitioner Clarence Muse in his attempt to stage an adaptation of *The Threepenny Opera* with a black cast. This attempt ultimately failed on contractual grounds (see Calico 2008, 81–83).
6. For further development of this tendency see also the plays under discussion in the chapter titled 'Rightwing Radicalism in Germany After Reunification' in Haas 2003. For a discussion focused on white German and Austrian female playwrights' engagements with race see Kallin 2007.
7. For further discussion of Blackness in Fassbinder's films, see (O'Sickey 2001), (Laws 2010), (Layne 2012), and (Nagl and Blankenship 2012). On Kaufmann see Gaines 2017, 95–134.
8. The research project, 'Populäre Theaterkultur' (Popular Theater Culture), founded in 1983 by Manfred Brauneck included study of these diverse groups (see Sappelt 2000, 276).
9. For detailed analyses of this play see Landry (2012); Layne (2014); Moslund et al. (2019); Stewart (2017, 56–68); Voss (2014, 171–208).
10. In addition to Waktins' scholarship, scholars including Vanessa Plumly, Olivia Landry and Azadeh Sharifi have also published on black German theatre.
11. On this, see amongst others: Otoo and Sharon (2012) Sieg (2015); Sharifi (2016).
12. For more on this play see Sharifi (2018, 2020).
13. For a discussion of Black feminist thought in Black German theatre see Sharifi, 'Women of Colour Feminism' (2020, forthcoming). For an analysis of *Heimat, bittersüsse Heimat* see Watkins (2016b).

References

Ayivi, Simone Dede. 2018. 'Internationalität ≠ Interkultur': eine Schwarze deutsche Kritik. In *Allianen: Kritische Prais an weissen Institutionen*, ed. Elisa Liepsch, Julian Warner, and Matthias Pees, 74–83. Bielefeld: Transcript.

Barnett, David. 2005. *Rainer Werner Fassbinder and the German Theater*. Cambridge: Cambridge University Press.

Boran, Erol. 2004. *Eine Geschichte des Türkisch-Deutschen Theaters und Kabaretts*. PhD diss., Ohio State University.

Boswell, Marshall. 2013. Living Theater. In *Encyclopaedia of American Literature*, 3rd ed. Manly: Facts On File, by Inc. http://libproxy.lib.unc.edu/login?url=https://search.credoreference.com/content/entry/fofl/living_theater/0?institutionId=1724.

Brecht, Bertolt. 2001a. Fear and Misery of the Third Reich. Note on the Play of the Same Title, Unpublished in Brecht's Lifetime. In *Collected Plays: Four*, ed. Tom Kuhn and John Willett, 323–327. London: Methuen.

———. 2001b. Round Heads and Pointed Heads, or Money Calls to Money. Translated by Tom Kuhn. In *Collected Plays Four*, ed. Tom Kuhn and John Willett, 1–114. London: Methuen.

———. 2015. Verfremdung Effects in Chinese Acting. In *Brecht on Theatre*, ed. Marc Silbermann, Tom Kuhn, and Steve Giles, 151–158. London: Bloomsbury.

Bühnenwatch. http://www.buehnenwatch.com.

Calico, Joy H. 2008. *Brecht at the Opera*. Berkeley and Los Angeles: University of California Press.

Cronan, Tod. 2017. Class into Race: Brecht and the Problem of State Capitalism. *Critical Inquiry* 44: 54–79.

Dean, Jasmin. 2015. People of Colo(u)r. In *Wie Rassismus aus Wörtern spricht: (K)erben des Kolonialismus im Wissensarchiv deutsche Sprache*, ed. Susan Arndt and Nadja Ofuatey-Alazard, 597. Münster: Unrast.

Eddo-Lodge, Renni. 2019. *Warum ich nicht länger mit Weißen über Hautfarbe spreche*. Translated by Anette Grube. Stuttgart: J.G. Cotta.

El-Tayeb, Fatima. 2011. *European Others: Queering Ethnicity in Postnational Europe*. Minneapolis: University of Minnesota Press.

Erpulat, Nurkan, et al. 2012. *Verrücktes Blut*. Bel Air edition, DVD.

Fassbinder, Rainer Werner. 1985. *Plays*. New York: PAJ Publications.

Gaines, Malik. 2017. *Black Performance on the Outskirts of the Left: A History of the Impossible*. New York: New York University Press.

Gezen, Ela. 2018. *Brecht, Turkish Theater and Turkish-German Literature*. New York: Camden House.

Göktürk, Deniz, et al. 2007. *Germany in Transit: Nation and Migration, 1955–2005*. Berkeley: University of California Press.

Haas, Birgit. 2003. *Modern German Political Drama 1980–2000*. Suffolk and New York: Camden House.

Haas, Astrid. 2011. A Raisin in the East: African American Civil Rights Drama in GDR Scholarship and Theater Practice. In *Germans and African Americans: Two Centuries of Exchange*, ed. Larry A. Greene and Anke Ortlepp, 166–184. Jackson: University of Mississippi Press.

Hadar, Misha. 2019. Performing Multiculturalism: The Turkish Ensemble at the Schaubühne. *Theatre Journal* 71 (2): 135–152.

Kallin, Britta. 2007. *The Presentation of Racism in Contemporary German and Austrian Theater: Six Women Playwrights*. Lewiston: Edwin Mellen Press.

Kruger, Loren. 2004. *Post-Imperial Brecht: Politics and Performance, East and South*. Cambridge: Cambridge University Press.

Landry, Olivia. 2012. German Youth Against Sarrazin: Nurkan Erpulat's Verrücktes Blut and Clash as Political Theatre of Experience. *Türkisch-deutsche Studien* 3: 105–121.

Langhoff, Shermin. 2012. Wozu postmigrantisches Theater?. Interview by Irene Bazinger. *Frankfurter Allgemeine Zeitung*, January 15. https://www.faz.net/aktuell/feuilleton/buehne-und-konzert/gespraech-mit-shermin-langhoff-wozu-postmigrantisches-theater-11605050.html.

Laws, Page. 2010. Rainer and *Der weiße Neger*: Fassbinder's and Kaufmann's On and Off Affair as German Racial Allegory. In *From Black to Schwarz: Cultural Crossovers Between African America and Germany*, ed. Maria I. Diedrich and Jürgen Heinrichs, 245–261. East Lansing: Michigan State University Press.

Layne, Priscilla. 2012. Lessons in Liberation: Fassbinder's *Whity* at the Crossroads of Hollywood Melodrama and Blaxploitation. In *A Companion to German Cinema*, ed. Terri Ginsberg and Andrea Mensch, 260–286. Malden, MA: Blackwell Publishing LTD.

———. 2014. Between Play and Mimicry: The Limits of Humanism in 'Verrücktes Blut'. *Colloquia Germanica* 47 (1/2): 31–57.

Loher, Dea. 2004. *Unschuld. Das Leben auf der Praca Roosevelt*. Frankfurt am Main: Verlag der Autoren.

Maturi, Giacomo. 2007. The Integration of the Southern Labor Force and its Specific Adaptation Problems. Translated by David Gramling. In *Germany in Transit*, ed. Deniz Göktürk, David Gramling, and Anton Kaes, 31–33. Berkeley, CA: University of California Press.

Moslund, Sten Pultz, Moritz Schramm, and Sabrina Vitting-Seerup. 2019. Postmigration: From Utopian Fantasy to Future Perspectives. In *Reframing Migration, Diversity and the Arts: The Postmigrant Condition*, ed. Moritz Schramm et al., 227–248. New York: Routledge.

Nagl, Tobias. 2009. *Die unheimliche Maschine: Rasse und Repräsentation in Weimarer Kino*. Munich: Text und Kritik.

Nagl, Tobias, and Janelle Blankenship. 2012. 'So Much Tenderness': Rainer Werner Fassbinder, Günter Kaufmann and the Ambivalences of Racial Desire. In *A Companion to Rainer Werner Fassbinder*, ed. Brigitte Peuker. Malden, MA: Wiley-Blackwell.

Nobrega, Onur. 2011. 'We Bark from the Third Row': The Position of the Ballhaus Naunynstraße in Berlin's Cultural landscape and the Funding of Cultural Diversity Work. *Türkisch-deutsche Studien* 2: 91–112.

O'Sickey, Ingeborg Majer. 2001. Representing Blackness: Instrumentalizing Race and Gender in Rainer Werner Fassbinder's The Marriage of Maria Braun. *Women in German Yearbook*. 17: 15–29.

Otoo, Dodua, and Sharon. 2012. Reclaiming Innocence. Unmasking Representations of Whiteness in German Theatre. In *The Little Book of Big Visions. How to be an Artist and Revolutionise the World*, ed. Sandrine Micossé-Aikins and Sharon Dodua Otoo, 54–70. Münster: Edition Assemblage.

Öziri, Necat. 2017. Welche Welt bedeuten diese Bretter? *Nachtkritik.de*, November 1. https://www.nachtkritik.de/index.php?option=com_content&view=article&id=14570:debatte-um-die-zukunft-des-stadttheaters-xxxiv-necati-oeziri-bei-den-roemerberggespraechen-in-frankfurt-main&catid=101&Itemid=84.

Parker, Stephen. 2014. *Bertolt Brecht: A Literary Life*. London: Methuen Drama.

Sanyal, Mithu. 2019. Suddenly, it's OK to be German and to Talk About Race. *The Guardian*, September 18. https://www.theguardian.com/commentisfree/2019/sep/18/germany-race-conversation-afd-openness.

Sappelt, Sven. 2000. Theater der Migrant/innen. In *Interkulturelle Literatur in Deutschland: Ein Handbuch*, ed. Carmine Chiellino, 275–293. Stuttgart and Weimar: Metzler.

Schimmelpfennig, Roland. 2011. *The Golden Dragon*. Translated by David Tushingham. London: Oberon Modern Plays.

Sharifi, Azadeh. 2016. Institutioneller und struktureller Rassismus im Theater. In *Urteile: Ein dokumentarisches Theaterstück über die Opfer des NSU: mit Texten über alltäglichen und strukturellen Rassismus*, ed. Tunay Önder, Christine Umpfenbach, and Azar Mortazavi, 66–85. Münster: Unrast.

———. 2018. Dekolonisiert die Bühnen / Decolonizing the Stage. *Nachtkritik.de*, September 6. https://www.nachtkritik.de/index.php?option=com_content&view=article&id=15728:vorkaempferinnen-fuer-mehr-diversitaet-drei-schwarze-theatermacherinnen-stellt-die-theaterwissenschaftlerin-azadeh-sharifi-vor&catid=101&Itemid=84.

———. 2020. Women of Colour Feminism and Their Influence on the Contemporary Independent German Theater. (Forthcoming).

Sieg, Katrin. 2002. *Ethnic Drag: Performing Race, Nation, Sexuality in West Germany*. Ann Arbor: University of Michigan Press.

———. 2015. Race, Guilt and Innocence: Facing Blackfacing in Contemporary German Theater. *German Studies Review* 38 (1): 117–134.

Silbermann, Marc, Tom Kuhn, and Steve Giles. 2015. General Introduction. In *Brecht on Theatre*, ed. Marc Silbermann, Tom Kuhn, and Steve Giles, 1–8. London: Bloomsbury.

Stewart, Lizzie. 2013. Countermemory and the (Turkish-)German Theatrical Archive: Reading the Documentary Remains of Emine Sevgi Özdamar's *Karagöz in Alamania* (1986). *Transit* 8 (3): 1–22.

———. 2017. Postmigrant Theatre: the Ballhaus Naunynstraße Takes on Sexual Nationalism. *Journal of Aesthetics and Culture* 9 (2): 56–68.

Tatlow, Antony. 1977. *The Mask of Evil: Brecht's Response to the Poetry, Theatre and Thought of China and Japan: A Comparative and Critical Evaluation*. Bern, Frankfurt am Main, Los Angeles: Peter Lang.

Theodor, Michael. 2017. *Black German: An Afro-German Life in the Twentieth Century*. Translated by Eve Rosenhaft. Liverpool: LUP.

Tsui, Chiann Karen. 2015. Brecht's Guter Mensch in Sichuan: Recontextualizing China. *The German Quarterly* 88 (3): 355–377.

Voss, Hanna. 2014. *Reflexion von ethnischer Identität(szuweisung) im deutschen Gegenwartstheater*. Marburg: Tectum.

Watkins, Jamele. 2016a. *The Drama of Race: Contemporary Afro-German Theater*. PhD diss., Amherst, MA.

———. 2016b. Rearticulating Black Feminist Thought in *Heimat, bittersüße Heimat*. *Women in German Yearbook* 32: 138–151.

CHAPTER 4

'Dangerous Dialogues': Questioning Constructions of Race in South Pacific Theatre

David O'Donnell and Shailesh Lal

1 Introduction

In considering the impact of race on the post-colonial Pacific, historian Jamie Belich recounts the role that racism played in European expansionism: 'Convictions of intrinsic superiority—not just intellectual and technological but also moral and even physical—steeled Europeans in their wars of conquest and made them confident of victory' (Belich 2014, 271). Given the overtly racist ideologies that created the modern Pacific, it is perhaps inevitable that much of the Indigenous theatre that has flourished in the South Pacific region since the 1960s has revealed and resisted this history of racism. As Diana Looser writes, contemporary Pacific drama emerges from 'the desire to reassert Pacific voices, perspectives, and performance techniques in ways that take advantage of, and also challenge, modify, or undermine Western theatrical conventions and their attendant cultural representations' (Looser 2014, 3).

In this chapter we consider ways in which two Pacific playwrights have modified Western theatre conventions, articulated racial thinking in the region and challenged dominant racist narratives and histories in the South Pacific. Both Larry Thomas (Indigenous Fijian and European) and Victor Rodger

---

D. O'Donnell (✉)
Victoria University of Wellington, Wellington, New Zealand
e-mail: david.odonnell@vuw.ac.nz

S. Lal
University of the South Pacific, Suva, Fiji
e-mail: shailesh.lal@usp.ac.fj

© The Author(s), under exclusive license to Springer Nature Switzerland AG 2021
T. Morosetti, O. Okagbue (eds.), *The Palgrave Handbook of Theatre and Race*, https://doi.org/10.1007/978-3-030-43957-6_4

(Indigenous Samoan and European) are of mixed descent—a position that often informs their playwriting, informing ironic representations of race and identity. This chapter focusses on Rodger's *Ranterstantrum* and Thomas' *The Visitors*, both of which were first performed in the context of high-profile arts festivals. *Ranterstantrum* debuted at the New Zealand International Festival of the Arts in Wellington, New Zealand, (2002) and *The Visitors* at the Pacific Arts festival in Pago Pago, American Samoa (2008). Each play begins with home invasion scenarios which (in very different ways) open up complex questions of race and identity in the Pacific.

2   PERFORMING RACE IN THE PACIFIC

The Pacific Islands are a charged space for examining issues of race and racism. As Teresia Teaiwa states: 'The immense diversity within the Pacific Islands region is demonstrated by its more than twelve hundred languages, more than seven million people (excluding the populations of Australia, Timor Leste, Hawai'i, New Zealand and West Papua) and fourteen independent or self-governing nations' (Teaiwa 2010, 112). This cultural diversity combined with centuries of migration and trade between islands and the devastating impact of colonial invasion inevitably foregrounds cultural difference and racially based confrontations.

Despite the historical and contemporary emphasis on racial issues in the Pacific, the term 'race' has become increasingly problematic, recognised as a social and political construct (Bamshad and Olson 2003; Loveman 1999). Segall argues that there are 'no biological barriers between 5.8 billion human beings alive today. External physical features previously used to distinguish "racial groups" are not reliable genetic markers because they represent relatively recent (over the past 20,000 years) adaptations' (Segall 2002, 6). He suggests that humans share a lot more genetically than the concept of race would suggest. Thus the general understanding about race is that it cannot be useful as a biological concept and that differences allocated to 'racial groupings' are arbitrary. Rainier Spencer has summarised scientific evidence to prove that no one can claim to be of 'pure' race. He explains that '[t]he scientific jury is in and has been for some time. Biological races don't exist, never have. Everyone is always already mixed' (Spencer 1998, 128).

In *Theatre & Race* Harvey Young gives an overview of the long engagement with the 'topic, question and "problem" of racial difference' throughout the history of Western theatre, from Ancient Greece to the present. Because theatre by its nature foregrounds the physical appearance of the actor and inherently involves one group looking at another, it has always been a particularly potent form for exploring issues of race. This act of looking contributes to 'racial thinking' which at its best 'can prompt sincere curiosity to learn about another's culture or background' and at worst 'merely embraces circulating stereotypes and caricatures' (Young 2013, 9). Young demonstrates how classifying people into different groups according to ethnicity is an act of power which establishes hierarchy and allows one group to dominate over others. He suggests that in the 'post-race' context of the twenty-first century where we theoretically 'possess the capacity to see beyond the rigidly defined racial categories of the past' (3), racial difference remains a *'difficult dialogue'* [emphasis in the original]: 'To talk about race feels dangerous' (3). This danger is implicit in the theatre dealing with the difficult conversations around racial identity and racism in the South Pacific.

3   FIJI: HISTORICAL BACKGROUND TO LARRY THOMAS' PLAYS

Ian Gaskell observes that 'The subject of race relations has been a recurring theme in most of the plays from Fiji' (Gaskell 2009, 142). This emphasis is due to the clear racial divisions which have become entrenched in Fijian politics since the colonial era: *iTaukei* (Indigenous), IndoFijian (the descendants of migrants from India)[1] and *Kailoma* (people of mixed Indigenous and European ancestry). According to de Bruce (2007), Fiji's racial form of classification was introduced by the British colonisers to ensure that the interests of the *iTaukei*, and in particular the colonisers, were protected and advanced. This resulted in clear demarcations of the *iTaukei*, the Europeans and later the Indians (de Bruce 2007, 115–116). The Indigenous *iTaukei* society is generally communal in nature with very close bonds formed within the family, fellow villagers and the land. The *iTaukei* articulate their sense of belonging in Fiji with ancestral history and provincial narratives. The *Kailoma*, also known as Part-Europeans or half-castes,[2] are the descendants of the early beachcombers who were 'escaped convicts, seamen sick of shipboard discipline, drifters and others who were marginal in their own societies' (Firth and Tarte 2001, 15). Later *Kailoma* families descended from European settlers who arrived in Fiji as respected planters and tradesmen. It is generally accepted amongst the *iTaukei* that these *Kailoma* children could not stake a claim to their *iTaukei* lineage. Since the *iTaukei* are a strictly patrilineal society, the ethnic marker for them is through an *iTaukei* father. Larry Thomas describes *Kailoma* as someone inside but caught in the middle. He elaborates that although *Kailoma* were insiders, they were still at the peripheries of the inner circle of the *iTaukei* hierarchy, close enough to observe but not enough to belong.[3] Despite this, the 1997 Fijian constitution classified Kailoma as 'Others', an umbrella category including the various ethnic groups that did not fit within the two most populous categories of Fijian (*iTaukei*) and IndoFijian. Being classified as 'Other' had a disturbing effect on Thomas for it suggested *Kailoma* were second-class citizens in their own country.[4]

IndoFijians are the descendants of Indian migrants brought to Fiji in 1879 by the British colonisers as part of the Girmit indenture system to establish the sugar industry. By the 1946 census the indentured labourers had numerically overtaken the Indigenous population. Even before this, an air of mistrust existed between the two 'races', partly due to the segregation policies of the British and partly because of their vastly differing cultures. The ethnic tensions in Fiji have become heightened since Fiji became independent from Britain in 1970 and came to the forefront in 1987 when Fiji experienced its first military coup de'état against an IndoFijian-backed government. Since then significant numbers of IndoFijians have emigrated to Pacific Rim countries like Australia, New Zealand, the USA and Canada (Lal 1992, 2008).

4 The Fijian Coups

On May 14, 1987, Lieutenant Colonel Sitiveni Rabuka led a coup de'état to remove the month-old National Federation Party (NFP)—Fiji Labour Party (FLP) coalition government. Despite the Coalition appointing an *iTaukei*, Dr. Timoci Bavadra, as its prime minister, there was an outcry by *iTaukei* nationalists who were concerned that the IndoFijian-dominated government would override *iTaukei* rights: 'In his early announcements, Rabuka had declared he had staged the coup for the paradoxical reason that racist elements within the Indigenous Fijian community (represented by the "Taukei Movement") were causing unrest. Later, however, his personal concern about increased Indian power was put forward as his real motive' (Ewins 1998, 8).

These events were followed by another coup on September 25 1987, enabling Rabuka to appoint an *iTaukei*-dominated government. The military coups of 1987 irrevocably damaged the relations between *iTaukei* and IndoFijians as not only did the coup 'thrust Fiji into the unwelcome glare of international notoriety, it had also brought to the surface previously harboured prejudices amongst the people' (Lal 1992, 269). From 1990 to 1999, Rabuka was the democratically elected prime minister of Fiji, eventually overseeing the abolition of his own 1990 constitution in favour of the multicultural 1997 constitution. He, along with IndoFijian leader Jai Ram Reddy formed a coalition to fight the 1999 elections together only to lose to the FLP which appointed Fiji's first IndoFijian Prime Minister Mahendra Chaudhry.

A little over one year after the FLP-led government came into power, Fiji experienced another coup on May 19, 2000. This was carried out by supposed Indigenous nationalists led by failed businessman George Speight with the assistance of a few highly trained military personnel from the Fiji military's Counter Revolutionary Warfare Unit (Van Fossen 2000). Chaudhry's cabinet and other opposition parliamentarians were taken hostage and the coup instigators received support from large numbers of the Indigenous population. Eventually, the government was dissolved, an interim government put in place and elections held. The interim government-led party won the elections and Fiji again had an Indigenous prime minister, Ratu Tevita Momeodonu.

In 2006, the military staged another coup and their Commander Josaia Voreqe (Frank) Bainimarama became Prime Minister. The main stated reason for this takeover was to eradicate corruption, nepotism and to improve race relations in the country (Fraenkel et al. 2009, 6–7). Bainimarama argued that previous governments had introduced policies that were leading to the marginalisation of a large sector of the Fiji population, namely the IndoFijians (Lal

2014). Citing Robbie Robertson, long-time Pacific politics journalist David Robie notes that 'For the first time in Fiji's history, Bainimarama steered the country closer to a "standard model of liberal democrac" and away from the British colonial and race-based legacy' (Robie 2018).

5   THEATRE IN FIJI

In Subramani's (1985) seminal work, *South Pacific Literature*, he comments on the slow progress of theatre in Fiji, citing a deficiency in production and theatrical skills and an absence of institutional support. When revising his book seven years later, Subramani acknowledges some improvement, particularly the contribution of Rotuman Vilsoni Hereniko as a playwright and director. Following his first play *Don't Cry Mama* (1977), *Sera's Choice* and *A Child for Iva* were produced in 1986 and 1987 respectively, both directed by Larry Thomas, who went on to write and produce his own plays. Hereniko wrote *The Monster* in 1987 as a response to the military coup, depicting two female beggars Ta and Rua (*iTaukei* and IndoFijian respectively) fighting over a basket of food as symbolic of the inter-racial contest for limited resources. Diana Looser comments that 'Ta and Rua reinforce political-ethnic divisions and frequently characterise each other in terms that emphasize racial and cultural difference in prejudicial ways' (Looser 2014, 206). Looser recounts that shortly before the premiere of *The Monster*, 'the military passed a decree banning all creative expression' and that plainclothes soldiers were planted in the audience (Looser 2014, 203). Despite this intimidating context, the play was performed without interference and due to the allegorical nature of its narrative, 'the soldiers had no context for political theatre and, Hereniko has surmised, simply did not connect the female cast and the non-naturalistic onstage action with the May coup' (Looser 2014, 204). This period also saw productions of plays by writers of varied ethnic backgrounds, including Hereniko and Teresia Teaiwa's subversive gender-based comedy, *The Last Virgin in Paradise* (1991), Sudesh Mishra's *Ferringhi* (1993) and Raymond Pillai's Hindi play *Adhuuraa Sapnaa—Shattered Dreams* (written in 1977 and performed in 1993).

6   *THE VISITORS*: 'THIS IS WHERE I BELONG'

Subramani (1992) comments that one of the most significant developments in Fijian theatre was the emergence of Larry Thomas, who has produced a substantial body of dramatic work that explores the complexities of ethnic tension and division in Fiji over a turbulent period of its history. Thomas was introduced to acting in 1973 as a year eight student at Marist Brothers School, Vatuwaqa. Attending theatre allowed Thomas to be amongst Europeans and to be transported away from the harsh realities and struggles of Raiwaqa, a multicultural suburb just outside Suva city where he grew up. It was in Raiwaqa that Thomas was exposed to a particular style of Fiji-English language with its distinctive mixture of English and *iTaukei* words, slang and a disregard for the rules of English grammar. His first play, *Just Another Day* (1988), introduced the audience to theatre with dialogues in Fiji-English, displaying the lives of urban-dwelling Fijians who were struggling to adapt to consumerism and a wage-based society. His second play, *Outcasts* (1989), was set in a squatter settlement where race relations and social stratification formed the core of the action. *Yours Dearly* and *Men, Women and Insanity* were produced as a double feature in 1991 (Thomas 1991). The former discussed personal relationships while the latter debated issues of racism, progress and education, using insanity as symbolic of the political upheavals triggered by the 1987 coups. *To Let You Know*[5] (1997) and *The Anniversary Present* (1998), both political commentaries on the state of the nation, were produced on the anniversaries of Fiji's 1987 coup. The following year, he produced *Searching for the Smile* (1999), which dealt with migrant issues. Since *The Visitors* (2008), Thomas has co-written two plays in the *iTaukei* language with Apolonia Tamata: *Lakovi* (2010) which presents the rituals of a traditional *iTaukei* wedding, and *Na iLululu* (2014) a play detailing the introduction of children to their mother's village within a traditional *iTaukei* setting.[6]

The Visitors was Thomas' first play to premier outside Fiji as the republic's performing arts contribution to the tenth Pacific Festival of Arts in Pago Pago, directed by Canadian Ian Gaskell who was Professor of Theatre Arts at the University of the South Pacific in Suva from 1997 to 2008. Thomas had to persuade the Fiji National Organizing Committee to enter this play in the festival as Fiji's representative because of the racial undertones and the negative image of the *iTaukei* it presented. Gaskell comments: 'With its unflinching depiction of racially motivated violence, *The Visitors* … undermines the idyllic pretence that Fiji is an island paradise peopled by happy, smiling natives' (Gaskell 2009, 143).

The Visitors is set in a Fijian city, in the home of an IndoFijian couple—Vishwa, a businessman and his wife Manjula (Manju), a history teacher.[7] In the middle of the night two *iTaukei* intruders (named Man 1 and Man 2) break into their house and terrorise the couple in their bedroom. At first it appears that the intruders are after valuables, but upon being offered the money and jewellery in the house, they reveal they are after something more, later revealed to be the wealth Vishwa has accumulated by illegal means. The play depicts a harrowing night of torture and blackmail as the intruders interrogate Vishwa and subject Manju to emotional, physical and sexual abuse as they try to discover how much she knows. During the course of the invasion, Manju learns a series of unpleasant revelations about her husband. In addition to having conducted affairs with other women, he has financed a rival gang of home invaders robbing occupants of their jewellery and cash, amassing a stash of gold and cash which he intends to use to start a new life in Brisbane with Manju and their children. It is also revealed that Vishwa was one of the businessmen who had helped finance the coup in 2000. The unwanted visitors eventually find the stashed jewellery and money they had been looking for and leave.

The home invasion narrative enables Thomas to illuminate the deep under-lying racial tensions that caused the coups, and the competing claims to belong in Fiji. The *iTaukei* intruders feel that they own the country therefore do not need to justify their intrusion into an IndoFijian home. Man 1 states, 'We are the taukei, the owners, you do not question us' (Thomas 2008, 42). Man 2 follows up with another scathing attack: 'This is my country! It belongs to us. You people never seem to understand that' (43). In response to these claims, Manju emerges as a very strong-willed individual, who does not give in to the intruders despite the abuse she suffers. The home invaders not only shatter the security of her serene domestic world, but also expose her cheating husband as a fraud. Despite these revelations, Manju is able to retain her sense of self and her confidence that she belongs in Fiji. She tells the intruders, 'This is where I belong. No matter what anyone says I have the right to be here' (43). She expresses a history that highlights the contributions IndoFijians have made to the development of post-colonial Fiji. This is evident when Manju eloquently traces the history of IndoFijian labourers, lamenting the adversity they endured:

> My great grand parents came to this country not of their own free will, but through cunning and force. They came and they worked like slaves, like all the other indentured workers. … When the girmit was over they chose to stay. … They had to wake up at four o'clock in the morning to start work. They worked in the hot sun and their weekly ration was barely enough to feed one person. My grandparents and those indentured workers and their descendants built the roads, the factories, the schools, they cleaned the streets and collected the sewage just so their children could have a better education and a decent life. (41)

The struggles of the indentured Indian labourers have been well documented (Ali 1979; Gillion 1962; Lal 1983; Mayer 1963; Sanadhya 1991). Through Manju, Thomas addresses the concerns of those IndoFijians who feel that their ancestors' long periods of suffering and hard work do not receive the recogni-tion and appreciation they deserve in Fiji. It is because of her deep affiliation with Fiji that Manju resists her husband's plan to emigrate and finds it difficult envisaging themselves living elsewhere. Manju explains to Man 2: 'I have fought with my husband many times because he wants to migrate and I keep saying no, we should stay because this is a beautiful country, this the country my ancestors came to and chose to live despite the suffering and hardship. … I have worked hard for this country and people like you not gonna make me leave' (30). For an *iTaukei* audience that may struggle to understand an IndoFijian perspective, Manju's argument emphasises the attachments migrants can develop for an adopted country over generations.

Vishwa represents an alternative IndoFijian opinion that contrasts strikingly with that of his wife. While Manju believes that they belong to Fiji so need to stay, Vishwa, like many IndoFijians, feels that any resistance to the *iTaukei* campaign to dominate Fiji politics and society is pointless: 'Why fight when you know you on the losing side? Why should we Indians stand around idly and be bullied. No matter what we say, we will never be taken seriously because in the end we will never be accepted, we are still visitors, never mind the work our girmit ancestors did to build this country' (28).

Despite this, he also feels a strong connection to Fiji. On being confronted by the intruders on his true feelings for Fiji and why he cares, his decisive response is 'because it's my life' (40). Vishwa represents those IndoFijians who have emigrated in response to the political upheavals but still remain emotionally connected to Fiji. On the other hand, Vishwa is accused of deceit and profiteering from the coups. Thomas based Vishwa's character on the shady businessmen who were claimed to be behind Fiji's coup of 2000.[8] A scene in *The Visitors* where a badly beaten up Vishwa is helped onto a seat by his assailants resembles the media images of a heavily bandaged businessman Ballu Khan being carried into court by police officers in November 2007.[9] In *The Visitors*, Manju and Vishwa reflect contrasting IndoFijian perspectives on their connectedness to their identity and to Fiji. Actor Michelle Reddy, who played Manju, states, 'they both represent the dreams and the concerns and the worries of being an IndoFijian in a country such as Fiji. And it is legitimate because a lot of people I know feel the same way.'[10] Reddy elaborates that many IndoFijians remain transients as they are constantly deciding on whether to migrate or remain.

The title of the play reflects the complexity of ethnic politics in Fiji. In both *iTaukei* and Indian cultures, relationships with visitors are highly valued. For the *iTaukei*, the *vulagi* (visitor) is seen as an esteemed member of an extended family who is treated with great respect. Similarly in Hindu culture the *atithi* (visitor) is seen as a representative of God and is treated with reverence (Mishra 2012, 10). However, there remains the understanding that the visitor is only welcome to stay for a prescribed time. The title of the play can be interpreted as a reference to the *iTaukei* home invaders as unwelcome 'visitors' who break all of the normal conventions of respect between visitors and their host. On another level the title refers to the arrival of Indian indentured labourers over a century ago. What happens when the visitor becomes a permanent citizen? The play dramatises the destructiveness of race-based competition and claims to belong.

The play's characters and the politics of Fiji both reveal that *iTaukei* and IndoFijians are closely intertwined. The intruders are initially portrayed as racist thugs skilled at intimidation, but during the course of the play they articulate their political purpose more clearly. Man 1 defines his Indigenous status in terms of his connection with the land: 'I feel it as I walk and the pulse of the land vibrates through my body and we are one, in the vanua [land] it's the spirit which binds us together. That is something you will never understand' (40). However Man 1 resists Vishwa's persistent questioning about his knowledge of Fiji, suggesting that his knowledge is limited. Late in the play, Man 2 opens up to Manju and Vishwa in a moving monologue:

You want to know about my history? (*pause*) I don't know my history. They never teach me that, they just expect me to know it ... one thing I can tell you, my history is not feeding me, my history is not looking after me. I don't hate you guys ... It's hard to see that in my own country, I am nothing, that people like you are better off than me. (48–49)

In contrast to Manju's full description of the history of the migrant Indian workers, this *iTaukei* character knows little of his culture, and his racial thinking has become a habit that stems from this ignorance coupled with a sense of grievance at IndoFijian affluence. This scene demonstrates how destructive racial thinking stems from a lack of understanding of the past. Paradoxically, the close encounter between the home invader and his victims has sparked a connection which, although it remains unfulfilled in the play, contains the seed of understanding and reconciliation.

Once Vishwa's illegal activities are revealed, there remains little sympathy for him. Although initially portrayed as a victim, Manju emerges as the strongest character by the climax. She remains steadfast in that knowledge and does not allow physical and emotional disturbances to overshadow her belief in herself and her country. Manju introduces us to a new form of Fijian nationalism that emerges from one's contribution and commitment to the nation rather than her ethnicity. She suggests that traditional and hereditary significances are not the only means of belonging to a place. Her loyalty to Fiji and genuine concern for its people helps break the negative stereotypes associated with IndoFijians as opportunistic transients.

Director Ian Gaskell recalls that upon reading *The Visitors* in early June 2008, the committee in Suva deliberated that the play was unsuitable for the festival, thus would not form part of the contingent. Thomas implored the committee to see how the play reflected the realities of life in a fast-changing Pacific. He argued that the issues dealt with in the play needed to be vigorously and consciously discussed and that theatre was one of the most effective media by which such awareness could be achieved. The Committee finally endorsed the play, but on opening night in Pago Pago, it was received with significant discomfort from the leaders of Fiji's delegation who made a hasty exit from the auditorium immediately after the play ended. Thomas later confided that a High Chief had expressed his displeasure about the play, lamenting that it was presenting a negative image of Fiji.[11] Gaskell suggests that: 'just as the play depicts a marginalised section of the Fiji population—the "visitors" of the title—and interrogates their sense of belonging, when it came to the Festival the production itself did not belong. It was an unwelcome visitor spoiling the party; its sense of "Pacificness" ran counter to the accepted version' (Gaskell 2009, 145).

In an article on defining the scope and mission of Pacific Studies, Teresia Teaiwa argues that 'Indigenous violence, corruption, neglect and obfuscation shall be critiqued as rigorously as the sins of colonialism and imperialism' (Teaiwa 2010, 117). In this spirit, Larry Thomas' play balances a critique of

Indigenous nationalism with an expose of the corrupt practices of an IndoFijian businessman. Through this racially based confrontation, the play creates some sense of catharsis and suggests the possibility of a potentially more harmonious future, as expressed by Manju.

7 VICTOR RODGER AND THE SAMOAN DIASPORA

While Larry Thomas' plays depict the troubled racial politics of an independent Pacific nation, Victor Rodger's work reflects the inter-racial tensions resulting from the Pacific diaspora which has accelerated since the Second World War as large numbers of Pacific peoples have migrated to the Westernised nations in search of employment and better economic opportunity. While many Pacific migrants have settled in Australia and the USA, Aotearoa/New Zealand has the greatest numbers and Auckland has become the largest Polynesian city in the world. The most significant Pacific populations in New Zealand are Samoan, Tongan, Niuean, Cook Islands Māori, Fijian and Tokelauan. Cluny MacPherson argues that the common experience of racist discrimination, particularly in terms of finding employment and accommodation was a trigger for increased political unity among the different island groups: 'Prejudice … was directed en bloc at "Pacific Islanders" and made no distinction, for instance, between Niueans and Samoans' (MacPherson 2012, 186).

Unlike Fiji, the infrastructure and funding for theatre is well developed in New Zealand, and Pacific theatre practitioners receive support and encouragement from the national scriptwriting agency Playmarket and training institutions like Toi Whakaari, Te Auaha and the (now disestablished) Pacific Institute of Performing Arts. Victor Rodger, a Christchurch-born playwright of Samoan and Scottish ancestry, is just one of dozens of playwrights of Pacific descent working in New Zealand professional theatres.[12] Samoan playwright Oscar Kightley's *Dawn Raids* (1997) deals explicitly with racial discrimination against Pacific Island migrants (Kightley 2017). It is a fictionalised account of the mid-1970s dawn raids when the government instigated home invasions on Pacific households in the early hours of the morning in a concerted campaign to arrest and deport Pacific people residing in New Zealand without a working visa. The raids remain one of the most visible instances of anti-Pacific Island racism in New Zealand. Kightley's play focusses on a Samoan family who are hiding the pregnant girlfriend of their son in their home, showing the trauma and emotional impact of the raids on Pacific communities in Auckland.

Victor Rodger has examined race and racism more than most New Zealand playwrights, including the identity politics of his own *afakasi* (mixed-race) status in semi-autobiographical plays like *Sons* (1995) and *At the Wake* (2012). In *My Name is Gary Cooper* (2007) a young *afakasi* man, named after the Hollywood movie star, tracks down his white father who abandoned his pregnant Samoan mother in the 1950s. The *afakasi* Gary Cooper enacts an ironic revenge on his unsuspecting father by systematically seducing his wife and children. The play refers to and in some ways reverses the plot of the Gary Cooper movie *Return to Paradise* (1953) which was filmed on location in Samoa. Several of Rodger's plays feature gay protagonists negotiating their doubled 'otherness' within the predominantly white, straight society in New Zealand. For example, *Black Faggot* (2013) uses humour to explore gay and transgender identities within Samoan culture. The confrontational title refers to a term of abuse which is both racist and homophobic. Thus Rodger's plays consciously address the marginalisation of and prejudice against Pacific Island people in New Zealand society.

8   *RANTERSTANTRUM*: 'THE LONE BROWNIE AT THE BALL'

Ranterstantrum was first performed at the 2002 New Zealand Festival of the Arts, directed by one of New Zealand's most respected directors Colin McColl.[13] The play's title suggests anger, a combination of a 'rant' and a 'tantrum'.[14] Similar to *The Visitors*, the play is a realist work where the characters' backstories are gradually revealed over the course of the play. Rodger skilfully manipulates this form to create a play with significant surprises and plot twists. *Ranterstantrum* begins with a trick—a violent scene where a Polynesian home intruder terrorises and prepares to rape a young woman that we assume is 'real' is later revealed to be a play-within-the-play.[15] This fictional drama intercuts with another 'real' scene in which a *Pākehā* (white) middle-class couple Lee and Max witness a fight outside their home between a Polynesian boy and girl. Lee complains, 'Why are they all like that? Why are they so angry?' (Rodger 2016, 12). This immediately puts the focus on racially inflected *Pākehā* stereotyping of Polynesian people as an 'other', a homogenous group who are expected to behave aggressively and anti-socially.

The majority of the action takes place at a middle-class dinner party, a housewarming hosted by two *Pākehā* actors, Bridge (Lee's sister) and Scott. Following an accident where Scott trips and smashes a glass table, drenching Lee and Max with red wine, he has been sent to hospital. Dressed only in their underwear, Lee and Max return to the dining room to find a Polynesian man, Joe, finishing off the rest of the chicken. Assuming he is an intruder, they attack him, threaten him with a knife, Lee slaps him and Max ties him to a chair. When Bridge returns, she explains that they have made a terrible mistake. Joe is a late dinner guest, not a burglar, so Lee and Max release him, explaining that they have been victims of a home invasion by a Polynesian man, and that they mistook Joe for that man. We discover that Joe is an actor, currently playing a rapist in a play with Bridge and Scott, the same play which we saw scenes from earlier. Thus Rodger creates a confusion in the audience between Joe's role in the fictional play and his role as the dinner party guest, reflecting a wider social confusion about the role of race and racial stereotypes in New Zealand society.

As the situation clarifies for the audience, this scenario enables Rodger to foreground ways in which *Pākehā* New Zealanders stereotype Polynesian men. The play theatricalises what Young refers to as 'racial projection' (Young 2013, 16), whereby one person makes racist assumptions about a person based on their appearance. Young writes, 'When we apply a racial projection across another person's body, we implicitly broadcast our assumptions about a person's various habiti' (Young 2013, 16). Bridge says to her sister, 'Didn't I say Joe might be coming?' and Lee replies, 'Yes, but you never said that he was—' (28). Lee stops short of using a racial descriptor, but it is clear that she assumes that a guest at a *Pākehā* dinner party will be white. Max apologises to Joe, 'We're so sorry. Honestly, you looked just like him' [the criminal who invaded their home] (29). Joe explains that he is often mistaken for famous islanders including actor Robbie Magasiva (29).[16] Thus Joe's experience reflects that when racial thinking informs the act of looking at another person, the learned assumptions of the viewer mean that they see a 'race' not the person.

More extreme racist stereotypes are revealed through the character of Scott who abuses the multi-racial staff in the hospital Accident and Emergency Department, complaining about 'Fucking Arabs' and staff who 'smell like curries' (40). When he returns to the dinner party he calls Joe a 'big black poof' (51). Scott's provocative comments are often intended to be humorous, and generate nervous laughter in the audience. A reviewer commented that 'this is a comedy where we all dance on the knife edge in terms of what is safe to laugh at' (Amery 2002). In laughing spontaneously, or making the decision to laugh or not to laugh, audience members are forced to confront their own casual or unconscious bias about race. However Scott is not the only character to use racist terms. Bridge calls Joe a 'coconut' (39), and Max subjects a Polynesian KFC worker to an unwarranted tirade of verbal abuse (37). Thus the play illustrates the casual, habitual racism that pervades white society in New Zealand, and invites the audience to consider their complicity with this. Joe appears to play along, referring to himself as a 'nigger' and when Lee objects to his use of the word he remonstrates that 'it's been reclaimed' (41). As this suggests, Joe's frequent references to racial stereotyping are laden with irony, both a cutting critique of the racial assumptions of his white peer group and a coping strategy to survive in white society. Thus Rodger draws attention to the difficult space Polynesian people face when they are the only non-white person in the room. Joe sees himself as 'the lone brownie at the ball and so I become the voice and the face of Polynesia, by default. Spokesperson and dartboard all in one' (70).

The given circumstances of the play frequently have political resonances beyond the domestic context of the play's setting. When Lee tells Scott that she has apologised to Joe several times for her mistake, Scott jokes, 'Fuck, white people'll apologise for anything these days' (54). This is a reference to a number of well-publicised apologies for race-based colonial wrongdoings. For example, in 2002 the New Zealand Prime Minister Helen Clark issued a formal apology to the people of Samoa for acts of violence and negligence committed by the New Zealand government during the years Western Samoa was a colony of New Zealand (1914–1962). Scott's joking about white apology displays a cynicism towards such apologies which raises questions about their integrity and efficacy.

Rodger frequently uses irony and black humour to highlight his themes. The fact that Lee and Max are in their underwear when they attack Joe emphasises their whiteness, and also suggests that the play will 'expose' their prejudices. Once Bridge has clarified the situation and restored order, Lee and Max reluctantly dress in Hawaiian shirts and lavalavas,[17] because their own clothes are still wet and there are no other clothes available. Joe jokes, 'You look like a couple in an ad for a trip to a Polynesian paradise' (28). The couple's discomfort in Polynesian clothing emphasises their deep unease about their place in the Pacific. Joe asks if they have ever visited the Pacific islands. Lee says 'Never', and Joe replies, 'You should, don't know what you're missing' (28). This moment highlights the reality that *Pākehā* society in general is ignorant and uninformed about their closest neighbours in the Pacific. Pacific Studies scholar Damon Salesa writes, 'Pākehā New Zealanders live on Pacific Islands but many—perhaps most—still describe themselves as "Europeans", even if the Pacific has been their home for generations' (Salesa 2017, 9). As the play was initially performed in an international arts festival where the patrons were primarily white, Rodger issues a clear challenge to *Pākehā* New Zealanders to look beyond racial projections and to see Pacific Island cultures as distinct and relevant to their lives. When Joe mentions the legendary All Black rugby player Jonah Lomu, Lee instantly responds with a racist stereotype: 'A Neanderthal who didn't know how to look after his money' (47).[18] She assumes Lomu was Samoan, but Bridge corrects her with the fact that he was Tongan. This emphasises that many *Pākehā* people struggle to differentiate between the different Pacific cultures living in New Zealand, even when the example is someone with such a high public profile as Lomu. Joe responds that Lomu was: 'Embraced by everyone as a good old true blue brown kiwi. But the first whiff of trouble he was just another no good dirty Tongan' (48). This speech reflects the ambiguous and peripheral space Pacific migrants inhabit in New Zealand society, and the tendency to fall back on racial stereotypes when Pacific people fail to live up to the expectations of the dominant society.

As Emma Cox writes, 'theatre of migration is at its most basic level implicated with, and troubled by, power relations within the broader society' (Cox 2014, 27). Rodger draws attention to wider social realities such as racially segregated suburbs in New Zealand cities. We discover that sisters Lee and Bridge were raised in the affluent suburb of Brown's Bay on Auckland's North Shore, far removed from the Polynesian hub in Auckland's industrial south. Lee recalls that their father would not let them date 'island boys or Maoris', reflecting the racial prejudice of an older generation (42). When Joe comments that they would not have had much to do with 'darkies' on 'that side of town' (42), Lee makes another race-based assumption, asking Joe if he's from South Auckland. He replies that he's from Ponsonby, an inner-city suburb which had a large Polynesian community in past decades but has since become gentrified as property prices rose. Salesa argues, 'we cannot avoid the fact that Auckland is a racially ordered city. … a mosaic comprised of often highly segregated or concentrated neighbourhoods, of ethnoburbs and suburbs. Unfortunately, these neighbourhoods, if they are Pacific neighbourhoods, are likely to experience "extreme concentration" and deprivation' (Salesa 2017, 52–53). Thus *Ransterstantrum* alludes to broader social histories that have led to an increasing geographical segregation of races in New Zealand cities. Joe challenges Lee: 'You mean that we should all sound like we're from a cul de sac in Browns Bay and speak the Queen's English, like. But we—'us'—we're not all like that. Can't be. Ever' (49). The play invites us to consider how conceptions of race cause social divisions in New Zealand and foregrounds the underlying racist assumptions in the uncritical use of pronouns such as 'they' and 'us'. Lee questions why Joe identifies so strongly with black American culture, saying, 'It's not of New Zealand. It's not "us"' (47). Joe responds: 'No, it's just not "you." But "us"—it's an interesting word these days. "Us." I have a funny feeling when you say "us" and you're talking about Kiwis, you're not imagining the same sort of people that I am' (47).

The play calls attention to the increasingly multicultural nature of New Zealand society, and the discomfort of white people with this. Joe observes that Lee's aggression towards him appears to be inherited racism from her parents and attributes it to 'fear of a motherfucking black planet' (62). Salesa argues that New Zealand is becoming less white by the day, noting that in Auckland, 'one of every four babies born is of Pacific descent; one out of four is Asian; and around one in five is Māori' (Salesa 2017, 7). He attributes the unease felt by *Pākehā* New Zealanders about being part of the Pacific as part of 'a legacy of colonialism and decolonisation overseas that it has never properly come to terms with' (Salesa 2017, 8–9). The production of Victor Rodger's play in a major arts festival is part of that process of coming to terms with the inherent racism in white society represented by the *Pākehā* characters.

In a final-act revelation, we discover that Max was raped by the Polynesian intruder who invaded Lee and Max's home, mirroring the plot of the play-within-the-play but changing the gender of the victim. This explains the couple's antagonism towards Joe at the beginning of the play, and why they have such a negative view of Polynesian men. In giving the *Pākehā* couple some dramatic motivation for their prejudicial attitudes, Rodger complicates the dialectics of the play. It presents a disturbing picture of a society divided along racial lines, where racially motivated violence is the norm. Given the metatheatrical framing with a play in which Joe portrays a Polynesian rapist, it implies that non-white actors can be complicit in their own stereotyping. We learn that Joe met Bridge and Scott while playing the role of Othello: 'Please: call me Mr Thick Lips', he jokes (55). Three out of five characters are actors, and this emphasis on acting in the play highlights the role that representation plays in building racial projections. Joe refers to a number of Hollywood movies featuring black actors, including *In the Heat of the Night*, in which Sidney Poitier's Mr. Tibbs character contests the prejudices of the racist cop played by Rod Steiger. When challenged on contributing to racial stereotypes by playing a criminal, Joe replies, 'Gotta pay the bills. Gotta eat. Can't eat my principles' (45). This raises the question of to what degree a non-white jobbing actor can afford to maintain his political integrity in the face of a highly competitive job market. It also draws attention to the constant compromises Pacific migrants need to make in order to function and survive in the dominant white culture of New Zealand.

In the final scene of the play, Joe tells the others that he plans to learn the Samoan language. He quips, 'can't even speak Samoan. Been playing one long enough. Bout time I came up with the goods' (78). This is a poignant, telling moment in the play. Rather than being secure in his Samoan identity, Joe presents it as a role he has been playing. This calls attention to the sense that racial identity is expressed as a performance. Ric Knowles argues that critical race theory brings to intercultural theatre 'an acute, historicised awareness of race as constructed, or more properly, performed; of racial and cultural identity and difference as fluid; of the intersectionality of social identities' (Knowles 2010, 50). In *Ranterstantrum*, Rodger is well aware of this intersectionality, and probes it to deepen our understanding and empathy for Joe's position. Joe is Samoan in a white society, he has a relatively privileged job as an actor, he is gay among a cast of straight characters, he is well aware of the different roles he plays, in life as well as on stage. His very presence in the play undermines and critiques the black-and-white binaries expressed by the *Pākehā* characters.

Reviewers recognised the innovative quality of the play's mix of drama and black comedy, and its intense and provocative engagement with racial issues: 'The play is a fiery challenge to decades of playwrighting that have seen only occasional nods to the complexities of our race relations as a young country' (Amery 2002). In 2016 Rodger revised the play, updating topical references and re-titling it *Ranterstantrum Redux*. This version was performed in a new production directed by Vela Manusaute at The Basement Theatre, Auckland in August 2017. One reviewer commented on the ambiguity and shock value of the racially inflected dark comedy: 'At times, it is hard to know whether to laugh or gasp' (Sills 2017). Despite the passage of time, one reviewer found the play 'essentially remains an ever-timeless inquiry into the ongoing issues of racism and sexual violation' (Smythe 2017). This reviewer's response reflects the way that the play challenges the spectator to examine their own personal responses to race and racism: 'the most confronting issue that Rodger's script raises in my mind has less to do with racism and sexual abuse themselves, but rather how a sensitive observer can respectfully and constructively respond to them' (Smythe 2017). As this reviewer suggests, the dramaturgy of the play inherently challenges spectators to actively review their attitudes to race and racism.

9   Conclusions: Performing Race in the South Pacific

Both *The Visitors* and *Ranterstantrum* create dangerous dialogues that grapple with the troubling race-based histories in the post-colonial South Pacific. Their home invasion scenarios carry the symbolism of the European colonialisation of the Pacific, as well as the legacy of specific histories such as the dawn raids.

In each case, the security and sense of belonging in the home is violently disrupted as a metaphor for racial insecurities in the nation. *Ranterstrantrum* is unapologetically told from Joe's point of view, depicting the struggles of diasporic islanders to find a place of equality within white society. In Thomas' play Manju emerges as a sympathetic character who, despite her desperate circumstances, unfailingly proposes a vision of Fiji where all cultures can live in harmony. This reflects the vision in Tongan writer Epeli Hau'ofa's iconic essay 'Our Sea of Islands', where he emphasises the symbolic importance of the ocean in establishing a common identity for Pacific islanders and proposes the possibility of a united regional identity. Hau'ofa contests the colonial 'belittlement' of the Pacific, stressing the largeness of the region and its connectedness as a 'sea of islands' not 'islands in a far sea' (Hau'ofa 1993, 7). Hau'ofa's 'new and optimistic' view celebrates kinship, connection and autonomy of Pacific peoples, proposing a vision of the Pacific which is 'hospitable and generous' (Hau'ofa 1993, 16).

While making theatre in very different contexts, both writers bring an awareness of the social construction of race to their plays, and are skilled in revealing the contradictions and fluidities of race and identity through the embodied storytelling of theatre. As mixed-race playwrights, they provide a multi-layered view through balancing perspectives of characters of different ethnicities. Edwards, Ganguly and Lo argue that:

> in genetic terms, all of humanity is mixed; that biologically race is always already mixed race. In such a reading, mixed-race, rather than appearing as a transgressive site or a marginal mode of cultural belonging, can be conceptualised as a global arena of ancestral and cultural genesis. This could then allow us to read dual or multi-ethnic ancestries not as in-between, crossed, marginal or transgressive, but as a primordial site/mode of human belonging in this world. (Edwards et al. 2007, 2)

Following this argument, these playwrights who identify as 'mixed-race' are the norm rather than the exception in the Pacific. Their plays vividly evoke the race-based conflicts that are the legacy of colonisation, and expose the boundaries that are the legacy of racial thinking as an illusion. Young argues that the very act of attending theatre helps to create a sense of community (Young 2013, 18–19) and that this 'momentary community enabled by performance' creates a sense of solidarity among spectators and helps audiences 'to recognise themselves as active members of the society in which they live' (Young 2013, 19). In this context, Manju's appeals for an integrated Fijian society, or Joe's isolation as 'the lone brownie at the ball' have great potential to activate audiences to expose, question and heal racial rifts in the Pacific. The plays invite audiences to question and re-consider their habitual racial thinking, and to become socially active in dispelling the damaging consequences of race-based conflict. Both plays demonstrate that theatre has been and continues to be an effective public forum for exposing and contesting racially based behaviours and assumptions in the South Pacific region.

NOTES

1. There have been various terms employed to represent the descendants of Indian labourers in Fiji, the most common being Fiji Indians and Indo-Fijians. The former places emphasis on the Indian part of identity which we feel is inaccurate. The latter hyphenates the term to show movement from Indian to Fijian aspects of identity. In this chapter we use an unhyphenated IndoFijian to symbolise the merging of the two cultures in producing the IndoFijians of today.
2. The titles provided to the *Kailoma* have constantly changed. Lucy de Bruce (2007) argues that these labels have applied more to their geographical location or social status rather than racial genealogy and that the half-caste label may also be employed to celebrate, reclaim or to resist their status.
3. Larry Thomas, personal communication, March 22, 2015
4. Larry Thomas, personal communication, April 5, 2015.
5. *To Let You Know* is a highly political play that premiered on the tenth anniversary of the May 14 1987 coup. See Diana Looser's *Remaking Pacific Pasts* (226–236) for a detailed analysis of this play.
6. Thomas has also produced a series of documentaries that address social issues in Fiji: *Compassionate Exile* (1999), *A Race for Rights* (2001), *Bittersweet Hope* (2005), and *Struggling for a Better Living: Squatters in Fiji* (2007).
7. In the premiere production Vishwa was played by co-author Shailesh Lal, whose experiences as an actor have informed the discussion of the play in this chapter.
8. Larry Thomas, personal communication, March 29, 2015.
9. Controversial businessman Ballu Khan was a known supporter of Prime Minister Laisenia Qarase. He was arrested on November 3, 2007 on suspicion of plotting an assassination of coup leader Bainimarama. He was assaulted by police after they claimed he had resisted arrest and had to be carried to the court.
10. Michelle Reddy, personal communication, April 2, 2015.
11. Larry Thomas, personal communication, March 29, 2015.
12. New Zealand-based Pacific playwrights include Oscar Kightley, Erolia Ifopo, Makerita Urale, Dianna Fuemana, Toa Fraser, Albert Wendt, Fiona Collins, Tanya Muagututi'a, Vela Manusaute, Tusiata Avia, Miria George, Suli Moa, Louise Tu'u, Moana Ete, Michelle Johansson, David Mamea and Leki Jackson-Bourke.
13. McColl has been Artistic Director of the Auckland Theatre Company since 2003. This analysis is based on David O'Donnell's viewing of McColl's production and on the revised script supplied by the playwright.
14. Rodger took the title from a 1980s dance work by New Zealand choreographer Douglas Wright (with Wright's permission).
15. Tom Stoppard uses the same convention in the opening scene of *The Real Thing* (1982).
16. This is an in-joke. Robbie Magasiva played the role of Joe in the 2002 *Ranterstantrum* production.
17. A lavalava is a wrap-around rectangular piece of fabric, worn like a skirt in Samoa and other Pacific islands.

18. Jonah Lomu (1975–2015) was the youngest person to become an All Black test player and became a legend in world rugby circles, but his later life was marred by financial difficulties and a kidney disease which caused his premature death at the age of 40.

References

Ali, Ahmed. 1979. Girmit: Its Significance in Fiji. *Indian Horizons* 28 (4): 25–30.

Amery, Mark. 2002. Comedy Aimed at Racial Jugular. *Sunday Star-Times*, March 10.

Bamshad, Michael J., and Steve E. Olson. 2003. Does Race Exist? *Scientific American* 289 (6): 78–85.

Belich, James. 2014. Race. In *Pacific Histories: Ocean, Land, People*, ed. David Armitage and Alison Bashford, 263–281. Houndmills: Palgrave Macmillan.

Cox, Emma. 2014. *Theatre & Migration*. Houndmills: Palgrave Macmillan.

de Bruce, Lucy. 2007. Histories of Diversity: Kailoma Testimonies and 'Part-European' Tales from Colonial Fiji (1920–1970). *Journal of Intercultural Studies* 28 (1): 113–127.

Edwards, Penny, Debjani Ganguly, and Jacqueline Lo. 2007. Pigments of the Imagination: Theorising, Performing and Historicising Mixed Race. *Journal of Intercultural Studies* 28 (1): 1–13.

Ewins, Rory. 1998. *Colour, Class and Custom: the Literature of the 1987 Fiji Coup*. 2nd ed. Canberra: Australian National University.

Firth, Stewart, and Daryl Tarte. 2001. *20th Century Fiji: People Who Shaped the Nation*. Suva: University of the South Pacific.

Fraenkel, Jon, Stewart Firth, and Brij V. Lal, eds. 2009. *The 2006 Military Takeover in Fiji: A Coup to End All Coups?* Acton, ACT: ANU Press.

Gaskell, Ian, ed. 2009. Truth, Identity and a Sense of 'Pacificness'. *Australasian Drama Studies* 55: 132–149.

Gillion, Kenneth L. 1962. *Fiji's Indian Migrants: A History to the End of Indenture in 1920*. London: Oxford University Press.

Hau'ofa, Epeli. 1993. Our Sea of Islands. In *A New Oceania: Rediscovering Our Sea of Islands*, ed. Eric Waddell, Vijay Naidi, and Epeli Hau'ofa, 2–16. Suva: University of the South Pacific.

Kightley, Oscar. 2017. *Dawn Raids*. Wellington: Playmarket.

Knowles, Ric. 2010. *Theatre & Interculturalism*. Houndmills: Palgrave Macmillan.

Lal, Brij V. 1983. *Girmitiyas: The Origins of the Fiji Indians*. Canberra: The Journal of Pacific History.

———. 1992. *Broken Waves: A History of the Fiji Islands in the Twentieth Century*. Honolulu: University of Hawaii Press.

———. 2008. *A Time Bomb Lies Buried: Fiji's Road to Independence, 1960–1970*. Canberra: The Australian National University E Press.

———. 2014. In Frank Bainimarama's Shadow: Fiji, Elections and the Future. *The Journal of Pacific History* 49 (4): 457–468.

Looser, Diana. 2014. *Remaking Pacific Pasts: History, Memory, and Identity in Contemporary Theater from Oceania*. University of Hawai'i Press.

Loveman, Mara. 1999. Is 'Race' Essential? *American Sociological Review* 64 (6): 891–898.

MacPherson, Cluny. 2012. Empowering Pacific Peoples: Community Organisations in New Zealand. In *Tangata o le Moana: New Zealand and the People of the Pacific*, ed. Sean Mallon, Kolokesa Māhina-Tuai, and Damon Salesa, 179–199. Wellington: Te Papa Press.

Mayer, Adrian C. 1963. *Indians in Fiji*. London: Oxford University Press.

Mishra, Sudesh. 2012. 'Bending Closer to the Ground': Girmit as Minor History. *Australian Humanities Review* 52: 5–16.

Robie, David. 2018. Coups, Globalisation and Fiji's Reset Structures of 'Democracy'. *Asia Pacific Report*. https://asiapacificreport.nz/2018/01/28/coups-globalisation-and-fijis-reset-structures-of-democracy/. Accessed 30 October 2019.

Rodger, Victor. 2016. *Ranterstantrum Redux*. Unpublished Playscript.

Salesa, Damon. 2017. *Island Time: New Zealand's Pacific Futures*. Wellington: Bridget Williams Books.

Sanadhya, Totaram. 1991. *My Twenty-One Years in the Fiji Islands and the Story of the Haunted Line*. Suva: Fiji Museum.

Segall, Marshall H. 2002. Why Is There Still Racism If There Is No Such Thing as 'Race'? *Online Readings in Psychology and Culture* 5 (1). https://doi.org/10.9707/2307-0919.1045.

Sills, Ethan. 2017. Packs a Powerful Punch. *New Zealand Herald*. https://www.theatreview.org.nz/reviews/review.php?id=10449. Accessed 30 October 2019.

Smythe, Nik. 2017. Engaging and Confronting Psychological Inquest. *Theatreview*. https://www.theatreview.org.nz/reviews/review.php?id=10441. Accessed 30 October 2019.

Spencer, Rainier. 1998. Race and Mixed-Race: A Personal Tour. In *As We Are Now: Mixblood Essays on Race and Identity*, ed. William S. Penn, 126–139. Berkeley: University of California Press.

Subramani. 1985. *South Pacific Literature from Myth to Fabulation*. Suva: The University of the South Pacific.

———. 1992. *South Pacific Literature from Myth to Fabulation*. Rev. ed. Suva: The University of the South Pacific.

Teaiwa, Teresia K. 2010. For or *Before* an Asia Pacific Studies Agenda? Specifying Pacific Studies. In *Remaking Area Studies: Teaching and Learning Across Asia and the Pacific*, ed. Terence Wesley-Smith and Jon Goss, 110–124. Honolulu: University of Hawai'i Press.

Thomas, Larry. 1991. *3 Plays: Outcasts; Yours Dearly; Men, Women and Insanity*. Suva: University of the South Pacific.

———. 2008. *The Visitors*. Unpublished Playscript.

Van Fossen, Anthony. 2000. George Speight's Coup in Fiji and White-Collar Crime in Queensland. *Queensland Review* 7 (1): 1–11. https://doi.org/10.1017/S1321816600002026.

Young, Harvey. 2013. *Theatre & Race*. London: Red Globe Press.

CHAPTER 5

Staging the Ambiguities of Race: Polymorphous Indigenous Dramaturgies in Canada

Marc Maufort

1 Introduction

This study of the representations of the Indigenous 'other' in contemporary Canadian First Nations dramaturgies radically departs from the Enlightenment and nineteenth-century understanding of race as tied to rigid biological categories.[1] Like Ali Rattansi, I subscribe to the cultural constructedness of race, while foregrounding its ambiguities and fluidity. As Rattansi mentions, the Enlightenment's reliance on 'The Idea of Progress' paradoxically led to racist assumptions involving 'descriptions of bestiality and ideas of the closeness of American Indians and Africans to wild apes' (Rattansi 2007, 25). Further, Rattansi points out that in the nineteenth century, there emerged a 'science of race', relying on several principles, namely: 'that each race was innately associated with distinct social, cultural, and moral traits. [...] that the races could be graded in a coherent hierarchy of talent and beauty, with whites at the top and blacks at the bottom' (31).

A similar judgement arguably characterised European views of Indigenous people in North America. However, as Rattansi further documents, these views came increasingly under attack in the course of the twentieth century, especially with the introduction of the notion of the phenotype, a term referring to 'features such as skin colour and shape of the nose' (72). Rattansi concludes that '[g]iven [...] the failure of phenotypical features such as skin colour, hair

M. Maufort (✉)
Université Libre de Bruxelles, Brussels, Belgium
e-mail: mmaufort@ulb.ac.be

© The Author(s), under exclusive license to Springer Nature Switzerland AG 2021

T. Morosetti, O. Okagbue (eds.), *The Palgrave Handbook of Theatre and Race*, https://doi.org/10.1007/978-3-030-43957-6_5

81

type, or shape of the nose and skull to provide a systematic and coherent taxonomy of races, the concept of race is now regarded by the majority of biologists as having no credible scientific foundation' (75). Cultural race theory has further stressed the cultural features of the outdated concept of 'race'. As Ric Knowles indicates, this theoretical school privileges '[…] an acute, historicised awareness of race as constructed, or more properly, performed, of racial and cultural identity and difference as fluid' (Knowles 2010, 50). Moreover, the Indigenous playwrights under consideration here de-essentialise both Indigeneity and whiteness, in as much as they examine their enmeshment in contemporary North America.

The polymorphous dramaturgies devised by First Nations playwrights in the late twentieth and the early twenty-first centuries provide an excellent vantage point from which to observe the multiple ways in which Indigenous artists have depicted race/ethnicity in their innovative works. This is particularly noticeable in the works examined in this chapter, Tomson Highway's *The (Post)Mistress*, Drew Hayden Taylor's *God and the Indian*, Marie Clements's *Tombs of the Vanishing Indian*, and Yvette Nolan's *The Unplugging*. I contend that their multi-faceted depiction of Indigeneity reflects what Caribbean essayist Édouard Glissant called 'creolisation'. Glissant initially regarded creolisation as a feature typical of the Caribbean region but subsequently viewed it as a global phenomenon. Glissant construes creolisation as a flux of cultural relations, which counters the totalising and binary vision inherent in the racial theories inherited from the eighteenth and nineteenth centuries. In *Poétique de la relation* [*Poetics of Relation*], Glissant draws from Deleuze and Guattari's notion of the rhizome in order to articulate his vision of creolisation:

> Gilles Deleuze and Felix Guattari [...] propose the rhizome, an enmeshed root system, a network spreading either in the ground or in the air, with no predatory rootstock taking over permanently. [...] Rhizomatic thought is the principle behind what I call the Poetics of Relation, in which each and every identity is extended through a relationship with the Other. (Glissant 1997a, 11)

The fluidity of creolisation amplifies the more static notion of *métissage*: 'if we posit *métissage* as, generally speaking, the meeting and synthesis of two differences, creolization seems to be a limitless *métissage*, its elements diffracted and its consequences unforeseeable' (34). In *Traité du Tout-Monde*, Glissant extends creolisation to the fluidity of cultural globalisation: 'My proposition is that today the entire world is becoming archipelized and creolized' (Glissant 1997b, 194).[2] Having applied the creolisation model elsewhere in a South African context,[3] I wish to suggest in these pages that the non-binary, indeed sometimes 'atomised', representations of the cultural differences of Contemporary Indigeneity echo Glissant's concept of 'creolisation', a phenomenon that has received little (if any) critical attention so far. Moreover, as my case studies will make clear, this cultural creolisation is matched with a concomitant creolisation of aesthetic devices. The Indigenous aesthetic operating in the plays analysed moves well beyond the classic 'trickster' template of the early phases in the development of Indigenous dramaturgies.

Cree playwright Tomson Highway championed the figure of the Trickster in his highly successful plays of the 1980s. In his introduction to *The Rez Sisters* (1986), he clearly voiced the importance of the Trickster/Nanabush in his playwriting: 'The dream world of North American Indian mythology is inhabited by the most fantastic creatures […]. Foremost among these beings is the "Trickster" […]. Essentially a comic, clownish sort of character, he teaches us about the nature and the meaning of existence on the planet Earth' (Highway 1988, xii). In *The Rez Sisters*, the mythical creature of the shape-shifting Trickster is concretely enacted by a dancer. However much of a classic *The Rez Sisters* became (and justifiably so), the presence of a fantastic trickster in Indigenous playwriting in Canada turned into an over-used trope, verging on stereotyping.[4] In a 2002 article, playwright Drew Hayden Taylor already regretted this excessive reliance on literal trickster figures, both on the part of artists and academics (Taylor 2002, 28). In a similar vein, Kristina Fagan deplores that 'The trouble was that the trickster archetype was assumed to be an inevitable part of Indigenous cultures, and so the criticism paid little attention to the historical and cultural specifics of why and how particular Indigenous writers were drawing on particular mythical figures' (Fagan 2010, 3). This trickster theory, Fagan continues, became 'overgeneralised' (8). She further argues that Native people cannot be seen 'as the passive recipients' (9) of an 'essentializing […] trickster criticism' (9–10). Like Fagan, I would contend that in the 1980s and 1990s, critics came to expect Indigenous plays to conform to the trickster template (4). In the second decade of the twenty-first century, the trickster trope is increasingly replaced by polymorphous forms of thematic and aesthetic expression.

Analysing Indigenous works for a white scholar is inevitably a difficult task, a limitation readily acknowledged. I naturally remain an 'outsider inside' who does not purport to deliver definitive and authoritative cultural interpretations of Indigenous material. Although I use primarily Western critical tools, my analysis seeks to carefully take into account the heterogeneity of Indigenous identities. By and large, I concur with Alan Filewod who claimed in one of his seminal writings about Indigenous dramaturgies that as a non-Native critic, he could only write about his 'response' to Native drama (Filewod 1992, 17). However, I would likewise tend to agree with the perspective of Americanist Birgit Däwes, who pointed out in response that this 'acknowledgment of the colonialist gaze may lead to an impasse of silence' (Däwes 2007, 56). Like Däwes, I would argue that my positioning as an outsider may shed fruitful, albeit necessarily limited, light on Indigenous texts (19). Finally, I also acknowledge a debt to Chadwick Allen's groundbreaking study, *Trans-Indigenous. Methodologies for Global Native Literary Studies*. Allen invites scholars to consider what they can 'understand differently by juxtaposing distinct and diverse Indigenous texts' (Allen 2012, xix). Allen thus favours 'multiperspectivism' (xxii). In this chapter, I shall endeavour to achieve such a goal by examining play-texts from different North American Indigenous cultures, thus practising what Allen describes as 'reading across and through texts 'close together placed' rather than "together equal"' (xxxiii).

2   Transcultural Reframings
of the Trickster Template

The recent career developments of Northern Manitoba Cree playwright Tomson Highway perfectly illustrate the creolisation of race matters. In *The (Post)Mistress* (2013), Highway clearly moves away from the 'trickster' aesthetic of his earlier career. *The (Post)Mistress* is structured as a one-woman monologue, a typical postcolonial dramatic form,[5] which bespeaks resistance against the colonial gaze. This monologue-like play echoes the technique of Indigenous storytelling, as the (post) mistress shares significant stories about her life experiences with the audience. Further, *The (Post)Mistress* is conceived as a musical, a typically Western genre, for a single female character, Marie-Louise Painchaud. The combination of the Western form of the musical with Indigenous storytelling constitutes a first degree of aesthetic creolisation. This is further emphasised through other technical features: the insertion of images of Canadian stamps between the different parts of the printed version of the play as well as the almost expressionistic use of 'a gridwork of small, square aluminum boxes—the mailboxes [...] of a small country post office as seen [...] from the perspective of the post-office workers' (Highway 2013, n.p.). The stage also includes the presence of a 'celestial orchestra' (n.p.), comprised of a grand piano and a saxophonist. Moreover, the book's cover shows us a crowned postmistress, resembling the image of Queen Elizabeth on a Canadian stamp. This ironic touch introduces a transcultural, postnational motif into the play: how could the Queen of England still embody the multiple identities of a contemporary creolised Canada? In addition, the play is frankly multilingual: originally written in English, it was translated into French by Highway and Raymond Lalonde, under the title *Zesty Gopher s'est fait écraser par un frigo* (n.p.). Moreover, the lyrics sung by the postmistress are written in Cree, English, and French.

From a thematic point of view, the creolisation of racial signifiers can be perceived from the start. In a squarely metatheatrical opening, Marie-Louise Painchaud notices the presence of the audience: 'What are you doing here? [...] How long have you been sitting here watching me like that?' (Highway 2013, 2) Highway's choice of a non-Indigenous female character as his main protagonist can only destabilise the expectations of a public used to watching trickster-style Native plays. Marie-Louise quickly introduces herself as a postmistress whose family hailed from Quebec. However, her racial background is partly Indigenous, as her great-grandfather, Lucien Boulanger, 'married a Cree Indian woman from somewhere up north' (3). Marie-Louise's friend Sylvie Labranche is 'Métis—part Cree from Manitoba, part French from here' (5), a further marker of creolisation. Moreover, Sylvie has a secret lover from Brazil, Barbaro Botafogo, who studies Indigenous languages and knows an incredible amount of them (4–5). This extends the transnational and transcultural aspect of the work. In an amplification of Sylvie's story, Marie-Louise sings the first lyric of the play, a Cree love song, 'Taansi, Nimiss' [Hey, Big Sister], later translated into English. Punctuated in a creolised manner by a Brazilian samba rhythm, it expresses Sylvie's passion for her lover (4). Marie-Louise prolongs this mood of creolised singing in a 'Dixieland style', when she celebrates her friend Yvette Paquette's love for an African American man from New Orleans (10).

In the following scenes, the postmistress tries to detect secret love affairs by peering through the letters she is sorting. One therefore wonders if this does not reflect her own emotional frustration. Her next song is sung in French to a bossa nova rhythm, although translated into English: 'What I see in your eyes/is the reflection of those stars and the light of your love,/So, my dear, come and see me,/Let us dance arm in arm tonight' (17). Characteristically, she prefaces the song by lamenting: 'Oh, it's been so long since Roland [...] that's my husband [...] talked to me like this' (16).

The concluding tale/song of Act One introduces a clearly tragic mood, focusing on how Rosa Lee Johnson killed her partner Gus, who had violently abused her: 'In which second she grabbed something/Something sharp and made of steel,/She reached for his cold heart thus' (32). The first act concludes on a dissonant note: *Music (and singing) comes to a smashing, atonal end. [...] Rosa Lee Johnson's voice speaks out at us through the theatre sound system, steel-hard, bloodless, cold. [...]* Wipe that smirk off your face, you rat!' (33).

A softer mood marks the beginning of Act Two. When Marie-Louise tries to guess the content of a letter from Argentina, '*The bass line of a tango snaps on*', a Latino cultural reference which constitutes a further sign of creolisation (39). An embryonic magic realist atmosphere typifies this scene. Indeed, '[...] *the entire post office has been thrown into a time warp [...] it is as if she is moving inside a dream, or under water*' (39). She recites a love song entitled 'When I Was Last in Buenos Aires, Argentina', in which she dreams she had a secret Argentinian lover named Ariel. Her tango-like song could be likened to a sensuous elegy for lost love. As she imagines she would eventually leave her distraught lover, she ironically dubs herself a '(post) mistress' (45).

Her next story/song tells of the predicament of her friend Josephine Maurice, married to a Cree man, Zesty Gopher, who died crushed by a fridge (hence the title of the French-language edition of the play). Beyond the farcical implications of this story, Marie-Louise's Cree lyrics, translated into English and meant to be sung at the burial ceremony, are deeply moving. An Indigenous worldview is captured by this song, as the deep bond linking the living and the land reveals: 'We thank you, Earth,/for watching over us so well in this way/while we live here on this Earth/those of us known as humans' (49). Inspired by Indigenous epistemology, these lines blur the distinction between humans and non-humans. In a subsequent Berlin-style cabaret rap number (51), Marie-Louise recounts the ups and downs of her love relationship with her husband Roland, stressing the strong link keeping them united: 'things eventually do settle down' (61).

The final climactic scene of the play reinforces the magic realist overtones of the initial moments of Act Two. While there exists a considerable amount of scholarship on magic realism, in the limited framework of this chapter, I shall simply refer to Kim Anderson Sasser's recent theories in order to describe this mode of writing.[6] In *Magical Realism and Cosmopolitanism. Strategizing Belonging*, Kim Anderson Sasser, like many scholars in the field, regards magic realism as a mode of writing enabling the momentary alliance of incompatible aspects of human existence, such as the real and the magic or the supernatural. As Sasser remarks, '[…] magic adds to or builds on the realistic world. It is compatible with, or works alongside, reality in some way, while at the same time suggesting that a naturalist worldview is lacking' (Sasser 2014, 31). Magic realism suggests 'an amplified view of narrative reality, one in which magic might at any time "emerge" out of the real […] As magic "emerges" or "grows" out of the real, it is not antithetical or destructive to reality, but compatible with it' (32). As Sasser further indicates, '[…] magical realist narratives seem to claim of their magic that it is real too! Magical realism […] extends realist verisimilitude to the supernatural elements of its narrative, thereby inserting the magical […] into the real' (34). Magic realism, as a mode of writing, ideally captures the contiguity between different ontological realms such as the ordinary and the supernatural, which is a typical feature of Indigenous cosmologies.

At the outset of this magic realist climax, Marie-Louise tells us she is a ghost, having actually died from cancer a few years before. Because she previously kept the truth from us, she thus paradoxically qualifies as a trickster in human shape, a muted reminiscence of Highway's earlier aesthetic. She is now in charge of forwarding mail from the netherworld: '[…] now that I'm dead, I work in this great big post office up here in the sky handling mail between the dead and the living, letters they send to each other through their dreams—the human dream as the ultimate postal system' (Highway 2013, 64). She voices a message of universal peace: 'I hope that people will stop hurting each other and learn to laugh' (65). She then utters a *'gigantic'* magic realist laughter that sounds *'incredibly haunting, it is obvious that it comes from another world entirely'* (65). In the play's magic realist coda, Marie-Louise sends a love letter to her husband, who is still alive. She expresses her hope to be reunited with him after he dies, in a creolised song/missive again combining the Indigenous and English languages. As she climbs stairs into an imaginary sky, she intones a message of harmony, wishing Roland 'happiness on this Earth' (69). In a moment that establishes the connection between the ordinary and the beyond, her *silvery, miraculous voice* is heard one last time (70). In the final lines of the play, the tragic mood of the conclusion of Act One, as Sara Lee Johnson killed her partner, is serenely transcended.

In this play, Highway weaves together a magic realist aesthetic and the diffraction of creolisation. This enables a reinterpretation of conventional racial hierarchies, privileging a cosmopolitan stance anchored in the cross-pollination and enmeshment of ethnic constituencies. Thus, Highway manages to boldly affirm the positive potentialities of a non-essentialist understanding of race and of its cultural manifestations in artistic production.

3   NEGOTIATING THE RESIDENTIAL SCHOOLS TRAUMA ACROSS RACIAL AND GENDER DIVIDES

Ojibway playwright Drew Hayden Taylor (Ontario) has acquired a prominence almost equal to Highway's through his highly prolific dramatic output. Like his peer, Taylor articulates a fluid, creolised, non-homogeneous, understanding of racial Indigenous identities by departing from simplistic cultural binaries.[7] This phenomenon can be detected in the historiographic *God and the Indian* (2014). This play explores the traumatic past of the residential schools, in which the Canadian Government had decided Indigenous children should study and live in order to assimilate into white society. Forcibly separated from their families, these Indigenous children were often sexually abused by the priests who ran those institutions.[8] The difficulty of preserving memory and of witnessing constitutes a defining parameter of racial codes in contemporary Canada. Further, racial aspects are intertwined with gender issues, as Taylor wishes to show how the brutal system of these schools deeply affected both male and female children (Taylor 2014, 14).

Like Highway's *The (Post)Mistress, God and the Indian* concentrates on a non-Indigenous character, Assistant Bishop George, who is visited by a Native female character. This young woman turns out to be a former residential school student the bishop may have abused in earlier days. Moreover, the female character, curiously named Johnny, often describes herself as a 'ghost', whose racial identity has been negated and destroyed. This suggests a lack of Indigenous visibility in contemporary Canada. Aesthetically, the play could be regarded as a parody of the Christian ritual of confession, as both characters relive past traumas. In this process, simplistic cultural binaries are erased: Taylor focuses as much on the white settler's inner torture as on that of the Indigenous character. Like the representation of racial divides, the mood of the play is ambiguous. As Taylor points out: 'This an angry play. This is a healing play' (x).

The Native woman who visits Assistant Bishop George immediately creolises the dominant English linguistic register of the play when uttering in her Native language: '*Nintoogeewaan*. (I want to go home)', an implicit allusion to the family separation she endured at her residential school. Johnny prompts the bishop to remember what happened in her childhood. As he fails to acknowledge any involvement, she angrily racialises Christianity, 'I think you did a little better in life than me. I guess it helps when you are the same race as God' (10). Johnny further asserts her sense of emptiness when she compares herself to a ghost: 'It's like I'm a ghost, floating through the city, just a shadow of questionable actions. Sort of like the ghost of abuses past' (18). The trauma, however, is equally present in George's life: 'I should have faced responsibility and ... faced the evil ... And it's haunted me ever since' (29). Further, Johnny voices her guilt about the death of her brother in residential school, which further emphasises her ghost-like status: 'When my brother died, and my parents came to get us for the summer, they found out [...] I was supposed to look after him [...] my parents blamed me for not looking after him [...] I became just as dead to them as he was. That's why I am a ghost' (39–40). However, she affirms her desire to exist: 'I don't want to be a ghost anymore. I want to exist. To be seen. To be acknowledged by you. And to have you admit what you've done' (42). Act One concludes on an intensification of the desire for revenge, as Johnny points a gun at Bishop George.

However, at the outset of Act Two, a somewhat calmed-down Johnny recounts her ill-fated love affair with a young Cree man, who left her after making her pregnant. This suggests that the impossibility for many Indigenous people to lead a stable family life originates in the traumatic abuses they experienced. Because of Johnny's alcoholic addiction, the baby girl died at birth. As Johnny sadly concludes: 'ghosts can't have children' (53). She henceforth became sterile, which reinforces her racial invisibility. She attributes her decision to adopt a man's name to this incident (53). Her unsexing can be viewed as metonymic of the oppression of Indigenous people by white colonisers at large. Johnny's rage explodes when she 'fires a bullet at the [George's] family photograph' (66). Exasperated, the Bishop feigns to leave, at which point Johnny indicates that she will kill herself. This forces George to become conciliatory: 'Would that stop the nightmares? If I admitted to everything you claimed I did, would it make you sleep at night? Would it make you put down the gun?' (73). However, his full admission sounds contrived, and doubts about its sincerity subsist. As she realises this, Johnny '*weakens. Her resolve evaporates*' (76), which gives George the opportunity of placing the gun in a drawer. She accepts the failure of her attempts at securing a confession: 'I'm tired. I'm sick. I'm through with you. I don't need your confession anymore' (77). Although George seems to remember her real name, Lucy, before she leaves, Johnny denies the possibility of complete reconciliation. This somewhat contradicts Taylor's own assessment of *God and the Indian* as a play about healing: 'No goodbyes. [...] Lucy's dead. She's been dead for a very long time. I'm a ghost, remember?' (80). Johnny/Lucy does indeed disappear into thin air and George cannot even find any trace of the gun he hid in a drawer.

At this point, the reader/spectator realises that the reference to Johnny as a ghost was not simply metaphorical. This climactic moment suggests the whole play can be viewed as a magic realist nightmare. Indeed, in its linkage of the real and the supernatural, this work may constitute a projection of the Bishop's inner torments. It would be wrong, however, to assume that the Indigenous racial aspect of the play remains secondary. On the contrary, magic realism suggests the importance of a Native world view, predicated on a fluid relationship between different ontological realms. Taylor thus locates the source of the white clergyman's haunting in Indigenous epistemology. The playwright's depiction of this enmeshment between Indigenous and white races suggests their creolised, rhizomatic relationship cannot be reduced to a simple opposition between good and evil. Further, Taylor's creolisation even blurs gender differences, as Johnny's name indicates. Aesthetically, the magic realist background of the play encodes the polymorphous shapes of racial tensions.

4   Escaping the Prison of Stereotypes Through Racial Creolisation

The creolisation of racial dramatisations of Indigeneity is manifest in the experimental works of Métis playwright Marie Clements, including *Burning Vision* (2002), *Copper Thunderbird* (2007), and *The Edward Curtis Project: A Modern Picture Story* (2010).[9] In *Tombs of the Vanishing Indian* (2011), Clements even further amplifies her vision of Indigenous identities as fluid. Like Taylor's *God and the Indian*, this work seeks to come to terms with past trauma from a historiographic perspective. The play's geographical parameters are also broadened: moving beyond Highway's and Taylor's resolutely Canadian focus, Clements portrays Indigenous people from California. The play dramatises the plight of women from the Gabrielino-Tongva tribes, living on an island off the coast of Los Angeles, who were forcibly sterilised in the 1970s.

The legend of the 'Lone Woman', who haunts the play like a ghost, in a magic realist mode reminiscent of *God and The Indian*, constitutes the first historical layer of the play. As the introductory note by Virginia Carmelo indicates, the Gabrielino-Tongva lone woman was forced to leave the island of San Nicholas in 1835 to be housed in the Santa Barbara Mission on the continent. She escaped from the boat deporting her to return to the island, where her baby had been left. She survived 18 years alone on the island but failed to find her baby. When she was finally removed to California, she died within weeks. This legend thus establishes the importance of Indigenous kinship bonds (Clements 2012, n.p.). The second historical aspect of the play concerns the sterilisation of Native women, which as a prefatory note makes clear was a practice enforced by US authorities and made official through the *U.S. Family Planning Act* of 1970 (n.p.).[10] Third, the play also alludes to the U.S. assimilation policy of Indigenous people. Native Americans were encouraged to leave their reservation and to try to assimilate into the white urban world through the *Indian Relocation Act* of 1956 (n.p.).[11] By the end of the play, some measure of healing of these traumatic events is achieved.

Creating a link between the real and the supernatural, the first scene foregrounds the magic realist presence of the lone woman, who functions as a chorus of Indigenous voices: '*the voice of THE LONE WOMAN penetrates the space, growing louder, calling out from nothing as drums begin to beat, and a thousand Indian women's voices reach each other and echo down a long tunnel* (5). A re-enactment of the tragedy that provoked the lone woman's death and her separation from her three daughters follows these initial moments. Before she gets killed by policemen, the lone woman urges her daughters to remember her. She offers them a piece of rock, which could symbolise their attachment to the Indigenous land and to their mother (6–7). She later suggests that the rock might refer to her lost baby: 'I was playing on the beach with my son, my silly boy, my rock' (58). One of the sisters, Janey, laments the loss of her mother: 'She is gone, our center is gone, and like a triangle we descend into the vanishing' (8). Clements's unconventional aesthetic is not only detectable in her use of magic realism, it can also be perceived in the play's diorama stage set. Indeed, the three sisters live in these dioramas, a device meant to suggest their imprisonment in white culture as well as their isolation. Only towards the end of the play are they reunited. The diorama set also indicates how enslaved they are to white stereotypes of the Indigenous race, as if they were zoo creatures looked at in their cage: 'Each woman's Indian Room is decorated like set pieces in the diorama of a museum. The backdrops in each Indian Room fade in layers in a modern treatment of the Daguerre Dioramas shown in Paris in the 1820s. [...] each woman's Indian Room is encased in glass as if history is animating before the audience, untouchable, until the glass is broken and their stories are no longer separate or containable' (3). Being related to museum culture, the dioramas symbolise the demise of the Indigenous race, destroyed by the commodifying white gaze of the other characters and even perhaps of the spectator. The stories of the three sisters, Janey, Jessie, and Miranda, are recounted in counterpoint in the different scenes focusing on their respective dioramas. Throughout the play, until the sisters' narratives eventually merge, Clements emphasises the unfixed, indeed creolised, features of Indigenous identity. The Indigenous sisters are contrasted to three white male characters, whose attitude towards Indigeneity shows nuances ranging from hostility to understanding. The presence of a woman of mixed Jewish and Indigenous ancestry, Ruth, also contributes to de-essentialising racial parameters. In addition, the linguistic creolisation hybridises English through passages in the Gabrielino language, which often merges with Spanish.

In her diorama scenes, Janey, a street woman, reveals her traumatic experiences. We first discover her in a police interrogation room, as white detective Fullen tries to determine whether she actually murdered her baby. In a magic realist vein, she hears the voice of the lone woman/her mother, who speaks in glossed Gabrielino. As the lone woman affirms her emotional link with Janey, the latter answers in Spanish, probably because she was raised by a Chicano family (11). In a subsequent scene, the lone woman encourages Janey, in her Gabrielino language, to protect her child. In doing so, she emphasises the importance of the maternal womb: 'Hold him inside. Hold him close inside, inside. It is only from the inside, we are still mothers' (30). Detective Fullen quickly dismisses her maternal dreams as figments of her imagination, saying that her baby 'never was' (31). After having her examined by two interns,

Detective Fullen confronts her with the painful truth: 'You knew you were sterilized' (44). She pleads she always wanted to have a baby, comparing the womb to a means of escaping white oppression: 'To hide ... in the sky of a woman's body' (43). To a puzzled Detective Fullen, Janey replies: 'They think they took everything ... but you cannot take the sky' (61). Thus, she identifies femininity as a site of colonial resistance, while stating in a dream-like sequence she recreated her mother's imaginary island for herself: 'In my Indian Room, I constructed my own island. Like the Lone Woman before me' (61). In one of the last scenes, Janey remembers the episode when she talked to Jessie, a physician, about her inability to have children because of sterilisation. In a short meditative moment, the two women recognised each other as true sisters. Janey then shares a vision of home with Jessie: they both affirm their link with three desert boulders their mother used to draw their attention to. Says Jessie: 'Janey, baby, look. Don't you recognize them from home? Look how they stand' (70). Female agency is depicted as a way of countering Western oppression. A further twist in the racial creolisation pattern of the play is introduced minutes before the concluding scene, as Detective Fullen (whose grandfather collected things Indian) articulates a feeling of genuine kinship with Janey: 'I remember you ... I recognize you as a part of myself' (76). This notation, which betrays Fullen's sensitiveness as a white person, reiterates Clements's rejection of simplistic racial binaries in favour of a rhizomatic world vision. Janey's presence plays an important role in the concluding scene, to which I shall return after examining Jessie and Miranda's diorama stories.

Married to a white physician, Daniel, Jessie feels tormented about her disavowal of Indigenous culture. Being a physician herself, she is one of the first Indigenous women to have made it in the white establishment. Her cultural in-betweenness becomes manifest when she receives the visit of a Jewish Indigenous patient, Ruth. This character not only reinforces the creolisation of racial codifications through her mixed heritage, she also triggers Jessie's feelings of guilt about her cultural ambiguity. Ruth underlines the dangers of being a 'real, educated Indian woman', to which Jessie characteristically replies: 'I wouldn't call myself an Indian woman' (24). Ruth, who is in part a Gabrielino Indian, suspects that Jessie tries to repress a traumatic past: 'Sometimes history is too painful to remember, but we remember anyways because we are still working it out, aren't we?' (26). Jessie is later confronted with the painful issue of the sterilisation of Indigenous women, when a young patient, Sarah, comes to claim her allegedly promised womb transplant. When sterilised, it transpires, Sarah was falsely led to believe that this operation was only meant as a temporary way of stopping her multiple pregnancies. Jessie has to tell her that such a womb transplant is impossible. This episode introduces one of the main motifs of the play, the attempt by the white 'race' to eradicate the Indigenous one. Feeling betrayed, Sarah lashes out at Jessie's cultural in-betweenness: 'I don't trust your white paper, and I don't trust a woman who wears white and has brown hands' (48). The throes of cultural in-betweenness further resonate in a scene between Daniel and Jessie. Daniel, a benevolent white doctor, seeks to help abused Indigenous women, a feature indicating Clements's departure from simplistic ethnic binaries. The inner-city clinic he runs, says Jessie, is 'not exactly the cash cow your father had planned for you when you said you were going to medical school' (56). Jessie acutely becomes aware of her own cultural issues: 'Daniel, I never grew up with my heritage. [...] I'm telling you I had to forget the part of me that is Indian' (57). She later discovers names of sterilised patients in Daniel's locked filing cabinet, which threatens their love relationship. Outraged, Jessie throws the rock inherited from her mother at the wall: '*She looks at her glass wall covered with the names of women patients. Grabbing her rock, she throws it at the glass, breaking an opening*' (70). She confronts Daniel: 'When were you going to tell me you are sterilizing brown women. Indian women' (71), to which Daniel replies he meant to save these women from the poverty arising from multiple unwanted pregnancies. Feeling desperate, Jessie throws herself out of the window. The lone woman reappears in a concluding magic realist moment, soothingly suggesting that Jessie will be reunited with a 'river made of dreams' (74), that is, with the maternal figure symbolising her cultural roots.

Miranda's diorama story is similarly fraught with painful racial issues. Wishing to become a Hollywood star, she is working with a white director, Bob Stills, who holds highly stereotypical views of Indigenous people. This stance resurges in his movies, in which the Indian is always defeated. In a metatheatrical twist, we actually see the two characters rehearse a scene, in which Miranda is 'dressed as an Indian princess on a western movie set. She begins the long process of dying [...]' (26). However, subsequent sections of the play indicate that the racial divide is not that clear, as Bob Stills betrays his fascination with Indigenous people. In a near farcical moment, Miranda discovers a disguised Bob Stills, '*wearing a full Indian buckskin*' (37). As an Indigenous person, she finds this cultural appropriation particularly irritating. Stills awkwardly responds: 'I wish I was an Indian' (39). He nurtures an idealised vision of the 'Noble savage': 'An Indian gets to ride a wild horse, shoot bows and arrows; they get to tie people to stakes, and do the cool screams, scalp 'em, stab 'em, and dance, and sing, and smoke. That's a full afternoon of letting go if you ask me' (40). She vehemently opposes this sentimental view, indicating how she feels trapped by Hollywood stereotypes. In a gesture of creolisation of racial differences, Stills later reveals his awareness of exploiting racial binaries in his profession: 'I'm a fucking cliché, really. [...] when I do get my comeback, it's the same old crap that distorts history and the whole Indian-white man thing' (48). However, he persists in his errors. As he and Miranda have sex, he considers making a porn film out of the recording of their intercourse: 'I think I will call it...*Princess Redfeather*. Everybody likes to see an Indian getting fucked' (67). In counterpoint, Miranda asserts the relativity of cultural boundaries, ironically remembering that she was displaced to Los Angeles 'to become civilized like you' (66). Is civilisation really the privilege of the white race? As they fight for the possession of the infamous tape, Miranda is shot dead. In a magic realist moment echoing the conclusion of Jessie's diorama stories, the lone woman suggests that she has joined a 'river made of dreams' (75).

The last moments of the play, written in a distinctly magic realist mode, foreground the reunion of the three sisters, who have escaped their diorama boxes. They are now moving in the fluidity of a watery environment. As her sisters previously did: '*JANEY begins to move* [...] *towards the flow of the river*' (75). In a chorus, Janey, Jessie, and Miranda now deliver the last sentences of the play, which bespeak an immersion '[...] inside the waterways we called the tombs [...] And inside the dreams of Indians' (76). The allusion to tombs echoes the title of the play, while suggesting that healing of traumatic experiences can only be found in death. The mood of sadness dominates, as Janey observes: 'We didn't know the river rising beneath us was the tears of Indians' (76). In contrast to this atmosphere of mourning, the last stage directions suggest the sisters magically transform into the three boulders previously associated by their mother with their Indigenous home (77).

Like Tomson Highway's and Drew Hayden Taylor's, Clements's dramaturgies transcend the rigid template of Trickster playwriting. As I have shown, in *Tombs of the Vanishing Indian*, Clements devises a complex, non-linear and multivocal historiographic work, relying on a non-homogeneous, indeed creolised vision of racial identities, depicted in the flow of a continuous process. Clements emphasises the characters' inner contradictions, be they Indigenous or Caucasian. She also underlines their respective proximity to the other ethnic group in a way that de-essentialises binaries, debunks racial stereotypes, while simultaneously showing the dangers this cultural entanglement can bring about. This can be detected in Jessie's doubts of cultural in-betweenness, in Miranda's subjection to Hollywood stereotypes, Janey's sterilisation, as well as in Bob Stills's ambiguous attraction to the myth of Indianness, Daniel's misplaced desire to help Indigenous women, or Detective Fullen's humane approach to Indigeneity. Throughout the play, and particularly so in the concluding scene, an Indigenous worldview defying the Western gaze of colonialism is perceptible in Clements's reliance on magic realism, which undermines Anglo-American rationalism. This magic realist aesthetic is triggered by the female agency of the lone woman, which suggests a deep link between racial and gender formations.

5   Dystopian Futures: The Healing Power of Transcultural Synergies

Yvette Nolan's *The Unplugging* prolongs the themes of Indigenous survival and trauma healing from an ecological perspective, as it takes place in an undefined apocalyptic future. Like the earlier plays examined here, it foregrounds female agency as a potential source of regeneration. Like Highway's, Taylor's, and Clements's plays, *The Unplugging* relies on a non-homogeneous representation of race/ethnicity: Indigeneity is viewed in its creolised relationships with the white constituencies of society. Yvette Nolan is of mixed heritage herself, her mother being of Algonquin descent and her father an Irish immigrant. Written in a vein similar to Margaret Atwood's 'speculative fiction' in her *MaddAddam* trilogy, the play contains a strong ethical dimension: humans should behave responsibly towards nature and should act in a humane fashion with people from different ethnic groups.[12]

After the initial massive 'unplugging' of the world, that is a total collapse of modern technology, two Indigenous women, who can no longer give birth, are excluded from their community. One can assume the latter consists primarily of Indigenous people. However, it is also populated by white families, as the character of Seamus later exemplifies. After their banishment, the two women, Elena and Bern, are forced to learn how to survive in a harsh natural environment, first described as icy (Nolan 2014, 3), with the help of their improvised survival skills. They only have at their disposal such remnants of modern Western society as '*the hatchet, a lighter that still works, a couple of cans of vegetables, a package of noodles, a half box of salt, a roll of toilet paper, a box of wooden matches.*' As Rachel Ditor indicates in her preface, Yvette Nolan underlines 'our own digital dependence' and 'prompts us to think about our relationship to the land' (Ditor 2014, iii). In the first scene, 'Banished', Elena offers a more precise description of this apocalypse: 'Dead cars, dead stereos, dead computers, dead telephones, dead rockets, dead, dead, dead' (Nolan 2014, 7). In the second scene, entitled 'Survival', the female friends find refuge in a log-house and start accommodating to the harshness of life in the wild. They have to devise innovative ways of adapting to this unforeseen scenario. They lament the cruelty of their community, whose members seem to have become dictatorial, a sign that Nolan refuses to engage with the 'Noble Savage' trope.[13] Reflecting on their exile, Bern has to admit that Indigenous people sometimes had to behave in a cruel manner: 'In tough times—we—used to leave people behind' (14). I concur with Birgit Däwes when she affirms that Nolan in no way idealises nature (Däwes 2014, 39). The Indigenous women acknowledge the danger of their present predicament, realising they have lost their primordial link with nature: 'we were a nomadic people! We haven't lived like that in centuries' (Nolan 2014, 14).

The women's progressive re-familiarisation with the natural environment is dramatised through a sequence of scenes suggesting the co-existence of an Indigenous cosmology with a Western worldview. Indeed, the passage of time is evoked in each scene through allusions to the Indigenous names of particular months, which are immediately translated into English: Little Spirit Moon (December), Spirit Moon (January), Bear Moon (February), Snow Crust Moon (March), Pink Moon (April), Sucker Moon (May). This implies the importance of the cyclical rhythm of the seasons, with an emphasis on the regeneration power of spring, as we reach the last reconciliation scene. The moon also symbolically refers to the female agency inherent in the process of healing.

In the early scenes, as they learn how to survive with few resources, the women retrieve a sense of Indigenous respect for the food they eat. They also speak their native language again: 'Elena: [...] Thanks to the Creator for this meal. Thanks for this waaboos for giving himself to us for this meal. Bern: Meegwetch, waaboos. [...] Elena: [...] We need meat, Indians. It's in our blood' (23). In the scene called 'The Stranger', Bern discovers a young white man in the log-house, named Seamus. While she at first thinks he might be a rapist and feels suspicious, they eventually become friends. Bern shows him how she survived in her wild environment. She recounts how she and her female friend rejected the exploitation of nature typical of their former community: 'This is how we got into this situation in the first place, people indiscriminately taking and using and wasting without any thought to the future' (31). Seamus then reveals he is a second-generation immigrant from Ireland, introducing the motif of creolisation between Indigenous and Caucasian ethnic groups. Elena still fears Seamus is a spy sent by the old community to steal their survival skills. As we learn later, her suspicions are legitimate. Indeed, Seamus tells Bern that he escaped from the community because he was no longer interested in 'video games and Twitter', but instead wanted to learn how to live in harmony with nature, to discover 'what time of day it is from the sun, and what we can eat from the land and that mukwa means bear [...]' (42). This desire suggests his willingness as a white person to adopt what he naively believes to be an Indigenous lifestyle, an enmeshment pointing to Yvette Nolan's creolisation of racial positionings. At this point, ecocritics might wonder if Nolan does not advocate a simplistic return to an ancient Indigenous harmony with nature as a desirable outcome. On the contrary, I would argue that Nolan calls for a syncretic fusion of Indigenous and Western knowledges so as to ensure future potentialities. Although the play falls short of delineating the exact iterations of these creolisations, Nolan insists on innovative transcultural transformation. Indeed, as she has sex with Seamus, Bern suggests that all human beings have to morph into more aware creatures: 'We are all having to—become—something new' (54). At the end of the same scene, Elena wishes to ban Seamus from their place, which Bern refuses on ethical grounds. Victims can become perpetrators, Yvette Nolan suggests: evil resides in the heart of Indigenous and Caucasian people alike. As Elena feared, it next transpires that Seamus has indeed left the two women, probably a sign of betrayal. Bern defends Seamus in spite of everything, arguing that he may eventually teach the community how to adopt a more responsible lifestyle. The conclusion of the play confirms her hypothesis.

In the climactic scene, symbolically entitled 'Harvest', Seamus returns and explains he feels sorry for having considered abandoning the two women in the first place. Bern lashes out against him: 'you stole from us. I trusted you, I showed you how to survive, and then you stole food, you took snares, and matches [...]' (63). Seamus then indicates that he learned something extremely useful from them, and was therefore sent back by the community, 'To come in and talk. To make reparations. To ask you to come back to the community'

(66). Moreover, as Birgit Däwes judiciously points out (Däwes 2014, 39), he returns to the women in the company of Elena's daughter and grandson, in order to discuss 'possible futures' (Nolan 2014, 66). Thus, as a Caucasian, he encourages the two Indigenous women to reunite with their community, so that they can teach the skills they learned in the wild, perhaps in the hope of making both constituencies more resilient in the face of future disasters. This suggests an eventual creolisation of the racial divide separating Indigenous and Caucasian people. Only at that price, that is if the energies of Indigenous and white cultures merge, can the future of humankind as well as spiritual regeneration be secured.

As I hope to have shown, Yvette Nolan's *The Unplugging* moves further away from the trickster template than the plays analysed so far. The creolisation of conventional racial binaries becomes even more perceptible in this play: ultimate healing is only achieved through a collaborative enmeshment between Indigenous and white characters in the struggle for ecological survival. Female agency is foregrounded, as in the earlier plays examined, but the role of the white male protagonist is equally vital. One may wonder if the absence of magic realism, which so far had seemed to be an aesthetic marker of racial difference, is not precisely due to the urgency of the issues at hand. Whereas magic realism seems to encode meditations on the Indigenous past, this minimalist play privileges action to ensure a sustainable future for humankind and indeed our planet.

6   De-essentialising Indigenous Identities on the Canadian Stage: A Provisional Conclusion

Taking its cue from Chadwick Allen's invitation to place in conversation Indigenous texts from various cultural backgrounds (Cree, Ojibway, Métis and part Algonquin) (Allen 2012, xix), this chapter has examined some of the ways in which recent First Nations playwrights have dramatised the ambiguities of race. In their own idioms, the four case studies highlight the multi-layered processes of creolisation characterising contemporary Indigenous identity formations, from racial/ethnic, gender, (trans)cultural, linguistic, and aesthetic perspectives. Analysing these works, as Allen recommends, 'close together' rather than 'together equal' enables us to realise the full extent of their polymorphous dramaturgies (xxxiii). Their de-essentialised reinventions of racial/ethnic boundaries will hopefully generate further innovative creolisations of Canadian Indigenous drama in decades to come.

Notes

1. At the outset, I wish to sincerely thank Jessica Maufort for her insightful comments on earlier drafts of this essay. I am also grateful to Samuel Pauwels for his technical support.
2. I have used Julin Everett's English translation (Chancé 2011, 265).

3. See Marc and Jessica Maufort, 'A Fraught Process: Devising New State Idioms for Post-apartheid South Africa' (Maufort and Maufort 2020, 1–20); see also my essay in the same volume, 'Revisiting the Past, Imagining the Future: Aesthetic of Creolization in Post-apartheid South African Drama' (Maufort 2020, 183–205).
4. For a detailed examination of Tomson Highway's dramaturgies, see my book, *Transgressive Itineraries. Postcolonial Hybridizations of Dramatic Realism* (Maufort 2003, 148–157).
5. In this respect, see Helen Gilbert and Jacqueline Lo, 'Performing Hybridity in Post-colonial Monodrama' (Gilbert and Lo 1997).
6. The following works are perhaps the most widely acknowledged scholarly studies on magic realism: *Magical Realism. Theory, History, Community* (Zamora and Faris 1995) and *Ordinary Enchantments. Magical Realism and the Remystification of Narrative* (Faris 2004).
7. For a more exhaustive examination of Drew Hayden Taylor's dramaturgies, see my book, *Transgressive Itineraries* (Maufort 2003, 164–176).
8. For a historical examination of residential schools in Canada, see John S. Molloy. *A National Crime. The Canadian Government and the Residential School System 1879 to 1986* (Molloy 1999).
9. For a detailed analysis of these plays, the reader may turn to my earlier essays: 'Voices of Cultural Memory. Enacting History in Recent Native Canadian Drama' (Maufort 2013, 150–176), (*Burning Vision*); 'Celebrating Indigeneity: Contemporary Aboriginal Playwriting in Canada and Australasia' (Maufort 2011, 91–108), (*Copper Thunderbird*); 'Indigenous Playwriting and Globalization' (Maufort 2017, 284–295), (*The Edward Curtis Project*).
10. For a historical account of this phenomenon, see 'The Indian Health Service and the Sterilization of Native American Women' (Lawrence 2000, 400–419). More specifically, Lawrence alludes to the actual incident of an Indigenous woman who claimed a womb transplant from her physician, as the character of Sarah does in Clements's play. This case was first reported by Gail Mark Jarvis, 'Theft of Life' (Jarvis 1977, 30–32; quoted in Sasser, 400).
11. For more historical information about the relocation act, see Rebecca L. Robbins, 'Self-Determination and Subordination: The Past, Present, and Future of American Indian Governance' (Robbins 1999, 98–100).
12. For a detailed ecocritical analysis of *The Unplugging*, the reader should turn to Birgit Däwes's essay, 'Stages of Resilience. Heteroholistic Environments in Plays by Marie Clements and Yvette Nolan' (Däwes 2014, 21–45).
13. For a more detailed discussion of this stereotypical vision of the ecological Indian, see Greg Garrard, *Ecocriticism* (Garrard 2012, 129–145).

REFERENCES

Allen, Chadwick. 2012. *Trans-Indigenous. Methodologies for Global Native Literary Studies*. Minneapolis, MN: University of Minnesota Press.

Chancé, Dominique. 2011. Creolization. Definition and Critique. Trans. Julin Everett. In *The Creolization of Theory*, edited by Françoise Lionnet and Shu-mei Shih, 262–267. Durham, NC: Duke University Press.

Clements, Marie. 2012. *Tombs of the Vanishing Indian*. Vancouver: Talonbooks.

Däwes, Birgit. 2007. *Native North American Theatre in a Global Age. Sites of Identity Construction and Transdifference.* Heidelberg: Winter.

———. 2014. Stages of Resilience. Heteroholistic Environments in Plays by Marie Clements and Yvette Nolan. In *Enacting Nature. Ecocritical Perspectives on Indigenous Performance,* ed. Birgit Däwes and Marc Maufort, 21–45. Brussels: P.I.E. Peter Lang.

Ditor, Rachel. 2014. Preface to *The Unplugging,* by Yvette Nolan, iii–iv. Toronto: Playwrights Canada Press.

Fagan, Kristina. 2010. What's the Trouble with the Trickster? An Introduction. In *Troubling Tricksters. Revisioning Critical Conversations,* ed. Deanna Reder and Linda M. Morra, 3–10. Waterloo, ON: Wilfried Laurier University Press.

Faris, Wendy B. 2004. *Ordinary Enchantments. Magical Realism and the Remystification of Narrative.* Nashville, TN: Vanderbilt University Press.

Filewod, Alan. 1992. Averting the Colonial Gaze: Notes on Watching Native Theatre. In *Aboriginal Voices: Amerindian, Inuit, and Sami Theatre,* ed. Per Brask and William Morgan, 17–28. Baltimore, MD: Johns Hopkins University Press.

Garrard, Greg. 2012. *Ecocriticism.* London: Routledge.

Gilbert, Helen, and Jacqueline Lo. 1997. Performing Hybridity in Post-colonial Monodrama. *Journal of Commonwealth Literature* 31 (1): 1–19.

Glissant, Édouard. 1997a. *Poetics of Relation.* Trans. Betsy Wing. Ann Arbor, MI: University of Michigan Press.

———. 1997b. *Traité du Tout-Monde. Poétique IV.* Paris: Gallimard.

Highway, Tomson. 1988. *The Rez Sisters.* Saskatoon: Fifth House Publishers.

———. 2013. *The (Post)Mistress.* Vancouver: Talonbooks.

Jarvis, Gail Mark. 1977. Theft of Life. *Akwesasne Notes*: 30–32.

Knowles, Ric. 2010. *Theatre & Interculturalism.* Houndmills: Palgrave Macmillan.

Lawrence, Jane. 2000. The Indian Health Service and the Sterilization of Native American Women. *American Indian Quarterly* 24 (3): 400–419.

Maufort, Marc. 2003. *Transgressive Itineraries. Postcolonial Hybridizations of Dramatic Realism.* Brussels: P.I.E. Peter Lang.

———. 2011. Celebrating Indigeneity: Contemporary Aboriginal Playwriting in Canada and Australasia. In *Theatres in the Round. Multi-ethnic, Indigenous, and Intertextual Dialogues in Drama,* ed. Dorothy Figueira and Marc Maufort, 91–108. Brussels: P.I.E. Peter Lang.

———. 2013. Voices of Cultural Memory. Enacting History in Recent Native Canadian Drama. In *Indigenous North American Drama. A Multivocal History,* ed. Birgit Däwes, 150–176. Albany, NY: SUNY Press.

———. 2017. Indigenous Playwriting and Globalization. In *Literary Culture and Translation. New Aspects of Comparative Literature,* ed. Dorothy M. Figueira and Chandra Mohan, 284–295. Delhi: Primus Books.

———. 2020. Revisiting the Past, Imagining the Future: Aesthetic of Creolization in Post-apartheid South African Drama. In *Forays into Contemporary South African Theatre. Devising New Stage Idioms,* ed. Marc Maufort and Jessica Maufort, 183–205. Leiden: Brill/Rodopi.

Maufort, Marc, and Jessica Maufort. 2020. A Fraught Process: Devising New State Idioms for Post-apartheid South Africa. In *Forays into Contemporary South African Theatre. Devising New Stage Idioms,* ed. Marc Maufort and Jessica Maufort, 1–20. Leiden: Brill/Rodopi.

Molloy, John S. 1999. *A National Crime. The Canadian Government and the Residential School System 1879 to 1986*. Winnipeg, MB: University of Manitoba Press.

Nolan, Yvette. 2014. *The Unplugging*. Toronto: Playwrights Canada Press.

Rattansi, Ali. 2007. *Racism. A Very Short Introduction*. Oxford, UK: Oxford University Press.

Robbins, Rebecca L. 1999. Self-Determination and Subordination: The Past, Present, and Future of American Indian Governance. In *The State of Native America: Genocide, Colonization, and Resistance*, ed. M. Annette Jaimes, 87–121. Boston, MA: South End Press.

Sasser, Kim Anderson. 2014. *Magical Realism and Cosmopolitanism. Strategizing Belonging*. Houndmills: Palgrave Macmillan.

Taylor, Drew Hayden. 2002. Canoeing the Rivers of Canadian Aboriginal Theatre: The Portages and the Pitfalls. In *Crucible of Cultures. Anglophone Drama at the Dawn of a New Millennium*, ed. Marc Maufort and Franca Bellarsi, 25–29. Brussels: PIE Peter Lang.

———. 2014. *God and the Indian*. Vancouver: Talonbooks.

Zamora, Lois Parkinson, and Wendy B. Faris, eds. 1995. *Magical Realism. Theory, History, Community*. Durham, NC: Duke University Press.

CHAPTER 6

Representing the Roma Experience on the Contemporary Romanian Stage: The Intersectional Lenses of Giuvlipen's Anti-racist and Feminist Theatre Works

Diana Benea

1 Introduction

Exposing one of the most painful undersides of Europe's grand narrative of modernity, the existence of the Roma peoples has been historically threatened by countless forms of violence, from the denial of their culture and language to systematic discrimination and disenfranchisement, enslavement, segregation, forced expulsion, and near-annihilation during the Holocaust.[1] While the Roma are by no means a homogenous group, but rather 'a rich mosaic of groups' speaking various dialects of Romani, displaying significant cultural differences, and practising a number of religions, it has been argued that 'discrimination is sometimes the only thing that seems to unify the Roma' (Silverman 2012, 47). In contemporary Europe, the current status of the Roma is inextricable from a politics of 'double discourse' arguably promoting integration and equal rights, but largely failing to address the systemic discrimination against them, which is now legitimised by a three-pronged discourse

---

The author would like to thank Mihaela Drăgan, actress, playwright, and co-founder of Giuvlipen Theatre Company, for her kind support in documenting this chapter.

D. Benea (✉)
University of Bucharest, Bucharest, Romania
e-mail: diana.benea@lls.unibuc.ro

© The Author(s), under exclusive license to Springer Nature Switzerland AG 2021
T. Morosetti, O. Okagbue (eds.), *The Palgrave Handbook of Theatre and Race*, https://doi.org/10.1007/978-3-030-43957-6_6

101

highlighting their 'racialised de-Europeanisation, neoliberal undeservingness, and (dis)articulation of citizenship' (Kóczé and Rövid 2017, 684). As Kóczé and Rövid argue, despite living in Europe for centuries and possessing legal citizenship in their respective countries, 'by being racialised and less worthy from a neoliberal perspective, their political citizenship is not recognized, it is questioned and (dis)articulated' (693).

Given this history of structural violence and oppression, the Roma have very seldom been in the position to provide accounts of their experience or represent themselves in discourse, which amounts to their paradoxical 'epistemological erasure/invisibility' (Brooks 2015, 57) within the body of knowledge created about them. However, they have been 'known', portrayed, narrated, perpetually constructed, and reconstructed as an object of representation by the non-Roma, for whom the 'Gypsy' had to be 'invented' as the counterpart of 'the underside of the European cultural subject's invention of itself as the agent of civilizing progress in the world' (Bogdal 2012). In the quasi-absence of self-representations, the hetero-representations that have long dominated the production and reproduction of the Roma in various media, as well as in the public discourse, have reduced this identity to a repertoire of mostly negative stereotypes, 'usually behaviors and pathologies, such as criminality, nomadism, un-adaptability, faineancy, and secrecy, which create an incessant narrative of difference' (Fremlova and McGarry 2019, 91). Inhabiting this discursive space are a number of versions of the Roma as an exoticised or vilified ethnoracial and cultural other, ranging from the (noble/wild) savage living on the periphery of civilisation, to the eternal placeless nomad, to the carefree and joyful Gypsy musician, or to the more menacing contours of the thief, criminal, or child abductor, portrayed as an embodiment of lawlessness and a threat to the social order. While this constellation of images and motifs might be regarded as gender-neutral, the representation of Roma women has produced its own repository of tropes, which usually fall within two categories, 'the Romani woman as pregnant with many children around her skirt, and with an abusive husband—a prime example of unequal gender power relations—or Romani women as highly sexualized objects (like Esmeralda or Carmen) whose talents are enticing men as prostitutes or exotic entertainers' (Kurtić 2014, 12). Echoing an Orientalist discourse, the eroticised images at the core of the latter version picture the Roma woman either as a site of aggressive, threatening sexuality, which has to be regulated, or, by contrast, as containing the promise of submissiveness and availability.[2]

In the context of this ecstasy of representation embedded in an unsettling mix of fascination, contempt, and fear, opening up new spaces of self-representation becomes a political act in itself—a critical intervention that has become all the more timely in the current global climate of rising nationalism and xenophobia. As a space of self-making, with its unique mechanisms of display and audience engagement, theatre has provided a fertile medium for a reclaiming of previously suppressed Roma voices, thus contributing to the consolidation of a contemporary counter-narrative about the Roma experience. European theatre stages have witnessed in recent years a number of groundbreaking projects enacting such a reclaiming of the space of representation and creating a platform of visibility and empowerment for Roma voices.[3] The most acclaimed project of this kind is the visually spectacular *Roma Armee*, directed by Yael Ronen for Maxim Gorki Theatre in Berlin and featuring a transnational cast of eight actors who are Romnija, Roma, and Romani travellers from Austria, Serbia, Germany, Kosovo, Romania, England, and Sweden. The show brings to the fore a radical vision of Roma solidarity and resistance against racism and right-wing propaganda, by mixing documentary material drawn from the experiences of the cast with cabaret-style political critique. For Damien Le Bas (2017), who created the paintings and artwork for the performance together with Delaine Le Bas, the show becomes 'a voice and a weapon' to change perceptions of the Roma as 'the pariahs, the outsiders, public enemy number one, the thieves, the children of the devil, the cursed, the square peg that will never fit in the round hole', and to present them instead as 'the Kings & Queens of Gypsyland Europe'. Another noteworthy artistic project in this direction is the Roma Heroes International Roma Storytelling Festival organised by the Independent Theatre Hungary in Budapest, which has so far showcased, in its 2017 and 2018 editions, twelve contemporary plays by Spanish, Italian, Bulgarian, Romanian, British, Irish, and Hungarian artists, whose shared agenda lies in dramatising 'Roma heroes who are able to initiate changes in their own lives and in their communities' ('Roma Heroes' 2018).

On Romanian stages, the last few years have seen the emergence of a number of plays that significantly centre issues related to the Roma experience, such as Alexandru Fifea's *Voi n-ați văzut nimic* (*You Haven't Seen Anything!*, 2016), Alexandru Berceanu's *Privind prin piele* (*Skin Look*, 2016), Andrei Șerban's *Vi me som rom* (*I Am Roma, Too*, 2018), or Alina Șerban's one-woman show *Declar pe propria răspundere* (*I Declare at My Own Risk*, 2011) or her recent *Marea rușine* (*The Great Shame*, 2016), which is the first theatre play to address the question of Roma slavery in the Romanian principalities[4] and among the first to have been included in the season's schedule of a state-funded theatre (Excelsior Theatre, 2018). This chapter will focus on the most substantial, provocative, and aesthetically compelling site for such explorations of contemporary Roma identity on the Romanian stage (and beyond), namely the plays of Giuvlipen, the first Roma theatre company in Romania, which has also garnered significant international attention and recognition. Arguing that Giuvlipen offers an illuminating cross-section of recent European developments in Roma performance with its rich thematic scope and its interest in experimenting with diverse theatrical forms, this contribution will investigate the company's body of works as a productive case study.

2   GIUVLIPEN THEATRE COMPANY

Founded in 2014 by Roma actresses Mihaela Drăgan, Zita Moldovan, and Elena Duminică, the company has aimed to document the largely invisible experiences and history of the Roma population—the second-largest ethnic group in Romania—in an effort to articulate new understandings of contemporary Roma identity formation and to produce a change in 'the way of thinking of non-Roma people and their stereotypical views on Roma women, [in] the way of thinking of Roma men about the traditional roles of Roma women and most important, [in] the way of thinking of Roma women about themselves and their role in society', to quote from their manifesto ('Giuvlipen Theatre Company' 2016).[5] In a panel discussion after her performative reading of *Del Duma/Tell Them About Me!* at the 2018 PEN World Voices International Play Festival in New York City, Drăgan (2018a) talked about the impetus to found the company as stemming from a desire 'to reclaim a space with our voices and our bodies', which was all the more urgent in the context of the marginal position that Roma actors occupy on the Romanian stages, and the almost complete lack of substantial, complex representations of Roma experiences in the Romanian cultural discourse. As Drăgan (2017) also notes in an interview, Giuvlipen aims to build a Roma dramaturgy that brings to the fore 'an alternative to the way in which Roma people are portrayed in the media and in art', by rejecting all forms of hetero-representation whatsoever. Tellingly, in emphasising the crucial importance of self-representation, Drăgan (2017) goes on to clarify her uncompromising version of what critical race theory has called a 'voice of color': 'We have an entire history of oppression and silencing, so no non-Roma artist has any right to represent us in their project without asking us first.' Giuvlipen's plays may thus be regarded as originating in the painful awareness of a double consciousness similar to that famously defined by W.E.B. DuBois ([1903] 1996) as 'th[e] sense of always looking at oneself through the eyes of others' (5).

The group has been a pioneering force not only in terms of centring contemporary Roma lives in their discourse, but also as the first theatre collective to adopt a feminist agenda in their commitment to produce plays by, about, and for Roma women—portrayed through intersectional lenses as racialised, gendered, sexualised, and classed subjects facing multiple sources of oppression. Testifying to the groundbreaking nature of their work is the fact that the company members had to invent the Romani word 'giuvlipen', which translates as 'feminism' (by adding the collective suffix '-pen' to 'giuvli', the Romani word for 'woman'), as there had been no such word in their language. Informed by the theory and praxis of an increasingly visible and vocal Roma feminism, and by its various intersections with black feminism, third world feminism, as well as intersectional theory, the company members have always considered their artistic work as going hand in hand with their activism within the movement.

In exploring this case study through a close analysis of four of their plays, *Del Duma/Vorbește-le despre mine!* (*Del Duma/Tell Them About Me!*, 2013), *Cine a omorât-o pe Szomna Grancsa?* (*Who Killed Szomna Grancsa?*, 2017), *Corp urban* (*Urban Body*, 2018), and *Kali Traš/Frica neagră* (*Kali Traš/Black Fear*, 2018), this chapter aims to answer the following questions: what is the agenda of Giuvlipen's theatrical discourse of self-representation? What are the new narratives about Roma identity and the new concerns proposed by their plays? In what ways do these new narratives and images engage with the aforementioned repertoire of representations, contributing to a critical repositioning of the discourse on Roma identity? How can the theatrical means and formats employed by the company speak about such loaded issues—ranging from early marriage and Roma women's sexuality, to structural racism and social exclusion, to the atrocities of the Roma Holocaust—in a way that makes full use of the medium's strengths?

In a 2012 article on the groundbreaking work of Roma women activists in Central and Eastern Europe, Debra L. Schultz (2012) discusses the crucial issues that have been raised in less than a decade as a result of such activist efforts: from intersectional accounts of discrimination (based on race, class, and gender), to critiques of 'controversial issues that demanded looking within their culture: virginity testing and early marriage, domestic violence, forced prostitution, and trafficking' (37). As Schultz further notes, such a critical interrogation of the practices within their own communities implied breaking 'a taboo common to marginalized groups: never criticise your own people to the dominant society' (37). When Roma women do criticise such community-specific issues, they become, as Alexandra Oprea (2004) has argued, 'white', 'non-Roma', or 'gadjikane' (31). The issue of early marriage in traditional Roma communities raises a particularly intriguing dilemma in this context, given that such practices have been politically instrumentalised to legitimise a racist discourse. As Oprea (2012) and other scholars have demonstrated, this type of 'culturalist' discourse frames child marriages as 'primitive' practices ingrained in the Roma tradition, which has been employed to further reinforce their stereotypification as a 'backward' and 'misogynistic' culture, and, consequently, to render untenable any demands for integration or equality as long as there is no such equality in the Roma culture itself (15). The nuanced analyses emerging in recent years have nevertheless drawn attention to the fact that early marriage and childbearing is, indeed, symptomatic of patriarchy, yet 'cannot be addressed apart from poverty and racism' (Oprea and Silverman 2019, 310). Two plays in the Giuvlipen corpus have so far tackled this complicated topic, training their critical gaze upon questions of gendered power within the community, and in particular upon the practice (and the ramified implications) of early marriage.

3   *Del Duma/Vorbește-le despre mine! (Del Duma/Tell Them About Me!, 2013)*

Written in 2013 and widely presented on Romanian as well as international stages in Budapest, Berlin, and, most recently, in New York City, as part of the 2018 PEN World Voices International Play Festival, which showcases staged readings by ten of the world's most respected contemporary playwrights, *Del Duma/Tell Them About Me!* juxtaposes Drăgan's personal story as 'half

Romanian and half, the good half, Gypsy'—at least 'that's what I always say to annoy the racists' (Drăgan 2013, 1)—from a non-traditional family with the experiences of three Roma women from traditional backgrounds. In the panel discussion after her show in New York City, Drăgan (2018a) revealed that she had originally considered writing a piece about her identity, as a kind of 'coming out' story; however, after conducting interviews with the other Roma women whose experiences are dramatised in the play, she realised the larger significance and impact that such an exploration of a taboo topic might have, and her own role in making these frequently ignored stories visible for a broader audience. As she argues, 'I felt that these women's voices had to be heard, so it wasn't anymore my thing.'

Drăgan's (2013) light-hearted story about her failed romance with a Dutch DJ, an aficionado who knows everything there is to know about Roma people and treats 'the Romanian Gypsy girl' in exoticising terms, 'like a museum piece' (3), serves as a pretext for a meditation on her multiple freedoms as a woman from a mixed, non-traditional family. At the end of this opening section, she offers a provocative question and an equally provocative hypothesis: 'Would I have bothered with these idiots if I was a traditional Gypsy? I would have married a virgin at fifteen and would have been better off' (5). In the following three parts, Drăgan gives voice to three Roma women from more conservative communities, offering their stories for contemplation as possible answers to her question. Thus, the audience encounters Mariana, who married a virgin in her mid-twenties and whose previous status as a twenty-something unmarried woman had been regarded with scepticism by the middle-school Roma girls in her history classes. To her surprise, her thirteen-year-old students were not interested in such career-oriented women role models, but rather in starting families, raising children, and being housewives. 'You live the way you see' (8), Mariana concludes, calling attention to the power that gendered identities and hierarchies still hold in her teenage students' communities, before launching into an account of her own experience of the wedding night virginity ritual, which requires public proof that the newly married bride is a virgin. We then meet Calofira, the Adulteress, who married Bulibaşa's son as a young girl, and who was banished from the community after her husband's tragic death, on the assumption that she had started an affair with another Roma man even before her spouse's passing. Sent to her parents, without her children, the grieving young widow died soon after. While her guilt was never fully substantiated and her extra-marital relationship might have been only a case of platonic friendship, traditional cultures will nonetheless 'punish very hard in order to keep their balance' (11). Women who defy the patriarchal system are bound to experience retribution through social exclusion. Finally, we hear Roxana's story, a rebellious Joan of Arc of the Gypsies who resorted to a rather unusual tactic in order to circumvent early marriage: converting to another religion and thus managing to remain unmarried despite the fierce opposition of her family. Roxana's account traces her shift from despair over such practices and rage towards her family for not allowing her to go to school, to a more nuanced attitude acknowledging the impact of poverty and racism on the decisions of her community. In her own words, her stance gradually shifts from an understanding of her Roma identity as 'a problem' and 'a shame', to a vision of her mere existence as 'a revolutionary act in itself' (20). Working on a project as an educational assistant for Roma children, Roxana acquires first-hand knowledge of the lack of access to education and the school segregation practices resulting from systemic inequities and racist attitudes, among other factors. In her final monologue, Mihaela returns to her own 'character', pledging to produce the play so as to get Roxana's important message across—more specifically, her double revolt against her Roma community and the mainstream Romanian society. In doing so, the actress-playwright also hopes to reconcile her two ethnicities, Roma and Romanian, 'on the inside and on the outside' (20).

The three stories serve to highlight the ways in which patriarchal relations in the family and the wider community shape and limit the options of Roma women, prompting them to negotiate their position at the crossroads of several regimes of power. We therefore gain an insight into the challenges of forging a 'space of one's own' by learning to navigate between competing and frequently clashing discourses and cultural models—especially between a desire to be accepted in the community and an equally powerful urge to assert one's agency (at least) in matters pertaining to one's body, gender role, and sexuality. Is early marriage a quintessentially 'Roma tradition'? A practice that 'some stubborn Roma men' (9) want to maintain in order to preserve gender hierarchies? Or rather a mechanism of protection meant to ensure that young Roma girls remain shielded within the community, and thus avoid confronting the racism of mainstream society? The play provides no definitive answers in this respect, carefully juxtaposing these possible angles side by side and allowing the audience members to draw their own conclusions or create their own readings. Such a kaleidoscopic refraction of the topic creates a fertile ground for critical reflection and interrogation acknowledging the multiple layers of this taboo topic. Tellingly, Drăgan's account of audience response after performances of the play in Roma communities testifies to the importance of prompting a reflective, de-essentialising stance towards early marriages:

> I played in the Roma communities, in villages, in courtyards, and I was really afraid about their reactions ... because I am from an untraditional Roma family, and I don't want to come here to tell you [that] you should stop early marriage or give you lessons. ... I recognize my privilege. ... I mean, this is what I wanted to do, just raise some questions, not to be in the position to give lessons. And actually it was very interesting because many times in the Roma communities I received such a good reaction and I used to have a discussion with the people after every show and they even started to have polemics between the generations, the young ones started to argue with the old ones, "okay, we have to stop doing this, I don't want my daughter to be married, I want her to go to high school." (2018a)

4 *Cine a omorât-o pe Szomna Grancsa?* (*Who Killed Szomna Grancsa?*, 2017)

A more recent play produced by Giuvlipen, *Cine a omorât-o pe Szomna Grancsa?* (*Who Killed Szomna Grancsa?*, 2017), revisits the topic of early marriage, refracting the story of the protagonist through the prisms of several residents of the community, whose accounts provide a balanced juxtaposition of discourses—public and private, Roma and non-Roma, progressive and conservative, mutually enhancing or conflicting. Written by Mihai Lukacs and the company members, and based on the Rashomon effect of Ryunosuke Akutagawa's short stories, the play explores the possible causes and the aftermath of a real event, the suicide of seventeen-year-old Roma girl Szomna Grancsa, which shocked the rural community of Frumoasa, Harghita County, in 2007. 'I am the school'—these are the words that Szomna painted on the wall of her room before committing suicide, an act that was widely considered to be her *sui generis* protest against her family's decision to forbid her to attend high school while pressuring her to get married instead. The tensions within this mixed ethnic community are highlighted from the very beginning, via the perspectives voiced by two women, one Romanian, the other Roma, which serve to frame the play. The juxtaposition of these two accounts of the community draws attention, on the one hand, to the intense racialisation of the Roma, portrayed as thieves 'stealing all the wood in our forests' and causing 'all the disasters in the world' (Lukacs and Giuvlipen Company 2017, 1; my translation[6]), while revealing, on the other hand, the simmering resentment on the part of the Roma themselves, whose existence unfolds in a climate of 'racial hatred and that's what kills people' (2).

Structured as an assemblage of monologues and dialogues revolving around Szomna's life and death, the rest of the play functions as a dialogic or polyphonic production of knowledge about this character and the community itself, whose portraits emerge from the interplay of this multiplicity of accounts. Thus, with each new scene, the audience is presented with another interpretation of Szomna's suicide: her struggles with depression, her presumed fling with a high school colleague, and, perhaps most importantly, her family's poverty as a crucial factor in no longer allowing her to attend school. However, most of the accounts converge in arguing that Szomna was, indeed, a revolutionary figure in her community, driven by a strong desire 'to create her own path, leave the Gypsy ghetto, start a different life' (3), according to the village priest. In one of the most theatrically effective scenes in the play, we also get to hear and see Szomna speaking from beyond the grave about her impossible position as an outsider in both spaces, 'caught between two worlds and suffering because of each' (8), that is, from the lack of opportunities and the strictures imposed on her by her Roma family, on the one hand, and from always being relegated to the last desk in the classroom, on the other, which is symptomatic of the racist attitudes in her school. With regard to Szomna's status in the latter of these worlds, the play does a fine job at capturing the complex workings of racism and the insidious power of racialised representations, illustrated, for instance, by what the girl's classmates wrote about her as part of an assignment entitled 'What I like about you': 'She doesn't scream, she doesn't quarrel, she doesn't use swear words. This means she is well-behaved. She doesn't stink, she doesn't come to school barefoot, she is not dirty. This means she is beautiful. She does her homework, she doesn't steal. This means she is hard-working' (7). To paraphrase this textual pattern, what this means is that Szomna's portrait can only be constructed in relation to stereotypical representations of the Roma, by stressing the ways in which she departs from that repertoire of narratives. Along the same 'exceptionalist' lines, her teacher provides her own synthesis of these views, arguing that 'Szomna was a really normal teenager, despite the fact that she was Gypsy. It happens within their community; rarely, but it does' (7). Significantly, the teacher also supports the popular view on Roma integration that has dominated the Romanian public discourse for more than two decades, positing that education is the only way out for people like Szomna, without taking into account the multiple factors that might prevent their access to school, such as poverty. The final scene of the play returns to the duo from the beginning, now seen debating the possible impact of Szomna's act in their village. It is the Roma woman who states that Szomna 'did a great thing for our girls' (9), with her rebellion against two worlds, none of which supported her aspirations.

In her explorations of the 'utopian performative', Jill Dolan (2005) discusses the balanced intermingling of discourses in such plays as Moisés Kaufman and The Tectonic Theatre Project's *The Laramie Project* or Anna Deavere Smith's *Fires in the Mirror* as engendering the conditions for 'a conversation among people who might not otherwise have spoken to each other—or not spoken these words in this way—creating a new public sphere in which to scrutinize the events' (113). What Giuvlipen's *Del Duma/Tell Them About Me!* and *Who Killed Szomna Grancsa?* essentially dramatise in performance and wish to inspire in their diverse audiences is the constitution of a similar public sphere and of a particular experience of social inquiry in which to assess and reassess taboo topics related to Roma communities in a complex, layered manner, combining and carefully attending to multiple perspectives, thus radically departing from the frequently sensationalised, exoticised, or one-sided accounts in the mainstream public discourse.

5   Corp urban (Urban Body, 2018)

While *Del Duma/Tell Them About Me!* and *Who Killed Szomna Grancsa?* foreground the tight control over Roma women's bodies within patriarchal environments, Giuvlipen's 2018 production *Corp urban* (*Urban Body*) adds a more prominent intersectional dimension to this debate, placing such bodies beyond the determinations of their communities, that is, in relation to the mainstream Romanian society, within socioeconomic contexts defined by poverty, ghettoisation, and structural racism. As stressed by recent works of Roma feminism, an intersectional—gender-based, race-based, and class-based—analysis sheds light on the ways in which Roma women's sexual and reproductive rights are inscribed within different power regimes, both private and public, whose intersections and overlaps lead to multiple marginalisations and deprivations. The combined force of Roma and non-Roma discourses on Roma women's sexuality brings into sharp relief the unsettling paradox of regarding such bodies as 'on the one side, [...] bearing the obligation for the biological reproduction of their own ethnic group, and on the other, becom[ing] targets of racist fertility control and dehumanizing discourses according to which they give birth to children with less value than those of majority mothers' (Gheorghe et al. 2019, 161). The latter practices are by no means new, but rather part of a historical continuum in which Roma women's bodies have been the target of state-supported racism, 'from being incarcerated or killed as witches during the Middle Ages to being forcibly sterilized in the EU's Czech Republic and Slovakia' (Matache 2019, 20). Importantly, as Matache and others have argued, such racist practices have been legitimised by an arsenal of highly sexualised representations of Roma women.

Written by playwright Catinca Drăgănescu and starring Mihaela Drăgan, Zita Moldovan and musician Ardeja Fraga, the show fictionalises the stories of four Roma women through the very specific lens of their relationship with their body, in its multiple incarnations and instrumentalisations: the body as the site of motherhood, the body as a means of production, the body as a source of shame, the body as personal property. The show starts with a powerful manifesto on the significance of the body—as a site of the personal and the political—recited by each of the three performers, whose voices overlap and blend at times: 'When I no longer know who I am, I hold myself and feel myself, and I am this body that feels, vibrates, this body that has been with me forever and ever, and in whose flesh my history is written, my history and that of all those I have met.' From the very beginning, the body is therefore positioned as both the locus of individual personhood and the repository of a collective history of resistance and solidarity. This somewhat poetic imagining of the body is then reinscribed as part of a more pragmatic political agenda emphasising questions of rights, more specifically, 'the right each person has to know, to investigate, to explore, to decide what to do with their body' (*Corp urban* Performance 2018).[7]

This introduction sets the tone for the four stories to follow, which will delve deeper into the different political battlegrounds that Roma women's bodies have been turned into, as the racialised, pauperised, and hypersexualised objects of the double discourse mentioned above. Framed as songs on an album about life in the ghetto, the four pieces are effectively supported by Fraga's haunting live music, on the one hand, and, on the other, by a highly physical style of performing, which not only enhances the mood of the stories, but also reinforces the thematic concerns of the play. In fact, much of the force of the performance lies in the orchestration of Drăgan's and Moldovan's movement on stage, in the different relationships established between their bodies (working in unison, supporting, and complementing each other, but also subverting and clashing with each other at times), and in the ways in which this arrangement offers a movement-based commentary on the stories themselves. The first and fourth sections gravitate around the differential treatment of Roma women in state hospitals, throwing into focus the ways in which their reproductive rights are controlled and regulated by limiting proper access to healthcare. Through the lens of these stories, the pregnancy experience of such women unfolds against an institutional background defined by the lack of medical care in the ghetto (until the authorities decide to send a general practitioner there, 'because they're humans, too'), the informal fees that condition a smooth access to treatment, the dirty and crowded 'Gypsy' wards, the decisions taken without any prior consultation with the patients or their families, along with an often voiced racial prejudice against the Roma, who are portrayed as dirty and poor, hence dispensable beings not worthy of careful medical treatment. Left unattended for a long time, the protagonist of the fourth story dies on the surgical table, while her father-in-law is forced to sign a document stating that she refused medical care. In one of the most poignant scenes of the play, we hear the woman's final words blending with quotes from the Hippocratic Oath specifying the ethical standards which should govern any medical act. It is only in death that such women manage to leave the ghetto, a place that God seldom visits, given that 'maybe it's not that handy for him either' (*Corp urban* Performance 2018).

In the third section of the play, a racist discourse is employed to legitimise a doctor's refusal to provide treatment to a Roma woman who was a victim of domestic violence; the doctor 'knows the way we, the crows, are: now we fight, now we love each other, we'd better go home and solve our problems, because she's not in the mood for dealing with the Gypsy clans, not in the mood for scandal.' Having been denied access to medical services and to any kind of legal or institutional protection, the woman eventually stabs her husband and receives a twenty-five-year jail sentence. Finally, the second story dramatises the experiences of an elder sex worker who chose this particular profession in order to make ends meet. 'I have to get by somehow', the woman confesses and then launches into a celebration of her body, which has been 'kind to her', providing her with a means of livelihood (*Corp urban* Performance 2018). While she insists on not feeling sorry for her as this was her choice, one cannot help but wonder whether Roma women's otherwise limited access to the labour market might have come into play in choosing this line of work. As Vincze has pointed out, economic marginalisation affects Roma women differently from men, and this is due to the joint effects of 'their ascribed roles within the domestic sphere and the prejudices through which they are perceived by mainstream society' (Gheorghe et al. 2019, 166). What the sex worker nevertheless laments is the fact that the profession is not regulated, and, consequently, she benefits from no legal rights or protections on the part of the state.

The final scene of the piece returns to the political manifesto from the opening, celebrating the bodies on stage as sites of difference, of survival, of struggle, of solidarity: 'I am a live body whose color reminds me of who I am. I am part of the history I have survived, I am the memory of those who lived, struggled, and loved. I am part of them, of those who brought me to this point in my life.' In the context of a play revealing the systematic denial of rights that Roma women have to face in their daily lives, the final statement, uttered in turns by the three artists, amounts to an act of making rights claims—'to exist, to resist, to matter, so as to change, so as to change, so as to change' (*Corp urban* Performance 2018). It might be argued that such a struggle to claim (and enact) particular rights that are unauthorised or contested also implies a claim for 'the right to have rights', as recent studies on performative citizenship have underlined (Isin 2017, 517). Given the fact that the racialisation of the Roma has contributed to a kind of '(dis)articulated' political citizenship, the act of making rights claims emerges as a re-articulation of a performance-based notion of citizenship. The play not only explores the interactions of gender, race, and class that shape and constrain various aspects of Roma women's lives—in particular, their access to healthcare, to networks of institutional support, and even to the labour market—but also calls attention to the political potential of Roma women in mounting resistance to racism, class exploitation, and patriarchy, by claiming rights, justice, and recognition, while reimagining a more hospitable future in which, to quote again from the final scene of the play, 'neither the clothes I'm wearing, nor my ethnicity, nor my race, nor my sexual orientation make me less than I am. I am everything I want to be, everything I could be' (*Corp urban* Performance 2018).

A reimagining of the future is often inextricable from a retrospective process of working through any unresolved traumatic legacies—haunting historical injustices and suppressions—that are bound to erupt at any time in the present. As Avery Gordon (2008) has suggested in her explorations of several instances of haunting, such as the system of state terror known as *Desaparecidos* (The Disappeared) in Argentina, or the legacy of racial slavery in the United States, reckoning with and carefully attending to the ghostly or invisible events of one's history becomes a necessary step in understanding and restructuring the workings of our present-day societies, creating the possibility 'to conjure otherwise' in the future (28).

6   *Kali Traš/Frica neagră* (*Kali Traš/Black Fear*, 2018)

Departing from their previous focus on contemporary issues affecting Roma women's lives so as to reckon with the ghost of the most painful event in Roma history, the Holocaust, *Kali Traš/Frica neagră* (*Kali Traš/Black Fear*, 2018) gestures precisely in this direction. As Drăgan (2018b) clarifies in an interview for a programme on the National Romanian Television, Giuvlipen has been interested in examining historical themes ever since its founding: 'We were especially interested in Roma history, because this topic is so seldom talked about; as Roma actors, we felt this was our mission' (my translation). The show premiered on June 6, 2018, at the State Jewish Theatre in Bucharest, as part of a larger project entitled *Teatrul Rom nu e nomad* (*Roma Theatre Is Not Nomadic*), supported by the Administration of the National Cultural Fund. Loosely based on a survivor's memoir, Valerică Stănescu's *Cu moartea'n ochi* (*Looking Death Straight in the Eye*), alongside texts by Romanian writers Zaharia Stancu and Alexandru Sahia, and by the Polish Roma poet Bronislawa Wajs (Papusza), the show is the first Romanian theatre production, and still one of the very few pieces across the spectrum of the Romanian arts, to bear witness to the Roma Holocaust.[8] More specifically, the play engages with a historical event that has only recently gained visibility in the Romanian public discourse and is yet to become a part of our collective cultural memory: the deportation of around 25,000 Roma in Transnistria, under the regime of Ion Antonescu, from June 1942 to December 1943. According to the *Final Report* of the International Commission on the Holocaust in Romania (2004), 11,000 of these deportees died in the labour camps on the banks of the River Bug in extremely harsh conditions—most frequently, of hunger, cold, and disease (236). The title of the piece itself, *Kali Traš* ('Black Fear'), is one of the Romani phrases used to describe the Holocaust, alongside other equally evocative terms, such as *Porrajmos* ('the Devouring'), or *Berša Bibahtale* ('The years of misfortune') (Council of Europe 2013, 58).

In the same televised interview, Drăgan (2018b) offers an insight into the challenges and pressures attending the development of the play, particularly in what concerns finding the appropriate aesthetic strategies to represent such an unrepresentable event, whose magnitude amounts to a veritable crisis of aesthetic representation, as has been repeatedly argued about the Holocaust. In choosing the repertoire of images, representations, and performative modes for their new play, the major challenge was that of negotiating between the company members' various perspectives on the Holocaust, which essentially supported either a narrative of resistance or a narrative of victimhood. In this respect, Stănescu's memoir, the most important documentary source for the show, proved to be a fitting choice as it manages to strike a balance between the two.

Blending the matter-of-fact with the lyrical, Stănescu's account offers an insight into the deportation experience of a Roma Kalderash community of coppersmiths and fortune-tellers built around the leadership of his father, Bulibașa Urda. The story begins in the fall of 1942, with his father's premonitory dream about the imminent dissolution of his *șatra* (caravan), just days before the mayor of the village brings news about Antonescu's deportation order. Stipulating that Roma groups are to be rounded up and deported across the Dniester River, where they would be given houses and cattle and would work in the Soviet *kolhoz* (collective farms), the order sees Bulibașa's tight-knit community embark on a long and draining journey across Romania—a plunge into the unknown, punctuated with bad omens and invocations of God's grace, life-affirming celebrations as well as the first signs of dehumanisation. The bulk of the narrative is devoted to the hell endured by Bulibaşa's group in the Bug colony—a series of vignettes testifying to the horrors of the labour camps and the daily instances of looking death straight in the eye (ranging from starvation, to cholera and typhus, to summary executions), but also to their pledge to find ways to resist such atrocities and return to Romania, the land of their ancestors: 'if we all die, our tradition will die, too, our people will die, and nobody will know anything about our fate, and then we will have lived in vain on this Earth' (Stănescu 2007, 113; my translation). Some of the members of Bulibaşa's group do survive and make it back to their home country, where they resume their old ways of living; however, the author himself, the son born in the Bug colony, opts for a different life, leaving the *şatra* to go to school, and eventually mixing tradition (as a coppersmith) and modernity (as a writer).

The play dramatises the main stations of the journey to the Bug and the subsequent return to Romania in Stănescu's memoir—on the road, in the camp, on the train, at the Dniester, in the labour camp. Likewise, the narrative arc borrows some episodes from the book (the fortune-tellers casting spells to imagine their future life in Transnistria; Franz's execution after daring to demand an increase in the food rations at the labour camp; the famished protagonists eating rats lest they starve to death) as well as the verbatim transcription of several curses. However, this time around, the four protagonists are the members of a nomadic theatre group: Franz, the fiddler; Leanca, the fortune-teller; Diloda, the sword swallower; and Şopârla, the puppeteer. The rhythmic and colourful exuberance of the very first scene, in which the four performers introduce their routines to the audience as part of their folk theatre show, quickly gives way to a different register prefiguring the intrusion of another realm into the story, an invisible world of spirits and omens. In Şopârla's reading, the owl's hooting, traditionally interpreted as a bad omen, is juxtaposed with an image of physical extermination, of melting flesh and rotting bones, doubled by a vision of complete erasure from the collective historical consciousness: 'the greatest curse that has befallen us is oblivion.' Uttered again in the final scene of the show, this powerful statement serves as a frame for a play that in and of itself erects a monument against forgetfulness by recovering the haunted histories of those who have been physically exterminated and metaphorically suppressed from history, thus articulating a 'counter-memory' of their confrontation with 'black fear'. As the following scene in the play suggests, this act of resistance should be placed in the context of a longer history of surviving against all odds; just before learning about their imminent deportation, one of the protagonists remembers their struggle to survive the freezing cold and the ensuing famine in the winter of 1929. This history of resistance is reinforced several times throughout the play by a seemingly gimmicky but highly effective theatrical technique—the protagonists look death straight in the eye and sometimes even die, only to rise from the dead when one of the surviving colleagues utters the magic words 'get up!' (*Kali Traš/Frica neagră* Performance 2018).

Kali Traš/Black Fear bears witness to the Roma resistance in the face of a discourse that either criminalises ('gypsies are dangerous, they are capable of anything') or racialises them as non-persons or sub-humans ('we'll give you houses and cattle, so that you become humans'; 'so that you no longer wander from one village to another like stray dogs'; 'this country cannot get rid of you now, you've been reproducing like rats'). These lines are voiced time and again by the various authorities they encounter (mayors, gendarmes, police officers, soldiers), who also turn the performers into the exotic object of their fascinated gaze, by repeatedly taking photos of them. As one such figure implies, this racialised discourse constructing 'Gypsies' as 'impossible to assimilate', hence 'a serious threat to the constitution of Romanian blood', not only legitimises their deportation and extermination, but also divests the authorities of any responsibility; their racialised status therefore cancels the value of their lives and turns them into ungrievable subjects. This relentless politics of extermination is also considered in the play from the perspective of another state-supported practice, that is, the forced sterilisation of Roma women, legitimised by the same racialisation of the Roma as unworthy and eradicable. In one of the most heart-rending and aesthetically effective scenes of the play, Şopârla recounts having had her 'children house' removed from her body; the performative rendition and the duration of this scene, which is imagined as a prolonged act of dismemberment, suggest the ways in which such politics exhaust the bodies and endanger the lives of Roma women. Finally, another discursive trope employed by the authorities in this play in constructing a multi-layered narrative of difference is that of the Roma as a transnational community not moored to any particular state, hence entirely dispensable: 'You don't have a country, that's why we're kicking you out of Romania [...] To the Bug with you and your race!' (*Kali Traš/Frica neagră* Performance 2018). As Brooks (2012) has noted, the particular status of the Roma as existing 'in the interstices of the nation-state' has made the group 'vulnerable to its shifts in war, legal structure, and border making—yet without any true recourse to the international as a way of redressing the discrimination, displacement, and, at some points, genocide' (5).

Confronted with this pervasive discourse of othering and stigma predicated upon negative stereotypes that pathologise their identity as sub-human, nomadic, un-adaptable, or threatening, the protagonists repeatedly plead with the authorities to be allowed to live their lives as they have learned from their ancestors, peacefully co-existing alongside the Romanians. Emphasising their different histories and practices, on the one hand, while calling attention to their shared humanity, on the other, the four Roma performers mount a counter-discourse of resistance, pledging to contribute to the transmission of their heritage to future generations. This pledge is especially prominent towards the end of the play, in the scenes dramatising their return to Romania, which clearly emphasise the significance of each and every act of individual survival in the larger context of the collective survival of the Roma as a group—a collective resistance also reinforced by a choreography of procession-like movements that mirror each other or are performed in unison. 'The greatest curse that has befallen us is oblivion', thus ends the first Romanian theatre play to bear testimony to the systematic threatening into non-existence that has accompanied Roma existence (*Kali Traš/Frica neagră* Performance 2018). As Derrida (2006) suggests in the final pages of *Specters of Marx*, the purpose of opening the door to such long-suppressed ghosts is '[t]o exorcise not in order to chase away the ghosts, but this time to grant them the right, if it means making them come back alive, as *revenants* who would no longer be *revenants*, but as other *arrivants*, to whom a hospitable memory or promise must offer welcome' (220; emphases in the original). This is precisely what *Kali Traš/Black Fear* offers—a space in which to work through the largely invisible history of the Roma Holocaust by bringing it to light, making it part of our social life, and articulating a hospitable memory to Roma resistance.

7 Conclusion

As recent works in Roma studies have argued, with their unique position within and without their communities, Roma women's experience might offer the 'quintessential foundation' for a twofold anti-racist and feminist discourse, which should enable and legitimise them to serve as 'the primary architects' for politics and policies pertaining to race and gender issues (Oprea 2012, 19). Positioned on the frontlines of a Roma cultural revolution that challenges ethnic hatred, structural racism, sexism, social exclusion, and economic marginalisation, the works of Giuvlipen translate into artistic practice the political potential of Roma women as agents of social change. Mobilising a feminist and anti-racist agenda in each of their works, Giuvlipen's political labour lies in offering a powerful and thoroughly provocative counter-narrative to the tropes that have long dominated the representation of the Roma in various media by critically reimagining other scenarios for Roma history and especially for Roma women's existence. From *Kali Traš/Black Fear* to the plays investigating contemporary realities, Giuvlipen's body of works exposes the multiple facets of the discursive racialisation of the Roma, tracing its devastating effects in different historical contexts, from the *Porrajmos* to present-day forms of discrimination and social exclusion. Providing narratives and images of struggle and resistance, their plays call for the forging of new political subjectivities to challenge Romanophobia while also dismantling an internalised victimhood complex. As the analysis of the four plays has demonstrated, in this act of perpetual making and remaking, Roma identity emerges as an unfinished process that is inseparable from a political struggle for rights and recognition. In their act of (re-)claiming agency over the site of representation, this fluid identity, inherently political and always in the making, becomes Giuvlipen's answer to the static repository of hetero-representations that have perpetually othered the Roma.

The company's commitment to produce politically engaged contemporary Roma theatre addressing some of the most pressing concerns of the community is doubled by a commitment to experiment with a wide range of theatrical vocabularies, with new forms and formats in which to deliver their provocative political critique. This marked concern with formal experimentation has resulted in expanding their theatrical repertoire from one play to another—from documentary theatre in *Del Duma/Tell Them About Me!*, to the refracted perspectives of *Who Killed Szomna Grancsa?*, to an engagement with movement-based styles of performance in the concert-play *Urban Body*, and, finally, to examining historical topics while further exploring their interest in new modes of performativity in *Kali Traš/Black Fear*. It is due to such heightened theatricalisations that Giuvlipen manages to avoid the dangers of 'teaching lessons' or preaching—to both the converted and especially to the difficult-to-convert—via their plays. Predicated upon a belief that, without attention to the aesthetic, their works are less effective in producing the desired social change, Giuvlipen's theatrical practice thus achieves the rare feat of functioning as an aesthetically rewarding platform for staging identities, building community, and remembering suppressed histories, while creating a space for public discussion of vital issues pertaining to the Roma experience.

NOTES

1. Even though the exact number of the Roma victims of the Holocaust is difficult to estimate, historians have approximated that at least 500,000 and up to 1.5 million Roma perished at the hands of the Nazis (see, for instance, Hancock 1991, 20).
2. For recent analyses of such representations of the Roma in various media, see, for instance, the special issue of *Third Text* 22, no. 3 (2008) edited by Paloma Gay y Blasco, or the articles by Hadziavdic and Hoffmann (2017), Schneeweis and Foss (2017), Pușcă (2015), and Tremlett (2014).
3. For a survey of such contemporary developments in several European countries (Hungary, Romania, Spain, and France), see Drăgan (2019). For an account of recent developments in Roma theatre on the Austrian stages, see Grobbel (2015).
4. For an analysis of Roma slavery and emancipation in the Romanian principalities, see Achim (1998), especially chapters II and III.
5. Obviously, this manifold agenda raises different challenges pertaining to each of the three categories mentioned by Drăgan—not only in point of building diverse and responsive audiences, but also securing the material infrastructures for their projects. Positioning itself on the frontlines of such a threefold critique is no small feat for an independent theatre company which faces various limitations in obtaining the funding, the spaces, and the other resources that are vital to developing and producing their works. As Drăgan has repeatedly stated in interviews, one of the long-term goals of the company is to establish a state-funded Roma theatre, which will then take its long-awaited place among the otherwise surprisingly robust network of twelve ethnic theatres that have operated in Romania for several decades, consisting of nine Hungarian, two German, and one Jewish state-supported institutions (or separate sections within national theatres).
6. All subsequent quotes from this play as well as those from *Corp urban* and *Kali Traš/Frica neagră* are my translations.

118   D. BENEA

7. All quotes from *Corp urban* and *Kali Traš/Frica neagră* are transcriptions from the performances.
8. Also bearing witness to the Roma Holocaust is the exhibition organised in the lobby of the State Jewish Theatre in conjunction with the theatre show, entitled *Copiii nu uită … povestesc! Holocaustul romilor și povestea lui adevărată* (*Children do not forget … they tell the story! The Roma Holocaust and its true story*). Curated by the historian Adrian Furtună, the exhibition consists of drawings, photographs, and archival material as well as interviews with survivors.

References

Achim, Viorel. 1998. *The Roma in Romanian History*. Budapest: CEU Press.
Bogdal, Klaus-Michael. 2012. Europe Invents the Gypsies. The Dark Side of Modernity. *Eurozine*, February 24, 2012. https://www.eurozine.com/europe-invents-the-gypsies/.
Brooks, Ethel C. 2012. The Possibilities of Romani Feminism. *Signs: Journal of Women in Culture and Society* 38: 1–11.
———. 2015. The Importance of Feminists and 'Halfies' in Romani Studies: New Epistemological Possibilities. *Roma Rights: Journal of European Roma Rights Centre* 20: 57–61.
Corp urban. 2018. Script by Catinca Drăgănescu. *Performance at the National Museum of Romanian Literature*, Bucharest, September 11, 2018.
Council of Europe. 2013. *Human Rights of Roma and Travellers in Europe*. Strasbourg: Council of Europe Publishing.
Derrida, Jacques. 2006. *Specters of Marx: The State of Debt, the Work of Mourning and the New International*. Translated by Peggy Kamuf. New York and London: Routledge.
Dolan, Jill. 2005. *Utopia in Performance: Finding Hope at the Theatre*. Ann Arbor: University of Michigan Press.
Drăgan, Mihaela. 2013. *Del Duma/Tell Them About Me!* Unpublished Manuscript. Translated from Romanian by Claudia Câmpeanu. Mihaela Drăgan's Personal Archive.
———. 2017. Tell Them About Me. Interview by Valentina Iancu. *Revista ARTA*, June 2, 2017. https://revistaarta.ro/en/tell-them-about-me/.
———. 2018a. Interview by Author as Part of Panel Discussion at the PEN World Voices International Play Festival, New York City, April 16, 2018.
———, 2018b. Interview by Ilinca Ciobanu. *Identități* TVR 2, July 10, 2018.
———, ed. 2019. Roma Theatre in Europe. *HowlRound Theatre Commons*, March 10–14, 2019. https://howlround.com/series/roma-theatre-europe.
DuBois, W.E.B. ([1903] 1996). *The Souls of Black Folk*. New York: Penguin.
Fremlova, Lucie, and Aidan McGarry. 2019. Negotiating the Identity Dilemma: Crosscurrents across the Romani, Romani Women's and Romani LGBTIQ Movements. In *The Romani Women's Movement: Struggles and Debates in Central and Eastern Europe*, ed. Angéla Kóczé, Violetta Zentai, Jelena Jovanović, and Enikő Vincze, 88–108. London and New York: Routledge.
Gay y Blasco, Paloma, ed. 2008. Picturing 'Gypsies.' Interdisciplinary Approaches to Roma Representation. Special issue of *Third Text* 22, no. 3.
Gheorghe, Carmen, Letiția Mark, and Enikő Vincze. 2019. Towards an Anti-Racist Feminism for Social Justice in Romania. In *The Romani Women's Movement: Struggles*

and Debates in Central and Eastern Europe, ed. Angéla Kóczé, Violetta Zentai, Jelena Jovanović, and Enikő Vincze, 144–173. London and New York: Routledge.

"Giuvlipen Theatre Company, Romania." 2016. *East European Performing Arts Platform*, May 28, 2016. http://eepap.culture.pl/institution/giuvlipen-theatre-company-romania.

Gordon, Avery F. 2008. *Ghostly Matters: Haunting and the Sociological Imagination*. 2nd ed. Minneapolis: University of Minnesota Press.

Grobbel, Michaela. 2015. Crossing Borders of Different Kinds. Roma Theatre in Vienna. *Journal of Austrian Studies* 48: 1–26.

Hadziavdic, Habiba, and Hilde Hoffmann. 2017. Moving Images of Exclusion: Persisting Tropes in the Filmic Representation of European Roma. *Identities. Global Studies in Culture and Power* 24: 701–719.

Hancock, Ian. 1991. Gypsy History in Germany and Neighboring Lands: A Chronology Leading to the Holocaust and Beyond. In *The Gypsies of Eastern Europe*, ed. David Crowe and John Kolsti, 14–30. London and NY: Routledge.

International Commission on the Holocaust in Romania. 2004. *Final Report*. Iași: Polirom.

Isin, Engin F. 2017. Performative Citizenship. In *The Oxford Handbook of Citizenship*, ed. Ayelet Shachar, Rainer Bauböck, Irene Bloemraad, and Maarten Vink, 500–523. Oxford: Oxford University Press.

Kali Traš/Frica neagră. 2018. Script by Mihai Lukacs. *Performance at the State Jewish Theatre*, Bucharest, October 18, 2018.

Kóczé, Angéla, and Márton Rövid. 2017. Roma and the Politics of Double Discourse in Contemporary Europe. *Identities. Global Studies in Culture and Power* 24: 684–700.

Kurtić, Vera. 2014. *Džuvljarke Roma Lesbian Existence*. Niš: Ženski proctor.

Le Bas, Damian. 2017. Gypsyland Europa. Playbill for Yael Ronen & Ensemble's *Roma Armee* at the Maxim Gorki Theatre, Berlin.

Lukacs, Mihai and Giuvlipen Company. 2017. *Cine a omorât-o pe Szomna Grancsa?* Unpublished Manuscript. Mihaela Drăgan's Personal Archive.

Matache, Margareta. 2019. Foreword. In *The Romani Women's Movement: Struggles and Debates in Central and Eastern Europe*, ed. Angéla Kóczé, Violetta Zentai, Jelena Jovanović, and Enikő Vincze, 20–26. London and New York: Routledge.

Oprea, Alexandra. 2004. Re-envisioning Social Justice from the Ground Up: Including the Experiences of Romani Women. *Essex Human Rights Review* 1: 29–39.

―――. 2012. Romani Feminism in Reactionary Times. *Signs: Journal of Women in Culture and Society* 38: 11–21.

Oprea, Alexandra, and Carol Silverman. 2019. Concluding Remarks: A Book of Our Own: The Importance of Documenting Our Existence, Our Dissent. Promises and Prospects for the Romani Women's Movement in Central and Eastern Europe. In *The Romani Women's Movement: Struggles and Debates in Central and Eastern Europe*, ed. Angéla Kóczé, Violetta Zentai, Jelena Jovanović, and Enikő Vincze, 296–318. London and New York: Routledge.

Pușcă, Anca. 2015. Representing Romani Gypsies and Travelers: Performing Identity from Early Photography to Reality Television. *International Studies Perspectives* 16: 327–344.

"Roma Heroes—2nd International Roma Storytelling Festival." 2018. *Independent Theatre Website*. http://independenttheatre.blogspot.com/2018/04/roma-heroes-2nd-international-roma.html.

Schneeweis, Adina, and Katherine A. Foss. 2017. 'Gypsies, Tramps & Thieves': Examining Representations of Roma Culture in 70 Years of American Television. *Journalism & Mass Communication Quarterly* 94: 1–26.

Schultz, Debra L. 2012. Translating Intersectionality Theory into Practice: A Tale of Romani-*Gadže* Feminist Alliance. *Signs: Journal of Women in Culture and Society* 38: 37–43.

Silverman, Carol. 2012. *Romani Routes: Cultural Politics and Balkan Music in Diaspora*. Oxford: Oxford University Press.

Stănescu, Valerică. 2007. *Cu moartea'n ochi*. Bucharest: MarLink.

Tremlett, Annabel. 2014. Demotic or Demonic? Race, Class and Gender in 'Gypsy' Reality TV. *The Sociological Review* 62: 316–334.

PART II

War, Conflict and the Nation

CHAPTER 7

Race as Category in Nazi German Theatre

Anselm Heinrich

1 Introduction

When the Nazis assumed political power in Germany in January 1933 the theatre was high on their agenda. The Nazis were desperate to set themselves apart from performance practices during the Weimar Republic and offer a 'national' alternative. According to writer and cultural politician Hanns Johst, the theatre of the Weimar years had been characterised by 'ladies' underwear, sex, drunkenness, mental illness, decadence, materialism and bias' (qtd. Ritchie 1983, 101). All these 'experiments' were to end, repertoires were to be 'cleansed', the theatre was to become 'German' again (Hitler 1939, 284; Rosenberg 1935, 447). This turn to theatre's 'Germanness' linked it to wider racial discourses and concerned both theatre productions and personnel. In recent research, which has largely stressed the failure of the Nazis to establish their own dramaturgy, their own plays and their own aesthetics, their 'success' in cleansing the stage of unwanted plays and practitioners has tended to be sidelined. According to Uwe-Karsten Ketelsen, Nazi theories around their envisaged 'heroic theatre' were 'half-baked' attempts at a distinct dramaturgy not 'cohesive' (Ketelsen 1968, 38, 73). Günther Rühle summed up the dramatic output during the Third Reich as a mere 'gesture' of no substance (Rühle 1974, 62). Other leading scholars have similarly commented on how uninspired and ultimately unsuccessful the Nazis had been in their cultural policy (Dussel 1988; Rischbieter 2000; Gadberry 1995). However, it was in their destructive approach that Nazi cultural policy arguably had the most lasting effects.

A. Heinrich (✉)
University of Glasgow, Glasgow, UK
e-mail: Anselm.Heinrich@glasgow.ac.uk

© The Author(s), under exclusive license to Springer Nature
Switzerland AG 2021
T. Morosetti, O. Okagbue (eds.), *The Palgrave Handbook of Theatre and Race*, https://doi.org/10.1007/978-3-030-43957-6_7

123

Race was the key defining category throughout the Nazi years. It ordered German history and provided legitimacy to the Nazi present. It allowed Hitler's regime to move away from internationally accepted legal frameworks and establish their own based on *völkisch* considerations.[1] Heinz Kindermann, for example, eminent and respected scholar and Germany's leading theatre historian in a study on poetry written by Germans living outside the country's political borders in the late 1930s, questioned the validity of these borders (Kindermann 1938, 1940).[2] Geographically the focus of his book was on Eastern Europe and concerned areas which Germany had 'lost' after defeat in the First World War. He argued that the writing of these ethnic Germans expressed an allegiance with Germany and that it asked the motherland to fight for the extension of its current borders to incorporate those 'twenty million' who lived 'just outside the gates of the German Reich' (Kindermann 1940, 9). Kindermann thus invited his readers not to regard these political borders as permanent as the nation comprised of all Germans irrespective of where they happened to live (incidentally not a new discourse but one harking back to poet and author Ernst Moritz Arndt who in 1813 composed a song entitled 'What Is a German's Fatherland' in which he concluded that Germany was wherever the German language was spoken). Therefore in the current 'ethnic struggle' borders of states should be regarded as fluid, in fact they were artificial and petty constructs imposed on Germany by foreign politicians. Racially belonging to the German people, not 'arbitrary' political borders, had to be the defining factor of what constituted the German nation Kindermann argued, and he quoted Hitler in support: 'the power of the common blood is stronger than borders' (qtd. in Kindermann 1938, 10, 13). Hitler and Kindermann related to a discourse which had gained ground towards the end of the nineteenth century. Ernst Hasse, for example, had posited in 1897 that 'nations lasted longer than states'. The people (in the sense of their ethnicity or nationality) were the only fixed factor in history as political systems were constantly in flux (Hasse 1897). During the 1930s these kinds of discourses arguably pre-empted the outbreak of war in 1939 and provided legitimacy for far-reaching German geographical claims particularly in Eastern Europe (Kindermann 1943, 1944).

The application of the new racial order in the cultural sphere meant that only 'Aryans' were allowed to become members of the Reich Culture Chamber, which was founded in September 1933, and only members of the Reich Culture Chamber were allowed to perform. The ban extended to Jewish playwrights, composers, directors, choreographers, librettists, actors, musicians, dancers and so forth and it ended livelihoods in German theatres, orchestras and opera houses almost overnight. What often appeared as ad hoc measures in spring 1933 was put on a firm legal basis with the 1935 Nuremberg Race Laws. These laws decreed that the Jewish faith was not seen from a religious perspective but linked 'Jewishness' to race—so not a conscious decision of what religion one felt faithful to but a biological fact determined by blood and heritage. Hence, the Race Laws made it easier for the Nazi regime to determine who was Jewish, and who was subjected to attacks, pogroms and ultimate murder in the Holocaust.

The key reference points, which provided the Nazis with the alleged historical and biological justification in their racial policy, were Oswald Spengler's *Der Untergang des Abendlandes*, Joseph Arthur Gobineau's *Essai sur l'inégalité des races humaines* (1853), Houston Steward Chamberlain's *Die Grundlagen des 20. Jahrhunderts* and Hans F.K. Günther's *Rassenkunde* writings. These texts did not only stress the superiority of the Germanic/Aryan race and the need for this race to dominate others but also emphasised that any form of cultural expression was racially determined. According to Hitler, the Aryan race was the only race which was able to establish new cultures (*Kulturbegründer*) (Hitler 1939, 431–432). In his theories Hitler followed Oswald Spengler who related his attempt to 'predetermine history' to the one culture on earth which, according to him, at the beginning of the twentieth century 'had achieved perfection, i.e. the Western European/American', but which was now facing terminal decline (Spengler 1923, 3). Houston Stewart Chamberlain called for a 'rebirth' of the German nation based on a rediscovery of her Germanic roots. He posited that the 'entry of the Germanic race on the world stage [...] was nothing else than the salvation of an agonising humanity from the claws of timeless bestiality' (Chamberlain 1909, 550). Acknowledging the importance of both Spengler and Chamberlain, Hans F.K. Günther's studies provided the quasi-scientific basis for such claims of dominance. Günther asserted the superiority of the 'Nordic race'—residing primarily in Germany and Scandinavia—in relation to all others. The Nordic man was blond with blue eyes and taller than any other (Günther 1927, 83, 1933, 418–420), and the Nordic race had produced a disproportionally high number of highly gifted, pro-active and creative people (Günther 1926, 51–54; Hitler 1939, 433). Günther linked the particular courage and audaciousness he attributed to the Nordic race to aggressive expansion and conflict. According to his thinking, the eastward expansion of the German *Ritterorden* and the Hanseatic League in the eleventh and twelfth centuries and the 'movement of German citizens and peasants towards the East' where they 'founded the German power over the Baltic Sea' were entirely natural and, therefore, justified. Over the following centuries, however, a growing *Entnordung* (a process of becoming less Nordic) had taken place in countries where the Nordic race primarily resided. This was caused and further compounded by the influence of the Slavs and other 'inferior' Eastern races, although 'the German people resisted the Slavic blood for a long time' (Günther 1933, 402, 405). According to Günther, *Entnordung* was fatal as the racial deterioration would be followed by a social one with effects on the general character of societies. This would result in rising crime rates and soaring costs related to caring for people with lower abilities, productivity and health (Günther 1926, 198–199). For Günther and others these 'findings' made their research all the more important. Racial characteristics mattered because they did not only relate to issues of physiognomy but also to questions of character, two aspects which for him were inextricably linked. In a nutshell,

126   A. HEINRICH

Germany was in danger of social, political and economic decline following the reduction of the Nordic influence in its bloodstream, a fate similarly faced by other countries in history (Günther 1933, 51–60). In this context the influence of the 'Jewish race' was particularly 'dangerous' (Günther 1926, 72). *Entnordung* would, therefore, deprive the Germans of their most important racial 'ingredient' and reverse the development of the German nation from a role destined to rule to one doomed to disintegrate.

Looking forward, Günther saw two linked solutions: to increase the number of children of Nordic couples, and to reduce the number of children of couples with 'inferior hereditary dispositions', for example, by linking their access to health care and medical treatment to a 'racial hygiene' campaign, that is 'making them infertile' (Günther 1926, 201). Günther's theories were particularly dangerous as he did not only claim the superiority of the 'Nordic race' over others but also that it was under growing and increasingly debilitating pressure from an aggressively inferior racial influence. The extinction of the German nation seemed a very real prospect as Günther suggested a watershed moment in history (Günther 1933, 471). Germans were called upon to turn this development around quickly—nothing less than the survival of the nation was at stake (Hitler 1939, 432; Rosenberg 1935, 81–82). The Euthanasia programme of the late 1930s, the increasing anti-Semitic measures leading up to and including the Holocaust, and the military campaign for 'living space' in the East can all be linked to Günther's infamous theories of the 1920s.[3]

2   Race, Theatre and Performance

Theories of the Nordic man as both a born leader and as culturally productive, idealistic and intelligent proved a fertile ground for theories of German domination in the arts, too. Houston Steward Chamberlain dedicated a large section of his *Foundations of the 20th Century* to the arts (over 50 pages in the culmination of his second volume) and concluded that the Germanic man was the most musical human being on earth (Chamberlain 1909, 1143, 1145). Alfred Rosenberg in his *Mythus* dedicated half of his book to the 'Character of Germanic Art' and argued for the racial determination of any form of aesthetic expression (Rosenberg 1935). In turning his focus on the audience Heinz Kindermann linked the theatrical experience to aspects of race and blood, too:

> The communality of the blood along with the stirring dramatic idea and its realisation on stage, the rousing harmony of word and echo, of monologue and objection, of gesture and costume, of mask, mime and stage design, of light and colour, of rhythm and music, tantalise audiences which are of one race in equal measure for one evening, irrespective of where they came from emotionally, geographically or socially. (Kindermann 1943, 9–10)

By reflecting on theories of racial 'purity' Kindermann argued that only audiences of one single blood/race could truly come together as one, enjoy and experience an evening in the theatre properly and as a communal event. This also meant that the experience of going to the theatre was removed from an aesthetic discourse and instead became a biological issue. Witnessing a performance led to audiences experiencing their 'national soul', their belonging to the same national community—a discourse which proved powerful in relation to ethnic Germans in occupied Europe during the Second World War who—through theatre performances—'found' their German identity (Heinrich 2017). In 1943 Kindermann summed up the function of the German theatre as the first line of defence in the 'constant struggle for the preservation of our racial and *völkisch* being' (qtd. in Petersen 1941/42, 10).

Racial theories also influenced the way literary and theatre scholars discussed dramatists and their works. Shakespeare, for example, one of the mainstays in German repertoires, was interpreted as the archetypal Germanic, even 'Aryan' playwright (Wagner 1938, 13–14). His portrait was examined by 'racial experts' who conveniently proclaimed that this revealed 'solidly Nordic features' (Strobl 1997, 19). Theatre scholar Otto zur Nedden concluded in 1942 that racially Shakespeare 'undoubtedly' belonged to the 'Nordic cultural sphere' (zur Nedden 1943, 11). This and similar comments gave legitimacy to National Dramaturge Rainer Schlösser's assertion that no other nation had a similarly justifiable claim on Shakespeare—not even Britain (a claim which Gerhart Hauptmann had famously put forward in 1915) (Schlösser 1938, 22–24; Hauptmann 1915, xii). Linking to claims that 'race' was the determining factor in people's character Nazi commentators asserted that Shakespeare's 'Nordic genes' also resulted in his thinking and writing being *völkisch* (Braumüller 1937/38, programme no. 15). It was Hans F.K. Günther himself who attempted to provide the textual evidence for these claims in an academic article for the prestigious *Shakespeare-Jahrbuch* in which he considered 'Shakespeare's Girls and Women' from a eugenic perspective. It was vital for the survival of a people to make sure that the 'racially superior' members of the community chose similarly equipped partners in order for the race to 'improve' Günther claimed—and the behaviour of Shakespeare's characters provided the perfect template for this (Günther 1937, 85–86; Strobl 1999).

Productions of Shakespeare's plays across Germany began to be judged according to their 'racial merit' alongside their aesthetic and artistic qualities. When Heinz Hilpert opened his tenure at the famous Deutsches Theater in 1934 with *As You Like It* the production of this seemingly inconspicuous play was not only judged for its romantic interpretation, its playfulness and its talented cast, but also for its 'qualities' from a racial perspective. The reviewer in the radical *Völkischer Beobachter*, F. Grube, claimed that

> the poet shows us […] how the wholesome race, like superior blood, wins through against oppressive forces. Oliver, heir to baronial estates, deliberately neglects his brother Orlando, aims to vilify him as a mere servant in order to enjoy the substantial inheritance himself. But he gets it wrong. Orlando's noble blood rebels, he claims and ekes out a place beside his brother, who is eventually forced to give in and to share the inheritance with him. (*Völkischer Beobachter*, 13 September 1934)

128   A. HEINRICH

It may be debatable whether Hilpert aimed for such an interpretation, the key point here is that racial theories found their way into a performance discourse.

Shakespeare's protagonist in *Hamlet* was not only interpreted as a typically Germanic figure but also as a true *völkisch* hero (Türck 1937/38, programme no. 12). Friedrich Theodor Fischer regarded Hamlet's end as a victory of the race and as a symbol for the superiority of the nation over the interests of the individual as 'the people, the entity, the nation remains, the state is saved. And this is truly magnificent' (Fischer 1937/38, programme no. 14). In surveying *Hamlet* productions all over Germany the 1940 *Shakespeare-Jahrbuch* was relieved to report that, finally, 'Hamlet was not portrayed as a weakling or a nervous artist anymore, but as a youthful genius' (Papsdorf 1940, 254; Fechter 1941, 123–133). *The Merchant of Venice* was of particular interest for Nazi commentators because of the 'possibilities' it offered around the portrayal of Shylock and his daughter Jessica (Bonnell 2008). Her relationship to Lorenzo was no longer 'desirable' and so in October 1936 the writer and translator Hermann Kroepelin wrote to Sigmund Graff at the Propaganda Ministry with suggested 'improvements' to existing translations (German Federal Archives, letter dated 7 October 1936, file R55/20218, p. 73). By adding 'a mere three lines' and changing the play's ending 'ever so slightly' an easy 'solution' could be found

> not through an abatement of Jessica or through the bastardisation under her father's watch—in which case there would always remain the mother—but by contrast through a further logical development of Jessica's character, who after her father's collapse arrives at a new understanding of her familial links. This would ultimately make her relationship to Lorenzo impossible—as she follows her father's cry for help. Shakespeare himself provides us with the incentive for this development. In Act V, scene 1, line 90 Jessica says: 'I am never merry when I hear sweet music'. She thereby testifies to a particular intellectuality. Immediately following Lorenzo praises the same music, and just after that we include another line: Lorenzo: 'Do you cry, Jessica?' Jessica: 'Yes, I have to cry!' (BArch [German Federal Archives Berlin], file R55/20218, p. 89)

Another adaptation by the dramaturg Heinz Sailer, which made Jessica Shylock's foster child but not his biological daughter and eliminated all positive remarks about Jews in the play, was produced in Erfurt in 1939 (BArch, file R55/20194, p. 283). Even where the play's structure remained unchanged, it was used as an anti-Semitic vehicle. At the beginning of the war the *Shakespeare-Jahrbuch* was pleased to report that all new productions of the play now refrained from presenting Shylock in an 'apologetic' fashion (Papsdorf 1940, 247). The most influential war-time production of the play was Lothar Müthel's 1943 version in Vienna with Werner Krauß as Shylock. Richard Biedrzynski 'praised' Krauß for his ability to present Shylock as 'repugnant', 'alien', 'disgusting': 'Krauß plays the Jew in a way in which the Jew himself would never be able to due to his unimaginative character' (Biedrzynski 1944, 35).

Reviewing the same production Karl Lahm equally 'celebrated' Krauß's depiction of Shylock: 'The affected way of shuffling along, the hopping and stamping about in a rage, the clawing hand gestures, the raucous or mumbling voice—all this makes up the pathological picture of the East European Jewish type in all his external and internal human dirtiness' (Lahm 1943).

3   Thing Plays

While performances of the Shakespearean classics appealed to the educated German middle classes (the so-called *Bildungsbürgertum*) and productions such as the one by Lothar Müthel discussed above provided an opportunity to produce the established canon with anti-Semitic undertones, Nazi grass roots called for new forms of theatre altogether—particularly in the early years of the regime. These new forms, chiefly among them the so-called *Thing* theatre (*Thingspiel*), were based on racial considerations, too. The country's Germanic past became an important motif as the *Thing* movement aimed at creating a genuine National Socialist form of cultic theatre in open-air performance spaces for vast audiences. Reimar Volker has argued that the *Thing* movement was 'an attempt to at once establish and demonstrate a lineage to ancient Germanic culture' (Volker 2008, 46). It is important to note, however, that the *Thing* movement was based on ideas already formulated in Imperial Germany and had developed further during the years of the Weimar Republic. In the 1920s Wilhelm Karl Gerst became the driving force behind this movement. In 1924 he published his seminal study on amateur drama, in which he proposed plans for an increasing number of open-air stages and theatre festivals (Gerst 1924). After 1933 Nazi theorists seized upon Gerst's idea and attempted to turn open-air performances into political theatre with strong nationalistic undertones. The *Thing* plays combined some of the basic tenets Nazi commentators and practitioners agreed upon as characteristics of the new *völkisch* drama. It was to portray nothing realistic or individual but become symbolic and be driven by categories such as race, nation or providence. The term *Thing* had Germanic origins and denoted a gathering space of the people, in an outdoor setting, where judgement was spoken. Nazi theorists like Felix Emmel or Richard Euringer picked up on this historical function but added a cultic role for these sites—sites which should remind audiences of Germanic sacrificial altars 'on hills and in sacred groves' (Emmel 1937, 92–93). They labelled the plays performed in the 'plays of consecration' (*Weihespiele*), although this religious role of the Germanic *Thing* has no historical justification and is entirely fabricated. The venues offered space for thousands, sometimes tens of thousands, of people who assembled, or rather congregated, in the open air. 'In the depths of rural Silesia', in Annaberg, the Nazis built a *Thing* theatre for 50,000 people (Strobl 2009, 15). *Thingstätten* used natural settings, incorporating rocks, trees, waterfalls, ruins and hills of some historical or mythical significance. The first *Thingplatz* was built in 1934 near Halle, in East Germany, and more sites were erected according to a substantial building programme accompanied by intense propaganda. A preliminary report in the summer of 1934 stated that two *Thing* theatres were now finished, 18 were currently being constructed, and a further 66 had been approved (Brenner 1963, 99). In total some 1200 *Thing* sites were planned after 1933 (of which only 45 materialised, however).

The *Thing* movement remained relatively short-lived for a number of reasons and has been largely dismissed by the established literature as having been unsuccessful and with negligible influence. Bill Niven concluded that 'not much by way of even acceptable drama resulted from the amount of time and organizational zest invested in the creation of *Thing* drama' (Niven 2000, 54, 90). Jutta Wardetzky asserted that the failure of the *Thing* movement proved that the Nazis were 'kunstunfähig' (culturally inept) (Wardetzky 1983, 97; similarly Rischbieter 2000, 34–41). Reasons for the *Thing* movement's failure include its borrowings from other dramatic forms, for example, choric performances, mass workers' theatre and religious festivals. The changeable German weather also played a part as dry conditions could not always be relied upon. Predictable plots, slow-paced and lengthy performances, and poor audibility did not help either. Ultimately propaganda minister Joseph Goebbels pulled the movement from official support in 1936 (Heinrich 2013, 281–286). However, and importantly, for a time the *Thing* movement and its plays were not only officially endorsed but also immensely popular as tens of thousands of people witnessed performances in a brief window of two or three years. A 1933 writing competition for new *Thing* plays attracted some 10,000 entries, and Richard Euringer's *German Passion 1933* had a print run of 30,000 copies one year after it had been first performed (Brenner 1963, 100). This was, finally, a movement which promised social inclusiveness (provided one conformed to the preferred racial norm, that is) and a new ritualistic theatre experience (Berghaus 1996). The *Thing* plays also offered new aesthetic possibilities in terms of space, dramaturgy, costume and set design, as the constraints of the illusionistic middle-class proscenium theatre were replaced by unashamedly gigantic performance possibilities. With low ticket prices and an architecture without the established divisions between boxes, circles and pit, *Thing* theatre really seemed to be a theatre for everyone. And indeed 'large crowds [were— A.H.] flocking to the arenas' and they did so 'of their own accord' (Strobl 2009, 59). In 1933 some 60,000 people attended a performance of *Bread and Iron* at the Berlin Grunewald stadium which was enacted by 17,000 performers (Eichberg 1977, 61), and the opening performance of the *Thingstätte* in Koblenz with Heinrich Lersch's *Volk im Werden* (*Making of a People*) in 1935 attracted 20,000 spectators in a city with a population of 87,000. In 1934 and 1935 *Thing* audiences reached up to 58,000 for a single performance (Brenner 1963, 103). Audiences who might not have attended performances in established theatres now filled the new spaces (Strobl 2010, 380).

Thing plays often featured quasi-religious themes with a messiah figure coming to the rescue of a beleaguered and hopeless nation, for example, in Kurt Eggers' *Das Spiel von Job dem Deutschen* (*The Play About Job the German*),

Richard Euringer's *Deutsche Passion 1933* (*German Passion 1933*) or Kurt Heynicke's *Neurode: Ein Spiel von deutscher Arbeit* (*Neurode: A Play About German Labour*). Eberhard Wolfgang Möller's *Frankenburg Game of Dice* (*Das Frankenburger Würfelspiel*, first performed in Berlin in 1936) dramatised an uprising in the last Peasants' War in Upper Austria in 1625, which had been sparked by an attempt to forcibly reintroduce Catholicism in the region, as an anti-Austrian and anti-Catholic revolt against foreign and 'un-German' rule (Baird 2008, 180–184). In most of these performances lengthy and relatively simple plots developed around themes of redemption, spiritual rescue and national resurgence, performed by large casts with sometimes hundreds of extras, and a hero who transcended his individuality to serve his people, that is, sacrifice himself for the greater good. Overall, the new drama was intended to celebrate the racially pure national community and elevate each single human fate (both on and off stage) into higher spheres.[4] In this kind of theatre, social class, economic status in society, even gender did not seem to matter anymore; it was immaterial whether an audience was educated or not, rich or poor, young or old; what counted was their belonging to the 'Aryan' race and their belief in the unity which the performance created. Through this belief, audiences were supposed to experience the ideal *Volksgemeinschaft* (national community) there and then: they became part of a performance in which they took part. Euringer claimed that at *Thing* performances 'there are no spectators. There are no good seats. There is only a nation and a site' (Euringer 1936, 237). The unity between spectators, subject matter and performance also meant that only racially 'pure', that is, Aryan, performers and spectators were to be allowed into the *Thing* site. Wilhelm von Schramm, chief Nazi ideologist of the *Thing* movement, claimed that 'only free man with a natural nobility could be allowed to enter the inner ring of the *Thing* ... In the open air one demands [...] the visible embodiment of Nordic characteristics' (Schramm 1934, 62).

In his *German Passion 1933*, the *Thing* movement's first 'sensational success' (Brenner 1963, 100), Richard Euringer tapped into a wide-spread longing of a national 'rebirth' both after the Great War and the 'chaotic' years of the Weimar Republic. In the play an unknown and unnamed First World War soldier rises from a mass grave to return and save his people. In doing so he becomes the political and spiritual leader that both the cast in the play and the audience of the performance have longed for. The implication is that in a Germany changed by the 'revolution' of 1933 the legacy of the country's fallen soldiers was finally recognised—they had not died in vain—and with many theatre-goers these themes struck a chord. After years of economic depression, unemployment and hopelessness, here was a regime that seemed to be able to handle the problems and unite the country—and the *Thing* plays showed that it was 'belief' more than anything else which made all the difference. In *German Passion 1933* Euringer combined dramatic devices of mediaeval morality and Catholic passion plays and turned Christian motifs into *völkisch* ones. Erich von Hartz called this 'the incarnation of the Christian spirit into the German-Germanic body' (Hartz 1934, 28). The messiah figure was not a

132   A. HEINRICH

forgiving Christ but the 'unknown soldier of the Great War', a more or less straightforward reference to Hitler himself (as is even more obvious in the original German name of the character, *der unbekannte Gefreite des Weltkriegs*).[5] At the beginning of the play, the Jewish 'evil spirit' seems to triumph over the dead of the First World War:

> Night.—Night.—Blood-red night. They're quiet.
> Finally the end of the fight. The last one that turned
> around got his ribs smashed. His fate's been found.
> The war has come to an end. Peace has come again.[6]

But, when 'the mother' and 'the child' reply with their litanies,

> Want.—Want.—Want.—The hungry stay gaunt.
> A stove and no heat. The country in defeat.

the war dead become restless. Choruses of the dead call out from the depths, choruses of soldiers of the 'Young Germany' call from afar. As 'the unemployed worker' confirms the lamentations about a country which is economically crippled and taken over by foreign powers, the fallen 'unknown soldier' rises up—as the voice of warning and wearing a crown of thorns made of barbed wire—to suffer his 'passion' and to save his people. The 'evil spirit', a mixture of war profiteer, socialist revolutionary, traitor and capitalist, with more or less obvious references to his Jewish identity throughout the play, mobilises a campaign for total consumption and, to the applause of the (Jewish) 'major shareholder', goads the masses to attack the 'unknown soldier'. The indoctrinated masses, however, prove unable to capture the 'unknown soldier', and one by one they join his ranks. A new world of labour is born. Having completed his task, the 'unknown soldier' can then disappear while the 'evil spirit' sinks into the depths with great clamour. The dead of the Great War finally have their peace: their mission is accomplished; an Aryan Germany is reborn.

4   EBERHARD WOLFGANG MÖLLER'S *ROTHSCHILD SIEGT BEI WATERLOO*

Despite early significant successes and high-profile shows, and as noted above, the *Thing* movement ultimately struggled and was virtually stopped by Goebbels in early 1936. Instead of aiming to establish a radical new dramatic and aesthetic language with the *Thing* movement the regime returned to the established bourgeois theatre space. The new Nazi-dominated city councils were forced to realise that radical changes only alienated them from middle-class audiences as they returned to established formats.[7] Illustrative of these changes in official policy is the fact that in 1937 Möller's *Frankenburg Game of Dice*, heralded only a year earlier as the quintessential *Thing* play, was now presented in a reworked version for the traditional proscenium-arch theatre and performed at Bochum's municipal playhouse (Ketelsen 1999, 137). Euringer's *German Passion 1933*, too, was now produced indoors at the Berlin Theater des Volkes in 1935. One of the new *völkisch* plays to be written for the picture-frame stage was Eberhard Wolfgang Möller's *Rothschild siegt bei Waterloo* (*Rothschild is the Victor at Waterloo*, 1934), his most successful stage production (Drewniak 1983, 220–221; Panse 2000, 648–671; Gadberry 2000, 108–110).

This return to established formats, however, does not mean that political messages became less radical—on the contrary. Möller's *Rothschild* centred on a powerful anti-Semitic message. In it the Jewish banker Nathan Rothschild was presented as having made a fortune out of knowingly spreading false news about the Duke of Wellington's defeat against Napoleon at the London Stock Exchange in 1815 and causing despair and even death in the process. In the play Rothschild uses the disorder at the Stock Exchange to become enormously rich by buying huge quantities of momentarily worthless shares. In this fictional episode (though presented as historically accurate by Möller in the preface to the play) race, and the suggested racial attributes of all Jews, takes centre stage. It establishes a link between a radical capitalism which stops at nothing in order to make a profit and the 'Jewish character'. The centrality of this message is further underlined by Möller's own introduction to the play text, and it became the focus of contemporary performance reviews, too. Hans Gstettner's review of the 1936 Munich production, for example, lauded the play for its illustration of the 'soulless capitalism' associated with the 'eternal Jew' (qtd. in Panse 2000, 657). It seems that by the mid-1930s German theatre and its audience had firmly established its anti-Semitic stance as the common ground in German culture.

Möller's play was subsequently used for the equally anti-Semitic film *The Rothschilds* (1940), and the Rothschild topic was widely used for propaganda in other arenas, too. Although in relative terms the popular success of Möller's *Rothschild* remained limited it is illustrative of the fact that anti-Semitic discourses and measures had taken a firm foothold in German theatre. They appeared between the lines in the most successful and seemingly purely amusing comedies and operettas, they appeared in reviews of even the most politically harmless classical productions (see previously mentioned example of Shakespeare's *As You Like It*), and—perhaps most importantly—they manifested themselves in the 'cleansing' of repertoires and ensembles. For Jewish practitioners, the only hope of continuing to find employment rested with the Jewish *Kulturbund*.

5 THE JEWISH *KULTURBUND* THEATRE IN BERLIN

The organisation of the *Jüdischer Kulturbund* (Jewish Arts League) was an institution created by unemployed Jewish performers, who had been forced out of the established German theatre system after 1933, and with the consent of the Nazi regime. In an increasingly oppressive climate the *Kulturbund* attempted to offer a semblance of normality to its 70,000 members in 49 locations across Germany. The Nazis used the *Kulturbund* as a façade to hide oppression and persecution and at the same time succeeded in manifesting an obvious difference between Jewish Germans and gentile Germans as audiences became strictly separated. The *Kulturbund* put on theatrical performances, concerts, exhibitions, operas and lectures all over Germany, performed by Jewish entertainers, artists, writers, scientists and so on. Thus, Jewish performers could again earn their livelihood, however, scarce. With increasing persecution following the Nuremberg Laws in 1935 and, particularly, the 1938 pogroms, the situation at the theatre worsened considerably with emigration, arrests, further forced closures of companies such as publishing houses and artists' agencies and even closer control by the Propaganda Ministry. In September 1941, a few weeks after the German attack on the Soviet Union, the *Kulturbund* was closed down for good.

The Berlin *Kulturbund* theatre turned into the main theatrical outlet for Germany's Jewish community but its operation was strictly controlled and repertoire choices were limited. Unusual in the subsidised German theatre system the theatre was forced to run as a commercial venture. This appeared to have been a deliberate choice by the Nazi regime to stress even more that this was an 'atypical' playhouse. One of the key challenges for its directors was that the *Kulturbund* theatre was not only dependent on the wider political context but also on establishing personal relationships with the Nazis and a careful collaboration between theatre director Kurt Singer and *Staatskommissar* Hans Hinkel or the 'National Dramaturge' (*Reichsdramaturg*) Rainer Schlösser who oversaw the enterprise. Nazi repertoire and censorship policy, however, was far from consistent, and the censors 'appeared to make up the rules for theatres as they went along' (Rovit 2000, 195). The process of granting permission to produce a certain play was, therefore, often reduced to personal debate and wrangling.

In terms of both its repertoire and its audience the Nazis forced a Jewish identity on the *Kulturbund* which to many seemed alien. The strict focus on 'Jewish' plays and contents was a slap in the face for the Jewish community, which had largely regarded itself as German first and Jewish second, and had often moved away from practising their religion. Many members of that community were highly decorated WWI soldiers, they were (or had been) professors, judges, doctors—pillars of middle-class German society. What they strove for was a repertoire consisting of very much the same fare as was offered on other stages across Germany. The Nazi authorities, however, prohibited the performance of plays by gentile German authors and required a 'Jewish' programme. It is remarkable, however, that even concerning the aspect of the theatre's identity Nazi policy was inconsistent, as Schlösser did not want the *Kulturbund* to become 'too Jewish'. This, he feared, might prove dangerous, as it would present Zionism in too positive and even too powerful a light. The

Zionist minority within the Jewish community, however, supported the move towards a more characteristically 'Jewish' theatre, although until the last season of the *Kulturbund* this never materialised. It was largely due to the influence of the large number of liberal assimilated Jews educated according to Humanist concepts that the *Kulturbund* theatre continued with a 'pre-1933 bourgeois German theatre repertoire' (Rovit 2012, 97). Apart from the Greek classics, Shakespeare and modern classics such as Ibsen and Shaw, the repertoire increasingly consisted of light dramas and escapist comedies, which strikingly contrasted with the actual threats in real life outside the theatre. *Kulturbund* audiences saw plays by Schnitzler, Zweig, Molnar and Priestley, a fact, which 'in an ironic twist of logic' even appeared as 'a breath of freedom' (Rovit 2012, 207).

Overall, however, the *Kulturbund* theatre ghettoised Jewish cultural practices. It concentrated on Jewish dramatists, it was only open to Jews, and it was not allowed to publicise its activities. The exclusion of the Jewish influence on the arts in Germany was not only an injustice but also a travesty in a theatre which owed a significant debt of gratitude to Jewish performers, playwrights and benefactors. The establishment of the *Kulturbund* theatre was, then, another powerful illustration of the fact the German theatre after 1933 was divided and characterised along racial lines. In the wider context of German racial politics the *Kulturbund* also illustrated the radically worsening situation for Jews in Germany after 1938. Most of its protagonists were murdered in the Holocaust.

6 Conclusion

Race became *the* basis on which German theatre operated after 1933. A racially 'pure' Germanic theatre was the regime's ultimate goal—both onstage and offstage, and after 1939 across the whole European continent (Heinrich 2017). 'Non-Aryan' practitioners were forced off German stages immediately after the take-over, their plays, adaptations and translations banned, and replaced with 'Germanic' personnel and material. This represented a radical break which happened within a short period of time and had lasting effects. Yet, all too often research on theatre under the Nazis has concentrated on the poor quality of the new Nazi plays, on uninspiring performances, and the fact that the Nazis had not managed to establish their own distinct dramaturgy and aesthetic. Peter Gay, for example, claimed that the Nazis failed in their cultural policy and only managed to produce kitsch (Gay 1968, 120). More recently Birthe Kundrus claimed that the Nazi stages were characterised by an 'intellectual depletion' and did not warrant in detail exploration (Kundrus 2005, 93–157). Richard Evans added that 'public demand for comedies and light entertainment [...] depressed the standard of what the German stage offered' (Evans 2009, 568), and Hans Daiber posited that 'nothing remained of the Nazi drama. Much ado about nothing' (Daiber 1995, 143). In her history of the

Frankfurt theatre during the Third Reich Bettina Schültke admitted that she only reluctantly discussed the 'mediocre plays of the Nazi dramatists' (Schültke 1997, 12). These conclusions seem fair but they largely fail to recognise that despite their low quality most of the fair performed during the Third Reich was popular with record attendances. However even where this popular success is acknowledged it has all too often been dismissed following Thomas Mann's dictum that nothing produced between 1933 and 1945 deserved any attention. Crucially, in the context of this present research, the focus on dramaturgy and playwriting and conclusions of low literary quality have tended to sideline the fact that the Nazis did indeed 'succeed' in changing the make-up of the German theatre radically after 1933 with Jewish practitioners being laid off, Jewish works taken off repertoires, and Jewish actors, singers, composers, directors, musicians, designers, administrators and technicians being murdered in the Holocaust.

NOTES

1. The term *völkisch* derives from the German word *Volk* (people). It has strong romantic, folklore and 'organic' undertones, which, in its emphasising of the 'Blood and Soil' idea, combine with an anti-urban populism. The *völkisch* movement was also characterised by anti-communist, anti-immigration, anti-capitalist, anti-parliamentarian and strong anti-Semitic undercurrents.
2. Kindermann remained the leading German language theatre scholar for much of the twentieth century, and his studies form an integral part of performance studies libraries the world over.
3. Günther was of course part of a wider discourse and in his studies seemed keen to link his theories to a much wider field of *Rassenkunde* scholars.
4. For examples of Nazi theoretical positions concerning the *Thing* plays, see Rainer Schlösser, *Das Volk und seine Bühne: Bemerkungen zum Aufbau des deutschen Theaters* (Berlin, 1935); Wilhelm von Schramm, *Neubau des deutschen Theaters* (Berlin, 1934); Hans Severus Ziegler, *Das Theater des deutschen Volkes: Ein Beitrag zur Volkserziehung und Propaganda* (Leipzig, 1933); Richard Euringer, *Chronik einer deutschen Wandlung 1925–1935* (Hamburg, 1936); Heinz Riecke, 'Freizeitgestaltung und Spiele der Gegenwart', *Die Neue Literatur* 37 (1936), 22–32.
5. Hitler's rank in the Imperial German army during the First World War was *Gefreiter* (private), and this rank was regularly referred to by conservative critics of the Nazi party before 1933 to ridicule Hitler and his political ambitions. The equation *Gefreiter* = Hitler would have been made by theatre audiences as well, and it did not need further explanation.
6. Quotations from this play in English translation are taken from Eichberg/Jones, 1977, pp. 133–134.
7. The vast majority of German theatres were (and still are) municipal theatres (*Stadttheater*) which are owned and subsidised by city councils.

REFERENCES

ARCHIVAL SOURCES

Akademie der Künste Berlin, Heinz-Hilpert-Archiv 1.1 Regie/Sprechtheater, 1284.
Bundesarchiv (BArch) Berlin (German Federal Archives). Propaganda Ministry Files. R55/20218, R55/20194.
Herder Institut Marburg. Theater Posen. 34 VIII P120 Z23.
Stadtarchiv (Municipal Archives) Münster. Nachlass Vernekohl.

LITERATURE

Baird, J.W. 2008. *Hitler's War Poets: Literature and Politics in the Third Reich.* Cambridge: Cambridge University Press.
Barnett, D. 2008. Naturalism, Expressionism and Brecht. In *A History of German Theatre*, ed. Simon Williams and Maik Hamburger, 198–221. Cambridge: Cambridge University Press.
Berghaus, G. 1996. The Ritual Core of Fascist Theatre. An Anthropological Perspective. In *Fascism and Theatre. Comparative Studies on the Aesthetics and Politics of Performance in Europe, 1925–1945*, ed. Guenther Berghaus, 39–71. Oxford: Berghahn.
Bermbach, U. 2015. *Houston Stewart Chamberlain. Wagners Schwiegersohn—Hitlers Vordenker.* Stuttgart: Metzler.
Biedrzynski, R. 1944. *Schauspieler—Regisseure—Intendanten.* Heidelberg: Hüthig.
Bonnell, A.G. 2008. *Shylock in Germany. Antisemitism and the German Theatre from the Enlightenment to the Nazis.* London: IB Tauris.
Braumüller, W. 1937/38. Shakespeare—der Dramatiker der politischen Totalität. *Stadttheater und Kammerspiele der Städtischen Bühnen Münster* (14). Programme no. 15.
Brenner, H. 1963. *Die Kunstpolitik des Nationalsozialismus.* Hamburg: Rowohlt.
Chamberlain, H.S. 1909. *Die Grundlagen des Neunzehnten Jahrhunderts.* Vol. 1. 9th ed. Munich: Bruckmann.
Daiber, H. 1995. *Schaufenster der Diktatur. Theater im Machtbereich Hitlers.* Stuttgart: Neske.
Drewniak, B. 1983. *Das Theater im NS-Staat. Szenarium deutscher Zeitgeschichte 1933–1945.* Düsseldorf: Droste.
Dussel, K. 1988. *Ein neues, ein heroisches Theater? Nationalsozialistische Theaterpolitik und ihre Auswirkungen in der Provinz.* Bonn: Bouvier.
Eichberg, H. 1977. Thing-, Fest- und Weihespiele in Nationalsozialismus, Arbeiterkultur und Olympismus: Zur Geschichte des politischen Verhaltens in der Epoche des Faschismus. In *Massenspiele: NS-Thingspiel, Arbeiterweihespiel und olympisches Zeremoniell*, ed. Henning Eichberg, Michael Dultz, Glen Gadberry, and Günther Rühle, 19–180. Stuttgart: Frommann-Holzboog.
Eichberg, H., and R.A. Jones. 1977. The Nazi *Thingspiel*: Theater for the Masses in Fascism and Proletarian Culture. *New German Critique* 11: 133–150.
Emmel, F. 1937. *Theater aus deutschem Wesen.* Berlin: Georg Stilke.
Euringer, R. 1936. *Chronik einer deutschen Wandlung 1925–1935.* Hamburg: Hanseatische Verlagsanstalt.

138   A. HEINRICH

Evans, R. 2009. *The Third Reich at War. How the Nazis led Germany from Conquest to Disaster*. London: Penguin.

Fechter, P. 1941. Deutsche Shakespeare-Darsteller. *Shakespeare-Jahrbuch* (77).

Fischer, F.T. 1937/38. Shakespeares 'Hamlet'. *Stadttheater und Kammerspiele der Stadt Münster* (14). Programme no. 14.

Fischli, B. 1976. *Die Deutschen-Dämmerung. Zur Genealogie des völkisch-faschistischen Dramas und Theaters*. Bonn: Bouvier.

Gadberry, G. 1995. *Theatre in the Third Reich, the Prewar Years: Essays on Theatre in Nazi Germany*. Westport, CT: Greenwood.

———. 2000. The History Plays of the Third Reich. In *Theatre Under the Nazis*, ed. John London. Manchester: Manchester University Press.

Gay, P. 1968. *Weimar Culture: The Outsider as Insider*. New York: Harper & Row.

Gerst, W.K. 1924. *Gemeinschaftsbühne und Jugendbewegung*. Frankfurt: Verlag des Bühnenvolksbundes.

Günther, H.F.K. 1926. *Rassenkunde Europas*. 2nd rev. ed. Munich: Lehmann.

———. 1927. *Adel und Rasse*. 2nd rev. ed. Munich: Lehmann.

———. 1933. *Rassenkunde des deutschen Volkes*. 16th ed. Munich: Lehmann.

———. 1937. Shakespeares Mädchen und Frauen. Ein Vortrag vor der Deutschen Shakespeare-Gesellschaft. *Shakespeare-Jahrbuch* (73).

Hartz, E. 1934. *Wesen und Mächte des heldischen Theaters*. Berlin: Langen Müller.

Hasse, E. 1897. Deutsche Weltpolitik. *Alldeutsche Flugschriften* 5.

Hauptmann, G. 1915. Deutschland und Shakespeare. *Jahrbuch der Deutschen Shakespeare-Gesellschaft* (51).

Hausmann, F.-W. 2003. *Anglistik und Amerikanistik im 'Dritten Reich'*. Frankfurt: Klostermann.

Heinrich, A. 2012. 'It is Germany Where He Truly Lives': Nazi Claims on Shakespearean Drama. *New Theatre Quarterly* 28 (3): 230–242.

———. 2013. Germania on Stage. Nazi Thing Theatre. In *Germania Remembered 1500–2009: Commemorating and Inventing a Germanic Past*, ed. Nicola McLelland and Christina Lee, 273–288. Tucson: Arizona State University Press.

———. 2017. *Theatre in Europe under German Occupation*. London: Routledge.

Hitler, A. 1939. *Mein Kampf*. 434th–443rd ed. Munich: Eher.

Ketelsen, U.-K. 1968. *Heroisches Theater: Untersuchungen zur Dramentheorie des Dritten Reichs*. Bonn: Bouvier.

———. 1999. *Ein Theater und seine Stadt: Die Geschichte des Bochumer Schauspielhauses*. Köln: SH-Verlag.

Kindermann, H. 1938. *Rufe über Grenzen. Antlitz und Lebensraum der Grenz- und Auslanddeutschen in ihrer Dichtung*. Berlin: Junge Generation.

———. 1940. *Die Weltkriegsdichtung der Deutschen im Ausland*. Berlin: Volk und Reich.

———. 1943. *Theater und Nation*. Leipzig: Reclam.

———. 1944. *Die europäische Sendung des deutschen Theaters. Wiener Wissenschaftliche Vorträge und Reden 10*. Vienna: Rohrer.

Kundrus, B. 2005. Totale Unterhaltung? Die kulturelle Kriegführung in Film, Rundfunk und Theater 1939–1945. In *Das Deutsche Reich und der Zweite Weltkrieg, Band 9: Die deutsche Kriegsgesellschaft 1939 bis 1945, zweiter Halbband: Ausbeutung, Deutungen, Ausgrenzung*, ed. Joern Echternkamp. Stuttgart: Deutsche Verlags-Anstalt.

Lahm, K. 1943. Shylock der Ostjude. *Deutsche Allgemeine Zeitung*, May 19.

7 RACE AS CATEGORY IN NAZI GERMAN THEATRE   139

Malkin, J.R., and F. Rokem, eds. 2010. *Jews and the Making of Modern German Theatre.* Iowa: University of Iowa Press.

Niven, W. 2000. The Birth of Nazi Drama?: *Thing* Plays. In *Theatre Under the Nazis,* ed. John London, 54–95. Manchester: Manchester University Press.

Panse, B. 2000. Zeitgenössische Dramatik 1933–44. Autoren, Themen, Zensurpraxis. In *Theater im "Dritten Reich": Theaterpolitik, Spielplanstruktur, NS-Dramatik,* Henning Rischbieter, 489–720. Seelze: Kallmeyer.

Papsdorf, W. 1940. Theaterschau. Shakespeare auf der deutschen Bühne 1938/40. *Shakespeare-Jahrbuch* (76).

Petersen, H. 1941/42. Was wir uns erwarten. *Blätter der Reichsgautheater Posen.*

Rischbieter, H. 2000. NS-Theaterpolitik. NS-Theaterpolitik als Prozeß. Theatermetropole Berlin. Die deutsche Theaterlandschaft 1933–44. In *Theater im "Dritten Reich": Theaterpolitik, Spielplanstruktur, NS-Dramatik,* ed. Henning Rischbieter, 9–277. Seelze: Kallmeyer.

Ritchie, J.M. 1983. *German Literature Under National Socialism.* London: Croom Helm.

Rosenberg, A. 1935. *Der Mythus des 20. Jahrhunderts: Eine Wertung der seelisch-geistigen Gestaltenkämpfe unserer Zeit.* 53rd–54th ed. Munich: Eher.

Rovit, R. 2000. Jewish Theatre: Repertory and Censorship in the Jüdischer Kulturbund, Berlin. In *Theatre Under the Nazis,* ed. John London, 187–221. Manchester: Manchester University Press.

———. 2012. *The Jewish Kulturbund Theatre Company in Nazi Berlin.* Iowa: University of Iowa Press.

Rühle, G. 1974. *Zeit und Theater, vol. 3: Diktatur und Exil 1933–1945.* Berlin: Ullstein.

Schlösser, R. 1938. Der deutsche Shakespeare. *Shakespeare-Jahrbuch* (74).

Schramm, W. 1934. *Neubau des deutschen Theaters.* Berlin: Schlieffen-Verlag.

Schültke, B. 1997. *Theater oder Propaganda? Die Städtischen Bühnen Frankfurt am Main 1933–1945.* Frankfurt: Kramer.

Spengler, O. 1923. *Der Untergang des Abendlandes. Umrisse einer Morphologie der Weltgeschichte.* 53rd–59th ed. Munich: Beck.

Strobl, G. 1997. Shakespeare and the Nazis. *History Today* (47).

———. 1999. The Bard of Eugenics: Shakespeare and Racial Activism in the Third Reich. *Journal of Contemporary History* 34: 323–336.

———. 2009. *The Swastika and the Stage: German Theatre and Society, 1933–1945.* Cambridge: University of Cambridge Press.

———. 2010. Making Sense of Theatre in the Third Reich. *History Compass* 8 (5): 377–387.

Türck, H. 1937/38. Hamlet, eine eminent tatkräftige Natur! *Stadttheater und Kammerspiele der Stadt Münster* (14). Programme no. 12.

Volker, R. 2008. Herbert Windt's Film Music to *Triumph of the Will*: Ersatz-Wagner or Incidental Music to the Ultimate Nazi-*Gesamtkunstwerk*? In *Composing for the Screen in Germany and the USSR: Cultural Politics and Propaganda,* ed. Robyn Stilwell and Phil Powrie, 39–53. Bloomington: Indiana University Press.

Wagner, J. 1938. Was ist uns Shakespeare? *Shakespeare-Jahrbuch* (74).

Wardetzky, J. 1983. *Theaterpolitik im faschistischen Deutschland: Studien und Dokumente.* Berlin/East: Henschel.

zur Nedden, O. 1943. *Drama und Dramaturgie im 20. Jahrhundert. Abhandlungen zum Theater und zur Theaterwissenschaft der Gegenwart.* 2nd rev. ed. Würzburg: Triltsch.

CHAPTER 8

Māori Theatre in Not-Quite-Post-Colonial Aotearoa New Zealand

Sharon Mazer

I understood that Māori theatre can only be a hybrid, as in traditional Māori society the concept of a 'theatre' was foreign. I also realised that, because our theatre had to be a hybrid, I should understand and hold firm to my traditions and Māori point of view. Otherwise, the theatre I created would become purely generic.
—*Hone Kouka (2007: 241)*

1   Introduction

First performed as part of the 1996 New Zealand International Festival of the Arts in Wellington, Hone Kouka's ground-breaking play *Waiora* opens with the sound of waves rushing the beach. Four *tūpuna* (ancestral spirits) quietly appear. After a moment or two, they sing.

> *Taukuri e...   Aue rā, e te hau kāinga*
> *Mākukū ana I aku roimata*
> *Taukuri e...Te ūnga o te tāngaengae*
> *E kukume noa nei te ate*
> (Kouka 1997: 15)[1]

The *waiata* (song) is a lament, reflecting the sadness of Māori who left their homelands to seek work and a different kind of prosperity in the cities in the middle of the twentieth century.

S. Mazer (✉)
Auckland University of Technology, Auckland, New Zealand
e-mail: sharon.mazer@aut.ac.nz

© The Author(s), under exclusive license to Springer Nature
Switzerland AG 2021

141

T. Morosetti, O. Okagbue (eds.), *The Palgrave Handbook of Theatre and Race*, https://doi.org/10.1007/978-3-030-43957-6_8

Ranginui...	*E tū nei titiro kau iho*
	Ki ahau e whakarere atu nei
I a Papa...	*Kia kāewaewa noa rā*
	Kia tika ai ko te kimi oranga.
	(Kouka 1997:15)[2]

As they sing, the *tūpuna* move gently through the performance space, weaving together the spirit world, the imagined world of the play and the real world of an audience that is still settling into its seats. The lyricism of the play's first moments is abruptly broken by the arrival of the *whānau* (family)—father Hone/John and mother Wai/Sue, with their children Amiria, Rongo and Boyboy—who have come for a picnic. The year is 1965. Having moved from their rural homeland on the North Island to the more urban East coast of the South Island so that Hone can find factory work, they are celebrating Rongo's 18th birthday with her Pākehā (i.e., non-Māori)[3] teacher, Louise Stones. They are also looking forward to welcoming Hone's Pākehā boss, Steve Campbell, who they hope will confirm that Hone has been promoted to foreman. Throughout the play, the Māori *whānau* and their Pākehā guests will laugh and sing, bicker and embrace, tell stories and reveal truths, come to blows and tee-ter at the edge between the living and the dead, while the *tūpuna* glide through the shadows, seen only by Rongo as she is overcome by yearning for her deceased grandmother and lost home.

Socially, theatrically and linguistically, *Waiora* is a hybrid, set between Māori and Pākehā ways of performing, and oscillating between ritual and theatre. The dramatic action at its centre is underscored by the history of colonisation and reflects contemporary tensions between Māori and Pākehā at the same time that its theatrical structure is vested in the tenets of Ibsenian realism. Its char-acters are grounded in carefully crafted social and psychological conditions, and their dialogues are driven by suppressed, sub-textual, and powerful, secrets that are revealed as the play unfolds. But it is the spirits of the ancestors, who set the stage and linger, an immanent and potent presence throughout the performance. These figures, the *tūpuna*, do more than shimmer at light's edge; they act upon the *whānau* by performing elements of the Māori cultural reper-toire, and the play reaches its resolution only when the *whānau* take up the performative challenge with a *haka* (dance) that recalls Rongo from the sea to the world of the living.

This chapter looks at how Māori theatre negotiates with the history of European colonisation and the idea(l) of a post-colonial, bicultural Aotearoa New Zealand. At centre are analyses of two pivotal plays by the prominent Māori playwright/director Hone Kouka: *Nga Tangata Toa* ('The Warrior People', first performed in 1994) and *Waiora: Te Ūkaipō—The Homeland* (performed first in 1996).[4] Hone Kouka was not the first playwright to make use of Māori language and culture in New Zealand theatre, but these plays were the first to circulate widely on New Zealand's mainstages. They can be seen both to represent the culmination of Māori challenges to the dominant theatrical culture from the previous decades and to have established a platform for what came after. In this, *Nga Tangata Toa* and *Waiora* are indeed classics, innovative theatre works that have settled into the canon of New Zealand dramatic literature, representing touchstones in social history and prompting overlapping waves of plays by Māori, Pasifika and other others that have emerged since.

Weaving elements of Māori protocol—*karanga* (call), *karakia* (prayer), *wero* (challenge), *whaikōrero* (oratory), *waiata* and *haka*—through Ibsen-inspired dramaturgies, *Nga Tangata Toa* and *Waiora* were produced at a critical juncture in New Zealand theatre history and set the stage for much of what we see now. While this chapter looks closely at these two signal achievements in Māori theatre history, it also surveys some of the social, cultural, theatrical and dramaturgical movements that led to and emerged from Kouka's ground-breaking work, paying particular attention to: the role of Kapa Haka, as an 'invented tradition' (Papesch 2015), in promoting the restoration of *te reo* and *tikanga* Māori (Māori language and culture); the idealisation of 'theatre marae',[5] exemplified in plays like *Michael James Manaia* by John Broughton (1991), as a way of dislocating and decolonising the stage from its Euro-dominant form; and the next generation of Māori playwrights, including (e.g.) Miria George and Albert Belz.

New Zealand theatre historian Diana Looser cautions against viewing the emergence of a distinctively Māori theatre in linear terms. Rather, she conceives of its trajectory 'as a spiral, a Māori framework for historical understanding that encompasses both cyclical and lineal movements by repeatedly acknowledging the past as it moves into the future' (2014: 114).[6] Over time, Māori theatre has confronted the challenges of the present moment by calling on older cultural practices, circulating them through whatever's new on the international stage, and coalescing the results into a relatively stable collation of generic, theatrical and dramaturgical conventions that can be readily recognised as 'Māori' in an increasingly multicultural Aotearoa New Zealand. Its influence can be seen everywhere: in adaptations of plays from the Euro-American tradition—in particular, Shakespeare—and in works by Pacific, Asian and other theatre artists seeking to represent their sense of belonging in this not-quite-post-colonial island nation.

2   Historical Perspective

Māori are the indigenous people of Aotearoa. In the thirteenth century, their ancestors sailed in *waka* (boats) across the South Pacific from Hawaiki—the legendary homeland of the Polynesian people—and became *tangata whenua* (the people of the land). By the time of European contact in the late eighteenth century, Māori were clustered in *iwi* (tribal groups) on *marae* (tribal home-lands), and together they built *te ao Māori* (the Māori world), moving fluidly throughout the islands that together form the heart of the country now known as Aotearoa New Zealand. The costs to Māori, the losses and the degradations caused by colonisation were massive, and the injuries endured are ongoing. But the world they created has also been remarkably resilient: from the earliest encounter with European explorers, beginning with Captain James Cook in 1769 and the signing of the Treaty of Waitangi in 1840, through the long period of active colonisation and the even longer period of suppression, to the movements towards revitalisation of language and culture that arose alongside the political actions that led to the establishment of the Waitangi Tribunal in 1975 and the commencement of the long process of claiming compensation.

Today Aotearoa New Zealand is a bicultural nation. *Te reo* Māori is recognised alongside *te reo* Pākehā (English) as an official language; it is spoken in Parliament (albeit not to such a degree as English) and in other public as well as private institutions (including universities[7]), where bilingual signage is now the norm, and formal proceedings are often framed by *tikanga* Māori. However, to say that New Zealand is past—or post—the colonial is to whitewash the ongoing depredation of Māori sovereignty, the still accumulating losses of economic and social capital, and the policies, practices and prejudices that continue to impede the progress of Māori individuals and communities towards full parity with Pākehā.

Throughout this history, the theatre has played a double role: both implicated in colonisation and a platform for the pursuit of social justice. It landed in New Zealand with the British settlers at the beginning of the nineteenth century. Performances of Shakespeare's plays by touring groups were highly popular, imported as a way both of preserving an increasingly idealised attachment to their homeland and of cultivating an evermore idealised image of themselves as a civilised people in contrast to the Māori whose lives they were industriously displacing. There were home-grown entertainments as well, which went further towards inculcating an imagined community (Anderson 1983) in which the presence of Māori—both Māori performers and Pākehā actors in brownface—literally served as a bit of local colour on the colonial stage as a way of constructing, marking and capitalising on, the exoticism of the place in which these new New Zealanders found themselves. The coloniser's whiteness was theatrically contingent, it seems, on the performed brownness of the colonised.[8]

As the settlers settled, subsequent generations of Pākehā theatre makers turned away from plays that conserved their British identities by representing the strangeness of a new land for the people they had left behind and began to explore ways of telling more local stories in their own voices. Māori characters still frequently featured, especially in the ground-breaking theatre work of Pākehā playwright/performers Bruce Mason and Mervyn Thompson, and still served as markers for what is distinctively New Zealand. But increasingly the figuration of Māori became individualised and politicised, based on the personal experiences of the Pākehā artists and/or crafted in collaboration with Māori artists, and staged as a way of beginning to reckon with colonisation, albeit without fully facing their own complicity. The voyeurism of earlier plays didn't fully disappear, but the sense of putting Māori on show in order to shore up Pākehā identity was diminished somewhat.

As community theatres proliferated across New Zealand and, over the course of the twentieth century, gradually transformed into professional theatres, so did new ways of performing Māori identity and culture. As Margaret Werry demonstrates in her book, *The Tourist State: Performing Leisure, Liberalism and Race in New Zealand* (2011), the spectacle of 'Maoriland' was central to the formation of a distinctive New Zealand identity. Whether in tourist ventures or at world's fairs and expos around the turn of the twentieth century, Māori were put on show, and they also constructed shows for consumption by non-Māori both in New Zealand and abroad. These shows were composed of set pieces, songs and dances adapted from the ritual and cultural repertoire—in particular, the protocols of *pōwhiri* (the ritual of encounter) and the pleasures of the concert party. In dressing themselves in 'traditional' costumes and performing a cultural show and tell—effectively 'this is a famous song that tells the story of' or 'this is the dance performed by warriors before battle'—Māori entrepreneurs created a distinctive way of presenting themselves to outsiders as Māori while also preserving essential components of their ways of being Māori. The distance between performing *waiata*, *poi* and *haka* for tourists and incorporating such performance practices into plays about New Zealand, at least in the early years of the nation, might not have been much. Both genres would have exploited racial and cultural differences to benefit the self-regard of the (presumptive) non-Māori spectator. Both have evolved considerably over the intervening years.

This evolution is in no small part due to the entrance of Kapa Haka onto the national stage in 1972. Writing from the perspective of someone who was on stage for that first Polynesian Performing Arts Festival in her 2015 doctoral thesis, *Creating a Modern Māori Identity Through Kapa Haka*, Te Rita Papesch reflects on her career as a prominent performer, composer, judge and commentator. She makes a case for Kapa Haka as an 'invented tradition'; however, unlike Rustom Bharucha (1989), from whom she borrows the term, she argues that creating a new composite performing arts practice provided a platform both for the revitalisation of language and culture and for political debate at a critical time in New Zealand history. In Papesch's words

> Kapa Haka has not only become a way for Māori to preserve and develop our language and cultural practices, but just as importantly, through our performances we could speak to each other in ways that remained relatively intact and outside mainstream Pākehā discourse, even though we were no longer on the marae in the way we used to be. (Papesch 2009)

Now called Te Matatini (the many faces), the biannual national Kapa Haka festival attracts a wide audience: thousands of, predominantly Māori, spectators in the arena and many millions more, much more mixed, viewers via a broadcast that is livestreamed by Māori TV and accessible worldwide. Teams of

30–40 men and women take the stage to perform. Each group represents their particular *iwi* (tribe) or *rohe* (tribal region)—although increasingly, festival audiences see also teams made up of diverse tribal identifications drawn from cities in New Zealand and Australia. This is a competition, modelled in part on the Olympics, for trophies and honours that are awarded according to criteria that have been rigorously debated in the months leading up to the main event. Each team reaches the national stage only after prevailing at a series of fiercely contested regional competitions. The time frame is strictly enforced, and the components of the performance are prescribed: *whakaeke* (entrance); *mōteatea* (chant, or lament); *waiata-ā-ringa* (action song); *poi* (a women's dance with balls on string); *haka* (men's dance); and *whakawātea* (exit). The challenge for performers is to impress the judges by balancing respect for the ritual and cultural origins of each item with theatrical innovation.

Kapa Haka is a popular performance practice, now widely embraced by non-Māori and Māori alike,[9] and as such it can be seen everywhere, in particular in schools and universities as well as on marae and in ex-patriot groups who maintain their cultural connections in communities overseas. Kapa Haka is intrinsically political, having been constructed and performed by activists who were at the same time agitating for the restoration of rights and land in the 1970s. It was, and remains, particularly performative, as every song, every dance is aimed towards sustaining Māori identity into the future. The performance is entirely in *te reo* Māori, which means that while it occurs in plain sight, it is relatively opaque to non-Māori spectators. The public performance provides, in effect, a private place for presenting diverse sides of the ongoing discussion of how best to achieve social justice for Māori by Māori (Mazer 2011).

Like Kapa Haka, Māori theatre brings key elements of ritual and cultural practices onto the secular stage without necessarily sacrificing their potential to invoke the sacred. In the 1970s and 1980s, a number of playwrights and directors experimented with the concept of a 'marae theatre' or 'theatre marae'—described by Diana Looser as 'a boldly syncretic form that sought to diverge from and subvert Western dramatic frameworks by deploying the spatial, linguistic, rhetorical, and gestural vocabularies of the *marae*, especially the protocols of the *hui* (ceremonial gathering)' (2014: 55, italics in original; see also McCallum 2011). Looser, following Balme (1999), notes the ambivalence in the invocation of 'theatre marae', which was seen to introduce ritual elements without rocking the foundations of the theatre, and the potential of 'marae theatre' insofar as it might trouble the idea of the theatre itself 'by turning the performance space into a *marae* through protocols, consecration, choice of venue, or a combination of those' (2014: 55, italics in original).

Of these experiments in bringing the marae onto the theatre stage, perhaps Jim Broughton's one-man show *Michael James Manaia* (1991), as performed by acclaimed Māori theatre artist, Jim Moriarty, can be seen as most exemplary for the way it plants the soil of the *marae* on the theatre stage and makes use, in particular, of the structures and cadences of *whaikōrero* in the tortured monologue of a mixed race veteran at war with himself (Parker 2007: 116). An early solo play by Hone Kouka, *Mauri Tu* (1991), is included in Looser's list of Māori plays that can be seen to sit well within the 'marae theatre' model. The relationship between theatre—as a colonial artefact—and *marae*—as *tūrangawaewae* (a place to stand) remains uneasy in not-quite-post-colonial Aotearoa New Zealand.

3   Hone Kouka

Of Ngati Porou, Ngāti Raukawa and Ngāti Kahungunu descent, Hone Kouka is one of the pioneers of Māori theatre. Trained as an actor in the late 1980s, he quickly became known as an innovative playwright, and he is now also a prominent director, producer and champion of emerging Māori theatre artists.[10] Both *Nga Tangata Toa* and *Waiora* can be read as experiments. Deliberately constructed at the nexus between the theatrical and the social, they were first produced in the early 1990s at the point of convergence between Māori political activism and the coming of age of New Zealand theatre. William Peterson writes that Kouka's 'most acclaimed and well-travelled works, *Nga Tangata Toa* and *Waiora*, grapple with core issues and concepts that Māori playwrights and writers have been dealing with since the late 1970s, when contemporary Māori writing was forged out of the growing protest and land rights movements of the time' (2001: 15).

The emerging evocation of ritual and *marae* protocol on the stage echoed and expanded upon the reclamation of *reo* and *tikanga* outside the theatre in ways that can be traced to the activism, for example, of Sir Apirana Ngāta in the early twentieth century and to the first national Kapa Haka festival in 1972.[11] Kouka was one of many Māori theatre artists and others who were insistent that Māori culture had its own, intrinsic theatricality, to be found in customary performance practices on the *marae* and, as such, potentially transferrable to the theatre—not as the sort of exotic window dressing in the way earlier Pākehā playwrights and producers were seen to have done, but as meaningful in and of themselves.

Looking back at his own achievements and that of his contemporaries in his 2007 essay 'The State of Contemporary Māori Theatre', Hone Kouka presents the values underlying his first turn to Ibsen for inspiration, taking *The Vikings at Helgeland* as the model for *Nga Tangata Toa*. He begins by calling the play and its first production in 1994 at Taki Rua Theatre, 'a landmark in my career and in terms of Māori Theatre' (2007: 241). Acknowledging his collaboration with director Colin McColl and business manager Tony Burns (both Pākehā), he outlines their development of 'a kaupapa (philosophy) to re-position Māori theatre' as follows:

> We meant to enhance all elements and have Māori theatre sit comfortably within mainstream theatre. We had proven that we were worthy storytellers, but our focus was now to lift production values, acting, design, technical aspects etc. The production proved to do this and, in hindsight, I feel that it shifted Māori Theatre

148   S. MAZER

from the domestic towards the epic: our theatre was beginning to come of age. (2007: 241)

The tension between the epic and the domestic is both politically and socially generative for Kouka and other Māori theatre artists. The dynamic intertwining of Māori and Pākehā personal and social histories is expressed in the weaving together of ritual and theatre. The spirits of the ancestors are invoked to animate the drama at hand, revealed as still powerful forces, capable of disrupting the complacencies of the mundane social order and exposing the continuing irresolution of the colonial problem.

In both *Nga Tangata Toa* and *Waiora* the human figures at centre are seen to be surrounded by forces beyond their control. In the first play, they succumb, with tragic results; the outcome in the second is more ambivalent, hopeful of a spiritual conciliation. Much of what is recognised these days as 'Māori theatre' has been built on the platform provided by these powerful experiments in bringing Māori ritual and traditional performance onto post-colonial New Zealand stages.[12] In both plays, the struggle to reckon with the effects of colonisation are represented in fiercely intimate conflicts between Māori and Pākehā characters and marked at the points where English gives way to *te reo* Māori, often shifting from prose to verse and back again (Peterson 2001). While the characters are driven by desires that can be investigated and activated in Stanislavskian terms, the language is oddly formal, the scenes abruptly broken: by private reverie; by figures, ghosts, *tīpuna*[13] or inexplicable 'strangers'; by *karanga, waiata, haka* and *whaikōrero*. Where text-based, psychologically grounded characterisation appears to fail to bring the text to life, we can begin to see, and perhaps experience in some visceral way, how uneasily the veneer of the European drama overlays the rituals at the heart of Māori culture.

Diana Taylor begins her discussion of *The Archive and the Repertoire* by recognising that 'we learn and transmit knowledge through embodied action, through cultural agency, and by making choices.' Performance, she continues, 'functions as an episteme, a way of knowing, not simply an object of analysis' (2003: xvi). Taylor's identification of performance as a locus for cultural knowledge and transmission in the wake of colonial suppression is set in the context of the Americas, but her core question is readily transferable to post-colonial Aotearoa New Zealand: 'What tensions might performance behaviors show that would not be recognized in texts and documents?' (2003: xviii). Both *Nga Tangata Toa*, in its more epic dramaturgy, and *Waiora*, as a domestic drama, enact divergent, contradictory theatricalities. On the one hand, the plays appear to adhere to the tenets of realist theatre: particularly in the construction of characters driven by secrets and confronted with the legacy of the past, and in explicit references to the effects of heredity, to Darwinian ideas of survival of the fittest, and to the family unit as embodiment of the larger social unit. On the other hand, these plays deploy distinctive scenographies and innovative staging practices drawn from *pōwhiri* and also Kapa Haka, bringing Māori protocol into the European dramaturgical frame in ways that are alternatively seamless and disruptive of the status quo.

The effect of this juxta-positioning for an audience is not Brechtian, but the reverse—a kind of hyperrealism that is mystified and heightened through direct engagement at the spirit(ual) level, potentially provoking a deeper empathetic response. The structural alignment between the form and content, the byplay between European Realism and Māori ritual, in *Nga Tangata Toa* and *Waiora* makes Kouka's political perspective on the cumulative effects of colonisation visceral, experiential and inescapable for audiences as well as performers. At the same time, such kinaesthetics open a space for a vitalised critique of the European theatre tradition in which New Zealand audiences—Māori and Pākehā alike—have been steeped. The naturalness of Naturalism and the real-ness of psychological realism are called into question as cultural constructs, and the socio-ideological underpinnings of the relationship between individual identity and social role in theatre as in life are given a productive materiality in performance.

4   *NGA TANGATA TOA*

Set at the end of the First World War, in 1919, *Nga Tangata Toa* aims for the epic and the tragic, interweaving (almost) realistic dialogue and psychologically motivated characters, with silent action and tableaux, protocol and ritual. It begins with a *haka pōwhiri* (ritual welcome) and *whaikōrero* and concludes with a *karanga* by the *tūpuna* who call Rongomai to the sea. The original stag-ing of *Nga Tangata Toa* in 1994 explicitly recalled the *marae* in ways that also suggested a Viking hall, as described here by William Peterson:

> Dorita Hannah's set for *Nga Tangata Toa* quoted the features of the marae and offered spectator/participants the opportunity to plant their feet firmly in the 'black sand' which is characteristic of the East Coast of the North Island where the events of the play took place. Set in 1919 at the close of World War I, the play incorporated many of the performative rituals embedded in the culture of the marae. (2001: 18)

The drama conflates the domestic with the dynastic in form as well as con-tent. It begins with 'Arrival': the return of the heroic soldier, Taneatua, who comes face to face, silently, uneasily, with his wife, Te Wai, on the wharf as a *haka pōwhiri* is performed by the other company members. Observing the way the play is structured into episodes, many with titles reflecting Māori ritual and customary practices, Peterson notes that 'while the length of the exchange is compressed for theatrical effectiveness, the basic protocol of the pōwhiri is fol-lowed' (2001: 18) in this first scene.

In contrast, the second scene, 'Discovery', is dialogic, an exchange between sisters-in-law Rongomai and Rose that also serves as exposition, revealing the convoluted plot, the conflicts and secrets that will drive the rest of the play:

Rongomai's father was left to drown in the sea by Paikea (Rose's father-in-law, Rongomai's uncle) who then became *rangatira* (chief)[14]—an evil act that Rose brings to light in order to drive her sister-in-law to revenge. This scene offers the appearance of realism as a relatively intimate scene between two young women, one Māori, the other Pākehā. Each has a powerful secret, is full of desire and rage in equal parts, and wants from the other more than she is willing to give. The intimacy between the two women, and their fierce antagonism, signals a failure to reconcile the worlds they represent: Pākehā and Māori. Both are tainted in some way by having married outside their race. Like the settlers from whom she is descended, Rose—the disgraced interloper—cannot be at home on the marae, nor can she return to her own people. Rongomai, too, is exiled, stranded between her Pākehā husband and the Māori man she truly loves.

The mundane world is stirred by the mystical: Rongomai picks up Rose's revelation and finishes the story of her father's death as if seeing it in her mind's eye:

ROSE:	How did you know? It says he told no one.
RONGOMAI:	I have magic, I dreamed of this long ago. But as a child. So I dismissed it. *Pause.* I hid it from my memory, now you bring it back. Why?
ROSE:	It was a letter from my husband. He was at war.
RONGOMAI:	You didn't have to tell me. Why come here?
ROSE:	I thought you should know.
RONGOMAI:	How caring. You've never thought of me before. So why now? Well, sister-in-law?
ROSE:	I had nowhere to go.
RONGOMAI:	Well you have no place here. Get out!
ROSE, *quickly*:	Revenge.

(Kouka 1994: 11)

As it sets the scene for the destruction that follows, the dialogue in this scene and in the play that follows is far more formal than it appears on the surface—'I have magic'—almost to the point of being stilted. This formality brings with it a feeling of historic import, that the action is in the past and perhaps even now only half present; it implies an act of translation, from Māori to English, from the old ways to the (almost) new and all that troubles this time of transition. This way of speaking and being carries within it the simmerings not only of restrained desires and barely leashed antagonisms, but also of uneasily hemmed in spirits or forces.

As the play progresses, old grievances are stirred by new revelations. Wi (short for William), Rongomai's Pākehā husband, admits to having won her hand in marriage on false pretences: his best friend, Taneatua, entered her tent under cover of darkness, allowing Rongomai to believe it was Wi who had embraced her. Rongomai's shame at this revelation is what ultimately drives her towards the play's scorched earth conclusion. What was love between the Māori woman and the Pākehā man turns to spite. The *marae* is burnt to the ground, and violent death claims the characters one by one until finally Rongomai is called by the *tūpuna* into the sea. The drama is at once familial and dynastic, domestic and epic. The colonial conflict is largely implied in the uneasy presence of the Pākehā characters on the *marae*, who are caught up in the same sorts of contradictory desires as their Māori counterparts. The destruction is wrought as much by forces beyond human comprehension and control as it is by individual psychology. Nevertheless, by setting his play into such a definitive historical moment—the end of the First World War, when New Zealand is said to have come into its own as a nascent nation—Kouka ensures that the audience bears witness to the harsh fate faced by Māori communities, no longer sustained by the old ways of being and doing, turning on each other, ill-equipped to fight forward.

The stage on which *Nga Tangata Toa* is to be performed is something more than the locus of representation, following the European tradition. It is that, of course. But Kouka's use of the stage reflects the Māori tradition, wherein the word for stage, *atamira*, also refers to a platform for the dead, the place of mourning and of spirits. The play, performed, offers the audience a kind of *tūrangawaewae*, a way of retracing steps to where Māori once stood whole as a people. Just as the characters are seen to be moved by their circumstances, histories and desires to act and interact in ways that we can recognise 'as if' they were real people, so too they can be seen to enact something beyond mimesis, to conjure and contain the life force of the *tūpuna*, and to bring forth their stories as a kind of *whakapapa*, a genealogy that, along with the play's evocation of *tūrangawaewae*, can serve as a point of orientation and identification, even for those at a far remove.[15] As the play proceeds inexorably towards its tragic outcome, the uneasy swinging between ritual-like and real-like modes of performing, and between Māori and Pākehā ways of being, offer us the opportunity to come to understand—as performers and as spectators—something about the destructive legacy of colonisation and to question what remains to us here and now.

5 WAIORA

On the surface at least, *Waiora* appears less like *The Vikings of Helgeland* and more like *The Wild Duck*—albeit with a reprieve from tragedy at the end. Kouka says: 'Another personal milestone was the play *Waiora*, set in 1965. It is basically a play about immigrants—unfortunately, the immigrants in the play are Māori, displaced in their own country. ...It also confirmed for me a method of creating work relying on a Māori kaupapa' (2007: 241).

Following close on the heels of *Nga Tangata Toa*, but set almost 50 years later, *Waiora* directly takes on the problem of (post)colonial estrangement. It mirrors *Nga Tangata Toa* in many ways, with, superficially at least, realistic scenes that are closely intertwined with episodes of ritual performance: from the welcoming *waiata* sung by the *tūpuna*, seen only by Rongo, as the *whānau* enters the stage for the first time, to the *haka* performed by Hone, her father, to call her back from the sea and the *waiata* that closes the play.

Many of the stylistic differences between the two plays can be traced, perhaps, to the different time periods they represent. The further past-ness of *Nga Tangata Toa* is imbued with a kind of formality, the sense that the pre-colonial might still have been within reach, whereas in the almost now-ness, not-quite-post-colonial-ness of *Waiora*, the family is cut off from its *tūrangawaewae* and, singing Beatles' songs, slipping into the colloquialisms of the 1960s. In her 'Foreword' to the published version of *Waiora*, actor/writer Roma Potiki tells us,

> Māori theatre is a theatre that constantly remembers the past. I cannot recall having seen a play by a Māori writer that did not make some reference to tūpuna. The emanations/spirits of the dead most certainly rattle our bones. It is our ancestors who remind us of who we are, where we belong, and why we have been given the gift of life. Tūpuna and ngā Atua Māori are all central to the way in which *Waiora* is structured. These Atua steer the play through the stormy passage of change. The whānau are beached, far away from the support of their relations and the safety of their tūrangawaewae. (1997: 9)

In *Waiora* the Pākehā characters appear to be more grounded—or at least unthinkingly in place—than the Māori characters. In Steve's words:

> Me, I was born here; it's home, part of me. Three generations of Campbells have lifted their eyes to this place. Three. One of the first to come here. Started with nothing. Just like you. (*beat*) Ya spend enough time anywhere and the place'll own ya, take ya over. This place owns me and my family. My grandfather's buried here, so we're always a part of it now. The land. When I look out, see the mountains, the hills, I see him. (*beat*) We were farmers before we got into timber. It's the land, ya understand that …the bond with the land. It's home when ya work the land. (Kouka 1997: 64–65)

Steve's claim to the land—three generations, starting with nothing!—is specious from the Māori point of view. The 'Just like you' is an affront to Hone, whose people have been in this place for over 1000 years and who can only respond 'I understand. Thanks' (65). He is the one who must carry on, politely, waiting for Steve to give him the one thing he most needs: the promotion that, he will learn, has been handed to a less-qualified Pākehā man due to the unwillingness of the workers to take direction from a Māori man. Even so, by the end of the play the Pākehā have been pushed to one side as the performance of ritual restores a provisional sense of being at home to the *whānau*.

Waiora is deceptively simple in its characters and plot, especially in comparison to *Nga Tangata Toa*: a Māori family is joined by a schoolteacher and the owner of the mill where the father works for a *hangi*/picnic on the beach; the clamour of disappointments, losses and squabbles arising from their alienation and isolation grow so loud that they fail to hear the *tūpuna* calling (see Edmond

2007). In the course of the play, what is exposed is the shallowness of the Pākehā characters, their limited ability to comprehend the world inhabited by their Māori friends and their complicity in not-quite-post-colonial oppression. Because they are shown to be well-intentioned, caring people, both Louise and Steve are not beyond the audience's sympathies—especially for the Pākehā audiences who were critical to the play's early success. At the same time, Kouka invites our exasperation with their blundering efforts to retain a sense of themselves as good people and our impatience to see them do more than make nice.

Roma Potiki points directly to the struggle between Māori and Pākehā world views, and to the costs of colonisation still playing out in contemporary Aotearoa:

> [Rongo] has the chance of aligning herself with the forces of nature and whakapapa so that a kind of healing—the reunification of the whānau—can take place. Death of mauri, of memory and of self is the alternative. A kind of genocidal amnesia is proffered by Pākehā society and to some degree accepted in the uneasy, ritualised relationships between the Māori family and the Pākehā mill owner and school teacher. (1997: 9)

But as oppressive as the situation may seem, Māori ritual proves resilient; it restores agency to the family and averts the tragic ending. As the unhappiness deepens, Rongo is drawn by the voices to the sea and drowns, or seems to, before her father calls her back with a *haka*. The *whānau* pull together, and Pākehā characters are cast to one side, as Rongo sings a *waiata* to farewell the *tīpuna*, and Hone offers a final *karakia* (prayer).

Like *Nga Tangata Toa*, *Waiora* is suffused with Māori language and ritual performance, woven through the English and against the apparent realism of the play in ways that reflect the tensions of colonisation and the oppressive conditions faced by Māori then and even now. While the dialogue between characters is actable in psychological-realist terms, the otherworldly hovering of the ancestral spirits demands a different way of being onstage and perhaps off. The scenes of Rongo on her own by the water mix subtext with text, *te reo* with English, *haka* with monologue, *waiata* and pantomimed reverie in ways that are challenging even to imagine, let alone to act. Here Kouka imagines an environment that seems simultaneously mimetically real and theatrically mythical, only half in the lived world:

> RONGO *is down at the beach. The* TĪPUNA *are with her. Water laps around her feet and in her hand a shell, a stone, something to remind her of the old woman, her grandmother. She is silent, but her mouth is moving. Slowly, the waiata she is singing fades up and we hear it. The waiata is 'Tawhiti'. The* TĪPUNA *have quietly raised their voices with her. ...She finishes the waiata and begins to speak. The* TĪPUNA *gather around her.*
>
> *Rongo* Did you like that Nanny? It is one of the wai that you taught me. Kei te mahara ahau ki ngā pao, ngā waiata, ngā haka arā te katoa. E hika! Kei te

makariri te wai.[16] *(beat)* I am standing in the water so I can touch home. (Kouka 1997: 30)

In both plays, realism as a dramaturgical structure seems to come to stand in for colonisation as a social reality. Both theatricalise the failure of Pākehā structures to resolve the tragedies of the Māori experience of contact with the European and what came after. To call up the *wairua*, or spirit, of the Māori characters is to invoke their power in the secular space of the theatre; once summoned, they may well remain.

6   Māori Theatre in the Twenty-First Century

It can be hard to recall how radical the introjection of *te reo* and *tikanga* Māori into otherwise conventional (i.e., European) theatre settings was in the 1990s. To wait in the foyer until summoned by *karanga*, or to enter the auditorium through a *haka pōwhiri*: these are not uncommon experiences for New Zealand theatre goers in the twenty-first century.[17] Kouka's theatrical experiments have served as starting points for emerging Māori playwrights, who have embraced and pushed against the foundations he, and others of his generation, established. Some common themes and dramaturgies can be seen in contemporary Māori plays: in particular, the interweaving of past and present, of spirit and human worlds, of ritual and theatre, and of the domestic and the epic, in order to create an *atamira* for perceiving the festering injury of colonisation as an ongoing challenge to social well-being.

In Albert Belz's *Te Karakia* (2008), for example, what begins as a kind of *Romeo and Juliet* inspired love story between two young people—one Pākehā, the other Māori—quickly runs into a retelling of the violent protests that erupted in response to the tour by apartheid South Africa's rugby team, the Springboks, in 1981.[18] This is a rough, uneasy play, one that seeks to reproduce the polarising effects of the original event while inviting reflection on more contemporary conflicts—albeit without the comfort of a common perspective. Throughout the play snippets of ritual—both Māori and Christian—are invoked and just as quickly disrupted or diverted, trampled and soiled by the rush of events. A *karakia* is a prayer, an act of placation or healing. But there is no reconciliation in Belz's play: not for a nation shaken by the surfacing of colonial shame, nor for the Māori and Pākehā families struggling to live in peace on the land. Instead, in its final tableau, the former lovers stand isolated in separate pools of light, estranged, irrevocably desiring and militantly opposed to each other. The play closes with a lament:

> Ma wai ra e taurima.
> te marae i waho nei?
> Ma te tika.
> ma te pono.
> me te aroha e.[19]

Only the values of *Māoritanga*—respect, integrity and, above all, love—can forestall the continuing depredations of colonisation.

Where Kouka and Belz cast their characters into New Zealand's troubled past, in *and what remains* (2005), Miria George[20] imagines a near future, a mere five years ahead, in which a final solution is being implemented. The play is set in a departure lounge, where the last Māori woman of childbearing age, Mary, will flee the government's sterilisation programme. She holds her suitcase close; it contains dirt from her family's farm, the land she must now forsake. Her well-meaning Pākehā husband attempts to dissuade her, unsuccessfully; unable to comprehend what it is to her to be Māori, he refuses to come with her, claiming (like Steve Campbell in *Waiora*) an attachment to a land that is not his to claim. The personal and the political are intertwined in the liminal space of the airport, a place of transit and tradition, through which travellers of diverse cultural identifications pass, largely indifferent to the central conflict. In this play, Māori ways of speaking and doing, *reo* and *tikanga*, have been almost entirely effaced, replaced by rituals of arrival and departure which are performed as ordinary—that is, deracinated—acts in an extraordinary—post-post-colonial—situation. In this play, Miria George poses a radical question: what if Māori ceded the land and flew away? The question of what might remain is left in the air as Mary departs.

7 CONCLUSION

Hone Kouka's declaration that 'Māori theatre can only be a hybrid' (2007: 41), like the now customary pairing of 'Aotearoa' with 'New Zealand', sets the stage for an indigenous genre of performance that reflects rather than refuses the ongoing tensions of a not-quite-post-colonial nation. At their best, instead of 'decolonising the stage', plays like *Nga Tangata Toa* and *Waiora* perform anti-colonial acts in staging the continuing impact of the colonial encounter. They demonstrate the fallacy of any claim to post-coloniality in Aotearoa New Zealand and, in so doing, engage their communities performatively without being at all utopian. The social order they represent remains uneasy, the present nation's historical injustices as-yet unreconciled, still a work unevenly in progress. When the machinery of the theatre, and the dominant culture it represents, gives way to the performance of *tikanga*, the audience experiences the power of ritual, cultural and social acts as resistance to repression. The play goes on, as does the history, relentless. The call to remember lingers.

NOTES

1. 'Alas...I cry for you my place of origin / now left saturated in my tears // Alas...the place where my umbilical cord is still / attached and pulls at my heart with almighty strength' (Kouka 1997: 110).

2. Ranginui…Bear witness upon me as I leave behind all I know, all I am, including…// Papa…Land walked upon by generations many before me / As I now wander (seemingly) aimlessly in search of well-being (Kouka 1997: 110).
3. Pākehā generally refers to the descendants of the British settlers such as these characters. Another, more literal, term for non-Māori is 'tauiwi'—that is, outsiders, or not of our tribe.
4. This chapter builds on my earlier discussion of these two plays in 'Here as Elsewhere: Thinking Theatrically/Acting Locally' (2014).
5. *Marae* are the traditional facilities—for meetings, dining and sleeping—at the centre of Māori tribal communities and institutions.
6. See Looser's (2014) survey of Māori theatre history. On post-colonial drama more generally, see Gilbert and Thompkins (1996). For a survey of New Zealand theatre and performance, see Maufort and O'Donnell (2007).
7. While outside Māori faculties, schools and departments, English remains the dominant language of instruction, students can legally submit work for assessment—from undergraduate essays to PhD theses—in *te reo* Māori. Most New Zealand universities, including my own, have established *marae* as well.
8. It is possible to see the legacy of this practice even now in so-called colour-blind or non-traditional cast productions of classical plays, such as a recent Auckland Theatre Company version of Anton Chekhov's *The Cherry Orchard*, which was set in 1970s New Zealand, with Māori actors in the roles of Lopakhin and Varia, and in the Pop-up Globe's 2017/2018 production of *A Midsummer Night's Dream*, in which Māori actors featured in the roles of Theseus/Oberon, Hippolyta/Titania and Puck (see Mazer 2019).
9. There are some notable detractors. See *Te Whare Tapere: Towards a New Model for Māori Performance Art*, the influential PhD thesis by Te Ahukaramū Charles Royal (1998). It appears that Royal has recently tempered his criticism, judging by his new website: http://www.charles-royal.nz/whare-tapere.
10. For further biographical information, please see the NZ Book Council website: http://www.bookcouncil.org.nz/Writers/Profiles/Kouka,%20Hone. For a glimpse of Kouka's current work as a producer, see the Tawata Productions website: http://tawata.wordpress.com/about/.
11. See Papesch (2015); also see Mazer (2011).
12. See Peterson (2001), Edmond (2007), Carnegie and O'Donnell (2007), and Kouka (2007).
13. *Tūpuna* and *ūpuna* both mean ancestors. Kouka uses the first in *Nga Tangata Toa* and the second in *Waiora*.
14. The echoes of *Hamlet* are deliberate here.
15. For an excellent discussion of these concepts, see Selwyn Te Rito (2007).
16. 'I remember the pao, waiata, haka, everything. Oh! The water is cold' (Kouka 1997: 30).
17. To call an audience in has become customary also in dance performances, a practice pioneered by Atamira Dance Collective with its production of *Ngai Tahu 32* in 2004 (Mazer 2007).
18. Albert Belz is of Ngāti Pouro, Ngā Puhi and Ngāti Pōkai descent.
19. Who will take responsibility / on the marae now? / There can be justice / and truth / only if there is love (*New Zealand Waiata* n.d.).
20. 'Miria George is of Te Arawa, Ngāti Awa, Ngāti Kuki Airani (Rarotonga and Atiu) descent.'

REFERENCES

Anderson, Benedict. 1983. *Imagined Communities: Reflections on the Origin and Spread of Nationalism.* London and New York: Verso.

Balme, Christopher. 1999. *Decolonizing the Stage: Theatrical Syncretism and Post-Colonial Drama.* New York: Oxford University Press.

Belz, Albert. 2008. *Te Karakia.* In *The Intricate Art of Actually Caring ... and Other New Zealand Plays,* ed. Sharon Mazer, 145–223. Calcutta: Seagull Books. 2018.

Bharucha, Rustom. 1989. Notes on the Invention of Tradition. *Economic and Political Weekly* 24, 33 (19 August): 1907–1909 + 1911–1914.

Broughton, John. 1991. *Michael James Manaia.* In *Southern Stage,* ed. Gary Henderson. Wellington: Playmarket. 2018.

Carnegie, David, and David O'Donnell. 2007. Māori Dramaturgy and *Nga Tangata Toa.* In *Performing Aotearoa: New Zealand Theatre and Drama in an Age of Transition,* ed. Marc Maufort and David O'Donnell, 219–236. Brussels: P.I.E. Peter Lang.

Edmond, Murray. 2007. Te Kaainga/Where the Fire Burns—Hone Kouka's Trilogy: *Waiora, Homefires* and *The Prophet. Australasian Drama Studies* 50: 91–110.

George, Miria. 2005. *and what remains.* In *The Intricate Art of Actually Caring ... and Other New Zealand Plays,* ed. Sharon Mazer, 331–402. Calcutta: Seagull Books. 2018.

Gilbert, Helen, and Joanne Thompkins. 1996. *Post-Colonial Drama: Theory, Practice, Politics.* London: Routledge.

Kouka, Hone. 1994. *Nga Tangata Toa.* Wellington, NZ: Victoria University Press.

———. 1997. *Waiora: Te Ūkaipō—The Homeland.* With waiata composed by Hone Hurinhanganui. Wellington, NZ: Huia Publishers.

———. 2007. The State of Contemporary Māori Theatre. In *Performing Aotearoa: New Zealand Theatre and Drama in an Age of Transition,* ed. Marc Maufort and David O'Donnell, 237–246. Brussels: P.I.E. Lang.

Looser, Diana. 2014. *Remaking Pacific Pasts: History, Memory, and Identity in Contemporary Theatre from Oceania.* Honolulu: University of Hawai`i Press.

Maufort, Marc, and David O'Donnell, eds. 2007. *Performing Aotearoa: New Zealand Theatre and Drama in an Age of Transition.* Brussels: P.I.E. Lang.

Mazer, Sharon. 2007. Atamira Dance Collective: Dancing in the Footsteps of the Ancestors. In *Performing Aotearoa: New Zealand Theatre and Drama in an Age of Transition,* ed. Marc Maufort and David O'Donnell, 283–292. Brussels: P.I.E. Lang.

———. 2011. Performing Māori: Kapa Haka on the Stage and on the Ground. *Popular Entertainment Studies* 2 (1): 41–53.

———. 2013. A National Theatre in New Zealand? Why/Not? In *Theatre and Performance in Small Nations,* ed. Steve Blandford, 107–122. Bristol and Chicago: Intellect Books.

———. 2014. Here As Elsewhere: Thinking Theatrically/Acting Locally. *Antipodes* 28 (1): 35–45.

———. 2019. A Bicultural *Dream* in Aotearoa New Zealand: (De)Colonising Shakespeare? *Te Kaharoa* 12 (1): 1–14.

McCallum, Rua. 2011. Māori Performance: Marae Liminal Space and Transformation. *Australasian Drama Studies* 59: 88–103.

New Zealand Waiata. n.d.. http://folksong.org.nz/ma_wai_ra/.

158   S. MAZER

Papesch, Te Rita. 2009. *Kapa Haka: From the Margins to the Mainstream*. Paper Presented at the New Zealand Postgraduate Conference, Victoria University, Wellington, 20–21 November.

———. 2015. *Creating a Modern Māori Identity through Kapa Haka*. Unpublished PhD thesis, Canterbury University.

Parker, George. 2007. *Actor Alone: Solo Performance in New Zealand*. Unpublished PhD thesis, Canterbury University.

Peterson, William. 2001. Reclaiming the Past, Building a Future: Māori Identity in the Plays of Hone Kouka. *Theatre Research International* 26 (1): 15–24.

Potiki, Roma. 1997. Foreword. In *Waiora: Te Ūkaipō—The Homeland*. Wellington, NZ: Huia Publishers.

Royal, Te Ahukaramū Charles. 1998. *Te Whare Tapere: Towards a New Model for Māori Performance Art*. Unpublished PhD thesis, Victoria University of Wellington.

Selwyn Te Rito, Joseph. 2007. Whakapapa: A Framework for Representing Identity. *MAI Review*. Accessed 10 June 2010. http://www.review.mai.ac.nz/index.php/MR/article/viewFile/56/55.

Taylor, Diana. 2003. *The Archive and the Repertoire: Performing Cultural Memory in the Americas*. Durham and London: Duke University Press.

Werry, Margaret. 2011. *The Tourist State: Performing Leisure, Liberalism, and Race in New Zealand*. Minneapolis: University of Minnesota Press.

CHAPTER 9

Racial Nationalism and the Serbian Theatre: From *Radovan III* to DAH

Dennis Barnett

1   INTRODUCTION

This chapter has, as its focus, the theatre of the former Yugoslavia, more specifically, Serbia, and the ways in which it responded to and was affected by 'racism' just prior to the country's dissolution, and how it might seem to have changed following it.[1] To do this, we will look at three very different theatrical events, one from 1972 and two from the first decade of the following century.

Though this area of the world has been in a state of flux from the beginning of recorded history, in the period under examination that flux has been particularly drastic; beginning with the counter-cultural movement of the late 1960s, which helped spark protests against the powerful communist party and its leaders, through the brutal war and Bosnian genocide of the 1990s, dividing the country into six different nations (with a seventh, Kosovo, always on the verge of breaking away), and, lastly, to the onset of democratic socialism, driven by the pressures of a still nascent capitalism. These changes were all fed by or were partly in response to a pendular process of racialisation, the treatment of a non-racial category of people (in this case, national identity), as if it had a racial component. This process has also swung from one extreme to another; from its enforced, yet schizophrenic suppression during communism to its violent explosion during the war and, today, to a dissimulated construction of it as something that has passed.

D. Barnett (✉)
Coe College, Cedar Rapids, IA, USA
e-mail: dbarnett@coe.edu

© The Author(s), under exclusive license to Springer Nature   159
Switzerland AG 2021
T. Morosetti, O. Okagbue (eds.), *The Palgrave Handbook of Theatre and Race*, https://doi.org/10.1007/978-3-030-43957-6_9

160   D. BARNETT

As for the theatre's role in all of these, the plays/performances we will look at are examples of what seems to be the predominant attitude towards 'political' theatre in this culture, namely, that of addressing an issue without naming it, through primarily connotative strategies. The first one, *Radovan III*, was a commercial blockbuster on the Belgrade stage in 1972, a product of the mainstream theatre machine; the other two, *Crossing the Line* (2009) and *In/Visible City* (2005), come from an entirely different artistic milieu. Created by DAH Theatre, a performance group founded and run by a few women artist/activists at the beginning of the war, these pieces are the product of improvisation and montage, with a detailed and specific movement vocabulary. *Crossing the Line* was performed in smaller, more intimate houses, and *In/Visible City* was created to perform on a city bus. *Radovan III* was played to thousands during its decade-long run in Belgrade; the others to no more than a hundred people at a time for, at the most, five or six performances a year.

As we endeavour to understand the racialisation that existed over this span of time in the former Yugoslavia, we will explore the ways in which these performances engaged with it. They will present us with snapshots of two different moments in history and two different ways in which the Yugoslav (and now Serbian) theatre has worked to expose and, in some ways, ameliorate its effects.

2   RACIAL NATIONALISM

Howard Winant wrote an overview of race theory in 2000, in which he noted that, historically, as social attitudes changed, theoretical perspectives changed, as well. He argued that the time for the next change was overdue (Winant 2000, 178–180). Though his plea has been supported and encouraged by others since then, to this day nothing new has emerged. Critical Race Theory (CRT) has maintained its hold on the discussion since it emanated from the field of Critical Legal Studies in the 1980s.

Through more than thirty years of scholarship, little has been produced in CRT that ventures significantly from its original thrust, delimiting its scope to the socio-historical and political reality within one country, the US. It recognises that racism is simply one 'structure of inequality' amongst many and that for a fuller understanding we must unravel the intersectionality at work, both historically and in the present, and that disempowerment is a product of multiple systems of oppression and discrimination, for which race alone cannot account (Crenshaw 1989). Still, 'race', as CRT defines it, never strays beyond the classification of people by physical characteristics. The former Yugoslavia, for the most part, is a relatively homogenous area. Most of its population is descended from Slavic tribes that arrived in the Middle Ages and have no distinctive physical characteristics to set them apart. For this reason, beyond the treatment of and systemic discrimination against the Roma, a population that is universally oppressed, there is scant evidence of 'racism' in the former Yugoslavia as defined by CRT. In order to bring the insights of CRT to bear on this topic, therefore, we will need to expand its disciplinary limits.

The sociologist, Melissa Weiner, recognising that CRT has, thus far, not been formally exercised on a global scale, has made a tenuous foray in favour of that effort. She defines race as 'ascribed physical, biological, *and/or cultural differences*[2] that are essentialised'. These differences, then, get used to define 'resources, choices, and opportunities based on social representations of inferiority/superiority' (Weiner 2012, 333). She proffers the idea of a 'racialised world system' that dominant nations use to frame the value of a particular group to 'justify exploitation and genocide and finance their own economic supremacy' (Weiner, 335). This is a near-perfect description of the dissolution of Yugoslavia, determined by an ideology that Weiner calls 'racial nationalism' (Weiner, 336). Interestingly, the same term has been used to describe the policies of Donald Trump and was defined as an ideology wherein 'each country is associated with a race, a people or a religion' and is 'threatened by the arrival or rise to power of different people' (Saunders 2018).

As Ernest Renan elucidated, there are a number of concepts that we speak about that lack any sense of monolithic definition: race, culture, ethnicity, and nation (Renan 1882, 11). All of these overlap and get redefined (or not) each time they are used. Homi Bhabha in his *Location of Culture* (1994) also explodes any sense of unitary meaning, describing his liminal 'third space' as the negotiation that occurs in our agreement to communicate at all (Bhabha 1994, 36–39). In that process, walls of meaning get built, defining you as 'other' than me, black as 'other' than white, and Croat as 'other' than Serb. It is a simplistic reading perhaps of the racialisation process, but there's nothing that necessarily demands it to be complex.

This concept of 'racial nationalism' has begun to crop up within a variety of disciplines, though, as yet, there seems to be no concurrence on how to define it. For our purposes, however, with Renan and Bhabha in mind, let us keep it simple: 'racial nationalism' will be, for us, how we refer to the racialisation process when applied to the arbitrary construction of difference based on one's equally arbitrary self-identification by nationality. Henry Louis Gates helps move us in that direction, as well:

> Race has become a trope of ultimate, irreducible differences between cultures, linguistic groups, or adherents of specific belief systems which—more often than not—also have fundamentally opposed economic interests. (Gates 1986, 5)

Therefore, the 'trope' of race, for our purposes, represents the extreme sentiments of nationalism in the former Yugoslavia, grown out of and expressed through all three of the perceived differences Gates lists above, and nationalism, of course, has been a ubiquitous factor in the Balkans for most of the last millennia.

The six countries that came into being following the dissolution of Yugoslavia are Serbia, Croatia, Bosnia-Hercegovina, Macedonia, Montenegro, and Slovenia.[3] The ways in which these nationalities reached their independent states were varied. Serbia held onto the name Yugoslavia the longest,

162   D. BARNETT

struggling to maintain unity. Montenegro and Macedonia remained Serbia's allies and parted from the Republic later than the others and without conflict. Slovenia was the wealthiest and least affected by the Ottoman influence. When they declared their independence, Slobodan Milošević, the Serbian President, mounted a weak and short-lived objection. It was Croatia and Bosnia-Hercegovina that he fought for, and in them we can see the most fervent examples of 'racial nationalism'.

The 'differences' that Serbs, Croats, and Bosnians have used to racialise each other range in significance from the obvious religious divisions to the geographical claims of homeland to the subtler differences in language and dialect. All of these differences existed in the former Yugoslavia, but Communism, and particularly, as we'll see in the next section, Yugoslavian Communism, hid those differences under the guise of unity.

3   NATIONALISM AND TITO

Following World War II (WWII), the region that for centuries had served as the 'third space' between Europe and Asia, the dividing line between Byzantium and Rome, between Roman Catholicism and Orthodoxy, between the Latin alphabet and the Cyrillic, for the first time seemed assured of finding unity under the name of the Federal Republic of Yugoslavia. Out of the war emerged the leader and the myth that would meld the dissonant parts into one. His name was Josip Broz, affectionately known as Tito.

Tito, who ruled Yugoslavia for thirty-five years, purposively, through his policy of 'unity and brotherhood' (*bradstvo i jedinstvo*), drew a veil over all tendencies to racialise each other on the basis of nationalist identity. Some of these tendencies had formed centuries earlier out of geographical, religious, and imagined ethnic differences, while others stemmed from more immediately retributive impulses, due to atrocities committed during WWII.[4] Having the support of a narrative that created him as the warrior who single-handedly drove the Nazis out of Yugoslavia, brought communism to his people, and stood up to the hegemonic advances of the Soviet Union empowered Tito and the Communist Party to literally mandate that the nationalist enmity between peoples would be transcended. History would be rewritten to integrate all into his vision of a unified Yugoslavia, as the memories and grudges causing the divisions were relegated to silence, thus furthering the narrative that constructs Tito as the man who single-handedly held the Balkans together (Mijić 2018, 138).

An assurance of minority rights was included in the first Yugoslav constitution. In practice, Tito's approach to the various nationalities made this statement deeply ironic. To prevent the tribal and internecine rivalries of the past from diminishing the strength of his federation, Tito went to extremes to refrain from appearing biased in his treatment of the various nationalities.

In order to restore the balance after 1945, Tito's tactic was to throw hatred into history's deep freeze by enforcing communal life on the three communities using repression, and if necessary, violence. Tito believed that only drastic measures could erase the memory of hatred. As a consequence, until the late 1980s, if a Bosnian Serb were tried in Sarajevo for political crimes, then surely, in a few weeks, there would be a trial of a Bosnian Croat and a Bosnian Moslem regardless of whether the latter two had been involved in any political activity or not (Glenny 1990, 148).

Obviously, besides being a mockery of human rights, this practice embroiled the country in a policy of dissemblance. Tito's heavy-handed tactics buried the various nationalist urges into an effective dormancy, a dormancy that would be maintained only through coerced complicity with the Communist Party line. Over Tito's thirty-five years of autocratic rule, the racial nationalism remained ostensibly invisible.

When war broke out in 1991, racialism again erupted. Though, over the next decade or so, it would tear at every individual Yugoslav, the greatest damage may have been inflicted on the Yugoslav family. In truth, Tito's efforts at unity had nearly been successful. Many families were products of intermixed marriages, and a large percentage of the younger generation had embraced 'Yugoslavism' because they themselves were a combination of those nationalities. Now, overnight, many Yugoslav parents turned into Serbs, Croats, and Bosnians, and the Yugoslav husband you had one day suddenly became a Serb the next, and the fact that you were now a Bosnian or a Croat made you his enemy.

4   Tito and *Radovan III*

During Tito's rule, the arts in Yugoslavia enjoyed more freedom than they did in the Soviet bloc countries. According to Misha Glenny, Tito's 'system could only function with two absolute political taboos: overt nationalism and the active participation of the masses in politics' (Glenny 1996, 32). Therefore, the words 'Serbian', 'Bosnian', or 'Croatian' were never used. 'Yugoslav' was the only national reference allowed, assuring that the theatre would reinforce Tito's construction of unity. Playwrights wishing to subvert his wishes had to depend on more connotative strategies. No one proved more skilled at doing this than the Serbian writer, Dušan Kovačević.

A good example of it can be seen in *Maratonce trče počasni krug* (*Marathon Runners Run a Victory Lap of Honor,* 1972), Kovačević's first play, which he wrote as a student at the University of Belgrade. In it, the Topalović family has been running a corrupt undertaking business through five generations, all of whom are still living. The head of the family is 120 years old. Tito and most of the Communist Party members at the time were veterans of WWII and in their 60s or 70s. Younger Yugoslavs were often not welcomed into the Party, which was an important step towards being successful at the time. Though there is

164   D. BARNETT

nothing in the text that openly ties the Topalović family and their dishonest and illegal ways to Tito and the Communist Party, the parallel was evident to most audiences.

    Shortly after *Marathon Runners*, came the equally successful *Radovan III* (*Radovan Treći*). Though *Radovan III* helped secure Kovačević's fame, much of its success is attributed to Zoran Radmilović, a Serbian theatre 'legend', who played the title role. He had been a Belgrade favourite for a number of years, having portrayed Hamlet at the Belgrade Dramatic Theatre in the 60s. Today a statue of him in his role as Pere Ubu in Jarry's *Ubu Roi* stands in the court-yard at Atelier 212, the theatre that presented many of Kovačević's early works. Radmilović brought his impressive talents at improvisation to the role of Radovan and, with Kovačević's blessings and to some degree his collusion, altered the original text nightly, eventually filling his performances with thinly disguised references to the daily politics of Yugoslavia. By the time Radmilović died in 1985, after 299 performances as Radovan, the play had become his rostrum.

    Both *Maratonce* and *Radovan III* ran in repertory for much of the next fourteen years. If Kovačević had stopped writing then, undoubtedly, he would still have been the most successful and popular Serbian playwright of the time. Today, half a century later, those two plays remain iconic representatives of the Yugoslav and Serbian stage. However, Kovačević is a highly prolific writer, and since 1972 the Belgrade theatre scene has never been without at least one of his works in repertory, and often as many as three or four. Outside of the former Yugoslavia, translations of his plays are widely available, and productions have been mounted throughout the world. His greatest international success came for his screenplay for Emir Kusturica's *Underground*, an adaptation of Kovačević's play, *Spring into January*, which won the prestigious Palme D'Or at Cannes in 1996.

    Kovačević says that to have referred to his characters as Serbs or Croats (or any other of the region's constituent nationalities) during Tito's lifetime would have resulted in having his plays banned, and criticising Tito could have ended in imprisonment. Treading on this ground obviously presented a fine line he had to negotiate; how to communicate connotatively to his audience, while still denoting the official line. He insists, however, that avoiding jail was a secondary reason for the care he took. According to him, to have written more explicitly about nationalism or Tito would also have made for 'bad art'. He had no desire, he says, to write a polemic or be a pamphleteer (Kovačević 1997, Interview).

    This begs the question: Can theatre, in general, address issues of nationalism or, for that matter, the racialisation of anything other than physical characteristics, without resorting to agit-prop? It seems there have been very few blatant (or even denotative) references to nationalism in the theatre of the former Yugoslavia. Is that due to the assessment that such work is inferior? Certainly, for theatre to address traditional racism, one identifying race by appearance, casting black or white actors often is all it takes to communicate an idea or attitude about race. But in a world where physical differences are not prevalent and where the racialisation that goes on is tied to alternative groupings of people, is it possible that agit-prop (i.e., 'bad art') is the only choice?

Radovan III, to which we'll turn now, revolves around the title character's daughter, Georgina, who has been pregnant, waiting to give birth, for five years. To avenge his family's dishonour, Radovan forbids her from giving birth until she is married. Immediately, Kovačević's stylistic trademarks are apparent: darkly comic extravagances, infused with incisive cultural critiques, often within the same action. Here we see his use of absurdity to expose the patriarchal forces at work in his culture (incidentally, another one of CRT's 'structures of inequality'). The subordinate role of women in Yugoslav society plays an important role in most of Kovačević's early work, though he is more humanist than a feminist; and as a theme in *Radovan III*, it plays a subordinate role. As we will see, in spite of Tito's taboos, his main target, ultimately, is racial nationalism.

In addition to his daughter's predicament, Radovan is fixated on the fact that his 'enemy' lives in the same apartment building and on the same floor; in fact, they are seven stories up, living in contiguous flats and have built a barb-wire fence between their two balconies. They are the Vilotić family, and they can be heard taunting Radovan through the wall. In the following exchange, Rose, Radovan's wife, has just reminded him that the Vilotićes come from the same region as his family:

> ROSE: They are your countrymen. Your people, more or less.
> RADOVAN: They aren't "my people." My people lived on the other side of the mountain. We don't have anything in common with the Vilotićes. They've always been traitors and riff-raff. For the last five wars, our families fought on different sides. I know what you're thinking: yes, once we were one tribe, but we separated from each other a long time ago. Everything that was good and honest came to our side. Everything that was ugly, corrupt, and spoiled, stayed on their side.
> ROSE: They say the same thing about you.
> RADOVAN: Yes, I know. That's because we didn't rip out their tongues when we had the chance. (Kovačević 1973, 10–11)

Of course, there is no mention of being Serbian or Croatian, but both the attitude displayed towards the other family and the fact that they were once 'one tribe' would have made the nationalist divide obvious for the Belgrade audiences. Željko Djukić, who translated and directed the play for its American premiere in 1993, suggests that this was reinforced just by naming the main character 'Radovan', which all Yugoslavs would identify as the prototypical Serbian male.

At another point, Radovan requests that Rose make uniforms for everyone, so he can distinguish the members of his family from the enemy,

166   D. BARNETT

foreshadowing both the inevitable conclusion of the play and the racialisation that would tear his country apart twenty years later. To further exacerbate the affront to Radovan's family, the father of Georgina's child is a Vilotić. One by one, the members of Radovan's family desert to join the invading Vilotić 'hoard', until Kovačević's final 'joke' must be told. Radovan and his family turn his apparent defeat into a victory by joining his enemy. The only family member left in Radovan's apartment is his daughter, Georgina. As the play ends with the long-awaited birth, mother and child are about to be slaughtered by an army of 'others', composed of their own family members. Following the war, these scenes from twenty years earlier shake with a haunting resonance.

This tragic and ironic joke emanates from a contradiction at the heart of the culture; that the similarities between the three groups inevitably expose the arbitrary construction of their differences and the racialisation process. This contradiction is deeply woven throughout each of Kovačević's plays. It is the joke that rises from the remnants of any naturalised construction that has been too explicitly dissimulated. In the Yugoslavian culture, the overt nature of this construction was supported and supplemented by a doubling process. When Tito dictated the ideology of Yugoslavism, he further exposed the constructedness of nationality. But in the Balkans, the nationalist, ethnic, and religious constructions are tied to an equally constructed past, and the cohesion such ties allegedly engender is emphasised to such extent that nothing is explicit enough to prevent the building of arbitrary boundaries—the same boundaries that Tito just as arbitrarily attempted to remove. Here we have what Bhabha refers to as 'the disrupted dialectic of modernity' (Bhabha 1994, 18). It is the dry sand in the mouth of a desert sojourner who has ventured too close to a mirage. In Kovačević's work, we see the modern proponent of one of these nationalisms swallowing the grit of postmodernity as if it were the 'pause that refreshes' (Barnett 1997).[5]

5   AND THEN TO WAR

After Tito's death in 1980, the succeeding administrations attempted to continue his policies under the slogan 'After Tito—Tito' (Crnobrnja 1996, 83). However, after thirty-five years of forcing its citizenry to swallow their national identities, the Yugoslavian government, without Tito, no longer had the power to keep them out of the public sphere. Tito's celebrated motto of 'brotherhood and unity' was about to be stood on its head. As part of his erasure of the individual nationalisms within his country, Tito had attempted to also erase the damage that Serbs and Croats had done to each other during WWII. After his death, research into detailed accounts of these matters 'became one of the platforms for the relaunch of nationalism' and 'rival nationalist interpretations of history were propounded' (Clark 2002, 25).

If the reintroduction of nationalism into the public sphere had been the only change facing the people in Yugoslavia at the time, it might not have exploded with such vehemence and purpose. But it coincided with the transition towards

9 RACIAL NATIONALISM AND THE SERBIAN THEATRE **167**

a more capitalist system that made the ultimate dissolution inevitable; changes that confronted citizens with an onslaught of adjustments, such as

> the political democratization, and the introduction of multi-party government; transfer of the state property to private ownership; collapse of both public and private sectors; waves of hyperinflation and the galloping devaluation of labour; amassing of private capital accompanied with illegal operations in legal businesses, etc. (Šentevska 2018, 46)

In addition, the wealthier areas, Slovenia and Croatia, felt burdened by the needs of the poorer, more rural areas, Montenegro, Macedonia, and Bosnia. When we add to all of these the historical penchant for nationalism, we see how the country had become a virtual powder keg. All of these became fertile ground for the leaders of the three factions, Slobodan Milošević (Yugoslavia, then Serbia), Franjo Tuđman (Croatia), and Alija Izetbegović (Bosnia), who saw their opportunity and, by inflaming the racialisation process with dissimulations of their own, were able to garner support for agendas that were certain to enrich themselves. Ultimately, Croatia's and Bosnia's moves towards becoming an independent state, as well as Serbia's efforts to hold the Republic together, were merely the formation of teams to compete for capitalism's holy grail (for many, just another dissimulation that would become all too real).[6]

During the war, the usual impulses of theatrical activity maintained a wide array of possibilities; from complete denial a war was going on (the most prominent strategy), to not-so-subtle derangements of classical works, forcing square pegs into the round holes of wartime analogies.[7] Though funding for theatre remained high, in an effort, particularly in Serbia, to once again dissimulate the appearance that the war and international sanctions weren't having any effect, there were plenty of examples of where programming had to be adjusted and where individual theatre artists were made to suffer. When Borka Pavičević attempted to schedule a performance at one of several state-funded theatres in the city, the Belgrade Dramatic Theatre, of a play by the Croatian author, Miroslav Krleža, she was told:

> that we did not need Krleža ... at that time.... One day, I came to the theatre and saw that an entire display case, containing photos of Tito and Krleža...had been completely demolished [and] we would receive letters addressed to our freelance actor, Rade Šerbedžija, saying that he should go back to Croatia. (Pavičević 2018, 38–39)

She also details how the wife of another one of her non-Serbian actors, while he was performing in the theatre, had a gun held to her head in the apartment where they were staying (39).

These are the ways that racial nationalism crept into the mainstream theatres during the war. These, of course, were theatres that relied on state-funding to survive. One of the fringe theatres, on the other hand, took a clear-eyed,

168 D. BARNETT

anti-war stance, a choice that destined them perhaps to remaining on the fringe but also allowed them the freedom to speak their truth to the onslaught of violent power around them.

6 DAH THEATRE

In 1991, Slobodan Milošević sent the Yugoslavian army into a war with the separatist armies from Croatia and Bosnia. Around the war, however, he and his government created a public zone of silence. There was nothing about it on the news and open discussion of it drew nervous looks. However, Milošević was no Tito. Tito's Machiavellian dissemblance was finely mastered to maintain the good will of the majority of Yugoslavs. Milošević, by comparison, was an amateur. It seemed obvious something was going on; men were being drafted at an increased rate, and many were returning in coffins.

Coincident with this, a small group of artist/activists, having been in Denmark to train with Eugenio Barba at the Odin Theatre, returned to Belgrade and found their own theatre. With Barba's focus on movement and montage as their main approach, this theatre, called DAH (meaning 'breath'), was initially envisioned as an apolitical venture. Confronted with the obvious dishonesty of their government, however, DAH's directors, Dijana Milošević (no relation) and Jadranka Anđelić, were compelled to head in exactly the opposite direction. Using Brecht's poetry as their primary source, they bravely mounted their first performance on the streets of Belgrade, daring the government to deny what was obvious to all. Since then, DAH has been an outspoken voice of opposition to war, nationalism and inequality of all kinds, carrying the message of diversity and inclusion, peace and love, throughout Eastern Europe, as well as to the rest of the world.

Of course, there are significant differences between DAH and Kovačević. Because of Tito's mandates during that period, Kovačević tackled issues besieging his public by developing a way to talk around them and say what had to be said through connotation only. His apparent love for his culture and the people of Yugoslavia ameliorates the starkness with which he makes fun of them, and, perhaps, what serves his purpose best is that most of his works are comedies. Black and, at times disturbing, ultimately they provide his audiences with great comfort in being allowed to laugh, subliminally, at their government and at themselves. DAH's works, on the other hand, have been predominantly serious works. The comfort that a DAH audience feels is often accompanied by tears. Whereas Communism shaped Kovačević's ultimately traditional and discursive style, his power as a writer grew through his opposition to it, but DAH never perceived themselves as a political theatre, rather as a theatre of heart and compassion, expressed primarily through their visual poetry and the power of their abstract and mostly non-discursive style. The obligation they felt to 'speak truth to power', to say those things that under Tito had to be left unsaid, is what led them to a political stance. And lastly, the theatres Kovačević worked in were supported entirely by government grants. Most of DAH's funding, though they've applied and received minor assistance from the Serbian government, has come from other sources (most notably the European Cultural Foundation and the Rockefeller Brothers Fund), leaving them free to speak their truths.

As different as DAH and Kovačević are stylistically and generationally, they have a surprising number of things in common. Neither have any interest in producing agit-prop screeds to promote specific political agendas, as they both want to be responsive to and reflective of Serbian current events, and care deeply about human rights, equity, and the condition of their homeland; their vehicle for effecting change is not politics, but art, which for them leaves a deeper mark on the hearts and minds of their audiences.

So, in a way, the fact that neither of them have wanted to directly address the nationalisms in their world, to call them by name, as it were, makes sense and does not imply anything about theatre in general in the area. The fact that they tackled the subject, no matter how indirect their approaches were, makes them stand out in their respective eras. Kovačević was one of a kind while he had the Communists to push against, and his work during the war, particularly *Five-Star Dumpster* (*Kontejner sa pet zvezdica*) (1999), was indirectly, yet severely critical of the Milošević regime. But once the war ended, his work, though still popular and highly entertaining, lost much of its political bravado. In fact, most of the former Yugoslavian theatre world continues its perceived obedience to the various governments, which have all, as in many countries, become dominated by nationalist sentiments, which prevent the theatres from taking any political risks.

Though the research here cannot claim an absolutely exhaustive view of Serbian theatre, it does stem from twenty-five years of close attention to it, and it seems, during that period, that there have been very few plays or productions that speak openly about or depict characters from any of the racialised nationalities; the rare exceptions, actually, are plays that are mostly self-referential, Serbian authors critiquing Serbs and Croatian authors exposing the brutality of Croatian forces.

In Serbia and Kosovo, in 2015 at the National Theatre in Belgrade, followed by a run in Priština, Miki Manoljović directed a production of *Romeo and Juliet*, wherein the two families were of two different nationalities: Serbian and Albanian. As with productions in the US that conceptualise the families similarly, only using black and white performers, Shakespeare's text was used to point out the tragedy of racism, and both Serbs and Albanians were equally blamed. The hope was to contribute to the process of reconciliation. And in Croatia, one of the more controversial plays of the last decade, written and directed by Oskar Frljić, who is Croatian himself, was called *Aleksandra Zec*. Based on a true account, it was about a Serbian girl and her family who were brutally murdered by Croatian forces during the war. This was premiered in Zagreb in 2014. The Croatian forces in this play were the instigators, and no effort was made to protect the Croatian audiences from that fact (Sarić 2019). The fact that of the two examples uncovered in my research, one of them comes from Croatia seems safe to presume that the open identification of nationalist images in Serbia, and particularly in the mainstream theatre, is rare.

DAH, on the other hand, who has purposively remained on the fringe, saw the emotional and economic toll that the war took; saw the pain and residual anger on people's faces; and went to work.

7   GENOCIDE BY RAPE

It has been well documented that, in the 1990s, numerous war crimes occurred in the former Yugoslavia. Many of the perpetrators from all sides were brought to the Hague for trial, and, according to the website of the United Nations International Tribunal for the former Yugoslavia (ICTY), there were ninety convictions. Most of them were Serbs. The Hague is careful to differentiate between different types of war crime, but arguably, there are no greater than those they labelled 'genocide'. Genocide was first codified as an international crime by the United Nations General Assembly in 1946. At that time, rape was considered merely an unavoidable side-effect of war; it was not even deemed to be an independent crime of war, much less an act of genocide. That began to change with the analysis that followed the Yugoslavian war, in which it was determined that rape had been a tactical strategy, directed from the top with genocide as one of its clear aims.

Unlike the Nazis, who believed that any Jewish blood was a compromise in purity, Milošević and his generals approached genocide with a decidedly more arrogant practicality. To them, it was Serbian blood that was going to purify the population. By peopling the Bosnian countryside with Serbian 'bastards', they would diminish the presence of Muslims and Croats. The Bosnian Serb Army, more or less a separate force supported by Milošević, for instance, didn't stop at mere rape, but purposely impregnated their victims and held them prisoner until they were far enough into the pregnancy that abortion was impossible. This had the dual effect of creating more Serbs and dividing the families of their enemy by 'defiling' their wives and daughters. Today, the website for the Office of the UN Special Adviser on the Prevention of Genocide claims that 'the systematic rape of women which may be intended to transmit a new ethnic identity to the child or to cause humiliation and terror in order to fragment the group' is just as surely an act of genocide as any massacre.

Though they seem like disparate and unconnected acts, banning Croatian directors from Serbian stages and the genocidal rapes that occurred during the war come from the same basic urge to racialise an entire nationality. Though the sad and dark idiocy of war has many faces, in this one the arbitrary racialis-ing of an entire group of people who look, act, and speak just like you, who you cannot pick out of a crowd of distant relatives (just as Kovačević predicted in *Radovan III*), exposes the dissembling to such a degree that when the war ended and the governments ceased to indulge in nationalist rants, the racialis-ing seemed to melt away, as Shakespeare says, 'like a hailstone in the sun' (*Coriolanus* 1.1. 170–171).

8 Opposing Racial Nationalisation

In 2006, while Slobodan Milošević was deteriorating in a Hague jail cell, DAH Theatre presented a performance called *Crossing the Line*. It was based on *The Women's Side of War*, a publication of letters and diary entries written by women from all sides of the war whose lives were forever altered. It featured three actresses, who, though they were meant to represent broadly all women, the audiences had no problem identifying as Croatian, Serbian, and Bosnian, respectively. While they spoke directly from the women's writings, their segments were illuminated further by the movement and sounds of the other actors, as well as a recorded score of voices, music, and projections.[8]

Crossing the Line also avoided any mention of the different nationalities. It was not meant to cast blame on or defend any side within the war. Its sole aim was to offer and perform a rite of healing for the many people who had been raped or injured, lost loved ones, homes, villages, friends—and ultimately an entire country to the ravages of racialised nationalism. As in *Radovan III*, though without the humour, it also focused on the absurdity of fighting a war over such arbitrarily constructed differences. At different points, the women trade garments, until each actor is wearing a combination of nationalities; and in one passage, they speak one word at a time. Three different words for bread, three different words for milk, three different words for mother, all of which used to belong to one language,[9] now torn apart and labelled with their own nationalities; yet, as this piece so poignantly points out, two words they all shared were the words for love (*ljubav*) and war (*rat*). *Crossing the Line* was performed throughout the former Yugoslavia (as well as in the US and Europe) for the next seven years, to audiences filled with women from every region. Many of them were visibly moved and demonstrably grateful for hearing their wartime experiences finally being given voice. The act of witnessing that this performance embodied and the healing it offered are examples of the goals to which DAH believes theatre must always aspire.

In/Visible City is a DAH performance that first premiered a year prior to *Crossing the Line* in 2005 and has remained in their repertory ever since. It is their longest running and, arguably, most internationally successful project. Funded by the European Cultural Foundation, amongst other organisations, it was specifically conceived to help combat the racialisation process. *In/Visible City* is a site-specific performance on a working bus that is a direct attack on nationalism, without ever seeming like it.

It begins at the starting point of a bus route and continues till that route is completed. As people board the bus on their way to or from work, unwittingly they become an audience. The performers speak lines, sing songs, and present traditional dances that have been chosen to focus on the neighbourhoods they are travelling through. In Belgrade, for instance, during the summer of 2017, the bus passed through Jewish, Roma, and Hungarian areas to name a few, and as it passed through them, DAH entertained the passengers while simultaneously reminding them of the contributions made by the Jewish, Roma, and

Hungarian residents of Belgrade throughout history. It is a subtle and painless approach, to be sure, but nevertheless cleverly opposes at every step any tendency to racialise these groups. After they have completed the route in one direction, they usually begin at once performing again, only this time the neighbourhoods come in reverse order. In addition, of course, each performance is distinctive and has to be prepared anew for each location.

DAH has performed *In/Visible City* with as many as ten or twelve performers, including props, costume changes, and live musicians. In one version, they included a trombonist; in another, a segment was rapped and amplified; and in 2011, at their twentieth anniversary festival, DAH included a parkour artist from England, who jumped off the bus at one stop and ran through the park they were passing, doing jump rolls and other acrobatic stunts. They have performed *In/Visible City* throughout Serbia, in Macedonia, Italy, Sardinia, Denmark, Norway, and England. A version of it was adapted for Rio de Janeiro, as well.[10]

9   Conclusion

This chapter is being written in 2019. The government of Serbia would like everyone to believe that the nationalistic fervour that tore this region apart at the end of the twentieth century has 'melted away'. It is easy to look at the repertories of the Belgrade theatres, read the local papers, watch the TV, and converse with people in this area today, and believe it to be true; but it is deceptive. Some Serbians, for example, say that, though they welcome their Croatian neighbours and harbour no resentment, they feel that the sentiment is not reciprocated, that Croatians still treat all Serbs with suspicion. One must wonder if Croatians are saying the same about the Serbs? Possibly. This sense of peaceful cohabitation, it seems, is more due to the increased homogenisation of each nation-state than to any actual decrease in nationalist sentiment.

The years following the war have taken the people of these areas through times of hope, as democracy began to take hold, through abject horror that the nationalist forces would once again erupt, and eventually into a daily reality that seems best described as exhaustion; not denial per se, but a sense of resolution that their future seems out of their control—so, why talk about it? The fact that each nationality now has its own country and borders that are, for the time being undisputed,[11] may have relieved much of the tension that existed before, but the leaders of these countries, I am told, are just as nationalistic as ever. What this means for the future of the area is uncertain, but the desire of Serbia's President, Aleksandar Vučić, and his ruling coalition, to be part of the EU, should keep them focused on the changes they hope that it will bring. Whether any wealth or improvement in the quality of life ever reaches beyond the people in power remains to be seen (Ninković 2019).

Theatre, as may be expected, seems to reflect the same exhaustion. Whereas, before, Kovačević had Tito and Communism and a simmering nationalism to battle, today he has a 'democratically' elected nationalist in office and an audience worn out from winning battles, only to lose wars. His work, still attended by thousands and admired by most, has no political bite. It is pure escapism.

As for DAH, they continue to take their mission directly to the people who they feel need it the most. As of June 2017, 5000 refugees from the Mideast remained stuck in Serbia, due to the EU's decision in 2016 to close the route between Turkey and their member countries. Today, around 3000 of them remain in ten different camps. In 2018, DAH stepped directly into the centre of this controversy by spending much of the year, performing and providing workshops for refugees from one of them. Also, DAH is still performing *In/Visible* City as often as they can, in as many different locations as they can reach, entertaining passengers with stories of their communities' diverse histories. However, in an interview in 2019, Milošević described what she felt was an unmistakable animus from members of the audience, as a recent performance of *In/Visible City* began. Throughout the thirteen years DAH has performed this piece, she had never felt anything but a positive sense of community and acceptance. Though by the end of the performance, the animus had dissipated, it still presented for her a warning about what may be simmering in her country today (Milošević 2019).

As for their public performances in Belgrade, their most recent premieres have been well-crafted and researched explorations of revolution and revolutionary zeal throughout history: a piece about revolution in politics called *The Conundrum of Revolution* (*Zagonetka revolucije*, 2019), and one about revolution in the arts, *The Women of Dada* (*Žene dada*, 2017). Though the connection between these works and the activism of DAH is clear, the technique they bring to bear on these subjects remains formidable; though they contain moments of exceptional theatricality and beauty, similar to Kovačević's recent output, they seem to lack the political daring and immediacy of earlier works. Milošević partly attributes this to her efforts to continue growing as an artist, to her adamant desire to not repeat old tropes and conventions, and to continue the process of creating anew every time out, but it also may be connected to the changing face of the power structure in Serbia. Milošević claims that she and DAH are as resolute as ever about affecting their world and moving audience members closer to embracing each other's differences; but as their politicians have grown increasingly clever in disguising their nationalist intentions, DAH's battle against the disinformation has only grown more daunting.

Though mainstream theatres in this part of the world are never going to stand up against the government that is funding them, there will always be outliers. The members of DAH Theatre believe with every ounce of life in them that theatre should be on the frontlines in the battle against racism, against the racialisation of anyone, and against the tendency to treat other human beings with anything but equity and love.

Notes

1. Much has been written about theatre in the former Yugoslavia during the war itself. Though it is an important step in our overview, we will not dwell on it. For information on that topic, see Jane Dolečki, Senad Halilbašić, and Stefan Hulfeld, Eds., *Theatre in the Context of the Yugoslav Wars* (Basingstoke: Palgrave Macmillan, 2018); Silvija Jestrović, *Performance, Space, Utopia: Cities of War, Cities of Exile* (Basingstoke: Palgrave Macmillan, 2013); and Dennis Barnett, Ed., *DAH Theatre: A Sourcebook* (Lanham: Lexington Books, 2016).
2. Italics are the author's.
3. Kosovo, the section of Southern Serbia, primarily inhabited by Albanians, caught in a political no-man's land for nearly two decades, is likely to follow.
4. A number of Croatians, known as *ustaša*, collaborated with the Nazis, even to the degree of building and maintaining their own concentration camp in Jasenovac. There they executed many Jews, certainly, but they also included the Serbs in their list of undesirables. The estimates of Serb deaths at the hands of the *ustaša* vary from 33,000 to over a million, depending on whether the source is Croatian or Serbian.
5. Portions of this section are drawn directly from the author's dissertation.
6. These notions seem to almost be universally agreed upon by the members of the Serbian theatre community I have interviewed over the years, which, if it were only a critique of the Croatian and Bosnian leaders, could be seen to have nationalist leanings; however, the discussions I've had always start as critiques of their own government and then expand to include all governments. Ultimately, if any generalisation is to be made from these comments, it is that the theatre community in Serbia is far more anti-capitalist than nationalist.
7. According to Šentevska, this seemed to take one of two forms, either the blatant representation of war as a universal truth (therefore suggesting that what the audiences were enduring was somehow normal) or the complete abandonment of reality (51).
8. For a more detailed description of this performance, see the author's chapter, in Vessela Warner and Diana Manole, Eds., *Staging Postcommunism: Alternative Theatre in Eastern and Central Europe after 1989* (Iowa City: University of Iowa Press, 2019).
9. Most of these were traditionally referred to as examples of regional dialects—such as with milk: *mleko, mlijeko,* and *mliko*; but for bread, the separation was more arbitrary, with the Serbs now only using *hleb* and the Croats claiming its synonym, *kruh*.
10. With every new location, DAH needed to create a new version, arrange rehearsal time aboard a city bus not in use, and negotiate the commandeering of one of the city's working buses for each performance. *In/Visible City* has been performed 127 times, as of 2019. Here's a detailed list:

2005—five performances in Belgrade
2007/08—twenty-five performances throughout Serbia (Niš, Leskovac, Vranje, Inđija, Subotica)
2009—three performances in Novi Sad
2009—eight performances in Porsgrunn, Norway
2009/2014—ten performances in Belgrade

2011/13 as part of the EU project, twenty-four performances (Belgrade, Brighton in the UK, Skopje in Macedonia, and Ringebing in Denmark)
2014—six performances in Sassari, Sardinia
2015—twelve performances split between Belgrade, Indija, and Novi Sad in Serbia
2016—six performances in Porsgrunn, Norway
2017/18—ten performances in Belgrade
2019—eight performances in Faenza, Italy
2019—four performances in Subotica and Bujanovac, in Serbia.

11. There are two noticeable exceptions, of course, Kosovo and Republika Srpska (an area of Bosnia, inhabited almost entirely by Serbs and supported by the Serbian government). As the Serbian government grows increasingly closer to being granted a place in the EU, contrary to anyone's expectations following the war, Kosovo seems likely to gain its independence without much objection. The EU carrot will, in all likelihood, keep the Serbs from meddling much in Republika Srpska any more, either.

REFERENCES

Barnett, Dennis. 1997. *The World of Dušan Kovačević: An Intersection of Dissident Texts*. Ph.D. Diss., University of Washington.

Bhabha, Homi. 1994. *The Location of Culture*. London: Routledge.

Clark, Howard. 2002. *Kosovo Work in Progress: Closing the Cycle of Violence*. Coventry University: Centre for the Study of Forgiveness and Reconciliation. http://balkan-witness.glypx.com/.

Crenshaw, Kimberlé. 1989. Demarginalizing the Intersection of Race and Sex: A Black Feminist Critique of Antidiscrimination Doctrine. *University of Chicago Legal Forum* 139: 139–168.

Crnobrnja, Mihailo. 1996. *The Yugoslav Drama*. Montreal: McGill-Queen's University Press.

Gates, Henry Louis. 1986. Introduction: Writing 'Race' and the Difference It Makes. In *'Race', Writing, and Difference*, ed. Henry Louis Gates and Kwame Anthony Appiah, 1–20. Chicago and London: The University of Chicago Press.

Glenny, Misha. 1990. Rebirth of History: Eastern Europe in the Age of Democracy. In *New York*. London: Penguin.

———. 1996. *The Fall of Yugoslavia*. Third Revised Ed. New York: Penguin Books.

Kovačević, Dušan. 1973. *Radovan III*. Translated by Željko Djukić. 1993. Unpublished.

———. 1997. Interview.

Mijić, Ana. 2018. Don't Talk About the Elephant: Silence and Ethnic Boundaries in Postwar Bosnia-Herzegovina. *Human Studies* 41: 137–156. https://doi.org/10.1007/s10746-018-9457-9.

Milošević, Dijana. October 8, 2019. Interview.

Ninković, Goran. September 26, 2019. Interview.

Pavičević, Borka. 2018. *Theatre in the Context of the Yugoslav Wars*. Edited by Jana Dolečki, Senad Halibašić, and Stefan Hulfeld. London: Palgrave, 37–44.

Renan, Ernest. 1882. What Is a Nation? *The Limits of Nationalism*. Cambridge University Press, 2003.

Sarić, Irena. September 15, 2019. Interview.

Saunders, Doug. 2018. Donald Trump Proves Racial Nationalism Is Alive and Well. *The Globe and Mail*, April 30, 2016 (Updated May 16, 2018). https://www.theglobe-andmail.com/opinion/donald-trump-proves-racial-nationalism-is-alive-and-well/article29805755/.

Šentevska, Irina. 2018. Stages of Denial: State-Funded Theatres in Serbia and the Yugoslav Wars. In *Theatre in the Context of the Yugoslav Wars*, ed. Jana Dolečki, Senad Halibašić, and Stefan Hulfeld, 45–62. London: Palgrave.

Weiner, Melissa F. 2012. Towards a Critical Global Race Theory. *Sociology Compass*, 6/4/12: 332–350.

Winant, Howard. 2000. Race and Race Theory. *Annual Review of Sociology* 26: 169–185.

CHAPTER 10

The Palestinians in Israeli Theatre

Dan Urian

1 Introduction

A discussion of the social aspects of theatre demands several theoretical and methodological assumptions, the most important of which refers to the theatre as representing a social experience. It is accepted that while the theatre does not strictly reflect any given social reality, it does fashion it to its own particular needs, and in doing so, enables the theatrical disclosure of both hidden conflicts and overt dissension (Pavis 1985: 285).

One important aspect of the theatre's approach to 'public thought' is that of 'the public nature of drama', as George Lukács terms the circumstances of staging a play and its means of reception by the audience (Lukács 1969: 150). Theatre, after all, is carried out in a public place, much like a political performance. An additional factor is the number of addressees: the problem, dilemma or political argument is presented before audiences whose numbers, even for a mediocre performance, can reach tens of thousands. To this, we can add what John Fiske includes in 'vertical intertextuality': all those same articles and other information that accompany the play and are served up by the press and electronic media (Fiske 1987: 108–127). Consequently, plays taking a stand regarding a conflict central to Israeli society may have a powerful ideological effect. The combination of all these components illustrates the importance of the debate being carried out on Israeli stages over such problematic issues as the Palestinian-Israeli conflict.

D. Urian (✉)
Theatre Department, Tel Aviv University, Tel Aviv, Israel
e-mail: dan@hasolelim.org.il

© The Author(s), under exclusive license to Springer Nature
Switzerland AG 2021
T. Morosetti, O. Okagbue (eds.), *The Palgrave Handbook of Theatre and Race*, https://doi.org/10.1007/978-3-030-43957-6_10

Israeli culture has sought ways of presenting solutions to society's conflicts, particularly the rift between Jews and Palestinians. This was carried out at first by carefully reproducing the hegemonic status of the secular-western sector of society, for whom the institution of theatre served as a tool. Problems were raised and 'solved' on the theatrical stage during the first years of existence of the State of Israel. From the 1980s onwards, especially during the war in Lebanon (1982–1985), the Hebrew theatre began to feature biting revelations of hostilities, discord and contradictions, which it presented as insoluble. During the same period, 'mainstream' Zionist culture progressively weakened, as evidenced in many literary, theatrical and cinematic texts.

The process of 'absorption' of the Palestinian into Hebrew drama and Jewish Israeli theatre was slow and hesitant. It is significant that until 1985, no Palestinian characters were presented on the 'main' stage and their theatrical existence was mainly restricted to fringe theatre. Between 1973 and 1982, Palestinian characters appeared in 29 plays staged in Israel. Most of these characters played focal roles, which turned them, and the problem they were representing, into the major theme of the play. The culmination of this process occurred between 1982 and 1995, when Palestinian characters could be found in over 100 of the plays staged in the Israeli theatre, for the main part, representing the Palestinian side in the dispute.

Most of the plays that present Palestinians in the Israeli theatre are political texts that *use* the characters to deliver ideological claims. Occasionally a Palestinian character is written into a text in which the playwright fails to relate to him/her, but deals instead with his own difficulties as a Jew in a society undergoing a process of change. In general, the development of the Palestinian character is subordinated to the ideological or political statement, while at most other times he is an icon on the map of Jewish Israeli ideological consciousness. The majority of plays do not reflect reality as it is but, rather, they reflect the wish of their creators to take a stand and attempt to influence the situation. The repertoire of the Israeli theatre, in this respect, is one of the components of this reality; a factor that determines and fashions a historical reality alongside other elements: political, social, economic, religious and ideological.

Although the Jewish attitude towards the Palestinians underwent important changes from the end of the 1960s to 2020, the similarity between the characteristics of the Israeli theatre-goer and that sector of the Jewish population whose declared attitude to the Palestinians is a positive one is not coincidental: they are one and the same group or, at least, there is great overlap between them.

Israeli theatre has employed several strategies to circumvent social obstacles in presenting its position with regard to the Palestinian theme; these have included the choice of a suitable genre, such as through the 'back door' of satire, reflecting the secondary status given to the 'Palestinian Question' by Israeli society in the 1950s and 1960s. Then in the 1970s and 1990s, the place of the Palestinian among the *dramatis personae* changed and s/he became a central figure in many plays (these included *The Palestinian Girl*, 1985, and

The Jerusalem Syndrome, 1987, by Yehoshua Sobol, *Abir* by Hagit Ya'ari 1992, or *The First Stone* by Miriam Yachil-Wax, 1993). In recent years the more realistic stage portrayal of the Palestinian reflects the change from an ethnocentric and stereotypical approach, to one that is finally recognising the 'other', and attempting to come to terms with his humanity.

These changes were aided by another strategy, that of casting Palestinian actors in plays by Chekhov, Strindberg, Beckett or Athol Fugard which clearly relocated the plot within the Jewish-Palestinian conflict. Samuel Beckett's *Waiting for Godot*, staged by the Haifa Municipal Theatre (1985, 1994), became one of the most important plays regarding the Jewish-Palestinian theme. It was adapted/translated into Hebrew and Arab by Anton Shames who located it firmly in the Israeli Palestinian dispute. Its director, Ilan Ronan, gave a uniquely Israeli-Palestinian interpretation to the play, with the role of the master taken by a Jewish Israeli actor while those of the tramps went to Palestinian Israeli actors. The set became an Israeli building site. The choice of stage location was politically significant—Wadi Salib, in the heart of the Palestinian neighbourhood in Haifa. Performances with these elements of adaptation, casting, theatrical space, set design, props, costumes or music—all together or in combination—have commanded an important place in the Israeli theatre repertoire.

Despite these changes in both the Palestinian image and the frequency of its appearance in the theatre, no real change appears to have taken place in its actual *function* within the Hebrew dramatic narrative over the last 105 years. In most of the texts from 1912 to 2020, the same dualism can be found, whose source lies in the attraction/repulsion of the Jews towards the 'otherness' of the Palestinian: an image that is perceived on the one hand as noble and generous, and on the other as savage and violent. Such Palestinian characters first appeared in 1912, in *Alla Karim*, by L.A. Arieli-Orloff.

2   Palestinians in the Theatre, 1912–1997

A clear expression of how the Palestinians were perceived in the period of settlement (1881–1948), as culturally inferior, can be found in the stuttering Hebrew they are made to speak in the plays. Only those positive figures who support the Zionist enterprise speak correct, or at least intelligible, Hebrew. Violence, lies, deceit and servility characterise the traits displayed by Palestinians, both individually and as a group, in the plays of the settlement period. These reflect the stereotypes that, according to a study by Anita Shapira, were already common among the Jewish community (Shapira 1992: 94). The Palestinians were depicted as violent and aggressive towards their own people and as constituting a threat to the existence of the Jews; the Palestinian tradition of blood feuding was offered by playwrights as a clear example of their violent nature. *Alla Karim* is a love story between Naomi, Jewish Russian pioneer, and Ali, young Arab. Ali's character was fashioned through the colonial stereotype of the 'noble savage': primitive and violent but also generous and courageous.

180   D. URIAN

Ali's uncle is murdered by one of the Jewish pioneers, and Ali takes his revenge by the sword. This violence is generally one-sided: there are very few instances in which Jews demonstrate violence towards Palestinians. When a Jew does use violence against a Palestinian, he bewails his guilt and hastens to excuse his behaviour as unavoidable.

The plays published during the period of settlement were generally written by playwrights whose convictions were socialist or liberal and who desired peace. In spite of this, the plays contain an undercurrent that discloses a significant tension and hostility between Jews and Arabs, particularly echoes of the struggle of the Jewish pioneers who had reached Israel and found employment, thereby leading to the dismissal of Arabs from their workplaces. An additional dispute revealed itself in the struggle over land, which became a central theme in plays of the 1930s onwards. Conciliation is generally seen as imperative, both for mutual interests and to maintain the progress introduced by the Jews, as they see it, for the benefit of all—albeit in two separate communities.

The discrepancy between the disputed and hostile reality and the ways in which this has been presented in the Israeli theatre, with its profusion of texts dealing with the subject, is not as great as it would appear from repertoire statistics. Reading the texts, or watching their performance, will often reveal barely concealed expressions of fear and pessimism. The most common 'contradiction' is that between the spirit of conciliation in the text and its *almost always pessimistic ending*. This pattern is repeated too many times to be merely coincidental. Despite a desire for a peaceful situation, few of the plays see this as possible and their endings waver between the open-ended, the blocked and the pessimistic.

This is particularly prominent in love stories, which always end in either forced or voluntary separation. Many Israeli plays staged in the last 40 years feature love stories between Palestinian characters and their Jewish counterparts. There does not appear to be anything particularly unusual in this fact, for many dramas are 'love stories' which deal with the attempt to overcome barriers of race, creed and religion. The Jewish Israeli playwright generally treats the subject of intimate Jewish-Palestinian relationships with understanding and even a certain sympathy; despite such relations between Jews and Palestinians, male or female, having been considered against the norm by both peoples since the beginning of the Jewish settlement in Israel and up to the present time. The explanation for the frequent occurrence of this theme in Israeli theatre should therefore be sought in the world of the Israeli playwright; and perhaps perceived as a metaphor for the desire for conciliation—for there is nothing like a 'love story' to represent a yearning for peace.

An interesting example of this is *The Return* by Miriam Kaney (1973), the first among many Israeli plays in which the character of a male Palestinian is presented as 'acceptable' for intimate relations with a Jewish woman. However, his 'acceptability' is conditioned by the blurring of his Palestinian identity and his cultural assimilation into Jewish society. A fluent and even literary Hebrew is allotted to these Palestinian characters in the course of their legitimisation on stage as fitting partners for Jewish women. They are educated members of the free professions, and their female Jewish partners are generally of western background, liberal-minded, students, or well-educated professionals. The relationship formed between them is one of real love, with a tendency to motifs of love conquering all barriers of enmity, such as that of Romeo and Juliet.

The character of Riad in *The Return* is the prototype of the Palestinian as lover. He speaks like a lawyer and dresses like one, drinks whiskey and not arak, and bears other signs that lend Hebrew similar to that of the Jewish characters, neither illiterate nor artificially rhetorical. The objection of Riad's father to the liaison and Riad's own loyalty to his Palestinian village are the reasons given for the eventual separation. In many other plays, the separation also follows social or family pressure. In this way, the Israeli playwright achieves a double goal, by suggesting that although relationships are possible between Palestinian and Jew, they will encounter psychological and social barriers. Beyond merely telling the story of certain individuals, these plays deal with the problematics of Jewish-Palestinian relations in general, including the fear of an apparently powerful rival who might appropriate the place of those Jews whose power has diminished. The message of these love stories is generally a pessimistic one, for the barriers cannot be lifted—only in one play, *Flatmates* by Shmuel Amid (1985), does a couple succeed in doing so. However, there are no happy Jewish-Palestinian families in the Israeli theatre.

The perception of the Palestinian as the 'other' began to become particularly acute only after the 1967 War, with the growth of the Palestinian population under Israeli rule, when those in the occupied territories joined Israeli Palestinians, to form one national identity. The issue of the territories and the establishment of Jewish settlements appears in *The Governor of Jericho* by Joseph Mundi (Cameri Theatre, 1975), a play that confronts the occupiers with the occupied and sharply denounces the logic and justice of occupation. The play rehearses claims such as 'We are sitting on their lands and claim that historically they are ours!' and the response of the 'superior-separatist' ideology: 'So what? This is a desert, the land belongs to those who till the soil and fertilize it. He who exploits it properly is its legal owner' (Mundi 1975: 52). The play also voices the supremacist Israeli-Jew's fears of the Palestinian: 'They hate us ... and these bastards have patience' (ibid.: 18); 'They will destroy us all. There will be a massacre, a terrible massacre' (ibid.: 25). 'This land is part of me', says the nationalist Palestinian who embodies the nightmare. 'We don't want you here... it may take a year, two years or even fifty years. But I know that you will go away from here, you are all strangers here!' (ibid.: 51).

The process of 'inclusion' of the Palestinian 'other' started and intensified in the Israeli theatre with the Lebanon War, 1982–1985. A joint work by Palestinians and Jews that was performed close to the outbreak of the Lebanon War represents the turn. *They*, by Miriam Kaney and other playwrights including the Palestinian playwright Riad Masrawa (1948–2016) (1982), directed by Joseph Chaikin (1935–2003), presented a collage of texts on the topic of the conflict between Jews and Palestinians. Unlike the plays that had promoted 'coexistence' in the 1970s, this text presents acute problems, which take place against the background of the Lebanon War; the mutual fears of Palestinians and Jews are presented in a 'competition of suffering' between two actors—a Jew and a Palestinian, Sinai Peter and Ghassan Abbas:

> Sinai: Well, now listen to me carefully. A third of my people were exterminated in the Holocaust.
> Gessan: What's true is true. Mine hasn't been yet. (not published)

In the 1980s the Palestinian 'other' became a major figure in Israeli theatre, albeit mainly on the fringe. In many plays the playwright warns the spectators about the potential uprising of the hundreds of thousands of exploited and oppressed Palestinians. Avraham Shoshner in *Oil* (Akko Festival, 1986), for example, presents a dystopic vision of an *Intifada* of Jews against Palestinians; this *Intifada* takes place in a State where the Palestinians are the rulers and the Jews are slaves, exposed to humiliating interrogations of identity and physical abuse. Functioning here as a 'traditional' Palestinian, the Jew adopts the 'characteristics' of the latter, in particular, the Palestinian's grovelling. Similar to other theatrical texts which presented the Palestinian as lacking identity, in *Oil,* Jews are presented merely as Jew A, Jew B. Both sides escalate the conflict; the Jewish rebels promise that 'within a decade there won't be left a single Palestinian in the world' and the Palestinians promise the Jews that they will 'obliterate them from history' (Soshner 1986: 42, 44).

The first *Intifada* broke out on December 9, 1987, a few days after the first performances of *The Jerusalem Syndrome* by Yehoshua Sobol (Haifa Theatre, 1987). The juxtaposition of the apocalyptic destruction of the Second (and the Third) Temple in the play with the ongoing events in the territories might have been contributed to making public acceptance of the play difficult (Urian 1989: 75–97). It offended those spectators who understood the play as questioning the value of the Jewish heroic myth ethos; this myth had served many politicians in justifying a relentless and even extreme policy towards the Arabs, while the rebellious Palestinian was concomitantly establishing a new saga of heroism. Sobol may not have foreseen the actual outbreak of the uprising during rehearsals for the play, but he may well have imagined such a reality: 'While I was writing *The Jerusalem Syndrome* I imagined the land as being swept by metaphors inciting anxiety and hatred (the "two-legged animals", the "doped cockroaches"...), addicted to its fears and overcome by violent and destructive instincts' (ibid.: 96). Even earlier, in *The Palestinian Girl* (Haifa Theatre, 1985), Sobol had presented two of the extreme figures who embody a nightmare for Israeli spectators: a Jew and a Moslem, both of whom practise religious bigotry and individual terror. The *Intifada* transformed images and increased fears, and the latter became even more acute when the conflict reached the stage characterised by Baruch Kimmerling as 'personal yet also total conflict, in which each of the two communities transfers the dispute to all spheres of life, both as whether as the injurer or the injured' (Kimmerling 1993).

Following the outbreak of the *Intifada* in 1987 additional changes began to occur in the image of the Palestinian character. He/she was no longer an Israeli Palestinian but in many texts had become a Palestinian from the Occupied Territories. Research by Kalman Benyamini (1990) reveals that young Israeli Jews perceived the Palestinians as negative and frightening. Palestinian society, as portrayed in the plays of the 1990s, reflects this, particularly among young playwrights. In several of these plays the knife as a theatrical prop represents the violent side of Palestinian society. In *Masked* by Ilan Hatzor (1990), set in a butcher's shop against a backdrop of a dirty and bloodstained wall, an *intifada* activist stabs his brother to death for collaborating with the Israeli authorities. The link between knife and Palestinian also appears in Israeli satire. In *Hey Rimona* by Ilan Hatzor and Ilan Sheinfeld (1992), the voice of a Palestinian is heard offstage even before he enters: 'To cut or not to cut, that is the question.' Similar traits are also attributed to Palestinian characters by Israeli Palestinians: in *The First Stone* by Miriam Yachil-Wax (1993), based on detailed research by both the Jewish playwright and the Israeli Palestinian actress Salwah Nakara-Hadad, the autopsy report is read out of a young Palestinian woman who was brutally murdered because she wanted a divorce from her elderly husband.

At first glance these plays appear to complicate the inherent difficulty in reaching a possible settlement with the Palestinians and even seem to express an aversion to such conciliation. In fact, the texts constitute a late phase of a *structure* that has existed in the Israeli theatre since the 1970s, which bridges the apparent contradiction between the disputed and hostile reality existing between Jews and Palestinians, and the 'optimistic' trends of presenting this dispute in the theatre. In theatrical texts from the 1990s, the political message of the playwrights is even clearer: they are intent on instructing politicians to negotiate with the Palestinians. But the Israeli theatre of last decades reduced positive references to Arabs and criticism of the Jewish majority's prejudice towards them. Since *Murder* by Hanoch Levin (1997), Israeli theatre, especially mainstream, has avoided showing conflict with the Palestinians on stage. As Sammy Smooha, Professor of Sociology, specialising in the internal divisions in Israeli society, claims, however, 'The Jews have fears of Arab citizens and they feel disbelief', while Professor Ephraim Yaar, Public Opinion Polls specialist, said in an interview that 'it is no longer a shame today to say 'I hate Arabs'' (Fogelman et al. 2014).

3   *Murder*, 1997

Hanoch Levin (1943–1999) is an important and highly influential playwright in this direction. Unlike other playwrights he has seldom represented the 'Palestinian problem', until the turning point that came with the assassination of Prime Minister Yitzhak Rabin (1995), and was reflected in *Murder* (1997). This play differs from all his earlier plays in locating the conflict at the centre and incorporating a Palestinian figure, as well as differing in its fractured structure:

184   D. URIAN

Levin presents us with three interlinked episodes. In the first, three Israeli soldiers, in time of war, torture and terrorise a young Arab suspect before killing him. Three years later the father of the murdered man turns up at a Jewish family wedding and exacts his own private revenge. In the final section, with war again imminent, we see an urban mob turning on and savagely dismembering a pathetic peeping tom. The father of the original victim, meanwhile, roams the streets, still begging to know his son's final words. (Bilington 2001)

Murder is a text and performance in which incongruity is the central issue. There is order in the disorder and logic in the illogic of the play. The logic, which is beyond the pattern of the plot, design of the characters, dialogue or genre, is the murderous logic of the dispute with the Palestinians. Several of the critiques on *Murder* (both the play and its theatrical performance) expressed discontent with the play's disharmony, imbalance (in the representation of Israelis/Jews vs Palestinians), stereotyping, erratic structure and superfluous characters (Fuchs 1997). Levin, who had accustomed his audiences, critics and researchers to particular patterns in his plays-performances, had apparently failed to meet their 'aesthetic' expectations in *Murder*. This disappointment is understandable, as a playwright's success partly depends on posing questions that also get answered at the time of the performance. Yet *Murder* is a play without harmony, which both as a play and a performance highlights incongruity. It is not a 'tragedy' (as the late critic Shosh Weiz called it, Weitz 1997) in which incongruity, expressed as the disruption of prevailing order, gains a new balance at the end; in *Murder* there is no restoration of balance.

To relate *Murder* to a specific genre is problematic. The play, and particularly the performance, oscillates between two poles: that of satire, closely following reality, and that of mythical plays, brought together in the direction of Omri Nitzan. In attempting to understand *Murder*, one can be helped by Claude Levi-Strauss's perception of mythical narrative as an anxiety-reducing apparatus that alleviates the insoluble contradictions inherent to culture and human experience by translating them into concrete terms. 'The logic of the concrete' does not obliterate the polarity but does reduce the threat entailed in living with it. Myth, according to this perception, provides the tools for coping with polarity and enables one to come to terms with its existence in society. In myth solutions are suggested in the form of transcendental paradoxes/contradictions (gods or their messengers) or brought about by the device of improvisation to join disparate elements (*bricolage*) (Levi-Strauss 1967: 213–219, 229–230). In the reality of the dispute between Jews and Palestinians as represented in *Murder*, there is no transcendental solution; nor does the *bricolage* of the visionaries of the Oslo Accords (a set of agreements between the Government of Israel and the Palestine Liberation Organization (PLO), 1993, 1995).

The tension between the mythical and the 'real' is made particularly apparent by the stylised performance which, as reflected in Omri Nitzan's staging, creates a violent, quasi-theatrical ballet, detached from any realistic manifestation. *Murder* both resembles and differs from previous plays and performances in the Hebrew theatre that focused on conflict with the Palestinians. The resemblance is that of the pessimism prevalent in most plays and performances. Although the apparent 'naive optimism' of the Israeli theatre may appear to contrast with the attitude of most Israeli Jews towards Palestinians and 'the Palestinian conflict', the 'subtext' nonetheless repeatedly expresses Israelis' apprehension and rejection of the 'other'; in this way the plays complement their 'adjustment' on stage to the real conflict outside the theatre.

The implicit perception that those who suffer most from the conflict are the Palestinians is common to all such Israeli plays, from *Alla Karim* to *Murder*. Although the Jews pay a heavy price, they are shown to be the stronger side and in a position to suggest the solution. Since the late 1970s, and particularly in the 1980s, playwrights have been suggesting a compromise over the land and recognition of the national Palestinian entity as a solution. They have doubted, however, the capability of the Jewish-Israeli leadership to take such a direction. The playwrights, despite suggesting a 'murderous nature' of the Palestinians, have still maintained hope for a conciliatory solution. *Murder* differs from other plays because it does not offer any such solution. Two years after Rabin's assassination, the playwright and his politically loyal spectators appear to be left without hope.

Similar to previous plays in which Palestinian characters appear, *Murder* too confronts the 'Us' (the Jewish-Israeli public) with the 'others'. The 'Us' comprises three generations of artists and spectators whose group identity has been shaped in the public sphere as well as in the theatre. Dan Bar-On contends:

> As long as social consensus prevailed, and most of public attention was diverted to one dominant 'Other' (e.g., on the eve of the Six Day War) it was possible to manage the monolithic 'Us' in a fairly stable manner. Yet, when different 'Others' (Oriental Jews, Religious Jews and Palestinians) became dominant in different sections of the population (e.g. following the political turnabout of 1977, The formation of the first government by right-wing parties. During the Lebanon war in 1982–1985, or at the time of the first *Intifada* 1987–1993), the management of the monolithic 'Us' became more difficult and complex. (Bar-On 2000: 68, 79)

Since his first steps in the theatre Hanoch Levin has 'served' as a *transindividuel* to his audiences. A *transindividuel*, as determinated by Lucien Goldmann, is an artist who gives literary or theatrical expression to the *vision du monde* of his group; he represents the beliefs and opinions of a specific social group (Goldmann 1966: 151–165). Levin is such a *transindividuel* despite his image as an *enfant terrible* and despite the scandals that followed some of his plays. His audiences are middle class; some have grown up along the way with him since their early twenties; while others are Israeli yuppies who have adopted his sceptical-critical perception. In his plays Levin maintains slightly perverse complex relations with his audiences; already from the early plays these relations centre upon the theme of the humiliating versus the humiliated. He exposes a particular human and social mechanism, agonising over and playing with its theatrical expression in different variations. At the performance of *Hefetz* at the Haifa Theatre (1972), for instance, Levin 'confessed': 'Every person feels the need to humiliate others so that he alone can feel good. There is a hierarchy of humiliations. Humiliate as much as you can' (Bar-Kedma 1970). From the beginning of his career as a playwright he has voiced his reservations about his own group and about his theatre audience: 'I did not like before and I do not like now the audience and the public amongst whom I live ... My only purpose is not to please them. ... As far as I am concerned, the audience is an opponent. I regard the theatre as a wrestling match between the stage and the auditorium ... I feel the urge to strike them, to cause them harm, to show them how evil they are' (Bar-Kedma 1972). At the same time, Levin was nonetheless seeking respectable status in Israeli culture and was therefore probably less involved than other playwrights (including Yehoshua Sobol, Joseph Mundi and Hillel Mittelpunkt) in the conflict with the Palestinians and with the rifts in Israeli society in general.

Although he was among the first playwrights to put a Palestinian character on stage, Levin rarely presented the Palestinian problem. He was thereby probably reflecting the reservations of some of his spectators (the liberal intelligentsia) regarding the political reality. Presumably, they would have preferred, like one of his characters from *Murder*, a 'good, authentic Swiss boredom, ... since one doesn't have the strength to cope any more with the fascinating life of Asia' (Levin 1997: 115). One way or another, Levin was and still is (in his legacy) a loyal spokesman for the political subconscious of his plays' spectators, including their perceptions of the conflict with the Palestinians. In his early satirical works he exposed the economic exploitation of the Palestinians, as well as the desire for supremacy and the corruption of both politicians and army personnel. Only later did he recognise, as did his audiences, that the conflict was not only between two national groups, but also between each individual Jew and Palestinian. Levin and his audiences, who had believed in the possibility of peace following the Oslo accords, realised, after Rabin's assassination, that the conflict is insolvable. In *Murder* the playwright is not satisfied merely with his audience's agony; he himself joins them in a groan of recognition that the prophet shall be unheeded in his own country.

In 1970, the Palestinian entered the theatre by the back door, in Levin's 'satirical review' *The Queen of the Bathtub*. In the skit, 'Samatocha' the Palestinian is a waiter and dishwasher in an Israeli café; he is 'wise and obedient and harmless to Jews. He knows how to stand on his feet, just like us' (Levin 1987: 80). The Jews know that Samatocha does not place bombs and is not a terrorist, and they flatter themselves on not being primitives unable to distinguish between a Palestinian who places bombs and a Palestinian who does not. In this skit, the exploitation of the Palestinian is already juxtaposed with fear of this victim's violent response. Such response was to increase in the extra-theatrical reality and would be represented in the theatre as a consequence of the injustice of exploiting the 'other'. In an interview about the performance and the debate that followed, Levin spoke in the language of 'Us':

"I am not dumb. I am aware that without an army *we* [my emphasis] cannot survive. I am not spitting on the flag. Whoever watches *The Queen of the Bathtub*, and I mean the intelligent spectator, will understand that the play respects the military and the flag. I am against distortion, against fabricated images, against chauvinism that distorts patriotism." (Bar-Kedma 1970). The prominent representative of Israeli in those days, Moshe Dayan, who watched the performance, recognized the target of the playwright's dart and contended that: "In fact Palestinians are exonerated: the poor Palestinian whom we constantly slaughter, or brag about not slaughtering ... Sitting in the theatre, I felt that for Palestinians possessing a hostile view of the State of Israel, there couldn't have been a more encouraging play than this one." (Boshes 1970)

In *The Patriot* (1982) Hanoch Levin returns to the character of the exploited Palestinian. Machmoud sings 'an Eastern love song' to Fatima:

> Indeed, the Jews have a merciful heart.
> And none of them beats me.
> They divided the world between us.
> They shit and I clean up. (Levin 1987: 117)

The process of including the Palestinian 'other' in Levin's theatrical work then reached its climax in *Murder*. The very title of the play and its murderous beginning confound any possible expectation for denouement, alleviation or reconciliation. Playwrights use their plays' titles to voice the essence of their perceptions. 'A title is always a promise', states Jacques Derrida (1986: 115). Levin is generally outstanding in his choice of titles: *The Execution, All Wish to Live* and so forth. In *Ubu-Roi* Alfred Jarry uses the word *merdre* 33 times: the auditory affinity of the word *merdre* to *meurtre* ('murderous, deadly') creates a double entendre: murder and shit (*merde* is apparently camouflaged by the addition of 'r'. A number of spectators of *Ubu-Roi* in 1896, directed by Lugné-Poe in Theatre de L'Oeuvre, identified 'merdre' with 'merde' and interrupted the performance for about 15 minutes). In the opening scene of *Murder* a tanned soldier incidentally chants a verse about 'jolly shitting in a field of thorns' while killing a Palestinian youth (Levin 1997: 85).

The generic indetermination of *Murder* attests to the playwright's and (in particular) the director's deviation from 'the rules' in order to establish others more suited to a reality where there are none. The performance of *Murder* quotes excerpts of satires from the past and some of the play's scenes have none of a satirical nature. The play borrows from satire its sharpness, themes and even its characteristic 'incomplete' fragmented pattern. However, whereas satire is related to a distinct reality, to specific people and events, *Murder* is conceived as a play abstracting reality and, in its staged version, even 'poeticising' it. The result appears to be deliberate intentional generic ambiguity. Satire does not lend itself to a coherent pattern; it is usually a compilation of skits and of songs, loosely edited. In this respect, *Murder* inclines towards the satiric, as a coherent dramatic structure would be unsuitable for the representation of a chaotic history. Consequently, its structure is loose; with the exception of the Palestinian father and the returning soldier in Act III, all the characters in the play appear and then disappear; some are killed. The songs and the ironic tension between the lyrics and the nostalgic music (composed by Eran Dinur) contribute to the satiric nature of the play. *Murder,* however, is not only a satire but also a mixture of genres. Similar to the disharmonious plot, so too is the genre 'postmodern': a *bricolage* of genres that follow artistic needs rather than 'rules'. Nitzan, an experienced, capable and inventive director, created a performance about harsh reality, mixing realism with theatrical images set in segments of movement-sound-text.

Murder was performed after Rabin's assassination. Both playwright and director shared the disappointed hopes. It is these disappointments that dictate the main structure of both play and performance. Levin may or may not have borrowed the mechanism of confuting expectations from *Waiting for Godot* by Samuel Beckett. Godot never does—nor will—arrive; peace, according to Levin/Nitzan is slow in coming and may never arrive. The spectators watching the boy in *Waiting for Godot* and the messenger in *Murder* cannot fail to comprehend the futility of waiting. Levin, who knows his audiences and their mechanism of suppression and denial, adds an epilogue without a messenger, sealing the loss of any hope for peace.

In *Murder* the director maintains a 'dialogue' with Levinesque satires from the past. Nitzan, in coordination with the playwright, added two sections: to the end of Act I, after the entrance of the messenger who first foretells peace; and to the end of Act II, when the same messenger declares war. At the end of Act I the Palestinian youth murdered by the soldiers recites: 'My dear father, when you stand upon my grave don't say that you made a sacrifice / for the one who sacrificed was me', quoted from *The Queen of the Bathtub* (1970) (Levin 1997: 92); at the end of Act II the bride and the groom killed by the Palestinian sing: 'When we are taking a stroll, we are three / You and I and the next war' (ibid.: 30) quoting a song from the satirical cabaret *You and I and the Next War* (1968). Retrospection to the 1970s and the intertextual game activate the spectators, who know the passages and their context, and evoke a sense of déjà vu. Further 'retrospection' is presented in *Murder* by the Third Neighbor, the putative representative of the spectators, who counts: 'Every morning a new child is born / whose parents say: by the age of eighteen it must come to an end. And so eighteen years / and eighteen years more/ The more you expect to live—the less you do' (ibid.: 115). The passages quoted by the director are not only satirical, but also contain the mythical component of the performance: the monologue 'My dear father' evokes the sacrifice of Isaac. The performance of this monologue by the Palestinian actor, Norman Issa, recalls to mind the existence of Abraham's other son, Ishmael.

From the very beginning to its closing scene *Murder* is a series of violent acts. Although it echoes Levin's perception of the public debate in the 1970s and the 1980s over the wrongdoings of generals, settlers, the right wing, the media and so on, it deals mainly with the reality of the 1990s, with the terror

10 THE PALESTINIANS IN ISRAELI THEATRE **189**

of and by individuals. Its beginning is the *Intifada,* when Israeli soldiers abuse and kill a Palestinian youth. Its continuation is revenge, when the father of the murdered boy kills one of the men who might have been his son's killer (He is not totally wrong). The Palestinian then rapes the victim's bride and murders her too. This series of killings climaxes when a Jewish mob murder the poor Palestinian worker, who is both economically and nationally frustrated.

Murder is the first theatrical text in which Levin presents Palestinian figures as human being. In the performance Palestinian roles were played by the renowned and esteemed Palestinian actors Makram Khouri, Salim Dao and Norman Issa, chosen by playwright and director together. The Palestinians, nonetheless, like the other figures in the play, are images rather than characters. Levin does not manage to escape the dichotomous stereotyping that characterises the Hebrew theatre; the Palestinian is conceived either as violent, vindictive and threatening, or as a poor, victimised, grovelling, miserable creature. Levin, who so far had shaped the Palestinian 'other' as a miserable and exploited figure, now juxtaposed to this image the other face of the stereotypical Palestinian Janus his 'murderous' nature. It was the director's choice rather than the text that pointed to inclusion of the 'other' Palestinian. This was achieved through the tendentious casting of the actors and the addition of Isaac's song declaimed by Ishmael, which brought Palestinian bereavement to the Cameri theatre hall.

Many spectators left the performance of *Murder* confused, dumbfounded and shocked. Levin's attitude to the audience had remained ambiguous. He had continued to find stupidity and selfishness among his spectators and in the second act even 'invites them on stage', as represented by the wedding guests. Yet these were the very same spectators whom Levin had made his allies for so many years. Some have matured along with him and had learnt that the conflict results not only of the wrongdoings of the politicians, generals and settlers, but also from their own blindness to the damages of occupation.

The difficulty in containing the Palestinian 'other' was apparent in the response of both critics and spectators of *Murder.* Some critics and a number of spectators were speaking for a balance that cannot be found in reality. Gai Cohen, for example, voiced disappointment with the representation of the Palestinian in the play:

> There is a link missing in the chain of killings. The soldiers kill, because the Palestinian boy had killed before. I admit that it is impossible and unnecessary to know who exactly had begun it. The Palestinian father kills in retaliation and there is an act of terror—again, Palestinians against Jews—and in response, the lynch of the Palestinian worker. The missing link is our abuse of the Palestinians: closure, starvation, humiliation, confinement to enclaves of autonomy that rather look more like concentration camps, all in the name of the 'new Middle East'. This misery could have been articulated at the opening of the third act, before the act of terror. (Cohen 1997)

190   D. URIAN

In contrast, Sarit Fuchs claimed:

> The provoking problem is the measure of stereotyping, the pessimism and self-hatred in the text, which turn the play into a shallow one. The theatre's public relations promised symmetry between Palestinians and Jews, a sharing of the guilt for the endless killings in the region. It cannot go unnoticed that the Palestinians in the play, who respond to Jewish wrongdoing, are the only human beings ... Why do Palestinians have to be saints? Why is a revenging Palestinian more humane than a wicked Jewish soldier? (Fuchs 1997)

Levin responds to the reservations of both critics through the words of the Flushed Soldier: 'There's not too much reason here' (Levin 1997: 87).

Spectators interviewed after the performance of *Murder* were also divided in their responses:

> Michal, an estate assessor, explains (in a trembling voice): "This is a disgusting play. I am upset to see that all the cultural institutions fail to give sufficient backing to the soldiers. There is an unfair imbalance between the acts of the Jews and the acts of the Palestinians. The Palestinian in the play has a reason for revenge. We killed his son and this is understandable. In contrast, the Jews ruthlessly lynch someone, just like that. The Palestinian kills by shooting and we torture the living and desecrate the body. In my opinion, Levin totally missed the point. Had it been so important to clarify that the killing is unnecessary, he should have emphasized that any murder—of a Jew or of a Palestinian, left or right wing—is unjustified. I feel as if someone had taken a pistol and shot every Israeli through the heart."
>
> Shimon Zandhaus, a graphic designer: "This is a very powerful play. It does not speak of Palestinians or of Jews but about an existential situation, when violence and murder become the very essence of our being. Who is right is not the issue. In my opinion, this is the most important political play in the recent years."
>
> Nitza Rubin, an accountant: "The lust for murder in the third act was totally exaggerated. To see ourselves as a bloodthirsty people who enjoys it? I am a great fan of Levin—I haven't missed a play—but this time I think that he does injustice to truth. The lynch scene and the decapitation almost made me sick. It went beyond the limits of good taste. Both my husband and I served in the army—and Levin hurt us deeply."
>
> Her husband, Avi Rubin, an engineer, noted: "It is high time an Israeli playwright wrote a pro-Israeli play, in favor of the Jewish people. I am sick of constantly seeing the Palestinians as the suffering and the just." (Masat 1997)

The epilogue, which refers to the future, to the children, is the last nail in the coffin of any hope for peace while occupation, exploitation and hostility still prevail. *Murder* ends with mistaken identification, when a 'pale soldier', who had been previously blinded, errs in identifying the old man ('You are the father of the boy we killed') and answers the questions of the bereaved father from the first act: 'His last words were: "Have mercy on me, I want my father"' (Levin 1997: 121). Mistaken identity is often a comic device or a metonym for the disappearance of the father figure and of a defined authority, and for the malignant and capricious spread of the dispute.

Tracing the Palestinian image in Levin's works reveals a process of inclusion of the 'other' by both the playwright and his audience, who belong to the liberal intelligentsia. In *The Queen of the Bathtub* Levin put on stage a Palestinian who represents a problem that Israeli Jews have. In *The Patriot* Palestinians function in the confrontation between Levin and the Israeli bourgeoisie, in particular the Jewish settlers in the occupied territories. Only in *Murder* does Levin deal with Palestinians as characters in the same manner as Israeli Jews. Nitzan, as director, goes even further, in attempting to contain the Palestinian 'other' by means of Palestinian actors who represent their own group, for the first time in a Levin play. Salim Dao, who played one of the murdered Palestinians, also participated in a discussion on the play:

> Most people who complain say that the play is unbalanced since the Jews are the ones who turn out worse. They told me: the Palestinian at least had a reason to kill, whereas the Jews are brutes for no reason. I ask you: look at the terrible state we are in—what are we actually competing for? The horrors? What are we getting offended by? What difference does it make who does what? (Lahav 1997)

Indeed, some spectators, the Palestinians among them, felt that their inclusion had been expressed in *Murder*. As one of the Palestinian spectators noted: 'I feel something than I have never felt, that I am not a stranger' (Levi 1999).

4 Conclusion

One question that remains to be answered concerns the extent of the contribution of the Jewish Israeli theatre to coexistence with Israeli Palestinians and to a possible solution with to the dispute with the Palestinians. It can be said that in general, spectators at a theatrical performance find themselves simultaneously within the world of the stage and outside of it. They may therefore adopt a critical stand towards what is being shown on stage, both during and shortly after the performance, and connect its contents with extra-theatrical social and political referents. Regarding the Jewish-Palestinian conflict there is also the cumulative effect of the consistent rise in the number of plays dealing with the 'Arab Question' and, from the 1980s, with the 'Palestinian Question'. Racial attitudes in Israeli society displayed by Jews towards Arabs have fluctuated in response to the political climate, especially in the last 20 years, following the second intifada of 2000–2004 (Bar-Tal 2007). Despite this the theatrical repertory teaches us that both its creators and audiences are opposed to these trends, more passively in the central theatre scene and in a more active fashion in the fringe, to the extent of public opposition to racial attitudes (Urian 1995, 1997, 2013). All the factors that I have presented here, taken together, validate the assumption that the Palestinian image in Israeli theatre represents a wish to settle the dispute and has contributed to public thought by emphasising the strong desire of a group of Jewish Israeli spectators for conciliation with the Palestinian section of their population. The contribution of the theatre is especially important in the years during which a solution appears to be far off. In this respect, the theatrical texts that staged the Palestinian problem constituted an artistic avant-garde that urged and demanded the beginning of that difficult conciliation process with the Palestinians, which is still relevant today.

REFERENCES

Bar-Kedma, I. 1970. What's Wrong Mr. Levin. *Yediot Achronot* (July 16, 1970). (Hebrew).

———. 1972. The Ugly Humanity of Hanoch Levin. *Yediot Achronot* (April 14, 1972). (Hebrew).

Bar-On, D. 2000. Rabin's Assassination as a Final Step Towards the Breach of Monolithicness in the Formation of Israeli Identity. In *Memory in Dispute: Myth, Nationality and Democracy. Studies Following Rabin's Assassination*, ed. Lev Greenberg. Beer Sheva: The Humphrey Institute for Social Research, Ben Gurion University (Hebrew).

Bar-Tal, D. 2007. *Living with the Conflict: Socio-psychological Analysis of the Israeli-Jewish Society*. Jerusalem: Carmel. (Hebrew).

Benyamini, K. 1990. *Political and Civil Standpoints of Jewish Youth in Israel*. Research Report, Jerusalem: The Hebrew University of Jerusalem. Faculty of Social Sciences, Department of Psychology (in Hebrew).

Bilington, M. 2001. Murder. *The Guardian* (November 13, 2001). https://www.the-guardian.com/stage/2001/nov/13/theatre.artsfeatures1.

Boshes, H. 1970. The Foam that Strangled the Queen. *Haaretz* (May 22, 1970). (Hebrew).

Cohen, G. 1997. Duty. *Ha'ir* (August 8, 1997). (Hebrew).

Derrida, J. 1986. *Memoires: For Paul de Man*. New York: Columbia University Press.

Fiske, J. 1987. *Television Culture*. London and New York: Routledge.

Fogelman, S., H. Glazer, N. Darom, and H. Ahitov. 2014. Have We Arrived to the Break Line in Jewish-Arab Relations in Israel? *Ha'Aretz* (August 1, 2014). (Hebrew).

Fuchs, S. 1997. Evil in Search of Soul. *Maariv* (August 8, 1997) (Hebrew).

Goldmann, L. 1966. Structuralisme génétique et création littéraire. In *Sciences Humaines et Philosophie*, 151–165. Paris: Gonthier.

Kimmerling, B. 1993. Less Politics More Primitivism. *Ha'Aretz* (April 2, 1993). (Hebrew).

Lahav, G. 1997. Murder. *Yediot Achronot* (August 8, 1997). (Hebrew).

Levi, R. 1999. Film in *Yoman Hashavua*, Israeli Television, Channel I (March 26, 1999).

Levin, H. 1987. What Does the Bird Care?, Tel Aviv: Siman Kri'ah and Hakibutz Hameuhad. (Hebrew).

———. 1997. Murder. In *Those Who Walk in Darkness*, 81–121. Tel Aviv: Hakibutz Hameuhad. (Hebrew).

Levi-Strauss, C. 1967. *Structural Anthropology*. Trans. C. Jacobson and B.G. Shoepf. London: Allen Lane, pp. 213–19, 229–30.

Lukács, G. 1969. *The Historical Novel*. Trans. Hannah Mitchell and Stanley Mitchell, Harmondsworth: Penguin.

Masat, L. 1997. We All are Murderers, All Are Victims. *Yediot Achronot* (August 4, 1997). (Hebrew).

Mundi, J. 1975. The Governor of Jericho. Tel Aviv: Achshav. (Hebrew).

Pavis, P. 1985. Production et réception au théâtre: la concrétisation du texte dramatique et spectaculaire. In *Voix et images de la scène: Vers une sémiologie de la réception*, 233–296. Lille: Press Universitaire de Lille.

Shapira, A. 1992. *Land and Power, 1881–1948*, Tel Aviv: Am Oved. (Hebrew).

Soshner, A. 1986. Oil. *Iton 77*, 80–81, September–October 1986, pp. 36–45. (Hebrew).

Urian, D. 1989. The Ostrich Syndrome (Dan Urian Interviewing Jehosua Sobol). *Hetz*, No. 1, 95–97. (Hebrew).

———. 1995. *Palestinians and Israelis in the Theatre* (A Special Issue of Contemporary Theatre Review). London: Routledge.

———. 1997. *The Arab in Israeli Drama and Theatre*. London: Routledge.

———. 2013. The Occupation as Represented in the Arts in Israel. In *The Israeli Occupation of the West Bank and Gaza Strip: Implications for the Occupying Society*, ed. Daniel Bar-Tal and Izhak Schnell, 438–470. Oxford University Press.

Weitz, S. 1997. Murder Entails Murder. *Yediot Achronot* (August 1, 1997). (Hebrew).

CHAPTER 11

Faces of a Long Unspoken Collective Trauma: Theatrical Representations of Friendship, Love, Betrayal, and Pain in the Landscape of War in Contemporary Turkey

Deniz Başar

1   INTRODUCTION

This chapter analyses several plays about the impacts of ongoing Kurdish-Turkish war, or more precisely the war between PKK (Partiya Karkerên Kurdistanê—Kurdistan Workers' Party) and TAF (Turkish Armed Forces), from the alternative theatres of central İstanbul where Kurdish and Turkish artists work together, or in contact with each other, in two languages (sometimes simultaneously[1]) and produce political works that show the multifaceted damage inflicted by the war. One of the most important aspects of the alternative theatres, as the survey here demonstrates, is the solidarity bonds and artistic collaborations that independent Kurdish and Turkish theatre artists have established. The characters of these unconventional cross-border plays are made through collaboration and deal with the intangible divides in people's minds established by the war itself.

These invisible divides between people are not recognised—bureaucratically or diplomatically—within the borders of the nation state. This daily reality implants a constant paranoia of 'internal enemies' amongst both Turkish and Kurdish communities, which, torn by the war, are especially vulnerable to paranoia. The survey of plays in this chapter is chosen to include unorthodox

---

D. Başar (✉)
Boğaziçi University, İstanbul, Turkey

© The Author(s), under exclusive license to Springer Nature
Switzerland AG 2021
T. Morosetti, O. Okagbue (eds.), *The Palgrave Handbook of Theatre and Race*, https://doi.org/10.1007/978-3-030-43957-6_11

195

character representations or previously unstaged situations that represent a variety of people affected by the war to varying degrees. These people include the ones at the front lines of the armed conflict to people who live with the constant white noise of war in the superficially calm-looking Western urban centres of Turkey, and everyone in between these two ends of the spectrum: soldiers returning with a post-traumatic stress disorder (PTSD) or disability, people who lost relatives in the war, people who try to continue their daily lives in the war zone, and so on. The characters in these plays all need to deal with the toxicity of *betrayal* in all aspects of the micropolitics of their daily lives. The plays analysed in this chapter were all staged between 2010 and 2014 when I had the opportunity to be a part of the vital and political scene of İstanbul's alternative theatres as an emerging theatre researcher[2].

2   The Habitat: Alternative Theatre Scene of İstanbul

A significant episode in the contemporary theatre scene of Turkey began around 2008 (Başar 2014), when a generation of emerging young artists started renting small flats around the Beyoğlu district of İstanbul, which is known to be one of the most cosmopolitan, historical, and, possibly, the liveliest part of the city.[3] These artists were locked out of institutional theatre settings because of the lack of formal theatre education (most of them were trained in universities' theatre clubs while studying other things) or because of their ideological differences with the theatre institutions (Başar 2014, 152). In Beyoğlu, they began to create ensembles and write in the small black-box stages that they collectively made together. Only on these alternative stages and through their new plays, a variety of characters from contemporary Turkey (such as Kurds, LGBTI[4] characters, and urban women wearing head cloths[5]) started to appear on stage. This was a breath of fresh air in the theatre field of Turkey, circumventing the Leviathan-like bureaucracy of state theatres and municipality theatres, and the cheap populism of commercial comedy theatres and other private establishment theatres. The majority of the plays referred to in this chapter were created with a lot of devotion; most of the stages and ensembles, at least in 2011–2014 when I closely observed them, either had no state funding or received very little (below the survival level that would allow for the stable reproduction of their artistic work[6]) which made them dependent on the box office, therefore their audiences. In a way both theatre makers and audiences that were challenged by the norms of contemporary social life in Turkey have found each other in these theatre spaces.

It will be helpful here to explain briefly the context of Kurdish-language theatre in Turkey, where the development of theatre in Turkish and of theatre in Kurdish has been radically different. While Turkish-language theatre was institutionalised and strictly regulated by the state throughout the twentieth century (which since the early 1960s has prompted the creation of alternative theatre scenes as a reaction), Kurdish-language theatre—because of the ban on minority languages and political taboos attached to Kurdish—was never accepted and was immediately shut-down even after the language ban was lifted in 1991[7]. Still today making theatre in Kurdish in Turkey is a political statement, even when the play *text* doesn't have anything to do with Turkey—like the Kurdish Hamlet adaptation of Diyarbakır City Theatre in 2012 (see Verstraete 2018)[8].

The most nuanced, well-researched, and critically engaging scholarly work on Kurdish theatre in Turkey written in English[9] is Bilal Akar's MA thesis entitled 'Transformation of the Kurdish Theater Field in Turkey between 1991 and 2017', which examines this theatre and its establishment after the 1991 lifting of the language ban. Akar divides the period between 1991 and 2017 into two phases: 'emergence, development, and institutionalization of the Kurdish theater (1991–2002), and its expansion and emergence as an art field in the 2000s (2002–2017)' (2018, i). This second period is further divided into 'the period of struggle for autonomy from the mainstream Kurdish political movement (2002–2013), and the Kurdish theater as part of the alternative theater field in Turkey (2013–2017)' (Akar 2018, i), although the two are so periodised for the purposes of his research but are otherwise 'interwoven' (137). Although the plays I examine are from 2010 to 2014, they belong to the category that Akar defines as 'hybridization and the Kurdish Theater as part of the Alternative Theater Field' (121–126), which he roughly makes start in 2013.

I also want to note that only *locally written* plays (including free thematic adaptations) are analysed here, but there have been, in the alternative theatre scene of İstanbul, important stagings of Western texts that deal with similar war themes, directed and dramaturged to directly speak to the situation in Turkey. One example is *Fear and Misery* (Theater Deng u Bej[10], 2013–2014), a selection of four short plays from Mark Ravenhill's seventeen inter-related pieces on 'war on terror' collectively titled *Shoot/Get Treasure/Repeat*. In the translation of Ravenhill's text for the performance, both Kurdish and Turkish were used strategically to recall the situation in Turkey (Başar 2014, 145).

A researcher of the impact of the conflict on civilians, Burcu Şentürk writes that 'there have been a number of good [academic] studies in the context of this particular conflict between the Kurdish movement and the Turkish state, most of them deal with the position of the state or of the PKK as an institution' but 'the people who are directly exposed to the unwelcome outcomes of the conflict are missing in most of these works' (2012, 101). This is precisely why these plays are so important, because the characters in them are 'the voices of the people who are directly exposed to the undesirable results of the conflict [who] are not heard' (101) in the loud political debates and propaganda of an ongoing war. These plays document the emotional state of war-torn generations.

3 Context of the Armed Conflict: A Very Brief Summary

The Ottoman Empire lost land and control throughout the nineteenth century, but its ultimate collapse came, as known, in the years that lead to and followed World War I (WWI). Esra Özyürek explains that modern Turkey

> was born out of the ashes of the Ottoman Empire. The Late Ottomans fought against the Greek army and committed genocide against the Armenians and Assyrians. Atatürk, the founding "father of the republic," brought together Turkish and Kurdish forces to reestablish a state. After the foundation of the republic in 1923, he pushed the Kurds to the sidelines and attempted to Westernize the country with the iron fist of an authoritarian leader. Under his rule, Turkey adopted the Latin script, changed the weekly day of rest from Friday to Sunday, made men take off their fezzes and wear hats with brims, gave women the right to vote and to be elected to government, and established a state-sponsored industry that would create a Turkish-Muslim bourgeoisie. This period was also marked by enormous pressure being brought to bear on Islamic groups and lifestyles. (2019, 2–3)

Similarly, Meltem Ahıska emphasises in her study of Occidentalism in Turkey that '[…] the external border that separates Turkey from its East—that is, the Middle East—has been translated into an *inner border* that symbolically separates the West of Turkey from the "backward" East, contaminated by Arabic, Kurdish and other cultures' (2010, 15). Kurds, separated by this 'inner border' in the Turkish nation state, throughout the first two decades of the Republic of Turkey have rebelled for reasons related to religious or cultural oppression. As Şentürk again writes,

> An uprising led by Sheikh Said in 1925 was brutally suppressed by the central government. This was followed by the Ararat [*Ağrı*] rebellion by the Kurdish residents of this region between 1926 and 1930. In 1927, the Ararat Republic declared independence without any foreign support and international recognition. However, after bombardment by the Turkish Air Force, the Ararat Republic collapsed in 1930. The Dersim rebellion in 1937, initiated by the Turkish Armed Forces (TAF) especially by bombardments by the Turkish Air Force. Besides these uprisings, there were several other Kurdish rebellions up until 1938. However, all those rebellions, including the previously mentioned three big rebellions, were initiated by elites and remained fragmented and regional. (2012, 100)

These three rebellions were not interconnected and organised around defending a collective identity (especially considering that Sheikh Said and his followers were Sunni, whereas the Dersim rebellion was carried out by Alawis), but rather reactions to the newly forming and iron-handed Turkish Republic. And '[a]fter the violent suppression of these uprisings, there was no attempt to challenge the Turkish Republic in terms of the Kurdish issue until the 1970s' (Şentürk 2012, 100).

Following the establishment of the secular Turkish state in 1923 in the territory now known as Turkey, Turkish became the national language defined in the constitution. This provided people whose mother tongue was Turkish with a significant institutional privilege, justifying institutional violence and assimilation politics towards people with different mother tongues. These constituted a large portion of Turkey's population since the country was established after the collapse of a multicultural empire, and given a good portion of Muslim/Turkish people in Western Turkey were forced immigrants from the Balkans and Greece. Since the Army has been the founding organisation of Republic of Turkey, mandatory military service was established as a duty for all healthy men in the country. However, later in the century, after the vibrant years of the 1968s student movements, many left-wing groups went underground and started armed resistances worldwide. Kurdish university students began discussing the Kurdish question in the late 1960s but until a decade later the context of discussion was centred around '"regional backwardness," seen as the outcome of the feudal system, "lack of education," which could be eliminated through educating people, and "underdevelopment," which required investment' (Şentürk 2012, 100). This has changed with the establishment of PKK in 1978 when Kurdishness (through language, culture, and shared identity) became a definitive aspect of the resistance. One of the major differences between PKK and the previous Kurdish uprisings in early twentieth century was that PKK was a grassroots resistance organisation (especially at the beginning) and did not come from the power holds of Kurdish tribes or elites[11] (see Şentürk 2012, 109).

In 1980 Turkey experienced the bloodiest military coup in its history, and the military rule continued for three years, ending in 1983. This has also been the most important breaking point of the armed conflict between PKK and TAF. The level of inhumanity and brutality in military prisons, especially the Diyarbakır prison, ignited the fire of the previously scarcely initiated armed conflict between PKK and the Turkish state. The 'low intensity armed conflict' (as it is referred to in international politics) that has continued since 1984 resulted in an estimated number of 40,000 people's deaths; as Özyürek has affirmed, 'In their fight against the insurgents, the Turkish state has penalized virtually all of its Kurdish citizens, forcefully removing them from their villages in security operations, creating terror in Kurdish-majority cities, and subjecting them to disappearances that still await justice' (2019, 3–4).

In the last decade of the Cold War, fears of communism have led to many military coups and wars all around the 'developing' world and the 1980 military coup in Turkey was one of them. The oppression of the coup not only made the armed conflict between PKK and TAF what it is today, but also enforced Islamic politics as an antidote for any kind of left-wing resistance to capitalist state system. The era that opened after 1983 was tainted with global neoliberalism, which turned Turkey into a cheap labour market and pushed thousands of Kurds as forced immigrants in the peripheries of big cities to work in 'mushrooming sweatshops' (Özyürek 2019, 4). Following the 1980–83 military junta, the 1990s were marked by deep economic crisis, high inflation rates, and intensifying war against the Kurds (4), as especially those living in southeast of Turkey were heavily targeted by the TAF[12]; this resulted in a generation of Kurdish youth witnessing or being directly influenced by state brutality, which, according to first-hand accounts of PKK members' families, led to many young people join the PKK (Şentürk 2012, 111).

The peace-negotiation process started in 2012 between the Turkish government and PKK was ended brutally in late 2015, when TAF attacked Kurdish settlements and civilians in Southeast Anatolia; the attack resulted in the complete abolishment of some settlements, mass displacement, and, in cases like Cizre and Nusaybin, mass murder, creating scenes of state violence and propaganda similar to those of the 1990s. This led, in early 2016, to public outrage from activists and intellectuals, such as Academics for Peace,[13] who became the new targets of the government and, in some cases, resulted in the imprisonment or exile of these public intellectuals and academics.

4 Impact of the War on the Micropolitics of Daily Life

The war has affected the micropolitics of life in many ways, setting the background for the plays analysed in this chapter. First of all, war shapes the public psyche in a way that makes people prone to believe in conspiracies and seek for 'internal enemies' amongst their social circles, creating a toxic aura of expectation of betrayal in all interactions. Kimberly Theidon (2013) describes this when discussing *intimate enemies* in the context of Peru, which I find useful for my analysis: the paranoid psyche of living intimately with enemies is grounded in the collective trauma of a society that is divided by the ongoing war. I also agree with Kellerman that

> Similar to radioactivity, the emotional trauma cannot be seen or detected [...] Collective trauma remains hidden in the dark abyss of the unconscious [...]. While on the surface things may look quite normal, the very absence of something that was there before–the void or empty space–will have a psychological effect on anyone who visits the disaster area and reveals its hidden secret. (2007, 33)

The 'unconscious' is an important keyword here since it refers to a state of seeing the world through a particular bias that is shaped by experience, and most importantly doesn't allow individuals to assess its impact from outside. Therefore collective trauma appears invisible to the consciousness of its sufferers by never allowing a critical distance from the effects of experience. This trauma has been documented in the last two decades in oral history research projects such as Burcu Şentürk's research, in which she has interviewed the close relatives of 'martyrs' of both sides: TAF soldiers and PKK guerilla. Unsurprisingly Şentürk's research shows that relatives of both sides of this armed struggle see themselves as the rightful side and construct very different narratives about what is happening based on very different ideological frameworks. What might be surprising to an outsider, though, is that both sides of the conflict insist that they have no hatred towards civil people based on their ethnicities. This is where a concept like 'intimate enemies' comes handy to understand this scenario:

> It can be suggested that Kurdish and Turkish people are not as polarized as their politically represented identities may suggest. The common history, common religion and intermarriages between these ethnic groups cannot be overlooked. The claims of families that they do not have feelings of hatred for Kurdish/Turkish people show that for them the problem is not between the Kurdish and Turkish people. Through their narratives, it was clear that none of the family members consider this conflict an ethnic conflict between Kurds and Turks. Furthermore, due to universal conscription into the military, many of the TAF soldiers who lost their lives are ethnically Kurdish. (Şentürk 2012, 114)

In the context of this chapter, each character from the analysed plays can be placed in one of four concentric circles based on his or her level of intimacy with the ongoing war. In the centre circle are the people who fight on the front lines—men on their mandatory military duty sent to Southeast Anatolia and members of the Kurdish guerilla (PKK). In the second circle are the civilians living in the Southeastern regions of Turkey who directly witness and suffer the war. The third circle is for the people who are physically located outside the war zone (out of the Southeastern regions of Turkey) but whose loved ones serve their military duty or have people in their lives who either returned injured from the war, or died, or got 'lost' in the war zone. In the most outer circle, war appears as a distant background, akin to a white noise that constantly reminds the characters and the audience about its existence.

5 A Survey of the Plays (2010–2014)

5.1 Front Lines of the Conflict—The Inner Circle

Disco No 5 is one of the first productions of the Kurdish theatre company Destar,[14] which, founded by Mîrza Metîn and Berfîn Zenderlioğlu in 2008, collectively run the Şermola Performans stage in Beyoğlu since its inception in 2010.[15] They created their theatrical language through a synthesis of their praxis-based political theatre background, physical theatre, and the Kurdish musical storytelling tradition called *dengbej*[16], against a backdrop of magic realism. The group used Kurdish in their productions and presented their plays with Turkish surtitles; amongst their many important and well-received productions, *Disco No 5* remains legendary, comparable perhaps to Grotowski's

1962 *Acropolis*, which dealt with the holocaust (see Romanska 2012). 'Disco' was a term used amongst prisoners and guardians as an ironic slang for referring to the military wards under the military rule between 1980 and 1983. *Disco No 5* brings the state brutality of the 1980 Diyarbakır prison on stage without showing graphic violence and through the solo performance of Mîrza Metîn's solo, who transforms himself into seven different characters: the prisoner, the torturer-guard and the animals in the prison cell—the spider, the fly, the rat, the dog of the guard, and the snake. The torturer-guard's dog's name in the play is 'Co' (read as 'Jo' in Turkish), which was also the name of the dog of the real life general Esat Oktay Yıldırım, who was repeatedly reported to enjoy torturing prisoners in Diyarbakır (Tosun 2011)[17]. The stage design is simple: a human-sized red spider net in the background, a hanging thick red rope in front of it, and a chair. A thin layer of still water on the ground, supported by a wide plastic cloth, is the central part of the stage design, coming to represent bodily fluids throughout the play: blood, urine, sweat, tears, and so on. As the dehumanising tortures cut back from the humanity of both the prisoner and the guard, the animals in the story, especially the spider and the fly, create an allegorical representation of the relationship between the state and the individual. The latter is identified with the fly caught in the spider's net, whereas the spider is the state insisting on negotiating the terms of how the fly should betray his own species (family and friends) for his own survival by helping the spider.[18]

And then, of course, there is the other side of the war represented on stage—the young men who are involved in the armed conflict through mandatory military service and asked to do inhuman things under circumstances that they cannot break free from, just like the allegorical fly caught in the allegorical spider net. In 2010, nü.kolektif staged *Becoming a Man Through Crawling*,[19] a play based on the research of Pınar Selek, which dissects the military masculinity of Turkey (including the larger effects of it on the society), and its establishment through mandatory military service. Selek's book is based on the sociological analysis of fifty-seven in-depth interviews of men reflecting on their mandatory military service experience. nü.kolektif's (2010–2015)[20] choice of using Selek's text is not a coincidence: Selek,[21] one of the ground-breaking antimilitarist-feminists of Turkey, was imprisoned by the Turkish government and made to suffer through extended court trials, which eventually led to her exile. Her prosecution started because of a PhD study in which she conducted interviews with PKK members; therefore, in turning her text into a play, nü.kolektif also demonstrated their solidarity by providing a public platform to her viewpoint at a moment when the state was brutally trying to stop her from speaking to any audience in Turkey.

nü.kolektif's core members, Ülfet Sevdi and Nicolas Royer-Artuso, were educated in Brazilian theatre practitioner and theorist Augusto Boal's methodology and use techniques of Theatre of the Oppressed through their playmaking. Their highly performative theatre, in with narratives of the propaganda are included in the text, manage to criticise militarism by using its own language and constructing physical-mechanical movement and soundscape on stage that, alongside the clownesque make-up of the performers, highlight the absurdity of naturalised military training and mindset. The director and adapter of the text, Sevdi, says about *Becoming a Man Through Crawling* that

> It is an entertaining comedy about military service including songs and music. It [the play] has a structure that constantly develops through layering. I tried to construct a play where the audience would not know where to look, in which nothing is repeated again and where everything transforms into machinery. We can't imagine this play as a separate entity from the country's [Turkey's] military history. The questions of how I can bring this historical process on stage has took me to mehteran ceremonies [Ottoman army music], miniature paintings, and fasıls [Ottoman entertainment music, generally accompanying the drinking culture]. It resulted in a movement pattern that does not have any depth, which I call 'the movements that evolve into miniatures'. (Sevdi 2011)

This two-dimensional miniature dramaturgy was established through the theoretical reading of Beliz Güçbilmez, who suggests that realist theatre in Turkey had subconsciously developed its depictions of reality following the realism of miniature paintings. In her ground-breaking work, *Time, Space and Appearance: the Form of Miniature in the Turkish Realist Theatre* (2006, revised in 2016), Güçbilmez proposes that miniature aesthetics in Turkish theatre have developed over the last century in a very organic way, differently from the Western dramatic form that has made perspective paintings opening from a focal point their visual reference. Through Güçbilmez's theoretical reading, many theatre practitioners, including Sevdi, have consciously started engaging with miniature aesthetics to further clarify and sharpen their topics.

Another interesting choice is the use in the play of female performers, who were made to deliver the viewpoint of the interviewed men changing their perspective from first to third person (turning, e.g., the statement 'I became more of a man through my military service' to 'He said he became more of a man through his military service'). Using women on stage also allowed for a more accurate portrayal of military culture, as the toxic masculinity that this culture creates does not only affect men, but also (or more so) impact the women who share their public and private lives. The play was also one of the few verbatim play experiments of Turkish theatre at the time.

More directly absurdist examples looking into military mindset include Aydın Orak's *Daf* ('Trap' in Kurdish, 2012) by Theatre Avesta, with Destar one of the very first Kurdish theatre companies created in İstanbul in 2003 by Orak and Cihan Şan. Orak was born and raised in the Kurdish border-settlement of Nusaybin (in the city of Mardin); Syria was seen from there immediately over the border, and the area in between was 'heavily salted with landmines' (Baş 2015, 327). *Daf* reflects on Orak's personal life-long experience of the threatening reality of the Turkish-Syrian border; reminiscent of Beckett's *Waiting for Godot* (and maybe even *Woyzeck* or *The Good Soldier Švejk*), the play is set in the middle of a no-man's land. Two soldiers on the opposite sides, Apol and Miran, protect two different countries in physical proximity of each other. While Apol is patriotic, speaking in the language of nationalistic propaganda, Miran does not care about nationalism or militarism even though circumstances forced him to protect a border that he does not believe in. Throughout the play the two men establish a fragile relationship, but '[a]t the end of the play, borders destroy friendship as Miran shoots Apol and Apol fires back' (Baş 2015, 330). Baş clarifies how an allegorical shadow-play telling an animal-based story (similar to *Disco No5*), object theatre, *dengbej*, and even Kurdish rap are used throughout the play to provide a nuanced understanding of the situation in which the two characters are stuck in, their different backgrounds, and worldviews.

In his thoughtful critique of Baş's comments on *Daf*, Akar (also as a first-hand audience of the play in 2012) objects that the significant epic elements in the play are not conducible to the *dengbej* tradition (2018, 14–15). That the play's authors should claim a link to *dengbej* (Baş's analysis is based on her interview with Orak) reveals a desire to be in continuity with a wider cultural scene and, perhaps, a wish to gain social capital as carriers of tradition.[22]

5.2 Civilians Influenced by the War–Second Circle: Direct Influence

Nerde Kalmıştık? ('Where were we?' in Turkish) is probably the only play written in Turkey that deals, with naturalistic approach, with the post-traumatic stress disorder (PTSD) of a retuning soldier. *Nerde Kalmıştık?*, written by Ebru Nihan Celkan, was first staged in 2012 under the direction of Mîrza Metîn in Şermola Performans. The play shows how shallow understandings of a supposedly 'distant' war are not changed by the alienation and silence of the traumatised returning soldier Umut. Only at the end of the play Umut, drunk at a family, gets to tell the story of how he was chosen to kill eight 'terrorists' in a village house only for him to realise later that this was only a family with women and children. The main problem with the play is that, despite the local jokes (referring to events in 2010–2011, when the play was written) and the academic research behind it, it feels like copying a stereotypical Vietnam-veteran-soldier story of Hollywood. It should also be noted that there are no Kurdish-identifying characters in the play and that characters are generally flat, failing to articulate the physical and emotional impact of the war.

Gor ('Tomb' in Kurdish) is another play by Destar written by Metîn. The play follows dead characters in their monologues, which overlap and intertwine accompanied by a nocturnal soundscape. Stylistically, *Gor* has absurdist and Brechtian elements, from Beckett's *nowhere-forever* landscapes to the white-painted faces of the performers echoing the first stagings of Brecht's *Man Equals Man* (Silberman 2012, 180). However, the *dengbej*-style performative musical storytelling is the central structural element of the play. In *Gor*, the souls of the people killed from both sides of the same unnamed war share the same tomb (perhaps, a mass grave)—the state and regional feudal sides of

11 FACES OF A LONG UNSPOKEN COLLECTIVE TRAUMA   205

Kurdish culture being criticised at the same time. The play has only one female character (since at the time there was a lack of Kurdish actresses) and each male character is presented as having harmed her (purposefully or not), because of either their traditional beliefs or political ideals. They all feel guilty and almost none of them can look her in the eye; one of the characters is a feudal man who used to beat his wife and children, another is a soldier who lost his humanity after surviving the snow-covered mountains alone after an attack, another is a Kurdish guerrilla soldier who accidentally killed his own sister when he bombed a bus full of civilians.[23] One male character only is not scared to look at the woman, and this is the writer, who represents an alternative type of masculinity: not violent, abusive, or insecure.

The second play by nü.kolektif analysed here is also based on a project involving testimonies and oral historiography: Rojin Canan Akın and Funda Danışman's book *It Is Not as You Know It: Growing Up in 1990s in Southeast Anatolia* (2011). The book was made into a play in 2012 in collaboration with Kurdish theatre collective Teatra Densal.[24] This was a truly verbatim play, based on a narrative structure where performers give voice to the testimonies of four Kurdish people who, growing up in the 1990s in Southeast Anatolia, witnessed unimaginable state atrocities. The play was one of the few staged projects in the 2010s that used Kurdish and Turkish languages together.[25] Ironically enough, an important Kurdish part of the play, performed by İsmail Yıldız, needed to be cut out after the very first performance as Yıldız was arrested for his journalism on the Kurdish regions of Turkey on 20 December 2011 ('Basın', 2011). In the play, performative elements of the Turkish *meddah* storytelling tradition are integrated with the Kurdish *dengbej*. Nicolas Royer-Artuso composed original music for the play with lyrics were written and sang by Dengbej Xalide. The stage was divided by a white curtain, with the two musicians and the *dengbej* behind it, who, with the light coming from behind them, appeared as shadow figures reminiscent of the Ottoman traditional shadow puppetry.[26] This made the musicians (or rather their disembodied music and shadows) a visible representation of subconscious collective memory (and amnesia). On the other hand, the four performers telling their stories were placed on the front stage, their rather static storytelling being made theatrical through music and soundscape. The performance was accompanied by the projection onto the performers (as well as onto the white screen behind hiding the musicians) of miniatures by artist Canan depicting the stories told on stage. The projection of these miniature paintings allowed for these personal stories to become visible without indulging into violence pornography. nü.kolektif therefore showed a development in how to use miniature aesthetics since their very first experiment in *Becoming a Man Through Crawling* and tailored it here to documentary theatre, using miniature painting that seems to create a multiplicity of viewpoints around the central theme.

Another play, *Antigone2012*, is a free rewriting by Berfin Zenderlioğlu of the original Greek tragedy, equally engaging with the God-given right to bury the dead. *Antigone2012*, staged by Destar (in Kurdish) at Şermola Performans in 2012, continued into the following season as *Antigone2013*. The play opens with a newly married couple entering their bedroom to have sex for the first time; the woman convinces her new husband to play a sexual game where she would tie his hands and feet to a chair. Once this is done, she reveals her true identity: she has been seeking revenge for her brother who was killed by her now-husband, then a soldier, in front of her very eyes as a child. The woman tortures her husband by forcing his head into a fish tank to make him confess where her brother is buried; as the story slowly progresses, the audience learns that the husband has always known of her real identity through his access to the state archives but that he let her go ahead with her plans because he actually likes her. The play ends with the woman leaving and the man tied to the chair, as she feels deceived and defeated at the list of the possible mass graves her brother might be in.

Despite the minimal stage design (a fish tank and shadow screens amplifying performers' shadows at certain moments of the play), this is one of the few theatre pieces by Destar, known for its history of well-crafted direct addresses to audiences, that utilises a somewhat permeable fourth wall. The ethical conflict that the tragedy of Antigone represents is essentially a confrontation between the people who chose to obey their oppressive regimes. In the original play, Kreon wins over Antigone because of the silence of the people who knew that Antigone was right but chose to keep silent because of their fears and conformism. Between Hrant Dink's political assassination in 2007 and the state's brutality resurgence in 2013 (culminated in the Gezi Park Resistance for the non-Kurdish parts of the country, too), the theatre field of Turkey experienced an Antigone 'phenomenon'.[27] Many companies, including commercial, institutional, and alternative theatre, repeatedly reproduced Antigone, with a similar phenomenon happening in Latin America (Werth 2010) and Africa (Chanter 2011).

Pelin Temur's 2014 *Kuyu* ('The Well' in Turkish) deals with the collective amnesia of people in Turkey and themes of memory of the war and loss. It is important to note that this is also the only play that was staged outside İstanbul, at the Mek'an in Ankara (which is also the capital of state theatres, making it a city with very strong theatrical orthodoxy)[28]. In the play three women slowly break through collective amnesia with their narrative-ritualistic performance; the dimness of the stage adds to the play's holistic tone, which particularly serves the overarching tone of mourning. They are the survivors of the war and witnesses of the war crimes; the well, which is used as a central leitmotiv, refers to the actual reality of wells being used as mass graves in Anatolia since the Ottoman Empire[29]. As a central image, the well is also a direct allusion to the acid wells that were used for mass murder by the JITEM[30] (a highly controversial counter-terrorism branch of gendarmerie) in the 1990s in Southeast Turkey, and the performers embody the women who have lost their loved ones in these wells. However, the well also signifies the stillness of the memory with almost no traces left on the surface. The play uses ritualistic staging, which aims to

11 FACES OF A LONG UNSPOKEN COLLECTIVE TRAUMA

help healing the amnesia and embody the memory to allow both performers and audience to eventually accept and confront the realities of war crimes.

5.3 Civilians Influenced by the War—Third Circle: Indirect Influence

This circle—which is inevitably linked to the *second circle*—also includes the scenarios in which 'time has passed' and, therefore, civilians directly influenced by war are expected by society to 'get over' their traumas and naturalise their experiences. Plays in this circle look into what happens when time has passed after a trauma but no justice is achieved: How can civilians live with the wound of an old injustice? What vulnerabilities do they develop and what triggers them?

Lemonade is a 2011 production of İkincikat company, and one of the very first staged plays of now established playwright Sami Berat Marçalı. It is a soft-spoken, urban, middle-class, family drama where the audience only sees the central family in its home and in the most domestic state of mind. Ege, the middle child in the family, lost his ability to walk during his mandatory military service when he was sent to the Southeast Anatolia. Even though Özlem, his mother, suffers from memory loss, she still has a sense of time and place, except for her perception of Ege; her mind has built a universe where her two other children, the oldest daughter Müge and the youngest son Melih, are adults, but Ege still goes to primary school. Throughout the play, whenever she is confronted with the existence of Ege, she goes back to a liminal zone of denial: 'Ege is at school', 'Ege is playing with his friends outside', 'Ege is studying Math for his exam', and so on. Müge has the central care-giver role in the family, as she sacrifices herself for the well-being of Özlem and Ege, while Koray, one of the most interesting characters in the play, is the gay lover of Ege (who, we learn, only came out after his return from the war). Throughout the play the audience gets a sense that Müge is trying to blame the physical and psychological trauma of the war to his brother's 'becoming' gay. On his part, Ege wishes his lover Koray to reject the military service, something that is done only by devoted political activists, and which Koray feels he can't do. At the end, Koray declares to Ege that he will do his military service but promises to come back—which, we sense, is an empty promise.

İkincikat's *Üst Kattaki Terörist* ('The Terrorist Upstairs' in Turkish, 2014) is the most humorous play mentioned in this chapter. Adapted by Marçalı (the writer of *Lemonade*) after the story of the same title by Emrah Serbes,[31] the play deals with questions essential to contemporary Turkish society: how does a person become a fascist? And under what circumstances may this person change their mind?

The play is centred around a boy named Nurettin, who is about twelve years old. Nurettin's older brother has died in Southeast Anatolia stepping on a landmine when Nurettin was only five; the boy doesn't cry at his older brother's funeral and reproaches his mother for mourning publicly as this would make

'terrorists happy'. The newspapers and TV channels present at the event, however, present this as an 'act of heroic altruism of a little boy for his grand
nation'. As Şentürk puts it,

> [...] in the media, these families are represented as "families of the nation," who
> bestow their children on the nation and their homeland. The usual media
> representation of these families consists of mothers and fathers in tears shouting
> *vatan sağ olsun* [long live homeland]. While the poverty of these families is
> highlighted by these representations, it shows audiences that even though these
> people do not have anything, they love their country/state/nation enough to
> sacrifice their beloved sons. (2012, 107)

Nurettin, in this sense, acts exactly like the national media may be expecting,
and it is made clear in the play that he indeed enjoys this validation and short-
lived national fame, thinking he can stretch this by continuing not to mourn
for his brother's death. The play has a very dark humour typical to Serbes's
stories, as it opens with the twelve-year-old Nurettin calling a national news
outlet to remind them that he still hasn't cried for his brother and that they
should cover this in their news sooner or later.

Nurettin lives in a lower-middle-class Turkish nationalist neighbourhood,
feels the need to actively engage with the nationalist movement, and uses various forms of hate-speech when referring to Kurds. He is deeply traumatised,
even though he denies this by acting in a pretended, but widely approved,
machismo. His circumstances guide and shape his ultimate hatred against
Kurds (actually, against everyone), but the story takes a twist as a form of
brotherhood is built between Nurettin and the Kurdish university student who
moves into the flat upstairs. The name of the play, *The Terrorist Upstairs*, is how
Nurettin refers to this student, while their interaction transforms Nurettin's
grudge and the Kurdish university student slowly replaces his dead brother.

5.4 White Noise of the War—The Outer Circle

Iska (*Missed Target* in Turkish) written by Fuat Mete, staged at Krek right
before this was closed in late 2014, saw the stage separated with an aquarium-
like glass surface turning the fourth wall into an actual physical barrier with the
audience, who were given headphones at the entrance to live-listen to the play.
In *Missed Target*, six characters appear side by side, in colour-coded cubicles, to
tell their stories in sometimes overlapping monologues. All are from the urban
centre of İstanbul, but belong to different classes and have different motivations;
the one thing in common that brought them into these near-absurdist
confession cubicles is that each one of them has a conflicted story related to
mandatory military service. One character is a female lawyer that has sent her
drug-addict brother to military service because of her inability to handle him,
but who now fears that he might die. The second character is a lower-class
religious woman whose beloved husband is doing his military service, as she

prays for his return and hopes to have children. There is also a retired public officer who lost an arm in a traffic accident and fears to lose his son in the war, just like his arm. There is a young girl waiting for her boyfriend; a nurse waiting for her son's return; and, lastly, a football hooligan who believes his masculinity is reduced since he did not get into the front lines of the armed conflict as his military service brought him outside the Southeast Regions. It is through this last character that the audience gets an unexpected insight into military service as he reveals his regret for not defending a Kurdish boy in his camp when almost everyone, including some high-ranking soldiers, were abusing him (the boy later shot his own foot to be sent to hospital and get away from emotional torture).

Finally, there are plays in which no major character is directly affected by the war, but that show the constant buzz of the ongoing war. The best example of this is Ahmet Sami Özbudak's *Trace*, staged at GalataPerform in 2013. The action takes place in the ghettoised zone of central İstanbul called Tarlabaşı, in a house where, like in many others in the neighbourhood, three generations of marginalised people have lived and left their legacy. The play feature a brief but important scene in which a Kurdish guerrilla soldier nicknamed 'Dağlı' (which literally means 'the [one] from the mountains') comes to visit his Kurdish cousin Rizgar who is staying with his transvestite sex-worker lover. Sevengül, Rizgar's lover, accepts Dağlı into her home and gives him green beans to clean for dinner as they wait for Rizgar, who, on his arrival, greets Dağlı in Kurdish (since Dağlı does not know Turkish). This is the only scene in the play where Kurdish is used, and even though the scene is very short, it evokes the existence of another language sphere somewhere very close. The scene ends up with Rizgar taking his cousin Dağlı out after discussing the irony of Sevengül immediately making a mountain guerrilla soldier 'who hunted many men' useful in a domestic context. This also subtly humanises Dağlı, subverting the monstrous image of the Kurdish guerrilla drawn by the mainstream Turkish media.[32]

5.5 Human Contact in the Landscape of Betrayal and Embodied Taboos

All the characters described in this chapter are deformed by the war, and their psyche is damaged by the constant fear of betrayal and/or conscious/ unconscious forms of denial. Through these characters, it is possible to see a nuanced representation of war and its long-term effects; the most important potential of these plays is in making the neutralised state of mind distorted by collective trauma *visible* and, therefore, questionable and possibly changeable. Making the unnaturalness of the current situation emerge is the most important long-term political goal of these plays.

This is also precisely why all these plays use very different aesthetics, which makes it possible to tackle taboos that are ingrained in education and get reinforced by daily media imagery to eventually become internalised beliefs contributing to group identities (such as 'Turkishness') if they are never contradicted from a variety of rhetorical and aesthetic directions. Challenging taboos from different angles erodes the very adaptability of the taboo, shaking the widely distributed and controlled linguistic and semiotic codes that allow individuals to tiptoe around such taboos. Once they are seen under a different light, or placed in an unconventional frame, the absurdity and irrationality of these taboos, was previously invisible in the propaganda that first created and established them, become apparent. Each theatre piece in this survey also challenge taboos by revealing situations, characters, and emotions that are not allowed in the public sphere, challenging biased and prejudiced encounters the tragedy of which is exposed.

It is important to remember that the environment of theatre-making in the alternative theatre scene of Turkey, particularly İstanbul, is key to the political relevance and experimental quality of these plays. These small and collectively owned black-box theatre spaces, mostly surviving completely on their own and sometimes even despite direct authoritarian interventions, managed to create an audience for themselves who desired to engage with difficult taboos but did not know how to do so. From what I have witnessed between 2011 and 2014, I can say that both my own understanding of reality and that of a remarkable portion of other active participants have shifted through this theatrical experience. This is even more so considering that what is on stage (especially on a tiny black-box stage) is an intimate confrontation with the 'other' (or othered) side of the same reality that makes internalised bias less likely to hide back into the subconscious or collective amnesia.

Contemporary alternative theatre in İstanbul is still an intense experience where audiences hold the artists constantly accountable for their work, even after the military-coup attempt in 2016 that created a new wave of state-orchestrated witch-hunts that continues to this day.[33] Since these independent theatre spaces have (quite literally) no backdoors for the artists to escape after the show, and that artists are available to talk to audiences almost always, before and after the plays, the interaction with audience members, above all if regulars, can often extend to pubs and cafes in Beyoğlu (in my case), as in other areas, where the discussions about 'what just happened' continues. This I find quite similar to Habermas's description of literary circles and coffee houses of London in the eighteenth century, as these public interactions are theorised as a 'public sphere' that is key to 'literary publicness' (Habermas 2001), as literary works are further discussed in newspapers and journals to enlarge the conversation. In my 2014 MA thesis on the subject, I have similarly described the alternative theatre scene of İstanbul as 'performative publicness' (Başar 2014) in which the key element of engagement (from both artists and the audience) comes through being present in a theatre space and making/witnessing a play that opens a much-needed and timely discussion.

11 FACES OF A LONG UNSPOKEN COLLECTIVE TRAUMA   211

NOTES

1. There were also non-verbal plays such as *Cerb* (In Kurdish: Experiment) of Destar (later known as Şermola Performans), which was performed between 2010 and early 2013. Performers were Mîrza Metîn, Alan Ciwan, Engin Emre Değer, Mozes Dagil, Berfin Zenderlioğlu, and Sevgi Turan.
2. I specifically worked on the alternative theatre scene of İstanbul between 2011 and 2014, but some of the plays I analyse in this chapter premiered in 2010.
3. In 2005, Garajİstanbul, one of the first black-box stages in İstanbul, was established with the efforts of a group of avant-garde theatre artists working since the 1990s in different self-sustained theatre troupes. Dot Theatre, also established in 2005, was another first-wave black-box stage that settled in central İstanbul in a place that was five minutes away from Garajİstanbul. Starting around 2008 and flourishing after the 2010s, there was a second generation of ensembles made out of young and idealist people who started renting spaces in Beyoğlu and making their own plays. For more information, see Başar 2014, 41–109.
4. LGBTI is the acronym that is used by the activists in Turkey. 'I' stands for intersex.
5. 'Headcloth' is the term used in Turkey to describe Islamic headwear (generally a scarf) that practicing Muslim women wear to cover their hair.
6. Some of these companies, such as Destar (owner of Şermola Performans stage) and İkincikat, lost their small funding in 2013–2014 season, right after they gave open support to Gezi Park Uprising in June 2013. For more information, see Başar 2014, 171–172.
7. For more information on the lifting of the language ban, see Watts 2011, 54.
8. Diyarbakır City Theatre was closed in late 2016 after State of Emergency was declared on 20 July 2016; following the failed military coup attempt on the 15th. For more information: İnce 2017.
9. Additionally a particularly good study written in Turkish is the PhD thesis of Duygu Çelik, which investigates how *dengbej* tradition has influenced the aesthetics of contemporary Kurdish theatre (2017).
10. A short-lived theatre collective that was unique, being established by two Kurdish female theatre practitioners, Gülistan Yüce and Özlem Taş, in a period when modern Kurdish theatre was suffering from a lack of Kurdish-speaking actresses. See Başar 2014, 226.
11. For a detailed account of the formation of Kurdish resistance and its relations to the Turkish left throughout the second half of the twentieth century, see Bozarslan 2012.
12. 'While the situation of human rights in Turkey is not very good in general, the position of Kurdish people is particularly fragile. The Human Rights Watch Report *The Kurds of Turkey: Killings, disappearances and torture* (1993) focuses on human rights violations perpetrated against Kurdish people during 1990s. According to this report, Kurds in Turkey have disappeared and have been killed and tortured at an appalling rate, while many villages with mostly Kurdish inhabitants have been brutally attacked by the security forces and forcibly evacuated. It is stated in the report that, in 1992, 74 people—34 in the southeast—were shot and killed in house raids by security forces and that "the evidence suggests that the killings were deliberate executions"' (Şentürk 2012, 110).

13. To understand the Academics for Peace movement and the serious backlash they have got from the current government of Turkey, please see 'CALL FOR', 2017.
14. All of the plays mentioned in this chapter, with the exception of *Kuyu* [*The Well*], are produced in physical proximity to each other in the Beyoğlu district of İstanbul. When *Kuyu* toured to İstanbul from Ankara, it was also staged at Şermola Performans, sharing the same audience.
15. Şermola Performans was sold to another theatre company in 2016 because of financial difficulties. Destar later adopted their stage's name (Şermola Performans) as their ensemble name since they realised they were more known among their audiences by their stage's name. They still continue their work as an ensemble and perform in a variety of alternative stages in İstanbul.
16. For more details on meaning and influence of *dengbej* tradition in contemporary life of Kurds, see Hametlink 2016.
17. I thank Bilal Akar for bringing up this point after reading a draft of this chapter.
18. More information on *Disco No 5* can be found in Elif Baş's 2015 article 'The Rise of Kurdish Theatre in İstanbul'. The article also provides a substantive historiography of Kurdish theatre in the alternative theatre scene of İstanbul after the 2010s.
19. There are different translations of this book's title, such as *Leading a Dog's Life: Masculinity* or *Being a Man Through Creeping*, but I think the verb 'becoming' is the one that actually captures the constructed nature of the masculinity that Selek is dissecting in her study, therefore I am using my own translation here: 'Becoming a Man Through Crawling'.
20. nü.kolektif was particularly active between 2010 and 2014 but they had some theatre activities in 2015, too.
21. To find out more about the activist and intellectual Pınar Selek and her case with the Turkish state, see 'Pınar Selek'.
22. After generations of suppression of the Kurdish language and physical barriers posed against live Kurdish drama for most of the twentieth century, it is more than understandable that Kurdish theatre practitioners want to re-imagine the roots of Kurdish drama and invent their own tradition, which is also an affirmation of cultural agency. These efforts mean to create historical narratives where their work can be read as a part of a genealogy. For further debates of this issue, see Scalbert-Yücel 2009 and Çelik 2017.
23. After my encounter with Bilal Akar's thesis, I can't stop thinking that a particular thread in the story—a young woman being killed in a bus bombing—is an allusion to the death of Helîn Başak Kanat, a Kurdish woman theatre practitioner who died very young in similar circumstances in 1994. These kinds of allusions are only available to audience members who would know such references, and at the time I wasn't one. Kanat's death is briefly mentioned in Akar 2018, 77. I found a little more information in informal web resources, which were the only ones I could reach.
24. Teatra Demsal was established by Rojbin Elban, İsmail Yıldız, and İhsan Gümüşten in 2010 and became the fifth Kurdish theatre company in İstanbul at the time after the theatre branch of Mesopotamian Culture Center, Seyri Mesel, Destar, and Avesta.
25. Perhaps the first Turkish-language play that had Kurdish language in it in the twentieth century was Erkan Yücel's documentary play *Earthquake and*

Persecution that he made in collaboration with Kurdish artists. It was performed in 1978 before being banned (Çelik 2017, 150-512 & Akar 2018, 43).

26. This type of shadow puppetry, namely, *Karagöz and Hacivat*, is known as 'Turkish shadow puppetry' in scholarly literature but for the context of this chapter perhaps calling it 'Ottoman shadow puppetry' would be more accurate; since shadow puppetry wasn't specifically oriented to Muslim-Turkish people's practices but was made by the cosmopolitan and imperial human landscape of Ottoman İstanbul with many practitioners of the art form and characters on stage coming from various ethnic and religious backgrounds.

27. One of the important *Antigone* re-imaginations from this period was Şahika Tekand's *Euridice's Cry* (2006). In the article that Serap Erincin wrote about the play, she brings forth the relevance of the play's context to contemporary Turkey:

> Since the 1990s, the same thing has been happening with the Kurdish situation. A newspaper article of 2008 tells the story of a woman whose son joined the PKK, the armed Kurdish separatist group internationally recognized as a terrorist organization. Meanwhile, the woman's brother was a member of the Turkish military that has been fighting the PKK. She was afraid that her son would end up fighting his own uncle. Another news item described the agony of a family from the city of Bitlis: one of their sons died while fulfilling his military service—which is compulsory for every male citizen—and another joined the PKK. So, considering this history and the current situation, it is easy to see why the event preceding the opening of *Antigone*, and *Eurydice's Cry*, for that matter, would be remarkably significant for spectators from or interested in Turkey. The parallels between a Thebes under the rule of a military man after a period when brothers have killed one another, and Turkey's recent history, is striking. (2011, 183)

28. In 2014, Mek'an was one of the very few alternative theatres in Ankara, along with Farabi Stage.

29. In the early seventeenth century one of the high-ranking Ottoman Pashas was literally nicknamed as 'Murad Pasha, the Well-Digger' for using wells as mass graves for Alawis he killed while suppressing Celali Uprisings.

30. Jandarma İstihbarat ve Terörle Mücadele—Gendarmerie Intelligence and Counter-Terrorism.

31. From Emrah Serbes's short-story book *Erken Kaybedenler* (*The ones who lose early [in life]*, 2009).

32. Emine Fişek has written a remarkable article about *Trace*, which I mostly agree with; except her reading of the scene with Dağlı. Fişek states that the scene is 'left unexplained [...] mostly serve[ing] as comic relief' (Fişek 2018, 385). I think the scene is not unexplained but is actually a suggestion towards the absence of something, and what Fişek reads as comic relief, I read as humanisation.

33. State of Emergency ended in 2018 but its legislative impact continues to this day.

214   D. BAŞAR

References

Performances

Antigone2012 [later Antigone2013]. By Berfin Zenderlioğlu. Directed by Berfin Zenderlioğlu. Şermola Performans, İstanbul. 2012. Performers: Berfin Zenderlioğlu, Mîrza Metîn. Performance language: Kurdish with Turkish surtitles.

Bildiğin Gibi Değil "90'lı yıllarda Güneydoğu'da çocuk olmak." ["It Is Not as You Know It": Being a Child in 90's in Southeast Anatolia]. Adapted from the interviews conducted by Rojin Canan Akın, Funda Danışman in the same-titled book by Ülfet Sevdi, Bilge Açıkgöz, İsmail Yıldız, and Deniz Karaca. Directed by Ülfet Sevdi. Apr. 2012, Şermola Performans, İstanbul. Performers: Havin Funda Saç, Gülistan Sarbaş, Hevidar Bakır, İsmail Yıldız / Musicians: Dengbej Xalide, Barış Dodanlıoğlu, Nicolas Royer-Artuso, Murat Karadağ / Miniatures: CANAN. Performance language: Kurdish and Turkish.

Daf [Trap]. By Aydın Orak. 2012, Cihangir Sahne, İstanbul. Performers: Aydın Orak, Remzi Pamukçu, Dilan Güçer. Performance language: Kurdish.

Disco 5No'lu [Disco No.5]. By Mîrza Metîn. Dir. Berfin Zenderlîoglu. Şermola Performans, İstanbul. 2012. Performer: Mîrza Metîn. Performance language: Kurdish with Turkish surtitles.

Gor [Grave]. By Mîrza Metîn. Dir. Mîrza Metîn. Şermola Performans, İstanbul. 2013. Performers: Alan Ciwan, Berfin Zenderlioglu, Mensur Zîrek, Mîrza Metîn, Sadin Yeşiltaş. Performance language: Kurdish with Turkish surtitles.

Iska [Missed Target]. By Fuat Mete. Dir. Berkun Oya. Krek, İstanbul. 2013. Performers: Bilge Önal, Gülce Oral, Hare Sürel, Metin Coskun, Nazan Kesal, Ushan Çakır. Performance language: Turkish.

İz [Trace]. By Ahmet Sami Özbudak. Dir. Yesim Özsoy. GalataPerform, İstanbul. 2013. Performers: Okan Urun, Burak Safa Çalış, Batur Belirdi, Bertan Dirikolu, Yeşim Özsoy Gülan, Ceren Demirel, Görkem Dogan. Performance language: Turkish (Kurdish is spoken briefly in the play).

Kuyu [The Well]. By Pelin Temur. Dir. Ahmet Melih Yılmaz. Mek'an, Ankara. 2014. Performers: Sezen Keser, Beste Tunçay, Özge Bozdoğan. Performance language: Turkish.

Limonata [Lemonade]. By Sami Berat Marçalı. Dir. Murat Mahmutyazıcıoğlu. İkincikat, İstanbul. 2011. Performers: Deniz Türkalali, Heves Duygu Tüzün, Banu Çiçek Barutçugil, Tevfik Şahin, Barış Gönenen, Sezgi Mengi. Performance language: Turkish.

Nerde Kalmıştık? [Where Were We?]. By Ebru Nihan Celkan. Dir. Mîrza Metîn. Şermola Performans, İstanbul. 2013. Performers: Ararat Mor, Bahar Selvi, Barış Gönenen, Cem Uslu, Ceren Kıran, Doğan Keçin, Engin Aydın, Fulya Aksular, Fatih Özkan, Mertcan Kayretli, Merve Engin, Sadi Celil Cengiz. Performance language: Turkish.

Sürüne Sürüne Erkek Olmak. [Becoming a Man through Crawling]. Adapted from Pınar Selek's same named study and directed by Ülfet Sevdi. Nov. 2010, Kooperatif Art Performance Hall, İstanbul. Performers: Jülide Durmaz, Güray Dinçol, Gülsün Odabaş and Mustafa Çiçek. Performance language: Turkish.

Üst Kattaki Terorist [The Terrorist Upstairs]. Adapted from the short story of Emrah Serbes by Sami Berat Marçalı. Directed by Sami Berat Marçalı. İkincikat Karaköy,

İstanbul. 2014. Performers: Denizhan Akbaba, Banu Çiçek Barutçugil, Bedir Bedir, Gözde Kocaoğlu. Performance language: Turkish.

SECONDARY SOURCES

Ahıska, Meltem. 2010. *Occidentalism in Turkey: Questions of Modernity and National Identity in Turkish Radio Broadcasting*. London: Tauris Academic Studies.

Akar, Bilal. 2018. Transformation of the Kurdish Theater Field in Turkey between 1991 and 2017. Master's thesis, Koç University.

Akın, Rojin Canan, and Funda Danışman. 2011. *"Bildiğin Gibi Değil" 90'larda Güneydoğu'da Çocuk Olmak*. İstanbul: Metis Yayinlari.

"Ankara'da Yeni Bir Alternatif Sahne: Mek'an Sahne!" [A New Alternative Theatre in Ankara: Mek'an Stage!] Mimesis. Last modified October 30, 2014. Accessed October 26, 2018. http://www.mimesis-dergi.org/2014/10/ankarada-yeni-bir-alternatif-sahne-mekan-sahne/.

Baş, Elif. 2015. The Rise of Kurdish Theatre in İstanbul. *Theatre Survey* 56 (3): 314–335.

Başar, Deniz. Performative Publicness: Alternative Theater in Turkey after 2000s. Master's thesis, Bogazici University, 2014. Accessed October 31, 2018. https://www.cademia.edu/7942915/Performative_Publicness_Alternative_Theater_in_Turkey_After_2000s.

"Basın Açıklaması: 'Bildiğiniz Gibi Değil!'" [Press Release: "It is not as you know it!"]. Mimesis. Last modified December 23, 2011. Accessed October 25, 2018. http://www.mimesis-dergi.org/2011/12/bildiginiz-gibi-degil/.

"Bildiğin Gibi Değil nü. kolektif ten Yeni Oyun" ["It is not as you know it"—new play from nu.kolektif]. evetbenim. Last modified December 15, 2011. Accessed October 25, 2018. https://evetbenim.com/bildigin-gibi-degil-nu-kolektif-ten-yeni-oyun/.

"bildiğin gibi değil_ teaser." Video file. Vimeo. Posted by Guliz Saglam, 2012. Accessed October 25, 2018. https://vimeo.com/36695447.

Bozarslan, Hamit. "Between integration, autonomization and radicalization. Hamit Bozarslan on the Kurdish Movement and the Turkish Left." Interview by Marlies Casier and Olivier Grojean. In "Ideological Productions and Transformations: the Kurdistan Workers' Party (PKK) and the Left," special issue, *European Journal of Turkish Studies—Social Sciences on Contemporary Turkey*, no. 14 (2012).

Büyükuysal, Deniz. "Kuyu ya da dikici bellek" [The well or the sewing memory]. Gezite. Last modified October 28, 2014. Accessed January 30, 2016. http://gezite.org/kuyu-ya-da-dikici-bellek/.

"Call for Targeted Academic Boycott of Turkey." *Academic Boycott of Turkey DO NOT BE A PARTY TO CRIMES IN TURKISH HIGHER EDUCATION* (blog). Entry posted June 7, 2017. Accessed October 26, 2018. https://academicboycottofturkey.wordpress.com.

Çelik, Duygu. Dengbejlik Geleneği ve Türkiye'deki Kürt Tiyatrosuna Etkileri [Dengbej Tradition and Its Effects on Kurdish Theatre in Turkey]. PhD diss., İstanbul University, 2017.

Celkan, Ebru Nihan. 2013. *Toplu Oyunları*. Taksim, İstanbul: Mitos Boyut Yayınları.

Chanter, Tina. 2011. *Whose Antigone?: The Tragic Marginalization of Slavery*. Albany: State University of New York Press.

216   D. BAŞAR

Erincin, Serap. 2011. Performing Rebellion: Eurydice's Cry in Turkey. In *Antigone on the Contemporary World Stage*, ed. Helene P. Foley and Erin B. Mee, 172–184. Oxford: Oxford University Press.

Fişek, Emine. 2018. Palimpsests of Violence: Urban Dispossession and Political Theatre in İstanbul. *Comparative Drama—Special Issue: Performing Turkishness* 52 (3-4): 349–371.

Frantz, Gilda. 2014. Individual and Collective Trauma. *Psychological Perspectives* 57: 243–245.

Güçbilmez, Beliz. 2016. *Zaman / Zemin / Zuhur: Gerçekçi Türk Tiyatrosunda Minyatür Kurgusu [Time, Space and Appearance: the Form of Miniature in the Turkish Realist Theatre]*. 2nd ed. Ankara: Dost Yayınevi.

Habermas, Jürgen. *The Structural Transformation of the Public Sphere: An Inguiry into a Category of Bourgeois Society*. Translated by Thomas Burger. Edited by Thomas McCarthy. 12th ed. Cambridge: MIT Press, 2001. First published in 1962 in German, first published in English in 1991.

Hamelink, Wendelmoet. 2016. *The Sung Home: Narrative, Morality, and the Kurdish Nation*. Leiden; Boston: Brill.

İnce, Elif. "Turkey's state of emergency puts Kurdish theatre in a chokehold." ifex. Last modified January 5, 2017. Accessed July 29, 2019. https://ifex.org/turkeys-state-of-emergency-puts-kurdish-theatre-in-a-chokehold/.

Keleş, Şükrü. "Kuyu: Bütün bunlar ne garip!" [Well: How awkward all these things are!] Evrensel. Last modified March 1, 2015. Accessed January 30, 2016. http://www.evrensel.net/haber/106349/kuyu-butun-bunlar-ne-garip.

Kellermann, Peter Felix. 2007. *Sociodrama and Collective Trauma*. London: Jessica Kingsley.

"Kürt Tiyatrosu'nda Yeni Bir grup: Teatra Demsal" [A New Theatre Group in Kurdish Theatre: Teatra Demsal]. Mimesis. Last modified December 5, 2010. Accessed October 25, 2018. http://www.mimesis-dergi.org/2010/05/kurt-tiyatrosu%E2%80%99nda-yeni-bir-grup-teatra-demsal/.

Leveton, Eva. 2010. *Healing Collective Trauma with Sociodrama and Drama Therapy*. New York: Springer Pub.

"nü.kollektif 'Bildiğin Gibi Değil'" [nü.kollektif "It is not as you know it"]. Facebook. Last modified April 2012. Accessed October 25, 2018. https://www.facebook.com/events/807928545964413/.

Özyürek, Esra. 2019. Introduction to *Authoritarianism and Resistance in Turkey: Conversations on Democratic and Social Challenges*. In, ed. Esra Özyürek, Gaye Özpınar, and Emrah Altındiş, 1–8. Cham, Switzerland: Springer.

"Pınar Selek." Pınar Selek ile dayanışma [Solidarity with Pinar Selek]. Accessed October 25, 2018. https://www.pinarselek.com/public/destek.aspx?id=45.

Porgebol. "#KUYU'dan cikanlar" [the things that come out of the #WELL]. wordpress. Last modified September 25, 2014. Accessed January 30, 2016. https://porgebol.wordpress.com/2014/09/25/kuyudan-cikanlar/.

Romanska, Magda. 2012. *The Post-traumatic Theatre of Grotowski and Kantor: History and Holocaust in Akropolis and the Dead Class*. London: Anthem.

Scalbert-Yücel, Clémence. 2009. "The Invention of a Tradition: Diyarbakır's Dengbêj Project." Abstract. *European Journal of Turkish Studies* 10.

Selek, Pınar. 2008. *Sürüne Sürüne Erkek Olmak*. İstanbul: İletisim Yayınları.

Sevdi, Ülfet, "Sürüne Sürüne Erkek Olmak." Interview. Pinar Selek. Last modified February 28, 2011. Accessed October 25, 2018. https://www.pinarselek.com/public/page_item.aspx?id=1271.

Sevdi, Ülfet, Nicolas Royer-Artuso, Bilge Açıkgöz, and Havin Funda Saç. Last modified December, 2011. "nü.kolektif: Bu "nü" Bildiğin "nü" değil!" Interview by Öykü Gürpınar and Nihan Acar. Mimesis. Accessed October 25, 2018. http://www.mimesis-dergi.org/2011/12/nu-kolektif-bu-nu-bildigin-nu-degil/.

Silberman, Marc. 2012. Bertolt Brecht, Politics, and Comedy. *Social Research* 79 (1): 169–188.

Somasundaram, Daya. 2014. Addressing Collective Trauma: Conceptualisations and Interventions. *Intervention* 12 (1): 43–60.

"SUMMARY OF THE BOOKS." Pinar Selek Solidarity Platform. Accessed October 25, 2018. https://www.pinarselek.com/public/page_item.aspx?id=246.

"surune surune erkek olmak / nu kolektif." Video file. Vimeo. Posted by Guliz Saglam, 2010. Accessed October 25, 2018. https://vimeo.com/17466274.

"Sürüne Sürüne Erkek Olmak, Tiyatro Sahnesinde" ["Becoming a Man through Crawling" is on Stage]. Bianet. Last modified November 26, 2010. Accessed October 25, 2018. http://m.bianet.org/bianet/kultur/126273-surune-surune-erkek-olmak-tiyatro-sahnesinde.

Şentürk, Burcu. "Invisibility of a Common Sorrow: Families of the Deceased in Turkey's Kurdish Conflict." In *Cultural Difference and Social Solidarity: Critical Cases*, by Scott H. Boyd and Mary Ann Walter, 99-116. Newcastle: Cambridge Scholars, 2012.

Şermola Performans. Accessed November 9, 2018. https://www.sermolaperformans.com/.

Theidon, Kimberly Susan. 2013. *Intimate Enemies: Violence and Reconciliation in Peru*. Philadelphia: University of Pennsylvania Press.

Tosun, Funda. "ERMENİ DEVRİMCİ DEMİRCİOĞLU'NDAN DİYARBAKIR CEZAEVİ 'Bir Canavarmışım Gibi Subaylar Beni Görmeye Geliyordu" [DIYARBAKIR PRISON FROM ARMENIAN REVOLUTIONARY DEMİRCİOĞLU "Officers were coming to see me as if I was a monster"]. *Agos* (Istanbul, Turkey), May 28, 2011. Accessed May 28, 2020. https://m.bianet.org/biamag/azinliklar/130311-bir-canavarmisim-gibi-subaylar-beni-gormeye-geliyordu.

Vardar, Nilay. "Nerde Kalmıştık?" [Where were we?] Bianet. Accessed January 26, 2016. http://bianet.org/bianet/sanat/141486-nerde-kalmistik.

Watts, Nicole F. 2011. *Activists in Office: Kurdish Politics and Protest in Turkey*. Seattle, Washington DC: University of Washington Press.

Werth, Brenda G. 2010. *Theatre, Performance, and Memory Politics in Argentina*. New York: Palgrave Macmillan.

CHAPTER 12

Staging Race in White South African Afrikaans Theatre

David Peimer

The two primary ideologies of totalitarianism…; one that interpreted history as
class struggle, one that interpreted history as a natural fight of the races…are
core to imperialist policies.
—Hannah Arendt (1994: 206–207)
The most potent weapon in the hands of the oppressor is the mind of the
oppressed.
—Steve Biko (2002: 43)

1 Introduction

This chapter seeks to broaden scholarly discussion on the ways race is represented in contemporary South African theatre from a white Afrikaner perspective. The chapter extends Steve Biko's (2002: 43) observation that the most powerful 'weapon for the oppressor is the mind of the oppressed', asking if, logically, it follows inversely that the most powerful weapon for the oppressed is the mind of the oppressor. This opens up inquiry into ways in which critical analysis of theatrical imagery and narrative can illuminate both the construction of the oppressor's mind among racialising processes of stereotyping the Other and how this is subverted or dismantled. To this end, the chapter uses a critical matrix which incorporates Homi Bhabha's critique of racial politics, Hannah Arendt's on race and totalitarianism and Megan Lewis's on the Laager

D. Peimer (✉)
Edge Hill University, Ormskirk, UK
e-mail: Peimerd@edgehill.ac.uk

© The Author(s), under exclusive license to Springer Nature
Switzerland AG 2021
T. Morosetti, O. Okagbue (eds.), *The Palgrave Handbook of Theatre and*
Race, https://doi.org/10.1007/978-3-030-43957-6_12

219

in Afrikaner memory, culture and identity construction, to explore three selected plays by Reza de Wet, translated from Afrikaans.

2   BHABHA AND PROCESSES OF STEREOTYPING

Homi Bhabha (1994: 64) provides an analysis of how legacies of race and racism have been and continue to be located at the core of much ideological and societal structuring in the colonial and post-colonial era. For Bhabha, racism is founded on the 'paradox of otherness' observed in the process of stereotyping. In essence, this process necessitates the exaggeration of the Other's perceived or projected difference, whether in physical appearance or essentialised psychological attributes, or both. However, the oppressor must stabilise this exaggerated difference, and assert it as natural, in order to justify it, and the actions that issue from it. This contradiction produces anxieties, as the dominant group and individuals within it oscillate continuously between a reified, othered account of essential difference, and endless attempts to contain contradictions arising from encounters with un-co-operative and complex social realities. This produces a resort to repetition on the part of the oppressor, as a further device for containing anxieties. Bhabha further suggests that containing oppressor anxieties by repetition generates a recurring resort to a racialised discourse of fixity. In short, fixity is needed to try to contain this resultant anxiety or condition of ambivalence, and repetition is the method. As Bhabha notes, ambivalence is 'one of the most significant psychic strategies of discriminatory power' (1994: 66). Further: 'The stereotype operates in relation to the objective of fixity: the stereotype...vacillates between what is always "in place", already known, and something that must be anxiously repeated...as if the essential duplicity of the Asiatic or the bestial sexual license of the African needs no proof, and can never be proved' (Bhabha 1994: 66).

For Bhabha, the anxious repetition of the stereotype is a necessity which results from, and points to an inability on the part of the oppressor to transcend insecurities produced by their performance of the dominant role. In short, the stereotyping process produces anxiety because of the oscillation between two irreconcilable polarities: exaggeration of difference and the attempt to fix racial hierarchy as stable. For this reason, stereotyping is less an issue of 'the ready recognition of images as positive or negative' (Bhabha 1994: 67) and more a function of the dynamics of acts of stereotyping. As he notes, 'the anxiety of difference can never be...eliminated, but can only be briefly assuaged before it (must be) again repeated as part of the stereotyping process...and...because of this...the same old stories must be told (compulsively) again' (Bhabha 1994: 77). Finally, Bhabha recognises that protecting myths of racial purity and origin is essential in the othering process—the 'myth of historical origination' (Bhabha 1994: 74)—that is, the prioritisation of one's own racial type as necessarily superior to that of others.

3 Lewis and the Laager

In her seminal work on the representation of white Afrikaners in South African theatre, Megan Lewis notes: 'performing whitely connotes…a state of being, an ideology, a set of behaviours…an enactment…or staging with distinctly white attributes' (Lewis 2016: 11). Lewis focuses on the *laager*—the circle of ox wagons that signified safety for Afrikaners trekking inland to avoid the advancing British—as a metaphor for Afrikaner self-definition. Rather than submit to British rule, they packed some belongings in their wagons, left their farms and livelihoods, and trekked into uncharted territory in northern South Africa. Arendt contends that:

> The Great Trek, to escape British rule, and leave their homes and farms, suggests how they became rootless, a part of nature, a tribe roaming…rather than accept the limits imposed on them by British rule…they left all their material possessions behind…and even the gold rush did not interest them. They feared the 'Uitlanders (Outsiders)' more, and trekked further into South Africa. (Arendt 1994: 256)

She argues, further, that 'they perceived themselves as the Chosen Race of Africa with a Covenant with God to rule the African…whereas British colonialism utilized race and bureaucracy which grew out of ruthless military discipline… race was focussed on by the Boers in their fear of and desire for Africa' (Arendt 1994: 241–242). As Lewis notes, the laager consisted of two contradictory parts: the circle of wagons, seemingly impermeable; and the spaces in between the wagons, the sites of vulnerability and potential contamination. 'Like whiteness, the laager must maintain a belief in its infallibility to remain intact and powerful and, like whiteness, it becomes vulnerable to anxiety when its porousness is revealed' (Lewis 2016: 28). Lewis reminds us that the Afrikaner laager from its inception in the early nineteenth-century Great Trek, to its culmination in the 1948 elections that brought Afrikaners to power with the institutionalised racism of apartheid, embedded itself as a core notion in Afrikaner identity and mythology.

After the Afrikaner defeat in the Anglo-Boer war, Lewis notes, 'how Afrikaner nationalists transformed their defeat into a foundational myth, imagined a unified volk (Afrikaans for nation) out of a group of disparate Boers [Afrikaans for farmers]' (Lewis 2016: 25). This was helped by romanticising the 1830s Great Trek and the 'role of the laager in differentiating them from the other' (Lewis 2016: 25). In the construction of memory and national identity, Afrikaner narratives combined white patriarchy—'rugged masculinity and docile femaleness' (Lewis 2016: 43)—Calvinism, the notion of the 'Chosen Race of Africa' and the icon of the Volksmoeder ('Mother of the Nation') who 'preserves civilisation and light amid the brutality and darkness of Africa' (Lewis 2016: 44).

4 Reza de Wet

Reza de Wet (1952–2012) was an Afrikaans playwright (Middeke et al. 2015: 146) who won more awards in South Africa than any other dramatist. Her plays subvert and dismantle notions of Afrikaner identity, by deconstructing singular, historically framed narratives of Afrikaner myths of identity. Her dramaturgy exposes narratives located in white racism in relation to both themselves and the black other. And when the dismantling of the mind of the oppressor is staged, audiences may grasp the dynamics of racist social processes. Her dramaturgical aesthetic can be characterised as magic realism in its use of grotesque parody and satire, interweaving aspects of Western tradition—Lorca, Genet, Chekov—with the certain features of ancient African storytelling: ancestral, 'other-world forces', ritual, non-verbal and verbal storytelling, and quick transformations of character, space and time. Although mostly set in the early twentieth century, her plays' intertextual aesthetic—brings into focus contemporary Afrikaner identity.

De Wet often deploys Genet's strategy of staging gender and parent/child role-play, to explore the 'brutality and innocence of childhood...in an authoritarian society...primal drives...isolated farm lands...naivety and cruelty with a strong mystical bent...She sees Afrikaners as an indigenous tribe moulded by their experiences in Africa and her plays are grotesque parodies of Afrikaner society, Afrikaner Calvinism, authoritarian repressive forces' (de Wet 2005: 21). Anticipating Bhabha's notion of the paradox of racism, Arendt contends that the Boers 'were the only European group who, in complete isolation, lived in black Africa with a fright of something like themselves, yet ought not to be like them...their ideology incorporating notions of racial superiority, God, church, Chosen Race' (de Wet 2005: 21).

5 The Plays: *African Gothic*

The play was first performed in the Apartheid era (1985) and revived Post-Apartheid in 2005. The dramatic action is set in the desolate rural landscape of a ruined farm, where, although remnants of former grandeur suggest a vanishing era, two young adults, brother and sister, Frikkie and Sussie, live in a flea-ridden, decaying farmhouse. They sleep all day and dig for water in the muddied main room of the house each night. The laager has become a decaying myth of dismantled fantasy; Afrikaners desperately try to assert racial superiority and difference, but this has imploded under the weight of anxieties resulting from struggles to maintain it as a stable concept. This metaphorical world is a devastating subversion of Apartheid ideology. After urinating in her 'tattered nightgown' (de Wet 2005: 23), Sussie's first words in the play are:

> Sussie: Ssh...I still sleeping. I'm dreaming.
> Frikkie (*in a vest, faded shorts, mud on his legs and feet*): Did the fleas bite you too? (de Wet 2005: 43)

Outside, we hear the sounds of rain, wind and wild, howling jackals. Each night the siblings also role-play both themselves as children, and their parents. Early in the play, we note:

Sussie: Let's play our stories.
Frikkie: I know all the stories.
Sussie: …. Pa called me his little doll…put my legs…and…
Frikkie: Let's play…Ma…and me. (de Wet 2005: 44–45)

5.1 *The Laager and the Family in* African Gothic

Later the brother and sister role-play themselves as children 'listening at Ma and Pa's bedroom door' (de Wet 2005: 24), they hear Ma accuse Frikkie of wetting his sheets. This had led to a whipping from his father. We witness the emergence of violence in the father/son context in response to the collapse of the stabilising process required to produce stereotypes necessary to maintain the 'superior white' myth:

> Sussie (*as their mother to Frikkie who plays himself as a child*): You've messed your sheets again…These things are of the devil! You think about girls…Repent!…Your father will thrash it out of you. (de Wet 2005: 26)

Alina is an elderly African lady who was the servant for their parents and now for them. As we slowly discover, Frikkie and Sussie killed their parents when they were children, and though they imagined they were liberating themselves from authoritarian brutality, actually affirmed it as their characteristic condition. When Grove, a white Afrikaans lawyer from the city, arrives at the gate to discuss their inheritance from an aunt, Sussie instantly changes to her child-like state and asks:

> Sussie: Is he coming to see Ma and Pa?
> Frikkie: Ma and Pa aren't here!…Look what's out there…mangy cow, two chickens, rusted plough, broken tractor. (de Wet 2005: 26)
> Then Sussie shifts to being her mother:
> Sussie: He's a visitor…must have tea. Old Alina! Frederick, get dressed, for visitors, like after church (de Wet 2005: 30)
> Grove enters:
> Grove: Mr, Ms Cilliers. I'm Mr Grove, from Bloemfontein…If you forgive me from saying…I've never seen white people living like this (de Wet 2005: 32)
> After a brief pause, Sussie, role-playing her mother, calls Alina:
> Sussie: Alina! Have you lit the lamps? Bring them. At once! (Middeke et al. 2015: 149)
> A short while later, Grove, watching Alina, says:
> Grove: Look how she does it! …they hate us. They'd like to kill us. You can see it in their eyes
> Alina (*glares at him…violently speaks*): Sooka!
> Grove: What did you say? Watch yourself! (*to Frikkie*) …dangerous, … the black woman… don't trust her…brutal murderers. (Middeke et al. 2015: 148)

Kruger suggests that *African Gothic* is a 'powerful critique of the myths entrenched in traditional views of white Afrikaner identity' (Middeke et al. 2015: 148). The 'superior race' notion is revealed to be a set of brutal, cruel authoritarian attributes and inherited notions of the psychological laager—family, parent/child, Calvinist ideas of 'purity' of religion, masculinity, femininity, the Fatherland, the Volksmoeder and the 'Chosen race'—are dismantled as myth, and shown to be about racial hierarchy, land, incest, family taboos, murder, hate. Alina avails of the porousness of this mythical laager, to watch from inside its boundaries, and audiences are enabled to observe, through her eyes, the cruel, yet anxious attempt to repeat tropes of the 'superior white race'. As its fear of the 'inferior' black other is staged and exposed, Bhabha's account of the racialised dynamics of the stereotyping process is revealed. Alina is not the stereotyped 'noble black person', but rather a silent observer, witnessing the dismantling of notions of 'superior' race to reveal their foundational barbarity. Racism plays out as a grotesque parody of its own myths, and child-like role-play, shows the mind of the oppressor, in its ruthless selfishness, and incestuous introversion, to pursue power at all costs, as superiority over the other. The play is in fact a 'parody of the Afrikaner pastoral novel' (de Wet 2005: 34) which portrays idyllic illusions of a past of peace-loving, paternalistic landowners, benignly disposed to persons of different skin pigmentation, and heroic Davids, resisting the Goliath of British colonialism. De Wet gives us a dramaturgy of the 'destruction of this derelict paradise...with the comedy and horror of Gothic drama' (Middeke et al. 2015: 148). Scenes of increasingly crude racism towards Alina, and of visceral shock—including public urination, allusions to incest, eroticised whipping and murder—strip unflinchingly the thin veneer of self-serving, self-deluding myth concealing a brutal past.

5.2   Afrikaner Identity and Calvinism

Within the psyche of their laager, the siblings play out rituals of behaviour which deconstruct almost every myth they were brought up to believe. Frikkie and Sussie play out being the children they once were and subject to extreme Calvinism, hierarchy, belief in being part of the Chosen Race, rugged masculinity and submissive femaleness, with the whip being used by their parents. An example of the depth of Calvinism is:

> Sussie (*looking at a picture of Grove's wife*): She's got red nails and a red mouth...Bad...My mother says that women who want to improve on God's work are wicked and damned...powdered face, blood red nails...are of the devil. (de Wet 2005: 43–44)

They also re-enact how they murdered their parents in an act of rage against the strictures of authoritarianism and role-play games suggestive of incest entangled with role-playing their parents. The effect of all this in front of Alina further reveals the dismantling of the myths of superiority, harsh barbarism and what happens when the 'ambivalence or anxiety of racism' breaks down in characters set up to be constructed by a particular sense of culture, memory, family and nationhood. We, and Alina, also observe Sussie as both the 'demented child-like sister and at times, their terrifying Calvinist influenced Volksmoeder' (de Wet 2005: 49) when Sussie reverts to role-playing herself as a child with her mother:

> Sussie: Ma will be angry...Ma will say I'm a bad girl...'A disgrace to our family and God' ...Wicked! Wicked!...Bad, bad girl!And later, Sussie, as a child, says to Frikkie:
> Sussie: Let's play Ma asks Frikkie about wetting his sheets...
> Frikkie: Have I done something wrong Ma?
> Sussie (*as his mother*): These are devil thoughts, ...your father will thrash it out of you
> Frikkie (*as child*): I sometimes...think about girls.
> Frikkie: She looked like you Ma!
> Sussie: You're bad, wicked! Pa will thrash. (de Wet 2005: 39)

Then, suddenly, they switch to role-playing Sussie as a child and Frikkie as her father:

> Sussie (*child's voice*): Can I ride you Pa? ...Pa's little girl...his little doll...kiss me Pa... (de Wet 2005: 54)

Frikkie has the brutality of his father and the primal innocence of boyhood. In short, both siblings move between fantasy, memory and reality as they live out their deconstructed identities. This dramaturgical aesthetic not only employs magic realism as a form, but also shows the breakdown of their assumed entitlement of racial 'superiority', and the collapse of the identity contradictions that Bhabha notes. The theatrical device of employing a silent Alina heightens this observation for us, the audience. Instead of focusing primarily on the conflict between black and white characters, de Wet viscerally subverts the white Afrikaner identity, showing it as embodying the anxious, contradictory attributes of the colonial, post-colonial and apartheid 'superior white' oppressor.

Further portraying this is the character of Grove, who is a 'modern', Westernised, educated, seemingly 'civilised' city lawyer. He comes to visit Frikkie and Sussie in the farmhouse and verbally denigrates the siblings, showing the notion of homogeneity within the laager to be a purist myth:

> Grove: How can you live in a derelict house without furniture? The farm...in rack and ruin...making no effort to improve the situation...a Boer (white Afrikaner farmer) always makes a plan! (de Wet 2005: 56)

As the narrative evolves, he becomes increasingly arrogant and frightened and reveals his crude racism towards Alina. As Bhabha might suggest, he exaggerates difference more and more with a verbal assault illustrating the master/

226   D. PEIMER

servant set of contradictions. And the more he tries to normalise or stabilise his stereotyping of the racialised other, the harsher his racism emerges in his attempt to try to contain his unconscious anxious contradictions through repetition of attitude.

5.3   'Superiority', Incest and Authoritarianism

Frikkie and Sussie exhibit less anxiety in their assumption of the exaggerated difference between themselves and Alina. Grove, however, begins with a slight assumption of superiority but, with de Wet's parodic irony, he becomes much harsher in his attitude towards Alina. We observe this process as he loses his ability to control his 'anxiety or ambiguity of ambivalence' towards her as the pressure from the way the siblings threaten and terrify him increases. He shows shock and fear of Frikkie and Sussie with their living in 'filth' and sees them as 'mad', but towards Alina, he reveals a hateful, cruel, master-like attitude which repeats itself with increasing viciousness. Alina's reactions to him are physicalised and minimally verbalised, and the dramaturgical effect is to heighten our empathy for her. The siblings do not pretend to inhabit masks of a 'civilised demeanour' whereas Grove does. When this collapses under the weight of his contradictions, his arrogant and brutal assumption of being her 'master' emerges repetitively, together with his assumption of being part of a 'Chosen, superior race'. In short, his descent from charming civility to barbaric hypocrisy enrages her and the audience/reader. His assumption of superiority towards Frikkie and Sussie is based on how 'degraded and neglectful' they have become, but his attitude to Alina is based purely on a racial categorisation and through this the notion of racial purity of origin is exposed.

The further dismantling of the myth of Afrikaner 'superiority' is suggested as de Wet alludes to connections between incest and authoritarianism. Sussie says to Grove:

> Sussie: Ma taught me to be nice to guests.... sleep on the bed with me.... Pa's dead so you can use his pillow. (de Wet 2005: 57)

Sussie then softly sings a song about the thousands of children who died in British concentration camps during the Anglo-Boer war. The dialogue at this point shifts to observations of the farm and Afrikaner longing for an idealised sense of belonging to the land:

> Grove: There is nothing out there...I've never seen such desolation.
>   Frikkie: Rain doesn't come... sun burns into me...But, it's...where I belong.
>   Grove: ...faithful to our forefathers. (de Wet 2005: 59)

From nostalgic yearnings, the dramaturgy moves back to notions of violence and authoritarianism:

> Sussie: The sjambok...grandpa....pa used it on us...make a man of Frikkie.

12 STAGING RACE IN WHITE SOUTH AFRICAN AFRIKAANS THEATRE   227

Grove: .... yes, my little boy...knows the difference between right and wrong. (de Wet 2005: 59)

Later, the conversation changes as the siblings play out more child/parent games and Grove gets angry:

Grove: Stop behaving like this! Like a child! You're a grown woman...this is ridiculous! (de Wet 2005: 68–69)

Frikkie gets the rope he will soon tie Grove up in to whip him to death, and ominously replies:

Frikkie: You made my sister cry. (de Wet 2005: 9)

The argument increases, then subsides briefly and Grove tries to sleep. First, he orders Alina:

Grove: I'm talking to you! Understand? Wake me up...morning!
Later, lying in the bed, Sussie calls out to Frikkie:
Sussie: He touched me!
Frikkie: Filthy...disgusting...animal!
After a short while Grove sleeps, they tie the rope around him. He wakes up and they role-play with the terrified Grove:
Sussie: Ma and Pa scolded us...did things...Just like you...
Then she suddenly switches to role-playing her mother:
Sussie: You will burn in hell!...Pappie's little doll...Evil...your father will flay you both alive.... You are not my children...you ...touch each other...so much.... Spawn of the Devil...
Then the role-play switches:
Sussie: Frikkie and Sussie put Ma and Pa away...We play it every day...our best game. (de Wet 2000: 145)

Finally, tied up, Grove is helpless, and Frikkie whips him to death, with blood everywhere.

5.4   *Gender and Role-Play*

During the play, Grove, unaware of the contradiction, idealises his white Afrikaner wife as the loving, docile woman and strong Volksmoeder. By contrast, regarding Alina, he implicates/problematises gender in his racialising of the other. In this paradigm, Grove, suggestive of the white Afrikaner psychic laager, tries to accommodate numerous classes, levels of status and sophistication, but the 'vulnerable gaps' in the circle of wagons must try to keep the racialised Other from entering. In Bhabha's thinking, Grove is trying to help contain the anxiety resulting from his 'exaggeration of difference' between self and Other in the stereotyping process.

Ironically, as Arendt suggests, Afrikaner myths inform identity but the more they trekked away from British control of their 'freedom', the closer they got

228   D. PEIMER

to being part of the nature they despised and desired in the way they defined persons as being 'inferior because of how close they are to nature' (see Arendt quote on p. 3). Nature, ancestors, the spirit world are seen as closer to myths of Afrikaner identity than that of white English-speaking South Africans. Thus, the laager is shown to be delusional in being constructed to 'keep whites in and blacks out' and thereby colonialism and apartheid operational. It is porous, 'vulnerable to anxiety' and through this process, the racialising of identity is represented. It is also ironic that it is not Alina, but the siblings who subvert Grove's racial assumption of superiority as they shock, disgust and terrify his sense of 'performing whiteness'. The laager is not only porous to the black Other, but its own internal white other. Unknown to Grove, Frikkie damages Grove's car engine and he cannot get back to the city and his 'ideal' family. That night Grove walks outside in the rain and dark, surrounded by wild jackal sounds, to try to get to the neighbouring farm. He gets lost and returns to Frikkie and Sussie's filthy farmhouse and asks them if he can stay the night. During the night, they role-play their parents and themselves as children, and taunt, mock and scare him, eventually accusing him of inappropriately touching Sussie. Later, they tie him up and whip him to death with a sjambok (a short whip). Throughout, Alina watches, silently or occasionally softly singing a Sotho song, observing, and we sense her thoughts while the notion of the 'superior white Afrikaner' is subverted. Furthering this, all the white characters treat Alina as a servant, inferior and only capable of manual labour. With her aesthetic of combining dream-like worlds, role-play, the desolate landscape, de Wet's sense of magic realism is employed to enhance the illusion of a circle of psychological wagons and the subversion of the notion of 'superiority'.

The importance of religion in the colonising project is shown in the play by the way Calvinism informs the myths of Afrikaner identity and nationhood. De Wet develops this by linking it to gender and the maintenance of hierarchy in the stereotyping process. Calvinism is also observed in relation to notions of maleness and femaleness. Frikkie is the rugged, wild, uneducated, 'uncivilised', physical farm male who repeats the harsh authoritarianism—framed as religiously determined—of his father, while Grove is represented as the Calvinist observing, law-abiding, educated, sophisticated male. Sussie role-plays her mother's Volksmoeder authoritarianism under the yoke of religious control. This severe repression drives the child-like and real Sussie into contrasting impulses of repression and rebellion. Most importantly, all three characters see Alina as a servant devoid of femaleness, individuality, motherhood, part of a cultural history of thousands of years, a childhood, having her own family. In short, a character defined in a singular way, a stereotype whose difference is highly exaggerated and must be kept in that position and repeatedly, as Bhabha would suggest. Yet, the more they define Alina as only a servant, a body with no other qualities, the more we perceive the processes of their harsh racism. Extending this notion, we observe the depth of Sartre's insight into the Self/Other relationship: 'The Jew is the invention of the anti-semite' (Sartre 1995: 74). From Sartre, we can extrapolate the question: Is the black subject the invention of the racialising white subject?

5.5 Breathing In

The play—written in 2000 but this chapter is based on a 2005 performance—is set in a cowshed on a desolate farm in the last days of the Anglo-Boer War (1902). It is night, and candles, saddles, leather horse belts fill the space. During the play, the 'sound of soft, soaking rain is often heard' (de Wet 2000: 149). The badly injured, dying Boer General lies on a wooden feeding trough covered in animal skin. Throughout the play we hear him make breathing and gasping sounds with very few words, suggesting his fevered, delirious state. Anna and her daughter, Annie, appear to be tending to him, but know it is pointless. Annie is thin and very pale. The dramatic action focuses on Annie who has kept her youth and beauty by breathing in the last breath of dying men who her mother persuades to be murdered for her as they fall under her 'spell' of beauty, youth and innocence. This seemingly absurd premise works because de Wet creates a world that combines a sense of ordinary familiarity with that of the frighteningly strange (de Wet 2000: 147–148)—a Gothic tale imbued with magic realism, the horror of a wartime reality interwoven with the dark comedy of a world of long-forgotten ancestral ghostliness. This intertextuality of worlds is key to de Wet's aesthetic and strikingly different to the great tradition of anti-apartheid Protest theatre in the way cultural stereotypes and the oppressor/oppressed relationship is represented.

5.6 Gender and Identity Parodied

Brandt is the young soldier who arrives to give dispatches to the General and await his orders. His narrative is of the soldier who obeys all of a higher rank, believes in the Afrikaner myths of duty, loyalty, patriotism and sacrifice of life for the fatherland. Anna has experienced starvation, disease and the deaths of thousands in the British concentration camps, plus the burning of many Boer farms by the British army. She no longer embodies the Volksmoeder type and ridicules all the inherited myths of Afrikaner identity. In essence, she parodies and mocks the notions of self-sacrifice, fatherland, patriotism and the insular world of the laager concept. Anna dismantles Afrikaner patriarchy with matriarchal domination—the soldier, the General are mocked as being naïve. She subverts their notion of Afrikaner masculinity in the way she 'turns Brandt's ideal of self-sacrifice against himself' into sacrificing his life for his 'love' for Annie's apparent love and beauty.

> Annie: Everything led me here…where you could find me…I've been lost…so lost and alone…
> Brandt: Your face…beautiful…your hand…so small…cold…
> Very gently, he kisses her face and hand
> Anna enters
> Anna: Mud under my nails…I'm filthy…my girl, thank the Adjutant for being so good to you. (de Wet 2000: 154–155)

230   D. PEIMER

Parodying Plato's sense of a 'soulmate' and the ancient Jason myth, de Wet employs dark comedy in how Anna turns Brandt against obeying his internalised Afrikaner myths and his General, into self-sacrifice for the 'purity' of love, not the purity of the 'Chosen Race' or tales of Afrikaner 'purity of origin'. If Alina in *African Gothic* enables us to strip away the layers of Afrikaner national myths, here, Anna is the catalyst for a similar function.

In both plays, it is the female principle that is core to de Wet's dramaturgical strategy of ridiculing and subverting national mythologies that construct white Afrikaner identity to be 'superior 'with the 'laager' myth being central. The process of racism is seen to thus require defining the black other's exaggerated difference as 'inferior' and servile. Further, while Anna parodies the insular myth of the laager, all she wants is money from people who stay with them. This is her only way to survive the war and keep her daughter youthful and alive, through the dying breath of young men. Survival is all that matters. However, we also note Anna's self-interest:

Anna: You're all I have in the world. You're everything to me. If you leave me... I'll be all alone
    Suddenly the General feverishly shouts:
    General: I'll never surrender...Take cover!.... Here they come!...Our fatherland....
    Without sentiment, Anna retorts:
    Anna: It's war. Now don't start feeling sorry for him...His breath is rancid! It reeks of fever! Well, it's no use dwelling on these things. What's past is past and there's an end to it...we don't have time to waste...everything's difficult these days. (de Wet 2000: 184)

And when Brandt enters, he immediately defines himself as loyal to the General and the Afrikaner myths which construct his identity:

Brandt: Open the door. It's Adjutant Brandt! I have urgent business with the General.
    Anna: I told you I would take care of him. I certainly hope you'll give us a little reward...I have to make a living.
    Brandt: You want me to pay you?
    Anna: I have to get by somehow. These are hard times.
    Brandt: For   nursing   the   General?...He's   lost   his   son, wife...farm...Everything...He's given up everything for his fatherland and you want me to pay you?
    Anna: If I perform a service, I should get paid. It's only right.
    Brandt: Do you know what we suffer? No sleep...food...giving everything. But what can I expect from you...a homeless, rootless...parasite! You don't know the meaning of patriotism.... the war...
    A bit later Anna offers him a dead British soldier's boots as his are soaked. Brandt replies:
    Brandt: What do you take me for? ...I'm defending my country...
    Anna: You can do that much better if your feet are dry!

Brandt: I would rather die than touch those boots! Get away from me...you carrion cow!

Anna: And what are we to live on? All the farms are burnt to the ground.

Brandt: ... excuses...(*softly*) Feels... as if the war... has been going on forever...

Again, de Wet employs the parody as the General feverishly shouts:

General: Shoot them.... Deserters!

Anna: Oh be quiet! I've had enough of you. (de Wet 2000: 185)

5.7 *Myths Subverted*

From this position of matriarchy, we observe the deconstruction of many myths which constitute Afrikaner identity—Calvinism, fatherland, Chosen Race, self-sacrifice, gender roles, racial and national 'purity'. In this way, we note how the mind of the oppressor functions in relation to difference, both within the contradictions employed in the formation of identity and in relation to the black other. On a stage of dark comedy, ancient Gothic literature and ancestral worlds of spirits, Annie seems other-worldly and complicit with her mother in needing to murder young males to inhale their last breaths in order to be nourished. She is not the docile female of Afrikaner mythology, and nor is her mother the Volksmoeder. Overall, it is the male characters who romanticise and glorify Afrikaner mythology and the female characters who subvert all. This process enables us strip the white Afrikaner mythical identity of its core beliefs. In the end, this process renders the project of racialising difference to be profoundly critiqued through ridicule.

Outside the cowshed, we hear the sounds of the desolate African landscape, howling animals, rain and the war. The latter grounds us and Anna in a brutal reality, the former in a sense of non-exotic, ancient worlds. As in *African Gothic*, this aesthetic shows the inherited legacy of Afrikaner nationhood mythology to be absurd and its contradictions revealed. Thus, once the mind of the oppressor is understood, the notion of race—foundational to its identity—is seen to be dismantled. At the end of the play, Annie has been restored to beauty and life by the dying breath of the young soldier, and the General's dying breaths are heard in the dark. It is a grotesque, parodic image of the last breath of Afrikaner rule and mythology; Calvinism, gender stereotypes, fatherland, sacrifice of life for patriotism and 'Chosen Race' of Africa. Brandt of course first resists, calls Anna 'insane...mad...a murdering bitch' (de Wet 2000: 185) but in the end gives in as Anna says to Annie, 'He loves you more than his own life' (de Wet 2000: 186). Finally, tied up while he has been sleeping, he is desperate, and screams, tries to fight to get away, but cannot.

Brandt: You bitches from hell...Trapped me! Tricked me... (de Wet 2000: 185)

But he cannot escape and Anna strangles him as Annie takes in his slow dying breath. Bold and strong, laughing with 'lips as red as cherries' (de Wet 2000: 185), Anna says:

Anna: He knew about war and honour but he didn't know you

232   D. PEIMER

> Annie: What a pity! All the fighting...and where did it get him? (de Wet 2000: 186)

5.8   Beliefs Dismantled

Interestingly, the primary conflict in the play is between Anna and her relentless mocking and dismantling of every one of Brandt's beliefs that construct his identity—an ironic twist of Bhabha's notions. We witness his increasingly desperate attempts to justify his paradigm of inherited national myths as he tries to use repetition to contain his anxiety at the contradiction between exaggeration and naturalising or stabilising them. As his paradigm of beliefs is stripped bare by Anna, he resorts to discriminating against her and racism is revealed to be at the core of Afrikaner identity. In *African Gothic*, Alina is the catalyst of this process, and in *Breathing In*, it is Anna. Either way, the mind of the oppressor is revealed. As Lewis might suggest, the circle of wagons of the laager is porous from outside forces and from forces within. No matter how much fixity in the laager is sought, the identity formation of the 'superior' (in discriminatory behaviour) can never be sustained as stable or fixed; it is forever subverted, resisted and dismantled whether from within it by an other white Afrikaner, or from without by the racialised black Other. Further propping up the laager mentality is an adaptation of Burke's notion that the English colonial has an 'entitled inheritance and that inequality is the basis of English society' (Arendt 1994: 230). As portrayed in the play, a sense of Boer entitlement to the land and inequality in relation to the 'black other' has been dismantled.

It is not by chance that de Wet locates the action of the play during the Anglo-Boer War. In the relationship between Brandt and his General, we observe this link to the Afrikaners' perception of themselves as the 'Chosen Race' of Africa, who entered into a Covenant with God to 'rule the African'. That is part of the reason they engage in the war against the British for three years knowing their 50,000 farmer fighters cannot defeat over 200,000 British troops. Anna knows this and it further informs her reasons for ridiculing Afrikaner myths, and she will kill anyone so that she and her daughter survive. Life experiences have taught her to understand that colonial and Afrikaner national identities reflect Goethe's trinity of war, trade and piracy; the rest is inherited ideology arranged to justify this through beliefs of 'superiority' and its resultant discrimination

> Anna: This place will be the death of us. And we can only survive if we keep moving. (de Wet 2000: 190)

Crossing (Performed in 1995 in South Africa and 2000 in London)

12 STAGING RACE IN WHITE SOUTH AFRICAN AFRIKAANS THEATRE

5.9 A Too Narrowly Defined Reality

Similar to the other plays, *Crossing* is set in the decaying room of an old farm-house in rural, isolated South Africa. The house is at the crossing of a large river. As in most of de Wet's plays, the dramatic action is located in the past, here, in 1930. Again, by using the metaphor of a historical period, de Wet gains a certain distance from her subject matter and is able to cast a more critical eye on contemporary Afrikaner mythical notions of identity and the discriminatory thinking that informed it. The aesthetic of the play is a combination of 'old fashioned mystery and ghost stories of magic realism and Gothic drama' (Middeke et al. 2015: 150). As she notes in the introduction to the play: 'the characters should be so pale that their faces appear almost mask-like…and…sensitive orchestration of the effects is of the utmost importance…the mood and atmosphere…suggest sounds of Africa…and …a rushing river…rain…the howling wind outside' (de Wet 2000: 187).

This atmospheric aesthetic is captured in the opening lines of the play:

> Hermien: Thought you were sleep-walking again. You look like you've seen a ghost
> Sussie: I had a dream…
> Hermien: You mustn't let dreams disturb you…visions…premonitions…they are different. (de Wet 2000: 60)

Hermien is the older sister and is strict and controlling, yet combines her control of her younger hunchbacked sister, with deep caring. Her sister, Sussie, is pale and fearful, and the play embodies how they are isolated in a vast landscape and are profoundly dependent on each other in a multitude of ways. The play shifts between an apparent realism and subtle dream-like worlds. This interweaving process creates an aesthetic that deepens our engagement with the subject matter of the play and not dismiss it as naïve fantasy. The premise of the narrative is that the sisters see their mission as warning people not to cross the river when it is in flood. Most do not heed their warning and drown; the sisters believe it is their duty to fish out the corpses and bury them. It appears vital that they know the names of the dead who they then partly interact with as spirits.

They play a game to remember the names of the dead they have buried:

> Sussie: Lukas! River stones in his pocket…the current was so strong it had torn off his clothes
> Hermien: Washed away his shoes.
> Hermien: Wish we could have kept him.
> Sussie: I'm tired of lifting heavy wet bodies out of the water…Tired of digging graves…
> Hermien: Why complain? The earth is soft after the rain
> Sussie: Why don't we just leave them where they are?

234   D. PEIMER

Hermien: That's not how our mother brought us up...we bury them with their Christian names on a cross. (de Wet 2000: 67)

And later, Hermien shows her control and care for her disabled sister:

Hermien: I've always been good to you... I stroke your hump when it aches
Sussie: Its always...Hermien this, Hermien that...like our mother.
Hermien (*tenderly stroking her hump*): There...there...We always sleep together...in one bed...one day we'll lie side by side forever...like them...same gravestone... (de Wet 2000: 67–68)

Ironically, this interaction seems grounded and not dream-like; this results in a contradictory sense of 'conscious trance' which helps make these parts of the play more believable for a contemporary audience. As de Wet describes her aesthetic: 'the world created for each play .... remains consistent to its own peculiar logic...I wished to lend fantastical situations the quality of irrefutable truth.... (as some of the) characters try to escape the confines of a too narrowly defined reality' (de Wet 2000: 71–72).

5.10   *Dreams Parodied or Believed?*

During the night, Maestro, a 'sinister Svengalian hypnotist' arrives with his obedient partner, Ezmerelda, and Sussie hovers between being hypnotised and infatuated with him. He wears a 'cloak and a high black hat...hair dark and wet...eyes...deep'. He rides in a 'carriage...two horses...rain howling in the wind'. He scorns the sign: 'Beware! Do not cross the river when it's in flood' (de Wet 2000: 61). He transforms Sussie such that she seems to believe she has wings hidden in her hump and dreams of flying like a beautiful angel. Reminiscent of mediaeval miracle plays, she performs the innocent young woman seduced by the charismatic and mysterious stranger.

Maestro (*gently touching her hump*): You have wings there...tightly folded...one day they will burst through...you will spread your wings...such lovely hands...delicate...what do you desire?
Sussie: To go away...far from here...see other places
Maestro: Then we shall go on a journey...swifter than breath...you will float out the window.
Hermien: That's a pretty story.... My sister's not a child...she knows she is deformed.
Maestro: ...believe me.... (de Wet 2000: 61)

But it is all a fantasy, a dream. Shifting in and out of 'realism', the darkness and rain persist. Maestro and Ezmerelda eventually leave and drown in the river and the sisters find their bodies and bury them. They had warned them:

Hermien: The river is in full flood... Hear it!

Maestro: There is nothing to fear
Hermien: That's what they all say…there are rapids and cross-currents to suck you under…
Ignoring her, he proclaims:
Maestro: I am a celebrated hypnotist…I make dreams come true…Everyone searches, but few find…. (de Wet 2000: 65)

Crossing has numerous thematic concerns which are similar to *Breathing In*. Again, the female principle of Hermien does not conform to the embodiment of the Volksmoeder, but serves as the catalyst to subvert the 'superior and inferior' racial myths in Afrikaner identity construction. Her hunchbacked sister, Sussie, embodies the psychological 'deformity' of what happens when the subject's paradigm of contradictions breaks down and individuation becomes imaginary 'wings', a flight of fantasy, an unlived dream. Sussie wishes to, but cannot, escape the Afrikaner myths of the docile, obedient, Calvinist defined female role in the laager. Hermien, like Anna in *Breathing In*, reveals the porousness in the laager and dismantles the dominant myths that attempt to frame the Afrikaner female. Hermien could escape this world with its singular narrative of oppressive behaviour, but she chooses to stay to look after her sister (and control her) and to live out her vocation of burying travellers who try to cross the river when it is raining and in flood and drown. The metaphor of her burying other characters connects to the 'drowning', under its own contradictions, of the myths of the Afrikaner construction of a racialised, national identity.

5.11 Memory and Myth Deconstructed

Staging the play in the post-apartheid era, de Wet employs memory and metaphor to reveal the constituents of the national myths that manifested themselves, and still do, in Afrikaner culture. And, always implicit in the exaggeration of difference is the notion of the 'inferiority' of the Other—the racialised identities required to maintain Afrikaner self-definition and its attendant notion of assumed authority over the Other. Hermien, like Anna in *Breathing In*, deconstructs the logic of the stereotyping process of the white Afrikaner. From within the laager, she sees how it is located on the exaggeration of difference and the need to repeat the difference endlessly to try to contain the internal contradictions. In essence, the mind of the oppressor contains within itself, within its own laager, an Afrikaner Other who subverts its own mythologies.

What is interesting and different to the other plays is the character of Maestro. As his name implies, he is a trickster, a con artist with the charisma of the entertainer. He knows he is role-playing, and that the myths of Afrikanerdom are parts to be performed and which can hypnotise his nation. One senses how he enjoys being both serious and parodic about these myths. Hermien sees this in him, yet she knows he remains unconscious of perhaps the deepest myth; the assumed power or authority of the male principle and his belief in his power over nature—the rain, flooding river, African night, Ezmeralda and the racialised Other. This assumption of masculine authority ultimately leads to his downfall and literal death. De Wet suggests that the seeds of the Afrikaner process of stereotyping, of superiority and inferiority, and all its attendant identity myths, construct the mind of the oppressor. But what makes her dramaturgy attain deep insight is her perception that within those seeds resides the subversion and ridiculing of this process—the downfall or 'drowning'. Finally, de Wet suggests that the downfall of racism in South Africa is contained in the centuries of colonially arranged, religiously informed, racialising of identities. This downfall is suggested in Hermien's final, ironic, metaphor-laden comment:

Hermien: We must order more crosses. (de Wet 2000: 65)

6 Conclusion

De Wet thus contends that fixity is illusion and the stereotyping process at the heart of racialising identities is a set of contradictory polarities which cannot be sustained no matter how often the narratives are endlessly repeated. Her plays further suggest that the white Afrikaner coloniser and apartheid paradigm of national and historical myths are revealed to be parodic and cannot resist the inevitable collapse brought on by its own processes of stereotyping—the laager is an incubator of its own illusionary contradictions. Her plays viscerally strip the mind of the oppressor bare and dismantle its assumption of power. As Bhabha (1994: 67) notes: 'Power is thus portrayed as the range of differences and discriminations that informs the practices of racial hierarchization....Its (Childs and Williams 1997: 75) objective is to construe the colonized as a population of inferior types on the basis of racial origin, in order to justify conquest'.

References

Arendt, Hannah. 1994. *The Origins of Totalitarianism*. London & New York: Penguin.
Bhabha, Homi. 1994. *The Location of Culture*. London & New York: Routledge.
Biko, Steve. 2002. *I Write What I Like*. Chicago: University of Chicago Press.
Childs, P., and P. Williams. 1997. *An Introduction to Post-colonial Theory*. London & New York: Harvester Wheatsheaf.
Lewis, M. 2016. *Performing Whitely in the Postcolony: Afrikaners in South African Theatrical and Public Life*. Iowa City: University of Iowa Press.
Middeke, M., P. Schnierer, and G. Homann, eds. 2015. *Contemporary South African Theatre*. London: Bloomsbury.
Sartre, Jean-Paul. 1995. *Anti-Semite and Jew*. London: Penguin.
de Wet, R. 2000. *Plays One*. London: Oberon Books.
———. 2005. *Plays Two*. London: Oberon Books.

PART III

Blackness and the African Diaspora

CHAPTER 13

In the Prison of Their Skins: Performing Race in Caribbean Theatre

Osita Okagbue

1   INTRODUCTION

This chapter is premised on the understanding that race is neither ontologically valid as a concept, nor is it useful or reliable as a term for marking difference between peoples or social groups. This position is informed by/aligns itself with other views, from that of Julian Sorrell Huxley and Alfred Cort Haddon who in 1935 suggested that 'the term race as applied to human groups should be dropped from the "vocabulary of science as it had lost any sharpness of meaning"' (quoted in Les Back and John Solomos 2000, 2009: 62), Robert Miles, whose neo-Marxist view is that race is a socio-political construct, 'an ideological effect, a mask that hides real economic relationships' (Miles 1984 in Back and Solomos 2009: 7) and often deployed as an instrument for social regulation, to then American President, Bill Clinton, who in 2000 while receiving the final Report on the Human Genome Project quoted the genomics researchers' unanimous conclusion that there is no race in our genes, that human beings are the same everywhere (cited by Sandra Soo-Jin Lee in Karim Murji and John Solomos eds. 2015: 26). However, although it is now generally accepted within scholarship and other 'informed' social and political spaces

---

This title makes a nod to George Lamming's influential novel, *In the Castle of My Skin*, which was published in 1953.

O. Okagbue (✉)
Department of Theatre and Performance, Goldsmiths, University of London, London, UK
e-mail: o.okagbue@gold.ac.uk

© The Author(s), under exclusive license to Springer Nature Switzerland AG 2021

T. Morosetti, O. Okagbue (eds.), *The Palgrave Handbook of Theatre and Race*, https://doi.org/10.1007/978-3-030-43957-6_13

240   O. OKAGBUE

and contexts that 'race' is a problematic ideologically constructed term for marking difference, it is also true that it has real material effects because, according to Robert Miles (1982: 42), of its reality as a tool for analysis as well as an impetus for human behaviours and actions. Nowhere is this affective materiality of race more evident than in the lived realities of the characters from the three Caribbean plays selected for analysis in this chapter, *Dream on Monkey Mountain* by Derek Walcott (first performed 1967 and published 1970) from St Lucia, *An Echo in the Bone* by Dennis Scott (first performed 1974 and published 1985) and *Old Story Time* by Trevor Rhone (first performed 1979 and published 1981), both from Jamaica.

An important question which this chapter would like to explore is why it is that despite its porousness and its unreliability, race is still used in constructions and demarcations of identity by many individuals and social groups and, allied to this, why it is that the word black or white or yellow bring forth certain associations in the minds of those who the terms are mentioned to or used to designate. The chapter intends to explore this in the context of Caribbean society, especially through its theatre. I have chosen to do this because the Caribbean is one of those few areas in the world where colonialism and trans-Atlantic slavery played a significant role in their founding; and trans-Atlantic slavery and colonialism were also the two historical events in which race, both as an idea and a practice of human relations, was very much in evidence. The characters in the selected plays, black, white and mixed or 'brown' (as Mama/Miss Aggy, one of the major characters in *Old Story Time* designates Margaret, the mixed-race girl she wanted her son, Len, to marry), demonstrate the racialised nature of Caribbean societies which the characters live in and which the plays explore. The reality is that while there are claims that race no longer is the key determinant of the social structure and thus of human relationships in the Caribbean, the same slave, colonial and imperial notion of race still influences people's lives, often determining where individuals find themselves on the social ladder. One therefore can state categorically that race still determines where and what kind of lives people live in the Caribbean. As John Thieme (2007) points out in his essay on Scott's *An Echo in the Bone*, in

> the era in which Walcott and Dennis Scott, were coming of age, slavery remained *the* unspoken *Ur*-narrative of Afro-Caribbean life, as well as a crucial sub-text underlying the experience of Caribbean peoples of other ethnicities... (p. 5)

It is in fact difficult to see how the experience of slavery can ever be exorcised from the collective unconscious of Caribbean peoples, especially those of African descent for whom the negative impact of slavery seemed to have been greater. Thus although Walcott, Scott and Rhone wrote their plays in the late 1960s and 1970s, immediately after the Caribbean countries achieved political independence from their former European colonial and slave masters—events which unsurprisingly elicited widespread optimism that total freedom from the socio-political effects of their slave past would follow for the descendants of the formerly enslaved Africans—evidence unfortunately suggest that this has not been the case and that the early euphoria and hope have since gone and the long tentacles of their slave past are still present in much of contemporary Caribbean society. Even plays written decades after this immediate post-independence period confirm that the plight of a majority of peoples of African descent has not changed significantly from what it was when Walcott, Scott, Rhone and their contemporaries wrote their plays.

One needs to state from the outset that although the term race will be used in the chapter, it is important to restate/indicate a positioning from above that recognises the problematic, contested nature and therefore inadequacy of the term as a marker of human difference, a standpoint that was also strongly indicated in the introductory chapter to the book. But having said this, the chapter unfortunately acknowledges that for many, especially peoples of African descent who globally have disproportionately been at the rough end of consequences of racist behaviour by and treatment from the white European Other, as are some of the characters in the plays, race remains a lived reality in contexts in which although they constitute a majority population in the Caribbean, they remain the poor, oppressed and marginalised.

The colonial and slave history of the Caribbean was a deeply impactful fact of life, and the imprint of this history is still seen and felt coursing through the different strata of society. The Caribbean islands are made up approximately by 70 per cent of peoples of African descent who are the descendants of previously enslaved Africans who were forcibly brought to the Caribbean to provide labour for the plantations—in fact, peoples of African descent represent the majority group in most English-speaking former colonies in the Caribbean with Jamaica actually having close to 95 per cent of its population having some degree of African ancestry (Rex Nettleford 1974, 1978). The remainder of the Caribbean population—approximately 20–25 per cent—is made up of peoples of European descent (i.e. the descendants of the former enslavers/plantation owners) and those of Asian descent (descended from the indentured servants and labourers). Given, as pointed out earlier, that theories and the deployment of the term race was mainly a colonial and imperial strategy used to differentiate between coloniser and colonised and between slave owners and the enslaved, it is not surprising that race played a major role in the social, political and economic organisation of the Caribbean colonial and slave society. Thus Caribbean society was and in many ways still is a perfect illustration of the fact stated above that although the idea of race is a myth, yet it is a myth which has real physically and psychologically felt effects on the lives of many who had to live under its surreptitious purview as we will shortly see in the plays.

The social structure left behind across most parts of the New World, and the Caribbean in particular, when trans-Atlantic slavery ended was one that graded and to a large extent still continues to grade people up along the social ladder from black, through brown to white. According to Elsa Goveia, Caribbean peoples, 'belong to a universe in which it is accepted that the upper class should be people of white or lighter complexion as the lower class should be people of dark complexion' (Goveia 1970: 10). There is evidence though that suggests that it was not always the case that there was this strict hierarchy among the many groups that made up Caribbean society at the onset of trans-Atlantic slavery or that Africans were perceived as inferior or placed lowest in the social scale. As revealed by Gunnar Mydral in 'Racial Beliefs in America':

> When the Negro was first enslaved, his subjugation was not justified in terms of his biological inferiority.... The historical literature on this early period also records that the imported Negroes—and the captured Indians—originally were kept in much the same status as the white indentured servants. (in Back and Solomos 2000, 2009: 112)

But as already pointed out, race only came into reckoning as part of the attempt by ideologues of the imperial, colonial and trans-Atlantic enslavement enterprise to justify the two practices. The slave system was not new to Africans, and slaves were first and foremost seen and treated as human beings, unfortunate may be to be slaves. It is well-known that slaves in Africa could buy themselves out of slavery after a while and so the state of being a slave in some instances was temporary, with some notable former slaves buying their freedom and later rising to become leaders in the societies in which they had been previously enslaved. Moreover, when European slave traders first arrived on the West African coasts, because they needed partners to trade with or to supply them with their human cargo, they recognised and accorded respect to the chiefs and factors who controlled all coastal trade. The key point to note however is that Europeans came to Africa for slaves because it was cheap and the African slaves were good workers who could endure the harsh conditions of the plantations. The idea of Africans and black people as belonging to an inferior race was therefore a later invention which, as I have argued elsewhere, was used to justify the inhuman treatment and the denial of rights that the enslaved Africans received from European slave owners in the New World (see Okagbue 2009: 1–18).

Porous and spurious as it is, this introduction of a discriminatory racial element into the relationship between Africans and Europeans in the Caribbean has had a deep and long-lasting effect on the social structure of Caribbean societies as Goveia highlighted above. It is hardly surprising that as a result of this pervasiveness of race as a basis for social placement, that it also plays a significant, and in fact a defining role in perceptions and constructions of identity by many people in the Caribbean. Race had underpinned social organisation and relations during the era of slavery in the Caribbean, and unfortunately, it continues to do so in contemporary post-slavery and postcolonial Caribbean society; there is abundant evidence of this in Caribbean plays as we shall see later in the chapter. With this experience of race as a major factor in the way people lived, were treated and as it continues to determine placement and treatment and life experiences, one is not surprised that it also affects very much how people perceive themselves in relation to themselves and to others. In comparing identity formations in African and Caribbean theatres, I suggested that whereas African characters tended to identify themselves along class lines—those who have and those who do not have—identities in the Caribbean are based more on racial origins than they are on class affiliations or belonging—people perceive themselves as their "race" as opposed to their class' (Okagbue 2009: 88). Thus, many Caribbean plays explore the theme of self and of survival in an environment in which that sense of self is seriously in question. Most of the characters in much of Caribbean theatre seem to be in a struggle to see to what extent they are able to rise above the limitations imposed on them by the colour of their skin and racial origins. We will see how these are the key concerns in *Dream on Monkey Mountain, An Echo in the Bone* and *Old Story Time*.

2 Caribbean Theatre and Its Social Context

According to Maria Shevtsova (1993: ix), 'no matter where it is constructed, the theatre vibrates with the movements of its society'. This means that theatre, wherever and in whatever form it exists and in whichever context it is produced, it always captures and resonates with the internal rhythms as well as the physical/material dimensions, processes and reality of that context. Theatre, therefore, does not lie as it is a good barometer for accessing the pulse and dynamics of the society out of which it has emerged. As we will see in discussing the selected plays, the theatre in its dialectical and mutually affective relationship with society acts as a repository of the history, culture, memory and social processes of its context; Victor Turner (1990: 8–18) sees this as the theatre acting as a 'cultural-aesthetic mirror' that affords society the opportunity for self-reflexivity, and a platform within/on which 'the central meanings, values and goals of a culture are seen "in action" as they shape and explain behaviour' (p. 1). Caribbean theatre is no different, and in fact in the view of this chapter, Caribbean plays perform this function quite well as they, more than any artistic or historical representation of and from the islands that make up this geographical place, are able to capture as well as reflect the deep imprints of Caribbean racial and cultural history.

Caribbean society during the period of plantation slavery was one in which the line between slave and master was drawn along racial lines; the slaves were peoples of African descent and the masters were mainly peoples of European descent; the slaves were 'black' while the masters were 'white'. There were of course the native Indians, mixed-race (mulattoes), European and later Asian indentured workers/servants. As I have pointed out, Europeans did not introduce slavery into the African continent:

> Slavery as an institution was not new to Africans, what was new and different was the treatment given to the slaves. The slave in Africa was never seen as an inferior person in any way; unlucky maybe, but never the non-human that he/she became in the New World. In the Caribbean and the Americas, he/she lacked the humanity which would have linked him/her to the master thereby making the inhuman treatment received from the latter unacceptable... (Okagbue 2009: 10)

However, of significance to the theme of this chapter is that trans-Atlantic slavery signalled the onset of the uprooting, subsequent humiliation and, ultimately, the collective alienation of peoples of African descent in the Caribbean. Having been forcibly removed from their ancestral homes in Africa and thrown into a bewildering and often physically and emotionally hostile plantation environment of the New World entirely dominated by European slave masters, the enslaved Africans became aware for the first time of their blackness. But not only that, they also realised that the terrible life and experiences which they faced in the New World was because of the colour of their skin (Okagbue 2009: 21) as the European enslavers seemed bent on de-culturising and emasculating them to the point of denying them the rights to their cultures, their names and languages.

So, in order to justify the enslavement of Africans and the inhuman treatment meted out to them, myths of African barbarity, savagery, atavism, bestiality and primitivism were created and pervasively circulated to present trans-Atlantic enslavement as an act of saving or elevating Africans from these horrible and low conditions of existence. Thus, although African and Europeans had traded freely as equal partners on the African coasts before the trans-Atlantic slave trade began, but once the trade started and progressed, the racial myths of denigration were created and deployed by European enslavers and their imperial backers, not only to justify the inhuman trade, but also to maximise their economic profit as making the slave non-human meant that they could not expect to be paid a human wage for their labour.

This binary that balanced the superiority of white people against the inferiority of black people had significant implications, not only in the ordering of Caribbean society but actually in the constructions of identities by the various peoples of the Caribbean. In relation to the latter, unfortunately, the racist myths used to underpin trans-Atlantic slavery did have an effect on the enslaved Africans; it did resonate in them after a sustained period of time and use. As Albert Memmi (1974) surmises in his portraits of the coloniser and colonised, what is surprising about the negative portrait of the colonised is the

> echo that it excites in the colonized himself. Constantly confronted with this image of himself, set forth and imposed on all institutions and in every human act, how could the colonized help reacting to his portrait?... Wilfully created and spread by the colonizer, the mythical and degrading portrait ends up being accepted and lived with to an extent by the colonized. It thus acquires a certain amount of reality and contributes to the true portrait of the colonized. (p. 87)

The enslaved Africans could only think of their 'race' whenever they thought of themselves because it was the only reality they had because of its materiality in their lives; every experience of theirs in the New World was impacted upon by the colour of their skins—the treatment they received, their placement on the social ladder and their relationships with the other social groups with whom they shared their environment.

However, in spite of the concerted and sustained effort of the enslavers to deprive the enslaved Africans of their cultures and the worlds and practices embodied by these cultures, that they were able to cling on to some elements of their different African cultures was, as Emmanuel Obiechina (1986: 101–160) argues in his essay, 'Africa in the Souls of Dispersed Children', a testament to their indomitable wills which refused to die in the face of the relentless and merciless onslaught from their enslavers. This indestructible will to survive and protect their culture has remained and is a major factor in articulations and contestations of race and culture politics in the Caribbean. It also explains as we shall see later on why race remains a major consideration and theme in Caribbean life, literature and theatre.

3   Race and Place in Caribbean Theatre/In the Prison of Their Skin

Although colonialism and trans-Atlantic slavery have both ended a long time ago—for slavery about a century and half ago, and more than half a century for colonisation—the racism which they engendered remains a lived reality for the descendants of the formerly enslaved Africans in the New World. There is no doubt that race played and continues to play a part in social placement in Caribbean society and thus has a significant impact on identity formation in the Caribbean; and the characters in the three selected plays demonstrate the full extent of this importance as they represent the different ways in which different peoples in the Caribbean see themselves and how that perception affects the way they live and the way they interact with other people, both within their putative racial group and those from outside it.

In general, being black in the Caribbean means being poor, disenfranchised and often having to struggle and work hard to escape or rise above the limitations placed on the individual by belonging to this racial category; conversely, being white very often guarantees a higher placement on the ladder with attendant resources and privileges. One area in which there is a continuation of the socio-economic structures from the slave period is in matters of land rights, a theme which Scott explores in *An Echo in the Bone* as we shall see later; this we see is also the theme of David Edgecombe's *Kirnon's Kingdom*, a play written decades later in 2001. Although written twenty-seven years apart, both plays deal with the issue of ownership and usage of land. In Scott's play, Crew, as a descendant of a formerly enslaved African, has a tiny piece of land which borders the large expanse owned by Master Charles, the descendant of a former European slave owner. Although Crew owns this land, he unfortunately is not allowed to use it as freely as he wished because of Master Charles' desire to either force him out or compel Rachel, the former's wife to come work as his servant in the Great House. While in Edgecombe's play, Harold Kirnon, an African descendant of slaves, is a sharecropper on a vast cotton estate owned by Mas James. In his own case, the lack of right to land actually means a lack of the right to participate in the political process as one cannot vote if one does not own land. Thus the play highlights the failure of an equitable distribution of land after emancipation and political independence many decades later. Thus, although Kirnon and his family sow and tend the cotton, they have no rights over the product of their labour, just as their slave ancestors. Therefore, being black and poor sits in sharp contrast to being white and privileged, with the mixed and other 'races' in between, just as it had been during the period of enslavement and colonisation. These sharply contrasting positions in society are amply demonstrated in many of the plays in Caribbean theatre.

Because race was and still is a major factor in Caribbean social arrangement, and because race also plays a central role in identity formation for many people in the islands, the issue of race is a recurring theme in Caribbean plays. Two attitudes/responses to race can be identified in the three selected plays; the first is the attempt by characters to escape the limitations of race and the second is confronting and overcoming race. Walcott's *Dream on Monkey Mountain* is a play whose central character, Makak, represents a good example of an individual of African descent who, having for a long time endured the deprivation, denigration and indignities which his Caribbean society meted out to him on account of his racial origin, decides to escape and make a return to Africa, a former homeland where it is revealed in his dream that he was descended from a line of kings and great peoples. The mental journey which Makak eventually makes is also for the mixed-race policeman, Corporal Lestrade, who hates himself intensely for being partly black and thus rejects his African/black identity. However, Lestrade's alienation is made worse by that fact that although he rejects his African self, his white European side does not accept him either, so he occupies an in-between space of identity of being neither black nor white.

As is often the case in Caribbean plays and literature in general, one way race is explored is through the theme of characters who embark on a quest to understand the self and their position in society, and Makak and Lestrade with their companions, Tigre and Souris, undertake such a quest in the play; the group of black characters in *An Echo in the Bone* makes a similar mental journey during the Nine-night ritual wake for the dead Crew. Mama in *Old Story Time* without embarking on any journey is also forced to confront her anti-black prejudices which had made her treat her son, Len, and his wife, Lois, the way she did. *Dream on Monkey Mountain* opens with Makak in jail overnight for disorderly behaviour; and while in jail he meets two other black habitual criminals, Tigre and Souris, and all three prisoners are being guarded by Corporal Lestrade. Prior to his time in jail, Makak had been having deep psychological problems arising from his perception of himself because of his being a black man of African descent in the Caribbean—he sees himself as ugly, socially marginalised and lives as a recluse on Monkey Mountain with only Moustique, his business partner, as his only friend. Makak feels so alienated and negative about who he is that he would not look at himself in the mirror for fear of being confronted by the image of 'this old man, ugly as sin'. He tells Tigre, Souris and Corporal Lestrade:

Sirs, I am sixty years old. I have lived all my life
Like a wild beast in hiding. Without child, without wife.
People forget me like the mist on Monkey Mountain
Is thirty years now I have look in no mirror,
Not a pool of cold water, when I must drink,
I stir my hands first, to break up my image. (Walcott 1970: 226–227)

But to compound his problem of racial alienation and self-hate, he lusts after a White Apparition or the famed Daemon Woman of Caribbean mythology—in the play she is represented by a white mask which Makak uses to act out his race fantasies—who appears to him in his dream to tell him that he is not that ugly. The irony however is that the appearance of this woman actually reinforces the depth of his ugliness for him because he knows, as does the audience, that she is unattainable. As Corporal Lestrade reminds him in the centre of the forest when Makak is made to pronounce judgement on her, together with other well-known white characters from history who stand accused of race crimes against black people:

She, she? What you beheld, my prince, was but an image of your longing. As inaccessible as snow, as fatal as leprosy.... She is the wife of the devil, the white witch, she is the mirror of the moon that this ape look into and find himself unbearable. She is all that is pure, all that he cannot reach.... She is lime, snow, marble, moonlight, lilies, cloud, foam and bleaching cream, the mother of civilization, and the confounder of blackness.... She is the white light that paralysed your mind, that led you into this confusion. (Walcott 1970: 318–319)

Walcott, in my view, is advocating two things in the play. The first is that Makak's longing to physically return and claim his African ancestry and Lestrade's initial claim to whiteness and subsequent extreme advocacy of his black identity are just dreams which are as futile as the former's desire for 'racial improvement' through love and acceptance by the white daemon woman and the latter's paranoid and vigorous rejection of his African identity through his enforcement of 'white law'; both courses of action or state of being, the play argues, provide no solution to the racial problem faced by the black person in the Caribbean. The second is that the desire to pay homage to Africa is necessary, but should not be an end in itself. The play's message seems to be that the feelings of inferiority and self-deprecation of characters like Makak, Souris and Tigre or of superiority at first and later inferiority and confusion of the mixed-race Lestrade are products of their imaginations which they have to exorcise in order to come to terms with their true African-Caribbean identity.

As Walcott (1974) writes, '[i]n the subconscious there is a black Atlantis buried in a sea of sand' (1974, 1998: 58). Each person or character has to search for this Africa in their souls, either as individuals or as a collective. Makak manages to get the other characters to undertake this journey of cultural retrieval with him. It is significant that the two central characters at the conclusion of the meeting in the forest find themselves. Makak exorcises the debilitating hold of the white apparition who had held him captive, by chopping off her head, and Lestrade is able to 'achieve self-knowledge and to discover his identity by going into his subconscious. This is the only way he can discover the beautiful depth of his blackness' (Ginette Curry 2007: 219). It is therefore not by accident that Lestrade calls Makak 'old father' and later 'grandfather' in that final scene when he comes to accept his 'cultural and racial identity' (Okagbue 2009: 36) and significantly too Makak responds: 'Now he is one of us.... They reject half of you. We accept all' (Walcott 1970: 299–300). The same can be said of the group of African-Caribbean characters who ultimately discover themselves and answers to their slave past through the wake in honour of Crew in *An Echo in the Bone*.

Scott's play is set in an old sugar barn behind Crew's cottage in the present, nine nights after the killing of the white estate owner, Master Charles and the disappearance of Crew himself; the latter is suspected of having carried out the killing. Crew's wife, Rachel, has organised a Nine-Night ritual ceremony to commemorate her dead husband; but in reality this is a device by the dramatist to enable the African-Caribbean characters to get to the bottom of what had transpired between Crew and Master Charles that led to the killing. During the ritual Crew's first son, Sonson, becomes possessed by the spirit of his father, and through him racial memory is evoked and all of them are able to go back in time to experience the entire history of black people in the Caribbean and their oppressive experiences as slaves in their relationship with white slave owners over the centuries. The action of the play effortlessly traverses time and space, enabling the playwright to present contrasting facets of African-Caribbean history; and through this mechanism the racial tensions that have always coloured the relationship between black and white people are graphically essayed and conclusions reached about the rightness or wrongness of Crew's action.

The setting of *An Echo in the Bone* recreates the social structure of Caribbean society during the slave era in terms of social space and place for the various groups, and Caribbean society now, in terms of ownership and control of material resources. In the play, Master Charles is the only white character but he disproportionately owns and controls most of the land and therefore the economy of the place as it were, while the other characters who are all black live on the margins of his large estate and make do with whatever little he allows to trickle down to them. This is what was pointed out at the beginning that although race is imperfect and intellectually imagined, but that it still affects people on a daily basis in the Caribbean as the position of Crew, his family and their friends and neighbours who are of African-Caribbean descent illustrate. The underlying story of the play is that Crew, an ex-slave or a descendant of slaves, has a small piece of land which he had inherited and which for him is a symbol that he is no longer a slave. However, his land borders the expansive holding of Master Charles, who for some reason as it emerges during the trance sequence had diverted the water flow away from Crew's land thereby rendering it useless for him. Crew, a very proud man, humbles himself and goes to the

Great House to beg Master Charles to allow the water back through his farm, but instead of helping him out as requested, Master Charles pushes Crew down the steps in an attempt to humiliate him further. Of course, Crew loses his temper and strikes out with his machete at Master Charles, killing him in the process. Realising what he had done and not wishing to be tried and hanged for what he considers a provoked act of self-defence and justified retaliation for an injustice on his person, Crew runs away and later takes his own life.

Like *Dream on Monkey Mountain*, *An Echo in the Bone* also explores a psychic journey that takes the black characters who are in the barn to participate in the wake for Crew back to the beginnings of African-Caribbean history; and like similar plays by Caribbean dramatists of African descent, the journey inevitably leads back to trans-Atlantic slavery. It is a journey into the communal psyche and racial memory of African-Caribbean peoples, which is where their Caribbean history, as Walcott says, began: 'For us in the archipelago the real memory is salted with the memory of migration... [the] degraded arrival [which] must be seen as the beginning, not the end of our history' ('The Muse of History', 1974, 1998: 41).

All black people in the Caribbean are products of the slave encounter between Africa and Europe and, thus, deeply etched in the collective and individual unconscious of every Caribbean person of African descent is 'the painful memory of the "middle passage" and any excursion into the self inevitably brings the individual face to face with this racial scar' (Okagbue 2009: 36). At the heart of the narrative in *An Echo in the Bone* is, on the part of a majority of the black characters, a deep sense of cultural and racial origins, so an awareness of racial and cultural roots and the implications arising therefrom is an underlying theme; 'it underpins the conflict between Crew and Mr Charles, his oppressor and descendant of the slave master' (Okagbue 2009: 37). Every African-Caribbean person in search for identity, for roots and routes, almost always ends up with that archetypal image of the slave being ground down by the oppressive sugar cane farms and mills of the plantations, and this image/scene is graphically played out for the reader/audience in *An Echo in the Bone*. The play unfolds as a series of scenes which on the surface are disconnected, but which by the time the last scene/episode unravels reveal the racial history and rage which drove Crew to kill Master Charles. At that moment in the play when the white man pushes the begging black man down the steps—the action freezes—that image is designed to recall centuries of maltreatment and hurt which black people had suffered in the hands of white people in the Caribbean. The effect of this freezing is that it completely transforms Crew's individual act of murder into a collective rising up by black people to take revenge on Master Charles who also becomes a representative of his own people/race. The confrontation between them is transformed into the archetypal confrontation between black and white, between slave and master. The play's final message seems to be to remind the reader/audience of African-Caribbean peoples of the need for them to recover and repossess their racial pride which will enable them to reclaim and repair their humanity that had been bruised and battered by their colonial and slave experiences.

The final play to be discussed in the chapter is Rhone's theatrically experimental play, *Old Story Time*. Unlike the two previous plays discussed, *Old Story Time* centres specifically on contemporary Caribbean life, and in particular, experiences of the highly racialised relationships which still exist in the society. On the surface, there appears to be a change in the social structure reflecting instances of upward social mobility among black people arising from educational achievement by some of the characters; this is a situation that is completely absent from the other two plays. However, in spite of this, the fact remains that a majority of the black characters in *Old Story Time* occupy a lower position relative to the few white characters who by contrast are at the top. It is worthy of note that in a play with eight main characters—Len, his wife Lois, his mother, Mama (Miss Aggy), Pa Ben (the narrator), Pearl, George, Margaret and Estate Developer—George and probably Margaret and the Estate Developer are the non-black characters but they are at the top in terms of their financial standing and social status. Len is highly placed because of his high educational achievement—he is the most educated character in the play; whereas his mother Mama and Pa Ben are poor and on the lower scale with Pearl because they are black, and also because the first two being of the older-generation blacks who did not have the opportunity to improve themselves through education as Len and Lois had been able to do; Lois also joins the upper class because of her marriage to Len and because prior to her meeting and marrying Len, she had been one of the very few blacks to have been offered a decent job as a teller in a bank. George, who was her manager at the time, reminds her of how newsworthy and ground-breaking it had been then for a black person to have been offered a job in a bank. Although it still did not stop him from looking down on her as a person.

However, of more significance in relation to the theme of the chapter is the perceived and lived attitude to race by the characters. For Len, being black does not seem to have posed any problems for him in the long run, although that is not to say that the racism that being black attracts had not touched him; after all, he was roundly humiliated by George and his racist friends because he had stupidly sent a love letter to the beautiful mixed-race Miss Margaret who eventually became George's wife. Pa Ben and Pearl seem also to be comfortable in their skin and 'racial' background whereas for Mama, being black is a different matter altogether and is a condition she has struggled with for a long time. Mama belongs to a group of black characters (the group includes Lestrade and his famous speech in *Dream on Monkey Mountain* and many others from other Caribbean plays by dramatists of African descent) who have a problem with their race because they bought into the pervasive imperialist and colonial theory of the 'evolutionary backwardness of black peoples' (Okagbue 2009: 47). These characters are almost always running away from themselves, escaping the shadow of their skin colour.

Mama believes strongly and accepts this notion of 'negro' inferiority to the point that she beats Len mercilessly when she catches him playing with Pearl, a 'little dutty black gal' when she ideally wants him to befriend and marry Miss Margaret, 'a nice brown girl with hair down her back'. Her deeply ingrained negative perception of self, accompanied by a deep-seated hatred for blackness, leads her to yearn for her son to improve himself and the family line by marrying a fair-skinned woman and governs everything she does in the play. But irrational as her behaviour may seem to others, for her what she is doing is the right thing, and when her friend and close confidante Pa Ben reminds her that Len's father was black and suggests that the boy perhaps had married Lois because he wanted a wife who looked like his own mother, she replies:

> Mama: Black was good enough for me. It not good enough for him. There was better for him (*To herself*) What happen to Miss Margaret?
> Pa Ben: The boy make him own choice
> Mama: What happen to Miss Margaret? (*She continues bemoaning the loss of Miss Margaret*). (Rhone 1981: 23)

Mama hates herself as a black person and because of that, and like Makak in *Dream on Monkey Mountain*, she idealises white people, trusts them and values their judgements above that of black people—this may be why it took her so long to accept that George was, in fact, a fraudster who had conned her out of her savings; however, she also, unlike Makak, hates other black people and in the play she sees them, black women in particular (first Pearl and later Lois), as threats or obstacles to her dream of seeing her son progress and improve his lot by marrying a white or fair-skinned woman. Mama shares with Makak and Lestrade a desire to lose themselves in 'a white mist' which they see as a way out of their racial predicament. Other characters of African descent in the play, in their different ways, try to point out to Mama the foolishness and wrongness of her attitude to her culture and racial origins. But it is not until the end when his duplicitous nature is revealed to her that she realises that George was 'the evil wretch' who had persecuted her son to the point of forcing him to run away from school and that it was Lois and her dead father who were the good Samaritans that took him in and cared for and persuaded him to go back to school and complete his education.

Another character whose attitude to race in the play is worth noting is George. He plays the typical racist from the colonial and imperial script. He knows his 'nigger' who, in his view, is of limited intelligence, emotionally immature and so can be easily handled or swindled as in the case of his dealings with Mama. For George, Mama was just a foolish old black lady who could easily be separated from her money; the latter, because of her disposition and thoughts about race is the perfect foil for that scenario to play out. And George's history with Len while they were at school showed how racist and full of himself he was and apparently still is. The full extent of his racism is explained

252   O. OKAGBUE

by Pa Ben's bitterness while watching George haughtily strut about in his riding gear while ordering and racially abusing Len:

> George: [*On buggy riding away*] Giddy up
> Pa Ben: You should see them, just sneering down on the world, them head way up in the sky, drunk with power and authority…
> [George *struts around still dressed in his finery.*]
> George: Here, boy. [Len *hesitates*] On the double, boy. Move! [Len *hurries*] Clean my shoes, burnish it till you see you big black ugly face in it, boy! [*Len goes on all fours and starts to polish* George's shoe. George *is enjoying himself immensely. He uses* Len's *back as a foot-rest for his free foot, his riding crop poised over* Len's *backside.*] And boy, don't forget we need you for the Easter play. We have you down for three part—Judas Iscariot, one of the thieves, and both ends of the donkey. Ha, ha, ha! [*He straddles* Len, *riding and whipping him.*] (Rhone, 49–50)

Even when he was in trouble having been caught out in his fraudulent scheme and he had come seeking to get assistance from Len, he is still condescending in his attitude to Len, trying to pull the wool over the latter's eyes with false and over-inflated figures which he thought Len was not going to spot. But Len had soused him out and was in fact out to expose him for what he had done to his mother with his bogus housing scheme. He and his friends had been so incensed that Len had the nerve to send Margaret a love letter; she at the time was George's girlfriend, and they beat the hell out of him to teach him a lesson not to aspire to a relationship with a fair-skinned girl. They also made fun of Mama on one occasion when she visited Len in school and brought him food. Thus George's overall attitude is that blacks and whites should not intermix; in fact, he believes that it was a mistake to give out scholarships which enabled a poor black boy like Len to attend such a privileged school as they were attending. Moreover, George also feels that admitting black people to his former school was negatively affecting the educational and sporting standards of the school. However, one suspects that subconsciously this attitude arises from a fear of the social mobility which such access to quality education as is available to white people would lead to, with Len's success and social rise a case in point.

4   Conclusion

The three plays looked at in this chapter illustrate the fact that although, as the essay argues, race is a social construct that pretends to be based on a biological/scientific truth, that unfortunately in the context of their Caribbean setting, it has considerable material effect on the lives of people of all races. Caribbean society, built as it was on a foundation of colonialism and trans-Atlantic slavery, operated a racial ideology in which a majority of the population who were of African descent were enslaved and because of that occupied the lowest rung of the social ladder, while a minority who were Europeans and slave masters occupied the highest rung. Colonialism needed this social ordering to make it work and be profitable as well. Thus a concept of race in which superficial biological differences, such as skin colour and texture of hair, were used to construct ideas about difference that assigned arbitrary values to black, white, yellow and other colours. However, in all this, the most significant was the binary opposition that became established between black and white; black was inferior, white superior, black was primitive while white was civilised and so forth. This ultimately became the measure used to justify the maltreatment and harsh inhuman conditions under which enslaved Africans and their descendants lived in the plantations and have continued to do so afterwards.

What the plays demonstrate is that although slavery and colonialism ended, the social structure left in their wake is still visible/operational today, both in the placement of people on the social ladder and the nature of the relationship between the various peoples of the Caribbean. The plays reveal that Caribbean society retains a structure in which a majority of people who are black are poor and at the bottom just as in the days of slavery and during colonial times, while a majority of those who are rich are white or are of fairer skin. The plays also reveal that the practice of keeping the races apart is still very much intact, with, in the main, black people living with black people and white people living with white people, and the other groups locked in their separate locations or sides of towns. Makak in *Dream on Monkey Mountain* longs for a white woman but he was not likely to get her; Mama in *Old Story Time* hoped that her son, Len, would marry Miss Margaret, but as we saw, this crossing of racial boundary/barrier was anathema to George and his friends; and Master Charles in *An Echo in the Bone* lives alone in the Great House and only allows blacks like Rachel, Crew and others to come to serve his needs and return to their hovels on the margins of his huge estate. This all goes to show that the idea of race is very alive in the Caribbean, contrary to claims otherwise by the politicians and the tourist industry.

Finally, what the plays also reveal is that racist thinking exists on all sides. It is particularly pertinent to point out that in the representation of characters, there appears to be racism against white characters at two levels, by characters and by the dramatists. There, for instance, appears to be a form of silencing of the white characters by both the dramatists and the characters, apart from George in *Old Story Time* (Miss Margaret and Estate Developer are mentioned by other characters in flashback scenes, but never make a physical appearance), and thus representations of white characters are from the perspective of black characters. So all these representations are just constructions of whiteness by blackness. A good case in point being Master Charles in *An Echo in the Bone* who never appears in his own right but is represented by one of the black characters during Sonson's period of possession. Similarly, no white character really is presented in *Dream on Monkey Mountain*, rather the impression of a whiteness is given by the mask of the White Apparition which Makak has created and plays with. Thus throughout the plays, and this is true of other plays in Caribbean theatre, there is no real voice of whiteness in the plays; rather what there is, is how blacks see whites through the purported behaviour of whites towards blacks.

References

Banton, Michael. 2000 & 2009. An Idiom of Race: A Critique of Presentism. In *Theories of Race and Racism: A Reader*, ed. Les Back and John Solomos, 51–63. London and New York: Routledge.

Curry, Ginette. 2007. *"Toubab La!": Literary Representations of Mixed-Race Characters in the African Diaspora*. Newcastle: Cambridge Scholars Publishers.

Goveia, Elsa. 1970. The Social Framework. *Savacou* 2: 7–15.

Lee, Sandra Soo-Jin. 2015. Race and the Science of Difference in the Age of Genomics. In *Theories of Race and Ethnicity: Contemporary Debates and Perspectives*, ed. Karin Murji and John Solomos, 26–39. Cambridge: Cambridge University Press.

Memmi, Albert. 1974. *The Colonizer and the Colonized*. London: Souvenir Press.

Miles, Robert. 1982. *Racism and Migrant Labour: A Critical Text*. London: Routledge and Kegan Paul.

Miles, R. 1984. 'Marxism Versus the "Sociology of Race Relations"?', *Ethnic and Racial Studies* 7 (2): 217–37

Mydral, Gunnar. 2000 & 2009. Racial Beliefs in America. In *Theories of Race and Racism: A Reader*, ed. Les Back and John Solomos, 87–104. London and New York: Routledge.

Nettleford, Rex. 1974. *Mirror Mirror: Identity, Race and Protest in Jamaica*. Jamaica: William Collins & Sangster Ltd.

———. 1978 & 2004. *Caribbean Cultural Identity: The Case of Jamaica*. Kingston, Jamaica: Ian Randle Publishers.

Obiechina, Emmanuel. 1986. Africa in the Souls of her Dispersed Children: West African Literature from the Era of the Slave Trade. *Nsukka Studies in African Literature* 4: 101–160.

Okagbue, Osita. 2009. *Culture and Identity in African and Caribbean Theatre*. London: Adonis and Abbey Publishers.

Rhone, Trevor. 1981. *Old Story Time and Smile Orange*. Harlow, Essex: Longman Caribbean Writers.

Scott, Dennis. 1985. An Echo in the Bone. In *Plays for Today*, ed. Errol Hill. Harlow, Essex: Longman Caribbean Writers.

Shevtsova, Maria. 1993. *Theatre and Cultural Interaction*. Sydney, Australia: Sydney Association for Studies in Culture and Society, University of Sydney.

Thieme, John. 2007. Re-possessing the Slave Past: Caribbean Historiography in Dennis Scott's *An Echo in the Bone*. https://www.academia.edu/972995/Repossessing_the_Slave_Past_Caribbean_Historiography_and_Dennis_Scott_s_An_Echo_in_the_Bone. Accessed 28 April 2020.

Turner, Victor. 1990. Are There Universals of Performance in Myth, Ritual and Drama? In *By Means of Performance: Intercultural Studies of Theatre and Ritual*, ed. Richard Schechner and Willa Appel, 8–18. London and New York: Routledge.

Walcott, Derek. 1970. *Dream on Monkey Mountain and Other Plays*. New York: The Noonday Press, Farrar, Straus and Giroux.

———. 1974 & 1998. The Muse of History. In *What the Twilight Says: Essays*. London: Faber and Faber Limited.

———. 1974 & 1998. What the Twilight Says. In *What the Twilight Says: Essays*. London: Faber and Faber Limited.

CHAPTER 14

Black Women in Post-revolutionary Cuban Theatre

Lilianne Lugo Herrera

1 Introduction

Several studies in Cuban culture use the body of the mulata as a productive site to analyze issues of colonialism, sexuality, gender, and race. For Alison Fraunhar, for example, the mulata body has occupied 'over the last two centuries in Cuba and its diaspora' three main positions: 'as national allegory; as the embodiment of Catholic and Yoruba spirituality; and as the intensely feminine erotic body of pleasure' (Fraunhar 2018, 214). The mulata is the perfect figure to embody both the racialised and exoticised Caribbean body, but creolised through a process of miscegenation that guarantees that it is not entirely white nor black. This in-betweenness of the mulata body has proven to be a rich site for scholarly analysis.[1] However, much less attention has been brought to black women's bodies and their depictions in cultural products. If miscegenation is key to signal national identity, and 'the mulata epitomizes the in-between-ness of cultural hybridization' (Arrizón 2002, 145), how can we then think about the bodies of black women—that body that ostensibly does not show traces of racial mixing? Can it escape the markers of objectification and commodification? For example, a frequently anthologised poem by Nancy Morejón, 'Mujer negra', is read by Arrizón as 'a counter-revolutionary act against male objectification'. Morejón strategically historises a black woman's poetic voice and 'in this process, her body foregrounds not the oppression of objecthood as a sexual victim, but her capacity for survival' (Arrizón 2002, 146). However, no

---

L. Lugo Herrera (✉)
University of Miami, Coral Gables, FL, USA
e-mail: lilianne@miami.edu

© The Author(s), under exclusive license to Springer Nature Switzerland AG 2021
T. Morosetti, O. Okagbue (eds.), *The Palgrave Handbook of Theatre and Race*, https://doi.org/10.1007/978-3-030-43957-6_14

255

study has yet addressed how black female bodies appear in Cuban theatre after the Revolution, nor the ideological implications of their representation in the cultural imaginary.

Most of the authors who analyze the Cuban mulata trope include the importance of nineteenth-century *teatro bufo* in the creation of the mulata stereotype as a hyper sexualised body. Yet few studies actually address other examples of how theatre has shaped the image of black women in Cuban and Caribbean culture.[2] In this chapter, I analyze several important plays that, since the triumph of the Cuban Revolution, have privileged black women characters as protagonists. These characters often represent ideological positions in regards to the Revolution, either as embodiments of the pre-revolutionary past or as signs of the Revolution's failure in its ideal of promoting—and enacting—racial equality. I am most interested in showing some of the patterns and strategies of characterisation that were used during the first years of the Revolution, as well as how they reappear in the twenty-first century with different intentions. Certain stereotypes resurface in the representation of black women in theatre, which is, unfortunately, a sign that despite the Revolution's discourse about racial equality, inequality and racism persist in Cuban society.

Different methodological perspectives have been used to engage with issues of race in Cuban theatre. What has been called a *teatro negro* [black theatre][3] in Cuban scholarship has not always meant the same. At times, the idea of a black theatre has responded to the playwright's race. On other occasions, the question of race and black theatre has been associated with the appearance within the plays of cultural traits that belong to Afro-Cuban culture, which includes elements of religion, music, masks, and dances. Martiatu Terry's anthology *Wanilere Teatro* is an example of this last approach. For instance, Armando González-Pérez's *Presencia negra: Teatro cubano de la diáspora* indistinctly draws as parameters for the anthology the use of Afro-Cuban deities and symbols, the authors' race, and the characters' racial features. Most scholarship focuses on the first two possibilities—for instance, Nancy Morejón, Martiatu Terry, and Alberto Curbelo, among others, have described the works of black playwrights and how their plays utilise their Afro-Cuban cultural heritage.[4] Yet the characteristics and strategies of representation of black characters in Cuban theatre have received much less attention. For these reasons, I focus on the depiction of black female bodies, and the strategies of representation used by these groundbreaking playwrights. Also, in general, the works of Cuban female playwrights have been scarcely published and studied, a fact that sparks my interest in analyzing here the plays of Maité Vera, Georgina Herrera, and Fátima Patterson.

2   Theatre After the Cuban Revolution

The Cuban Revolution officially promulgated the total equality of its citizens, though, in reality, diverse forms of racism persisted in society.[5] This chapter analyzes plays whose black characters problematise race, gender, and sexuality in Cuban stages. Through the study of the characters created by Maité Vera, José Milián, Eugenio Hernández Espinosa, Alberto Pedro, Rogelio Orizondo, Georgina Herrera, and Fátima Patterson, it is possible to analyze ideological notions in regards to how racism affects family, economic survival, and the professionalisation of these women through the years. In particular, I am interested in analyzing how the Revolution influenced certain attitudes and perceptions of race in the social imaginary.

Immediately after the triumph of the Cuban Revolution during the early 1960s, the recently created government aimed to integrate the black population to the revolutionary society. Many initiatives were taken to dismantle marginal neighbourhoods and integrate black workers to the state's labour force.[6] Government support helped develop educational and cultural programmes. Among these was an explicit and visible attempt to acknowledge the religious and cultural practices of black residents, including their religions, dances, myths, and music. It is during this decade when the Escuela Nacional de Arte (ENA) (National Art School) and Casa de las Américas were founded. While the ENA had the purpose of preparing the next generation of artists, musicians, and theatre makers of the country, Casa de las Américas became an epicentre for international culture, both promoting Cuban literature and art, and bringing back international recognition, visibility, and support from artists and intellectuals from elsewhere.[7]

Another fundamental institution from the decade was the Teatro Nacional de Cuba, which galvanised many projects in all artistic genres and directly affected theatrical production through the creation of the Seminario de Dramaturgia del Teatro Nacional [Playwriting Seminar of the National Theatre]. Many of the most important Cuban playwrights from that generation were formed at the Seminar, including Gerardo Fulleda León, Eugenio Hernández Espinosa, Tomás González, Maité Vera, and José Milián, among others. While the Seminar ceased its courses in 1963, the playwrights that emerged from it have continued working for several decades and become important figures in the panorama of Cuban culture.[8]

One of the authors who emerged from the Seminario de Dramaturgia was Maité Vera. Her comedy *Las Ulloa* (1963) focuses on the Ulloa family, a mixed-race family whose main concern is that its youngest member, Magali, can marry a white man. Magali's light skin colour can help her pass for white, which the family sees as her opportunity to succeed. But the hopes around Magali's future complicate when she falls in love with Julián, a black young man that she has met in school. Magali's character relates to *Cecilia Valdés*, the foundational novel of nineteenth-century Cuban literature. In the novel, Cecilia is a very light-skinned mulata with aspirations of passing and marrying 'up', but she is hindered by tragedies. This tragic mulata formula has reappeared in the many versions of Cirilo Villaverde's novel, and in many other texts and contexts.[9] In *Las Ulloa*, in contrast, the main conflict is not between a society that does not accept interracial unions, but between Chela, Magali's grandmother, the only black woman of the play, and Magali, who represents the younger generation formed within the Revolution.

The Ulloa family has had interracial marriages for two generations, starting with Chela, who feels eternally grateful to her dead husband, a white man who renounced his family's inheritance in order to marry her. Interraciality continues with Magali's parents, Esther and Rafael; he is mulato and she is white. Chela's two daughters, meanwhile, never married, since they would consider only white men that, in the end, were never what they expected or loved. Chela seeks only the best for Magali, which for her would be the possibility of passing, and having a family that can stand as a white family, therefore avoiding all the anti-black prejudices.

In *Las Ulloa*, all characters—at least all adults—are presented as flawed: they are resented either because they were discriminated against, or because they have internalised racism to the point of not seeing how their lives are shaped by the notion of 'racial improvement'—meaning that their racial markers, such as skin tone and hair, can be similar to those of a white person. The Ulloas are so concerned with passing that they forget all other aspects of life. Life in the family is bitter, and nobody is doing anything to change it: except for Magali. Despite its didactic tone, *Las Ulloa* is a good attempt to portray the particularities of race in the Cuba: where the visible features of blackness are much more important than the black heritage itself. It is not about not being black—but to pass, to seem white. In the context of the play, the conflict is resolved only because Magali belongs to a different generation: she is being educated in a school system that promulgates equality, and feels safe to take her decision of having a relationship with Julián. The optimism of the play is remarkable and signals the general enthusiasm of the 1960s, when the Revolution's promises of change were a quick *deus ex machina* that promised to solve all conflicts— inside *and* outside the theatre. The generational conflict between Chela and Magali, then, can also be understood as a symbolic racial representation of the changes introduced by the Revolution, which gives the play that didactic quality.

At the end of the play, Chela dies, and Magali decides to reconcile with Julián. The couple discusses their love in a park while comparing their relationship to the play that they had just read in school, *Romeo and Juliet*. In a final coda, Magali naively affirms that she believes in only one race: that of all colours (Vera 2010, 264). Since Chela's old mentality and resentment cannot be changed, the character dies. It is a way of signalling the conflict between old and new ideologies, which was one of the main overarching strategies of the Cuban Revolution's ideological discourse: 'old' meant what belonged to pre-1959 Cuba. Everything that had been a symptom of that capitalist era had to be erased and substituted with the 'new'. Remarkably, one of the driving ideological notions that emerged during the 1960s and supported revolutionary discourse was precisely Che Guevara's 'new man'. In a way, even though *Las Ulloa* was written two years before the publication of Che Guevara's *El socialismo y el hombre en Cuba* (1965), the play anticipates this idea of a new generation that thinks and acts differently, a generation that is, in other words, revolutionary. In that context, a black woman like Chela—who cannot overcome her prejudices and the traumas from her experience as a black woman in pre-revolutionary Cuba—needs to die, so that the next generation can have its space.

Another play from an alumni of the Seminario de Dramaturgia del Teatro Nacional is José Milián's *Vade Retro*.[10] *Vade Retro* presents a conflict of pre-revolutionary Cuban society—its premise is to show how racial discrimination was a fundamental and systemic problem of capitalism. Its protagonist, La Coreana, is probably one of the most pathetic characters of Cuban theatre: she is a black, poor, crazy woman who is mocked by everyone. *Vade Retro*—a sort of tragic farce—metatheatrically alludes to a circus performance on Christmas Eve, and it explicitly signals the contrast between the joyous character of the festivity for a few characters, while La Coreana miserably suffers the mocking, scorn, and humiliation from all the people that she encounters. At a moment of supposed generosity and solidarity, she is constantly despised. At the end, there is a flashback in which she remembers how even her mother assured her that her only future was to find a rich man or to become a prostitute. She repeats the same to her so-called son: a black rag doll that she carries constantly. La Coreana had once been the lover of a white man, but he abandoned her while she was vulnerable and pregnant, thus ensuring her madness. Finally, in the last scene of the play, La Coreana kills herself. As she repeats several times in the play, there is no future. Life is a circus in which black women like her have no other place than to be observed, and mocked, once her sex appeal has faded.

At the beginning of the published version of the play, the author's statement emphasises the existence of La Coreana as a real person, who was 'abandoned by her lover, by her family, and by the society where she had to live. Victim of the misery and madness generated by chronic hunger, this deranged woman, with her symbolic rag son on her back, is a terrible example of that distant past of our country, which, unfortunately, is a reality of some countries that are still victims of underdevelopment and capitalist exploitation' (Milián 2010, 511). By situating the context of the play in Cuba's capitalist past, Milián defers any debate about race in contemporary society. Since this problem purportedly no longer exists in the present, the play functions as a mere reminder of how the past was, and how life continues to be—according to the playwright—in other capitalist countries. Like Vera, Milián relies on the Revolution's promise of a better present and future, using the past as a mere contrasting element: a past that has been happily overcome. Social change and individual improvement seem to be all in the hands of a larger ideological revolutionary process.

La Coreana's abject situation—despised by everybody, and conscious of her status as black, poor, and marginal—is consistent with other depictions of black women in a pre-revolutionary context. For instance, the first story of the film *Soy Cuba* (1964), a famous Soviet and Cuban co-production, also depicts a black woman who is forced by her poverty to dance and prostitute herself in a bar during the fifties.[11] But, since the official discourse of the Cuban Revolution was precisely the eradication of prostitution, no prostitutes or women of dubious morals reappeared on Cuban stages until the twenty-first century, in some cases alluding to women who married foreign men and emigrated to European countries after the fall of the Eastern Bloc. Then, without the economic support of the Soviet Union during the 1990s, the Cuban economy totally collapsed, and the black population was especially affected. Tourism emerged as the main source of income for the country, and with it prostitution visibly flourished, especially in touristic cities. Examples of such processes appear in *Las lágrimas no hacen ruido al caer* [Tears do not make noise when falling] (2003), by Alberto Pedro, and Eugenio Hernández Espinosa's *Chita no come maní* [Chita does not eat peanuts] (2002),[12] since both plays present black women living in foreign countries—Lithuania and Italy, respectively—married to foreign men.

Eugenio Hernández Espinosa is one of the most prolific Cuban playwrights. He is also an accomplished director, and one of the Cuban intellectuals who, over the course of his career, has consistently explored the topic of race in Cuban theatre and society. Among his most significant titles regarding the issue of race are *María Antonia, Emelina Cundiamor, Tíbor Galarraga*, and *Chita no come maní*. As a tragedy written in 1964 and that premiered in 1967, *María Antonia* is Eugenio Hernández Espinosa's most famous play. María Antonia is the tragic heroine par excellence: her passion for Julian, excessive and fatal, leads her to death, despite her godmother's efforts to invoke positive forces that could take her away from her *fatum*. Here, Afro-Cuban gods and men go hand in hand, and María Antonia's destiny is marked by these gods. But this woman does not rely on a revolutionary ideological change, nor expects one. She dares to defy authority, in this case her religion, to accomplish her desire and pride. The polemic raised by its premiere, directed by Roberto Blanco, was so intense that the play was finally censored by Cuban authorities. According to Martiatu Terry: 'For the first time it was a woman, a black woman (not a mulata), a transgressor, who starred not in a vaudeville or in a comedy, but nothing less than in a tragedy. *Santería* was shown not as witchcraft, but as a religion that is an expression of wisdom...' (Martiatu Terry 2005, 23). *María Antonia*'s performance was a smash hit with audiences, but the play introduced a world that had seemingly disappeared thanks to the Revolution. By 1967 this world of religion, violence, ignorance, gambling, and poverty was not considered appropriate to the Ministry of Culture. And, since this play did not reflect the new directions of society, it was censored and canceled. *María Antonia*'s censorship was an early symptom of the cultural policies of the 1970s.[13]

Beginning in the late 1960s, and especially during the next decade, later known as *Quinquenio gris* or *Decenio negro* [the gray five years, or the black decade], many Afro-Cuban artists, homosexuals, or those with a relatively differing political view, were taken from the cultural life of the country, and some were sent to the Unidades Militares de Ayuda a la Producción (UMAP) work camps. Some black intellectuals were accused of attempting to foment a 'black power' in Cuba.[14] For many of these authors, there is a considerable gap in their productions or publications during those years. Also, black characters and plays with Afro-Cuban components decreased significantly. Ileana Sanz explains:

> The vigorous creative effervescence of the Sixties, which stimulated the exploration and re-evaluation of the African component, languished in the following decade. Sustained in the priority of safeguarding the unity of the nation, cultural policy promoted the image of a culture and identity without tensions, which equated the unitary with the national, and dismissed the exaltation of one of the components, in this case the African. (Sanz 2003, 171)

Dramatic production during the 1970s diminished considerably, mainly because of the separation of many playwrights and creators from their positions in state-owned cultural institutions—and by that time the state was the sole workforce employer. Another phenomenon that also affected dramatic production and its authors was the emergence of the so-called *teatro nuevo* [new theatre], a tendency that aimed to bring theatre to non-traditional performance spaces: streets, factories, and rural communities. The *teatro nuevo* opposed the *teatro de sala* [theatre in venues] which was perceived as conventional and bourgeois. As a result of the *teatro nuevo* movement, moreover, important experiences with the audiences and with new forms of dramaturgy emerged—not necessarily availed by a conventional dramatic structure—as the examples of Teatro Escambray and the Cabildo Teatral Santiago attest.[15] For these groups, racial conflicts were not a main concern, and the lack of black characters during this period demonstrates how the focus was geared towards other ideological concerns of the time, such as revolutionary participation and social integration in all spheres of society.

3   Theatre in the 1980s and 1990s

The next decade, the 1980s, was marked by the creation of Havana's International Theatre festival, and the first graduation of the Instituto Superior de Arte (ISA), in 1976. ISA was the first—and still is—the only university for the arts in Cuba. Its Facultad de Arte Teatral (Theatre College) for the first time offered as majors the specialties of Theatre Criticism and Playwriting, which ever since have formed most of Cuban playwrights and theatre critics. This new generation not only studied, questioned, and participated from the theatrical life of the time, but they were also responsible for creating new aesthetics and incorporating new topics to their plays. According to Carrió, the 1980s was marked by two different aesthetic tendencies: on one side a group of young creators were experimenting with the body and scenic discourses that do not necessarily respond to a written play—with Victor Varela, Marianela Boán, and Teatro Buendía as its main examples—and, on the other side, there was a group of playwrights who were producing what has been called as 'the juvenile tendency' (Carrió 2002, 39). This juvenile tendency 'often superficial, hypercritical and paternalistic' (Pogolotti 2002, 99) also did not address race as a main concern, much more preoccupied by a new generation of people who had grown under the Revolution and were not responding to their parent's or to social expectations. Again, the conflict between the old and the new was present on Cuban stages, but not associated with race, since racism was considered solved long time ago.

By the early 1990s, however, the fall of the Eastern bloc and the Soviet Union drastically affected Cuba in all areas. With its main political and economic ally gone, Cuba fell in a deep crisis—euphemistically called *Período Especial* (Special Period). In regards to race, despite the official discourse of racial equality in Cuba, and especially after the Special Period, the black population had less access to opportunities of better economic advantages, and more police repression and harassment. Historian Alejandro de la Fuente has consistently studied this problem and has argued that by 1986 'significant progress had been made toward building a nation that was truly for all' (de la Fuente 2001, 337), with more inclusion in government representation, and similar standards of living to the white population. However, during the Special Period, black workers were excluded from the emergent economy that actually offered the opportunity of earning a decent living.

> Thus the crisis of the 1990s resulted in growing social and racial tensions. Based on racially charged notions such as "good presence" and "cultural level," Afro-Cubans have been denied opportunities in some of the most lucrative sectors of the economy, particularly in tourism. As is usually the case, the intensity of racist prejudices is related directly to the desirability of the sector in which the discrimination is taking place. Afro-Cubans' strategies of adaptation, which frequently involve participation in illegal activities such as prostitution, black-market activities, or plain robbery, are in turn used to demonstrate their alleged natural inferiority. Such inferiority is further evidenced, so the argument goes, by the fact that after four decades of socialism and antidiscrimination efforts, Afro-Cubans make up the bulk of the so-called criminals and *marginales*. Given these perceptions, it is not surprising that blacks are singled out as potential suspects by the police, as a journalist claims. (de la Fuente 2001, 328–329)

After the profound moral and economic crisis of the Special Period, and the relative ideological opening of the first decade of the twenty-first century, the question of race would be brought up front and discussed again in the space of the theatre. This return of the *marginales* that de la Fuente explains is verifiable in the plays that I will further discuss. In post-Special Period Cuba, black women were frequently left out of opportunities—which was, in a way, a return to their social position before the Revolution—to judge from the similarities between the modes of representation of such characters in some of the plays from the 2000s.

4 Twenty-First-Century Theatre

In *Chita no come maní* [Chita does not eat peanuts] (2004),[16] Eugenio Hernández Espinosa focuses on a black woman living in Italy with her husband. *Chita* is a one-act play that could be characterised as a comedy, due to its irony and constant scenic games, despite its quite tragic dramatic situation. Chita, the Spanish name for Cheeta, a chimpanzee that accompanied Tarzan in many of its movies, is the nickname that Giácomo has given to his wife, Niurka, a black woman that he met in Cuba and who now lives with him in Italy. Giácomo is devoured by jealousy, and encloses Niurka in a cage. He gives her bananas and peanuts and calls her Chita. Upon arriving in Italy, despite her initial excitement of finally leaving behind the poverty of her family, Niurka found that Giácomo behaves erratically and violently, and has even asked her to stay in a cage and behave as an animal for the viewing pleasure of his friends. The situation of the play is profoundly disturbing: Niurka is in the cage, arguing with Giácomo, who criticises her, her family, and her country. According to Giácomo, Cuba is so miserable that he 'bought' her from her father with just 50 dollars and a bottle of olive oil. She responds by talking about love, but he says that there was never love, only her desire to escape Cuba. Giácomo is frustrated because finally he acknowledges that he took advantage of the poverty of a country where black women are discriminated and forgotten, even inside their own country:

> GIÁCOMO. I am not crueler than your country, which ignores you. Or don't you remember that every time we would go out an officer would unexpectedly come up, asking for your ID? Don't you remember the day that, right before my eyes, you were loaded to a truck as if you were garbage, and you were taken away from me? ... Do you want to return to a country where they say that you are part of a minority, when the thousands of thousands of Cubans who have left are white? (Hernández Espinosa 2009, 318)

Niurka attempts to defend herself, arguing with Giácomo, and finally succeeds in getting out of the cage and locking him on it. But the whole situation finally releases their inner truths: she acknowledges that she had never loved him in Cuba and that she faked love to marry him. They end up embracing, and the stage directions assure that they are finally doing it with 'Love'.

Overall, Hernández Espinosa's play is highly problematic, not only because of its depiction of a black woman in a cage, imprisoned by a white man in a foreign country, but because it was performed in Cuba, to a Cuban audience, where the government fails to acknowledge the existence of prostitution in the country, and the demographics involved in it, which are mostly black women. Hernández Espinosa gives a space on the stage to those prostitutes who are not named by the state, and places them in a situation where, rather than succeeding in total happiness, as they assure when they return—according to the public imaginary—they are coerced by two impossibles: these women cannot live outside Cuba, with husbands that do not respect them, but neither can they return to a country where all doors seem closed for them. It is under this context that plays such as *Chita no come maní* emerged, making visible at the theatre these new *marginales* that emerged after the 1990s social reconfiguration of the country.

As I previously mentioned, Alberto Pedro's *Las lágrimas no hacen ruido al caer* [Tears do not make noise when falling] (2003), also presents a woman trapped in a foreign country—this time Lithuania. The solo show, interpreted by Monse Duany and directed by Miguel Abreu, premiered in September of 2013 in Havana and has been touring intermittently for several years. Osiris, the protagonist, takes refuge in the music of Cuban diva La Lupe and in her religion to survive the coldness of Lithuania and racism in Europe. At the end of her monologue, Osiris hopes to arrive in Miami somehow. If she escaped San Pedrito—her little town in Eastern Cuba—and survived a post-Soviet Lithuania, she might be able to get to the United States. Osiris uses her memories—and the spirits who accompany her, including La Lupe—to affirm her values, her uniqueness, and her desire to live beyond her circumstances. She sings, she reminisces and finally decides to arrive somehow in Miami. This final resolution is problematic: another country will not necessarily solve her problem, but her momentum to arrive there at least provides her with the agency that she has lacked over the years in Lithuania to change her life. Contrary to Hernández Espinosa's Chita—who reconciles with her abusive husband—Osiris is willing to take the risk of leaving her husband and make a life of her own. Notice how the protagonist's name evokes the Egyptian God of the dead, of resurrection and fertility. Alberto Pedro's Osiris uses her power—the spirit of her dead, and her strength—to give the leap of faith towards Miami.

Another play that presents a black woman character, also in a marginal and abject position, is Rogelio Orizondo's *Vacas* [Cows] (2008).[17] *Vacas* has three women on stage. One of them, Betina, is a black woman who, despite being educated, had the back luck of being born in an old building that has collapsed. Since Betina has nowhere to live, she sleeps on the back of a nightclub where she dreams of singing one day, and begs for cigarettes. There she meets Liuba, a woman who dreams of going back to Russia, her mother's native country. Liuba invites Betina to her house, where she lives with her girlfriend Eva. Liuba finally decides to leave for Russia, leaving Eva with Betina, since they are now lovers. At the end of the play, Betina has landed a new job and has found meaning and love in her life. Here, the sex appeal of Betina's black body is not dismissed, since it propitiates Betina's integration to the queer family, but it is not the centre of her participation in the play. Actually, when Liuba takes her to her home, Betina is bleeding and lacks a tooth, that she has lost due to the aggressiveness of a man in the street. Liuba's intentions are an expression of solidarity and fraternity, not the result of her sexual attraction to Betina. It is Eva who falls for Betina, not Liuba.

Betina was an educated woman, a well-known publicist, but when the building falls, she has nowhere to turn. Like her house, her world has fallen apart. Her work is not a solution, since a state salary in Cuba cannot provide the sufficient means for survival. Betina realises that there is no future for her, and since she knows that she will not have support from the state—nor is she waiting for it—she resigns herself to live on the streets until she finds refuge with a queer family. This situation had been unthinkable to the theatre of the 1960s, so full of promises and hope, both because this kind of situation of poverty and marginality was considered eliminated from the country, or at most it was seen as a remnant of a capitalist past; and also since homosexuality was penalised and considered a capitalist aberration as well. But in the Cuba of the twenty-first century, black women like Betina have found themselves with a career and no money to repair their houses, or to buy food or clothes.

Vacas is also a search for origins: Liuba goes back to Russia in search of her mother's roots, and Betina, who used to do publicity campaigns for African issues that she never quite understood, ends up searching for her African origins, way back in time. Obviously she cannot know who her real ancestors were in Africa, but once she finds love with Eva, she is able to create her own mythology of her past. At the end of the play, Betina tells this story to Eva: 'I made a white cake. And I put our names on it. When my ancestors were left alone in Africa because the slavers took all the strong blacks, they formed The Tribe of the Moon. They would tattoo a moon on their foreheads and on full moon nights they would love each other, releasing their internal fire until the camp fires were lit... On full moon nights my ancestors were the happiest on earth. They all became goddesses and could give rise to fire and love' (Orizondo 2008, 54). Betina legitimises her love for Eva in an impossible past. And that past makes her proud, and full, and happy. The past liberates her and fulfills her dreams of having a new family, a new tribe, her own personal Tribe of the Moon, symbolised in the cake that she has baked for Eva.

Betina is presented by Orizondo with a certain degree of abjection: she lives on the street, she urinates frequently—and as a sign of rebellion—in front of the man who watches that nobody enters the building where she once lived, and begs for cigarettes. Like in Milián's and Hernández Espinosa's plays, here a black woman is somewhat abject for the rest of the characters and for the spectators, but here, instead of presenting a world with no exit or future, Orizondo places the hopes and new life of the character in a queer life. Orizondo is the youngest author I analyze in this chapter. Graduated in 2009 from the University of Arts (ISA), in Havana, his plays both formally and ideologically have a queer sensibility and political irreverence. In Orizondo's work, the didacticism and optimism of the previous decades is all gone. Rather, his plays are infused with the possibility of those new forms of affiliation, which are visible through the desecration of language, sexuality, and political correctness.

Another strategy of presenting black women characters in the twenty-first century is by going back to a different time, but while the plays from the 1960s used that context to show the conflicts that had been overcome thanks to the Revolution, these playwrights propose new forms of attachment and the recognition of historical black figures that had been stereotyped in a specific condition. That is the case, for example, of *Penúltimo sueño de Mariana* [Mariana's Penultimate Dream], by Georgina Herrera.[18] Herrera situates as her protagonist a very important historical figure in Cuban history: Mariana Grajales, the mother of the Maceo brothers. The Maceo brothers participated in the Independence wars, and especially Antonio was one of its main leaders. Mariana Grajales' is mentioned in Cuban schools, most notably as an example of Cuban patriotism, as she sent all her sons to the war, regardless of her own pain. In Cuban schools, however, little is said about her as historical figure, and much less about what exactly it was like for a black woman to be immersed in political issues in nineteenth-century Cuba.

In this play, Mariana is about to die in a foreign land: Jamaica. There, her daughter Dominga takes care of her. In a dream-like state, she remembers how before the beginning of the War of 1968, her family heard the news of a possible rebellion and embraced such possibility, and how she constrained her feelings in order to survive the continuous news of the wounds and death of her sons. The presence on stage of Yemayá, with its drums, chants, and dances, guarantees a type of action that it is not necessarily literal, but an embodiment of the spirituality of the characters. Yemayá is a goddess from the Yoruba Afro-Cuban religion, and here the playwright attributes to her being the 'mother' (protector saint) of Mariana Grajales. Yemayá is also a connecting force between her and Fermina Lucumí, another character who exemplifies rebellion and feminine force. Fermina was a slave who led a rebellion in her sugar cane plantation. She was imprisoned and shot, along with her enslaved male companions. The event occurred in 1843 in Matanzas, one of the areas with a larger concentration of slaves in nineteenth-century Cuba.

On her deathbed there is not much that Grajales can do, but she encourages her daughter to continue dreaming of freedom, a dream that has to be conquered by force. Grajales knows that similar to the struggle to emancipate enslaved peoples, Spain would not peacefully concede Cuban independence. The only way to achieve that freedom is through rebellion, and from her deathbed, she dreams of it. The dream situates Mariana in an abject state—she does not belong to the living nor to the dead. She sees her dead sons, she reminisces and talks about moments from the past, before the war for independence. At times she is completely lucid and talks to her daughter about what it was like to experience the loss of most of her family and the pain of living in a foreign land. But through this abject state she finally recognises the horrible pain that she endured throughout her life, and therefore, she can be seen as a human being, fragile and courageous at the same time. Herrera humanises Grajales' historical figure, which has been seen by Cuba historiography as a mere embodiment of the exemplary mother who sacrifices her own sons for the nation.

In *Penúltimo sueño de Mariana* history and fiction go hand to hand: both Grajales and Lucumí are historical characters, but the link with Yemayá is a fictional element created by Herrera. Here, the playwright proposes new forms of affiliation and historical influences that go beyond the traditional narratives of historiography. Though there is no evidence of a relationship between both women, the play creates a spiritual link that leads to rebellion, resistance, and pride. The dream-like state of the play—with Mariana Grajales and Fermina Lucumí connected via Yemayá—allows the presentation of new forms of attachment between two historical black women who dared to be rebels, but who, despite their sacrifice, have been forgotten—or stereotyped—by Cuban historiography.

Similar to *Penúltimo sueño de Mariana*, Fátima Patterson's *Iniciación en blanco y negro para mujeres sin color* [Initiation in black and white for colorless women] (2011), attempts to create new forms of attachment through religion, music, and spirituality. *Iniciación en blanco y negro para mujeres sin color* takes the form of a ritual, both in terms of dramatic structure and because of the relationship established with the audience and with space. When the spectators are still outside the theatre, the actors purify the room with the smoke that comes from burning some aromatic herbs and then invite the audience to 'clean up' at the entrance of the theatre with the scented water of a recipient (this type of ritual is typical of Yoruba ceremonies). The entrance to the theatre also occurs with the accompaniment of musicians, as if it were a procession. The musicians remain onstage for the rest of the performance, providing the soundtrack behind a curtain that says 'Initiation'. The notion of the play as ritual ends when both musicians and actors leave the stage at the end of the play and invite the spectators to join them in a carnivalesque retreat with music and dance. Patterson's performance invites the audience to participate in the ritual, which demands on the spectator another level of physical and mental presence. The spectator is being part of an experience that is also spiritual and energetic, not just artistic. The powerful smell of herbs, the music, and the water with which spectators wash their hands when entering the space, create another degree of awareness towards the action on the stage.

In *Iniciación en blanco y negro para mujeres sin color*, Patterson positions a white woman (Blanca) and a black woman (Negra) as leading characters, in addition to a group of women that act as a chorus or in various roles along the different scenes. The play does not develop a narrative single argument. Instead, several small conflicts and stories are weaved, with the help of the powerful live music of the drums on stage. Both lead characters: Blanca and Negra, reflect on the ways in which women have been historically stripped away from power. They also wonder about the ancestors that they had and are unknown to them—due to the lack of documentation for many slaves and in black families in general. Finally, they imagine a rebellion. If at the beginning there was some discrepancy about the forms and objectives to do so, they end up agreeing about the need for a rebellion against patriarchy. The reasons to do so, as Negra affirms, are many: 'For the tears shed, for the children lost on the road, for the dress ripped away from the wounded body, for respect for myself, that's why I scream' (Patterson 2011, 4).

The ritual—besides its relationship with the audience and the use of musical instruments and chants that are used in Afro-Cuban religious ceremonies—also frames the action in other ways. The notion of death–life–resurrection appears as a common trope within the dialogues: for Afro-Cuban religions ancestors and other dead are part of the life of the living. A spiritual family—invisible to many—is part of the everyday life of these women. There are also other elements of religious practices that appear in the play, such as a scene in which Erzili—a Haitian Vodou goddess appears in a trance. The actresses perform a scene of trance that is common in religion—but not in theatrical spaces. Erzili's scene connects the experience of women during the Haitian Revolution with the Cuban stages—evoking not only the Haitian Revolution as a historical landmark in the Caribbean, but also to connect the black women experience beyond the Cuban island, and towards a Caribbean solidarity.

Patterson takes advantage of the fragmented structure of the piece to rely on the poetic capacity of dialogue and delves into language and its meanings, hence the emphasis on certain words such as 'seed', 'belly', and 'death'. Instead of one single character and its individual conflicts, Patterson presents a collective character in which several black women discuss the modes of a revolution, a revolution that has to start with language: 'It is up to us, nobody but us, to find the word that will unveil the mystery; to us because we are instruments, containers of something bigger than ourselves, bigger than all of you. My word comes now, the word denied for so long, the wet word, not by distance but by mourning, the word drowned but not wrecked' (Patterson 2011, 11). Through a poetic language and accompanied by the movement and the music of the drums, the women deconstruct the language that has fixed them as stereotypes of procreation and sex, denying them the agency to change their lives and act upon the world.

Now joined together through the ritual, black women and white women can finally start the change. To do so, they have a certain memo: 'First: it is strictly forbidden the participation in satanic activities that detract from moral and good conduct of our class. Second: it is forbidden to recall events that ridicule and/or minimise us. Third: it is forbidden to express oneself with an inappropriate or coarse language that might be associated with episodes of yesteryear, which could be used in a destructive way' (Patterson 2011, 15). Change must start with language, since language is the expression of a symbolic order. By creating new forms of affiliation between black and white women, Patterson also situates in the ritual the potentiality of change, of sisterhood, and the possibility of overcoming, together, the stereotypes and oppression of patriarchy.

5   Conclusion

While this is not an exhaustive archive of black female characters in Cuban theatre, it helps delineate some types of characters and the stereotypes associated with them. Also, I have pointed out some of the strategies that have frequently been used in the characterisation of black women, such as sexualisation, abjection, and the importance of mother figures. Unfortunately, many of the stereotypes associated with black women are still used in their theatrical representation. While Cuban intellectuals are arguing for more spaces for open discussion about race in Cuba, and for more opportunities for black people within spaces of power in Cuban society, it is still difficult to overcome the stereotypes associated with blackness in the social imaginary.[19] As a playwright, I have also attempted to create plays in which black women are represented beyond stereotypical notions of femininity, motherhood, or as a sexualised body. Two of my plays incorporate black women who struggle to find their place in a society that hardly accepts its inherited colonial attitudes and its rampant racism: *My vernicle*, a fictional work inspired by the life and works of black Cuban artist Belkis Ayón, and *Museo*,[20] in which the younger generation of a black family ends up leaving the country due to their lack of opportunities to live a better life. As a white Cuban woman, I recognise my limitations to represent the black Cuban experience, but both as a scholar and playwright, my aim is to contribute to an ongoing conversation about race and theatre in Cuba and abroad.

In this chapter, I have explored how, if in the theatre of the 1960s racism and marginality were portrayed as consequences of a capitalist and unequal society, the theatre of the 2000s showed that these problems were not solved after more than forty years of Revolution. By representing women that had to leave their country to provide sufficient means of survival for them and their families, even as they faced new challenges and potential discrimination abroad, or by showing how the state was unable to provide for their black women despite of being professionally educated, the playwrights signalled the need to recognise new forms of racism in contemporary Cuban society and suggested that alternative forms of solidarity, love, and empowerment are being created outside the state's heteronormative paradigm. Also, these playwrights present ritual and religion as those alternative ways of spiritual connection, agency, communal affiliations, and as a possibility for change.

In general, the bodies of these black women stand for the ideological notions of the context in which they were created. In some cases, they embody the hope for a revolutionary future and its promise of ending systemic racism, poverty, and the notion of whiteness as markers of superiority; but after the Special Period crisis, these hopes were certainly diminished, if not all gone. Then, the need to represent the social problems and the increasing marginalisation of the black population was primordial, and as such, the bodies of these black women were a powerful sign to prove so. Also, these plays are a powerful reminder of the ways in which the historiography of the Revolution has left aside, in some cases by simplification and in others outright erasure, historical black women that were fundamental to achieve slave emancipation and eventually Cuban independence. Finally, through the sacred space of the ritual and its communal character, *Iniciación en blanco y negro para mujeres sin color* offers the possibility of imagining and starting to create new forms of representation of black women in the social imaginary, one that privileges empowerment and agency over sexualisation and abjection.

Notes

1. See Fraunhar, *Mulata Nation*; Jill Lane, *Blackface Cuba, 1840–1895* (Philadelphia: University of Pennsylvania Press, 2005); Vera Kutzinski, *Sugar's Secrets: Race and the Erotics of Cuban Nationalism* (Charlottesville: University Press of Virginia, 1994); Raquel Mendieta Costa, "Exotic Exports: The Myth of the Mulatta," in *Corpus Delecti: Performance Art of the Americas*, edited by Coco Fusco, 43–54 (New York: Routledge, 2000); Alicia Arrizón, "Race-ing Performativity through Transculturation, Taste and the Mulata Body," *Theatre Research International* 27, no. 2 (July 2002): 136–152.

2. *Teatro bufo* was a nineteenth-century theatre form that used blackface to identify its black characters. It has been considered the cradle of a Cuban national theatre, and an important milestone for the formation of a Cuban cultural identity. Some historians, such as Inés María Martiatu Terry, have criticised statements that uncritically situate the *bufo* as a 'national theatre', without considering the ways in which black characters were portrayed, and what kind of 'nation' this theatre was representing since there was impersonation despite no representation. Inés María Martiatu Terry, *Wanilere Teatro* (La Habana: Letras Cubanas, 2005): 13–14.

3. All translations are mine.

4. Morejón, Nancy. 2005. *Ensayos*. La Habana: Letras Cubanas and Curbelo, Alberto. 2012. La absurda realidad del ser. *Tablas* 3: 37-48.

5. Other scholars have consistently studied this problem. See Alejandro de la Fuente, *A Nation for All: Race, Inequality, and Politics in Twentieth-Century Cuba* (Chapel Hill: University of North Carolina Press, 2001); Zuleica Romay, *Elogio de la altea o las paradojas de la racialidad* (La Habana: Casa de las Américas, 2014).

6. This process of social integration was reflected in plays such as *Santa Camila de La Habana Vieja*, by José Ramón Brene, *Andoba*, by Abraham Rodríguez, and Cuban film *De cierta manera*, directed by Sara Gómez, among others. José Ramón Brene. "Santa Camila de la Habana Vieja." (*Re-Pasar el Puente*, La Habana: Letras Cubanas, 2010), 43–132.

7. Today both institutions still operate under the same premises.

8. One of the projects related with the Teatro Nacional was Ediciones El Puente, an editorial project that aimed to promote the works of young writers and playwrights. Due to ideological conflicts within Cuban institutions, though, Ediciones El Puente ended in 1965. Two of the plays analyzed in this chapter, *Las Ulloa* and *Vade Retro*, were featured in an anthology that could not be published by El Puente during the 1960s and were finally completed by Inés María Martiatu. See Inés María Martiatu, *Re-Pasar El Puente* (La Habana: Letras Cubanas, 2010), 41.

9. Other versions of *Cecilia Valdés* include the novel *La loma del ángel*, by Reinaldo Arenas, and the plays *La virgencita de cobre*, by Norge Espinosa, and *Parece blanca*, by Abelardo Estorino. For Cecilia Valdés' versions in post-Soviet Cuba, see David Lisenby, "Frustrated Mulatta Aspirations: Reiterations of 'Cecilia Valdés' in Post-Soviet Cuba," *Afro-Hispanic Review* 31, no. 1 (2012): 87–104.

10. Mikhail Kalatozov. *I Am Cuba: The Ultimate Edition*. Harrington Park: Milestone Film & Video, 2007.

11. *Vade Retro* had its premiere on October 21, 1967, by the Conjunto Dramático de Camagüey, directed by Pedro Castro.
12. It had its premiere on April 2, 2004, interpreted by Monse Duany and Nelson González, under Hernández Espinosa's direction.
13. After its censorship in 1967 *María Antonia* was not restaged until 2011, when Hernández Espinosa himself directed it. For him, restaging the play 40 years later was a proof that the original conditions that gave rise to the play remained essentially the same. That is, despite all the projects that had supposedly solved the dilemma of blacks in Cuba, the marginal world not only exists in Cuba, but it actually grows within the current conditions of life, and the country's deteriorating economy, values, and education. Eugenio Hernández Espinosa, *María Antonia*. (La Habana: Letras Cubanas, 1979).
14. For more information on this matter, see Inés Martiatu Terry Tomás González: "el autor como protagonista de su tiempo" (*Tablas* 3–4, 2008), 139–143. and Lillian Guerra, *Visions of Power in Cuba: Revolution, Redemption, and Resistance, 1959–1971*. (Chapel Hill: University of North Carolina Press, 2012).
15. See Raquel Carrió, "Teatro y Modernidad" (*Tablas* LXX, 2002), 33–39; Graziella Pogolotti, "El Teatro Cubano En Vísperas de Una Nueva Década" (*Tablas* LXX, 2002), 98–102.
16. It had its premiere on April 2, 2004, interpreted by Monse Duany and Nelson González, under Hernández Espinosa's direction. Eugenio Hernández Espinosa, "Chita no come maní," *Quiquiribú Mandinga* (La Habana: Letras Cubanas, 2009), 307–326.
17. Rogelio Orizondo, *Vacas* (La Habana: Ediciones Unión, 2008).
18. The date of its writing is unclear, but it was performed in 2004 by the Compañía Rita Montaner and the Grupo Espacio Abierto, under the direction of Xiomara Calderón. Georgina Herrera, "Penúltimo sueño de Mariana" (*Wanilere Teatro*, La Habana: Letras Cubanas, 2005), 277–315.
19. In that regard it is important to mention the works of Zuleica Romay, Roberto Zurbano, Alberto Abreu Arcia, and the group Cofradía de la Negritud, among others.
20. Lilianne Lugo. *Museo* (La Habana: Ediciones Alarcos, 2011).

References

Arrizón, Alicia. 2002. Race-ing Performativity Through Transculturation, Taste and the Mulata Body. *Theatre Research International* 27 (2): 136–152.

Brene, José Ramón. 2010. Santa Camila de la Habana Vieja. In *Re-Pasar el Puente*, ed. Inés María Martiatu, 43–132. La Habana: Letras Cubanas.

Curbelo, Alberto. 2012. La absurda realidad del ser. *Tablas* 3: 37-48.

Carrió, Raquel. 2002. Teatro y Modernidad. *Tablas* LXX: 33–39.

Fraunhar, Alison. 2018. *Mulata Nation. Visualizing Race and Gender in Cuba*. Jackson: University Press of Mississippi.

de la Fuente, Alejandro. 2001. *A Nation for All: Race, Inequality, and Politics in Twentieth-Century Cuba*. Chapel Hill: University of North Carolina Press.

González-Pérez, Armando. 1999. *Presencia negra: teatro cubano de la diáspora*. Madrid: Betania

Guerra, Lillian. 2012. *Visions of Power in Cuba: Revolution, Redemption, and Resistance, 1959–1971.* Chapel Hill: University of North Carolina Press.

Guevara, Ernesto. 1965. El socialismo y el hombre en Cuba. *Marxists: Archivo Che Guevara.* https://www.marxists.org/espanol/guevara/65-socyh.htm.

Hernández Espinosa, Eugenio. 1979. *María Antonia.* La Habana: Letras Cubanas.

———. 2009. Chita no come maní. In *Quiquiribú Mandinga*, 307–326. La Habana: Letras Cubanas.

Herrera, Georgina. 2005. Penúltimo sueño de Mariana. In *Wanilere Teatro*, ed. Inés María Martiatu, 277–315. La Habana: Letras Cubanas.

Kutzinski, Vera M. 1994. *Sugar's Secrets: Race and the Erotics of Cuban Nationalism.* Charlottesville: University Press of Virginia.

Lane, Jill. 2005. *Blackface Cuba, 1840–1895.* Philadelphia: University of Pennsylvania Press.

Lisenby, David. 2012. Frustrated Mulatta Aspirations: Reiterations of 'Cecilia Valdés' in Post-Soviet Cuba. *Afro-Hispanic Review* 31 (1): 87–104.

Lugo, Lilianne. 2011. *Museo.* La Habana: Editorial Alarcos.

Martiatu Terry, Inés María. 2005. *Wanilere Teatro.* La Habana: Letras Cubanas.

———. 2008. Tomás González: el autor como protagonista de su tiempo. *Tablas* (3–4): 139–143.

———. 2010. *Re-Pasar El Puente.* La Habana: Letras Cubanas.

Mendieta Costa, Raquel. 2000. Exotic Exports: The Myth of the Mulatta. In *Corpus Delecti: Performance Art of the Americas*, ed. Coco Fusco, 43–54. New York: Routledge.

Milián, José. 2010. Vade Retro. In *Re-Pasar el Puente*, ed. Inés María Martiatu, 509–541. La Habana: Letras Cubanas.

Morejón, Nancy. 2005. *Ensayos.* La Habana: Letras Cubanas.

Orizondo, Rogelio. 2008. *Vacas.* La Habana: Ediciones Unión.

Patterson, Fátima. 2011. *Iniciación en blanco y negro para mujeres sin color.* Manuscript.

Pogolotti, Graziella. 2002. El teatro cubano en vísperas de una nueva década. *Tablas* LXX: 98–102.

Romay, Zuleica. 2014. *Elogio de la altea o las paradojas de la racialidad.* La Habana: Casa de las Américas.

Sanz, Ileana. 2003. Desde los márgenes: la literatura oral afrocubana invade el discurso letrado. In *Rito y representación: los sistemas mágico-religiosos en la cultura cubana contemporánea*, ed. Yana Elsa Brugal and Beatriz J. Rizk, 167–172. Madrid: Editorial Iberoamericana/Vervuert.

Vera, Maité. 2010. Las Ulloa. In *Re-Pasar el Puente*, ed. Inés María Martiatu, 225–264. La Habana: Letras Cubanas.

CHAPTER 15

Black Performances and Black Artists Performing in Contemporary Brazil

Victor Hugo Leite de Aquino Soares
and Roberta K. Matsumoto

1 INTRODUCTION: SOCIOHISTORICAL CONTEXTUALISATION AND BRAZILIAN BLACK PERFORMANCES

The history of black performance in Brazil follows that of the country in its formation. During the colonial period, a large contingent of enslaved Africans of diverse ethnic groups arrived in Brazil. These African peoples can be associated with a variety of knowledge, cultures and ways of life that profoundly influenced the cultural complexity that characterises today's Brazil. To evoke that complexity and the diversity of the African continent and its ethnic groups, we have in fact chosen to use a plural, Africas. The cultural richness of Brazil, however, does not equate to that peaceful celebration of harmony between peoples and the three main ethnic groups—Indigenous, black/African and white/European—known as 'racial democracy'. This definition intends to celebrate an allegedly peaceful integration between ethnic groups, masking the relations of violence and rape that characterised the clash between different cultural matrices during the formation process of Brazil. As is well known, this has been relentlessly denounced by many black thinkers, notable among them, Abdias Nascimento in *O Quilombismo* (2019, 38).[1]

The cultural diversity of Brazil is grounded in relations of tension, as well as 'negotiation and conflict', aptly captured by the title of a work by João José Reis and Eduardo Silva (1989), *Negociação e conflito: a resistência negra no*

V. H. Leite de Aquino Soares (✉) • R. K. Matsumoto
University of Brasília, Brasília, Brazil

© The Author(s), under exclusive license to Springer Nature
Switzerland AG 2021
T. Morosetti, O. Okagbue (eds.), *The Palgrave Handbook of Theatre and Race*, https://doi.org/10.1007/978-3-030-43957-6_15

Brasil escravista (*Negotiation and Conflict: The Black Resistance in Slave Brazil*), which covers the resistance of the enslaved and their tradition of rebellion which deconstruct notions of passivity and acceptance of manorial impositions during slavery. Domination involved enslavement, genocide, exploitation, war, rape and racism, all of which, despite some groups trying to deny or understate these facts, are inscribed in our history, their 'updated' practice continuing to occur in the contemporary world.

The moment of our history characterised by the transit, traffic and trade of black people between Africa and the Americas was marked by the development of resistance strategies, including the maintenance of African traditions, as the people faced the imposition of Eurocentric and ethnocentric domination—a range of values, knowledge and ways of life imposed by the colonisers as the only acceptable form of existence, thereby relegating all others to subalternity. In the struggle for survival, the very existence of the enslaved was accompanied by an exacerbation of their culture as a constitutive and ontological element. As resistance was mainly against the erasure of the enslaved Africans' sociocultural constitutions, black performances can be seen today as a process of affirmation of these people's humanity, as they feed a specific culture threatened by the dehumanisation connected with racism and colonialism. As Leda Maria Martins explains,

> Africans forcefully transplanted to the Americas through the Black Diaspora had their bodies and their corpus landless. Ripped of its familiar *domus*, this body, individual and collective, was occupied by the emblems and codes of the European, who took possession of him as lord, in him writing his linguistic, philosophical, religious, cultural codes, his vision of the world. [...]. Nevertheless, the colonization of Africa, the transmigration of slaves to the Americas, the slave system, and the division of the African continent into European ghettos failed to erase the African/African *body/corpus* of cultural, textual, and complex and symbolic constitution founders of their alterity, their cultures, their ethnic, linguistic diversity, their civilization and history. (Martins 1997, 24–25)

The passage above highlights the dialectical process of confrontation between coloniser and colonised, as well as the permanence of the African symbolic universe and culture despite colonisation; in response to this, black performance has been one of the ways of maintaining African and Afro-Brazilian culture and integrity. It is possible to understand the black body, as well as the black *corpus* in performance as a reterritorialisation of the culture, the history and the memory of these African civilisations forcibly transplanted in the Americas. The black body/corpus in performance can give life to a multiplicity of forms of resistance, maintaining their origins and features to impact on the black scene in contemporary Brazil.

Wishing to clarify further how this process of erasure and resistance took place, the following sections will highlight some significant moments of the arts scene in Brazil to analyse and understand some of the characteristics of contemporary performance, to then concentrate on specific black theatre groups.

2   Between Stigma and Stereotype: The Representation of the Black

At the beginning of the colonial period, as Cristiane Sobral tells us in her book, *Teatros negros e suas estéticas na cena teatral brasileira* (*Black Theatres and Their Aesthetics in the Brazilian Theatrical Scene*, 2016), the presence of black and Indigenous people characterised the early performing scene. Indigenous and black people appeared as performers (and/or characters) in marginalised, supporting and subordinate roles, without that specific characterisation or detailed history, culture, or memory that we find in some complex characters. During the eighteenth and nineteenth centuries, theatre companies with black actresses and actors resorted to whiteface (hands and face) to represent white characters. This was a serious indication of an attempt to erase the black character from the national theatrical scene, except in forms of subordination and objectification, as indicated by historian Joel Rufino dos Santos (2014). In much of Brazilian theatre, black was synonymous with slave and it was with this colonial perspective that the black characters of our dramaturgy were written and inscribed. In the theatrical practice, the condition of subjection promoted by colonial domination would only be transformed by updating the representation of blacks as no longer slaves, but servants/employees in more contemporary examples. The stigma around black people related to this subaltern social position of blacks in Brazilian art ranges from a distorted reproduction of reality to the forging of a stereotype almost impossible to overcome. As in other countries touched by diaspora, slavery and colonialism, we find menial figures such as those of Aunt Anastasia and Uncle Barnaby, or Mommy and Uncle John, in *Sítio do Picapau Amarelo* (*Yellow Woodpecker Ranch*), a famous children's work by Monteiro Lobato, adapted for a television series in the 1970s and 1980s. According to Mendes (1993):

> The old 'Father John' in total exercise of subordination, without defying the limit imposed by the ignorant bosses, reinforcing the hypotheses of black intelligence; The kind and loving 'black mothers' and the dedicated' 'mucamas', figures presented without subjectivity, with naive wisdom, full of affection and sweetness [...].

In the twenty-first century, we continue to come across many of these types; there are still maids, drivers, caretakers and other servants who commonly appear in Brazilian soap operas. Characters such as those of rogues or black Cariocas, associated with vagrancy, marginality and deviation, posit themselves between social imaginary and cultural production to form and shape thoughts and ideas about black people in the country today. The common trait these representations of black people have, regardless of the century, is the lack of detail or specificity with which these figures are portrayed in these dramas.

Black performers usually play a supporting role, and there are no indications or circumstances that can delineate their subjectivity, as black characters are presented as objects—reflecting an image that is the legacy of slavery: people without history, memory, culture, affectivity, epistemologies or intellect—as part of a wider project of erasure and genocide.

These brief considerations provide us with a basis to pursue our discussion of black performances and black artists in contemporary Brazil. These premises on Brazilian social imaginaries, the condition of the country's black population and the resistance engendered in the exercise of black cultural expression, are the background to our analysis of artists, theatrical presentations, performances and groups of the Brazilian black diaspora.

3 THE BLACK EXPERIMENTAL THEATRE (TEN): PERSPECTIVES AND LEGACY

Our choice to present and reflect on the trajectory of the Black Experimental Theatre (TEN) in the history of the national theatre and the black movements in the country is in order to highlight the importance and influence of the discussions raised and promoted by this group. We highlight the group's commitment in the poetic and political struggle for the recognition of the Brazilian black population as a contributor and mobiliser of national history and culture.

TEN appeared in Rio de Janeiro in 1944, founded by Abdias Nascimento,[2] with the participation of several Brazilian black artists such as Ruth de Souza, Marina Gonçalves, Lea Garcia Teodorico dos Santos, Aguinaldo Camargo and other people involved in the foundation of the company, or who later joined it. One of the reasons behind the foundation of TEN can be traced to the staging in Peru of Eugene O'Neill's *Emperor Jones*; on this occasion, Nascimento saw a black-painted white actor performing the role of a black character (see Nascimento 2004). Nascimento then started to strongly oppose both the idea and practice of blackface, which, originated in minstrel shows in the United States as white performers painted themselves as blacks to ridicule and caricature black people, was adopted in Brazilian soap operas. A contextualisation and criticism of this practice are present in the documentary *The Negation of Brazil* (2000) by Brazilian black filmmaker Joel Zito Araújo as well as in the film *Bamboozled* (2000) by the African-American filmmaker Spike Lee. As blacks were seen as not able to interpret characters with dramatic complexity, TEN fought for the representation of our own stories and those of others, claiming dignity for the Brazilian black population and aiming at the disruption of racial-colonial models of domination on the Brazilian theatrical scene. The basic goals of TEN were

> (a) to reclaim the values of African culture that have been, by prejudice, marginalized to the mere folkloric, picturesque or insignificant condition; (b) through a structured pedagogy in the work of art and culture, to try to educate

the "white" ruling class, recovering it from the ethnocentric perversion of self-esteem of European, Christian, white, Latin, and Western superiors; (c) to eradicate from the Brazilian stages the white actor made up of black, a traditional norm when the black character demanded dramatic quality of the interpreter; (d) make impossible the custom of using the black actor in grotesque or stereotyped roles as brats carrying bruises or carrying trays, black washing clothes or scrubbing the ground, mulatinhas de requebro, domesticated Father John (Uncle Tom) and tear-black Black Mothers (mammy); (e) unmask as inauthentic and absolutely useless the pseudo-scientific literature that focused on the black, with very few exceptions, as an exercise beautician, or diversionist, were purely descriptive academic essays dealing with history, ethnography, anthropology, sociology, psychiatry, etc., whose interests were far removed from the dynamic problems that emerged from the racist context of our society. (Nascimento 1978)

TEN, being a practical example of a project with an anti-racist fight for art, went beyond the sphere of theatre as its only field of action. Its sociopolitical reach was directly related to Nascimento's multiple experiences, with an impact on many fields: as he was an actor, director, teacher, poet, plastic artist and politician, he brought numerous contributions to the aesthetics, performances and black movements of Brazil, and he also worked in the Black Front, an important organisation of the national black movement. This demonstrates his dedication to the re-insertion of the black population in Brazilian society, as he mobilised aspects, such as the recognition of the culture, citizenship, identity, dignity and humanity of Brazilian black people. When considering TEN's shows, it is noticeable that there were no innovative or inventive proposals in the formal aspects of the works, but rather a shift in focus.

Sobral (2016) explains how the dramatic texts followed canonical forms but contained changes in the thematic issues, as subjects that concerned the African and Afro-Brazilian memory, history, culture and society were approached. Evani Tavares Lima in his doctoral thesis entitled *Um olhar sobre o teatro negro do Teatro Experimental do Negro e do Bando de Teatro Olodum* (*A Look at the Black Theatre of the Experimental Theatre of the Black and the Theatre Bando Olodum*, 2010) indicates that there may have been, in maintaining forms of white-European theatrical representation, an attempt to stress how black interpreters, as well as white, can perform quality work, thus fighting against the general idea that black people couldn't really act. This was a key concept in TEN's objection to blackface, as well as to the constant disavowal of black subjects on the scene, who were put in check or discredited in their abilities of representation.

It is through this lens that we can look at the black dramas that were put on the scene by TEN through appropriating classical and/or canonical theatre texts, such as Shakespeare's *Othello*, Nelson Rodrigues' *Black Angel* or Eugene O'Neill's *The Emperor Jones*. Sobral again points out that in these dramaturgies it is possible to identify the collapse of some stereotypical patterns that were common in the representation of black characters in Brazil. One can see, for example, a reaffirmation of humanity that means characters escape binary, Manichaean divisions.

A further concern of the group was that the black population could participate in the theatrical event on and off the stage. At the time, the few black people present in the theatre spaces occupied positions like general services or cleaning, and TEN was interested in the democratisation of theatre as a cultural asset. Unfortunately, one of the objections one may raise against TEN is that, even as a great visionary project, it was not able to reach significantly the Brazilian black population, having only involved a small number of people because of the difficulty of maintaining and making feasible the ideological-political stands Nascimento himself endorsed. We personally do not dismiss this process because of its narrow reach, however; rather, we prefer to visualise it as a starting point: as a crossroad, a land of multiple paths. It is also possible to see it as an invitation to the continuity of this very project or, why not, the beginning of others, depending on one's ethical and aesthetic choices, or place in the world. Black diaspora subjects that were drawn from the African continent in a process of forced migration had to creatively engage in multiple survival strategies; they had to create and invent to continue to exist. TEN was a way to follow some of these paths, and suggest others, its aesthetic effort involving several moments in which one could be put face to face with their choices. It was, and is, a continuous process of forging what it means to be a black person and artist in the diaspora. Starting from these premises, we now proceed to talk about black performances and black performers in contemporary Brazil.

4   Contemporary Brazil: Black Performances and Performers

The contemporary Brazilian black scene is mobilised by several artists who provide, in one way or another, a multitude of presentations of the diverse ways in which their experiences as black people in diaspora can be organised, elaborated and reflected. These poetics, which link aesthetics and politics, are weaving examples of resistance to the unfair contours of racism, providing escape routes from the impositions of a system of colonial-racial domination that still prevails in the Brazilian theatrical scene. Blacks, in these examples, are 'insubmissible'[3] in exhibiting their potentialities, which, day-by-day, break down the social constraints that have relegated them to denial, marginality and subalternity. The attempt now is to shift from the margin to the centre, or to the centre of the margin at least, revealing the racism that is hidden behind racial democracy and/or the illusion of a reality that is factually shaped by the interests of elites, sometimes elaborating on the denied, persecuted subjectivities of the humanity usurped by slavery (see Flor do Nascimento 2014). Black performances are based on 'erasures in the canon' now read by 'black retinas' (Sobral 2014): the subject who was previously seen as object can now share her/his views of the world, in their own black perspective, a process that has to do with the recovery of humanity and the appreciation of its subjectivity. This opens multiple possibilities for black and diaspora artists that intertwine with the modes of re/presentation of reality in poetics of resistance.

5   OLODUM THEATRE BANDO

One of the options open to contemporary black theatre is the rescuing of the aesthetic dimensions of African and Afro-Brazilian cultures; this was one of the goals of TEN, and can now be observed in the work of a group from Salvador (Bahia), Olodum Theatre Bando, one of the largest and oldest theatre groups in contemporary Brazil. This company, which celebrates 30 years of activity in 2020, evokes black cultural expressions in many of its theatre shows. The group began as an educational enterprise in 1990 through a partnership between the Olodum cultural group—an Afro-Brazilian bloc presided over by João Jorge Rodrigues—and Márcio Meirelles, who wanted to merge the language of performance with the racial, social, cultural and political issues of the daily lives of people in Bahia. After an audition, those chosen to participate in the project received qualified training with a team of already experienced artists that had established in the 1980s. The project was launched with the show, *Essa é nossa praia (This Is Our Beach)*, which premiered in 1991 in the Pelourinho, the historical centre of Salvador. Other shows include *Ó Paí, Ó!* (1992); *Woyzeck* (1992); *Bai Bai Pelô* (1994); *Zombie* (1995); *Eré pra toda a vida—Xirê (Eré for All Life)* (1996); *Ópera de três mirreis (Three-Mirrored Opera)* (1996); *Cabaré da Rrrrraça (Cabaret of Race)* (1997); *Dream of a Summer Night* (1999); *Áfricas* (2006) and *Bença* (2010). In a dialogue between *butoh* and Afro-Brazilian cultures, the company also did *Dô* (2012) in partnership with Tadashi Endo.

Bando is a great school of art and life for the artists who are part of it. Throughout these years, it has trained several actresses and actors in the field of black performance and racial relations—among them, Lázaro Ramos. The group is grounded in affirmative actions, the positive affirmation of black identity, the struggle for racial equality, social justice and citizenship; their poetics of resistance aiming, therefore, to corroborate the insertion of blacks in Brazilian society. Although these actions are in harmony with the legacy and the trajectory of TEN, we can see that, unlike TEN, Olodum Theatre Bando has been able to mobilise larger sections of people in the local and national scene, expanding their dialogue about race with great part of their audience, inside and outside the arts, involving black and non-black alike, thus elaborating what the researcher Regia Mabel da Silva Freitas calls a 'social politics in scene'. We can take as an example the shows *Onovomundo* (1991), *Eré para toda vida—Xirê* (1996), *Áfricas* (2006) and *Bença* (2010), which use aesthetic elements of Afro-Brazilian religions for the composition of the play and the dramaturgical translation of the thematic axes of the works. In *Onovomundo* (1991), for instance, wheels are used to represent the rites of popular black cultural expressions, with specific reference to the elements of nature—earth, fire, water and air, each referring to African ethnicities and nations of *candomblé* (*jeje, nago, candomblé de caboclo* and *bantu*, respectively). These elements and the tales derived from them can be associated with the peoples that came to Brazil from Africa and used orality as a way of maintaining their traditions. As Freitas (2014) points out, these narratives and elements were coupled in this particular show with an extensive, sensitive and serious field research, in intense dialogue with the peoples of *candomblé*, and with a view to avoiding the exoticisation or folklore of black cultures.

In *Erê pra toda vida—Xirê, Áfricas* and *Bença*, the themes of *candomblé* and African/Afro-Brazilian elements are also a constant presence; this logic of recovery and nurturing of these cultural elements transcends the dimension of theatre, though, and becomes the modus operandi of the group when (in the backstage) it greets the *orixá* Oxalá, a Yoruba-derived divinity, before each show, singing to 'Oni Saurê'.[4] In *Erê para toda vida—Xirê*, the director, Freitas (2014), points out that the movements in the show were to be interpreted as prayers for African gods. The story of the play blends aspects of the Afro-Brazilian universe with issues of abandonment and extermination of black boys—in allusion to the children of Afro-Brazilian cults—in the big cities. In this, we see an employment of syncretism between the Yoruba twin deities, the Ibejis, and the Catholic saints, Cosme and Damian, both children. Syncretism can be read as a strategy of resistance by Brazilian black people, who had to camouflage and infiltrate their own deities in Brazilian society disguised as other religious images of European and Christian ancestry, so that their forms of worship could be kept alive, if re-edited, thus escaping from the persecution and violence that were directed at the practice of African cultural expressions.[5]

Áfricas, Bando's children's theatre show, draws on African myths to unveil images and symbolic universes that are little explored in Brazilian social imaginary. The show promotes the expansion of aesthetic and historical repertoires on the continent that shelter diverse peoples and ethnicities. In this way, it includes references beyond the white/European stories that surround black children and young people in Brazil. Despite being a show aimed at a specific type of public, *Áfricas* has the power to embrace people of different generations, who can humorously walk through the various dimensions of the work, between visuality, dance, musicality, orality and play. This show thus embodies the living word, as understood by Hampaté Bâ (2010): the word makes the movement of the inner forces to be exteriorised, reminiscent of the secrets of the mythical and magical processes of creation of the world, a cosmology that elevates the word to the dimension of the sacred, through the colour, form, rhythm that overlap in the staging of the work. Thus, the actors and actresses, in performing the word, resemble the *griot* figure, the 'word artist', the storyteller, the diffuser and the archivist of knowledge for the people of West Africa. As the critic Sérgio Cumino (2010) has observed,

> Whenever there is a spectacle that comes to mind in the release of stories from the African myth, a set of conventional stage elements comes to mind, in the form of

legends with traditional candomblé elements, orixas' garments like those of rituals, without saying in the cantigas used in the ilê, all these elements within a cult, are the ritual composition of mythology. When taken to a show it becomes an allegory. While the myth points to something indescribable that is beyond itself, the allegory in the theater is just a story or image that teaches a practical lesson. The AFRICAN spectacle subverted this system, coming out of the conventional reading of African myths, surprising the audience by taking the scene, the myth, inducing the audience to transcend the relationship with the present, and almost in a trance led us to a whole mythology that pulsates in our subconscious rescuing our archetypes in a scenic rite creating a synergy in the collective unconscious of all. We learn from African mythology that everything in the universe exists in us, all elementals. What impressed was the Bando's sensitivity to transform this concept in a scenic way, this is the magic of the show. Actors turning into a river, with no recourse, only with their bodies, and the public actually visualize the river.

In many of its productions, the Olodum Theatre Bando masterfully achieves this mythical celebration by recovering the Afro-Brazilian and African aesthetic dimension on stage. This communion is something exquisite that makes rite and myth intertwine, orchestrating the 'living tradition'[6] in the contemporary black Brazilian scene.

6   *Salina, the Last Vertebra* (2015)—AMOK Theatre

An encounter between rite and myth can also be seen in the work *Salina—a última vértebra* (*Salina, the Last Vertebra*, 2015), staged by the group AMOK Teatro, directed by Stephane Brodt and Ana Teixeira. The Rio de Janeiro group, AMOK Teatro, was founded in 1998 and is directed by Ana Teixeira and Stephane Brodt. The award-winning group combines theatrical research, aesthetic innovation and training of actresses and actors in dialogue with diverse cultures and traditions. An influence that can be noticed in AMOK's work is that of Théâtre du Soleil, a French company directed by Ariane Mnouchkine, in which Stephane Brodt had acted. In these 20 years, Brodt has performed in several shows such as *Letters from Rodez, The Executioner, Macbeth, Kabul, The Dragon, Savina, Family Stories, Salina*, and *Kindzu Notebooks*. At the AMOK house (the group's workspace) the company often hold workshops on from actor to character and training for improvisation—further details can be found in the group's website.

The astonishment of the audience, still latent in Brazil when confronted by a cast completely formed by black artists on stage, cannot be denied, and it gets worse when these same people appear in roles that are not in the list of stereotyped and/or caricatured options through which blacks are commonly represented. That is why we believe that TEN's efforts to increase and professionalise actresses and black actors in Brazil so that the stage could become more and more black are still relevant today. We also appreciate the importance and the sociopolitical and aesthetic strength in including numerous black performers not only in *Salina*, and the AMOK group generally, but also in shows from the Olodum Theatre Bando, for example. This is a choice that permeates both form and content, and one wonders whether mere black visibility without any contents would stir up critical thinking about the social condition of the black. This is a question that challenges us, and to which we should not give fixed answers, as its solution depends on the situation, the quantitative presence of black actresses/actors and their impacts on the scene, addressing racial issues.

Salina, the Last Vertebra is based on the homonymous text of the Frenchman, Laurent Gaudé, and features elements of Greek tragedy and African epic; it presents a mythical Africa, an ancestral setting for the extremely human trajectory of the character Salina, and involved a long process of scenic research, training and exchanges. These elements refer to the extensive mosaic of African and Afro-Brazilian cultures in the diaspora, with a demarcated influence of other cultures, as evidenced by the group's intercultural nature. AMOK also profits from the participation of and collaboration with Jorge Antônio dos Santos, master drummer of the Congado[7] dos Arturos (from Minas Gerais). The show has circulated widely, touring various regions and festivals and gaining important nominations and awards from the Brazilian theatrical scene, as well as reaching China on the international stage.

Once more, we can see this work is influenced by African and Afro-Brazilian cultures in a dialogue between two cultural expressions, *congado* and *candomblé*, that inform the staging, bodies and corporealities, the rhythms and musicality of characters, in a process of recovering and re-editing an invented Africa, with aesthetic polyphonies and ritual and mythical aspects. These are often present in the work of AMOK Theatre; another factor worth highlighting is the extreme sensitivity with which each character is presented and detailed by the performers, turning to the humanity of these black figures, previously reduced to stereotype by the national dramaturgy.

The subjectivity and the high dramatic complexity of the characters that perform in *Salina* outline an important feature in the range of possibilities that the contemporary black scene provides, as we have an expansion of the image of black people and their world in Brazilian theatre. The characters in *Salina* are not romanticised and do not follow a binary logic. The unfolding of the process of composition of the work also traces social-political questions, relating to the idea of what it means to be black in Brazil today. AMOK is in this heavily influenced by the legacy of Théâtre du Soleil, with stress on actor training, intercultural dialogues, technical rigour and methods of improvisations in confluence with the presence of the elements of the theatrical staging integrated to the process of composition of the show (Féral 2010). All these articulations are present in *Salina*, as well as the pieces of the Olodum Theatre Bando, both relating to the dreams of Nascimento, Ruth de Souza and so many other TEN members and black artists. With a stage dominated by black performers representing complex roles, thus surpassing dualisms such as good and evil, black and white, coloniser and colonised, this theatre effectively goes beyond the reductions of the racist spectrum.

7   Lázaro Ramos and Grace Passô

Breaking the stereotypes and expectations imposed by racism is to locate oneself in the condition of 'being in spite of' (Lispector 1998, 26).[8] Being black is linked to diverse expectations of what this does or may mean, both for racist thinkers and for the black and political struggle movements known as 'militancy'. Lázaro Ramos in *Na minha pele* (*In My Skin*) reflects on these issues. A native of Salvador (Bahia), he is an actor, writer, director, presenter and filmmaker of national recognition. He was for many years a member of the Olodum Theatre Bando, for which he directed in 2018 a film about them entitled *Bando, um filme de*. He began his career in Bando at the age of 16, making his debut in 1994 with the piece *Bai, bai, Pelô* (directed by Marcio Meirelles), participated in several pieces, including *Cabaré da Rrrrrraça* (directed by Marcio Meirelles) and *Ó paí, ó* (Meirelles and Chica Carelli), and starred in the film under the direction of Monique Gardenberg. In 1988, at the age of 10, Ramos played with Mário Gusmão in a Christmas special called *The Boy and the Old Man*; with Gusmão he would also star in 1995 in the show *Zumbi*, in which they play the homonymous protagonist and the character Ganga Zumba; he then successfully toured the country with the national success *The Machine*, a show directed by João Falcão. In the cinema, at the age of 21, he starred in *Madame Satã* (2002, directed by Karim Aïnouz), *Ó Paí, Ó* (directed by Monique Gardenberg) and several other films; for television, he starred with the character, Foguinho, in *Cobras & Lagartos* (2006). In 2015, he appeared with Taís Araújo in the premiere of the piece *O Topo da Montanha*, related to the last speech of Martin Luther King, a production that is still in circulation today. Between 2015 and 2018, Ramos starred with Tais Araújo in the TV series *Mister Brau*, and he is now the presenter of the programme *Espelho*, in which he interviews personalities, talking about culture, race relations and various subjects. Planned for release very soon is his first fiction feature film as a director, *Medida provisória* (*Executive Order*), with Alfred Enoch, Tais Araújo and Seu Jorge in the cast.

Grace Passô is another important name that contributed in putting into the picture issues alike to those mentioned before. She is a native of Pirapora (MG) who moved early to Belo Horizonte (MG) where she lived in the Alípio de Melo neighbourhood. Passô is an actress, director and playwright who in 1994, at the age of 13, joined the Center for Artistic Technological Training. Since her graduation, she has been part of several theatre groups, among them Espanca!, in which she participated in shows such as *Por Elise, Amores Surdos, Congresso internacional do medo* (in partnership with Theatre XIX); she was the director of *Contractions* (Group of 3) and *Well-Intentions* (LUME Theatre), Ricardo Alves Júnior's *Elon Does Not Believe in Death* and Lucia Murat's *Paris Square*; she also featured in the movies *Season* (by André Novais Oliveira) and *In the Heart of the World* (by Gabriel Martins and Maurílio Martins). Recently, she has toured several regions with the award-winning solo show, *Vaga Carne*. In her career of excellence, she has won awards such as the Shell Prize for best playwright, the Leda Maria Martins for best performance and best text, the São Paulo Association of Art Critics (APCA) for best playwright, the Cesgranrio for best national novel and best actress in Rio. Passô is critically acclaimed as one of the best actresses of contemporary Brazil. Both Lázaro Ramos and Grace Passô reflect and engage with the process of being black people and artists in the diaspora, and/or generally with the processes of 'being in spite of', alongside with the implications of James Baldwin's famous statement 'I am not your negro'.[9]

Race is a contradictory category that, in its multiple directions, imprisons and liberates us at the same time. Knowing yourself means dealing with these issues, and while there is no room for choice, there is a time when one can discover oneself as a black artist. Ramos observes: 'Even when we try to forget that we are black, someone reminds us' (2017, 94). Baldwin's statement itself advocates for a freedom to be who you are (and who you want to be), in spite of—being black. The expression is used by the character, Lóri, in *Uma aprendizagem ou o livro dos prazeres* (*An Apprenticeship or the Book of Delights*), a work of the Brazilian writer Clarice, Lispector (1998). In his flow of thought, Lóri notes:

> One of the things I learned is that one should live in spite of. In spite of, one should eat. In spite of, one should love. In spite of, one must die. It is often the same in spite of that pushes us forward. It was the in spite of that gave me an anguish that, unsatisfied, was the creator of my own life.[10]

We have quoted this passage to highlight how, in many instances, the right of black people to be 'in spite of' has been denied. This literary excerpt brings us to the apex of a person's subjectivity, and it is this stage of being and possibilities of existence that we wish to touch upon when talking about the contemporary black scene, echoing the voices, trajectories and performances of artists like Passô and Ramos.

The invisibility and negation of black characters on the national theatre scene was one of the reasons that prompted the actress Passô to get beyond the authors. In the audiovisual series *Afronta*[11] (2017) by Juliana Vicente, a Brazilian filmmaker, the actress affirms: 'This was so that I could see myself and see mine in the art that I did'. Still in the video, Passô talks about the feeling of not performing characters of classic texts of the European canon which she had encountered in her training process: 'The imaginary that was behind those classic texts, those characters, those clothes were completely alien to me. None of this was part of my symbolic imagery' (ibid.). However, the actress confronts racism in her own writing through a plurality of individualities that she represents in her work, an example being her first play *Por Elise* (*For Elise*, 2012) in which figures from ordinary life emerge. As Passô says, 'this was a desire to see a symbolic universe of my life within a theatre that I would do. And to make that text and shed light on what really mattered to me, I had to drive, you know?'[12] Another choice that stands out is the wish to cross the alterities of the canons of whiteness and Eurocentrism to compose characters that are not part of the author's own universe, a choice she comments on by citing Leda Maria Martins:

> Leda Maria Martins spoke the other day in a lecture, like this: 'As a Brazilian Negro, we are obliged to speak at least three languages, right? You have to fight, too, to deal with and overcome the other's language.' So in that sense, at school, I once again tried to conquer the language of the other. Understanding these classics, run after understanding how my body makes an aristocrat [...][13]

The frictions and tensions of the encounter between coloniser and colonised are presented by Passô and Martins to give an overview of the complexity of the difficulties met by black artists in challenging the contradictions and images embedded in the country's training processes. How often does art speak for what it says? Playwrights often comment on how discourses in art are aligned with power and narrative disputes, like Passô when she describes aspects of black performances:

> There is no way for you to be black and do not have a very strong relationship with memory. The memory survived; it survives in our bodies. Since it [the story] was officially told by those who tried to destroy these bodies. So, there is a lot that is rooted, that has to do with this diasporic course, thus, the black communities, right? So it is so deep a mixture, it is a mixture of those who experience, or had to experience everything and from there produced something else that I do not know the name, thus, that is in another time already, that is exactly the opposite of this perspective of the colonizer, which is one, right, that is the one who comes to kill and catch. It is a perspective of who is on the other side, is the one who received the colonizer, survived him, learned his music, did not let his culture die, fell in love with the colonizer, spit on him, is running behind to take care of what happened in the past, at the same time here in the future, knows that everything is together. They are polyglot bodies, so full of reference and more resistant, right? There is no other option.[14]

These 'polyglot bodies', black and in diaspora, have found multiple forms of agency on the national territory. Passô observes that these bodies are in the past as in the future, 'all together'. Many marks of the colonial and slave trajectory are updated and embedded in the dynamics of the contemporary strategies of resistance and invention. Time articulates memory and events, to erect, beyond the chronologies, the archaeology and architecture of the sociohistorical and political processes of the course of the black population to contemporaneity.

Passô's work encompasses these contradictions, shuffles our social and aesthetic imaginaries in the implosion of categories proposed by both the colonial domination systems and black movements. In the solo show, *Vaga Carne*[15] (2016), in which she is an actress and a playwright, her character is only a voice. Ironically, a black woman, the locus of so many processes of social oppression and silencing, materialises and presents a voice on the scene, becoming the very place of speech,[16] of enunciation: a discourse, which accumulates the loads of historicity, affectivity, commonality of black people and her feminine gender, and takes and overflows the body, skin and political-social limitations to present a voice in its subjectivity and existence. The ritual character of the show is informed by the sense of sharing of the theatrical moment between audience and actress, in between representation and existence. The expectation, as Passô comments, is that the voice can take all that is present, 'that the play be a field of living experience of the body. And it's not just who's on the scene, but the audience as well. The ability to make a scene, a scenic event, [in] a collective experience, kept in due proportion and, with the awareness that it does not even compare to that, but for me it is the size of certain rituals of *terreiro* that you go, you see?'[17] One becomes a voice that takes bodies in collective contamination. The contents of the work permeate the body as a social construct and from this leads the audience to reflect on its role in this context. The actress reveals:

> [...] It is the first play I touch, subtly and objectively, to the fact that my body is a black body, as if my body said: 'read me'. I will not tell its story [her body], I will not tell. And start asking about the other's gaze on this body. More than a play idea, it's just, like, about the things I've been doing in the theatre, you know? Through certain language strategies, I seek to create a field where my existence, it can be full, where my body can be full.[18]

Vaga Carne is a speech that reverberates aesthetic movements into and out of race relations, performing arts and Brazilian society. It breaks with the expectations and images that the national scene had already woven on blacks and more specifically on black women; the show is about freedom to go through these 'language strategies' to invent and compose a dramatic space for the full representation of marginal bodies in the social and theatrical scene of Brazil. You may have dared not be the 'black man of anybody', to echo James Baldwin, or an 'unsubmissive' black woman, but this is, as Conceição Evaristo (2016) tells us, exactly what Passô bravely does, causing a collapse in the forms of representation that we are adopting, both from within and outside (in sociohegemonic contexts).

On his part, Ramos in *Na minha pele* (*In My Skin*, Ramos 2017) discusses various racial and social issues in Brazil. With regard to his career as an actor, he operates and takes inspiration from a multiplicity of ideas already present in the work of Bando, TEN and Passô, which are a foray into being a black actor/actress and how these social imaginaries inform actions. A striking phrase from *Na minha pele* is 'Your place is where you dream to be' (Ramos 2017, 62), which well describes what he, Passô and others mean by pursuing a universe of full existence for us, our bodies and our stories, as black diaspora subjects. Ramos points out, from his trajectory, to the aesthetic and ethical choices that locate him as a black actor who places himself in the commitment of positive affirmation of black identity, who does not deny or abdicate black form, or his place in the world. Thus, consequently, we see again the effort, in life as in art, to make categories of race not a prison but a form of articulation of black consciousness.

8 Conclusion

The trajectories of the artists and groups presented in this chapter only constitute a little portion of black performances in contemporary Brazil, but their relevance is in how contemporary they are in increasingly cracking structures and assumptions about blackness, by promoting a poetics of resistance that reveals the contours of racism, shaking the canons (Sobral 2014) of Eurocentrism, and weaving inventive ways through which to put themselves on the scene, while and by proposing other images of ourselves and other worlds.

Notes

1. For the formation of the Brazilian people and the contradictions that the process of colonial exploration entails, see Ribeiro (2015), founder of the University of Brasília.
2. In order to respect the author's wishes as expressed to the Ipeafro, the institute that created and now houses his collection, we have chosen to spell the name as he signed it, Abdias Nascimento, rather than using his official citation name, Abdias do Nascimento. See the note to the 3rd edition of Nascimento (2019).
3. 'Insubmissos' here makes reference to the work of Evaristo (2016) that deals with the process of resistance and un-submission of black women to various structures of oppression that surround them both daily and historically.
4. The text is as follows:

   Oni saurê
   Aul axé
   Oni saurê
   Oberioman
   Onisa aurê
   Aul axé baba
   Oberioman
   Onisa aurê
   Baba saurê
   Aul axé

Baba saurê
Oberioma
Baba saurê
Aul axé baba
Oberioman
Saul axé
Man Man Man
Man Man Man
Man Man Man
Man Man Man

(Saudação iorubana para Oxalá. Hino do Bando de Teatro Olodum. In Freitas 2014).
5. For syncretism as a strategy of resistance and as a form of black agency, see Sodré (1988).
6. This expression is used by historian Amadou Hampaté Bâ to discuss the dynamism of the oral tradition of African peoples and how this influences their historicity and epistemologies. See Bâ (2010).
7. The *congadas* or *congados* are Afro-Brazilian religious cultural manifestations that stage the coronation of Congo kings; for the study on black performances and these *folguedos*, see Martins (1997).
8. Original passage translated by Ane Karoline.
9. Baldwin was a black and homosexual writer from the United States, who became well known for his work *Giovani's Room* written in Paris during his departure for Europe because of the difficulties and persecutions he faced in the process of civil rights in the United States and also for being homosexual, a fact that added to the complexity of his blackness. Baldwin was considered by political personalities as the ambassador of the blacks, for having a versatility of dialogue between blacks and whites and also among blacks that defended currents of thought and lines of action that were opposed to, for example, those of Martin Luther King Jr and Malcolm X, which the author had very close. 'I am not his black', never finished by the author, was a motto for Raoul Peck's homonymous documentary that discusses these questions that we present.
10. Ibid. Translated by Ane Karoline.
11. *Afronta! #12—Grace Passô*. (Websérie. Direção: Juliana Vicente. Duração: 13min52s. Brazil, produced by de Juliana Vicente e Preta Portê Filmes, 2017). https://www.youtube.com/watch?v=UiQCtYshfXA. Accessed 16 April 2019.
12. *Afronta! #12—Grace Passô*. (Websérie. Direção: Juliana Vicente. Duração: 13min52s. Brazil, produced by Juliana Vicente e Preta Portê Filmes, 2017). https://www.youtube.com/watch?v=UiQCtYshfXA. Accessed 16 April 2019.
13. Ibid. Original passage in Portuguese translated by Ane Karoline.
14. Ibid. Original passage translated by Ane Karoline.
15. Trailer available in: https://www.youtube.com/watch?v=QZkDBYHnyfo. Accessed 16 April 2019.
16. This notion of place of speech can be seen in Ribeiro (2017) and more widely in Foucault (1979).
17. *Afronta! #12—Grace Passô*. (Websérie. Direção: Juliana Vicente. Duração: 13min52s. Brazil, produced by Juliana Vicente and Preta Portê Filmes, 2017). https://www.youtube.com/watch?v=UiQCtYshfXA. Accessed 16 April 2019.
18. Ibid. Original passage translated by Ane Karoline.

References

Araújo, Joel Zito. 2000. *A negação do Brasil*. Documentário. Direção: Joel Zito Araújo. Duração: 92 min. Brasil, co-produção Casa de Criação. https://www.youtube.com/watch?v=PrrR2jgSf9M. Accessed 16 April 2019.

Bâ, Amadou Hampatê. 2010. A tradição viva. *História geral da África, 1*. Brasília: UNESCO. Secad/MEC, UFSCar, pp. 167–212.

Cumino, Sérgio. 2010. Crítica "Para não dizer que falei das flores—Bando de Teatro Olodum termina temporada em São Paulo e deixa saudades" encontrada no blog do grupo. http://bandodeteatro.blogspot.com/2010/04/para-nao-dizer-que-falei-das-flores.html. Accessed 16 April 2019.

Evaristo, Conceição. 2016. *Insubmissas lágrimas de mulheres*. Rio de Janeiro: Editora Malê.

Féral, Josette. 2010. *Encontros com Ariane Mnouchkine: Erguendo um monumento ao efêmero*. São Paulo: Editora SENAC São Paulo: SESCSP.

Flor do Nascimento, Wanderson. 2014. Orí: A saga atlântica pela recuperação das identidades usurpadas. In Edileuza Penha de Souza (Org.), *Negritude, Cinema e Educação*, vol. 3, 134–146. Belo Horizonte: Mazza Edições.

Foucault, Michel. 1979. *Microfísica do poder* (Roberto Machado, tradução). Rio de Janeiro: Graal.

Freitas, Régia Mabel da Silva. 2014. *Bando de Teatro Olodum: uma política social in cena*. Recife: Ed. Universitária.

Lee, Spike. 2000. *Bamboozled*. Direção: Spike Lee. Duração: 135min. Estados Unidos, produção de John Kilik, Spike Lee e co-produção de Kisha Imani Cameron.

Lima, Evani Tavares. 2010. *Um olhar sobre o teatro negro do Teatro Experimental do Negro e do Bando de Teatro Olodum*. Tese de Doutorado. Campinas, São Paulo: Universidade Estadual de Campinas, Instituto de Artes. http://repositorio.unicamp.br/handle/REPOSIP/283930. Accessed 16 April 2019.

Lispector, Clarice. 1998. *Uma aprendizagem ou o livro dos prazeres*. Rio de Janeiro: Rocco.

Martins, Leda Maria. 1997. *Afrografias da memória: o Reinado do Rosário no Jatobá*. Belo Horizonte: Mazza Edições.

Mendes, Miriam Garcia. 1993. *O negro e o teatro brasileiro*. São Paulo: Hucitec.

Nascimento, Abdias. 1978. *O genocídio do negro brasileiro: Processo de um Racismo Mascarado*. Rio de Janeiro: Editora Paz e Terra.

———. 2004. Teatro Experimental do Negro: trajetórias e reflexões. Estudos Avançados, vol. 18, n° 50, pp. 209–224. São Paulo January/April. http://www.scielo.br/pdf/ea/v18n50/a19v1850.pdf

———. 2019. *O Quilombismo*. São Paulo: Editora Perspectiva.

Passô, Grace. 2012. *Por Elise*. Rio de Janeiro: Cobogó.

———. 2017. em *Afronta! #12—Grace Passô*. Websérie. Direção: Juliana Vicente. Duração: 13min52s. Brasil, produção de Juliana Vicente e Preta Portê Filmes. https://www.youtube.com/watch?v=UiQCtYshfXA. Accessed 16 April 2019

Ramos, Lázaro. 2017. *Na minha pele*. 1ª edição. Rio de Janeiro: Objetiva.

Reis, João José, and Eduardo Silva. 1989. *Negociação e conflito: a resistência negra no Brasil escravista* (p. 71). São Paulo: Companhia das Letras.

Ribeiro, Darcy. 2015. *O povo brasileiro: a formação e o sentido do Brasil*. Global Editora e Distribuidora Ltda.

Ribeiro, Djamila. 2017. *O que é lugar de fala?*. Belo Horizonte: Letramento.
Santos, Joel Rufino dos. 2014. *A história do negro no teatro brasileiro*. Novas Direções.
Sobral, Cristiane. 2014. *Só por hoje vou deixar o meu cabelo em paz*.
———. 2016. *Teatros negros e suas estéticas na cena teatral brasileira*. Dissertação de Mestrado. Brasília: Universidade de Brasília, Programa de Pós-Graduação em Arte. http://repositorio.unb.br/handle/10482/21400. Accessed 16 April 2019.
Sodré, Muniz. 1988. *O terreiro e a cidade: a forma social negro-brasileira*. Vol. 1. Petrópolis: Vozes.

CHAPTER 16

Lackface: Blackface Masking in Contemporary US Theatre

Kevin Byrne

1 Introduction

At the top of Branden Jacobs-Jenkins's 2010 play *Neighbors*, the audience is introduced to the Crow Family, unloading boxes at their new suburban home in the dim half-light of the stage. Out of a semi-darkness, a figure is suddenly revealed in a bright spotlight:

> *Topsy, a picanninny in blackface—sackcloth dress, nest of pigtails, big juicy red lips— reaching for a white baby doll. Startled, little Topsy looks up at the light. Annoyed, she sucks her teef, rolls her eyes.[…] [S]he attempts to move on, stepping out of her spotlight and into—KATHUNK!—another one.* (Jacobs-Jenkins 2012, 311)

This is a shocking reveal of blackface, a conscious drawing upon the symbols and iconography of the stereotype, an exaggerated metatheatricality which is both performative and critical of its performativity, and an attempt at evoking an uncomfortable mix of enjoyment and disgust. The show's opening tableau already offers a series of striking contrasts between darkness and light, the human and the doll, the ersatz blackface of Topsy and the idealised white of the toy. Topsy attempts to flee but, finding herself trapped in the Beckettian spotlight that prods, demands, and judges, is forced instead to perform. She begins dancing to a crude version of 'Dixie':

K. Byrne (✉)
Independent Scholar, San Marcos, TX, USA
e-mail: kjbyrne@hotmail.com

© The Author(s), under exclusive license to Springer Nature
Switzerland AG 2021
T. Morosetti, O. Okagbue (eds.), *The Palgrave Handbook of Theatre and Race*, https://doi.org/10.1007/978-3-030-43957-6_16

291

> *The dance ends with Topsy mooning/flashing everyone, naughtily: she curtsies deeply,*
> *too deeply, lifting her dress completely over her head, flashing the crowd with her*
> *pubescent goodies. It's cute. It's repulsive. But there is a pattering of recorded*
> *applause. Topsy loves her audience. The audience loves her.* (312)

The simultaneous performance of so many racist sights and sounds is both playful and overwhelming: Topsy, from Harriet Beecher Stowe's *Uncle Tom's Cabin*; 'Dixie', the anthem of the Confederacy; the blackface makeup and motley dress; dolls and sexuality. Without a word of dialogue yet spoken, the play has already thrown minstrelsy's long history into the current state of race relations and formations in the US. The scene mixes the tragic and comic and employs blackface without explicitly critiquing or condemning it as a stereotype of black identity. This is illustrative of the aesthetic and political uses of blackface in US theatre today; it captures the tensions around racial identity in a country both widely multicultural and deeply riven with racist contradictions.

Taking a cue from the energy of such plays and performances, the 'lackface' title of this chapter is intended as glib and self-effacing, which is something that these shows do at their most cunning. Lackface connotes the way blackface as a material effect can maintain its racist baggage while being decoupled from the idea of race; blackface as neither a distorted image nor an inverted negative of blackness. The works here, in various ways, reflect a belief that racial construction is unconnected to anything biological or inherited. Race is rather a function of culture, something ideological that is infinitely and anxiously re-inscribed. This blackface hollowness, sustained over centuries as an endlessly repeatable racist glyph signifying difference and oppression, is employed to force open new opportunities of racial understanding. Uncoupling the blackface mask from any essential or measurable fact and tossing it into such rough discursive waters grants these playwrights the freedom to toy with it as an idea.

Blackface continues everywhere in US culture. This, in itself, is a fascinating and strange phenomenon. And these performances' snatch both historical and contemporary racisms and, pell-mell, mash them together to illustrate the freighted history of race and blackness as concepts. This chapter is a snapshot of the current conversations happening over race, blackness, and the legacy of minstrelsy. A list of works to be discussed include Jacobs-Jenkins's *Neighbors* and *An Octoroon* (2014); Young Jean Lee's theatrical assemblage *The Shipment* (2009); and the musical *Passing Strange* (2008), with lyrics and book by Stew, music by Stew and Heidi Rodewald. The plots of these works have little direct connection. *Neighbors* follows the disruptions caused by the Crows after their arrival next door to a mixed-race family. Jacobs-Jenkins adapted Dion Boucicault's nineteenth-century melodrama *The Octoroon* about 'life in Louisiana' for *An Octoroon. The Shipment* is a collection of skits thematically organised around black identity. And *Passing Strange* is a classically constructed bildungsroman about an African American artist. These are all voices in a loud conversation and I will be tracing some common characteristics of blackface in the twenty-first century. Other playwrights who dramatise racial slippage and blackface materialism at this time include Thomas Bradshaw (*Southern Promises*), Jackie Sibbles Drury (*We Are Proud to Present a Presentation about the Herero of Namibia, Formerly Known as Southwest Africa, From the German Sudwestafrika, Between the Years 1884–1915*), Robert O'Hara (*Barbecue, Booty Candy*), and Suzan-Lori Parks (*Father Comes Home from the Wars (Parts 1, 2 & 3)*). In these works, race is defined, sometimes simultaneously, as fact, fiction, narrative, history, and culture; as material object, mask, and phenotype; and as performance, embodiment, gesture, and hail. It is understood that race is not a biological or quantifiable element. This groundlessness allows the performances to explore an unmoored and unfettered feeling of racial construction.

Contemporary uses of blackface in US theatre are not just critiquing black stereotype nor are they specifically concerned with lampooning anti-black social norms. They are undermining the belief in any material or measurable aspect of race formation which serves the US's entrenched racism. These plays confound expectations through their intentional fakery and explicit realness, jumping over the uncanny valley of aesthetic realism. They also confuse expectations by provoking uncomfortableness in their audience through assaultive visual and verbal displays or crass, shocking jokes and situations. They expose and explode well-meaning but assimilationist liberal pieties, stretching to the limit a position of tolerance that disallows freedom of identity. These plays employ racist types to undermine the foundations of essentialised identity formation, undercutting the stereotypes' reason for existing. This negation through presentation is central to their operations.

A key term to this investigation is 'post-black', which neither ignores the history of blackness nor argues for an equivocating, non-racial perspective to social understanding, but rather builds the black identity on social grounds. As Harvey Young explains, 'post-black critical writings… place an emphasis on variable, multiple black identities that willfully reengage with the history and logic of race' (Young 2013, 294). The term post-black had antecedents in race theorisations and had been used before the election of Barack Obama, but his victory caused it to be used and applied more broadly. Harry Elam directly reflects upon the post-black idea in performance in his essay 'Black Theatre in the Age of Obama'. He writes, 'The post-black represents a new black that is simultaneously free from, and yet connected to, the legacies of the black past.' Specifically referencing the 'already so overdetermined' (Elam Jr. 2013, 259) power of blackface, he notes that post-black plays which use the masking intend 'to overturn stereotypes by overtly employing these same stereotypes' (266). Elam details a set of conditions for blackface minstrelsy in the contemporary moment. A post-black definition of black performance emphasises blackface's materiality as a fiction of blackness rather than its realness or even its opposite. The mutability of race categorisations is built into the dramaturgy of plays which frustrate easy conclusions or solutions.

For example, Lee's *The Shipment* playfully introduces race, visuality, and – face as signifier by having the character Stand-Up Comedian discuss 'poop-face'. This early section of the play is structured as a black comic's stand-up routine but the direct pleasures and humorous anecdotes endemic to the form quickly move to darker and more uncomfortable territory. Stand-Up Comedian, in a twisty, surreal, funny, angry monologue, swerves almost inevitably, or without really even wanting to, to the topic of African American identity. Early on in his routine, he balances race against foeces (while also rhyming race with face):

> Shit, there ain't nothin' funnier to me than poop. When I'm at home that's practically all I wanna talk about. My wife, she can't take it.[...] But I still needed an outlet to express my feelins, so I came up with the poop FACE.
> *He makes the poop face.*
> But I can't talk about poop. Nope. I gotta talk about RACE because white people be some stupid-ass muthafuckas. (Lee 2012, 217)[1]

Through the leitmotif of excrement and race, Stand-Up Comedian continues: 'If I was to take a shit onstage, use my own shit as blackfacepaint, fuck a human brain until I came, suck my come back out of the brain, and spit it at the audience... I don't really know where I'm goin' with this' (219). The dominant dramaturgical conceit of *The Shipment* is to use a number of theatrical tricks to simultaneously expose and undermine racial assumptions. Poopface is ridiculous and the show dares the audience to look at Stand-Up Comedian and think not about race and blackness but shit instead. Because shit is funny! And the show as a whole deems a failure its own project to not see race or have the audience aware of it.

In an essay on slavery's depiction in contemporary theatre that focuses on *Neighbors* and *The Shipment*, Ilka Saal writes of the 'affective force' that results from theatricalising such minstrel stereotypes (Saal 2019, 140). Saal notes that the 'self-reflexive foregrounding of the mediality of theater... seeks to provoke reflection on representational techniques of blackness' (147). The works analysed here are able to create affective moments when they are at their most interesting. In fact, the scenes of weakness or glibness in these works, such as the endings of *Neighbors* and *Passing Strange*, are due in part to abandoning of such affective potentialities. *Neighbors*, *An Octoroon*, *The Shipment*, and *Passing Strange* present an especially daring and dangerous way of looking at race and blackness in the US. They employ a wide variety of styles, tones, and techniques, but all discuss, enact, or display minstrelsy. My analysis of them highlights both the possibility and dangers in such an extreme gambit of including racial stereotypes in a live event and granting them agency and the chance to speak. These are but a sampling of the blackface scripts available by playwrights which have similar characteristics and ideologies around race's theatrical depiction, as well as other aspects of personal and communal identity such as sexuality and gender.[2] A few commonalities, connections, and patterns emerge. I would like to explain four key techniques, not uncommon in themselves to contemporary theatre and performance, which are used by all the plays to some degree. They all are metatheatrical, have biographical or autobiographical elements, incorporate media forms, and acknowledge blackface as a thing and object. These techniques give contemporary theatre the ability to critique a racist ideology while still employing its rhetoric.

2   METATHEATRICS

The first technique to examine is the metatheatrical quality of the shows, the self-aware aspect in which they call attention to themselves as theatrical illusion and fictive construction. As with all of the qualities to be discussed here, there does not seem to be any especial reason why a live theatre piece with blackface would need to also be a metatheatrical one, but every one of the shows does so. Metatheatricality provides the audience with critical distance between themselves and the action of the drama and also calls dramatic tropes into question. In *Neighbors*, metatheatrical devices puncture the shock of meeting a family of black stereotypes. The play opens and closes with the blackface characters surveilling the audience while in a blatantly theatrical setting. *An Octoroon*, Jacobs-Jenkins's other play with blackface, is rife with metatheatrical elements, beginning with its very existence as an adaptation of a famous nineteenth-century melodrama. Jacobs-Jenkins anticipates a knowledge of the source text, which centres on the tragic love between a mixed-race slave and a white plantation owner, or at least a felt understanding of melodramatic tropes.[3] In addition to using the genre's histrionic acting conventions in a way both parodic and deeply suspicious of its racial conventions, the play has a number of metatheatrical ways of undercutting itself to destabilise the audience. In the opening lines of the play, the character BJJ walks onstage nearly naked and says directly to the audience: 'Hi, everyone. I'm a "black playwright." (*Beat*.) I don't know exactly what that means' (Jacobs-Jenkins 2015, 7). This metatheatricality is combined with autobiography and self-critique. The metatheatrical goofing continues as the next character to appear onstage is Dion Boucicault himself, whose arrival is punctuated by the two screaming 'Fuck you!' (13) at each other. This moment is both metatheatrical and autobiographical, and this combination is also key, with 'BJJ' singularly identified by his initials and Boucicault granted the grander epaulet of 'Playwright' in the stage directions and cast list.

Another element which is emphasised in the stage directions and dialogue of *An Octoroon* is the hammy and overly expressive acting style. This intended unnaturalness translates to the audience as a forced amateurness, which then is in parodic contrast to the earnest emotiveness of the dialogue itself. According to Rosa Schneider's essay 'Anyway, the Whole Point of This Was to Make You Feel Something', 'Jacobs-Jenkins manipulates melodramatic structures—such as the sensation scene, tableau, and… melodrama's gaze—that play upon and reimagine the history of melodrama in the US. These changes not only alter the way slavery's violence is portrayed on stage but make melodrama comprehensible to a twenty-first-century audience unused to the genre's demands' (Schneider 2018, 1). Certainly, a parody of melodramatic acting is something as old as the form itself, but the use of it in *An Octoroon* is calibrated to play off other elements of postdramatic theatre and racial understandings to reveal the racial tensions at the centre of Boucicault's text.

Lee also uses the tactic in *The Shipment*. The play is a series of seemingly unconnected performance genres acted by a group of African Americans: a dance, a comedy routine, a 'message play', a song, and a realistic domestic drama. The metatheatricality is especially intense in the message play, which is about the evils of selling drugs. It has, like *An Octoroon*, intentionally bad acting and stilted presentational dialogue. The actors are reduced to black types. For example, one actor plays the following four characters: Mama, Drug Dealer Mama, Video Ho, and Grandma from Heaven. The stage directions dictate that '*none of the performers should put on any kind of "black-sounding" or "white-sounding" accent. They should deliver their lines and move as flatly as possible*' (Lee 2012, 222) in delivering subtext-less lines of dialogue, such as:

> Drug Dealer Desmond: I'm going to rob people and shoot them and also sell drugs. You should do it, too.
> Rapper Omar: But I don't want to be a drug dealer. I want to win this rap competition (*pulls out flyer*) and get a recording contract. (225–226)

What is happening throughout this section of the play stretches well beyond an easy send-up of sanctimonious 'don't do drugs' public service announcements. Coming after the 'poopface' comedy routine and before the naturalist drama, the piece presents the performative aspects of false stereotyping by these actors and characters to force the audience to confront their own assumptions about black culture. In addition to befuddling expectation and engaging in postmodern gamesmanship of undermining the author, incorporating metatheatrical critiques in blackface plays specifically chips away at the audience's inherent racial biases.

In similar fashion, the staging of *Passing Strange* (Lee 2009) emphasises the sense of identity fluidity and metatheatricality in a number of ways, from the presence of the band and cast onstage at all times, the lack of a constructed set, and the actors playing multiple characters. In addition to the alienating effects, these techniques add layers to the show's themes of personal growth and collective racial identity. A number of songs throughout the show repeat the motif of masks and masking, especially when the protagonist, Youth, is experiencing his crisis of self in act two. A character, Desi, pleads with him to 'come down now/ remove your mask' so they can experience real love with each other. In a response to her plea, the next major song of the show, 'Work the Wound', opens with the lyric, 'Every day I build a mask/ up to the task./ Another song, you see' (Rodewald and Rodewald 2008). The standardised metaphor of 'false masking' is given an added wrinkle of certain racial components and complexities.

3   Biography and Autobiography

All of these blackface performances incorporate elements of documentary, biography, or autobiography. In contrast to the pressurising falsity of the racist blackface mask, these plays have at some level and in some way an aspect of the real, authentic, or deeply personal, utilized to specifically interrogate race, blackness, and the blackface mask. By evoking true cases of racially charged incidents which then also incorporate blackface masking, these works present blackness as lived experience and not a quantifiable or imposed label.

Passing Strange mines autobiography in story and song, and the added dimension of music conveys a playful dynamic of racial construction. Based upon Stew's life, the musical follows his avatar Youth, who leaves his California home to travel around Europe in a journey of self-discovery. (In another combination of autobiography and metatheatricality, the original production featured Stew onstage and performing for the whole show. He served as narrator, sang several numbers, and interacted performatively with his doppelganger.) The show most forcefully enters the territory of post-black investigations of race construction, along with both the cultural underpinnings of blacks and the exoticising assumptions to be made about a racial minority, in the juxtaposition of the songs 'Identity' and 'The Black One'. The contrast between the two is striking, both sonically and lyrically. At this point, Youth has embarked for Berlin and attempted to ingratiate himself with the city's radical punk scene. In 'Identity', the 'chains of identity' are being broken as he flees from his 'own people'. The music is percussive and synth-driven, giving the song a jackhammer-like quality in connection with the central figure's emotions. And, yet, the identity that he is splitting apart—the personal identity or ego—is then subsumed racially by the social circle in which he lives. With 'The Black One', Youth becomes exoticised and eroticised by his Berlin friends and participates in his otherness by playing up his minority status to near-minstrel proportions. The score labels the tempo 'Vaudeville Shuffle' (Rodewald and Rodewald 2008) as a way of further highlighting that Youth is on display and performing a character. The song's call-and-response nature begins as a series of questions, the answer to which is inevitably, and comically, 'the black one': 'Who lends the club that speakeasy air?' and 'Who dances like a god and has *wunderbar* hair?' The lyrics quickly get more baldly racist. Youth is asked if he is 'a postmodern lawn jockey sculpture'. And, in a nice bit of internalised racism, when another character sings, 'He's dancing in a cage,' Youth responds, 'But I'm the one with the key' (Rodewald and Rodewald 2008). This loopy non-freedom reflects the deeply ambiguous and personal questions about race by the show's creators. This is the most theatrical and exuberant moment in *Passing Strange*, when Youth is splintering apart and confronting his blackness and black Americanness while overseas. In contrast, the musical concludes on a more conventional note. With shades of Dorothy, Youth realises just a moment too late that the realness he was seeking was at home, all along. But it is notable, both within this specific show and in conversation with the others discussed here, that the most exciting and jarring moment, at least compared to traditional narratives and conventional narrative structure, involves a layering of stereotyping and the main character's use of them for personal and selfish aims.

As a particular and specific variation on the metatheatrical practice of both establishing and destabilising author and authorship, details about the personal history of the actors or playwright are mined for drama. This ideally foregrounds connections between race and identity central to these projects, as in the opening lines of *An Octoroon*, which tantalises and shocks with both its directness and its ambiguity. BJJ is called a black playwright and he doesn't know what that means. But which description is he unsure of? Playwright? Black? Playwright who is black? BJJ's self-critique at the start of the show takes on a number of dimensions as the play progresses. He begins the play depressed, lonely, and yelling at himself in the mirror. This moment of post-black performance involves race, metatheatricality, and an auto-critique that borders on flagellation. (Similar to Stew's appearance in *Passing Strange*, Jacobs-Jenkins was in the cast of the original production. He was not BJJ but rather appeared as a mystical and only semi-explained rabbit that stalked the stage at key moments (Sellar 2014). This adds another layer of both masking and autobiography to the performance.)

The autobiographical and personal impetus of Lee's *The Shipment* drives the show's structure as well as its content. In the Author's Note, she describes that the play's 'first half is structured like a minstrel show—dance, stand-up routine, sketches, and a song'. She puts her African American cast into format of the centuries-old black racist delivery system for much of the show's duration. The minstrel show has always been an entertainment format which is explicit about brutally policing racial and gender boundaries on the US stage, even with the addition of black performers, who became minstrel stars after the Civil War.[4] In the contemporary moment, though, it is quite a crucible to put your performers into such a structure, even willingly. Lee explains her reasoning, saying that she wrote the first half in this way 'to address the stereotypes my cast members felt they had to deal with as black performers'. There is an incredible tension in these two statements. On the one hand, Lee is responding to racisms which were expressed to her by a group of black actors—itself a chilling and vulnerable position to be in[5]—and then chooses to exorcise that stereotyping through the minstrel show itself. Upon this tension between playwright and actor, Lee colludes with the cast to destabilise the audience: 'The performers wore stereotypes like ill-fitting paper-doll outfits held on by two tabs, which denied the audience easy responses (illicit pleasure or self-righteous indignation) to racial clichés' (Lee 2012, 212). The outfit metaphor echoes the white baby doll from the top of *Neighbors*. And it also implicates the assumed audience responses of either enjoyment or anger. In this note, Lee states what she does *not* want the audience to feel; she leaves unarticulated what she *does* want them to experience. In layered moments of multiple racial signifiers, *The Shipment* destabilises earlier forms of racial ideology and theatricalises an alternative and unessentialised racial grounding. Biographical and autobiographical elements in post-black minstrelsy open up possibilities of racial construction and new methods of group and self-identification.

4   Mediatisation

These plays evidence an interesting and strange pattern through their use of media and mediatisation. This is an element of performance common to theatre in the contemporary moment but is provocative and assaultive when combined with minstrelsy and blackface. Mediatisation can be the use of photos or video, the acknowledgment of screen or filmic technology, or anachronistic references to mass culture.

This technique is a further alienation and destabilisation to race categorisations in these live performances. Examples are widespread across these plays but some of the most direct are from *Neighbors*, starting, most obviously and glaringly, with the Crow Family of minstrel stereotypes which moves to the neighbourhood: Topsy, Mammy, Sambo, Zip Coon, and Jim Crow. The play is also full of pop culture references, whose intended effect is to comically disrupt the audience's sense of time and place. In an early scene, Mammy says to Jim, 'You didn't think we was just gonna be sittin' up in here in big ole fancy house just watching Tyler Perry movies and doing the Electric Slide all day?' (Jacobs-Jenkins 2012, 323). The effect is comedic for several reasons. A stereotype living in the present day is inherently comedic, and then Jacobs-Jenkins audaciously gives the stereotype-specific access to Tyler Perry films. The Perry film and television empire hinges on the character of Madea, played by Perry himself in drag, and he has repeatedly been accused of embracing stereotype and pandering to his audience. Also, at regular points during the show, each of the family members is given an 'interlude' during which they perform a solo comedy pantomime. All are full of physical comedy and are wildly, uncomfortably profane. Mammy's interlude is called her '*Gone with the Wind* tribute' (394). In the scene, Mammy accidently starts a fire with a carelessly flicked cigarette, in an homage to the book and film's burning of Atlanta. Her solution: '*She opens up her shirt, takes out her behemoth breasts—which are probably not real breasts—and proceeds to put out the fire with an ungodly amount of breast milk*' (Jacobs-Jenkins 2012, 386). She then suckles a pair of white babies on those breasts, twirling them like tassels on pasties. The comic grotesquerie of the scene is parodic but Jacobs-Jenkins is doing more than just attempting to cause offence. He neither minimises nor humanises the stereotype; rather, he inflates it to fantastic proportions—a la Rabelais's Gargantua and Swift's isle of the Brobdingnags.[6] The audience confronts the racist blackface portrayal and recognises how the mediated images through white-authored books, white-directed films, and white-created pancake advertisements have affected their perception of African American womanhood.

These works engage with current institutionalised racisms through the intrusions of the contemporary world. More than quick laughs, these are incongruous jolts to keep the audience on edge and remind them of the stakes in shows which required the playwright to employ blackface in the first place. The intrusions in *The Shipment* are no less jarring than *Neighbors*. Similar to the way Jacobs-Jenkins's references are more than mere allusion, the song choices and their placement in the show are crucial to the multiple, theatrical ways it complicates and undermines black identity formations and assumptions. Even if the audience does not grasp Lee's subtle mapping of the minstrel show onto the performance, other methods of theatricalising race make the intended destabilisation acutely felt. *The Shipment* has two distinct moments of juxtaposition involving pop music, which are mixed with other considerations involving blackface. The play opens with one such clash, that of a dance number with a rap track. The song 'F.N.T.' by Semisonic, a white rock band, plays in its entirety at the top of the show. The lyrics 'Fascinating new thing/ You delight me/ And I know you're speaking of me' (Semisonic 1996) is about surveillance and desire, which becomes glaring in this theatrical context. The song's earnestness is made uneasy and even sinister when coupled with the choreography: '*Dancer 1 performs a series of bordering-on-goofy choreographed moves that are unidentifiable in genre. Occasionally we'll see a flash of possible minstrel reference—a gesture, a bit of footwork. Sometimes Dancer 1 is smiling, sometimes not. It's difficult to tell what his relationship is to what he's doing and to the audience*' (Lee 2012, 213). The language here sets the tone and rules for the production without explicitly telling the audience how to feel about the show's description of race—because the show is entirely about the depiction of blackness despite never emphatically stating it. The flashes of 'possible minstrel reference' add unease and even condemnation to what is being observed. Though Lee does not specify the gestures or footwork, to be legible it must use the iconography derived from media that an audience would recognise: Jim Crow's dance, Mammy's glance, Al Jolson on bended knee. The lyrics of surveillance and desire implicates the audience in the stereotyping which the choreography teases.

This, in itself, would be enough of an introduction to the thematic concerns of racial assumption and cultural access to which the show succumbs, but Lee builds another smash intrusion before the show 'really' begins (which is, we are accustomed to believe, when an actor starts talking). The 'F.N.T.' song and dance sequence is immediately contrasted with hip-hop bombast, as the piece immediately switches to Lil Jon's rap track 'I Don't Give a Fuck' (Lil Jon and the East Side Boyz 2002). Stand-Up Comedian enters and 'mimes having sex doggy style' and shakes 'his booty like a stripper' before beginning his routine (Lee 2012, 215). This raw sexualisation is clearly juxtaposed with the 'F.N.T.' sequence and acts as an assaultive reminder of stereotyped assumptions of African Americans and the roles which US society expects them to play.

The second musical clash happens at the end of the message play, as three actors emerge and '*stand in line looking around at the audience in silence. They look at the audience for an uncomfortably long time.*' As they sing a capella version of 'Dark Center of the Universe' by the white indie-rock group Modest Mouse (2004), '*they continue to look around at the audience. They don't move or change expression, but they sing with feeling*' (Lee 2012, 238). A pop song presented a capella, in the middle of a show full of racial imagery and representation, accrues other resonances beyond the original. The opening lyrics, 'I might disintegrate into the thin air if you'd like / I'm not the dark center of the universe like you thought', is rather standard, shoe-gazing emo-rock, but now has racial overtones. The line, then, trades on racial assumption and negation. We know they aren't what we assume them to be, but not what they are.

Lee combines contrasting pop songs over incongruous action again in this moment. After a capella rock song, there is a transition into the play's final section. The stage directions explain: '*The Singers exit as Mary J. Blige's soul/pop song 'Ooh' begins. Stagehand 1 and Stagehand 2 enter carrying dollies. They are both white males over the age of fifty, wearing blue jeans. Stagehand 1 wears a lilac hooded sweatshirt and Stagehand 2 wears a blue T-shirt*' (239). The two stagehands say nothing and appear at no other point in the show. They are doing their job changing the scenery and, as is customary for theatregoers and their habitual practice of 'suspension of disbelief', the audience *ignores the stagehands*. We pretend they aren't really there or are invisible, as they should disappear into the task of setting up a scene so the 'real' actors in their 'fake' roles can come on and perform. The stagehands are both not there at all (invisible) and not acting (just working or labouring). But Lee is excruciatingly specific in what the stagehands look like and are doing. Those two white fifty-year-old men are onstage for an inappropriately long time, as the Blige tune is four minutes long, an eternity for a scene transition. Lee really wants you to notice the stagehands working. By having these men literally set the stage for the realistic drama that follows, the show features an explicit moment of racial duality that had been lurking at the frame of the production or just outside the theatre.

The combination of song and action is an interesting contrast to the 'Dark Side of the Universe' moment. 'Ohh' is a recording of a black female R&B singer, performing a love song about need and sacrifice. 'Ooh, what you do to me / Ooh, you're my everything' croons the chorus (Blige 2003), while the audience watches two white men setting up a couch, table, and snacks. Much as the racial mashup of the 'F.N.T.'/'I Don't Give a Fuck' moment was a jarring juxtaposition, so too is 'Dark Side of the Universe'/'Ooh'. These transitional points unsettle ideologies of race and racial construction. The mediatisation within these moments is a necessary ingredient to erode essentialist beliefs of race categorisation and forcing a definition of blackness into a mutable cultural realm.

5 Materiality

The final component to these shows foregrounds blackface as an object and material thing in the way that race and blackness are not. These post-black playwrights literalise and theatricalise a symbol of dominant racist ideology. As race itself is founded on phenotype and racism reiterates essentialised beliefs based in the visible, by smearing on a –face, these works simultaneously acknowledge and undermine biological racial determinism. By performing the materiality of black makeup and showing it to be false and easily applied, they playfully and sinisterly call attention to the anxious need for race difference and present an alternate conceptualisation of what it means to be black in the US.

The materiality or phenotypic assumptions about race in *The Shipment* are most present in the concluding scene, with a final punchline that retroactively distorts the rest of the play. Lee hints and feints at this final twist throughout the show through her attention to identity, poopface, pop music, and so on. The concluding scene provides one last variation on the idea of racial materiality. It is a miniature realist drama set in the living room which the audience has watched the stagehands assemble. In it, secrets are revealed among a group of co-workers and friends at a cocktail party. The dialogue is naturalistic and conversational, the acting style is psychologically driven and full of motivational subtext, and the plot is full of revelations about love, desire, and longing. There is no mention of race. The scene abruptly shifts to a discussion of black culture in the last moments. Some racist banter reveals that all the characters are white, though the actors are black and have displayed no visible or contextual trappings of racial impersonation. A crude racist joke forces the audience to reassess the assumptions they had made watching the domestic scene unfold. The last lines of dialogue are:

> Omar: I'm sorry. I'm sorry, but I have to say that I'm really uncomfortable with all of this. I just don't think we'd be doing this if there were a black person in the room.
> *Pause.*
> Desmond: I guess that would depend on what kind of black person it was.
> *Blackout.* (Lee 2012, 268)

With the abrupt revelation and equally sudden blackout to end the show, the audience is left contemplating a definition of race through the absence of material racial markers, such as how or if the actors were 'playing white' when they did nothing to symbolise it. This leads them further to think about the visible cues, vocalities, mannerisms, or cultural references that indicate whiteness. The final scene simultaneously highlights the necessary aspects of racial difference and the complete arbitrariness of such characteristics. The final line is ambiguous both within the context of the realistic playlet and for the overall meaning of the show. Though in this chapter I deride several works for abandoning affect in their concluding scenes, I find the abruptness, callousness, and uncertainty of this swift denouement a radically charged affective moment. The audience is given not enough time to assess their understanding of the play and instead must puzzle over it later. At that very instant when nothing more needs to be shown or said, the lights snap off.

Racial tomfoolery reaches absurd heights in *An Octoroon*, which uses a variety of –faces throughout to create dizzying and vertiginous levels of racial referents, all the better to undermine their material qualities. The overlap of actor and character is important to the play's racial critique. The stage directions specify that the actor playing BJJ is African American or black. In the first instance of racial impersonation in the show, he covers himself in whiteface: '*BJJ gets into whiteface—possibly tries to cover his entire body with it. This should go on for some time. After he is satisfied, he slowly turns around and, without taking his eyes off the audience, very, very slowly and very, very stoically gives himself an incredibly powerful wedgie*' (Jacobs-Jenkins 2015, 9).

BJJ then performs as the two white male characters of *The Octoroon*. The Boucicault stand-in Playwright is white and he puts on redface to play Wahnotee, an alcoholic Native American. And Assistant, a Native American or South Asian actor, plays the roles of two male slaves. A key stage direction highlights the slapstick madness of these races and – faces: '*Enter Paul, being chased by M'Closky, who is trailed by Wahnotee*' (23). The stage picture created is of a Native American actor in blackface being chased by a black actor in whiteface being trailed by a white actor in redface. No actual attempt at a convincing racial impersonation is made, as the audience has watched two of the actors/characters putting on racial makeup. The comedy of the moment derives from the cavalier way that such stereotyping is diminished to a violent silent film routine. The overt materiality of the – faces is a key component to the success of this tableau and how it can assess and critique racial constructions without falling into a reinforcement of stereotypes themselves. The masks' materiality divorces racist mimicry from the bodies of actors who belong to different racial categories but are not beholden to essentialised representations. Race's performativity and racism's materiality are contained in that one moment of theatrical excess.

In post-black plays, the materiality of blackface is undercut and the flow of racist ideals through culture is short-circuited through those selfsame symbols. The metatheatrical, autobiographical, mediated, and material are all important to post-black critiques. The conclusion of *Neighbors* highlights all of these qualities working in tandem. It layers many different levels of performance at once, as well as a number of tensions around the depiction of blackness. The unstableness of the scene, and a toxicity of blackface and a boundaryless-ness to race, grows beyond the performance's ability to contain it. The ending also offers no solutions or answers to the many questions the play raises; rather, in a disruption of conventional dramatic form, the play ceases. The borders of the performance are broken, between the two onstage families, the domestic drama and minstrel show, stage and audience, and the matrixed performance space and outside world.

The Crow Family is backstage before the start of their minstrel show. To calm the nerves of their youngest and newest member, Mammy says, 'Boy, don't you know they luvs us. They luvs evathang we does' (Jacobs-Jenkins 2012, 400–401). The 'they' of her statement is tantalisingly vague and remains so through the course of the scene. Mammy, Sambo, and Topsy list all the things 'they' love about the act, for over fifty lines of dialogue. The repetitive, mind-numbing list of stereotypes draws from the roots of the minstrel show and the contemporary media landscape. The terse and epigrammatic listing includes 'When we gets out our banjos' and 'guffaws and slaps our thighs', to more contemporary depictions, such as 'roll out necks and be lak, "I know you di-in't!"' and 'we acts all gay and vogue' (401). As a final word of advice, Mammy offers the wonderfully contradictory message, 'Be yo'self. It's just a show.' This adage, delivered by a mammy stereotype to another blackface character, turns the bromide of self-identity and appearance upside-down. The show is the self.

The wordless tableau the audience then encounters confounds expectation and pushes against the boundaries of performance.

> *The Crow Family [members] take their place on 'stage,' standing in a straight line. Minstrel music plays, but they don't move. Instead, they simply look into every face in the room. [...] The minstrel music finishes, and there is silence before the entire theater, stage and all, is ever so slowly and completely washed in amber light. It is awkward and goes on forever. We watch them. They watch us.* (Jacobs-Jenkins 2012, 402)

This combination of sights and sounds is deflating. The show has already been immobilised by silent surveillance. The idea of race that *Neighbors* presents is confusing and putrid. Stereotypes are humanised. Race is nothing more than racism. Blackness and whiteness are irreconcilable racial positions. The comedic irrelevant tone cannot change this basic conclusion, even as the ruthlessness of these basic assumptions is toyed with throughout the production.

The end of the play suggests a playwright backed into a corner, without answer or dramatic solution, who then pushes the actors and audience outside. The final stage directions stipulate an odd coda which adds both random chance and autobiography:

> Preferably there is no 'real' curtain call, and [The Actor Playing Melody] leaves with the audience. She goes outside and has a cigarette. She doesn't talk to anyone, waiting at the stage door, maybe with her mother. She looks different now, maybe, less like herself.
> *Eventually Jim comes out of the stage door to greet her. They hug and kiss. Maybe she gives him a cigarette, which he smokes. Maybe people catch this, maybe they don't.*
> Melody: How do you feel?
> *'We are Family' is heard blasting away over the speakers back in the empty theater, as The Actor Playing Jim Crow starts to tell her how he really feels.* (Jacobs-Jenkins 2012, 402–403)

This stage direction is impossible. The chance of anyone seeing it, and its improvisatory quality, and the seeming authenticity of the moment is in contrast to all of the falsity and illusion of the show. (And insisting the actor say how he really feels puts the burden of answering the questions of the show on his shoulders, which to me seems unfair.) This autobiographical, unmatrixed moment outside the theatre is the closest thing to relief that *Neighbors* offers.

6   Conclusions: Very Fine People

Blackface in the US isn't going away. It is at the bedrock of our culture and will continue to be used as a form of denigration and terrorism by citizens of this country against fellow citizens. The key theoretical text of post-black performance employed here is Elam's 'Black Theatre in the Age of Obama'. The Obama years are over and an openly hateful and contemptuous chapter has arrived in the US. It remains to be seen if the theatregoing public has a stomach for these works or if it was easier to pal around with stereotypes, however artfully, when racist vitriol was on a wane. The masquerades of racist coding have been removed in this country. It is old news to mention how President Donald Trump saw 'very fine people' on both sides of a white supremacist rally at which a protester was killed—a statement of such craven equivocation that I am reminded of the 'it depends' prevarications at the end of *The Shipment*. The policies, statements, attitudes, and paranoias of President Trump, aired and amplified through social media by his handlers and his sycophants, have made the US a significantly more dangerous place for black and brown people.

The lessons and experiments of these post-black works are complex, artistic, and humanistic. But a new era of US society and politics arrived with the seismic, caustic, and regressive shifts of both policy and polity under President Trump. The irony of the Obama era has given way to something else. Playwrights are finding new ways to express themselves, their voices, their anger, and protest.[7] It remains to be discovered if self-effacing, lackface theatre will continue to be funny.

Notes

1. A filmed version of the play's original production, directed by Lee, can be viewed at ontheboards.com.
2. A number of other '–faces' are present in contemporary theatre, as a way of challenging dominant ideological perspectives. These are racial, as in red-, yellow-, and whiteface, or are related to other identity categorisations, such as pinkface for gay stereotyping. All use the suffix –face as a way of aligning themselves with the historical precedent of blackface.
3. Lisa Merrill and Theresa Saxon's article specifically analyzes the adaptation of the Boucicault play. See Lisa Merrill and Theresa Saxon, "Replaying and Rediscovering *The Octoroon*," *Theatre Journal* 69, 2 (June 2017).
4. This was noted in the foundational minstrelsy history, *Blacking Up*. See Robert Toll, *Blacking Up: The Minstrel Show in Nineteenth Century America* (New York: Oxford University Press, 1974).

306   K. BYRNE

5. See the interviews in *The Routledge Companion to African American Theatre and Performance* with actors, producers, stage managers, and other artistic staff. Kathy A. Perkins, Sandra L. Richards, Renée Alexander Craft, and Thomas F. DeFrantz, eds., *The Routledge Companion to African American Theatre and Performance* (London: Routledge Press, 2019). This was also made clear to me in an unpublished essay written by my student Tiffany Gordon in 2020, titled 'Ain't It Funny: Marginalized and Mute'.
6. This is a very Bakhtinian moment. See M.M. Bakhtin, *Rabelais and His World*, trans. Helene Iswolsky (Cambridge, MA: M.I.T. Press, 1968).
7. It is indicative that Suzan-Lori Parks's *100 Plays for the First Hundred Days*, her response to the beginning of the Trump presidency, is primarily a document of disbelief and anger. See Suzan-Lori Parks, *100 Plays for the First Hundred Days* (New York: Theatre Communications Group, 2018).

REFERENCES

Bakhtin, M.M. 1968. *Rabelais and His World*. Trans. Helene Iswolsky. Cambridge, MA: M.I.T. Press.

Blige, Mary J. 2003. Ohh. In *Love & Life*. Geffen Records.

Elam, Harry, Jr. 2013. Black Theatre in the Age of Obama. In *The Cambridge Companion to African American Theatre*, ed. Harvey Young, 255–278. Cambridge: Cambridge University Press.

Jacobs-Jenkins, Branden. 2012. Neighbors. In *Reimagining A Raisin in the Sun*, ed. Rebecca Ann Rugg and Harvey Young. Evanston, IL: Northwestern University Press.

———. 2015. *An Octoroon*. New York: Dramatists Play Service.

Lee, Spike. 2009. *Passing Strange: The Movie*.

Lee, Young Jean. 2012. The Shipment. In *The Methuen Drama Book of Post-Black Plays*, ed. Harry Elam Jr. and Douglas Jones Jr. London: Methuen Drama.

Lil Jon and the East Side Boyz. 2002. I Don't Give a Fuck. In *Kings of Crunk*. BME Recordings.

Merrill, Lisa, and Theresa Saxon. June 2017. Replaying and Rediscovering *The Octoroon*. *Theatre Journal* 69 (2): 127–152.

Modest Mouse. 2004. Dark Center of the Universe. In *The Moon & Antarctica*. Epic Records.

Rodewald, Stew, and Heidi Rodewald. 2008. Come Down Now and Work the Wound. In *Passing Strange*. New York: Dramatics Play Service.

Saal, Ilka. 2019. Performing Slavery at the Turn of the Millennium: Stereotypes, Affect, and Theatricality in Branden Jacobs-Jenkins's *Neighbors* and Young Jean Lee's *The Shipment*. In *Slavery and the Post-Black Imagination*, ed. Bertram D. Ashe and Ilka Saal, 140–159. Seattle: University of Washington Press.

Schneider, Rosa. Fall 2018. Anyway, the Whole Point of This Was to Make You Feel Something. *Journal of American Drama and Theatre* 31 (1): n.p.

Sellar, Tom. 2014, May 21. Pay No Attention to the Man in the Bunny Suit. *The Village Voice*: 8.

Semisonic. 1996. F.N.T. In *Great Divide*. MCA Records.

Stew. 2008. The Black One. In *Passing Strange*. Ghostlight Records.

Young, Harvey. May 2013. Black Performance Studies in the New Millennium. *Theatre Journal* 65 (2): 289–294.

CHAPTER 17

Fighting Racism on the Contemporary Francophone Stage

Annette Bühler-Dietrich

1 Introduction

The title of my chapter is rather extensive; it could imply drama and theatre in the French overseas departments, in Canada, Asia, Africa and in Europe. Yet, for the purpose of this study, I will discuss plays which were written by Sub-Saharan African playwrights and by Black French playwrights, who, themselves, have different takes on and experiences of racism. I will focus primarily on plays, yet will refer to the theatre more generally as an artistic and institutional space where appropriate.

'Fighting Racism' is an activity all these plays carry out through their respective highlighting of and resistance against institutional and individual racist behaviour. Yet, the title is also meant to refer to a very specific type of fighting, namely boxing, to which I will turn in the latter part of this chapter. Between 1993 and 2014 three plays were published and performed which centre on Muhammad Ali. Of them, one is by Black British playwright Mojisola Adebayo, who writes in English. Since Muhammad Ali in her play becomes the pivotal figure just as in Dieudonné Niangouna's monodrama, and both plays interweave the life of Ali, autobiography and a critique of theatre as an institution, it seemed crucial to include Adebayo's play. Just as the mangled body of Emmett Till is a recurring symbol of racist violence, Muhammad Ali has come to symbolise the successful fight against institutional racism, and both icons appear in texts in English and French. Theatre is no closed-off space,

A. Bühler-Dietrich (✉)
Universität Stuttgart, Stuttgart, Germany
e-mail: post@annettebuehler-dietrich.de

© The Author(s), under exclusive license to Springer Nature Switzerland AG 2021
T. Morosetti, O. Okagbue (eds.), *The Palgrave Handbook of Theatre and Race*, https://doi.org/10.1007/978-3-030-43957-6_17

playwrights, performers and productions travel between countries and continents; how they discuss racism is inflected by these imaginary, virtual and real movements. If movements converge in the figure of Muhammad Ali, it becomes necessary to cross even a language border.

'Despite very different trajectories, what can be compared cross-nationally nevertheless is the confinement, the exclusion and the stigmatisation experienced by visible minorities who are poor and socially segregated in the USA, the UK and in France' (Body-Gendrot 2004, 156). The fact that plays on racism relate different countries and histories thus comes as no surprise.

2   On the Study of Racism in France

Racism and its origins in colonialism has become an important field of study for French researchers in fields such as sociology, political science, history, anthropology and cultural studies since the late 1980s (c.f. Taguieff 1987; Wieviorka 2004) but seems to have gained momentum during the last two decades when the relations between colonialism, memory cultures and Black French populations have been explored in research and in public discussion (c.f. Blanchard 2017a; Vergès 2006).[1] Even though French legislation deleted any reference to race (Blanchard 2017b, 222) due to the ideal of integration promoted by the French republic (c.f. Body-Gendrot 2004, 158), race enters through the back door via the claim to cultural difference (Blanchard 2017b; Bentouhami-Molino 2015). In spite of the heterogeneity of the Black French population, migrating to mainland France from French overseas departments as well as from former African colonies or having grown up in France all along, the experience of anti-black racism and police violence has created a Black French cohesion: 'The "We: Blacks of France" does not reflect a racial identity but a form of organisation, a series of actions and behaviours whose aim it is to destroy the mechanisms which reproduce inequality and oppression' (Etoke 2017, 160).[2]

Recently several publications in the realm of French cultural studies located in France and the US address this issue, among them Dominic Thomas's *Africa and France: Postcolonial Cultures, Migration, and Racism* (2013), *Black France / France Noire: The History and Politics of Blackness* (Keaton et al. 2012), *The Colonial Legacy in France: Fracture, Rupture, and Apartheid* (Bancel et al. 2017a) as well as monographs by political scientist Achille Mbembe, especially *Critique de la raison nègre* (2013) and *Politiques de l'inimitié* (2016).

These publications, as their subtitles indicate, shed light on the relation between French politics and its refusal to include the impact of French colonialism and the slave trade into French cultural memory on the one hand and the growing antagonism between the white French population and France's visible minorities on the other. Statements and measures by French president Nicolas Sarkozy in France and in African countries during his presidency 2007 to 2012 have aggravated the opposition between white and black France and impact cohabitation until today (c.f. Thomas 2013, 59–88). 'The fact remains that the postcolonial racism no one wants to hear about explicates the current situation' (Bancel et al. 2017b, 23). While the discourse on cultural difference already essentialised differences in the 1980s and 1990s (Thomas 2013, 62) and helped the extreme right-wing Front National to blossom (Crépon 2017), French national identity has been a contested issue ever since, encouraged and structurally implemented during Sarkozy but still living on. 'No longer capable of being inclusive, in fear of terror of outsiders, the national community now excludes' (Bancel et al. 2017b, 14; c.f. Blanchard et al. 2016).

One instance of exclusion is police violence, a prime-time media topic in May and June 2020 with demonstrations in the USA and in many other countries, notably France, where the movement 'La verité pour Adama' on 2 June 2020 organised a demonstration with 20,000 people in Paris, linking the death of Black American George Floyd on 25 May in Minneapolis with the death of Black French Adama Traoré. Relating the two deaths, the movement, launched by Traoré's sister Assa right after the passing of her brother in 2016, recalls the death of the 24-year old in police custody and the recent acquittal of the policemen responsible in its 2 June demonstration. Acts of police violence provoked the anthology *Marianne et le garçon noir* (Miano 2017), edited by novelist Léonora Miano, who focuses especially on the black male subject living in France. Her book combines articles by scholars in cultural studies as well as texts written by literary writers and performers. It starts out with the reference to incidents of police violence, namely the rape of Théo Luhaka in 2017 and the death of Adama Traoré, and highlights that rampant US police violence also happens in France. Although many of the articles on racism consider the category of race apart from other categories, artists in Miano's collection specifically evoke gender and sexuality. The violation of Luhaka by a French policeman abusing him with a baton (Etoke 2017, 158–159) shows how racism and sexual violence intersect. All contributions to Miano's anthology emphasise the heightened vulnerability of black male subjects; many of the contributors mention their personal experiences at airports, police stations and random controls. In her autobiographical essay, Michaëla Danjé, a black transgender performer, unfolds how racist and anti-male violence go together. Her experiences of racism cover explicit violence as well as nanoracism, a racism of the everyday. Mbembe sees an increase in nanoracism, which he defines as follows: 'Shameless dealings in words and deeds, symbols, and language' (Mbembe 2017, 365).

Danjé's text cuts across time and space, remembering the murder of Emmett Till as well as the arbitrary and racist execution of his father, Louis Till, by the American army he belonged to, in France (Danjé 2017, 71). Addressing LGBT concerns, history and racism, her text brings together issues that the plays I will discuss in this chapter raise in various ways.[3]

3   Contemporary Francophone Drama

To consider anti-black racism as a topic in contemporary francophone drama, two different contexts of writers, plays and performances need to be taken into account: Contemporary plays written by African writers from various countries, to my knowledge, do not primarily focus on individual experiences of racism in their countries. Whereas neo-colonial structural violence is an issue and leads to plots which focus on financial and structural exploitation (see Tansi 2002 [1977]; Méda 2018; Houansou 2019; Bühler-Dietrich 2019), what Mbembe calls nanoracism as a form of 'commonplace, banal' (Mbembe 2017, 365) interpersonal violence is less prominent in these plays. The exception to this are plays explicitly dealing with the colonial era either as historical drama or as parable; there colonisers are overtly racist (Dadié 1970; Guingané 1996).

If one looks at plays written for and within a European context by African or by Black French writers, the impression is different. Congolese playwright David-Minor Ilunga's recent monodrama *Délestage* (Power Cut) is set in a frame of police interrogation and attorney conversation. The two policemen do not beat their prisoner, but verbal abuse is frequent. In the play, the nameless character, an undocumented migrant in Brussels, tries to explain the realities in the DRC and his reasons for migration. Ilunga, writer and performer, chooses a comic register to convey his message. His character has the courage and power to speak up against the policemen; it is only when his attempts to make the attorney understand why he stayed in Brussels fail that he agrees to be deported (Ilunga 2016; Bühler-Dietrich 2019). In his play *Ombres d'espoir* (Shadows of Hope), a play commissioned on behalf of a German-Burkinabè cooperation, Wilfried N'Sondé, black novelist and playwright of Congolese origin, who grew up in France and spent several years in Berlin, discusses the fears and stereotypes surrounding the African migrant. N'Sondé shows exactly how nanoracism infiltrates everyday interaction, but also how solidarity could win out (N'Sondé 2012; Bühler-Dietrich 2018).

Before going on to talk about plays whose choice converges in the figure of Muhammad Ali, I want to discuss two plays recently written by Black French women playwrights.

With Eva Doumbia's *Le Iench*, the premier of which is scheduled for autumn 2020 at the CDN Normandie-Rouen, the experiences of contemporary black and PoC youth as well as police violence take centre stage.[4] *Le Iench* is anagrammatic for 'le chien' (the dog), an alteration typical of youth language in the play. The dog features as animal and metaphor; Doumbia's reversal of the word is directly connected to the skewed meanings the pet has for Drissa, the main character of the play, but also its meaning in the overall context of colonisation and migration.

The play opens with a prologue, which alludes to the end of the play without giving the ending away. The prologue details a quotidian scene in the life of the Diarra family, whose name, signifying lion, tells their Malian origin. Mother, daughter and younger brother go grocery shopping at a moment when Drissa has vanished and they are waiting to hear from him. Suddenly, Ramata, his twin sister, has a vision of him lying on the supermarket floor in a puddle of blood. Then, with the next scene, the main body of the play starts in one long flashback. The three-act play is interrupted four times by an interlude entitled 'Who will be next?' In these, a choir recalls the victims of police violence by name and in chronological order. Starting with Bouna and Zyed, whose deaths in 2005 lead to major riots in France that year (c.f. Thomas 2013, 63), the list closes with Adama Traoré. Citing the verbal abuse and the mortal fear of the victim when referring to Lamine Dieng, a young man who died of asphyxiation in police custody in 2007, the choir raises the thought that Drissa, the fictional character, might be the next victim. Doumbia's work of commemoration and mourning inscribes itself into projects like the website 'Urgence-notre-police-assassine en toute impunité' (Urgency-our-police-assassinates with complete impunity), which asks in fact the question 'who will be next?', or black musician Usher's video 'Chains' in which he projects photographs and names of victims of police violence (Usher 2015).

The play covers three moments in the lives of the family, especially of the twins: at age 11, age 18 and at the university. At age 11, the family buys a house and moves to the suburbs, apparently blending with their white French surroundings. There they get to know two boys, Karim, whose parents are Moroccan, and Mandela, a black boy born in Haiti, adoptive son to a white French mother. Both phases of French colonisation and the slave trade are hence evoked in these characters, who are ignorant of the immediate past: Both Karim and Drissa do not know who Nelson Mandela was and why the child Mandela, born on 11 February, would be named after him—a situation which points to a lack of communication on black liberation movements and the fight against racial segregation in both households. In act II, nanoracist treatment of the young adults is set in several situations: Ramata shaves her hair off, since first the boys in her class do not 'rate' her because she is black, then one of them even touches her hair. Mandela, instead of defending her, keeps silent to maintain his own invisibility. Drissa wants to go to a club but is refused by the black doorman who only works there because he needs to finance his family back in his home country. Obstinately, Drissa argues for getting in and is finally admitted without gratification. His desire to pass the door expresses just as much his desire for white normalcy as the desire to have a dog (Doumbia 2019, 29). In act III, Ramata and Drissa have passed their exams and attend university in contrast to their two friends, who have failed their baccalaureat. As to the requirements of fitting into a dominantly white society and fulfilling their parents' expectations, they have done everything right. Nevertheless, Issouf, the father, refuses Drissa's wish to keep the dog his friends gave him and instead beats his son violently. Only after Drissa has vanished does the father explain why he is opposed to dogs: To him they evoke the image of the black man killed like a dog (Doumbia 2019, 44). Doumbia shows a stifling mode of living, where the parents, especially the father, maintain traditional customs without arriving either here or there.[5] Drissa, discovered in his forest retreat by the police, is singled out by them as dangerous and treated accordingly. Sara Ahmed's important observation that '[t]here can be nothing more dangerous to a body than the social agreement that *that* body is dangerous' (Ahmed 2014, 211) is here confirmed. When his dog attacks the policemen, they kill the dog first and then him. The scene, consisting of Drissa's monologue, relates the memory of French colonial history to the failure of the French model of integration: 'To accept that I melt equally into would mean to recognise the error to have thrown me so deep down. / To accept to melt me equally into would make it necessary to ask for my forgiveness. / For one only forgives the one who asks for it' (Doumbia 2019, 46).[6] In contrast to his father, Drissa refuses to put up with permanent rejection. Yet the play ends on a note even more painful than Drissa's death. Ramata, after having organised a rally on behalf of her dead brother, just like Assa Traoré, immolates herself by lighting her hair. She refuses to comply with the fact that eventually the protests die down, after some small signs to the disadvantaged communities, while her own rage and loss prevail. Doumbia's precise analysis combines the individual pain of exclusion with structural institutional violence as suffered by Drissa and chronicled in the interludes and can be considered to be a successful transferral of socio-political discussions to the stage.

The 1980s and 1990s saw an upsurge of discussions on cultural difference and the incompatibility of cultures in France (Thomas 2013, 62). This is the period when Koffi Kwahulé wrote his play *Cette vieille magie noire* (This Old Black Magic), which I will discuss below, it is also the period when Franco-Senegalese writer Penda Diouf grew up in France. In her autobiographical monodrama *Pistes* (Trails; Diouf 2018)[7], Diouf draws on her personal experience of racism, growing up as the only black child in a French provincial town.[8] Written from the perspective of a black woman playwright, *Pistes* is as much about the fascination with a black sportsman as about a public and private history of discrimination and violence. This puts the play in a row with the plays discussed in the main body of the chapter.

In *Pistes*, Diouf remembers a series of incidents of nanoracism which determined her childhood and adolescence but also recalls the violent death of an uncle, a medical student, found dead in the Seine. Penda's, the character's, antidote is sports. Talented in athletics, she designates as her personal hero Namibian runner Franckie Fredericks, winner of silver medals at the 1992 and 1996 Olympic Games. Her interest in Fredericks eventually makes her travel to Namibia, especially the Namib desert, where she confronts the history of the eradication of the Herero and Nama people in a genocide perpetrated by the German empire in 1904 to 1907. She is also exposed to the aftermath of South-African apartheid, when she is considered to be in the wrong place upon entering expensive tourist lodges. Her trip to Namibia, which became independent only in 1990, connects her with a colonial past of large-scale racist violence and discrimination, yet also brings her closer to idol Franckie Fredericks:

> When I am on the trail, when I run, I try to find Franckie's large and fast strides. His slackening. His way of embodying the cool in order to swallow the trail. Swallow the strained muscles. Swallow the pain. Swallow the sweat. Swallow the lack of air. Swallow the lies. Swallow apartheid. Swallow the humiliations. Swallow the drowned bodies. Swallow the mourning. Swallow the tears. Swallow the world, in order to make place for another, better one. (Diouf 2018, 17)

The movement of running relates her to him, to their shared swallowing of physical pain, humiliation, mourning and racism. Swallowing includes both the remembrance of apartheid and today's refugees' plight in the Mediterranean and it points to another world. In his essay 'Kritik', Theodor W. Adorno writes 'What is wrong, once recognised distinctly and precisely, is already an indicator of what is right, better' (Adorno 1998, 10.2, 793). Diouf enumerates what is wrong and remembers what is painful in her own biography and in the history of Namibia in order to 'make place' for a new world. The play ends on this note of pain and courage: '"Courageous."... Others were courageous before me. I only walk in the footsteps of Franckie without ever catching up with him [...]' (Diouf 2018, 18), as she listens to the blues of Big Mama (ibid.) and concludes: 'I ran a lap, but I am far from having ended my journey' (Diouf 2018, 19). Neither her personal journey nor the history of violence has come to an end, yet the courage invested in this trip, after a severe personal crisis, strengthens her to carry on.

Diouf uses the metaphor of sowing to structure her play, to stitch together the elements of a personal and a national history which are not genealogically connected. 'To bring together the pieces of cloth of a scattered history, a patchwork sown of what's intimate. And to make a flag from it, a blood-stained cape to confront the world' (Diouf 2018, 4). Stretching the history of violence from France to Namibia, she points to structural continuities and confronts this history of violence in order to 'face the world'.

Diouf's combination of autobiography and national history is a recurrent feature in autobiographical monodrama. In the context of a discussion on racism, Diouf's turn to Frankie Fredericks as nodal point of another, complementary history to that of her own, is not unusual. In her list of renowned sportsmen and—women who have had an impact on race politics, she also mentions Muhammad Ali: 'In 1967, Muhammad Ali refuses to fight in Vietnam' (ibid., 17). Muhammad Ali, however, is a recurring figure in plays that discuss the fight against racism. More than any other sportsman, he seems fit to stand in for this fight. In the following, I want to discuss two plays which put Muhammad Ali at the centre, Dieudonné Niangouna's *M'appelle Mohamed Ali* and Mojisola Adebayo's *Muhammad Ali and Me*, in order to then turn to another play from the early 1990s, Koffi Kwahulé's *Cette vieille magie noire* which, in its main Ali-inspired character, already implicitly relates the question of the American Black to the French Black.

4   Two Plays on Muhammad Ali

In 2008 and 2013 respectively, two plays were put on stage which prominently figured Muhammad Ali, one by Black British playwright and performer Mojisola Adebayo entitled *Muhammad Ali and Me*, the other by Congolese playwright and director Dieudonné Niangouna, currently based in France, who wrote the play for the Burkinabè actor Etienne Minoungou, based in Belgium, and called it *M'appelle Mohamed Ali*. Both Adebayo and Minoungou performed the play themselves; just like Adebayo's play, Niangouna's text draws on biographical information, submitted by Etienne Minoungou, for whom it was written. Both plays, one in English, the other in French, not only flag Muhammad Ali in their title but tie together a story of personal battle with his biography. Even though the focus of this article is on francophone drama, I have decided to include Adebayo's play for comparison: while racism has specific national historical genealogies and specific articulations in specific countries, the similarities concerning violence and nanoracism are striking; hence, they justify a glance across national and language borders to find out what the person and the character Muhammad Ali bring to the discussion.

The idea to write a play on Muhammad Ali for Etienne Minoungou started with a physical likeness: people remarked that the Burkinabè actor (*1968) resembled the younger Muhammad Ali; a first conversation on the project during festival Récréâtrales in 2012 in Ouagadougou had Minoungou, then also director of the festival, talk about his life. The following year, the play premiered with a text written by Niangouna, toured in Europe and was finally shown in Ouagadougou during the Récréâtrales 2014, staged by Jean Hamado Tiemtoré. Alone on a bare stage, Minoungou changes between the personae of Ali and Etienne, often indicating Ali by the punches and jabs he makes. The physical likeness leads to a quick alternation between the performer speaking as Ali or incarnating his own role while speaking as 'himself'.

Muhammad Ali (1942–2016) is especially suited as a public persona to enter a play which interrogates the position of a subject in an adversarial environment. Even though both plays evoke him on stage, neither sets out to be a play only about the boxer. To the extent that the plays are about him, they are also about the character imagining him, changing into him. While Muhammad Ali's life has been discussed in a fair number of monographs, *The Muhammad Ali Reader* (Early 1998) also assembling essays and interviews on and with him, and film, the plays talk less about him than about the impact he has.[9] It comes as no surprise that the stages of his life—the initial successes, the Olympic Medal and the World Championships, the turn to the Nation of Islam, the refusal to fight in Vietnam and the subsequent ban from boxing, the comeback with the fights against George Foreman and Joe Frazier as well as the eventual suffering from Parkinson disease—make it into the two plays and reappear transformed in Kwahulé's play, too. Suffering from racist discrimination in the South even after he had won the gold medal, and being attacked by the press and watched by the FBI after officially joining the Black Muslims and then refusing to go to Vietnam, Ali is a perfect example of a black public persona who managed to resist all blows—in the boxing ring and outside—, stand in for his agenda and survive.[10] As such, he cuts across national belonging, gender and sexuality—he becomes an interlocutor not only for male Burkinabè Minoungou but also for queer female performer Adebayo.

In *M'appelle Mohamed Ali*, a male actor called Etienne waits in the wings to enter the stage. Although he enters the stage in act II, the very last lines of the play repeat those calling him on stage at the beginning: 'Étienne? / Yes. I'm coming' (Niangouna 2014, 10, 61). Even though he is on stage all the while, the action in act II could still be placed before an imagined performance and could be witnessed by the real audience but not by any intradiegetic spectator. The privacy of the scene, in which the private is highly political, gives rise to the encounter between Etienne and Mohamed Ali.[11] 'M'appelle Mohamed Ali' is an order, 'call me Mohamed Ali' (Niangouna 2014, 15) says Etienne, because he does not want to give away his name. Yet, Muhammad Ali also was his childhood idol, 'I was Mohamed Ali, all the days of my childhood' (ibid., 26); now, on stage, the 'Mohamed Ali who is in me' (ibid., 30) is released and the actor Minoungou alternates between Etienne and Mohamed Ali. Whereas Etienne's issue is the role of African theatre and his position as an actor—a topic the playwright Niangouna has treated in several essays (Niangouna 2013)—Mohamed Ali discusses slavery, racism, colour coding and asks for a black culture. He wants to revise history books and asks black people to stand in for themselves: 'We will refuse the financial aid, the agreements, the support; all of these forms of dependency which would throw us into a merciless misery' (Niangouna 2014, 24); he also asks white people to return the image of the black man to himself: 'Look at this Negro whom you've created thoughtlessly and render him to himself' (25).[12] In line with making Ali the spokesperson for African and African-American history, the play focuses especially on Muhammad Ali's refusal to be conscripted for Vietnam. Knowingly, the Ali character accuses Joe Louis of having collaborated with the military in order to show that only compliance with power permits a black boxer to be acknowledged, and he himself refuses to comply nevertheless. Although Ali's comments in court and outside concerning his refusal to go to Vietnam are well known, Niangouna includes only very few of the original remarks in Ali's long passages. His words cohere with the spirit of Muhammad Ali's refusal, yet his Ali character is as explicit as fits a fictional character on stage who can talk freely. Ali attacks press and court alike, highlights racism in America and elaborates on who is the real enemy. His French is sometimes colloquial, but his rhetoric is clear, arguing for his decision from several angles. After a brief further passage on boxing style, Ali finally talks about his fight with George Foreman and the expectations of the crowd. In his speech, he reads Foreman as the epitome of the stereotype of the dangerous black man and the fantasies of him:

> It is this Negro who kills a cow with a punch / It's this saturated Negro, abused by his stupidity, and reified by his very own muscular capacities. / The Negro one should only meet at the fair [...] The Negro on the tele, the Negro of the construction sites, the Negro of refuse collection, the libido Negro [...] the bad Negro: the monster. (Niangouna 2014, 53–54)

Niangouna's Ali reads the logic of this fight which Foreman is bound to lose and relates it to the white discourse on the 'Negro', this imaginary white construct of the black man.[13] This is independent of the real Muhammad Ali's comments on the fight which focus on strategies of fighting and expectations

(Playboy 1998, 134–135). Hence, Ali is further established as the diagnostician of a hegemonic white society. At the end, his vision—'We don't have a problem of colour, this is an illusion of memory. There are no people of colour. We need to leave the theatre, that's all' (Niangouna 2014, 58) remains without comment.

In Niangouna's play, Ali's utterances echo positions of Mbembe's *Critique de la raison nègre*. His part is to analyse and critique white society in order to point, as in Diouf, to something which lies beyond that. This point is taken up by Etienne: 'In this theatre, only the part of the future counts. It's a fight of the past. A fight which has been happening for thousands of years and which we act out ceaselessly in order to be able to hold close to the future' (Niangouna 2014, 58–59). His parts interrupt Ali's and all of them centre on acting and the theatre. As in Diouf, a situation of crisis, which is equally connected to his work as an actor and to his life, motivates the character. Impersonating whatever a director wants him to impersonate, he loses himself—'Oh well, our characters ate us up' (27). Yet now, acting the Mohamed Ali inside of him, the being behind the mask comes to the fore: 'And I allow the being behind the mask to appear, the bruised, the shamed, the irreverent, the injured [...]' (28). Etienne's utterances revolve around the position of theatre, its dependence on external funding, the expectations brought to it: 'I am not that actor, not that black actor whom one doesn't accept as soon as he asks the question, as soon as he goes to a place where you didn't expect him' (55). Just as Ali refuses to play the part society assigns to him as a black boxer, Etienne resists remaining within the confines of characters and positions assigned to him. Theatre and the boxing ring become interchangeable—'The ring is a dialogue and the stage a battle field' (58), both fight preconceived ideas on stage/in the ring and the political and financial structures which institutionalise these ideas. *M'appelle Mohammed Ali* thus allows Niangouna to fold the discussion on racism back into the institutional structure he and Etienne Minoungou are working in. Whereas Niangouna's essays on theatre openly address the challenges theatre in Africa faces, his monodrama allows him to include a site, the boxing ring, which is different but also very much alike. In a 2017 publication called 'Jouer l'Afrique. Résistance théâtrale' (Acting Africa. Dramatic resistance), he takes up the metaphor of boxing as the structuring principle of the essay: 'First round: [...] In order to make theatre in Africa you need to box the situation' (Niangouna 2017, 189). Theatre as the site of conflicting institutional, financial and political interests becomes an artistic battle ground. The metaphor is pervasive—Adebayo's and Kwahulé's plays both, too, in different ways, combine the ring and the theatre.[14] When Niangouna and Minoungou's successful production toured, theatres and festivals emphasised the discourse on Africa woven into the play: 'Today, in the middle of their lives, Minoungou and Niangouna call upon the famous boxer to reflect upon a modern Africa, for which the surmounting of challenges is still a daily act' (Les francophonies n.d.). In spite of the references to Muhammad Ali in the title and within the play, elements of his biography only enter the picture in as far as they make him refer to the institutional and discursive obstacles he needs to overcome on a daily basis. A 'modern Africa' is then, above all, one which resists the images and constraints imposed upon it—just like Muhammad Ali.

In contrast to Niangouna's play which focuses heavily on the spoken word, Mojisola Adebayo's *Muhammad Ali and me* is described by the playwright as 'a physical storytelling performance for three performers, with poetry, song, dance, British (or other) Sign language, ritual, music and movement, original fight footage, film and verbatim text by Muhammad Ali' (Adebayo 2011, 66). Adebayo dedicates it to Muhammad Ali and to Emmett Till and thus explicitly sets the frame for a discussion of racism. Just like *Pistes* and *M'appelle Mohamed Ali*, biographical information is an important element of the play, 'the play is and is in part *about* the merging of memory and imagination, biography and fiction' (70). The play recounts the character Mojitola's growing up as a black girl in a white neighbourhood, in a white foster home. 'The play is set within a fractured boxing gym, with elements of a boxing ring [...]' (69). The hybrid stage is as much a boxing ring as an open space which represents other locations, notably the private space of the foster home. The characters correspond to the logic of boxing, they are 'The Fighter, The Corner Man and The Referee' (71). These generic positions in a ring then take up the multiple roles in the play, keeping the underlying constellation transparent all along. Thus, the Corner Man sits in the corner of the ring with his towel when not part of the scene, and the Referee translates the entire play into Sign language, occasionally taking up a specific part. The story of growing up alone, prey to sexual abuse and nanoracism, is repeatedly being fractured by this boxing-ring setting.

Like Etienne Minoungou, Mojisola Adebayo plays Mojitola and Ali. Yet, while Etienne and Ali don't talk and the change between Ali and Etienne is only indicated by the quotation marks around Ali's phrases—or on stage by his boxing movements—Adebayo's play has her alternate as a performer between Ali and Mojitola, who might dialogue in the same scene. As indicated by her footnotes, Adebayo has done meticulous research on Muhammad Ali and most of his phrases in the play are statements by him quoted in the numerous publications on his life. Unlike Niangouna, Adebayo covers Ali's entire life, referring as much to his growing up as to his Parkinson disease. Whereas Niangouna's Mohamed Ali becomes a symbol of African(-American) resistance, Adebayo focuses on the individual. Ali's biographical trajectory is told in full in the play and is there to empower the girl Mojitola. Yet, when the Corner Man as 'Daddy Griot', the storyteller, narrates the story of young Cassius Clay, he also refers to the story of Emmett Till: 'Daddy Clay would show Cassius pictures / of Emmett, a boy the same age. [...] He looked like nothing human as he lay in that casket. [...] And from that moment on Clay would never forget / what kind of a place America was' (Adebayo 2011, 84). The Corner Man, playing a number of roles (see Adebayo 2011, 68), not only fulfils a specific function in boxing, he also corners Mojitola. Repeatedly she says: 'There's a man / who sits / in the corner of my life. / The corner man' (144). He represents cultural memory but also impersonates characters which limit and hurt Mojitola in one way or another and thus also stands in for an episodic memory of personal experiences of violence.[15] He is a shadow figure, related to the Shadow discussed below in Kwahulé's play.

Drawing on Ali's famous phrase 'What's my name?', used in the fight against Ernie Terrell in 1966, a boxer who kept on calling him Cassius Clay even though he had changed his name to Muhammad Ali, Mojitola is seen at school with another school child first making fun of her name and then hurting her even more when referring to her being abandoned by her parents. Adebayo's use of different language registers—prose, verse, biblical verse and prayer in citations from prayer books and the Old Testament—determine the play throughout. Here, the verse used by the School Child—'Did he cook a white girl in a pot to make you? / Mixed up with jollof rice and fufu? / Don't he like the taste of Danish pig stew? / Is that why he didn't want you' (105) emphasises the insult in the seemingly playful rhyme.

In the second round of the play, Mojitola has grown up to be a young woman in secondary school and Ali needs to face his trial for refusing to go to Vietnam. Just as he takes position, she learns to speak up for herself and even has the courage to report Jimmy, her foster Mum's son, for his sexual abuse. While Ali faces his first loss in the battle against Joe Frazier, she is not seen fit to play Hamlet because of her skin colour. Whereas in the first round, the main source of discrimination is her colour, in the following her gender and sexuality are being attacked likewise. The intersectional approach at work in the play, explicitly and implicitly addressing several parameters, also through the use of sign language, is displayed on the structural level—with the choice of cast and languages—as well as on the level of plot. Racism needs to be connected to sexism and ableism in order to uncover the intersection of these structures of discrimination (c.f. Kafer 2013). Adebayo is well aware of this. In this way, she situates herself within black Queer Studies (Johnson 2016). Furthermore, Adebayo's 'total theatre' (Goddard 2011, 12; Zenenga 2015) deconstructs hierarchies on all levels of the production: spoken language and sign language are equally present, popular music from the 1970s and 1980s features alongside church music, live action on stage is supplemented by existing or newly created video projections, citations from Muhammad Ali stand next to citations from religious sources, the boxing ring and all other locations blend into each other. The play, divided into two rounds and 30 short scenes, beginning with the child at age five and ending with the 40th birthday of Mojitola, adheres to chronology, yet also juxtaposes two different time lines—at one point she snaps at Ali: 'We're not even living in the same year, let alone the same physical place!' (Adebayo 2011, 136), contesting his possibility to help her. Adebayo's somewhat excessive use of various sign systems leads to a destruction of hierarchies and thus effectively defies hierarchical systems which support discrimination. The fact that she does this on stage, explicitly attacking its exclusionary mechanisms—'A black cannot play a white person. It's obvious, it's ridiculous, it's impossible!' (136) says a fellow student—highlights the theatre as a site of exclusion—and potentiality. Here again, as in Niangouna, the topic of the play folds back onto itself.

5 More Boxing

In 1992, well before the other plays, playwright Koffi Kwahulé received the 'Grand Prix Tchicaya U Tam'si' for his play *Cette vieille magie noire*, published in 1993 in French and, that same year, also in an English translation, *That Old Black Magic*, in New York, where the play had a staged reading in 1993. The play can be considered a classic among plays by African playwrights; in 2017, I had the occasion to repeatedly see a production of the play in Ouagadougou, Burkina Faso. It is interesting to note that the director, Mahamadou Tindano, went out of his way to cohere with the colour scheme of the play, which mixes black and white actors.

Even though Kwahulé does not mention Muhammad Ali in the title of the play, his discussion of boxing in the context of race evokes Ali; his reference to the illness of his main character at the end makes the link to the real Muhammad Ali the more present. *Cette vieille magie noire* takes place in the USA. Shorty, an exceptional black boxer, wants to retire from boxing. He prefers to act on stage, the play he is currently rehearsing is Johann Wolfgang von Goethe's *Faust I*. Yet, Shadow, his manager, refuses to release him from his contract. There might be something fishy about this contract and the figure of Shadow—a suspicion nourished by the *Faust* plot. If Shadow really is another Mepistopheles, however, is never entirely clear. Since Shorty signed his contract with blood, Shadow might be an incarnation of devilish power and control. In any case, he ties Shorty to his contract. Provoked, Shorty agrees to fight Todd Ketchel, the 'Great White Hope' (Kwahulé 1993b, 172),[16] yet, due to the influence of Shadow, Shorty kills his opponent during the fight. When Angie, Shorty's sister, sees the only possibility to free Shorty from the contract in a destruction of his reputation, she makes him victim to a doping scandal. Yet Shorty breaks down entirely under the journalists' attack and ends up in a mental hospital. There, in the end, Shadow visits him and brings a new set of boxing gloves and a robe. Now, everything might start all over again.

Kwahulé uses a musical score and a live jazz band to accompany the action on stage. The play opens with a play-within-the-play scene: Shorty and Shadow play Faust and Mephisto, the scene of the contract, yet in a boxing ring, with the utensils which reoccur at the end of the play: a red robe and red gloves. When the journalist-announcer sets out to describe the characters present at the opening party after the first night, he points to Shorty's exceptional boxing talent. Just like Muhammad Ali, he dances around his opponents, 'he seemed to float, to fly' (Kwahulé 1993b, 178). 'Shorty was not just a boxer, he was *the* Boxer' (178).[17] Thus, his leaving boxing is out of the question. In the context of the issue of racism, it is Shorty's position as a black boxer in the world of professional sports as well as his relation to white boxer Todd Ketchel which are paramount. First, all of his team are appalled when he suggests leaving boxing and Angie reminds him of his obligation towards black children: 'We're black in America ... anybody else can afford to lose, not us. There's no place for losers here. Don't forget where we come from. We come from a place where even hope is like suffering' (Kwahulé 1993b, 197). Still, Shorty does not take up the argument, one he seems to have heard all too often (196). Shorty's reluctance to keep the contract, his slackening during the fights and his eventual agreement to a sub-classification match allow for Shadow to bring out the mechanisms of Shorty's reception by the white audience: 'Why do you think the white audience keeps coming even though Shorty's matches are sloppier and sloppier? They don't come to see him win. They come to see him on his knees, the way they always imagined us on our knees' (213).

Maintaining Shorty as champion, Shadow fights the public's desire to see him fail. Yet even winning needs to be clearly orchestrated. When Shorty agrees to fight Ketchel, Shadow only accords on one condition: 'You're going to kill Todd Ketchel' (225). Ketchel needs to be killed, because, as Shadow rightly foretells, he will gain wealth and success even when losing the fight (227). Just before the fight, Suzy, Ketchel's wife, confirms this, when she mentions that 'Hollywood has already made him an offer' (242). Yet Shadow's premonitions as to white hegemony being enacted with all means during this fight are equally correct. In order to destabilise Shorty and to raise the public against him, an incestuous relationship between him and his sister is insinuated via the press. In the stylised fight, accompanied by Fauré's *Requiem* and Coltrane's *A Love Supreme*, Ketchel eventually collapses in the third round, just as Shadow predicted.

In the end, after a doping scandal and a nervous breakdown, Shorty is seen boxing in the ring/his hospital room. When Shadow repeats the lines 'Dance, Shorty, dance / Hit one for the kids / Dance for the little children / The ones whose dreams were broken […]' and the stage directions mention 'Shadow's voice is gradually covered by the increasingly violent music of the quartet' (265), the violence of Shadow's contract becomes visible once more. Being turned into 'The boxer', Shorty is not permitted to live apart from this ascription. The tenacity of Shadow, the impersonation of black suffering and black retaliation, shows that the success of the black hero cannot be separated from this s/Shadow.

Yet, Shadow is a queer character. His sexual relation to Shorty's sparring partner Mickey is alluded to in the play. Being queer makes him step out of a heterosexual logic which, in the play, is reserved for the white couple Suzy and Todd. Instead he pairs with Negus, an old former boxer, black and in a wheelchair. Both insist on Shorty's mission to be fulfilled and speak from a position of knowledge and experience. Even though we don't know why Negus is physically impaired, incidents of his life, in boxing or elsewhere, must have caused his impairment, inscribing the violence suffered by being black on his body. Shadow's queerness, his uncanniness and his embodiment of black cultural memory go together. Only by interfering in the hegemonic game of power by uncouth means can he fight the system.

Similar, yet different from Niangouna, Kwahulé destabilises the difference between the stage and the ring. In the end, the levels are blurred—the actors playing the staff at the hospital come to stand around Shorty's hospital room/ring and applaud after Shorty's boxing revival, and Shorty and Shadow bow, as if they have been performing all along.

In his list of the topics of francophone African diaspora plays in the 1990s, John Conteh-Morgan mentions two of Kwahulé's plays, one of them *Cette vieille magie noire*, as the only plays discussing racism, while all other plays address different topics (Conteh-Morgan 2010, 159). This, by itself, is an interesting result of his survey, taking into consideration that the topic has become a lot more prominent now, as mentioned above. In 2011, Kwahulé commented on his play in an interview and said:

> I couldn't write a play in a European space, I had to transfer it to the American space where the African-Americans had experienced the diaspora in a both violent and magnificent way. It was a way to redraw my new identity and to stage my concerns: I would not talk about Africa's Blacks but about the Black people of the New World. (Soubrier 2011)

It is worth noting that Kwahulé, who moved to France in the early 1990s, begins his writing in France with a play on boxing and racism in the USA. It is as if his experience of being black in France needs to be displaced to the US first before he starts to examine structures of exclusion and violence in France in further plays like *Jaz* (1998) or *Bintou* (1997).

6   Conclusion

Fighting racism on stage, the plays here discussed enact a work of commemoration and mourning as well as of resistance. This applies to Diouf's remembrance of a personal loss as well as of the brutal and inhumane treatment of Herero and Nama, to Doumbia's list of victims of police violence, and to the memory of Muhammad Ali's fight for dignity and against state authorities. Whereas almost all the plays eventually point to the hope for a different society, Doumbia's ending is desolate. The question 'Who will be next?' does not come to an end.[18]

All of these plays refuse any kind of straightforward storytelling. Instead, their discussion of discrimination and pain is subjected to a play of refracting mirrors which prevent Aristotle's 'imitation of an action that is serious, complete, and of a certain magnitude' (Aristotle, Ch. 6). Even in Penda Diouf's monodrama, the remembrance of suffering from racism needs the mirror or shadow of the Namibia plot to be told. In face of the monophony of racism, the plays create a polyphony of several voices and levels of diegesis. Cutting across national origins, interweaving stories from different places, they refuse to be tied to one place, to be fixed in one position. Kwahulé relates his refusal to be pinned down to diasporic consciousness:

I call diasporic consciousness the discovery of movement. There is a tendency to fix Africans. That is not only due to the Europeans or the Americans: we had to fix ourselves in our own quest for authenticity. By contrast, diasporic consciousness, by nature, doesn't permit its fixing: it moves, it invites to a spiritual and intellectual nomadism. And this awareness coincided with my discovery of jazz that had already explored this. (Soubrier 2011)

Kwahulé's diasporic consciousness as a structure of movement, not as a biographical, essentialist term, could then name a structure of thinking and being in movement, which counteracts racist attacks without claiming to prevent them.

Michaëla Danjé concludes her autobiographical essay with her conversion to being a trans woman after so many years of anti-male racism which she depicts in all of its harrowing details. She says: 'I quit one choreography in order to dance another one. I don't forsake the battle field, neither the one of my territory nor the one of my body [...] A black trans woman who will fight in France as long as one breath will animate my stride' (Danjé 2017, 74).

'To dance another [choreography]', in the context of this article, recalls Muhammad Ali's dancing in the boxing ring—dancing in order to confuse the opponent, to not be pinned down—just like the plays discussed here. 'Float like a butterfly, sting like a bee—his hands can't hit what his eyes can't see' is one of Ali's famous statements (quoted after Johnston 2016). Black playwrights turn his fighting strategy into their way of composition in order to attack racism effectively.

NOTES

1. The research on racism in France is extensive and diverse. A comprehensive overview would go beyond the scope of this article. Michel Wieviorka's publications on racism since 1991 are numerous.
2. Except for the published translations, all translations from French and German in the following are my own.
3. On Miano's anthology see also Bühler-Dietrich Forthcoming, where I treat Danjé's essay at some length, exploring the relation between gender, race and affect.
4. I would like to thank Eva Doumbia and Penda Diouf for having made their as yet unpublished texts available to me. Doumbia's text will appear in the autumn of 2020. Penda Diouf made me aware of Doumbia's text, I'm very grateful for that.
5. In a satiric novel, published in 2001 in face of the growing popularity of the right-wing Front National, Sami Tchak not only undertakes a biting deconstruction of racist stereotypes but also shows the distress of the immigrant father stranded in France with no hope of going back (Tchak 2001). Almost twenty years later, his observations still remain valid.
6. Doumbia here evokes the large political issue of the memory of colonialism and slavery in France. See Vergès 2006.

17 FIGHTING RACISM ON THE CONTEMPORARY FRANCOPHONE STAGE 323

7. A first staging of the play was shown at Théâtre Jean Vilar with Penda Diouf, director Aristide Tarnagda, in November 2019.

8. Danjé growing up as a Black boy shares certain experiences of racism and the ensuing permanent fear of and withdrawal from white society with Diouf. What distinguishes their experience is in fact the specifically anti-male violence Danjé suffers.

9. In a different vein, the *Rocky* saga likewise pays tribute to the impact of Muhammad Ali. In his fascinating reading, Jan Philipp Reemtsma shows how Rocky Balboa metamorphoses into Muhammad Ali in the course of the films (see Reemtsma 1997, 95) in spite of the initial modelling of Apollo Creed after Ali (90).

10. On Ali see the recent extensive publication by Eig (2017).

11. I will write Mohamed Ali when I refer to the character and Muhammad Ali when I refer to the real person.

12. In the following I will translate 'nègre' with 'Negro'. Both terms denominate a cultural construction of the Black man by the white man and the term is purposefully used by writers such as James Baldwin just as the term 'nègre' is frequently used by francophone writers to denote this colonial construct, see for example the French title of Mbembe (2013).

13. 'Negroes in this country—and Negroes do not, strictly or legally speaking, exist in any other—are taught really to despise themselves from the moment their eyes open on the world' (Baldwin 1993 [1963], 25).

14. Paul Zoungrana's homage to Burkinabè playwright Jean-Pierre Guingané likewise takes up the structure of the boxing match to show the battle between the author-character and his fictitious personae who have come to haunt him (Zoungrana 2016). One of the intertextual references of Zoungrana's play is Kwahulé's *Cette vieille magie noire* discussed below.

15. On the terminology see Assmann 2011, 181 and 199–200.

16. Reemtsma mentions that 'the great white hope' was the epitheton given to James Jeffries, who, after having retired from boxing, was called upon to fight Jack Johnson, the first Black heavyweight champion, in 1910 (see Reemtsma 1997, 16). Kwahulé refers to Johnson in the epigraph of the French edition of the play (Kwahulé 1993a, [5]). Johnson himself was an important early proponent of the fight against racism.

17. All translations of Kwahlué's play are taken from the published translation by Jill Mac Dougall.

18. Already in 1991 Michel Wieviorka did a sociological study on racism in the police and found that 'racism was prevalent throughout the police' (Wieviorka 2004, 61). It is appalling to consider that almost 30 years later the situation seems to remain the same.

REFERENCES

Adebayo, Mojisola. 2011. *Plays One*. Introduction by Lynette Goddard. London: Oberon Books.

Adorno, Theodor W. 1998. Kritik. In *Gesammelte Schriften*, ed. Rolf Tiedemann, vol. 10.2, 785–793. Darmstadt.

Ahmed, Sara. 2014. *The Cultural Politics of Emotion*. 2nd ed. Edinburgh: Edinburgh University Press.

Aristotle. 350 BCE. *Poetics*. Trans. S.H. Butcher. http://classics.mit.edu/Aristotle/poetics.1.1.html.

Assmann, Aleida. 2011. *Einführung in die Kulturwissenschaft. Grundbegriffe. Themen. Fragestellungen*. 3rd ed. Berlin: Erich Schmidt.

Baldwin, James. 1993 [1963]. *The Fire Next Time*. New York: Vintage International.

Bancel, Nicolas, Pascal Blanchard, and Dominic Thomas, eds. 2017a. *The Colonial Legacy in France. Fracture, Rupture, and Apartheid*. Trans. Alexis Pernsteiner. Bloomington: Indiana University Press.

———. 2017b. Introduction. A Decade of Postcolonial Crisis, Fracture, Rupture, and Apartheid (2005–2015). In *The Colonial Legacy in France. Fracture, Rupture, and Apartheid*, trans. Alexis Pernsteiner, 1–39. Bloomington: Indiana University Press.

Bentouhami-Molino, Hourya. 2015. *Race, culture, identités. Une approche féministe et postcoloniale*. Paris: Presses universitaires de France.

Blanchard, Pascal. 2017a. La France noire au regard de l'histoire de France. In *Penser et écrire l'Afrique aujourd'hui*, ed. Alain Mabanckou, 92–101. Paris: Seuil.

———. 2017b. Inequality Between Humans. From "Race Wars" to "Cultural Hierarchy". In *The Colonial Legacy in France. Fracture, Rupture, and Apartheid*, ed. Nicolas Bancel, Pascal Blanchard, and Dominic Thomas, trans. Alexis Pernsteiner, 220–230. Bloomington: Indiana University Press.

Blanchard, Pascal, Dominic Thomas, and Nicolas Bancel, eds. 2016. *Vers la guerre des identités? De la fracture coloniale à la révolution ultranationale*. Paris: La Découverte.

Body-Gendrot, Sophie. 2004. The French Dilemma of Race. In *Researching Race and Racism*, ed. Martin Bulmer and John Solomon, 150–161. London: Routledge.

Bühler-Dietrich, Annette. 2018. Unübersetzbarkeiten? *Ombres d'espoir* von Wilfried N'Sondé, eine Auftragsproduktion des Festivals africologne 2013. In *Kulturelle Übersetzer. Kunst und Kulturmanagement im transkulturellen Kontext*, ed. Christiane Dätsch, 153–169. Bielefeld: Transcript.

———. 2019. Formen des Miteinanders im frankophonen afrikanischen Theater. *Interculture Journal* 18 (32): 179–198. Interkulturelle Kommunikation in / mit Afrika: neue Perspektiven. http://www.interculture-journal.com/index.php/icj/article/view/377/433.

———. Forthcoming. How Gender, Sexuality, Race, and Affect Meet. In *Affecting Gender – Queering Affect. Essays Across Academia, Arts and Activism*, ed. Omar Kasmani, J.C. Lanca, Matthias Lüthjohann, Sophie Nikoleit, and Jean-Baptiste Pettier. Berlin b_books.

Conteh-Morgan, John with Dominic Thomas. 2010. *New Francophone African and Carribean Theatres*. Bloomington: Indiana University Press.

Crépon, Sylvain. 2017. Faces of the Front National (1972–2015). In *The Colonial Legacy in France. Fracture, Rupture, and Apartheid*, ed. Nicolas Bancel, Pascal Blanchard, and Dominic Thomas, trans. Alexis Pernsteiner, 341–350. Bloomington: Indiana University Press.

Dadié, Bernard B. 1970. *Béatrice du Congo*. Paris: Présence africaine.

Danjé, Michaëla. 2017. Et nous fûmes des écorces. In *Marianne et le garçon noir*, ed. Léonora Miano, 35–75. Paris: Pauvert.

Diouf, Penda. 2018. *Pistes*. Unpublished Manuscript.

Doumbia, Eva. 2019. *Le Iench*. Unpublished Manuscript.

———. 2020. *Le Iench*. Arles: Actes Sud.

Eig, Jonathan. 2017. *Ali. A Life*. Harcourt: Houghton Mifflin.

Etoke, Nathalie. 2017. Du noir dans le bleu blanc rouge. In *Marianne et le garçon noir*, ed. Léonora Miano, 149–164. Paris: Pauvert.

Goddard, Lynette. 2011. Introduction. In *Plays One*, ed. Mojisola Adebayo, 12–17. London: Oberon Books.

Guingané, Jean-Pierre. 1996. *Les lignes de la main*. Pièce de théâtre en trois tableaux. Ouagadougou: Éditions Gambidi.

Houansou, Giovanni. 2019. *La Rue bleue*. Cotonou: Les éditions du flamboyant.

Ilunga, David-Minor. 2016. *Délestage*. Unpublished Manuscript.

Johnson, E. Patrick, ed. 2016. *No Tea, No Shade: New Writings in Black Queer Studies*. Durham, NC: Duke.

Johnston, Chris. 2016. Muhammad Ali's Best Quotes: "Float Like a Butterfly, Sting Like a Bee." *The Guardian*, June 4. https://www.theguardian.com/sport/2016/jun/04/muhammad-ali-greatest-quotes-sting-butterfly-louisville-lip. Accessed 9 November 2019.

Kafer, Alison. 2013. *Feminist, Queer, Crip*. Bloomington: Indiana University Press.

Keaton, Trica Danielle, T. Denean Sharpley-Whiting, and Tyler Stovall, eds. 2012. *Black France / France Noire. The History and Politics of Blackness*. Durham, NC: Duke University Press.

Kwahulé, Koffi. 1993a. *Cette vieille magie noire*. Carnières/Morlanwelz: Lansman.

———. 1993b. That Old Black Magic. Trans. Jill Mac Dougall. In *New French Language Plays. Martinique. Quebec. Ivory Coast. Belgium*. Preface by Rosette C. Lamont, 169–266. New York: Ubu Repertory Theater Publications.

Les francophonies. n.d. M'appelle Mohamed Ali. http://www.lesfrancophonies.fr/M--Appelle-Mohamed-Ali. Accessed 9 November 2019.

Mbembe, Achille. 2016. *Politiques de l'inimitié*. Paris: La Découverte.

———. 2017. Nanoracism and the Force of Emptiness. In *The Colonial Legacy in France*, ed. Nicolas Bancel, Pascal Blanchard, and Dominic Thomas, trans. Alexis Pernsteiner, 363–367. Bloomington: Indiana University Press.

———. 2013. *Critique de la raison nègre*. Paris: La Découverte.

Méda, Ildevert. 2018. *Jasmin en flamme suivi de Adjugé !* Ouagadougou: Œil Collection.

Miano, Léonora, ed. 2017. *Marianne et le garçon noir*. Paris: Pauvert.

N'Sondé, Wilfried. 2012. *Ombres d'espoir*. Unpublished Manuscript.

Niangouna, Dieudonné. 2013. *Acteur de l'écriture*. Besançon: Les solitaires intempestifs.

———. 2014. *M'appelle Mohamed Ali*. Besançon: Les solitaires intempestifs.

———. 2017. Jouer l'Afrique. Résistance théâtrale. In *Penser et écrire l'Afrique aujourd'hui*, ed. Alain Mabanckou, 188–196. Paris: Seuil.

Playboy Interview. 1998 [1975]. Muhammad Ali. In *The Muhammad Ali Reader*, ed. Gerald Early, 132–159. New York: Harper Collins.

Reemtsma, Jan Philipp. 1997. *Mehr als ein Champion. Über den Stil des Boxers Muhammad Ali*. 3rd ed. Stuttgart: Klett-Cotta.

Soubrier, Virginie. 2011. Interview exclusive de Koffi Kwahulé par Virginie Soubrier. *The FrenchMag*, January 27. http://www.thefrenchmag.com/Interview-exclusive-de-Koffi-Kwahule-par-Virginie-Soubrier_a182.html. Accessed 9 November 2019.

Taguieff, Pierre-André. 1987. *La force du préjugé. Essai sur le racisme et ses doubles*. Paris: La Découverte.

Tansi, Sony Labou. 2002 [1977]. *La Parenthèse de sang suivi de Je, soussigné cardiaque*. Paris: Hatier.

Tchak, Sami. 2001. *Place des Fêtes*. Paris: Gallimard.

Thomas, Dominic. 2013. *Africa and France. Postcolonial Cultures, Migration, and Racism*. Bloomington: Indiana University Press.

Urgence-notre-police-assassine en toute impunité. http://www.urgence-notre-police-assassine.fr/123663553. Accessed 12 June 2020.

Usher. 2015. Chains. https://www.theverge.com/2015/10/16/9554541/usher-releases-an-interactive-video-targeting-police-brutality. Accessed 12 June 2020.

Vergès, Françoise. 2006. *La mémoire enchaînée. Questions sur l'esclavage*. Paris: Albin Michel.

Wieviorka, Michel. 2004. Researching Race and Racism. French Social Sciences and International Debates. In *Researching Race and Racism*, ed. Martin Bulmer and John Solomon, 52–65. London: Routledge.

Zenenga, Praise. 2015. The Total Theater Aesthetic Paradigm in African Theater. In *The Oxford Handbook of Dance and Theater*, ed. Nadine George-Graves, 236–251. New York: Oxford University Press.

Zoungrana, Paul. 2016. *To Be or Not To Be*. Ouagadougou: Œil Collection.

CHAPTER 18

'Though we are written into the landscape you don't see us' (Testament, 2018). Black Faces in White Spaces: Whiteness as Terror and the Terror of Un-belonging in *Black Men Walking*

Michael Pearce

1 INTRODUCTION

I am at the Nottingham Playhouse watching a performance of *Black Men Walking* in the theatre's studio space. Near the beginning of Act Two Ayeesha, a black female character described in the *dramatis personae* as '19 years old, Sheffield born and bred' (p. xv), delivers a monologue alone on stage. The scene is a flashback to the night before in an 'inner-city chicken shop' (p. 50). Blending spoken word with rap, Ayeesha describes the moment a drunk white man called her a 'nig nog' (p. 51). Outspoken and not easily cowed, she regales the audience with how she ridiculed him for choosing such an old-fashioned slur. But when a second man tells her: 'why don't you go back to your own country / You're not welcome here. / This is a white country, it's my country / We don't want no immigrants in' (p. 53), she admits she fled in tears.

The title is inspired by Caroline Finney's book *Black faces, white spaces: Reimagining the relationship of African Americans to the great outdoors* (Finney 2014).

M. Pearce (✉)
Exeter University, Exeter, UK
e-mail: M.Pearce@exeter.ac.uk

© The Author(s), under exclusive license to Springer Nature
Switzerland AG 2021
T. Morosetti, O. Okagbue (eds.), *The Palgrave Handbook of Theatre and Race*, https://doi.org/10.1007/978-3-030-43957-6_18

327

Throughout her speech Ayeesha looks directly at the audience. I wonder if she can see me. As the narrative slips between past and present tense, between her recounting the episode in the chicken shop and then re-enacting it, I lose track of time and my relationship to the story. Is she talking to me as an audience member? Or is she talking to 'the man'? I wonder if, as an actor, she is using any of us in the audience as substitutes for 'the man', as a technique to help her find the emotional truth of the scene. Am I 'the man'? As I slip between being fully involved in the performance and self-reflective, I am made to feel aware of my whiteness. I also become aware of the whiteness of those around me. I look around the small auditorium. As far as I can tell the audience are predominantly white. I become aware of me/us as white people watching (the actor playing) Ayeesha, and Ayeesha/the actor returning our gaze as she communicates her ordeal. Her monologue makes me think about entitled heterosexual masculinity and the numerous times I have witnessed similar instances where drunken white men feel safe enough in public to behave aggressively and in a racist manner towards another person without recrimination. I think about the many times I have watched similar portrayals of racial terror, as I am now, but without being led so forcefully to examine my relationship to the material as a white man. I wonder why. I wonder what it is about this performance that is different.

In this chapter, I discuss the representation of whiteness as terror in relation to *Black Men Walking*. I argue that in the West, black-authored dramas play an important role in challenging whiteness' authority and that the representation of whiteness as terror is a particularly effective means of achieving this goal. I also posit that theatre, as a medium that brings audience and performers together into a live encounter, provides ideal conditions to make whiteness visible and to (re)orient white audience members to their whiteness. The analytic approach is principally dramaturgical, drawing on both the play text and its performance as sources.

In this regard, the chapter represents a continuation of my past research which focuses on theatrical representations of race and racism on the British stage by black playwrights (Pearce 2017). Because the vast majority of plays by black British playwrights tend to be set in urban environments, *Black Men Walking* is particularly noteworthy for its exploration of these issues within a rural context. In addition to the dramaturgical analysis are some personal reflections of watching the play.[1] The incorporation of these moments acknowledges the impact of my personal experiences and background—in particular my positionality as a white male as well as an immigrant from Zimbabwe now living in the UK—on my understanding of the play. The intention is not to present a fully developed methodology but rather the beginnings of an approach sensitive to understanding how 'race' is constructed in theatrical performances through its representations and through the embodied experiences of the audience.

2 WHITENESS

Racialisation, the process of making 'race' a meaningful social and political category, has involved, in Paul Gilroy's words, 'elaborate ideological work' (1987a, p. 38). An overarching aim of critical whiteness studies is to make whiteness visible as a historically and socially constructed racial category and as a system of power. In the West, whiteness' dominance means that it has become normalised to the point of invisibility (Dyer 1997). As a result, white people tend not to perceive themselves as raced and structural advantages experienced by white people are not often explained through the lens of race (Dyer 1997; Frankenberg 1993; Garner 2007; Morrison 1992). Because white people are seldom made aware of their whiteness and the privileges that occupying this position brings, whiteness remains invisible or unmarked. In his book *White* Richard Dyer demonstrates the central role of cultural representations in securing whiteness' normative position and maintaining white hegemony:

> Research—into books, museums, the press, advertising, films, television, software—repeatedly shows that in Western representation whites are overwhelmingly and disproportionally predominant, have the central and elaborated roles, and above all are placed as the norm, the ordinary, the standard. Whites are everywhere in representation. Yet precisely because of this and their placing as norm they seem not to be represented to themselves *as* whites but as people who are variously gendered, classed, sexualised and abled. At the level of racial representation, in other words, whites are not of a certain race, they're just the human race (1997, p. 3).

The theatre can also be added to Dyer's list of industries culpable of constructing and consolidating white supremacist discourses. However, theatre, as Mary Brewer argues, also has the potential to make whiteness' power and dominance visible thereby contributing to a forward-thinking racial politics (2005, p. xi).

Black playwrights in the West routinely expose and undermine white hegemonic belief systems and modes of representation in their dramas. Strategies to decolonise theatre at the level of content and form have involved the incorporation of African-origin and black diasporic histories, myths, languages, cultural practices and performance traditions. By privileging black people's experiences these theatrical interventions attempt to rectify a representational legacy of invisibility, exoticisation, stereotyping and/or dehumanisation of black bodies on the stage. In doing so they also draw attention to the whiteness of the theatre industry, not only onstage but also backstage and in the auditorium. Sometimes black playwrights deliberately engage with whiteness, thematically and/or aesthetically. Such dramatic explorations and performative enactments occur in a variety of ways (whether through character, setting, time period, etc.) and reiterate that although whiteness is (usually) invisible to white people its 'exercise of power' (Garner 2007, p. 44) is acutely visible to those not racialised as white.[2]

330   M. PEARCE

Academic studies of representations of whiteness in black-authored dramas and those that employ critical whiteness studies as a framework are relatively uncommon (see, Brewer 2005; Carpenter 2014). Analyses that focus on whiteness risk marginalising the experiences that many black dramatists deliberately centre. However, as Faedra Chatard Carpenter reveals in her book *Coloring Whiteness: Acts of Critique in Black Performance* (2014), there is a long tradition of black artists—in this case African Americans—who have engaged performatively with whiteness. She highlights how performances of whiteness allow artists to 'express the intricacies of their own racial and cultural identities through (in relation to, and often because of) the social scripts and common tropes associated with whiteness' (p. 8). These enactments, she observes, 'animate' Du Bois' notion of double consciousness (p. 7), a term he used to describe how African American identity formation occurs in relation to whiteness:

> It is a peculiar sensation, this double-consciousness, this sense of always looking at one's self through the eyes of others, of measuring one's soul by the tape of a world that looks on in amused contempt and pity. One ever feels his twoness, - an American, a Negro; two souls, two thoughts, two unreconciled strivings; two warring ideals in one dark body, whose dogged strength alone keeps it from being torn asunder. (Du Bois, [1903]2016, p. 3)

Du Bois' description of the painful effects of whiteness on black peoples' sense of self is echoed by literary theorist bell hooks who highlights whiteness as a form of terror. She observes that although for many white people whiteness tends to be associated with qualities such as purity and goodness, 'whiteness makes its presence felt in black life, most often as terrorising imposition, a power that wounds, hurts, tortures' (hooks 1992, p. 341). For hooks, terror is the dominant trope in representations of whiteness 'in the black imagination' (1992). This does not refer to reactive stereotypical depictions of white people as 'bad'. Instead, hooks' focus is on representations of whiteness that are formed 'as a response to the traumatic pain and anguish that remains a consequence of white racist domination, a psychic state that informs and shapes the way black folks "see" whiteness' (1992, p. 341). Such representations are not limited to depictions of overt racial violence, although they do of course include these. They also encompass portrayals of the complex ways in which historic systems of racial discrimination and injustice continue to manifest in the present, socially, economically and/or psychologically, and how these signify a precarious future for black people for whom the threat of being terrorised always remains a possibility (1992, p. 345). Amidst claims we live in a post-racial society, where race is increasingly perceived as having less influence on peoples' lives, hooks emphasises the radical potential of critically examining black artists' representations of whiteness as terror. Doing so, she argues, provides a way in which to 'name racism's impact' and thereby to 'help to break its hold' (1992, p. 346).

The theatre provides an important space in which to realise the anti-racist political potential of making whiteness visible. Carpenter, drawing on the words of E. Patrick Johnson, argues that performances of whiteness provide an opportunity for black artists to deconstruct 'essential notions of selfhood' as well as 'provide a space for meaningful resistance to oppressive systems' (qtd in Carpenter, p. 6). Hooks, writing from a literary perspective, notes a similar potential while simultaneously highlighting the positive effect that representations of whiteness as terror might have on white readers or viewers. She argues that when white people are exposed to and engage critically with representations of whiteness as terror the possibility of challenging myths of whiteness and undermining its hegemony emerges. Arguably, because theatre brings audience members and performers together in a live encounter it provides a unique space for experimenting with how whiteness can be represented *and* experienced. As Mary Brewer posits, because theatre can make whiteness visible for the spectator in new ways it provides 'one of the cultural frameworks within which the spectator may recognize his/her location and level of complicity in the social conventions sustaining White power' (p. xiii).

3   BLACK MEN WALKING

Black Men Walking (2018) was written by Testament (a.k.a. Andy Brooks), a West Yorkshire-based hip-hop MC, poet and theatre maker. It premiered at the Royal Exchange Theatre in Manchester on 22 January 2018. The idea for the play was conceived by Dawn Walton, then Artistic Director of the black-led Eclipse Theatre Company which co-produced *Black Men Walking* with the Royal Exchange Theatre.

In the UK professional black-led theatre companies have played an important role in supporting and providing opportunities for black practitioners. In doing so they have been responsible for bringing a greater diversity of experiences and cultures to the British stage. Black theatre companies have also played a key role in driving debates about equality of access to British stages. But, despite a long history of operation in the UK and a period during the 1980s when black-led theatre companies flourished, funding cuts since the 1990s have dramatically reduced their numbers (see Chambers 2011). Eclipse Theatre, formed in 2003 and currently funded by Arts Council England as a National Portfolio Organisation (NPO), is remarkable for being one of very few professional black-led theatre companies still operating. The fact that the company is based in Sheffield also provides an important counterpoint to the plethora of black theatre and performance activity that occurs in London.[3] In fact, Eclipse Theatre was created with the intention of touring black theatre to middle-scale regional theatres.[4] Its formation responded to the need to extend access to black theatre and performance that has tended to be concentrated in large cities, particularly London, to smaller, regional cities such as Leeds and Nottingham that also have relatively sizeable racially diverse populations (Peacock 2015, p. 152).

The company's genesis can be traced back to the Eclipse Conference which was held in 2001 at the Nottingham Playhouse. The event aimed to expose and develop strategies to combat institutional racism in the theatre industry (Brown et al. 2001). The Eclipse conference organisers took their cue from the recently published Macpherson report which identified institutional racism in the police following the investigation of the murder of the eighteen-year-old man Stephen Lawrence in London in 1993. The name 'Eclipse' and its reference to light and shade reflects the company's aims 'to influence and instigate change that leads to a more diverse and equitable theatrical landscape' (Eclipse Theatre Company n.d.).[5] To date the company has produced a mixture of original works (e.g. *Michael X* by Vanessa Walters), adaptations (e.g. The *Hounding of David Oluwale* adapted from Kester Aspden's novel by Oladipo Agboluaje in 2009) and revivals of canonical plays (e.g. Lorraine Hansberry's *A Raisin in the Sun* in 2016) which fulfil the company's remit to diversify England's regional theatre landscape. *Black Men Walking* is the first play in Eclipse Theatre's 'Revolution Mix' initiative which signals a new direction for the company in its commitment to develop more new writing.[6]

Black Men Walking is a two-act play that follows Thomas, Matthew and Richard, three members of a black walking group, on a hike in England's Peak District National Park. The walk provides the city-based protagonists with an opportunity for physical and for psychological wellbeing. The men are guided by Thomas, the eldest of the trio and an amateur historian who is familiar with the park's landscape and the area's history of black settlement. The men frame their hike in political terms—'we walk for freedom' (p. 36)—positioning themselves as activist ramblers asserting their right to be in and to be empowered by a landscape in which black visitors are uncommon.

Thomas, Matthew and Richard's excursion begins benignly although there are warnings of bad weather. Not long into their trek strange looks from a passer-by and an encounter with a policeman leave the men feeling unwelcome in the park and their conversation turns to their experiences of racism living in England. At the end of Act One the trio become four when they meet Ayeesha who is seeking refuge in the park. Ayeesha is as surprised to discover that black people go hiking as she is to learn that black people have lived in England for centuries. Following her experience of racial abuse the night before in the chicken shop, Ayeesha does not feel she can fully call England home. When the weather deteriorates the group decide to return to their cars, struggling through fog and then snow. When the men fall down the side of a gorge the play almost ends in tragedy. But, in a magical moment Ayeesha is imbued with superhuman strength by the spirits of black people from Yorkshire's historical past and she manages to pull the men to safety. The quartet return home with a firmer sense of their identity as black and British.

The play was performed in an eclectic style. The scenes in the park were performed in a broadly social realist mode although the moments of walking were mimed. The two scenes set in urban locations (a fast-food outlet and a shop) were monologues delivered by Ayeesha which blended spoken word, rap and direct address. Intersecting these narrative scenes were six poems delivered by the Ancestors, described in the *dramatis personae* as 'the spirits of all the black people who have walked Yorkshire over the centuries' (p. xv). (The poems were voiced by the four actors who remained hidden from view during their delivery).

Black Men Walking is not *about* whiteness. Thematically, the play centres the representation of black people's experiences and history. Its portrayal of a black men's walking group speaks to the underrepresentation of black people in the countryside and in outdoor recreation. This theme of equality of access and barriers to participation in England's public spaces and the characters' experience of racism in and beyond the national park also paves the way for an interrogation of wider issues pertaining to national belonging. In addition, the Ancestors' poems reiterate the importance of historical knowledge as a means of challenging exclusionary narratives of national identity. Aesthetically, blackness is also centralised. There are no white actors in the play, none of the black characters takes on white roles and there are no other visual representations of whiteness (i.e. set, costume, props, masks or makeup). There are white characters, namely some passers-by, a policeman, a man in a fast-food outlet and a female shop assistant with whom the black characters interact; however, they are only visible to the black characters and not to the audience.

Watching the play, I could relate to its exploration of themes of migration and national belonging. But, although I could empathise with the black characters' treatment, their experiences were ultimately unfamiliar. It was this realisation—that I can 'pass' as English (my immigrant status is not something that can be known by simply seeing me) but the characters continue to be seen by some as outsiders on account of their skin colour—that my whiteness and the privileges this affords me came into focus. In turn this made me think about whiteness as an organising principle in the play and the context for the characters' 'terror' as they navigate the white spaces of the national park and the nation. I am aware that privileging whiteness as an analytic framework risks marginalising the experiences that the play deliberately centres. However, in this regard I agree with Sara Ahmed who argues that critiquing whiteness acknowledges how its power works and highlights that 'reification is not then something we do to whiteness, but something whiteness does' (2007, p. 150).

The word 'terror' describes extreme acts of violence against victims and their experience of fear. And although in a post 9/11 world the word has become powerfully associated with terrorism (i.e. The War on Terror), its usage in this chapter refers only to acts and consequences of anti-black racism. The belief in white supremacy has motivated countless instances of white brutality against black people across the world and the ideology of racism has been used to justify the implementation of systems of subordination and extermination, for instance the Atlantic slave trade, European colonisation of Africa and Jim Crow in the USA. Because whiteness describes the social, political and economic advantages that white people experience over black people and because these advantages are the result of these systems, whiteness can be understood as the historical legacy of acts of racial terror (Rasmussen et al. 2001, p. 12). Alongside extreme acts of physical white on black violence racial terror includes many other disturbing experiences, such as alienation, trauma and the imprint of past acts of racial hostility, default incrimination, fear and dread.

In *Black Men Waling* the representation of terror is subtle. It is most obvious when the group become lost in the blizzard and when Ayeesha recounts her experience in the chicken shop. Apart from these moments terror is not dramatised in an explicit way. The characters are not in a constant state of fear or danger. The men enjoy the countryside and their encounters with the police and passers-by are brief, although they spur lengthy discussions of feeling othered. Even Ayeesha is ambivalent in her re-telling of her experience in the chicken shop. She does eventually flee the shop in tears when the second man tells her to go home, but she also derides and mocks the first man for the ridiculousness of his choice of the word 'nig nog' as an insult. Instead, *Black Men Walking* engages with how the ideology of white supremacy manifests in the contemporary, supposedly post-racial moment, through individual and institutional racist acts and practices which terrorise black people on a daily basis, making them feel unequal, out of place and un-homed in England and as English.

4   White Spaces

Ayeesha: But we're not exactly FROM here are we?
[…]
Ayeesha: We're not really English are we?
Thomas: Are we not? How long do we have to be here to be English? (p. 71).

As *Black Men Walking* attests, there have always been people of colour living in (what is now) England. However, the country's racial profile changed significantly in the post-war period following mass migration of people from Commonwealth countries in Africa, South Asia and the Caribbean. The experience of racism and marginalisation of many of these first-generation post-war immigrants who arrived in the 1950s and 1960s and their children who grew up in the 1970s and 1980s has been well documented (Centre for Contemporary Cultural Studies 1982). In his seminal book, *There Ain't No Black in the Union Jack: The Cultural Politics of Race and Nation* Paul Gilroy demonstrates how visible minorities became scapegoated for the country's economic and social woes and, as a result, the words 'immigrant' and 'black' became interchangeable (Gilroy 1987a, p. 46). This racialised anti-immigrant discourse further cemented the association of English national identity as white, epitomised by the racist views of Conservative MP Enoch Powell during the 1960s: 'the West Indian or Asian does not, by being born in England, become an Englishman. In law, he becomes a United Kingdom citizen by birth; in fact he is a West Indian or Asian still' (1968).

In the UK successive governments have favoured multiculturalism as an approach to dealing with race relations. Although multiculturalism has never officially been codified in Britain, in the latter half of the twentieth century Britain has seen a process of 'multicultural drift', defined as 'a series of smallish adjustments and accommodations that added up to a quite substantial practice of multiculturalism' (Phillips 2007, p. 5). Multiculturalism does not simply describe people of different cultures living side by side. It is usually used in a way that emphasises the ideal of people of different ethnicities and races co-existing in a state of tolerance and equal opportunity (Crowder 2013, p. 3). Principles of multiculturalism have shaped a range of laws, policies and initiatives implemented to ensure social cohesion, often in response to inter-racial violence and civil unrest. In particular, the murder of Stephen Lawrence in 1993 which led to the identification of institutional racism in the police as well as the strengthening of the Race Relations Act. As the youngest character, Ayeesha, who is 'born and bred' (p. xv) in Sheffield, should ideally represent the successes of anti-racial discrimination efforts. But when she is called an immigrant in the chicken shop the moment highlights how, in Ahmed's words, 'having the 'right' passport [still] makes no difference if you have the wrong body or name' (2007, p. 162). Ayeesha's treatment uncomfortably echoes recent real-world scenarios, specifically, the surge in racist hate crimes that have occurred since the referendum to leave the European Union which took place on 23 June 2016.[7] In *Black Men Walking* the white men's public display of racism towards Ayeesha supports the view that the anti-immigrant rhetoric of the leave campaign emboldened racists by making them think they had majority support for their views (Versi 2016). Ayeesha's treatment exposes how for some people notions of race remain central to how Englishness is conceptualised and that the fantasy of England as white persists. As a result, black people continue to be vulnerable to being labelled as outsiders and subjected to acts of terror as visible minorities in a majority-white country. This representation of un-belonging as disorienting and frightening is a dominant trope in the play.

Black Men Walking can be located in a tradition of black-authored dramas that explore themes of national belonging as they intersect with issues of race and racism. However, the majority of plays in this cannon tend to be set in cities, mainly London. (Perhaps this is not surprising given that 98.1% of the black population live in urban areas (Office for National Statistics 2018, n. p.)). *Black Men Walking* is one of very few plays by a black playwright to feature urban and rural locations. The play's urban location, the city of Sheffield, is also noteworthy. At 1.5%, the region of Yorkshire and Humber where Sheffield is located has one of the smallest populations of people who identify as black in England and Wales (compared with London at 13.3%) (Office for National Statistics 2018, n. p.).[8]

By bringing together scenes in urban and rural areas *Black Men Walking* draws attention to the countryside as a space that is racialised as white and the implications this has for black people's sense of belonging in England/as English. In the scenes set in the Peak District Testament explores some of the challenges black people might encounter when navigating the English countryside. In the UK black people are underrepresented as visitors to the countryside and as participants in outdoor recreation.[9] As numerous scholars have argued, how the English countryside is represented plays a key role in terms of who accesses it (Cloke and Little 1997; Matless 1998; Sibley 1995). Representations of the countryside from high art to popular advertising campaigns have sustained the message that the countryside is a space designed for white middle-class peoples' leisure and pleasure (Agyeman 1990; Askins 2004; Neal 2002). For this dominant demographic the countryside is rarely perceived as being a space that is socially constructed which makes it unlikely that it is understood as a space that is racialised as white. Instead, it tends to be understood as a 'natural' and idyllic space (Chakraborti and Garland 2004). Meanwhile, as Eddie Chambers notes, for newly arrived immigrants from the Caribbean in the immediate post-war period, many of whom were relocating from rural areas in their homelands, the English countryside was 'an actual and notional space from which they as Black people were excluded' (2017, p. 55). This issue persists and studies have highlighted that the popular perception held by many people from black, Asian and ethnic minority (BAME) backgrounds is that the English countryside is a white and unwelcoming landscape (Agyeman 1990; Neal 2002). The extent to which a racialised urban/rural divide has been internalised and sustained across generations of black people is represented by Ayeesha. On discovering that a black men's walking group exists she exclaims: 'Black people really live in the cities, innit though? Countryside's not for us. I don't get it …' (p. 43). Ayeesha's belief that the men are stepping beyond the boundary of what is considered 'normal' practice for black people underlines how the association of the countryside with whiteness and certain urban inner-city areas with blackness (re)produces racialised identities and spatial practices (Sibley 1998). Julian Agyeman notes that the association of BAME people with certain inner-city areas sustains environmental inequality. He argues that by not facilitating equality of access to the countryside environmental policies and planning participate in a process that 'contains' BAME people to inner-city areas and impoverished living environments (Agyeman 1990, pp. 233–234). The notion of urban/rural racial segregation maintained by institutional racism and implicit bias was echoed in 2004 when then chairman of the Commission for Racial Equality, Trevor Phillips observed on the BBC Radio 4's *Today Programme* that a 'passive apartheid' existed in the countryside.

On the one hand, because *Black Men Walking* is based on a real-life walking group, the play presents an alternative vision of the English countryside.[10] Its depiction of a group of black men dressed in hiking books, thick trousers, waterproof jackets and beanies enjoying the outdoors challenges myths that black people do not engage in outdoor leisure and that the countryside is a racially homogenous space. As such it can be described as an act of resistance to dominant assumptions in its representation of black people's 'presence in the rural and their desire to be present' (Askins 2006, p. 3). Through the representation of the men attempting to transgress the reductive urban stereotype and the negative effects of inner-city 'containment' (Agyeman 1990; Sibley 1998) the play provides a re-imagining of black people's relationship to the countryside. On the other hand, despite the fact that in terms of social class the men (especially Matthew who is a doctor) are aligned with the majority demographic of visitors to national parks who are middle-class (Breakell 2002), and despite their attempt to blend in or 'pass' by wearing all the appropriate hiking kit, their visibility as racial 'others' draws unwanted attention and they are made to feel like interlopers. Therefore, through its depiction of the negative experiences of the play's characters in navigating the park the play also draws attention to 'the vulnerability of such contestation' (p. 3).

In *Black Men Walking* the whiteness of the countryside is made visible in the moments when the men come into contact with white people in the park. Sara Ahmed writes that 'whiteness becomes worldly through the noticeability of the arrival of some bodies more than others' (2007, p. 150). In the encounters with the invisible white characters the men's blackness becomes hyper-visible and the whiteness of the countryside and its terror are simultaneously exposed. When Thomas, Matthew and Richard pass a group of walkers they receive a strange look from a white woman:

> Thomas: Did you see her look at us then? Daft int' it? You'll be going about your business and someone will just look at you funny. Y'know, like the way you can feel security guards looking at you sometimes. I mean you forget, and then all of a sudden someone just looks at you funny (p. 18).

In this moment, Thomas, Matthew and Richard are made to embody their difference and made to feel like 'strangers' (Ahmed 2007, p. 162); not as people who are unknown to each other but as people whose bodies are seen in this setting as 'out of place' (p. 162). This dramatisation of how blackness is perceived as unusual in the park is developed when a policeman stops the three men to warn them about deteriorating weather conditions.

> Richard: I'm sure he approached us to genuinely warn us about the weather and the roads and so on.
> Matthew: Yes.
> *Beat.*
> Thomas: still you think, don't you?
> Richard: Yes.
> Matthew: Yes.
> *Beat.*
> Thomas: It's that feeling in't it?
> Richard: Y'know, before I came here I didn't really realise I was black? (p. 25).

The policeman is a familiar representation of white terror in black-authored plays. Hostile interactions between white police and black men in black dramas draw attention to a historically toxic relationship. The overrepresentation of black people in stop and search statistics (Lammy 2017) is a particularly contentious issue and indicative of the use of systemic terror to keep young black men subordinate. In *Black Men Walking* it is unclear whether the policeman stopping the men is an act of racial profiling—a rural equivalent of a stop and search. Ostensibly the policeman's motivation is concern for their safety; however, the men feel targeted as people who 'appear' foreign in this environment on account of their skin colour. The encounter is very brief. The fact the audience do not see the policeman (or passers-by) arguably reduces its impact. This emphasises the subtle ways in which racism can operate in certain contexts and how easily it can go unnoticed, especially by white people. As Matthew notes, 'most people probably wouldn't even register they are doing it' (p. 25). But the repercussions are evident in the text: each moment spurs lengthy conversations between the men about their everyday experiences of discrimination. In these moments of 'polite' racism the men become recipients of 'the "look" that "otherizes" racialized minorities as different, inferior, and out of place' (Fieras 2014, p. 133).

Scholars have emphasised that because 'popular constructions of rural England have perpetuated images of idyllic, problem-free environments', racial discrimination in these spaces is 'overlooked' (Chakraborti and Garland 2004, p. 383). The ambiguity of the men's interactions with the passer-by and the policeman highlights the difficulty of naming racism in a context (in this case 'polite' and middle-class) where supposedly it does not exist. This experience can be extended to thinking about how race and racism are perceived in the contemporary. Ruth Frankeberg notes the recurring figure of the 'disbelieving white liberal' as the white terrorist's counterpart in bell hooks' work (Frankenberg 1997, p. 26). Claims that the UK is a post-racial society and that racial prejudice is a decreasing issue alongside white people's refusal to see themselves as beneficiaries of a racialised social system maintains whiteness' invisibility by pushing issues of race and racism and their relationship to social inequality further into the background.[11] In its depiction of how the men are treated in the park *Black Men Walking* highlights how racism remains an issue in England but its form and modes of expression have changed (Redclift 2015). In doing so, the play raises questions about how to organise an effective anti-racist response in a context where racism's existence is denied.

The characters' experiences of unbelonging in the Peak District, which is one of England's national parks, opens up wider conversations about black people's marginalisation from Englishness. Access to and participation in England's natural heritage is perceived as a route to becoming English and being perceived as English. As one study highlighted, some BAME people felt confined to inner-city areas and that they 'were missing out on many benefits associated with the countryside, including a sense of belonging in England' (Countryside Agency 2005, p. 46). Although the explicitness of Ayeesha's encounter with racism is very different in tone from the coded racism experienced by the men, the moments are underpinned by the same impulse: the characters are fully acculturated into their particular social contexts, evidenced by the way they speak, dress, their cultural reference points and so on. Yet, despite being at home in their respective environments the characters are un-homed and treated as outsiders because of their skin colour. The rural and urban settings in which these incidents occur emphasises Testament's point that black people's experiences of racism in England are differentiated by context but nevertheless widespread.

In *Black Men Walking*, Testament draws a connection between the characters being perceived as unusual in the countryside and their being perceived as unusual to Englishness (Kinsman 1995, p. 301). Despite being a mainly urban society, there is a powerful and enduring equation of the rural with a version of English identity. The myth of the countryside as a rural idyll and the location where authentic or 'true' Englishness resides has been sustained in and through its depiction since the nineteenth century (see, e.g. Haigron 2017). However, this nostalgic version of England and Englishness excludes people of colour in favour of a vision of pre-war England as culturally homogenous and white (Neal 2002, p. 445). Sarah Neal makes the point that: 'The exclusion of minority ethnic people from English rurality in historical, cultural and symbolic terms can also be read as an exclusion of minority ethnic people from Englishness *per se*: the denial of a relationship to English pastoralism precludes *inclusion* in the nation' (2002, p. 445).

Black Men Walking highlights that although black people have been present in this landscape (and England more generally) since Roman times (since before England existed) their presence before the mid-twentieth century is rarely acknowledged. Instead, the symbolic starting point of multicultural and multiracial Britain is 1948, when the SS Empire Windrush docked at Tilbury carrying 492 Caribbean migrants who were relocating to the 'motherland' following the offer of employment. The play's implicit argument is that this narrative fixes the point of arrival of black people in England to a single moment of migration. The implication being that before 'Windrush' England was a 'white' country, a belief that continues to position black people as post-war arrivals. This historical narrative, the play suggests, needs to be altered if the association of black with immigrant is to be dislodged.

The historian Benedict Anderson defined the nation as an imagined community, arguing that because one can never know every person in the country, a sense of belonging is predicated on the idea of shared core values. In this regard, assimilation is possible: 'from the start the nation was conceived in language, not in blood, and that one could be 'invited into' the imagined community' ([1983]1991, p. 145). However, Anderson goes on to identify a 'paradox' in the way that nations operate. He highlights that although assimilation can occur belonging is also predicated on a sense of shared culture that is rooted in the deep past. In this way, 'seen as both a *historical* fatality and as a community imagined through language, the nation presents itself as simultaneously open and closed' (p. 146). Despite their performances of Englishness, the characters in *Black Men Walking* find themselves barred from entry into how the national community is imagined because it is historicised as white.

When the characters become lost in the snow (literally in whiteness) it is symbolic of their rootlessness. Their terror therefore becomes framed as an expression of what Paul Gilroy identifies as black people's 'banishment from historicity' (Gilroy [1987b]1992, p. 280). This state, Gilroy argues, is an effect of slavery. As a result, 'the recovery of historical knowledge is felt to be particularly important for blacks because the nature of their oppression is such that they have been denied any historical being' (Gilroy [1987b]1992, p. 280).[12]

Black Men Walking is part of a tradition of black-authored plays that emphasise the need for historical recuperation and revisionism.[13] However. *Black Men Walking* differs from typical black British history plays because, as opposed to the Caribbean or countries in Africa or even the imagined space of the black African diaspora, it positions England as the ancestral homeland. In *Black Men Walking* the homeland is not 'there' but 'here', in the countryside, in England. As Thomas tells Ayeesha: 'We are home. This is our home, don't you see?' (p. 68). The Ancestors' poems which splice the main narrative recount the 'forgotten' lives of four black people related in some way to Yorkshire: Septimius Severus, a Roman emperor who visited Britain and strengthened Hadrian's wall; John Moore, a black Freeman of the City of York; William Darby (later Pablo Fanque), a Victorian circus owner; and the so-called Ivory Bangle Lady, an upper-class resident of Roman York who lived during the fourth century and whose remains were found in 1901. The poems provide a context for the characters' presence in the landscape. History is the map that orients them to their collective past and assists them in finding their way in the future. The emancipatory potential of the recovery of this knowledge whitewashed from the historical record is illustrated at the end. It is only after Ayeessha finally accepts English history as part of her history declaring 'I am MEANT to be here!' (p. 75) that she is empowered by the Ancestors and pulls the men to safety.

Black Men Walking asks its audience to re-imagine the imagined community that is the nation (Anderson [1983]1991). What begins as a more or less realistic depiction of a ramble in rural England ends as a symbolic journey into the terrifying heart of white middle Englishness. Ultimately, *Black Men Walking* replies to William Blake's poem 'And did those feet in ancient time' penned in 1804 which has provided the lyrics to the hymn *Jerusalem*, arguably England's unofficial national anthem, by insisting black people have also walked 'upon England's mountains green' since ancient times. The play suggests that this historicism which provides a new perspective on the narrative of the nation can facilitate a re-orientation of black people to England as home. Furthermore, it can facilitate an important re-orientation for white people to understanding Englishness as not just white.

5   Spatialising Whiteness

Whiteness functions as something that is simultaneously visible and invisible. As Dyer highlights, if whiteness is to have any meaning, social currency and power then white people need to be seen as white. However, because whiteness has become normative, the benchmark against which everything else is measured, it has also become invisible or 'unseen' and must remain so if its power is to be maintained (1997, p. 45). But, as hooks reminds us, whiteness is highly visible to those not racialised as white and who experience whiteness as terror (1992, pp. 341–342). By including white characters who are invisible to the audience and visible to the black characters Testament theatricalises whiteness' defining characteristics.

This device facilitates Testament's representation of the white gaze and exploration of its effects on the characters' sense of self. The notion of the white gaze describes the historical and contemporary objectification and construction of black bodies body by whiteness. George Yancy highlights how the white gaze has attempted to fix and define black bodies along a contradictory spectrum as 'problem bodies, dangerous and unwanted bodies, desired and hyper-sexualized bodies, strange bodies, curious bodies' (2017, p. xiv). In *Black Men Walking* when the men encounter the passers-by the white woman's 'look' forces Thomas, Matthew and Richard to become aware of their blackness. It reduces them from just being men walking to become *black* men walking and inheritors of the gamut of stereotypical beliefs and assumptions associated with that term. Likewise, when the policeman stops the men he 'interpellates' them into a discourse in which black men are positioned as suspicious and guilty (see Young 2013, pp. 9–12). This act frames the men's presence in the national park as illicit. This is not, as Yancy describes, a passive process of seeing, but 'a process of racial ascription through a visual technology that "knows" the black body well in advance' (2017, p. 4). The encounters with white people in *Black Men Walking* recall Fanon's reaction to the moment a child sees him and says to his mother 'Look, a Negro! [...] Mama, see the Negro! I'm frightened' ([1952] 2008, p. 84). In this encounter Fanon describes being simultaneously seen as different on account of his skin colour, being understood in relation to historical white supremacist discourses of race and being defined and treated as an object of fear as a result. Echoing Du Bois' notion of double consciousness, the anecdote supports Fanon's point that: 'not only must the black man be black; he must be black in relation to the white man' (pp. 82–83). In this way, the play demonstrates how being stopped is both a political act—deliberately and unevenly employed against black people—and an 'affective' one—in that it 'leaves its impressions, affecting those bodies that are subject to its address' (Ahmed 2007, p. 161).

Each inter-racial encounter in the play illustrates how the white gaze intrudes upon the black characters' sense of self forcing them to perceive and embody their 'otherness'. The gaze is not only an act of appraisal or judgement, it is a transformative act which constructs its object with material ramifications.

Thomas compares being looked at by the passer-by to being 'like the way you can *feel* security guards looking at you sometimes' (p. 18 my italics) and he describes the implicit racism in the encounter with the policeman as, 'It's that *feeling* in't it?' (p. 25 my italics). Writing in the context of black people being watched closely by security guards in shops Yancy describes the impact of 'white surveillance' on black peoples' sense of self:

> The feeling of being seen/constituted as a criminal cannot be captured by what it feels like when one is casually mistaken for another. In such a case, one's personhood is not attacked. To be criminalised through white surveillance, though, is to be attacked at the level on one's personhood; it involves the invasion of the ontological integrity of one's sense of self, one's self-conceptualization. (2017, p. 55)

In *Black Men Walking* the way in which the white gaze criminalises its targets is evident in the men's reactions to the policeman. On sighting the policeman all three men 'change their demeanour' (p. 22). Their attempt to look less suspicious suggests their desire to conceal something which has the effect of making them appear guilty. Furthermore, when Thomas puts on his 'poshest voice' (p. 22) to greet the policemen his performance of middle-class Englishness indicates his belief that this 'version' of blackness, which mimics a stereotype of the dominant demographic of ramblers, will provide the most convincing appearance of their innocence and protection from being perceived as trespassers.

The play draws white audience members' attention to subtle forms of racism/ quotidian actions that perpetuate racism and of which white people may not be aware. For Ahmed whiteness is best understood as a form of orientation. She defines whiteness 'as an ongoing and unfinished history, which orientates bodies in specific directions, affecting how they 'take up' space, and what they 'can do' (2007, p. 149). Where whiteness is normative it occupies the 'absent centre' (Ahmed 2007, p. 157), orienting those not racialised as white in relation to it, as illustrated by the encounters between the black and (invisible) white characters. From this positionality whiteness is highly visible. In contrast, 'white bodies do not have to face their whiteness; they are not orientated "towards" it' (2007, p. 156). In order to make whiteness' power structures visible and begin the project of dismantling its hegemony 'whiteness needs to be made strange' to white people (Dyer 1997, p. 10). In the play's plot and through its staging *Black Men Walking* makes whiteness visible by re-orienting (white) audience members towards its exercise of power.

The play's representation of the characters' experiences of racism draws attention to whiteness as terror. These depictions unsettle white middle-class complacency of living in a post-racial society. The portrayal of the men's experiences in the national park challenge idealised assumptions of the countryside (like the symbolic associations of whiteness) as inherently good, benign and as a 'natural' environment. In thematic terms, therefore, the audience are exposed to unfamiliar representations of a familiar landscape and are therefore positioned to the material in a different way. However, the play takes this one step further through the device of the invisible white characters. The device not only draws attention to how the white gaze operates, it also implicates the white audience members in this power dynamic. During the play's performance there are key moments which open up a space for white people in the audience to be made aware of their gaze and to experience being gazed upon.

When the black characters acknowledge the invisible white characters (who are 'placed' in the vicinity of the audience) or in moments of direct address it establishes a relationship between performers and audience members in which whiteness becomes 'seen'. In the scenes involving the men in the Peak District the actors mime walking. They keep their eyes on the horizon and their legs move up and down in a march which gives the impression they are moving forward in space. The convention of miming other characters is established early on when they encounter the passers-by:

> *Spotting some passers-by.*
> Thomas: Morning.
> Mathew: Morning.
> Richard: Hello.

When the characters greet the passers-by in what appears to be a direct address to the audience the audience experience a moment of disorientation (some people laugh uncomfortably) before they understand that the men are not acknowledging them but other people in the park. Although in this and later moments the audience are never substituted for the invisible characters in the play the distinction between audience and invisible characters is left subtly ambiguous. As a result, the audience may feel implicated in the action at points. In these moments there is the potential for audience member to be made aware of their role as spectators and its relationship to the white gaze.

The play's theme of white people who 'look' and black people who are 'looked at' is uncomfortably echoed in the audience/performer relationship of the performance event. This is most striking during Ayeesha's monologue in the chicken shop. Ayeesha's monologue comprises description and re-enactment, with sections of Ayeesha recounting her experience as an anecdote and others of her delivering the text as though she is in the shop in real time. During the monologue the audience's relationship to the scene shifts and they become positioned in some sections as confidants (when they are being told something, as per the first line below) and as witnesses in others (when they are being shown something, as per. the rap section below):

> He mumbles something about there's too many of me now? Like blah, blah, blah...
>   (rap)

Nah, Then listen / Yes, I'm dark and Yorkshire! – Hendersons' / relish / Don't you ever forget it (p. 52).

At moments during this energetic and emotionally charged delivery the line becomes blurred between knowing whether as an audience member you are experiencing the monologue in the present or in the past and whether Ayeesha is addressing you or speaking to the man. In these moments it is conceivable that the white audience members, especially men, might feel implicated as 'the' man.[14] By directly addressing the audience Ayeesha returns the white gaze.

6   Conclusion

Because white people don't often experience being 'seen' as white, this experience has the potential to make white audience members, as described in my experience at the start of this chapter, aware of their whiteness and the whiteness around them. This is not achieved through guilt—the monologue is not accusatory—but through discomfort. Ahmed describes the relationship between whiteness and space in terms of comfort; in white spaces white bodies feel comfortable, at ease and at home (2007, p. 158). The theatre landscape might also be described as a comfortable space for people for whom it is most familiar, that is, the white middle-class demographic. For the regular theatre audience member the theatre will be comfortably accessible, its conventions will be familiar and, to some extent, so too will the way in which certain subject matter is represented, particularly in the mainstream. During the moments in *Black Men Walking* when the audience are made to feel uncomfortable the opportunity presents itself for critical self-reflection. Testament's spatialisation of whiteness through the theatrical device of including invisible white characters facilitates his representation of the effects of whiteness on his black characters'. It also creates a space for the white audience members to critically reflect on their positionality and privilege.

Hooks argues that the critical examination of whiteness represented as terror encourages white people to think about their positionality which in turn opens the possibility for white people to comprehend how 'their cultural practice re-inscribes white supremacy' (1992, p. 346). In other words, hooks advocates empathy as a crucial step in the process of deconstructing whiteness' hegemony. Hooks quotes the postcolonial theorist Gayatri Spivak who highlights the radical potential of problematising positionality: 'what we are asking for is that the hegemonic discourses, the holders of hegemonic discourses should de-hegemonize their position and themselves learn how to occupy the subject position of the other' (Spivak quoted in hooks p. 346). Occupying this empathetic position does not require white audience members to share the experience of whiteness as terror, or to understand it through comparison with their own experiences in such a way that emphasises 'we are all people'. Instead, being made aware of their 'orientation' (Ahmed 2007) to whiteness facilitates understanding of how whiteness operates, how its dominance is sustained and how white people are part of and benefit from a racialised system of inequality (Garner 2007, p. 12).

While watching the performance of *Black Men Walking* I am made mindful of my whiteness (my skin) and the privileges it gives me to access public spaces like the national parks without fear of discrimination; to pass through them without being watched or perceived as suspicious or dangerous; to encounter policemen with the expectation that the law is there to protect me and for my safety; to never be called an immigrant (even though I am one) unless I choose to tell someone of my heritage; and to open a history book and see people who look like me.

Notes

1. In total I watched the play twice: once at the Nottingham Playhouse in 2018 and at then at the Northcott Theatre in Exeter in 2019.
2. Examples of plays by black British writers that deliberately engage with whiteness include debbie tucker green's *stoning mary* and Roy Williams' *Sing Yer Heart Out for the Lads*.
3. Since the 1970s (and earlier) black theatre companies have emerged (and folded) across the UK, especially in larger cities such as Birmingham, Manchester and Leeds. However, black theatre activity remains concentrated in London.
4. Eclipse Theatre began as a company working with a consortium of theatres to bring black theatre to a regional audience. In 2008 Dawn Walton was appointed Artistic Director and in 2010 Eclipse Theatre Company was incorporated. For further details of their history, see: https://eclipsetheatre.org.uk/about/history
5. There is an interesting echo between the name Eclipse and the Dark and Light theatre company. The multiracial organisation was established in 1969 by Jamaican actor Frank Cousins and aimed 'to promote understanding between people of different races through the media of the performing arts' (qtd in Chambers 2011, p. 140). Dark and Light is notable as, in Chambers' words 'the first British theatre company with any continuous presence and its own base to be shaped and defined by black talent' (2011, p. 140).
6. With the development of seven new touring productions the initiative promises to be 'the largest ever national delivery of new Black British productions in regional theatres' (Eclipse Theatre Company Revolution Mix n.d.). *Black Men Walking*, the first of these seven productions, has so far been followed by Chinonyerem Odimba's *Princess & the Hustler* (2019) and Janice Okoh's *The Gift* (2020).
7. The increase in racist hate crimes has been reported widely in the press since the referendum (Boult 2016; D. Brown 2018; Travis 2016).
8. 7.3% of people in the region identify as Asian (the third highest in England and Wales) and 1.5% as Mixed. Approximately 10% of the region's population is not white compared with London at 40% (Office for National Statistics 2018, n. p.).
9. Despite comprising approximately 14% of the population of England and Wales (2011 Census) people from BAME backgrounds are underrepresented as visitors to national parks. Data collected by Natural England reveals that in addition to people from the most deprived areas, people from BAME backgrounds

participate in outdoor recreation less frequently than other groups (Natural England 2018). A visitor survey of the Peak District National Park revealed that 95% of visitors classed themselves as 'white', 3% as 'Asian', 0% as 'Black', 1% as 'mixed' and 1% as belonging to 'other ethnic groups' (Peak District National Park 2015).

10. The play was inspired by a black men's walking group in Sheffield. The group was formed in 2004 by Maxwell Ayamba, Donald Mclean and Mark Hutchinson.

11. For a collection of arguments in the media about the limitations of multicultural polities which position the UK as a post-racial nation, see Mirza (2010).

12. Here Gilroy draws on Orlando Patterson's articulation of slavery as social death.

13. The inclusion of Ancestors also locates the play within a tradition of black African and black African diasporic drama which feature Ancestral spirits who act as guides to assist the characters in the present (see, for example, Okagbue 2009).

14. This was my experience during the Nottingham Playhouse performance. A year later when I watched the production at the Northcott Theatre in Exeter I felt less implicated during the scenes when the actors interacted with the invisible white characters. This might be due to a combination of factors, including the fact the Exeter production took place in a much bigger space with the audience positioned further away from the stage.

REFERENCES

Agyeman, J. 1990. Black People in a White Landscape: Social and Environmental Justice. *Built Environment 16* (3): 232–236.

Ahmed, S. 2007. A Phenomenology of Whiteness. *Feminist Theory 8* (2): 149–168.

Anderson, B. 1983 [1991]. *Imagined Communities: Reflections on the Origin and Spread of Nationalism* (revised edition ed.). London: Verso.

Askins, K. 2004. *Visible Communities' Use and Perceptions of the North York Moors and Peak District National Parks: A Policy Guidance Document for the National Park Authorities*. Durham: University of Durham.

———. 2006. New Countryside? New Country: Visible Communities in the English National Parks. In *The New Countryside? Ethnicity, Nation and Exclusion in Contemporary Rural Britain*, ed. S. Neal and J. Agyeman, 149–172. Bristol: Policy Press.

Boult, A. 2016, July 1. Steep Rise in Racist Incidents After EU Referendum Cataloged by Worrying Signs Facebook Group. *The Telegraph*. Retrieved from https://www.telegraph.co.uk/news/2016/07/01/steep-rise-in-racist-incidents-after-eu-referendum-cataloged-by/

Breakell, B. 2002. Missing Persons: Who Doesn't Visit the People's Parks. *Countryside Recreation 10* (1): 13–17.

Brewer, M. 2005. *Staging Whiteness*. Middletown, CT: Wesleyan University Press.

Brown, D. 2018, May 12. UK 'More Racist After Brexit'. *The Times*. Retrieved from https://www.thetimes.co.uk/article/uk-more-racist-after-brexit-qb7hd7xl7

Brown, S., Hawson, I., Graves, T., and Barot, M. 2001. Eclipse Report: Developing Strategies to Combat Racism in Theatre. Retrieved from https://www.artscouncil.org.uk/sites/default/files/download-file/Eclipse_report_2011.pdf

Carpenter, F.C. 2014. *Coloring Whiteness: Acts of Critique in Black Performance*. Ann Arbor: University of Michigan Press.

Centre for Contemporary Cultural Studies, ed. 1982. *The Empire Strikes Back: Race and Racism in 70s Britain*. London: Hutchinson.

Chakraborti, N., and J. Garland. 2004. England's Green and Pleasant Land? Examining Racist Prejudice in a Rural Context. *Patterns of Prejudice 38* (4): 383–398.

Chambers, C. 2011. *Black and Asian Theatre in Britain: A History*. London: Routledge.

Chambers, E. 2017. *Roots & Culture: Cultural Politics in the Making of Black Britain*. London: I.B. Tauris.

Cloke, P., and J. Little. 1997. *Contested Countryside Cultures: Otherness, Marginalisation and Rurality*. London: Routledge.

Countryside Agency. 2005. 'What About Us?' Diversity Review Evidence - part 1. Challenging Perceptions: Under-represented Groups' Visitors Needs. Retrieved from http://publications.naturalengland.org.uk/publication/63060

Crowder, G. 2013. *Theories of Multiculturalism*. Cambridge: Polity Press.

Du Bois, W.E.B. 1903 [2016]. *The Souls of Black Folk*. Minneapolis, MN: First Avenue Editions.

Dyer, R. 1997. *White*. London: Routledge.

Eclipse Theatre Company. n.d.. About Eclipse. Retrieved from https://eclipsetheatre.org.uk/about/who-are-eclipse

Eclipse Theatre Company Revoltuion Mix. n.d.. About Revolution Mix. Retrieved from https://eclipsetheatre.org.uk/revolution-mix

Fanon, F. 1952 [2008]. *Black Skin, White Masks* (C. L. Markmann, Trans.). London: Pluto Press.

Fieras, A. 2014. *Racisms in a Multicultural Canada: Paradoxes, Politics, and Resistance*. Waterloo, Ontario: Wilfrid Laurier University Press.

Finney, C. 2014. *Black Faces, White Spaces: Reimagining the Relationship of African Americans to the Great Outdoors*. Chapel Hill, NC: North Carolina Press.

Frankenberg, R. 1993. *White Women, Race Matters: The Social Construction of Whiteness*. Minneapolis: University of Minnesota Press.

———. 1997. Local Whiteness, Localising Whiteness. In *Displacing Whiteness: Essays in Social and Cultural Criticism*, ed. R. Frankenberg, 1–34. London: Duke University Press.

Garner, S. 2007. *Whiteness: An Introduction*. New York: Routledge.

Gilroy, P. 1987a. *There Ain't No Black in the Union Jack': The Cultural Politics of Race and Nation*. London: Hutchinson.

———. 1987b [1992]. *'There Ain't No Black in the Union Jack': The Cultural Politics of Race and Nation*. London: Routledge.

Haigron, D. 2017. Introduction. In *The English Countryside: Representations, Identities, Mutations*, ed. D. Haigron, 1–31. London: Palgrave Macmillan.

hooks, b. 1992. Representing Whiteness in the Black Imagination. In *Cultural Studies*, ed. L. Grossberg, C. Nelson, and P.A. Treichler, 338–346. New York: Routledge.

Kinsman, P. 1995. Landscape, Race and National Identity: The Photography of Ingrid Pollard. *Area 27* (4): 300–310.

Lammy, D. 2017. The Lammy Review: An Independent Review into the Treatment of, and Outcomes for, Black, Asian and Minority Ethnic Individuals in the Criminal Justice System. Retrieved from https://assets.publishing.service.gov.uk/government/uploads/system/uploads/attachment_data/file/643001/lammy-review-final-report.pdf

Matless, D. 1998. *Landscape and Englishness*. London: Reaktion.

Mirza, M. 2010, September 22. Rethinking Race. *Prospect*. Retrieved from https://www.prospectmagazine.co.uk/magazine/munira-mirza-multiculturalism-racism

Morrison, T. 1992. *Playing in the Dark: Whiteness and the Literary Imagination*. Cambridge, Ma.: Harvard University Press.

Natural England. 2018. Monitor of Engagement with the Natural Environment: The National Survey on People and the Natural Environment. Retrieved from https://assets.publishing.service.gov.uk/government/uploads/system/uploads/attachment_data/file/738891/Monitorof_Engagementwiththe_Natural_Environment_Headline_Report_March_2016to_February_2018.pdf

Neal, S. 2002. Rural Landscapes, Representations and Racism: Examining Multicultural Citizenship and Policy-making in the English Countryside. *Ethnic and Racial Studies* 25 (3): 442–461.

Office for National Statistics. 2018. Regional Ethnic Diversity. Retrieved from https://www.ethnicity-facts-figures.service.gov.uk/uk-population-by-ethnicity/national-and-regional-populations/regional-ethnic-diversity/latest

Okagbue, O. 2009. *Culture and Identity in African and Caribbean Theatre*. London: Adonis & Abbey.

Peacock, D. Keith. 2015. The Social and Political Context of Black British Theatre: The 2000s. In *Modern and Contemporary Black British Drama*, ed. M. Brewer, L. Goddard, and D. Osborne, 147–160. London: Palgrave Macmillan.

Peak District National Park. 2015. *Peak District National Park Visitor Survey 2014 & 2015*. Retrieved from https://www.peakdistrict.gov.uk/__data/assets/pdf_file/0011/775325/Visitor-and-Non-Visitor-2014-15.pdf

Pearce, M. 2017. *Black British Drama: A Transnational Story*. London: Routledge.

Phillips, A. 2007. *Multiculturalism Without Culture*. Princeton: Princeton University Press.

Powell, E. 1968, [Online]. 16 November. Speech to London Rotary Club. Retrieved from http://www.enochpowell.net/fr-83.html

Rasmussen, B., E. Klinenberg, I. Nexica, and M. Wray. 2001. Introduction. In *The Making and Unmaking of Whiteness*, ed. B. Rasmussen, E. Klinenberg, I. Nexica, and M. Wray, 1–24. Durham, NC: Duke University Press.

Redclift, V. 2015. New Racisms, New Racial Subjects? The Neo-liberal Moment and the Racial Landscape of Contemporary Britain. In *New Racial Landscapes: Contemporary Britain and the Neoliberal Conjuncture*, ed. M. James, H. Kim, and V. Redclift, 1–12. London: Routledge.

Sibley, D. 1995. *Geographies of Exclusion: Society and Difference in the West*. London: Routledge.

———. 1998. The Racialisation of Space in British Cities. *Soundings* 3 (10): 119–127.

Testament. 2018. *Black Men Walking*. London: Oberon Books.

Travis, A. 2016, September 7. Lasting Rise in Hate Crime After EU Referendum, Figures Show. *The Guardian*. Retrieved from https://www.theguardian.com/society/2016/sep/07/hate-surged-after-eu-referendum-police-figures-show

Versi, M. 2016. Brexit Has Given Voice to Racism – and Too Many Are Complicit. *The Guardian*. Retrieved from https://www.theguardian.com/commentisfree/2016/jun/27/brexit-racism-eu-referendum-racist-incidents-politicians-media

Yancy, G. 2017. *Black Bodies, White Gazes: The Continuing Significance of Race in America*. 2nd ed. Lanham, MD: Rowman & Littlefield.

Young, H. 2013. *Theatre & Race*. Basingstoke: Palgrave Macmillan.

PART IV

Constructions of Whiteness and the 'Other'

CHAPTER 19

'A Wretched Caricature…Unworthy of America': Charles Mathews's Representation of the Yankee

Jim Davis

1 INTRODUCTION

Charles Mathews was renowned from 1818 to 1834 for his one-man shows which were known as 'At Homes'. These took the form of anecdotes and songs and a short drama called a monopolylogue, often built around autobiographical experience and/or journeys, and involved the representation of a cross-section of characters drawn from a range of national, regional and social backgrounds. Mathews's characters were based on a mixture of observation and imagination and he was often praised for his ability to differentiate characters within specific national identities, thus avoiding stereotyping and extreme caricature. From 1822 to 1823 Mathews visited America, performing not only selections from his 'At Homes' but also appearing in other dramatic roles, and on his return to England he performed a new one-man show, *Trip to America*. This was well-received in principle, although some Americans were critical. Mathews had previously made it clear that his American visit had been undertaken, in part, to gather material for his next 'At Home', although he had also been concerned not to give offence in the way he portrayed his American characters. For some contemporary scholars, a principal focus on his *Trip to America* has been his representation of black characters, particularly the fictitious slave Agamemnon and a black actor, possibly based on James Hewlett, playing

---

J. Davis (✉)
University of Warwick, Coventry, UK
e-mail: jim.davis@warwick.ac.uk

© The Author(s), under exclusive license to Springer Nature Switzerland AG 2021
T. Morosetti, O. Okagbue (eds.), *The Palgrave Handbook of Theatre and Race*, https://doi.org/10.1007/978-3-030-43957-6_19

351

352   J. DAVIS

Hamlet (Davis 2011; Lewis 2016). However, for commentators writing in the 1820s, it was Mathews's representation of the supposed Yankee, Jonathan W. Doubikin, that was deemed controversial, especially when this character—considered 'one of the happiest, most original, and most characteristic of Mr Mathews's personations in the present entertainment' (*Sketches* 1824)—was used as the basis for a farce, *Jonathan in England* by R. B. Peake.

Tracy C. Davis has argued plausibly that in *Trip to America* Mathews's 'inversion of British values was not invested in black characters; instead, African Americans recapitulated the social order of England, while Yankees stood in as the dystopic inversion.' For Davis 'Mathews performed a distillation of national, ethnic, and racialized characteristics, yet he pointed to the incommensurabilities of status and worthiness across class, racial, and national markers' (Davis 2011, 164). She argues that Mathews's 'ethnically inflected speech' in his entertainments was common across all classes and races and not directed specifically at any one group more than another (Davis 2011, 172). Davis suggests that *Trip to America's* 'editorial thrust was not towards racism, but instead a critique of the lower orders of white Americans. *Racialism* was his stock-in-trade, but that is not necessarily *racism*'(Davis 2011, 184). In her view, Mathews's target is not race but class and it is the failure of the white American lower classes to measure up to appropriate behavioural expectations that offends Mathews. As a result, it is the white American 'race', particularly as exemplified by the Yankee, which is the primary object of Mathews's satire, and that of this chapter.

2   MATHEWS'S YANKEE IMPERSONATIONS

Although Mathews toured extensively in the British Isles, visited France and twice visited America, he was not a good traveller. His letters home betray anxiety, irritability, hypochondria, an almost obsessive reaction to any form of discomfort and a snobbish regard for social hierarchy and due deference from underlings. Some commentators discussing his visits to America imply his transatlantic travel experiences were particularly challenging, but his reactions, if sometimes accentuated, are as much to do with his morbid levels of sensitivity as with any failings on the part of his American hosts. Nevertheless, the behaviour of the lower orders in America convinced him that, '[i]f this be the effect of a Republican form of government, give me a monarch even if he be a despot' (Mathews 1838–39, III. 307). Mathews is talking about the white working classes, all of whom he considered were 'born blackguards' and 'unendurable': 'There is not the slightest show of civility with them; a bow or a touch of the hat I have not seen once, or heard the words "thank ye" once used upon payment' (Mathews 1838–39, III. 309). He elaborated on this in a letter to his wife:

> The want of cheerfulness and civility is striking, and the egregious folly of the middle and lower orders in their fancied independence, is calculated to produce a

smile of thorough contempt rather than anger. It consists in studied sullenness, the determination never to be civil or apparently kind to a fellow-creature, and not to bow, or say thank ye, to a person they know to be their superior, for they affect not to believe in it. (Mathews 1838–39, III. 322)

The higher orders, by contrast, differed little from the English and were 'natural, easy and polite'. Mathews could not understand how the upper classes coped with such familiarity, although an American General reminded him that 'All such men have votes' (Mathews 1838–39, III. 323).

Since Mathews's American tour was in part predicated on his intention to gather material for his next 'At Home', his experience of ordinary Americans and reluctance to engage with the lower orders left him rather bereft of potential material. Writing from Philadelphia to James Smith, who was to co-author *Trip to America*, Mathews regretted that his observations of the American people were providing such little stimulus, complaining that, as well as a total lack of humour, 'there is such a universal sameness of manner and character, so uniform a style of walking and looking, of dressing and thinking, that I really think I knew as much of them in October as I know of them now in February'[1] (Mathews 1838–39, III. 381). Apart from the dull but worthy upper classes, Mathews largely interacted with Scottish, Irish and black Americans. As for the object of his study: 'I can't come at the Americans unless I go to porter-houses, and that I cannot condescend to do' (Mathews 1838–39, III. 383). Given that Mathews was also devoting considerable time to touring as an actor, it is impossible that his impressions of America were all derived at first hand; he and his fellow authors must have also relied on tropes made familiar by the extensive travel literature of the time (Jortner 2005, 71–76).

Despite Mathews's concerns, *Trip to America* enjoyed a very favourable reception when it opened at the English Opera House on 25 March 1824. The *London Magazine* (IX, April 1824, 43) thought the entertainment was 'more likely to conciliate the two nations, than a thousand books, although written by a thousand men as kind and as clever as Washington Irving'. The *Drama* (VI, 2 April 1824, 93) considered Mathews gave 'a fair account of the Americans. This is not only good acting—it is more. It is good feeling.' The *Morning Post* ('Mr Mathews At Home', 26 March 1824, 3) was equally benign, stating that Mathews 'never deals harshly either with the national manners, or individual peculiarities, and takes every opportunity of doing justice to the good fellowship with which he was treated'. The *Examiner* (28 March 1824, 200) was of a similar opinion believing that he had 'taken no greater freedom with American singularities than with those of his own country; and may revisit his republican friends again, without the slightest apprehension of a lower place in their esteem'. It also praised him for not following such monthly and quarterly journals as *John Bull* and the *Quarterly Review* in providing highly critical and untruthful reports on America. This issue was taken up by the *Morning Chronicle* (26 March 1824, 4), which also attacked travellers for their ignorant and distorted reports on America, particularly lambasting the *Quarterly Review*.

In contrast, Mathews had produced 'the most entertaining and correct picture of the habits, manners and characteristics of the Americans that ever was presented to Englishmen—exaggerated, occasionally, for effect—but never so caricatured as to leave any doubt of the truth of the portrait'. The *Chronicle* praised Mathews for his powers of observation and discretion displayed in *Trip to America*, although it was the claim to authenticity associated with Mathews's 'At Homes' which was later to be the basis for complaints about his representations. In particular, the Yankee Jonathan Doubikin was to be a central figure in these complaints, despite the *Examiner's* belief that he 'not only represents but individualises the New Englander' and that 'this portrait is from life'. Mathews had described the 'Yankee' in his letter to Smith: 'The Yankee is a term given by all the inhabitants of the other parts of the United States to those of the east exclusively. The larger cities boast of superiority in every respect, and speak of the Rhode Islander, and the Massachusetts man, exactly as the English speak of *all* Americans, and have a contempt for a Yankee' (Mathews 1838–39, III. 384). Jonathan Doubikin, who is referenced several times in *Trip to America*, was not the only Yankee character to be impersonated by Mathews, but he was certainly the most memorable. In Part II of the entertainment he delivers a long and rambling monologue about his Uncle Ben, who shoots a squirrel which Jonathan agrees to retrieve from a tree for a small payment, a 'trifle', which he never receives. Later, in the short play or monopolylogue which ended the performance and in which Mathews played all the characters, Agamemnon, a black slave sold to Doubikin by his Uncle Ben, enters in flight from his master:

> ([F]*inding his master is gaining ground upon him, he determines to get down the well and conceals himself until he has passed. Jonathan W. Doubikin, the real Yankee, enters with a gun, in pursuit of his runaway Negro. Jonathan tells a long story about his Uncle Ben, who sells Agamemnon. The bargain with his uncle was concluded nearly as follows*).
>
> JONATHAN. "Jonathan W., do you want a *nigger?*"—"Well, Uncle Ben I calculate you have a Nigger to sell?"—"Yes, I have a Nigger, I guess. Will you but the Nigger."—"Oh, yes! If he is a good Nigger, I will, I reckon; but this is a land of liberty and freedom, and as every man has a right to buy a Nigger, what do you want for your Nigger?"—"Why, as you say, Jonathan", says Uncle Ben, "this is a land of freedom and independence, and as every man has a right to sell his Niggers, I want sixty dollars and twenty-five cents. Will you give it?"—"Oh, yes!" (*Pause*) But the Nigger has proved a bad one: he is good for nothing, except eating, drinking and fiddling. Now I've lost the Nigger, Uncle Ben's got the money; but I'll not forget to tell him of that, and the small trifle he owes me too, the next time I see him. (Smith and Peake 2012, 213–214)[2]

Mathews provided Jonathan with an outlandish costume (including a large straw hat and a seal-skin waistcoat), based on an American farmer, with whom he travelled in a steam-boat from New York to Albany. In doing so he was striving for effect rather than verisimilitude, individuality rather than a stereotype.

How authentic was Jonathan Doubikin, the so-called 'real Yankee'? Edward Allen Talbot, who had migrated to Canada in 1818 and who published his account of his time in Canada, from which he had returned via New York, in 1824, saw Mathews's *Trip to America* in London. Since returning, he said, he had been asked continually about the fidelity of Mathews's representation of Americans. In only a few instances did he find the impersonations accurate, but one which he did think was true to life was Jonathan W. Doubikin:

> Mr. Jonathan W. Doubikin is in every respect a perfect, and by no means an overcharged, representation of the generality of Americans in the middle ranks of life, and especially of the Kentucky farmers.[3] The dress in which Matthews appears, when performing this character, is exactly that which is worn in America by agriculturists, as well in form and fashion as in material, except that a lighter stuff is used during the summer season. They carry a gun in the same manner. In their conversation they make use of the same phrases; and hold in equal contempt, and treat with similar cruelty, the poor Africans who have the misfortune to become their slaves, in the land of reputed liberty and independence. Indeed these two pretended attributes of their country, are a sort of convenient scape-goat for whatever enormities Americans, in their folly or their rage, may think proper to commit As they live in a land of liberty, they think they have liberty to do as they choose, without respecting the common rights of humanity, or any other rule of human conduct. And they also argue, that because they are made independent by the constitution of their country, no one has any business to prevent them from acting just as they please. (Talbot 1824, II. 319–320)

It is possible that Talbot, whose time in America was not that long, shared some of Mathews's concerns and prejudices, so this may by no means be an objective judgement. Talbot was far less convinced by the character of Mr Pennington, the sensible Yankee against whom, presumably, we should measure Jonathan. According to Talbot, Mathews's conversations with Pennington enabled him to praise the Americans for 'their liberality, hospitality, valour and wisdom', while Mr. Pennington quoted without acknowledgement the *patriotic* sentiments of Fanny Wright (Talbot 1824, II. 321). Fanny Wright had spent two years touring America from 1818 and became an advocate for the abolition of slavery and universal suffrage. Since she did not return to America until 1824, Mathews would have become acquainted with her views through such publications as *Views of Society and Manners in America* (1821) For the *London Magazine* (New Series IV, April 1826, 559), Mathews had also gone too far in his admonitions in *Trip to America*, especially through 'all the cant put into the mouth of Mr. Pennington.... It was about as ridiculous in Mr. Mathews to proclaim peace between the two countries; more especially as all the time he was holding one country up to the laughter of the other. In thus holding up foibles for fun, we see no harm; but when the act is mixed up with Mr. Pennington's speeches, there comes to pass a rare union of cant and twaddle.'

356   J. DAVIS

Jonathan Doubikin was one of Mathews's most popular characters in *Trip to America*. The dramatist R. B. Peake (a frequent collaborator on Mathews's *At Homes* and a successful dramatist in his own right) developed a short farce, probably in connivance with Mathews, *Jonathan in England*, featuring Jonathan (now surnamed Doubikins) as his central character. One of the earliest Yankee plays, David Humphreys' *The Yankey in England* c. 1815, published with a glossary of 'Americanisms', formed the basis for the farce, although the character of Humphreys' Yankee, Jonathan Doolittle, was more benign than the Jonathan Doubikins of Peake's farce. First performed at the English Opera House on 3 September 1824 and relying on comic intrigue caused by mistaken identity and the joke of the unwitting traveller abroad, the farce proved to be much more controversial than Mathews's vignettes in his 'At Home'. Doubikins intends to write a travelogue about England, but his observations on English life are riddled with misunderstandings. He claims, metatheatrically, that he's 'pretty considerable darn'd mad about that Mathers who I hear has taken me off at the playhouse, but I'll make the whole kingdom smart for it when my book is published'.[4] He has arrived in Liverpool with his 'help', the black slave Agamemnon, first encountered in *Trip to America*. Doubikins sings the praises of his home country and its superiority to all other nations, alluding to the fact that he and his relatives are all free born Americans. However, when asked by a Head Waiter to leave an inn after he has struck Agamemnon and caused a commotion, he complains: 'Do you call this a land of liberty where I cannot cane my own nigger—without being ordered out of the house—do explain to me the principles of the British constitution.'

Throughout the farce he continually seeks potential buyers for Agamemnon and, once ensconced in the house of a Mr Ledger, where he is mistakenly assumed to be an applicant for the post of postillion, he ends up in a conversation about politics with Ledger's butler. The butler describes liberty as 'a gift from Heaven, and the glorious privilege of Britons!', something which Doubikins ascribes to the global influence of America. However, when a black servant, Blanch, joins them at the table, Jonathan expresses his disapproval of the perceived British custom of 'keeping company with your niggers'. Doubikins assumes that this is a strange trait of the English political classes, having mistakenly assumed the butler is a politician. Meanwhile, the butler upbraids Blanch for giving money to Agamemnon, whom he assumes is a beggar, much to Doubikins' chagrin: 'Beggar!—no more a beggar than you are—he is my nigger—he is a slave, but not a beggar!'

Left alone with Blanch, Agamemnon is informed that

BLANCH   My good man—dere be no slave in dis country—moment you put your foot on shore here, in England, you free!
AG   Free? Free—what is dat? Me hear de name in America—but me don't know what it is. These two lines should be indented 'BLANCH....what is is.'

Moreover, she tells him that, if Jonathan tries to beat him again, he should complain to the constables at Bow Street.

Peake's portrait of Doubikins (abetted by Mathews's performance) reveals this particular Yankee in a rather unpleasant light. Doubikins is rude, brash, ignorant, talking up America as a land of freedom and liberty, while accepting slavery as perfectly normal. He also supports a somewhat problematic notion of economic liberty. He is proud of the way in which his Uncle Ben has inserted false information in a newspaper to reduce the price of stock he wished to buy in Baltimore, unable to understand that this fraudulent speculation is dishonest and unprincipled. Jonathan's views are not, however, shared by the only other American in the play, Delapierre, a suitor for Ledger's ward, whose fortune has been put in jeopardy by Uncle Ben's speculations. Prepared to marry the ward, whether or not she has a fortune, Delapierre receives the consent of the initially hostile Ledger. As for Doubikins, he gets his come-uppance when Agamemnon informs him that he is now a free man and that Doubikins can no longer lay a finger on him.

Reaction to the play was mixed. The *Morning Chronicle* (4 September 1824, 2) considered that Mathews was the first and only performer of the present day 'who has introduced upon the stage of this country the peculiarities of manner and accent, which characterise that remote, but important, nation'. However, the reviewer admits it is difficult to know how accurate or exaggerated Mathews's portraits were, seeing Jonathan as portrayed in the farce as 'little more than a transcript of his original *Yankee*, accommodated to other situations, and helped out by a variety of puns'. The *Examiner* (5 September 1824, 565) considered the farce was merely an excuse for Mathews to play Doubikin[s] again, although it wondered whether 'nettled at a little unreasonable cavil at his American portraiture, on the part of certain native zealots, Mr Mathews has given himself more license than heretofore'. In particular, it referenced the farce's approach to slavery and a hostile reaction among some audience members:

> The most pointed dart is turned against Negro slavery....[Jonathan's] complaint, that in a land of liberty he is prevented from beating his own *Niggers* is pleasant enough; and his indignation at being requested by the Alderman's butler...to sit down to tea with a Negro girl, naturally enough imagined. There was some difference of opinion in respect to a few of the innuendoes, especially at one in which the Negro is made to say, that he never witnessed anything of freedom in America but the name; the ayes, however, unequivocally prevailed.

The *New Monthly Magazine* ('The Drama', XII, October 1824, 430) also wondered whether the farce was a response to the hostile reception in some quarters of *Trip to America*, for 'in the manners and morals of the part, he is not so fair as he was in his own entertainment...for here "friend Jonathan" is as mean, avaricious, and cruel as the haters of independence could desire.' While acknowledging Mathews's performance as amusing, the review went on to complain that 'as a national satire it is palpably unfair. Indeed, America is too vast a country, and too much in infancy to be appreciated by a single specimen, which can only show some superficial, and it may be transitory, peculiarities of manner and expression.' The *European Magazine* ('The Drama', 86, September 1824, 272–273) considered the farce provided Mathews with an opportunity of 'raising a laugh at the strange phraseology of our transatlantic brethren', but that it went too far in introducing matter that 'by implication reflected reproach on American ideas of independence'. 'This illiberality,' it stated, 'was received with a strong expression of disgust. It is time that the custom of satirizing every country but our own should be banished from the stage.'

The *London Magazine* ('The Drama', X, October 1824, 420), which had responded favourably to *Trip to America*, assumed that Mathews had now resolved never to visit America again and had overcome any constraints imposed by American friends and visitors, so that we are 'no longer taught by him to believe that on the other side of the Atlantic, all is constancy, generosity and hospitality'. The change, in their view, was very much for the better and 'Jonathan in England was as unvarnished a caricature of impudence, stubbornness and *freedom* of a Yankee, as a lover of the ridiculous would desire to see.' Indeed, 'all the follies of all the odd characters throughout America, seem to be huddled in this one part, and the jumble is therefore considerably more humorous than natural.' Part of the problem lay not so much in whether Mathews's Jonathan was 'true to *observation*', but in the fact that he seemed 'true to *nature*. Whether it is absolutely *vrai*, we have happily never had the means of judging; but that it is strikingly *vraisemblable* no one who sees it can doubt.' This was one of the causes of Mathews's extraordinary success: 'his portraits are so absolutely true to nature, that you are convinced of their *likeness*, whether you have ever seen the originals or not.' While this may have been the case with British spectators, American spectators were not so easily convinced. Nevertheless, although some scholars have assumed that, on account of the offence and controversy it stirred up, the farce was not performed again, such a supposition is inaccurate. It stayed in the repertory and was occasionally performed as a benefit piece. Mathews also performed it in the provinces, expressing his surprise in a letter dated 31 October 1826, when he was performing in Liverpool, that 'Jonathan has gone capitally here—even—will you buy a nigger—notwithstanding the number of Yankees' (Mathews Family Papers, 1826).

Not long after the two productions an American writer, then resident in London, contributed an anonymous critique of Mathews's representation of Americans to the *European Magazine*. This was John Neal, who was determined to bring American literature and a more informed view of American life and customs to his British readers. He was also one of the earliest novelists to introduce dialect into American fiction and while resident in England published his novel *Brother Jonathan*. Neal claims he was the first American to contribute to monthly and quarterly periodical publications in England and had arrived in that country 'to take up the gage of battle, offered by the arrogant and supercilious writers of England' (Neal 1869, 275). He saw this as his 'mission' and stated that his 'chief object from the first was to bring together…two great nations with a common lineage, a common history, a common language, a common literature, a common purpose, and a common interest' (Neal 1869, 248). Sometimes he masqueraded as an English journalist, sometimes he wrote anonymously, although in certain circumstances he admitted himself to be a Yankee or 'Native'. As a New Englander and Yankee, he was particularly affronted by Mathews's audacious and blundering misrepresentation of the Yankee character.

In June and July 1824, *Blackwood's* published in two parts 'Speculations of a Traveller concerning the People of North America and Great Britain', both of which were anonymous but attributed to Neal. The first article (*Blackwood's Edinburgh Magazine* XV, June 1824, 692–696) referred to the 'many erroneous, mischievous, and, in some cases, very ridiculous notions' that the British and Americans entertained of each other, owing largely to 'political writers newspapers, and books of travels often hastily written, and too frequently by those who have gone from one country to the other, without a proper degree of inquiry and preparation'. Neal references 'the most absurd of laughable misrepresentation' in Mathews's entertainment as one instance of a general tendency, but senses that the English wish to appear friendly to the Americans and that, despite one being a monarchy and the other being a republic, the two nations are very much alike. In the second article (*Blackwood's Edinburgh Magazine* XVI, July 1824, 92), Neal elaborates further on Mathews's misrepresentations. Mathews does not sufficiently recognise the different language used in different parts of the United States so that his 'Yankees' 'come from no particular part of the Confederacy; and are evidently "made up", at second hand'. He wonders if the British would put up with a character who is a mixture of Welsh, Scottish and Irish characteristics, 'speaking a gibberish made up of Scotch, Irish and Welch, interspersed with provincial and cockney phrases?' Neal says that there are so many blunders in Mathews's composite rendering of the Yankee that, if he had not met Mathews in America, he would doubt if he had ever been there, so little is there 'in his "Trip to America" of that extraordinary truth and richness which characterise his trips to other parts of the world'. There are two exceptions to the rule, however: the story of Uncle Ben and the sketch of the Kentuckian, Jonathan Doubikin, whom Neal believed must have been drawn from life for

> nothing can be truer or bolder, than the canting of the Kentuckian about the land of liberty—where every man has a right to speak his genuine sentiments—and where, *therefore*, he is free to offer fifty-five dollars for that are [sic] nigger.' Neal felt this character was unexaggerated and would be instantly recognisable to any American—boastful of liberty; and speculating, at the same time, in the flesh of his fellow-men with a heartless or abominable indifference.

Jonathan in England, however, drew a much more critical response from Neal. Neal's championing of American literature and American identity in

Blackwood's Magazine had come to an end after he fell out with the publisher over the failure of his novel, *Brother Jonathan*; his critique of Mathews's representation of the Yankee character appeared in the *European Magazine* and was printed in full by Ann Mathews in her biography of her husband. She defended Mathews since he was 'only representing what *in* America is considered a fair subject of laughter and ridicule, like the *gascon* of France, and the cockney of England, which are quoted by the natives themselves as a fair specimen of ignorance, conceit and boasting' (Mathews 1838–39, III. 517). Neal clearly thought otherwise. In his rather long-winded polemic, 'Sketches of American Character. British Authorities Examined. Mr Mathews Trip to America. By an American', in which he argues for the diversity of the American nation while providing a less than flattering portrait of his countryman in proving his point, he accused Mathews of reducing the Yankee to something too exaggerated even for exhibition at Bartholomew Fair. Consequently:

> His portraiture of the Yankee is generally misunderstood here, and he knows it. He knows very well, that a wretched caricature, which he got up in a frolic, is received in a pernicious way by the multitude here, and yet he persists in multiplying the copies…his *Jonathan* is a very poor and very feeble counterpart, unworthy of America, unworthy of Mr. Mathews as an actor, and altogether unworthy of his country. (*European Magazine*, New Series, 1:4, December 1825, 373–380, 378, quoted in Mathews 1838–39, III. 526)

As a Yankee himself, Neal believed he and his fellow Yankees had been wretchedly caricatured. He also took exception to Jonathan's ridiculous costume, the inauthentic mixture of dialects in Jonathan's speeches, and the notion that a New Englander, born in Vermont (and thus a genuine Yankee), could be a slave-owner. For Neal, Mathews's transgression lay in his failure to provide an authentic portrayal of the Yankee rather than in any political or economic ramifications embodied in the character. It was almost as if as if Mathews has usurped Neal's own territory and affronted him by imaginatively concocting this generalised, inaccurate version of the Yankee.

Mathews felt compelled to respond to Neal in an article entitled 'Mathews Defence of his trip to America' (*European Magazine*, New Series, I:5, January 1826, 59–67, quoted in Mathews 1838–39, III. 532–549). He thought that he too had been misrepresented, but oddly enough he considered this was because the Jonathan depicted in the farce had been attributed to his authorship. He conceded responsibility for what he had uttered in *Trip to America*, but he was at pains to assert that Jonathan was an individual character, not 'a national portrait'. His responses are surprisingly defensive: he didn't write the play, Peake did; Humphries who wrote the play on which Peake based his farce must shoulder some of the blame; Mathews himself was obliged to appear in the piece because he was bound to do so by the terms of his engagement at the English Opera House. Finally, he returns to the representation in terms of the

19 'A WRETCHED CARICATURE... UNWORTHY OF AMERICA' 361

details to which Neal objected, such as the costume, arguing once more that Jonathan is intended as an individual—not a representative—portrait. After providing evidence directly from his 'At Home' as to his warm regard for America and Americans, Mathews concludes by stating:

> This is the first opportunity I have had of replying to calumny; and if, after this declaration, the Americans will not allow me to take the same liberty with their peculiarities (and which have literally not exceeded the ridicule of mere intonation and pronunciation) that I have with French, Irish, Scotch, Welsh, and, above all, the English (who are, I think, the most ridiculous persons in my "Trip,") I say, if they cannot afford to be laughed at a little, after all I have said in their praise, why, really, I cannot help it, and I do not care one *cent* whether they are offended or not. But I hope some one on their side of the water will assure the "Native" who defames them here, that they are not so weak. (*European Magazine*, New Series, I:5, January 1826, 67, quoted in Mathews 1838–39, III. 549)

Mathews's defence is perhaps rather naïve and self-justifying, but it raised interesting questions about the distinction between individualisation and stereotyping, especially when what the nation under scrutiny considers an inaccurate stereotype is perceived abroad as an authentic representation.

Neal published a response to Mathews, 'Reply to Mr Mathews. By a Native Yankee', in the *European Magazine* in February 1826 (New Series 2:6, 179–187). His argument is slightly repetitive, still focussed on the misrepresentation of the national character and suggesting that, given Brother Jonathan in America is as emblematic a national icon as John Bull in Britain, Mathews should have taken more care with the character and been more responsible in its execution. He reiterates his concerns over accuracy and detail and suggests Mathews's response to his first article has been both contradictory and disingenuous. Neal's overriding concern was with the generalising of the Yankee character and separation from its New England origins, despite Mathews's claims that he had individualised the character. In 1825 Neal had claimed that 'The New England Character bears the stamp not only of *nationality* but of *individuality*. You may know a Yankee anywhere. The language, dress, habits, usages, and manners, alike distinguish them from all their brethren, east, west, north, and south' (Quoted in Schäfer 2016, 231). According to Stefanie Schäfer, this individuality 'sets him [the Yankee] apart from national, regional, and colonial others, making him unique' and an 'embodiment of national character'. Even before Neal's representation of this figure, the Yankee had been a presence in American culture, but had occupied 'a precarious position': 'Ridiculed by travel writers, cautiously embraced by Americans, and imaginary from the very beginning, he impersonates one of the most controversial topics discussed by intellectuals on both sides of the Atlantic: the qualities and essence of this "new", predominantly white and male, North American culture'(Schäfer 2016, 231).

362   J. DAVIS

Nevertheless, Mathews's loose delineation of the Yankee—however individualised Mathews believed his performance to be—provided Neal with the means to emphasise what he saw as a limitation in Anglo-American understanding.

3   LATER CRITICAL RESPONSES TO MATHEWS'S YANKEE REPRESENTATIONS

Assumptions that Mathews's *Trip to America* provided the templates for blackface minstrelsy and the Yankee stereotype have long been discredited. Recent work on Neal, for instance, suggests that he and some of his predecessors and contemporaries had already been developing the Yankee prior to Mathews's representation (Watts and Carlson 2012). Thus, Francis Hodge's notion that Mathews, as the 'paterfamilias of Yankee theatre…set the pattern for low comedy in America' through his influence on James Hackett and that he 'was the progenitor not only of the Yankee but of all native American dialect comedy' is open to question (Hodge 1964, 60–61). Nevertheless, Hodge concedes that Mathews's *Trip to America* 'disturbed many Americans', perhaps because his satire was too broad, while *Jonathan in England* 'reflected Mathews' deep pessimism about the great experiment' (Hodge 1964, 77): '[T]here was something mean in this second piece, something not quite laughable, because it pointed out too blatantly the sharply defined incongruity between the idealistic expression of American freedom of the common man and the blight and ill-conscience of Negro slavery' (Hodge 1964, 72–73). Insofar as Mathews was arguably extending a supposedly realistic portrait of American life (admittedly within a farcical format), he had gone too far, turning Jonathan into 'an uncouth, stupid, witless, dishonest, stubborn, easily insulted, unmannerly braggart, lost in a civilised society, a Negro beater, and a mockery of true democracy' (Hodge 1964, 77). In her study of Brother Jonathan as an American icon, Winifred Morgan confirmed that Mathews had turned this figure into 'a cloddish boor' (Morgan 1988, 57). On the one hand, writes Morgan, the character represented pride in American 'difference', but in embodying 'the energy, the single-minded acquisitiveness, and the intransigent toughness of ordinary Americans' (Morgan 1988, 50) stage representations demonstrated the social tensions implicit in this figure.

The politics of Mathews's misrepresentation of the Yankee has been examined from a postcolonial perspective by Maura L. Jortner. She argues that in *Trip to America*, 'America is made foreign' and in *Jonathan in England* Americans are depicted as 'foreigner'. Both, she avers, 'rely on an Imperial vision, one which centers on "home", the "norm" and "the respectable subject" clearly on one side of the Atlantic' (Jortner 2009, 27). Relying on the clichés of contemporary travelogues and re-iterating already established stereotypes in *Trip to America* (in Jortner's view), Mathews misses the mixture of comedy and idealism in his American prototype, instead making him a slaveholder who mistreats his slave and a hypocrite who fails to realise that such behaviour is antithetical to the freedom and independence of which he boasts. The problem is heightened by the unequal relationship between England and America in 1824:

> The New World was the margin, the periphery to London's center.... Mathews was examining, seeing, and judging America through his imperial viewpoint. He was doing so, likewise, from within the center. His critique was aimed across the Atlantic at the post-colonial margin.
>
> Similar to contemporary travelogues, Mathews' work focused on the "strangeness" of both Other people and of Other places. He, like the traveller in written accounts, was always the "Self" experiencing the "foreign". (Jortner 2009, 33)

Jortner sees in Mathews's English 'Self' representing the 'Other' on stage a symbolic form of imperial conquest. This is further accentuated in *Jonathan in England*, in which Jonathan is used 'to condemn American claims to egalitarianism, independence and capitalism'(Jortner 2009, 41). Jortner provides a valuable comparative analysis of Humpreys's play *The Yankey in England* and *Jonathan in England*, convincingly demonstrating how such changes turned a sympathetic nationalist portrait into 'a vindictive pest'(Jortner 2009, 44).

The imperialist aspect of Mathews's performance resurfaces in Jenna M Gibbs's assessment of the impact of Mathews's Yankee on the British public, although flawed by its misunderstanding of the potential British audiences for Mathews's 'At Homes'. Gibbs claims that Mathews's shows were most popular at the Adelphi and Surrey theatres, which 'catered to audiences predominantly of the lower sorts' (Gibbs 2014, 153). She also claims that it was to the Surrey Theatre that Mathews first brought *Trip to America* in 1824 (subsequently and erroneously referred to as 1823), stating that 'Mathews's burlesque of black Americans and critique of American slavery was thus performed for plebeian audiences, stirred up by popular antislavery and the larger programme of human rights and political reform to which the cause belonged.' Thus Mathews, states Gibbs, 'may have been performing for racially mixed audiences, the white members of which were part of a working-class culture in which prejudice against and identification with non-white Londoners could co-exist' (Gibbs 2014, 157). The fundamental flaw in this argument is not only that Mathews did not premiere this piece at either the Surrey or Adelphi theatres but also that the assumptions made about their likely audiences are problematic. If Mathews performed at all at the Surrey, which tended to attract a socially mixed audience, in 1824, this would have been for only a short engagement. Mathews did not perform his 'At Homes' at the Adelphi until the late 1820s and there is no evidence to suggest this theatre attracted a specifically plebeian audience. Both *Trip to America* and *Jonathan in England* were performed at the English Opera House in the Strand, a theatre that was not particularly associated with a plebeian audience. Indeed, Mathews's 'At Homes' appear to have targeted the middle and upper classes and, on tour, Mathews recounts how the galleries tended to be the least full part of the house (Davis 2015, 244). Gibbs's surprise that Mathews drew the interest of reviewers who did not normally attend shows at minor theatres such as the Surrey is less of a surprise when we realise these pieces were premiered in the West End and that performances at the English Opera House were regularly reviewed in a range of newspapers and periodicals.

Gibbs argues that Mathews's Yankee impersonation can only be considered in relation to his representation of slavery, suggesting that Mathews 'held up African slavery in America as proof positive of the superiority of the British monarchy and empire' (Gibbs 2014, 154):

> What made his ridicule especially notable was its strong element of smug British chauvinism. This nationalism was also reflected in his decidedly unrepublican discomfort with American democracy's loss, in his eyes, of customary deference among its "lower sorts." Mathews's critique of American slavery thus stemmed more from his contempt for Americans' "absurd notions" of social equality than from any principled aversion to slavery. His burlesque of slavery was part of a patriotic boast about British 'monarchical "liberty." Nonetheless, he performed a rejection of slavery through his impersonation of Jonathan W. Doubikin, "a real Yankee," and his relationship to his "poor runaway Negro," Agamemnon, a character Mathews played comically but sympathetically. (Gibbs 2014, 159)

Whereas Mathews brought home to Britain his satire of American slavery and liberty, says Gibbs, Jonathan 'brought American slavery—in the person of his slave, Agamemnon—with him to Great Britain and in so doing provided a favourable commentary on British liberty' (Gibbs 2014, 162). This was still achieved, however, within an imperialist context.

There may also be scope for a socio-economic reading of Mathews's Yankee impersonation. Mathew Pethers suggests that a lack of respect for rank and social distinction was unsettling for Mathews and that his 'hatred' for American democracy may have been due to his 'ascent from a lowly background' (Pethers 2013, 95). *Trip to America*, in Pethers' view, portrays America as 'antithetical to English civilisation' and he quotes the *New England Galaxy* (May 1824) which condemned Mathews as a 'wretch who now seeks to fill his pockets by exerting his monkey faculties to beget and perpetrate national antipathies of the most mischievous nature' (Pethers 2013, 101). The notion of the Yankee New Englander as con-man, fortune-hunter and deceiver did not go down well with the American public. Interestingly, Pethers sees theatre as 'a primary site for the modelling and display of market relations' in North America and acknowledges that 'the comic interplay of the Yankee with African American characters' has been criticised in that it appears 'to reinforce racial stereotypes and strengthen a narrow conception of nationhood' (Pethers 2013, 84, 87). However, Pethers believes that this emphasis obscures 'the evolution of the Yankee into a figure of transatlantic significance' and that, following the War of 1812, 'it was the Englishman rather than the slave who became the primary dramatic foil for the Yankee'(Pethers 2013, 88). Mathews criticised Americans' 'inordinate appetite for gain' (Mathews 1838–39, III. 341) and as Jonathan

W. Doubikins in *Jonathan in England* demonstrated through his uncle's cheating on the New York stock market 'the Yankee tendency to deceive writ large' (Pethers 2013, 101).

4   Conclusions: Mathews's Return to America

Mathews was aware of the antagonism he had caused in America and had long wished to revisit the country if only 'to contradict the aspersions of vulgar and interested malice, which had accused him of ingratitude to the people who had used him so kindly' (Mathews 1838–39, IV. 187). In 1834, when in financial difficulties that had forced him to sell his home and his picture collection, Mathews was offered the opportunity to make a return visit, one which he hoped would also enable him to recoup some of the income he had lost. As it turned out, ill health dogged this American tour so that it was not to be the lucrative engagement he had envisaged. Nevertheless, he braved once again an American audience and even performed *Trip to America* while there. After the first performance Mathews appealed to the house to pronounce whether he was guilty of the charge of abusing the Americans in it, or not guilty? 'In answer to this, all the pit, and…every gentleman in the theatre rose, and in a thunder of voices, simultaneously shouted *"Not Guilty"*' (Mathews 1838–39, IV. 198). His address to the audience preliminary to the performance, written for him by his wife, provides a very full justification for the intention behind his 'At Homes'.

> My sketches are strictly those of *manners*; and as amusement is positively required of me, I naturally and necessarily seize upon those prominences of character most likely to afford it. In my several delineations of the English, Scotch, Irish, Welsh, and French, I have unhesitatingly delivered to them, upon their *own ground*, their respective peculiarities and manners, and have never, in a single instance, given offence. As I dealt with them, so I dealt with America: what I found a source of innocent amusement, I certainly made use of; but I never intentionally, or *with knowledge*, touched upon individual feeling with ill nature or a desire to wound. (Mathews 1838–39, IV. 199)

Interestingly, he does not refer to *Jonathan in England* in this rather disingenuous justification.

Mathews's performances as Jonathan W. Doubikin and Jonathan W. Doubikins raise many issues around on-stage representations of race and national identity, particularly when such representations are based on a mixture of external observation, imagination and possible exaggeration. Through his characterisation of the Yankee for his British audiences, Mathews created a calumny—in the eyes of some—that indicted white Americans as both a race (especially through their treatment of black slaves) and a nation (in terms of national identity formation) within a narrow, inaccurate and unrepresentative stereotype at a time when Anglo-American relationships required careful finessing. Michael Ragussis comments, in relation to the mid- to late-eighteenth century, how

366   J. DAVIS

Benjamin Franklin remarked on the way in which the British typically viewed America as an ethic dumping ground, with its "*mixed rabble of Scotch, Irish and foreign vagabonds.*" These movements of ethnic and colonial populations contributed to what I have called a crisis of acculturation and national identity, because as borders were crossed and recrossed and even remapped during this period, who was English or even British became fluid and periodically shifted. So, Franklin complained that the English viewed the American colonists "as unworthy the name of Englishmen," as if they were "*Englishmen by fiction of law only*". (Ragussis 2010, 24)

The evolution of the Yankee character had been slow in America and in the early nineteenth century was arguably still evolving, especially on stage. The bigoted, hypocritical, mean-spirited, slave-owning figure conjured up by Mathews was at variance with the Yankee Brother Jonathan image developing in America. Yet, as many of the British reviews attest, Mathews's Yankee was deemed authentic and true to nature by his fellow countryman, and indicative of white Americans in general. Whereas he was able to portray regional and national differences in his delineations of the French, the Irish or the Yorkshireman, his Yankee was too generalised and imprecisely drawn to win the approval of critics such as John Neal. It constituted a national and racial slur. Yet, just as blackface in the form of stereotyped representations by blacked up white minstrel troupes was to 'other' the African American population, especially from the 1840s onwards, so Mathews's Jonathan 'othered' the Yankee, also transforming him into a misleading cultural stereotype. Indeed, M. Alison Kibler considers that eventually 'the blackface minstrel, like the independent and patriotic Yankee and the manly and robust backwoodsman, served as an expression of American identity in defiance of European elitism' (Kibler 2008, 317). While Americans lauded the independence and individuality of the home-grown Yankee, Mathews's claim that his Yankee Jonathan was an individual rather than a type ran counter to the British reception of the character as an authentic generic portrait. For Mathews, there were no questions around his ownership and mediation of white American national and racial identity, perhaps because his representations of other national, racial and regional groups had not been so explicitly contested by his contemporaries. Yet, for all that, his Yankee had evidently touched a nerve, while also intervening in and impacting on future representations of this iconic character.

NOTES

1. Charles Dickens was later to have a similar view of the American people. See Dickens, *American Notes*, 289.
2. This quotation is taken from a compilation text based on the extant unauthorised texts published in 1824.
3. Although the Yankee is associated with the eastern seaboard and is usually a new Englander, Jonathan Doubikin is presumably representative of Yankees who have

migrated westwards to states such as Kentucky. However, in *Jonathan in England*, his uncle, from whom he has purchased the slave Agamemnon, is a citizen of Vermont, a New England state opposed to slavery.

4. All quotations are taken from the version of *Jonathan in England* submitted to the Lord Chamberlain. Add. Ms. 42868, British Library. The manuscript version of the farce reveals that it was allowed by the Examiner of Plays, George Colman the younger, after some omissions and alterations were made, but it is not clear from the text which of these may have been made by the dramatist in advance and which were required by the Examiner.

References

Davis, Jim. 2015. *Comic Acting and Portraiture in Late-Georgian and Regency England*. Cambridge: Cambridge University Press.

Davis, Tracy C. 2011. Acting Black, 1824: Charles Mathews's *Trip to America*. *Theatre Journal* 63 (2): 163–189.

Dickens, Charles. 1842, reprinted 1972. *American Notes*. Harmondsworth: Penguin Books.

Gibbs, Jenna M. 2014. *Performing the Temple of Liberty: Slavery, Theater and Popular Culture in London and Philadelphia, 1760–1850*. Baltimore: John Hopkins University Press.

Hodge, Francis. 1964. *Yankee Theatre: The Image of America and the Stage, 1825–1850*. Austin: University of Texas Press.

Jortner, Maria L. 2005. Playing "America" on Nineteenth-Century Stages; or Jonathan in England and Jonathan at Home. Doctoral thesis, University of Pittsburgh.

———. 2009. Throwing Insults Across the Ocean: Charles Mathews and the Staging of "the American" in 1824. In *Portrayals of Americans on the World Stage Critical Essays*, ed. Kevin J. Wetmore Jr., 26–49. Jefferson, NC and London: McFarland & Company, Inc.

Kibler, M. Alison. 2008. Performance and Display. In *A Companion to American Cultural History*, ed. Karen Halttunen, 311–326. Oxford: Blackwell Publishing.

Lewis, Robert Michael. 2016. Speaking Black, 1824: Charles Mathew's *Trip to America* Revisited. *Nineteenth Century Theatre and Film* 43 (1): 43–66.

Mathews, Ann. 1838–39. *Memoirs of Charles Mathews, Comedian*. 4 vols. London: Richard Bentley, Mathews Family Papers, Princeton University Library (5 November 1826).

Morgan, Winifred. 1988. *An American Icon: Brother Jonathan and American Identity*. Newark: University of Delaware Press.

Neal, John. 1869. *Wandering Recollections of a Somewhat Busy Life: An Autobiography*. Boston: Roberts Brothers.

Peake, Richard Brinsley. 1824. *Jonathan in England*, Add. Ms. 42868, British Library.

Pethers, Mathew. 2013. That Eternal Ghost of Trade: Anglo-American Market Culture and the Antebellum Stage Yankee. In *The Materials of Exchange between Britain and North America 1750–1900*, ed. Daniel Maudlin and Robin Peel, 83–115. Farnham, Surrey: Ashgate.

Ragussis, Michael. 2010. *Theatrical Nation: Jews and Other Outlandish Englishmen in Georgian Britain*. Philadelphia: University of Pennsylvania Press.

Schäfer, Stefanie. 2016. (Un)Settling North America: The Yankee in the Writings of John Neal and Thomas Chandler Haliburton. In *Traveling Traditions: Nineteenth-Century Cultural Concepts and Transatlantic Intellectual Networks*, ed. Erik Redling, 231–246. Berlin and Boston: De Gruyter.

Sketches of Mr Mathews's Celebrated Trip to America Comprising a Full Account of his Admirable Lecture on Peculiarities, Characters and Manners; with the Most Laughable of the Stories and Adventures, and Eight Original Comic Songs. 1824. London: J. Limbird.

Smith, James, and R.B. Peake. 1824/2012. *Trip to America* in *The Broadview Anthology of Nineteenth-Century British Performance*, ed. Tracy C. Davis, 163–215. Ontario, Canada: Broadview Press.

Talbot, Edward Allen. 1824. *Five Years' Residence in the Canadas: Including a Tour through Part of the United States of America in the Year of 1823.* 2 vols. London: Longman, Hurst Rees, Orme, Brown and Green.

Watts, Edward, and David J. Carlson, eds. 2012. *John Neal and Nineteenth Century Literature and Culture.* Lewisburg: Bucknell University Press.

CHAPTER 20

The Language of Blackness: Representations of Africans and African-Americans on the British Stage After *Uncle Tom's Cabin*

Tiziana Morosetti

1 Introduction

Victorian theatrical adaptations of *Uncle Tom's Cabin* (1852) are of particular interest in discussions of theatre and race, not only for the insight they offer into debates about slavery and racism in the nineteenth century, but also for the variety of stereotypes of both white and black Americans that they presented to British audiences. These adaptations provided a critical portrait of life in the United States that mainly responded to the political climate of Britain, and more generally participated in the frenzy surrounding Harriet Beecher Stowe's text. The novel was an immediate and unprecedented success, with nine theatrical versions staged in the 1850s in various American cities (Meer 2005, 105), and at least seven running in London between September and December 1852.[1] To these must be added the several British performances[2] that, by either mentioning the novel in passing or satirising what at the end of the year had already become Uncle Tom mania, substantially contributed to popularise both Stowe's novel and its protagonist in Britain.

Part of the research leading to these results has received funding from the People Programme (Marie Curie Actions) of the European Union's Seventh Framework Programme (FP7/2007–2013) under REA grant agreement no. 299000.

T. Morosetti (✉)
Department of Theatre and Performance, Goldsmiths, University of London, London, UK
e-mail: t.morosetti@gold.ac.uk

© The Author(s), under exclusive license to Springer Nature Switzerland AG 2021
T. Morosetti, O. Okagbue (eds.), *The Palgrave Handbook of Theatre and Race*, https://doi.org/10.1007/978-3-030-43957-6_20

369

When in T. L. Greenwood's pantomime *Dick Whittington and His Cat* (Sadler's Wells, 27 December 1852) a group of black extras enter holding placards that identify them as 'The Original Uncle Tom', 'The People's Uncle Tom', 'The Illustrated Uncle Tom', 'The Only Genuine Uncle Tom', 'The Author's Uncle Tom' and 'The Old Uncle Tom', or when Uncle Tom himself appears in William Brough's farce *Uncle Tom's Crib* (Strand, 14 October 1852) as the proprietor of 'a House of Call for Ethiopian Serenaders',[3] two intertwined things are happening. On the one hand, Uncle Tom has become an object of commodification that can be literally replicated on stage just like the many gadgets that followed the novel's publication; on the other, the blackface minstrel show has fused with Uncle Tom mania to become itself a portable set of references (to famous minstrel troupes and/or songs) used to convey to audiences an immediate association between black characters and 'fun'.

That the minstrel show should be so used is unsurprising. As Sarah Meer has affirmed in her *Uncle Tom Mania* (2005), 'Tom and Topsy would become images as ubiquitous as Jim Crow or Zip Coon and possibly even more long-lived. *Uncle Tom*'s characters would occupy some of the same structural positions in American and European culture as those of the minstrel stage: Uncle Tom and Chloe would take over not only literal shop windows but also figurative ones' (22). While it is not my interest here to assess whether or not the Uncle Tom tradition outlived that of Jim Crow,[4] this chapter argues that the former was instrumental to the survival of the 'minstrelised vision of the black' (Waters 2001, 39) as the inherently comic and grotesque figure promoted by the latter. If the minstrel show had been in the first place central in 'crystallizing and establishing certain stereotypes of blacks and black "racial" characteristics' (Pickering 2008, 118), the success of theatrical adaptations of *UTC* at a crucial moment in the history of British scientific racism—the 1850s and 1860s[5]—served to articulate stricter understandings of racial difference, while it further familiarized audiences with the aesthetic features of the 'minstrelised' black.

Amongst these features is the 'dialect' black characters are made to speak—a simplified and somewhat fictional version of African-American English Vernacular (AAVE) that had been popularized, before the minstrel show, by the impersonations of Charles Mathews (1776–1835). This was not an entirely invented language (Mathews having based the speech of his black characters on first-hand material that he had encountered on his trip to America)[6] but rather one that the minstrel show, a genre 'intended mainly for white audiences' and 'dominated by white performers and writers' (Rickford and Rickford 2000, 30), had approximated and fictionalized. Dillard, for instance, has illustrated how, while the language of blackface minstrelsy couldn't have been created 'out of whole cloth', 'minstrel-show writers may have been especially inept recorders of already existing dialects' (1972, 13). In their provoking article on the work of Dan Emmet, founder of the first American minstrel troupe, the Virginia Minstrels, Holmberg and Schneider have similarly evidenced how '[h]is spelling clearly documents correspondences to "Wes Kos" or West

African Pidgin English' (1986, 30); therefore, '[t]o maintain [as in earlier criticism] that Emmett included no genuine Afro-American phonology is [...] untenable. The argument that most of his work was calculated for theatric effect is more acceptable' (31). While retaining features of AAVE—such as 'the most well-known' of these—'the absence of the copula in the present before predicate nouns and adjectives, locatives and comitative phrases': 'He a friend. He tired. He over there [...]' (Labov 1977, 45)[7]—the language of the minstrel show cannot be described as accurate. 'Dialect', furthermore, would become increasingly absurd in the second half of the century, when 'a reaction set in against the sentimental caricature of the abolitionists, and a more derogatory stereotype of the Negro became more prevalent' (Lorimer 1978, 12). If in its early stages the language of black characters had not been 'as strained and forced' as later (Waters 2007, 30), towards the end of the century it would become near-incomprehensible, to make it funnier while immediately conveying an implicit (and by now perceived as incorrigible) inferiority the black. As Waters further explains,

> [f]rom [...] calling themselves 'me', they [the black characters] move to designating themselves as 'him', and, on occasion, as 'em'—a variant of 'them' and used variously for me, him, you. While 'me' may be a valid dialect usage, by the time 'em' is in play, the effect is to suggest near imbecility. There is, too, the all-purpose syllable 'cum' which is increasingly used and is inserted into every word of three syllables or more to suggest ignorance and pomposity in equal measure. (2007, 115)

Building on Tracy Davis's suggestion that language may have been, in this respect, a more effective 'marker' of blackness on stage than the employment of blackface (a hyper-visible and not always reliable device),[8] my chapter focuses on language as a main area of influence of *UTC* on later theatre—visible, for instance, in the several performances within the 'Robinsonade' tradition that have their Fridays anachronistically refer to Uncle Tom and regularly speak 'dialect'.

Central to my argument is the notion that the irreverent approach of Victorian theatre to Stowe's novel was paramount in creating a plethora of Uncle-Tom images, which, *detached* from their initial context, travelled from one performance to the next progressively losing their initial abolitionist implication. In this regard, I suggest a further distinction must be made between adaptations of *UTC* such as Mark Lemon and Tom Taylor's *Slave Life; or, Uncle Tom's Cabin* (Adelphi, 29 November 1852)—which at least expressed 'both the wish and the effort to preserve in the Drama the spirit which breathes through MRS. STOWE's pathetic pages' (Lemon and Taylor 1852, ii)—and farces like William Brough's *Those Dear Blacks!* (Lyceum, 19 November 1852) that merely use *UTC* as a pretest for satire. In these latter performances, in which the novel is reduced to a mere object that is variously handled and commented on by characters,[9] Uncle-Tom images are incoherently scattered, being consumed primarily through the lenses of the caricature or the performance-within-a-performance. This, however, substantially complicates readings of these images as merely transmitting racial stereotypes or mirroring changes in the political atmosphere. While theatre no doubt responded to 'a political climate that was less and less favourable to conceptions of black equality, black freedom or black capacity' (Waters 2007), a question must be asked as to how these derogative portraits of blackness should resonate with audiences when framed within *openly* farcical contexts.

In section 2 of this chapter I examine Lemon and Taylor's version in relation to the specific history of blackface minstrelsy in Britain, discussing 'dialect' in juxtaposition with Standard English (SE) to highlight ways in which the Victorian stage distinguished, through voice, between different 'types' of blackness. This distinction had already implicitly been promoted by abolitionism, as it 'appealed to race cosciousness by attempting to arouse a more intense concern for the evils of slavery through portrayals of "white" slaves' (Lorimer 1978, 85), and largely informed *UTC*; but it was perhaps made even more apparent by adaptations of the novel, as they inevitably reduced the complex subject of Stowe's writing to a few selected scenes. I read for example as highly significant the choice of Lemon and Taylor to replace in a central scene the juxtaposition between white (Eva) and black (Topsy) with that between (the fairer-skinned slave) Eliza and (the darker-skinned slave) Topsy. In section 3, Brough's *Those Dear Blacks!* and other 'light' performances will be examined to discuss the implications of the farcical nature of this theatre in terms of audience reception. In the final section, I will explore some performances belonging to the 'Robinsonade' tradition that reveal the infiltration of the 'minstrelised' black character and the widespread references to *UTC* and the minstrel show.

2   RACISM ON THE VICTORIAN STAGE: LEMON AND TAYLOR'S *SLAVE LIFE*

At the core of theatrical adaptations of *UTC*—which was conceived, in the words of Maurice Disher, 'with an eye for picturesque suspense which destined it for triumph when adapted to the stage' (1954, 3)—were three main elements: melodrama, moral drama and blackface minstrelsy. As Meer explains,

[m]elodrama conventions demanded an emphasis on scenery and spectacle [...]. Moral drama was created by transfiguring the novel's sentimental femininity into a theatrical picture of saintliness, with celestial imagery, blinding white lighting, and a soundtrack of heavenly choirs. And the pleasures of minstrelsy were invoked in song-and-dance scenes and comic interludes, sometimes in straightforward imitation of the minstrel stage, sometimes borrowing from the novel's blackface variations. (2005, 111)

British and American adaptations, however, differed significantly as to what the novel's 'theatricality' should entail. The American stage shared the notion that 'presenting *Uncle Tom's Cabin* in the theatre [...] was a potentially dangerous endeavor—one that at any moment during the performance incite an audience to riot in the auditorium or on the streets outside the theatre' (Frick 2012, 63). Hence only two productions of notice, George Aiken's *Uncle Tom's Cabin: or, Life among the Lowly: A Domestic Drama in Six Acts* (1852) and Conway's version at P.T. Barnum's Museum, had been produced by the end of 1853 (Frick 2012, 107). The more famous of the two, Aiken's version, adhered to the novel's plot, retaining some of the philosophical reflections of the characters and featuring a grand final scene emotionally revolving around Eva and Uncle Tom. A connection with the minstrel show was physically displayed in the choice of G.C. Germon, formerly of the Ethiopian Serenaders, as Uncle Tom, as well as in the inclusion of songs such as 'Ethiopian melody' and 'Old Folks at Home' by the Christy's Minstrels (Pickering 2008, 118). In a context in which audiences had complex understandings of blackness on stage, being used to a variety of performances from both black and white artists,[10] it is interesting to note how concerns regarding voice and makeup to convey an 'accurate' portrait of black characters were mingled with a preoccupation to stay 'faithful' to Stowe's novel. Cordelia Howard (1848–1941), the first actress to play Eva in Aiken's version when she was just four years old, recalls that

> Mrs. Germon was cast for Topsy, she holding the position of soubrette, or chambermaid, as it was then called, but she threw up the part, saying it was not worth making up for. It was quite short at first. There seemed to be no other woman in the company fitted for it, so my father was contemplating turning the character into a boy, and giving it to Asa Cushman, who had a good negro dialect, was funny, but had no pathos and was a tall, awkward, raw-boned fellow at that time. My mother was horrified at the idea, saying that it would ruin Eva's part and turn the whole thing into ridicule. Finally, she vowed she would play the part herself. At this my father was the one to be shocked, telling her that she could not possibly do it; that she was not familiar with the dialect, and that it was entirely out of her line. Heretofore she had played only leading parts, romantic heroines, etc. But she insisted on making the attempt, saying she could at least portray the interesting situation between the children: the influence of Eva's character on the savage nature of the negro child, so beautifully set forth by Mrs. Stowe. Well, her success is now a matter of theatrical history, and she played the part for many years. (1956, 268)

Alongside Topsy repeating her catchphrase, 'I'se so wicked', which even becomes a song in the hands of George Howard (Riis 1994/1852, xiii), Ophelia is also made to repeat the term 'shiftless' several times during the play for comic effect. But (in the case of white characters at least) this is done in line with the book, the humour of which, as Meer has observed, struck 'nineteenth-century observers' far more than later critics (2007, 131); given that '[Ophelia's] New England activity and fastidiousness are partially laughed at [by Stowe] as she frets about waste, tries to bring some order to Dinah's kitchen, or struggles with Topsy' (Grimsted 1970, 139), her comic turns in Aiken's interpretation do not disturb the rationale behind *UTC*.

British versions, on the other hand, 'generally content[ed] themselves with picking out some eight or ten of the most striking scenes and situations' (*Caledonian Mercury*, 2 December 1852, 1), which usually stressed the spectacular and the humorous over abolitionist concerns. This went to the detriment of the actual Uncle Tom, as his fate was often changed, and his presence limited, to expand instead on the misfortunes of George and Eliza, characters 'as white as she [Stowe] can make them' (Baldwin 2007/1948, 51), and on those of Topsy, whose catchphrase 'I'se so wicked' would become a recurring feature of her role.

The marginalisation of Uncle Tom on the British stage can be explained, to quote again from the *Caledonian Mercury*, with the protagonist's 'Methodism', which 'cannot be reproduced on the boards of a theatre' (1); Waters has similarly argued that 'Tom's journey is an inner one; it could not be expressed in the powerful, declamatory and expository style of 19th-century melodrama' (2001, 33). Far from involving *Uncle Tom's Cabin* exclusively, this process of simplification affected the adaptation, in Victorian Britain, of several other important books, the 'lone reflection, productive labour, and clever problem solving' of Robinson Crusoe (Gould 2011, 54) being similarly abandoned to make space for Crusoe's encounter with Friday and the 'natives', and introduce novel elements such as 'a motivating romantic interest' (56). In both cases, *Uncle Tom's Cabin* and *Robinson Crusoe*, it was the picturesque, the sensational and the comic that came to be highlighted on stage—Lemon and Taylor's drama providing audiences with unexpected action that was not included in Stowe's novel, but also with a live pony and two real dogs, in line with the Victorian taste for the spectacular and the 'realistic'.

The 'neutral Christianity of Uncle Tom' (Johnson 1999, 61) could also be argued to be substantially incompatible with the stereotype of the African-American as inherently amusing and childish that was being circulated by blackface minstrelsy. This genre had become extremely popular in Britain since T.D. Rice (1808–1860) first performed at the Adelphi and the Surrey in 1836 (Bratton 1981, 133). It is important to note, however, that the warm reception of American troupes like the Christy's Minstrels and the Ethiopian Serenaders was more due to the fact that they initially appealed to a huge, stratified audience (before the later gentrification of the genre)[11] than on its political implications, which always remained rather abstract for British audiences. As Jacky Bratton has observed, 'the most obvious difference between British and American popular consciousness [...] was, of course, that the average Englishman had no need of an art form which would help him deal with complex problems of identity and confrontation with a black population. He had no such problems, and experienced no such confrontation' (1981, 128). The success of the British minstrel show initially built then not on strong abolitionist feelings—if only because slavery had been officially abolished in 1833—but rather on 'the deep-rooted romantic feeling about the noble savage' (Bratton 1981, 133) expressed by Charles Dibdin and George Colman in their earlier dramas (see also Waters 2007).

Bratton discusses the experience of blackface minstrelsy within the wider frame of the several performances that shaped attitudes of the British towards the black throughout the century, quoting the 1810 exhibition of Sara Baartman or the 'Hottentot Venus', and those of the Zulus and the 'Earthmen' in 1853 and 1855 respectively, all motivated by a 'desire to gaze open-mouthed at strange specimens of humanity' (1981, 131). While these other examples feature real African people, a distinction should also be made between the early minstrel show and later representations of blackness; if the very act of staring at the 'strangeness' of the performer supported feelings of belonging and difference—blackface minstrelsy encouraging, in the words of Pickering, 'all social classes in Britain to think in racial categories' (2008, 109)—mid-century performances would articulate the criteria promoted by scientific racism in far more specific terms. Adaptations of *UTC* are no exception to this, as they

> created vehicles for an explicit antislavery message simultaneously with the means to portray openly racist standpoints. Minstrel audiences already accustomed to the manic misadventures of Jim Crow and the pretentious buffoonery of Zip Coon were *retrained* to think about blackface impersonation as tied to both abolitionist arguments and a range of pejoratively racialized and formulaically sentimentalized African American characters — clowns and zanies, but also sentimental heroines and patsies. (Davis 2013, 42; my emphasis)

The 'racialized' interpretation of black characters, however, is articulated very differently in the case of Topsy and Tom; whereas 'for many readers of the novel the impish humour of Topsy joined the religiosity of Uncle Tom as peculiar Negro characteristics' (Lorimer 1978, 84), I would argue that, in Lemon and Taylor's version at least, they represent two different stages of racialist thinking: one in line with the more 'benign', monogenist interpretation of 'race', the other showing an 'incursion of polygenic racism' (Davis, ibid.). By making Uncle Tom a devoted Christian, Stowe was employing a regular stereotype of blackness—as 'backward' but substantially redeemable through faith—that aligned early scientific racism with abolitionist ideas. As Curtin explains, 'English thought during the first three decades of the century was more generally favorable to Africans than it had been in the recent past or would be in the decades that followed' (1965, 235); while believing in the inferiority of black races, authorities 'left room for the operation of "moral causes"' (236), as they 'did not claim full equality for all races of men, only the minimum condition of monogenesis' (239). To the all-present question 'Am I not a Man and a brother?' '[a]ny monogenist [...] necessarily had to answer in the affirmative. With this point safely accepted, humanitarian pamphleteers could concede the inferiority of African culture and character' (ibid.). On the other hand, mid-century polygenist views such as those of Robert Knox (1791–1862) and James Hunt (1833–1869) posited that the 'African Negro', who in all classifications 'occupied the lowest position in the evolutionary scale' (Bolt 1971, 133), was altogether a different species, thus entirely alien and non-understandable.

This division is reflected in Uncle Tom and Topsy, as the former displays the two essential connotations of 'civilisation'—a Christian faith and a wish (if not an accomplished ability) to read and write—while the latter is beyond any chance of salvation, illiterate as she is and a 'heathen' (introduced as such both on page and on stage). If Topsy's catchphrase 'singl[ed] out her defiance of conventional piety as her most marketable characteristic' (Meer 2005, 39), her refusal to be in any way tamed suggested to both spectators and readers that she be located at the very bottom of the ladder of civilisation; a notion that is conveyed by Lemon and Taylor throughout their drama via the juxtaposition between her character and the fairer-skinned slaves George and Eliza.

In its several innovations at plot level,[12] Lemon and Taylor's drama is representative of the transformation of *UTC* on the British stage; described by the *Lloyd's Weekly London Newspaper* as not 'a mere Stage Version of the Tale, but a Play, in which free use has been made of many of her chief personages and most striking incidents' (5 December 1852, 9), *Slave Life; or, Uncle Tom's Cabin* sees (amongst other things) Eliza, Harry and Tom all end up being bought by Legree (I.1); Tom be stabbed by Legree (III.2) and be subsequently revenged by Cassy (Cassidy), who, in the final scene, kills Legree and flees to Canada with George, Eliza, Harry and Topsy (III.3). Eva and St Clare are entirely absent from the play, as are Ophelia and Emmeline—St Clare being interpreted perhaps, similarly to Uncle Tom, as too sophisticated and passive a character to adequately fit the melodramatic stage.

The assumptions surrounding the racialized black characters are made visible in two scenes in particular, I.1 and II.5, in which both visual and linguistic elements point to the difference between the displayed 'races'. The use of visual elements to this goal is already present in *UTC* and creates a conjunction between the novel and the contemporary science, as both use images 'to explain "race" to an American population increasingly interested in defining and maintaining racial differences. [...] By approaching racialized bodies as texts, racial science emphasized the power of visual images to codify what was arguably the most pressing—and nebulous—concern of the time: racial difference'(Reid 2008, 369). Voice, both on stage and on page, became another factor that conveyed such difference, as when black characters spoke SE they were generally regarded as of a higher status than those that spoke 'dialect'. In her *Racism on the Victorian Stage* (2007), Waters has illustrated at length how representations of blackness that do not solely stress the characters' dark complexion (as in dramas, like Boucicault's 1859 *The Octoroon*, that feature mulatto slaves) could still powerfully convey derogative portraits of blackness (130–154). However, the juxtaposition Waters takes into account in her analysis concerns exclusively the 'American' slave trope in its various articulations, from the darker-skinned 'minstrelised' black to the white-assimilated creole slave, without consideration of the alternative portraits of blackness that the Victorian stage provided at that point, and which were not related to this trope but rather to an 'African' stereotype.

The increased involvement of the British Empire in African affairs in the second half of the century meant that the public was exposed to a plethora of materials on and from the African continent, the 1879 Anglo-Zulu war especially bringing 'the Zulu people to the attention of the British public like no other African people before or since' (Parson 2003, 114). As I have illustrated elsewhere (Morosetti 2016) this involvement, which would culminate in the process known as 'Scramble for Africa' and its domination at the Berlin Conference (1884–1885), prompted several theatrical performances in which the portrait of the 'African' enemy differs from that of the black 'American' slave first and utmost in the language they speak: SE. The use of 'dialect' would have been out of question: since the stereotype promoted by the 'minstrelised vision of the black' was that of a childish and highly exaggerated—but substantially harmless—character, the fierce and 'difficult' African enemy could not possibly speak in the same way; SE was also generally the language of 'those to be feared or respected in some way' (Waters 2001, 30).

Examples such as E.G. Burton's *The Blind Child of Africa; or, the Last Prince of Abyssinia and the True British Seaman* (1851), in which a 'black cook' and the protagonist Achmet speak 'dialect' and SE respectively; or *Amakosa; or, Scenes of Kaffir Warfare* (Astley's, 1853), in which the 'Noble Kaffir Chief' Amakosa speaks highly dignified English ('thou hast spoken well') in striking comparison with the 'dialect' of Jawboo ('a Kaffir Boer'), reveal how by mid-century—both before and after *UTC*—the British stage was receptive of linguistic nuances, which were used to convey political and racial notions independently on the visual element. The encounter between the white *and* SE-speaking George and Eliza, and the black *and* 'dialect'-speaking Topsy in Lemon and Taylor's drama would then invite audiences to immediately arrange these characters in a hierarchy, while in the process recalibrating their own expectations accordingly.

Topsy is first introduced in the drama in I.1, a scene that combines several passages in chapter XX of the novel, during which Topsy is accused by Miss Ophelia of stealing a ribbon and, prompted to 'confess', then admits to stealing also what she hasn't actually taken; the reprimand is interrupted by the entrance of Eva, who is made aware of the accusations and then, in the novel,

> stood looking at Topsy. There stood the two children, representative of the two extremes of society. The fair, high-bred child, with her golden head, her deep eyes, her spiritual, noble brow, and prince-like movements; and her black, keen, subtle, cringing, yet acute neighbor. They stood the representatives of their races. The Saxon, born of ages of cultivation, command, education, physical and moral eminence; the Afric, born of ages of oppression, submission, ignorance, toil, and vice! (Stowe 1852, 180)

In this well-known passage, 'Stowe casts the difference between Eva and Topsy as biologically embedded but ultimately not entirely essential [...], argu[ing] in the mode of monogenesis, the view that all people descend from a common ancestor and that racial differences stem from environment' (Bernstein 2011, 44). When the privileged Eva exclaims '[p]oor Topsy, why need you steal? You're going to be taken good care of now. I'm sure I'd rather give you anything of mine than have you steal it' (Stowe 1852, 180), some socio-economic responsibility in the 'improvement' of Topsy's condition (and that of her 'race') is firmly put on the white child's shoulders, if framed within the usual narrative of patronizing condescension.

Different is the case with Lemon and Taylor's version; here, Topsy is rather abruptly presented to audiences in the very first scene, hence without most of the context in which Stowe locates her after almost two hundred pages of reflection on the slavery question; importantly, this is a context that audiences may or may not have had in mind when encountering the stage Topsy—as Meer has noted, not all spectators were familiar with the novel, and even for those who were 'the dramatizations functioned in part as mediating or exegetic texts, conditioning the way such audiences "read" the original, whether they did so afterward, remembered it in retrospect, or never did so at all' (2005, 105). The dialogue between Mrs Shelby (not Ophelia) and Topsy in the drama faithfully reports the accusations of having stolen the ribbon, and then focuses, as in the novel, on Topsy's nebulous origins and her status as an orphan seemingly without any notion of her own past. The compressed 'accuracy' of this dialogue, which sews together several moment in chapter XX, acquires, however, an entire new reading as Eva is replaced by Eliza, who also professes her love for Topsy and promises to 'take good care of her'; put in the mouth of a character that, albeit fair-skinned, is still a slave like Topsy, and with her has to flee a terrible destiny, the dialogue between the two loses the political implications it has in the novel, and only serves to align the fairer-skinned slave with her masters' view while stressing the visual and linguistic differences between the 'lowly' portrayed on stage.

Both in this scene, and in II.5, when Topsy meets George in a tavern (a scene without importance in terms of plot development), the darker-skinned enslaved girl is defined a 'monkey', a term that is used in the novel as well but which, in the economy of the dramatic action, emerges more distinctly. The term itself, as Jane Goodall has illustrated in her *Performance and Evolution in the Age of Darwin* (2002), was loaded with meaning, as it would have evoked for audiences notions surrounding the 'missing link' that—well before the publication of Darwin's *The Origin of Species* (1859)—were seen to influence performance at all levels. Blackface impersonators themselves, writes Goodall, played 'close to the human/animal divide upon which savages were supposed to be situated. Animal acts [...] were an essential component of variety programmes and had special prominence in minstrel shows', monkey images being particularly relevant (2002, 136). The connection between Topsy and blackface minstrelsy is, on the other hand, also reinforced by her singing 'Jim Crow' in the same scene—an inclination for music that later performances would only reinforce, as the inability of the 'minstrelised' black to utter meaningful sentences is highlighted not only by the use of 'dialect' but also by their inclination to interrupt the conversation to break into singing.

If in Lemon and Taylor's drama, compared to other examples, Topsy is given an unusually active role, taking part as she does in the plan that will eventually lead to the murder of Legree, she is still portrayed overall as a clumsy, noisy and 'half-clad savage'[13] (*Caledonian Mercury*, 2 December 1852, 1), whose behaviour, it is worth noting, contemporary commentators of the drama would have interpreted as substantially authentic. This notion was linked to the idea that theatre could provide *evidence* for anthropological, medical or scientific realities, above all if roles were performed by established and therefore 'reliable' performers; as I have noted in my discussion of the representation of the Zulu on the Victorian stage (Morosetti 2016), a self-nurturing circle was in place for which, as expectations of the 'foreign' and 'exotic' were met by performances, these were in turn seen as credible and truthful. Writing of Lemon and Taylor's drama, *The Morning Post* (30 November 1852) highlighted, for instance, that Mrs [Mary Ann] Keeley (1805?–1899), an established performer specialized in 'light' roles who played Topsy in the Adelphi production, 'gave us a most amusing picture of the lowest grade of the unfortunate genus "Nigger". Her "make-up" was perfect, whilst the peculiar humour which distinguishes genuine "darkies," and a struggle of an honest heart to make itself apparent through dense clouds of ignorance and prejudice, were portrayed with complete truthfulness' (5). Mrs Keeley's appearance was itself 'a signal for shouts of laughter and applause' (*Caledonian Mercury*, 2 December 1852, 1), as Topsy came to represent all that was funny and strange in the eyes of the audience.

All in all, as declared by the *Lloyd's Weekly Newspaper*, the 'effect' of watching Lemon and Taylor's drama was 'nearly the same as witnessing a French performance of one of Shakespeare's plays. You are so familiar with the beauties, that you are ready to cry out against the smallest alteration as an outrage' (5 December 1852, 9). The notation is interesting; on the one hand, it assumes that the original text had become so popular that every alteration of its plot would have been acknowledged, and possibly opposed, by the audience—who, as mentioned, may actually not at all have been familiar with Stowe's text. On the other, however, the firm success of *Slave Life; or, Uncle Tom's Cabin*, which remained on the play-bills 'for at least two hundred nights' (*Lloyd's Weekly London Newspaper*, 5 December 1852, 9), suggests instead that alterations were not only not opposed, but in fact welcomed by audiences. This seems for sure to be the case with performances like *Those Dear Blacks!* that only relate to *UTC* as a source of satire.

3   Brough's *Those Dear Blacks!* and the Conventions of Theatrical Blackness

Brough's farce revolves around the 'story of a "Yankee Nigger" [...] who, coming into an inheritance and travelling to England to find a white wife and white servant, is imposed upon by a penniless English clerk, Featheredge [...].

As might be expected, the black, Lillywhite, ends up in his rightful place as the servant, and Featheredge, whom he has hired, as his master' (Waters 2007, 177). Waters' analysis of this farce does not go much deeper than this; in support of her premise that this performance, alongside many others, provided a derogative portrait of the black in substantial continuity with that of the minstrel show, Waters quotes one review from the *Era* that describes in particular Lillywhite as 'preposterous' and 'ridiculous'. But, first, there were other reviews that actually show how Lillywhite's portrait may not have been taken quite so literally, the *Wells Journal* (27 November 1852) writing, for instance, that the farce 'is more laughable than pungent', showcasing 'the *conventional* eccentricities of the black' (my emphasis). Second, the text itself, *if read for what it is*, a farce, allows some complementary readings, as it is abolitionism that is being satirized here rather than the 'eccentricities' of the black alone.

Act 1 presents several passages in this direction, as when the protagonist Amelia, talking about her marriage to Featheredge, admits to her father that she can only be happy 'as we poor soulless creatures can be. We can't expect in this unsentimental latitude, such ardent all devouring love, as there must be in the fiery tropics' (3). She is later spotted duly reading *UTC*, but when Lillywhite arrives on the scene Amelia, taken aback by the encounter with a 'real' black person, reveals her own true nature in a dialogue that is worth quoting at length:

Lilly:	[...] Tell me, lubly white gal, could you lub de black man?
Amelia:	I dote upon them! (*looks up* [from *Uncle Tom's Cabin*]) Good Heavens—a Negro!
Lilly:	See dis Nigger on him knee!
Am:	If he had only chains on his hands, he'd be perfect!
Lilly:	You say you dote on black man—dote on this one!
Am:	If there was but a slave driver standing over him with a whip!
Lilly:	Oh! Don't you lub him?
Am:	Hear me, poor slave—
Lilly:	No, Missie, me no slave now. Me gentleman of poperty. [...] (*takes her hand*)
Am:	Release me! What impertinence! (*breaks from him*) Help! help!' [...] [Enter Mittimus]
Am:	Oh! Sir, I had sat down to read about those dear blacks, when that horrid Negro –
Mittimus:	Ah! Your tender heart feels for the poor suffering black man, far away, enchained, and treated like a beast of burden—but a black man speaking to you here!
Am:	Disgraceful, isn't it?
Mit:	Frightful! As well might we expect that the Philanthropist, who holds out the right hand of fellowship to the poor struggling working man, would let him take hold of that right hand, and with his dirty paw soil his benefactor's white kid glove! (9–10)

The very obvious satire of abolitionism in this passage shows an awareness of the fact that '[a]side from their self-righteousness, condescension, and sublimated guilt, some British abolitionists preferred to keep black people at a distance' (Nowatzki 2010, 56). On the other hand, this passage also echoes concerns about social issues in Britain; as Nowatzki has again noted, 'skepticism toward abolitionism was not [necessarily] based on racist or proslavery sentiments but on disapproval of abolitionism's indifference toward the suffering of the British poor' (65)—a subject that would soon become a central preoccupation of late Victorians, publications such as William Booth's *In Darkest England and the Way Out* (1890) bringing the attention on the inequalities of British society while establishing an overt connection between poor and 'savage'.

All this is not to diminish or dismiss the profound racism of the passage quoted above, as *Those Dear Blacks!* is genuinely painful reading for the reader of today; at all levels the black character (by the already meaningful first name of Adonis, which clearly mocks his 'horrid' appearance and of course evokes another supposed oxymoron: that of the 'Hottentot Venus' displayed forty years before) is presented as stolid, hopeless, repulsive and childishly optimist—his accent and malapropism strategically highlighting the ridicule of the character. When, at the end of Act 1, Featheredge agrees to being a servant to the richer (liberated slave) Lillywhite, but tricks him into calling him 'sir';[14] or when in Act 2, misunderstanding Amelia's intentions and believing she has agreed to marry him (and not Featheredge), Lillywhite repeatedly dances 'wildly' (Brough 1852a, 39 and 43), the caricature is aggressive to the point of being indigestible.

My point is rather that Brough's farce sits, as other performances that satirize *UTC*, on the edge between providing a stereotype of blackness as a condition that can never be equal to being white, and showcasing this as the product of a theatrical *convention*. Amelia's lingering on the images of the chains and the whip as conducive of an eroticized ideal of slave evokes not the 'minstrelised' black, but rather the ubiquitous abolitionist image of the supplicant slave, establishing an evident, if indirect, twofold comparison with Stowe's novel. On the one side, just as Topsy is loved by Eva *because* she has no family, no education and no hope, Lillywhite can only be loved by Amelia as a *dispossessed* slave that she knows not from first-hand experience, but rather from literature; he otherwise loses whatever appeal he may have as he steps in flesh, free and rich (before discovering he hasn't inherited a fortune after all), into Amelia's 'real' life. On the other, when she withdraws her hand, shivering away from Lillywhite's touch, Amelia clearly recalls Ophelia, who, as she herself admits in *UTC*, cannot bear to have Topsy touch her (Stowe 1852, 207). It is in their juxtaposition—and in the absence of an equivalent of Eva to complement Amelia's ideals with some sincere sympathy for the black—that Amelia and Lillywhite become specular stock characters: as she is the image of a 'typical' hypocrite abolitionist, Lillywhite cannot but be a projection of the stereotype of a slave. If *Those Dear Blacks!* therefore speaks to all-British, national concerns while providing a particularly vicious portrait of the 'minstrelised' black, it is also a text, I suggest, that by framing its stereotypes within an openly farcical context puts audiences, unlike adaptations of *UTC*, in a potentially more active and problematic position.

This is also the case with Frederick Neale's pantomime *Harlequin Uncle Tom* (Effingham Saloon, 27 December 1852), another of the several performances in the non-organic and non-homogenous 'repertoire' (Bernstein 2011, 13) generated by *UTC*. In Neale's piece Stowe's novel appears as an accumulation of disparate references and jokes. Legree is a Demon of Slavery attending to the chorus of demons, while the chorus of fairies is led by Fairy Beecher Stowe; *UTC* is again an object to be incorporated, mentioned as it is in the Fairy's lines (4); 'Great Britannia's just laws' are advocated for America (ibid.), and when the former is revealed on a throne there is also 'a slave in chains kneeling to her' (5). Linguistically speaking, the pattern is the usual juxtaposition between the SE spoken by the character Eliza, and the 'dialect' of Tom and Chloe, who are seen mainly discussing food and their master's generosity. In the final transformation scene, George and Eliza turn into Harlequin and Columbine, while Legree into Pantaloon.

The seemingly random use of elements from other artistic practices or genres was usual for a pantomime; one that had been staged two years before the publication of *UTC*, *Harlequin Alfred the Great; or, the Magic Banjo and the Mystic Raven* (Marylebone Theatre Royal, 26 December 1850) similarly included references to the minstrel show that also play on the image of the supplicant slave. The Ethiopians Serenaders are mentioned as a possible travesty for Alfred the Great, and in the first scene of the performance 'a little Nigger, in a kneeling attitude, rises through the Stage, holding a banjo' (10); in scene 4, Alfred plays the banjo himself, while two other characters play a large Concertina and the 'Inimitable Bones'; they also all sing 'Zip Coon', while wearing 'a black dress coat, with enormously long tails, white wristbands a good way up their arms, high white collars, black masks down to the mouth, and woolly skull caps' (19). In both cases, Neale's pantomime and *Harlequin Alfred the Great*, the absorption of external elements that are then re-arranged in metatheatrical fashion enhances the detachment of audiences, who are made potentially more aware of the mechanisms of representation and therefore, I suggest, of the *fictionality* of what is presented to them on stage.

If the freedom with which elements from the minstrel show and *UTC* are handled in mid-Victorian theatre may suggest that audiences had, by this point, accepted and internalized a certain stereotype of blackness—so that its ubiquitousness merely reflects its '*normality*'—I posit that the de-contextualisation of Uncle-Tom images later in the century implied their progressive shift from meaningful signifiers of racial difference to shells emptied of their initial relevance. An extravaganza such as J.C. Burnand's *L'Africaine or the Queen of the Cannibal Islands* (Strand, November 1865), in which the protagonist Selika speaks 'dialect' and to the accusation of being an 'outrageous heathen' answers in the negative as she is of 'the original minstrels, Christy'uns' (11);[15] or the already mentioned use of Uncle-Tom placards in Greenwood's pantomime, testify to the impoverishment and estrangement of these images. If, as Nowatzki has written, '[t]he concurrent rise of abolitionism and minstrelsy produced innumerable representations of black people' (2010, 1) that shared a 'fascination with [...] black bodies' (3), the *displacement* of these bodies from their original context meant that they could, on stage, be conveniently used as cheap and immediate ways to elicit certain responses from the audience. In their proliferation they contributed to the survival of 'minstrelised' black images well after the demise of the minstrel show—on the condition, however, of these becoming progressively incongruous.

4   LATER REPRESENTATIONS OF BLACKNESS: THE 'MINSTRELISED' FRIDAY

As Marty Gould has illustrated in his *Nineteenth-Century Theatre and the Imperial Encounter* (2011), the theatrical Robinsonade, which interests us here as another vehicle for the 'minstrelised' black on the late Victorian stage, changed considerably throughout the century, following shifts in mood and political atmosphere. In Pocock's *Robinson Crusoe, or the Bold Buccaniers, a Romantic Drama* (Covent Garden, Easter Monday, 1817) Friday's role as voice of Crusoe and intermediary with the island's native gives the audience 'an opportunity to applaud the assimilability of non-European peoples' and as such the play 'recasts Crusoe's colonial adventure as one of cross-cultural contact rather than of self-sufficiency' (Gould 2011, 56). However, since later in the century the approach to other 'races' becomes, as already noted, increasingly intolerant and aggressive, moving from 'sympathy to suspicion' (66), so does the representation of 'savages'—Friday in the case of *Robinson Crusoe* (from now on *RC*)—as narratives adopt the militaristic overtones of the imperialist mission. In this light, Crusoe is 'replaced by an imperialist adventurer who has no time to construct or to expand his settlement. Having shed his colonizing impulses, Crusoe begins to take less interest in cultural reform and instead uses his time on the island to subdue a hostile native force and establish British political hegemony over the territory' (ibid.). The transformation of Friday into a 'minstrelised' figure is part of this shift.

In his novel, Defoe already makes use of 'dialect', which, as Dillard has noted, was part of a wider eighteenth-century employment of 'pidgin English' to denote an association between black characters and the Transatlantic Slave Trade (1972, 21). In an early nineteenth-century drama like Pocock's, however, voice does not play a paramount role; while Friday speaks 'dialect' ('Massa! See da!', 1817, 20), he is only given a handful of lines, while the other main non-white character in the play, Pariboo or the Chief of the Cannibal Tribe, does not speak at all. Their 'otherness' is rather conveyed through appearance. Friday must feature '[b]lack body, arms, and leggings—a coarse stuff twisted about the upper part of the thighs and part of the body—short black curly wig'

(p. 9): he must, in short, resemble an 'African' black; Pariboo, on the other hand, is aligned to a Native American: he has '[d]ark red, brown, or copper-colour body, arms, leggings, &c.—[…] short petticoat, made of coloured matting—[…] twisted rows of beads round the arms, ankles, neck, and across the breast—black hair tied up very high in a top-knot, ornamented with beads and feathers—ear-rings of coloured beads—a tomahawk' (ibid.). While this opposition remains a constant of the stage *RC*—a pantomine like Henry Byron's *Robinson Crusoe or Harlequin Friday* (Princess's, 26 December 1860) also featuring alongside Friday, '*a very enlightened Negro, not to say a* lamp black', Hokee Pokee and Wanky Fum, two '*Vagabond Indians, all rage and tattoos*' (3)—the distance between Friday and Pariboo is articulated not in terms of the specific 'types' they represent, but rather in terms of their relation to the white master: Friday is presented as a faithful 'noble savage', not the exaggerated buffoon of later tradition, while the threat posed by Pariboo, who stays silent, remains abstract and unspecified. Similarly, in Pelham Thompson's melodrama *Jack Robinson and His Monkey* (Surrey, 20 August 1829) it is the relation and potential collaboration between Jack Robinson, a shipwrecked sailor, and his servant Muley, that is of interest, not their juxtaposition as representative of different 'races'; the two are shown in proximity as they conduct their life on an island in 'the Indian Sea' (3), and while Muley is in 'Negro dress' (2), he speaks SE.

In later examples, on the other hand, the infiltration of the minstrel show and the racialisation of Friday are made evident by the combination of 'dialect' as the *usual* feature for darker-skinned characters in combination with references to either blackface minstrelsy or *UTC*. In Henry Byron's burlesque *Robinson Crusoe* (Haymarket, 5 July 1867), for instance, a 'dialect'-speaking Friday thus cheerfully challenges his interlocutors:

Fri:	Who am I? Ha ha! That's a good'un that is.
Bones:	'P'raps Uncle Tom?
Cymbals:	Or Mr Calhaems Jacky.
Fri:	Or Mr Christy!
King:	Or Professor Blackie.
Fri:	Bah! Pooh! I'm Friday to spare your laughter Now guess! Ha ha! What Friday am come after? (6–7)

In James Willing's pantomime *Harlequin Robinson Crusoe and His Man Friday* (Standard 1874), Friday is made to appear, for the sake of comparison, alongside several other non-white characters: an Indian, a 'Thursday Night', and Okikeraboo, all of whom speak 'dialect' to utter basic sentences about their condition that have also become, at this stage, conventional ('Fri: Poor little nigger—De bad man beat me—and tear off my hair', 10). In John Francis Macardle and Frank W. Green's pantomime *Robinson Crusoe or Friday and His Funny Family*, this time at the Alexandra Theatre Liverpool (1878–1879), the grotesque and funny Friday is again accompanied by other equally alienated figures, as the list of characters features amongst others King Okojumbo, 'Monarch of the misty crinstel group [...] with a devouring passion for Missionaries. Friday, not by any means as black as he is painted—in short, a "good" Friday. His brothers Simple Saturday, who comes after Friday, and Black Monday, who follows close upon his brother'. Scene 4 of the text also jokes on the connection with the minstrel show:

Crusoe: What can you do?
Friday: Well, I can play de bones!
            And tambourine!
Crusoe: The startling fact he owns!
            The Christy's out of London *do* perform
            Sometimes, though here for their work it's too warm. (17)

Parallel to the proliferation of 'minstrelised' images in theatrical adaptations of *RC* is, it is worth noting, also the derivation and borrowing of visual elements and thematic concerns from other pantomimes, farces or extravaganzas; as Gould has noted, '[l]ater Robinsonades would look not to the novel but to earlier stage adaptations for inspiration and direction. What we see in the development of the genre is successive adaptations of an adaptation, a sequence of replication and revision that would ultimately yield a theatrical Robinsonade markedly different from its narrative source' (2011, 60). Late Victorian theatre generally shows this profound hybridisation, incorporating political and cultural notions as the century progressed while displaying a seemingly random absorption of elements from other traditions. This is the case, ultimately, also with *UTC* adaptations; as Riis has observed in his introduction to a 1994 edition of Aiken's drama,

> [t]he remarkably long life of *Uncle Tom's Cabin* on the stage was such that even in the 1890's, long after emancipation had been achieved, so-called Tom shows held the field against contemporary plays, in elaborately metamorphosed versions that challenged circuses and extravaganzas in their sumptuousness. Black jubilee choruses, wild animals, drill teams, and pugilists were employed to supplement the story. (xiii)

5   Conclusion

How should all these elements resonate with audiences it is not possible to know with any certainty; but it is not too absurd to imagine that the stratification of de-contextualized and sometimes contradictory elements should affect the fruition of these performances, as the displacement and incongruous arrangement of elements may have made audiences more aware of the fictionality of what was presented on stage. In short, the alienation of images such as those related to the minstrel show and the Uncle Tom tradition when framed in these multi-layered performances may have revealed them for what they were: theatrical conventions. This does not imply, however, that these should necessarily have been any less impactful in their racist potential; if not in their quality, certainly the *quantity* and variety of images surrounding blackness—from the subjected black slave and the equal-but-not-so-equal mulatto character to the ferocious African enemy—that assiduously bombarded audiences from all kind of stages must have affected their understandings of the 'African' and 'African-American' Other. Ultimately, all these images were, in their sum, *consistently* derogative.

Their nuances and differences, however, are worth noting, as later in the century a gap between images of blackness related to the 'American' slave trope and those referring to the 'African' stereotype came in place that meant that different associations and justifications for the British Empire's racist stances were suggested. Given that these overlapping images of blackness, each in their own trajectory, have substantially contributed to the derogative perception of black people and cultures that is still so much with us today, to understand the subtle differences through which racism could be articulated on the Victorian stage is, really, quite the minimum one can do.

NOTES

1. *Uncle Tom's Cabin; or, The Negro Slave* (The Standard, 8 September), *Uncle Tom's Cabin; or, the Fugitive Slave!* (The Victoria, 15 September), Edward Fitzball's *Uncle Tom's Cabin* (Royal Olympic Theatre, 20 September—then performed at Drury Lane in December), George Dibdin Pitt's *Uncle Tom's Cabin: A Nigger Drama* (Pavilion, 9 October), Richard Shepherd and William Creswick's *Uncle Tom's Cabin* (Royal Surrey Theatre, 27 October), T. H. Young's equestrian version of *Uncle Tom's Cabin* (Astley's, 22 November), and Mark Lemon and Tom Taylor's *Slave Life; or, Uncle Tom's Cabin* (Adelphi, 29 November).
2. These include William Brough's farces *Uncle Tom's Crib* (Strand, 14 October 1852) and *Those Dear Blacks!* (Lyceum, 19 November), Frederick Neale's pantomime *Harlequin Uncle Tom* (Effingham Saloon, 27 December), and T.L. Greenwood's pantomime *Dick Whittington and His Cat; or, Old Dame Fortune and Harlequin Lord Mayor of London* (Sadler's Wells, 27 December).
3. No pages are available for these manuscripts. *Uncle Tom's Crib* also includes amongst his characters a Mr Caesar Augustus Squashtop, 'a crossing sweeper and lecturer upon the rights of man and the wrongs of Africans', and others that hint to the Jim Crow tradition: Dandy Jim, Ginger Crow and Dark Ive ('Ethiopian serenaders'), and Dinah (Uncle Tom's daughter).
4. Waters has on the contrary stated that '[t]he craze for Uncle Tom, though intense, was much more short-lived than that for Jim Crow' (Waters 2001, 46–47).
5. See the founding of the Ethnological Society of London in 1843, the publication of Robert Knox's *The Races of Men* (1850) and James Hunt's 'The Negro's Place in Nature' (1863), and the setting up of the Anthropological Society of London (1863–1871), which signalled a rejection of the less virulent, monogenist opinions of the ESL and coincided mostly with Hunt's career (until he

died in 1869). The ASL would have merged with the ESL to become, in 1871, the Royal Anthropological Institute of Great Britain and Ireland.

6. However, this material mainly consisted of 'derogatory broadsides and snide newspaper articles' (Lewis 2016, 57), the racist spirit of which Mathews's impersonations may have absorbed.

7. For a discussion of AAVE and its usage and implications in the contemporary American context, see also John Baugh's *Beyond Ebonics: Linguistic Pride and Racial Prejudice* (2000).

8. I extend to later theatre a point that Davis makes in specific regard to Charles Mathews, who in his fast-paced shows 'must have indicated each character verbally (and possibly physically), but a change in makeup was impractical and a change of costume unwarranted. By this point, purely as an impersonator, without accoutrements, he had established conventions that indicated to his audience the contrast between characters' races. Through voice, syntax and pronunciation ("dialect"), and demeanor, he marked the distinctions' amongst the many different 'American' figures he brought to audiences (2011, 170).

9. A similar fate has *Robinson Crusoe*, which in William T. Moncrieff's *The Cataract of the Ganges* (1823), for instance, becomes a prop, as the protagonist Jack Robinson 'carries the novel from one scene to the next and gives the text voice by reading from it aloud' (Gould 2011, 38).

10. 'By the time black actors performed onstage during the 1850s and 1860s, minstrel audiences were used to the notion of counterfeit and rarely assumed that minstrel performers were black unless they were advertised as such' (Nowatzki 2010, 38), since 'the lack of makeup [in black performers] suggested that their performances of blackness were not constructed but real, and that, conversely, makeup signified counterfeit' (ibid.).

11. The minstrel show would later become 'more family-friendly and less proletarian, […] offer[ing] fewer opportunities for identification between white viewers and blackface characters' (Nowatzki 2010, 64).

12. To best appreciate the relevance of these innovations, it is worth keeping in mind the three main subplots around which the original story of *Uncle Tom's Cabin* revolves: the story of Tom and the St Clares, introducing Eva, Miss Ophelia and Topsy, and eventually Legree to the reader; the story of George, Eliza and Harry's escape to Canada, and their encounter with Tom Locker and the Quakers; and the story of Emmeline and Cassy. As noted in the novel, '[t]he separate incidents that compose the narrative are, to a very great extent, authentic, occurring, many of them, either under her own [Stowe's] observation, or that of her personal friends' ('Closing Remarks', *UTC*, ch. XLV); these separate incidents also had the function of illustrating the different aspects of the slavery problem and debate.

13. Clothes are another indicator of status, the 'whiteness' of Eliza and George being similarly conveyed by more refined attire (Thomas 2004, 50).
    Lilly: You's my serbant den. What your name?
    Fea: (*impressively*) Sir! –
    Lilly: What a funny name! Den I call you Sir, when I want you.
    Fea: Exactly! (…). (Brough 1852, 18)

14. Another piece of the same year, Arbuthnot's *L'Africaine or the Belle of Madagascar*, presents Selika as 'an Oriental Princess' who speaks SE.

15. See note 9.

References

Primary Sources

Aiken, George L. 1994/1852. *Uncle Tom's Cabin: or, Life Among the Lowly: A Domestic Drama in Six Acts*. London: Garland Publishing Inc. [Samuel French].

Arbuthnot, Captain. 1865. *L'Africaine or the Belle of Madagascar*. London: Thomas Hailes Lacy.

Brough, William. 1852a. *Those Dear Blacks! Farce in Two Acts*. British Library Western Manuscripts: Add. MS. 52936 C.

———. 1852b. *Uncle Tom's Crib, or, The Nigger Life in London: Dramatic Sketch in One Act*. British Library Western Manuscripts: Add. MS. 52935 J.

Burnand, F. C. 1865. *L'Africaine, or, The Queen of the Cannibal Islands: Extravaganza*. British Library Western Manuscripts: Add. MS. 53046 I.

Byron, Henry J. 1860. *Robinson Crusoe or Harlequin Friday and the King of the Caribbee Islands! A Grotesque Pantomime Opening*. London: Thomas Hailes Lacy.

———. 1867. *Robinson Crusoe: Burlesque*. British Library Western Manuscripts: Add. MS. 53060 J.

Greenwood, T. L. 1852. *Dick Whittington and His Cat, or, Old Dame Fortune and Harlequin Lord Mayor of London: Pantomime*. British Library Western Manuscripts: Add. MS. 52936 X.

Harlequin Alfred the Great; or, the Magic Banjo and the Mystic Raven. 1850. London: Thomas Hailes Lacy.

Lemon, Mark, and Tom Taylor. 1852. *Slave Life; or, Uncle Tom's Cabin: Drama in Three Acts*. British Library Western Manuscripts: Add. MS. 52936 A.

Macardle, John Francis, and Frank W. Green. 1878. *Robinson Crusoe or Friday and His Funny Family: Grand Comic Christmas Pantomime*. Liverpool: Daily Post & Journal Offices.

Pocock, I. 1817. *Robinson Crusoe, or the Bold Buccaniers: A Romantic Drama*. London: John Cumberland.

Stowe, Harriet Beecher. 1852. *Uncle Tom's Cabin or Negro Life in the Slave States of America*. London: George Routledge.

Thompson, Pelham. 1829. *Jack Robinson and His Monkey: A Melodrama in Two Acts*. London: Thomas Hailes Lacy.

Willing, James. 1874. *Harlequin Robinson Crusoe and His Man Friday*. British Library Western Manuscripts: Add. MS. 53144 I.

Secondary Literature

Baldwin, James. 2007/1948. Everybody's Protest Novel. In *Harriet Beecher Stowe's Uncle Tom's Cabin: A Casebook*, ed. Elizabeth Ammons, 49–55. Oxford: Oxford University Press.

Bernstein, Rubin. 2011. *Racial Difference: Performing American Childhood from Slavery to Civil Rights*. London: New York University Press.

Bolt, Christine. 1971. *Victorian Attitudes to Race*. London: Routledge and Kegan Paul.

Bratton, J.S. 1981. English Ethiopians: British Audiences and Black-Face Acts, 1835–1865. *The Yearbook of English Studies* 11 (II): 127–142.

Caledonian Mercury. 1852. December 2: 1.

Curtin, Philip de Armond. 1965. *The Image of Africa: British Ideas and Action, 1780–1850*. London: Macmillan & Co.

Davis, Tracy. 2011. Acting Black, 1824: Charles Mathews's *Trip to America*. *Theatre Journal* 63 (2): 163–189.

———. 2013. 'I Long for My Home in Kentuck': Christy's Minstrels in Mid-19th-Century Britain. *TDR* 57 (2): 38–65.

Dillard, J. L. 1972. *Black English: Its History and Usage in the United States*. New York: Random House.

Disher, Maurice. 1954. *Melodrama: Plots That Thrilled*. London: Rockliff.

Frick, John W. 2012. *Uncle Tom's Cabin on the American Stage and Screen*. New York: Palgrave Macmillan.

Goodall, Jane R. 2002. *Performance and Evolution in the Age of Darwin: Out of the Natural Order*. New York: Routledge.

Gould, Marty. 2011. *Nineteenth-Century Theatre and the Imperial Encounter*. London: Routledge.

Grimsted, David. 1970. *Uncle Tom* from Page to Stage: Limitations of Nineteenth Century Drama. *The Quarterly Journal of Speech* LVI (3): 235–244.

Holmberg, Carl Bryan, and Gilbert D. Schneider. 1986. Daniel Decatur Emmett's Stump Sermons: Genuine Afro-American Culture, Language and Rhetoric in the Negro Minstrel Show. *The Journal of Popular Culture* 19 (4): 27–38.

Howard Macdonald, Cordelia, and George P. Howard. 1956. Memoirs of the Original Little Eva. *Educational Theatre Journal* 8 (4): 267–282.

Johnson, Stephen. 1999. Uncle Tom and the Minstrels: Seeing Black and White on Stage in Canada West Prior to the American Civil War. In *(Post)colonial Stages: Critical & Creative Views on Drama, Theatre & Performance*, ed. Helen Gilbert, 55–63. Dangaroo: Hebden Bridge.

Labov, W. 1977. *Language in the Inner City: Studies in the Black English Vernacular*. Philadelphia: University of Pennsylvania Press.

Lewis, Robert Michael. 2016. Speaking Black, 1824:Charles Mathews's Trip to America Revisited. *Nineteenth Century Theatre and Film* 43 (1): 43–66.

Lloyd's Weekly Newspaper. 1852. December 5: 9.

Lorimer, Douglas A. 1978. *Colour, Class and the Victorians: English Attitudes to the Negro in the Mid-nineteenth Century*. Leicester: LeicesterUniversity Press.

Meer, Sarah. 2005. *Uncle Tom Mania: Slavery, Minstrelsy, and Transatlantic Culture in the 1850s*. Athens, GA: University of Georgia Press.

———. 2007. Topsy and the End Man. In *Harriet Beecher Stowe's Uncle Tom's Cabin: A Casebook*, ed. Elizabeth Ammons, 131–166. Oxford: Oxford University Press.

Morosetti, Tiziana. 2016. Constructing the Zulus: The 'African' Body and Its Narrative. In *Staging the Other in Nineteenth-Century British Drama*, ed. Tiziana Morosetti, 79–101. Oxford: Peter Lang.

Nowatzki, Robert. 2010. *Representing African Americans in Transatlantic Abolitionism and Blackface Minstrelsy*. Baton Rouge: Louisiana State University Press.

Parson, Neil. 2003. 'No Longer Rare Birds in London': Zulu, Ndebele, Gaza and Swazi Envoys to England, 1882–1894. In *Black Victorians/Black Victoriana*, ed. Gretchen Holbrook Gerzina, 110–141. New Brunswick; London: Rutgers University Press.

Pickering, Michael. 2008. *Blackface Minstrelsy in Britain*. Aldershot: Ashgate.

Reid, Mandy. 2008. Racial Profiling: Visualizing Racial Science on the Covers of Uncle Tom's Cabin, 1852–1928. *Nineteenth-Century Contexts* 30 (4): 369–387.

Rickford, John Russell, and Russell John Rickford. 2000. *Spoken Soul: The Story of Black English*. Chichester: John Wiley & Sons.

Riis, Thomas. 1994/1852. Introduction. In George L. Aiken, *Uncle Tom's Cabin: Or, Life among the Lowly: A Domestic drama in Six Acts*, xiii–xx. London: Garland Publishing Inc. [Samuel French].

Thomas, Julia. 2004. *Pictorial Victorians: The Inscription of Values in Word and Image*. Athens, GA: Ohio University Press.

Waters, Hazel. 2001. Putting on "Uncle Tom" on the Victorian Stage. *Race & Class* 42 (3): 29–48.

———. 2007. *Racism on the Victorian Stage: Representation of Slavery and the Black Character*. Cambridge: Cambridge University Press.

Wells Journal. 1852. November 27.

CHAPTER 21

Susan Glaspell's *Trifles* and *Inheritors*: White Settler Hunger, Debt and the Blackhawk Purchase Lands

Selena Couture

1 Introduction

In August 2018, I attended an academic conference event that staged scenes from Susan Glaspell's 1921 play, *Inheritors* in Boston. It was part of an opening session hosted by History Matters/Back to the Future, an organisation that promotes the study and production of plays by women-identifying playwrights prior to 1965 ('2018 ATHE Kickoff'). As a theatre historian who engages with performance, Indigenous lands, languages and constructions of whiteness, I was excited to see a staged reading of scenes from this work and I appreciated the organisation's efforts to bring it to wider attention. I was particularly interested to see how they might frame this work, specifically the first act, which has a white settler declare his conscientious objection to owning Indigenous land as his motivation to give a portion of it to found a college. Much to my surprise, this section of the play wasn't mentioned in the programme notes, nor was it staged. Instead, the organizers chose to focus on heroism of the young white settler woman who protests the abuse and exclusion of Hindu students

---

I express my thanks to the editors of this volume and to Bethany Hughes for feedback that helped me articulate more specifically the methodological concepts put forward in this chapter.

S. Couture (✉)
University of Alberta, Edmonton, AB, Canada
e-mail: couture2@ualberta.ca

© The Author(s), under exclusive license to Springer Nature Switzerland AG 2021
T. Morosetti, O. Okagbue (eds.), *The Palgrave Handbook of Theatre and Race*, https://doi.org/10.1007/978-3-030-43957-6_21

391

from the college her grandfather founded. While the engagement with anti-immigrant sentiments against racialized peoples was timely, the overlooking of the first act of the play, was once again an assumption of the 'always already' presence of settler coloniality.[1] This, alongside a conference-related excursion to the Boston Tea Party museum where I was handed a feather upon entering so that I could reenact the settlers 'playing Indian' (Deloria 1999, 185–187) as they tossed the tea overboard, reminded me once again of a particular blind spot in US exceptionalist rhetoric of revolutionary ideals. From my perspective as a western inhabitant and an 11th generation descendent of French settlers in the land currently known as Canada, these choices seemed oblivious to the history of violence against Indigenous people as well as the extractive relation to their land and resources that the USA has been built on. It also emphasized the continuing importance of attending to intersectionality when engaging in feminist analysis and performance.

In this chapter, I aim to intervene in the understandings of white settlers and non-Indigenous newcomers to the Americas who work with Susan Glaspell's oeuvre as part of the modernist movement in US theatre, and in particular, rectify the analysis that doesn't take up the necessary understandings of gendered violence in relation to Indigenous land theft. I argue that in addition to reading *Trifles* (1916) through a gendered analysis, attending to its Midwest setting nearby Glaspell's family home which was part of the Black Hawk Purchase and reading it in relation to *Inheritors* reveals a considerable underlying white settler hunger that can be related to ideas of whiteness as constructed through possession articulated by Indigenous scholar Aileen Moreton-Robinson (Quandamooka). As this chapter is part of a collection on theatre and race, I'd like to emphasize here that I am not discussing Indigeneity as a racialized construct in Glaspell's theatre. Instead, I am deploying methodologies from Critical Indigenous studies that take up critical race analyses to identify and deconstruct the racialized category of whiteness. These methods include grounding Glaspell's work in the Indigenous lands where she grew up and where she set both these plays, while also situating my theoretical frame in the Indigenous epistemologies from lands and waters I have lived on for decades. These are not new methods for Critical Indigenous studies, but they have not been applied to the study of Modernist drama in the USA. Glaspell is an ideal artist with whom to engage because, as this chapter will demonstrate, she herself was ambivalent and even critical at times of settler colonial project and was very aware of the precarity of it.

In the following pages I give a basic introduction of Susan Glaspell and how she was influenced by the mythologized figure of Black Hawk (actually Makataimeshekiakiak) in order to contextualize the reference to the Sauk leader in her play *Inheritors*. And, as white settler history is necessarily built on ignorance of Indigenous lives and land, it is also necessary to include (for the benefit of non-Indigenous readers) the story of the Sauk and Fox people's struggle for their land which was eventually sold to Glaspell's settler family. For those who may not be familiar with the two plays I'm discussing, I then give a brief overview of them and the recent analysis of them in Glaspell scholarship.

As an intervention into this scholarship, I expand on Una Chaudhuri's useful concept of 'geopathology' which foregrounds troubled (and at times gendered) theatrical depictions of relations to home or location and has fruitfully been used to analyse Glaspell's work. I look to Critical Indigenous Studies theory for a critique of the assumption of white possession of Indigenous lands to further set up an understanding of the precarity of white settler efforts as depicted in Glaspell's best known work, *Trifles*. Overall, in addition to expanding scholarship on Glaspell, this chapter aims to demonstrate a methodological intervention in reading settler colonial theatrical works using specifically situated Indigenous epistemologies as a lens to read works from elsewhere. This methodology, briefly stated, takes up a practice of situating—the artist, the aesthetic expression and the analyst engaged with these—in relation to Indigenous lands, waters and epistemologies.

2   SUSAN GLASPELL, BLACK HAWK AND MAKATAIMESHEKIAKIAK

Susan Glaspell (1876–1948) was a novelist, playwright, actor and co-founder of the influential Provincetown Players in 1916. She worked closely with Eugene O'Neill early in his career, and won the Pulitzer Prize for Drama in 1931 for *Alison's House*. Despite her influence and success during her lifetime, much of her work was ignored after her death until feminist critics revived it in the 1970s. The discourse on Glaspell's work is extensive and grows each year. Recent works including Linda Ben-Zvi's biography *Susan Glaspell: Her Life and Times* (2005), Noelia Hernando-Real's *Self and Space in the Theater of Susan Glaspell* (2011) and Emiline Jouve's *Susan Glaspell's Poetics and Politics of Rebellion* (2017) each engage to some extent with the significance of geography and land in Glaspell's works. Ben-Zvi discusses the importance of the pioneer women stories that Glaspell grew up on—which emphasize hard work, humour, courage, and the need for community. The precarious nature of that life is illustrated by Glaspell's story of the women in her grandmother's time who left a light on in their cabins at night—even though it exposed them to attacks by Indigenous people—so passing settlers might know they were welcome to stop for food or rest (2005, 6). Ben-Zvi also notes that Glaspell grew up listening to stories about Black Hawk (a Sauk leader)—who with Fox (Meskwaki) peoples held the land that comprises much of Iowa, Illinois and Wisconsin. Black Hawk was seen as exotic and regal when he was paraded through cities of the East after the defeat of 1832. Iowa settlers who had personal contact with him, described him as more fair-minded and brave than the federal government that won the land (although they benefitted from that victory). Ben-Zvi connects this to Glaspell's writing (particularly *Inheritors*) and her use of Black Hawk as 'not only a symbol of white injustice done to Indians but the standard against which subsequent generations must measure themselves' (2005, 7).

The US nationalist rhetoric about the figure known as Black Hawk that began in the early nineteenth century and continues to this day is very relevant to an understanding of Glaspell's works. Makataimeshekiakiak, an important leader of the Sauk people, has become immortalized as Black Hawk—and his name and image proliferate throughout the Midwest.[2] He is discussed as the leader of the last Indian War east of the Mississippi. The actual story, as Roxanne Dunbar-Ortiz explains in *An Indigenous History of the United States* (2014), is less a war than a massacre. When Makataimeshekiakiak led his people back to their homeland in 1832 the 'squatter settlers there claimed they were being invaded, bringing in both Illinois militia and federal troops. The "Black Hawk War" that is narrated in history texts was no more than a slaughter to Sauk farmers' (2015, 111–112). It ended with the Bad Axe Massacre on August 1–2, 1832, when Makataimeshekiakiak led the exhausted remnants of a band of Sauk people into the Mississippi River in a desperate effort to get back to Iowa after months of running from government forces. US soldiers fired on them from a steamboat and the riverbanks—killing hundreds of men, women and children. Soldiers took pieces of flesh as souvenirs. Makataimeshekiakiak escaped but surrendered to the army days later and became a prisoner of war who was then toured around on display throughout 1833 (Brown and Kanouse 2015, 2).

Elizabeth Maddock Dillon discusses this tour in *New World Drama: The Performative Commons in the Atlantic World, 1649–1849* (2014) in the context of Jacksonian-era necessity of creating white national US subject through performative embodying of Indigenous and black people. Makataimeshekiakiak was taken to the theatre in Baltimore, Philadelphia and New York where crowds came to see him. His tour was right after that of President Andrew Jackson (the architect of Indian removal) and in Baltimore they attended the same theatre on the same night. In Philadelphia he saw a Jim Crow performance,[3] and according to news reports paid no attention to the stage, sleeping through it, until the applause after the song Jim Crow woke him up, and he had to listen to four repetitions of it, when he cried out '"Peecabogo agankitchigamink pilcailazo"—when these barbarians come to visit me I shall treat them to a concert of wild cats' (Dillon 2014, 239–240). This extended performative display of a captured leader and prisoner of war undoubtedly fuelled the idea of Black Hawk that was passed on to Susan Glaspell who grew up on the Midwest land that her settler grandfather acquired through the 'Black Hawk Purchase'.[4]

3   TRIFLES AND INHERITORS

Emiline Jouve asserts the setting of *Trifles* in Glaspell's Midwest functions as a 'metaphor for isolation, alienation and disengagement', critiquing narrow-minded gender relations there and how they make the space of the house into a prison (2017, 36). She connects the 'geographical marginal position' with places of 'otherness' or as Foucault's heterotopia 'other places—outside of all places' and located in reality and 'something like counter-sites, a kind of effectively enacted utopia in which real sites—all real sites that can be found within the culture—are simultaneously represented, contested and inverted' (Foucault in Jouve 2017, 37). While most scholars of the theatre have been interested in the symbolic nature of the deployment of space/land on the stage, I am interested here in what can be understood about the construction of US whiteness by keeping attention on 'locating in the real'. Jouve also focuses on *Trifles* as a feminist classic (2017, 169) that demonstrates female solidarity through the metaphors of sewing and quilting enacted in the play as a form of resistance against patriarchal order (2017, 172). She attends to the final line which emphasizes 'knotting the quilt' and how it is both a homonym for 'not' and the knot of the rope that killed the husband (2017, 176). Jouve discusses *Inheritors* in relation to 'the reassessment of the measures taken by the government to compensate for the Indians' loss of their lands' as daring on Glaspell's part who could have faced charges of antinationalism under federal legislation at the time (2017, 87). She suggests Glaspell read Black Hawk's biography (first published in 1833), which asserts the Sauk and Meskwaki didn't receive any money for their land. She notes that this is represented differently in the play—Granny Morton says the Sauk received some money but not enough—and wonders if this was a way of getting past anti-American censorship that was circulating with the Lusk Committee (2017, 88). There are no Indigenous characters in the play and Jouve states that they are only 'alive through the white settlers who speak of them … literalizing the metaphor of social invisibility' (2017, 88). She discusses the founding of the college by the Morton family, but doesn't mention Silas's need to give the land back instead emphasizing that he founded the college for the 'aspiration to richer living' and freedom—quotes a section in which Silas declares planning a college on the hill is 'why we took this land!' (2017, 108). She also says that 'By ceding his land to the community and founding a college to "cultivate" minds, Silas keeps the Indian spirit alive' (2017, 109). There is a dark irony of imagining education as a liberatory action in relation to Indigenous people—in the context of boarding schools, assimilation and the harms done to Indigenous people through the dis-information passed on in settler colonial curriculums. The radical and possibly anti-nationalist nature of this work was recognized by Glaspell during her lifetime, as Jouve notes that she requested that it be removed from the repertoire of Hedgerow Theatre[5] during the second world war saying it was written for a different time and worried it would be seen as anti-war propaganda (2017, 118–119). Jouve's work is an extended engagement with both the poetics and politics of Glaspell's rebellious work—however doesn't consider deeply the implications of the precarity of Midwestern settlers who built their lives on Sauk and Meskwaki lands.

4 SPACE, GEOPATHOLOGY AND CONSTRUCTIONS OF WHITENESS

Noelia Hernando-Real's work does take up the significance of space in Glaspell's theatre and deploys Una Chaudhuri's concept of geopatholgy, defined as:

> the configuration of a stage space where place becomes a problem for the characters. Two principles integrate the dramatic discourse of geopathology. The first one is *victimage of location*, a principle that describes place as the protagonist's fundamental problem. This spatial problem leads the characters to acknowledge their need for the second principle which Chaudhuri calls *heroism of departure*. According to this principle, a character gains full independence and fulfills the creation of their own identity by disentangling themselves from the oppressive place they were fixed to. (2011, 18)

'Home' is a core part of the concept—and in the US materialism, there is an endless search to build a house to call home, but also the home leads to a fixity that undermines the myth of mobility (2011, 19). Hernando-Real asserts that the home as a gendered place—one which both restricts the feminine identity and confers it—is related to the common use of the domestic setting in US Realist theatre which aimed to represent 'environmental determinism that explained a character's psychological analysis' (2011, 22–23). This conception of geopathology which focuses on the problem of place is never discussed in specific terms of white settler precarity. Hernando-Real discusses *Inheritors*, which is set across the river from Davenport, Iowa, emphasizing that the Morton family in the play express their shame at owning the land—and acknowledging that the Sauk people's fight for it was reasonable, as Silas Morton says, 'To look out at the hill sometimes makes me feel ashamed' (Glaspell 1921, 111). Later he emphatically states, 'I know now. Why I can't forget the Indians. We killed their joy before we killed them […] I got to give it back—their hill. I give it back to joy—a better joy—joy o'aspiration […] Then maybe I can lie under the same sod with the red boys and not be ashamed' (1921, 118). Hernando-Real concludes that Silas's decision demonstrates he understands owning land is not the most important thing in life and his action is an attempt in 'reconciling with the Native Americans making the world a fairer and better place for everybody' (2011, 127).

While not taken up in Glaspell scholarship, Joanne Tompkins' engagement with Chaudhuri's geopathologies in her 2006 book *Unsettling Space: Contestations in Contemporary Australian Theatre* is useful to my analysis and expansion of land relations in these works. Tompkins comments that while Chaudhuri's *geopathology* characterizes modern Western theatre—Australian geopathology is aware of what is beyond the site of the theatre: 'Representational space performed in Australian theatre not only contests conventional Australian history and culture; it also stages alternative means of managing the production of space in a spatially unstable nation' (Tompkins 5). Unsettlement as she demonstrates through Australian theatrical and monumental works, recognizes the unstable nature of settlement and cultural anxiety about it (Tompkins 6). While the white settler relation to land in the USA is different than that in Australia due to myriad geo-historical specificities, the anxieties of possession of Indigenous lands underlies both societies. As Aileen Moreton-Robinson's *The White Possessive: Property, Power, and Indigenous Sovereignty* (2015) demonstrates, there is nothing more important for white settlers than owning Indigenous lands, indeed one cannot fully be white without this relationship to possession. Moreton-Robinson connects settler colonial nationalism with whiteness—through the various restrictions on non-white immigration that each put into place at key moments of their founding: the Australian Immigration Restriction Act of 1901; the US Naturalization Act of 1790, and ongoing documented preference in Canada and New Zealand for British citizens as immigrants (2015, xii). She takes this as illustrations that 'there are inextricable connections between white possessive logics, race, and the founding of nation-states'—and that this is 'materially and discursively linked' to the 'disavowal of Indigenous *sovereignty*' (2015, xii). She also emphasizes that while this may be hidden from white settler citizens, for Indigenous people 'white possession in not unmarked, unnamed, or invisible; it is hypervisible' (2015, xii). If you consider Indigenous sovereignty and the USA as a former colony that required the possession of Indigenous lands to anchor its capitalist economy, it becomes clear how essential this is to the nation-state. Moreton-Robinson connects her own work to African American scholar Cheryl Harris's theorizing of whiteness as a form of property in law and how 'White property rights were cemented in law through the appropriation of Native American lands and the subsequent enslavement of Africans'. Moreton-Robinson says Harris's work opens up whiteness studies for an Indigenous reading of white property rights and their connection to 'patriarchal white sovereignty in the form of the nation-state' (2015, xix). She defines whiteness as: 'a form of property, whiteness accumulates capital and social appreciation as white people are recognized within the law primarily as property-owning subjects. As such, they are heavily invested in the nation being a white possession' (2015, xix). She also discusses whiteness in relation to the discourses of security—economic, military, cultural protection—and the assumed threat to national security by Indigenous people and asylum seekers. In this way, white possession is tied to anxiety about being dispossessed by racial others (2015, 138). Moreton-Robinson emphasizes the patriarchal white sovereignty as at the core of the white possessive, and this aligns well with Two-Spirit and Queer analyses of the gendered violence embedded in settler colonial nationalism which emphasize even more the necessity for intersectional analysis when engaging in feminist critiques.[6] It makes sense that these would all be entwined in Glaspell's work—and also that this has been obscured or ignored as a critical lens up until this time because of the necessity of oblivion for the continuation of settler colonial subject positions and ongoing violent extraction.

5 A Situated 'Hungry' Reading of *Trifles*

Another part of the critical lens, through which I read these works is rooted in my experiences as an inhabitant of Coast Salish unceded, ancestral and traditional lands on the west coast of Turtle Island (currently known as Vancouver, British Columbia), or in the terms I've been discussing above, my own situated geopathology as an analyst.[7] In deploying this methodology, I am engaged with Donna Haraway's influential 1988 'Situated Knowledges' in which she aims to solve the problem of simultaneously accounting for the contingency of all knowledge claims while also remaining committed to accounts of the 'real' world (579). She suggests that a feminist objectivity 'is about limited location and situated knowledge, not about transcendence and splitting of subject and object. It allows us to become answerable for what we learn how to see' (583). This work has reverberated over greatly over the decades and feminist 'standpoint' theory has particular relevance to analysis of settler colonial feminist theatrical works that are themselves engaged with situatedness. Yet, as Aileen Moreton-Robinson (2013) explains:

> while feminist standpoint theorists acknowledge that all knowledge is socially situated, and therefore partial, they do not address their privileged relationship to the nation's sovereignty that underpins their situadedness and ontology, which enables knowing and the capacity to 'contract.' Canada and the USA colonised Aboriginal and Native American lands and they continue to do so. Feminist standpoint theorists' social location, subjugated knowledges, strong objectivity and socially situatedness of the knowledge are produced within post-colonising national contexts. (335–336)

In response to Moreton-Robinson's assertion, I foreground one of my relations to land and ontology as it has developed on these lands. I do not claim an Indigenous way of knowing for myself, but as Indigenous theorist and social scientist Kim Tallbear (Sisseton-Wahpeton Oyate) states, research questions occur to us 'out of our bodies and our histories... [and if people are] standing in multiple diverse places you're going to get a more robust approach to thinking about the way the world works (Tallbear)'. In this stance, I aim to both acknowledge my settler colonial relation and my indebtedness to Indigenous ontologies and lands.

I first read Glaspell's work as an undergraduate student in eastern Canada, and didn't return to *Trifles* again until I was teaching during the midst of my doctoral research on Indigenous performance, land and language and the construction of whiteness. As part of my research, I was permitted to study the həṅḋəmiṅəṁ language and learned that the word for white settlers in the language means the 'starving ones'. This is related to the history of a gold rush in the mid-nineteenth century in the area but has continued to be used by Indigenous people, and scholars such as Stó:lō ethnomusicologist Dylan Robinson to describe the hunger for Indigenous resources, knowledges and aesthetic expressions that continues to drive extractive settler colonial actions

(2016, 6, 2020, 47–50). Another key term for my teaching practice in Vancouver/Coast Salish territories has been the hən̓q̓əmin̓əm̓ word for visitor, which is composed of the word 'walk' with lexical suffixes meaning 'along-side' (Couture 2020, 197). This word guides my conception on how to behave in this territory—walking, a continual movement and present engagement with land that has minimal long term impact, and alongside—in relation to the people who are already present who are also in motion. The epistemological insights I gained from studying the language effected how I read Glaspell's work when I returned to it and inspired an effort to deploy such a way of thinking in a sort of 'alongside' position theoretically.

A 'hungry' reading of *Trifles* involves thinking of Mrs. Hale and Mrs. Peters as well as the accused murderer Minnie Wright as living in a society of 'starving ones'. There is much textual evidence in the play for reading it this way. The one-act play, which the Provincetown Players premiered at the Wharf Theatre in Provincetown, Massachusetts on the 8th of August 1916, opens with the Sheriff and his wife, the County Attorney and the neighbours, Mr. and Mrs. Hale[8] entering the kitchen of a farmhouse where John Wright was found strangled in his bed the day before. The Attorney chastises the Sheriff for not guarding the crime scene overnight, and the Sheriff defends himself saying that his deputy had to go to someplace nearby called Morris Center because of 'that man that who went crazy' (1916, 36). This is not the only mention of other violence besides the murder they are investigating: some of it is quite graphic and directed towards other-than-human beings (the strangling of the canary or the boy who takes an axe to Mrs. Peter's kitten when she was a child) (1916, 43). This opening and subsequent comments give us a sense of the anxious unstable society these characters live in.

Glaspell has set the play in winter, and includes constant references to the extreme cold. The characters talk about the fire going out and the hard, endless work of survival. The constant threat of starvation, exacerbated by isolation from others is also emphasized in Glaspell's setting. Key to this are the preserves; Mrs. Peters first real line[9] is when she responds to the Attorney finding the broken jars of preserves: 'Oh, her fruit; it did freeze. She worried about that when it turned so cold. She said the fire'd go out and her jars would break' (1916, 38). The men's response to this line, 'women are used to worrying over trifles' gives us the title of the play—pointing to its usual gendered analysis (ibid). A hungry reading of the play however, expands its importance further. The practice of preserving food—through smoking, salting, drying or canning—is in order not to go hungry during the winter. The preserves are returned to repeatedly by the women. Mrs. Hale remembers the heat of the day when she 'put up her cherries' including the difficulty of working in the summer to create the winter supplies (1916, 39). The women use the preserves as a way to comfort Minnie Wright—once they have a better understanding of her harsh home life—deciding to tell her the preserves haven't broken, and bring her the jar of cherries while she is in jail (1916, 44).

400   S. COUTURE

Another key practice of survival is quilting, which makes use of all remnants of fabrics in order to create warm blankets. The women's discussion Minnie's quilt-work, and whether she would quilt or knot it becomes another opportunity for the men to ridicule them (1916, 40–41). In the final exchange between the Attorney and Mrs. Hale before the curtain, when he makes a facetious joke that at least they found out Minnie wasn't going to quilt it saying, 'She was going to—what is it you call it ladies?' and Mrs. Hale—with her hand against her pocket where she's hidden the box with the Minnie's strangled canary replies, 'We call it—knot it, Mr. Henderson' (1916, 45).

In terms of the murder mystery the sewing box is very important: it is where the women find the evidence for Minnie's motive. But it is also important to examine the two sewing methods that the women are discussing when thinking about the play in terms of the starvation for human company. Knotting a quilt is a fast way to bind the layers together, it is a beginners' method, and one that would be done for expediency. It also indicates that the quiltmaker wouldn't have space or support to set up a quilting frame which stretches out the work, and on which many people can finish a quilt working at the same time (which is what happens during a quilting bee). The stitches one makes when quilting are also part of the artistry—either following or contrasting the colours and shapes of the fabrics. The women's statement that Minnie was going to knot it is part of their recognition of her isolation from community, and the lack of beauty in her life. It also works, of course, as a reference to the knotting of the rope she used to strangle her husband. Along with the only jar of cherries that hasn't broken, the women decide to bring Minnie her quilting so she can have solace in this work while she is imprisoned. By doing this, they'll also indicate to her that they've found her dead canary, and demonstrate their solidarity with her.

Their discussion of the silence after the singing bird was strangled, along with the description of the Wright place: 'down in a hollow and you don't see the road. I dunno what it is, but it's a lonesome place and always was' (1916, 42) and Mrs. Peter's comment on knowing what stillness means after the death of her 2-year-old child in Dakota (1916, 44) all accumulate to emphasize the hunger for human connection and the dangers that a lack of it creates.

6   Conclusion

This reading of the play that focuses on hunger doesn't weaken the gendered understanding of Glaspell's work, but expands it intersectionally. Reading Glaspell's work with an emphasis on the precarity of the settler's occupation of Indigenous lands can be part of a 'grounded' analytical approach. My 'hungry' reading comes directly from insights of relations between Coast Salish people and the settlers who came to their lands—yet still resonates with a work developed across the continent. A practice of learning from an Indigenous language in the place one inhabits and then applying that world view to interpretation of a theatrical work can expand understandings of the process of racialisation and the development of intercultural relations.[10] This, of course, would change depending on the location one inhabits and the local epistemologies. For example, in Tsalagi, the Cherokee language, the word for settler is *yonega*, meaning 'foam of the water; moved by wind and without its own direction; clings to everything that's solid' or in Dakota it is *wasicu*, 'taker of fat'. (Snelgrove et al. 2014, 17). Both of these words evoke observations of settler behaviour that Indigenous people found notable enough to name. The Tsalagi word could be understood as describing rootless, directionless people who are at the mercy of larger powers. The Dakota word seems to describe those who take the richest piece of meat—perhaps without concern for others. I have no way to access Sauk or Meskwaki languages or epistemologies from my distant position; however, doing so would be a way to directly intervene in the continuing colonial landscape that has grown in their land as referenced by Brown and Kanouse, in order to better understand the origins of the relationships between white settlers who live on Sauk and Meskwaki land. Approaching a work from a grounding of where you are also creates a heightened awareness of the setting of a play and, to expand Una Chaudhuri's concept of *geopathologies*, to go beyond the metaphorical stage to the real politics of the land. For *Trifles*, it brings an awareness to its setting on Sauk and Meskwaki land that had been part of the contentious Black Hawk Purchase. Glaspell returned to the unresolved precarity of living on the land her family settled on when she wrote about white debt and the theft of Indigenous land in *Inheritors* and created a 'starving' social world in *Trifles*.

Those of us who study and perform Glaspell's theatrical works are inheritors of the fraught relations that she expressed. Continuing to engage with them, without understanding the context of white possession, settler hunger and unpaid debts, is to work in a mode of settler colonial oblivion. This mode demonstrates how colonial violence is not an event of the past but a structure that needs to be propped up continuously by bureaucratic policies and also by cultural expressions that ignore whiteness. It is not within the scope of this chapter to fully analyse the extent to which Glaspell used Black Hawk and the theft of Indigenous lands to forward her own analysis of issues of social justice in the early twentieth-century USA throughout her extensive oeuvre. It is, however, clear that this is an area for further analysis, especially as Glaspell's work sits in the canon of US Modernism, being taught over and over again as a masterpiece of early feminist theatre, adding to the structured assumptions of the irrelevance of the theft of Indigenous lands.

Notes

1. The performance of *Inheritors* was in contrast with other efforts at the conference to respectfully 'guest' through engagement with Indigenous land and peoples. Specifically, the ATHE conference organizers led by Choctaw theatre scholar and artist Bethany Hughes, built relationships with Indigenous organisations in the Boston area which led to the speech by Elder Dedra Ko (Cherokee,

Haliwa Saponi, Mohawk), as part of the opening events and an excursion to Wampanoag Homesite at the Plimoth Plantation (Hughes 2019, E29–E30; E-25–E-27). Hughes defines 'guesting' as 'focused not on attaining or accreting, but on relationships, humility, and reciprocal nurturance. Guesting is an active and intentional practice of presence with the goal of honoring and supporting the Indigenous people and spaces that always already undergird, surround, and shape your life and work' (2019, E-23).

2. Consider, for example, the use of his name for the logo of the National Hockey League's Chicago Blackhawks. For an excellent discussion of this phenomenon throughout what they term the 'colonial landscape' of the Midwest, see Nicholas Brown and Sarah Kanouse's extended image-text essay collection *Re-Collecting Black Hawk: Landscape, Memory, and Power in the American Midwest* (2015). They foreground the 'Black Hawks' in the photos as floating signifiers with the aim to anchor them to continuation of 'dynamic Indigenous political geographies represented by the texts' (2015, 8). Following Brown and Kanouse, I will use the name 'Black Hawk' when referring to the mythic figure and 'Makataimeshekiakiak' when discussing the historical person (2015, 249).

3. Jim Crow performances began when a minor actor from Mississippi, Thomas Dartmouth Rice (1806–1860) was inspired by (or stole) a song and dance he observed an enslaved man performing on a plantation. Rice rubbed black cork on his face, dressed in rags and jumped about while he sang:

Come listen all you galls and boys,
I'm just from Tuc-ky hoe;
I'm goin' to sing a leetle song,
My name's Jim Crow.
Weel about and turn about,
And do jis so;
Eb'ry time I weel about,
I jump Jim Crow. (Lott 1994, 23–24).

This act was very popular with working class audiences in New York City in 1832; Rice then expanded the song and character into short plays, eventually spawning the tradition of blackface Minstrelsy (McConachie 2016, 318–322). Post Reconstruction era racial segregation laws which institutionalized economic, educational and societal biases against Americans were known as Jim Crow Laws and were named after this character. The 1833 performance Makataimeshekiakiak witnessed in Philadelphia would have been early in Rice's career.

4. After the slaughter of 1832, a treaty was signed and the US purchased six million acres of Sauk and Makweksi lands, the land was called the Iowa District and referred to as the Black Hawk Purchase (Wesson 2012).

5. The Hedgerow Theatre was founded by Jasper Deeter, a former member of the Provincetown Players, in 1923 in Moylan-Rose Valley, Pennsylvania (just outside the city limits of Philadelphia) (Jouve 118). The theatre is recognized as the 'Mother of all Philadelphia Theaters' and continues to operate. It has expanded to include training facilities, a children's theatre and a fellowship programme ('History: Our Story (Briefly)').

6. Cherokee Two-Spirit/Queer literary scholar Qwo-Li Driskill explains 'Sexual abuse must be seen with an understanding of the history of colonization, which uses sexuality as a tool to gain power over others and to control women's bodies […] It is no accident that white masculinity is constructed the way it is in the United States, as European invasion of the Americas required a masculinity that murders, rapes and enslaves Native and African peoples. It is a masculinity that requires men to be soldiers and conquerors in every aspect of their lives. A masculinity rooted in genocide breeds a culture of sexual abuse' (2004, 53). Scott Morgensen connects contemporary homonationalist ideas of US exceptionalism to 'settler sexuality: a white national heteronormativity that regulates Indigenous sexuality and gender by supplanting them with the sexual modernity of settler subject' (2010, 106). I don't engage in a queer reading of Glaspell's works in this chapter, but connect Moreton-Robinson's analysis to Driskill and Morgensen in order to demonstrate the expansive intersectional discourses of settler colonialism in relation to gender and sexuality.

7. The analysis I present in this chapter was initially developed while I was living and working on Coast Salish unceded territories. It does not (as yet) fully take up my relations to the Treaty 6/Métis Region No. 4 homelands on which my institution, the University of Alberta is located in Edmonton/Amiskwacîwâskahikan (in the nêhiyawêwin or Plains Cree language). One important source that has helped me situate myself in these lands has been Métis filmmaker Connor McNally's *ôténaw*. In this film, McNally documents Papaschase Cree Education scholar Dwayne Donald's walking tour of the river valley in the centre of Edmonton. While engaging with the river and shoreline, Donald relates historical knowledge and shares important concepts in the nêhiyawêwin language: wâhkôtowin—that humans are enmeshed in relationships with each other and all of the other-than-human world and that the highest form of human intelligence is attributed to one who acknowledges this. Donald also explains the history of violence and disputes between Indigenous people and settlers using the term e-mâyikamikahk meaning 'where it went wrong' to mark the development of differing understandings of communal resources and private property. An analysis of settler colonial relations to land in Glaspell's work could also be taken up using these concepts and would lead to different understandings.

8. Glaspell performed the role of Mrs. Hale in the premiere.

9. In the opening moments she says she's not cold when invited to come closer to the fire, expressing her discomfort at entering the house.

10. *Place in Research: Theory, Methodology, and Methods* (2015), edited by Unangan scholar Eve Tuck and environmental scholar from Canada Marcia McKenzie develops extended methods for place-based epistemological, ontological and ethical research in social sciences. They attend to the 'multidimensional significance of place(s) in social science research […] as sites of presence, futurity, imagination, power, and knowing' asserting that it is particularly important to do this now in contexts of 'globalization and neoliberalism, settler colonialism, and environmental degradation' (xiv). I am inspired by this work to develop methods of place-based inquiry that attend to the relationship of language and land in the humanities.

References

'2018 ATHE Kickoff Event Presented By History Matters/Back to the Future.' *History Matters/Back to the Future.* https://www.historymattersbacktothefuture.com/about/events/2018/08/2018-ATHE-Kickoff-Event-presented-by-History-MattersBack-to-the-Future/

Ben-Zvi, Linda. 2005. *Susan Glaspell: Her Life and Times.* Oxford: Oxford University Press.

Brown, Nicholas A., and Sarah E. Kanouse, eds. 2015. *Re-Collecting Black Hawk: Landscape, Memory, and Power in the American Midwest.* Pittsburgh, PA: University of Pittsburgh Press.

Couture, Selena. 2020. *Against the Current and Into the Light: Performing History and Land in Coast Salish Territories and Vancouver's Stanley Park.* Montreal: McGill-Queen's University Press.

Deloria, Philip J. 1999. *Playing Indian.* New Haven, CT: Yale University Press.

Dillon, Elizabeth Maddock. 2014. *New World Drama. The Performative Commons in the Atlantic World, 1649–1849.* Durham, NC: Duke University Press.

Driskill, Qwo-Li. 2004. Stolen from Our Bodies: First Nations Two-Spirits/Queers and the Journey to a Sovereign Erotic. *Studies in American Indian Literatures,* Series 2, 16 (2): 50–64.

Dunbar-Ortiz, Roxanne. 2014. *Indigenous History of the United States.* Boston, MA: Beacon Press.

Glaspell, Susan. 1916. Trifles. *Plays,* ed. C.W.E. Bigsby, 35–45. Cambridge University Press, 1987.

———. 1921. Inheritors. *Plays,* ed. C.W.E. Bigsby, 104–157. Cambridge University Press, 1987.

Hernando-Real, Noelia. 2011. *Self and Space in the Theater of Susan Glaspell.* Jefferson, NC: McFarland & Company Inc. Publishers.

'History: Our Story (Briefly): 95 Years in the Making.' n.d. *Hedgerow Theatre Company.* https://hedgerowtheatre.org/about/history-and-mission/. Accessed 16 December 2019.

Hughes, Bethany. 2019. Guesting on Indigenous Land: Plimoth Plantation, Land Acknowledgement, and Decolonial Praxis. *Theatre Topics* 29 (1): E-23–E-32. https://doi.org/10.1353/tt.2019.0013.

Jouve, Emiline. 2017. *Susan Glaspell's Poetics and Politics of Rebellion.* Iowa City: U of Iowa Press.

Lott, Eric. 1994. *Love and Theft: Blackface Minstrelsy and the American Working Class.* Oxford University Press.

McConachie, Bruce. 2016. Imagining a White Nation: Minstrelsy and U.S. Nationalism, 1840–1870. In *Theatre Histories: An Introduction,* ed. Bruce McConachie, Tobin Nelhaus, Carol Fisher Sorgenfrei, and Tamara Underiner, 3rd ed., 318–324. Routledge.

Moreton-Robinson, Aileen. 2013. Towards an Australian Indigenous Women's Standpoint Theory. *Australian Feminist Studies* 28 (78): 331–347. https://doi.org/10.1080/08164649.2013.876664.

———. 2015. *The White Possessive: Property, Power, and Indigenous Sovereignty.* Minneapolis, MN: U of Minneapolis Press.

Morgensen, Scott Lauria. 2010. Settler Homonationalism: Theorizing Settler Colonialism within Queer Modalities. *GLQ: A Journal of Lesbian and Gay Studies* 16 (1–2): 105–131.

Robinson, Dylan. 2016. Welcoming Sovereignty. In *Performing Indigeneity*, ed. Yvette Nolan and Ric Knowles, 5–31. Toronto: Playwrights Canada Press.

———. 2020. *Hungry Listening: Resonant Theory for Indigenous Sound Studies*. University of Minnesota Press.

Snelgrove, Corey, Rita Kaur Dhamoon, and Jeff Corntassel. 2014. Unsettling Settler Colonialism: The Discourse and Politics of Settlers, and Solidarity with Indigenous Nations. *Decolonization: Indigeneity, Education & Society* 3 (2): 1–32. http://decolonization.org/index.php/des/article/view/21166/17970.

Tallbear, Kim. 2018. Kim Tallbear on Situated Knowledges. *Just Powers vimeo*, August 23. https://vimeo.com/286431876

Tompkins, Joanne. 2006. *Unsettling Space: Contestations in Contemporary Australian Theatre*. New York: Palgrave Macmillan.

Tuck, Eve, and Marcia McKenzie, eds. 2015. *Place in Research: Theory, Methodology, and Methods*. New York and London: Routledge.

Wesson, Sarah. 2012. Makataimeshekiakiak: Black Hawk and His War. *Quad City Memory: Davenport Public Library*, February 7. https://web.archive.org/web/20120207012436/http://www.qcmemory.org/Page/Black_Hawk.aspx?nt=260

CHAPTER 22

Beyond the Peyote Dance: The Raramuri Tribe and 'Mexico' Representations in Antonin Artaud's Work

Luciana da Costa Dias

Yes, I am saying something bizarre, that contrary to everything we have been led to believe, the pre-Columbian Indians were a strangely civilized people
—Artaud 1988, 568

1 Introduction

Antonin Artaud (1896–1948) does not require any introductions. He is a 'well-known' French poet, director and actor. A former associate of Surrealist movement, his work is revolutionary for the francophone stage during the early twentieth century. Yet, his influence would grow worldwide over the next decades, until he became a key-name for current *Theatre and Performance Studies*. Nevertheless, the extent to which Artaud is truly 'well-known' is a problematic matter. His 'madness' is better known than his work. Some scholars even question if it is possible to separate his life from his work, given that his life has acquired a kind of 'mythical character'. As Jane Goodall points out, the myths around his life would develop in the late 1950s and early 1960s, with

This chapter was mainly written during my sabbatical year as a visiting research fellow at the Centre for Performance Philosophy at the University of Surrey (UK), granted by the Federal University of Ouro Preto (Brazil), where I work as an associate professor.

L. da Costa Dias (✉)
Universidade Federal de Ouro Preto, Ouro Preto, Brazil
e-mail: l.dias@ufop.edu.br

© The Author(s), under exclusive license to Springer Nature Switzerland AG 2021
T. Morosetti, O. Okagbue (eds.), *The Palgrave Handbook of Theatre and Race*, https://doi.org/10.1007/978-3-030-43957-6_22

the Beat Generation, notably the myth of a countercultural guru from a kind of sacred and violent theatre, as well as the myth of a 'mad writer', a *poète maudit*, whose psychotic and psychedelic experiences were exoticized. As she states, 'He is frequently referenced, less often quoted' (Goodall 1994, 2).

Not so well known (better saying, rarely discussed) is the impact that Mexico—the conceptions and misconceptions of its native culture and people—had on Artaud's work, creating racial dissonances that, as we intend to approach, resonate throughout his work. Mexico was the object of Artaud's theatrical fantasy long before he even visited the country. For instance, his *Second Manifesto* describes a play called *The Conquest of Mexico* (Artaud 1958, 126–132), that even under accusations that it is not performable (given the fact it sounds more like a surrealist poem than a play script), served to present Artaud's visceral notion that certain ancient cultures—like those of pre-Columbian Mexico—could embody a cosmic unity and vitality long lost in Western civilisation and Western theatre.

At first, the Artaudian perception on the decadence of European theatre would be heavily influenced by the physical style of a *Balinese Dance Company* that he saw at the *Colonial Exposition of 1931*, in Paris, whose 'actors with their geometric robes seem like animated hieroglyphs' (54). What Artaud admired in the Balinese dancers, as he wrote in 1931, is that they have nothing to do with 'entertainment', but, rather, 'possess some of the ceremonial qualities of a religious rite' (60). Artaud did not intend to be metaphorical when comparing actors to hieroglyphics. In fact, he assigns the same powers to the symbolic character of oriental languages as what he calls 'the pure theatrical sign'. What impressed Artaud was the immediacy of the performers, the sense that their performance was not a re-presentational act, but instead a kind of 'pure presence', concerning somehow a physical and gestural language lost in Western theatre (Bush 1994).

In *The Theatre and Its Double* (1938), his most known book, the concept of a primordial body-dependent language is articulated inside the vision of what he called the 'Theatre of Cruelty', a new theatre to be developed with its own, unique language—deeply embodied, something 'in between thought and gesture'. This book reunites many articles he wrote between 1931 and 1936, which laid out his vision on devitalisation and putrefaction of Western civilisation and its cultural and theatrical decadence. Artaud devoted his life to the attempt of rediscovering what would be such a 'lost' metaphysical/philosophical nature of theatre and its catalytic power—a task he was certain that could not be fulfilled within European borders. As Savarese explains,

> it can be taken as a veritable declaration of principles, especially when one considers the fact that his text *On the Balinese Theatre* was, of all the articles collected in *The Theatre and it's Double*, the first to be written. The last to be written, on the other hand, was the emblematically entitled *Oriental and Western Theatre* which Artaud wrote (...) shortly before his departure for Mexico. (2001, 52)

This chronology highlights that the 'the thinking which underlies one of the most important theatrical manifestos of the twentieth century' (52) began to take form, curiously, after Artaud saw a Balinese Performance at a 'Colonial Exhibition' in Paris—an event planned to 'promote the French colonial empire' (Hale 2008, 166) but which would affect Antonin Artaud in just the opposite way. Such a contact contaminated him in such an enormous way that it consequently led him to, later on, leave Europe behind for the depths of Central-America's canyons. If the pioneer impact from such a 'non-western' experience could in fact lead his work 'beyond western culture', as self-proclaimed, is a matter to be discussed elsewhere. The chosen line of investigation herein is how racial issues emerge and are vital to the development of his work. Nevertheless, his whole nine-month Mexican trip, usually treated as a footnote on Artaud's life, will be approached here as a turning point for his work. We agree with Jay Murphy (2017, 79), for who there was an Artaud before and 'a different one' after his journey to Mexico. As a basic framework for this paradigm shift, putting aside his so-called madness, we observe a metamorphosis within his work, ranging from his Theatre of Cruelty to the concept of 'Body-without-organs', an essential concept that only emerges in the last phase of his thinking. If such affirmation is correct, it is necessary to understand the reasons, emphasizing the impact that the one month living with the Rarámuri, 'a red Indian pure race' (Artaud's own words) had on his work.

2   ARTAUD AND PRIMITIVISM

In 1936, Artaud first travelled to Ciudad del México (Mexico City), under the Mexican Government's invitation, and then, deep inside Mexico countryside to Sierra Tarahumara, where he stayed with the Rarámuri tribe, taking part in one of their rites, later pictured in his book *The Peyote Dance and Other Writings* (see Artaud 1976). In this context, my aim here is: (1) to critically approach, in a post-colonial perspective, Artaud intentions of searching for a primal theatrical language; and (2) to interrogate how racial questions were problematized in such a search and how they reverberate through his work and beyond, radically changing it and affecting the Theatre and Performance Studies field.

First, before advancing with the discussion on Rarámuri racial representations, it is important to note that, to some extent, Artaud's view of the Balinese Theatre, as Lars Krutak exposes (2014), could be considered colonialist, in prizing it for its exotic and non-European character. Such a performance embodies quite different values from those of western society. Yet Artaud by no means, considers them inferior. Quite the opposite: to him, it embodies the spiritual and the natural, as a lost harmony between body and expression, something that, from his outcast point of view, could not be called primitive. Nevertheless, if 'Primitivism' were a trend within Modernism (a series of avant-garde movements in which Artaud could be inserted) it is interesting to note, that Artaud practically did not use the word 'primitive' in his texts, except, if not sarcastically, in a positive manner. He used other terms, such as 'ancient cultures' or 'original cultures', to avoid any progressive perspective, which he disliked. Indeed, he thinks of pre-Columbian Indians as a 'strangely civilized people'—but the weird part is: 'strangely' could actually mean 'even more civilized than westerns'.

It is necessary to bear in mind that the concept of primitive art originates from the very specific conception of art history as 'universal art history', that is, a conception born inside the same modern background as 'the notion of universal progress—of course, determined and realized by the west', and that within such a concept of history, 'there are peoples who are considered to be incapable of any modern progress by themselves, and this incapability is often attributed to racial differences' (Araeen 2005, 140). Furthermore, the so-called primitive would be, in such a perspective, the non-historical, and its works, a lesser object to art history.

In other words, the very idea of Primitive races (or cultures) presupposes an evolutionary process from such so-called primitive races until the 'civilized' Modern European [white] men and State, which is related to the modern idea of a linear 'universal history'—a linearity considered false by Artaud. Yet, Primitivism is a key-stone concept to modern art. 'The term Primitivism is used to describe the fascination of early modern European artists with what was then called primitive art—including tribal art from Africa, the South Pacific and Indonesia, as well as prehistoric and very early European art'.[1]

Under a critical review, such notion can, indeed, be considered as a kind of artistic idealisation that aspires to recreate or imagine what could a 'primitive' experience be. It can be seen in Picasso's influence by African Masks and in Paul Gauguin's use of Tahitian motifs, for example. Primitivism has often been criticized for reproducing racial (and racist) stereotypes concerning non-European peoples, and, it is important to remark, to a certain degree, it is also inside the same discursive scope that has also being used by Europeans to justify colonial conquest and racial superiority in general.

On the other hand, when taking under consideration that the search for the 'primitive' was also a search for the 'perimeters of civilisation', as suggested by Marianna Torgovnick (1990), a different light can be shed on such subject. She analysed the depths of the need for 'primitive' in western culture and places it deep inside the 'sense of collapse' which can be associated with the failure of Modern project, a widespread feeling after the First World War. To her, most of those 'explorers of the so-called primitive' were projecting their own sense of alienation and the feeling of being outsiders in their own lands to the subjects they explored. Antonin Artaud will fit such an assumption quite well, as we will see further on in the text. However, the importance of such an aesthetic phenomenon, that began with the avantgarde movements, independent of moral judgements, is enormous for Western culture to rethink itself alongside the twentieth century.

By discussing Modernism (avantgarde movements in general) under a Post-Colonial perspective, the book *Post-Colonial Studies: The Key Concepts* (Ashcroft et al. 2000, 129–130) critically approaches such a subject, since it connects the so-called primitive art and its 'revelation of an alternative view of the world in the form of African masks, carvings and jewellery—artefacts often stored in museum basements' with what they are: *a colonial loot*, as the dark token of modern European savagery. Still, Primitivism could, to a certain extent, be considered *a colonial insurgence*, as it had begun a radical critique, formulated by the reaction of artists as diverse as Jarry, Rimbaud and Artaud, whose work questioned the universal superiority of European art and civilisation and who, by doing so, ended up discussing the very concept of 'primitive' in their works. According to Julie Stone Peters, Primitivism should also be considered as a 'vehemently antiprogressivist and violently anticolonial [movement], with all the paradoxes of an anticolonialism that recognized its own dependence on the aesthetics of colonial exchange' (2002, 229).

On this behalf, Surrealism,[2] as an avant-garde movement, occupies a unique position in the cultural and intellectual history of the twentieth century. It marks the crisis in post-Enlightenment (modern) thought and is still in the heart of debates concerning modernism and postmodernism, as well as colonialism and postcolonialism. A former associate of the Surrealist movement, Artaud would partially share its vision, but only because he would be an eager critique of European modernity and its certainties of racial and cultural superiority compared to his peers. In the preface from *The Theatre and Its double* (entitled *The Theatre and Culture*), for instance, he wrote:

> Hence, our confirmed lack of culture is astonished by certain grandiose anomalies (…). Similarly, if we think Negroes smell bad, we are ignorant of the fact that anywhere but in Europe it is we whites who "smell bad." And I would even say that we give off an odour as white as the gathering of pus in an infected wound. (…) It can be said that everything excessive is white; for Asiatics, white has become the mark of extreme decomposition. (1958, 9)

In this regard, as observed by Stone Peters,

> In the writings that led up to Artaud's Mexican journey in 1936, one can find the intertwined themes of his era. Among these, perhaps paramount is the modernist primitivism produced in the fraught encounter with the first decades of the twentieth century, in the search to escape both the progressivist mythologies of the nineteenth century and its nostalgia for a preindustrial paradise lost, in recognition of the limits and failures of the empire and in the wake of the devastations of a world war that demonstrated just what "progress" would become. By the time of his voyage to Mexico, Artaud had broken with most "isms" of his generation, most notably surrealism and mainstream European Marxism (just another example of "*Barbarie Européenne*", he wrote from Mexico). (Stone Peters 2002, 228–229)

3 Artaud's Visit to Mexico

After this long *introit*, one can now finally ask: *Why did Artaud go to Mexico?* According to Krutak (2014), Artaud went to Mexico for different reasons: he was in search of what he called the 'primeval principles of the Cosmos' with which to cure himself and the Western World and Theatre from 'their rational disease'. He believed that he would find the 'natural secrets' that European civilisation had lost amongst the races of 'pure red Indians'. Artaud himself would answer that he was looking for a kind of 'primal theatrical language'—in other words, he had the intent of revising the paradigm of Western theatre by emphasizing its strong connection with life forces. But he was also in a quest for more. According to Tsu-Chung Su (2012, 2), 'Quest versus conquest, Artaud's envisioning of Mexico was influenced by his anti-colonialist and anti-imperialist stance, as shown in his scenario of *The Conquest of Mexico*, in his last manifesto for the Theatre of Cruelty'.

> *The Conquest of Mexico* poses the question of colonization. It revives in a brutal and implacable way the ever-active fatuousness of Europe. It permits her idea of her own superiority to be deflated. (Artaud 1958, 126)

Critically confirming such a perspective, Ayanna Thompson, in her book *Performing Race and Torture on the Early Modern Stage*, points out that *The Conquest of Mexico* script emerged after Artaud's decision of adapting John Dryden's *The Indian Emperor or the Conquest of Mexico by the Spaniards*, a play from 1665, by totally inverting its original meaning and purpose. Such a decision had an intrinsic logic, given Artaud 'explicitly linked depictions of cruelty/torture with depictions of racialized subjects', given 'Artaud was explicitly [and precursory] challenging the racist justifications for these colonial projects' (Thompson 2008, 1), as well as challenging the 'superiority' of Western 'white' civilisation, whose members, the colonizers could not be considered superior at all by him. In his own words,

> By broaching the alarmingly immediate question of colonization and the right one continent thinks it has to enslave another, this subject questions the real superiority of certain races over others (...). It contrasts the tyrannical anarchy of the colonizers to the profound moral harmony of the as yet uncolonized. (Artaud 1958, 126–127)

Artaud[3] arrived in Mexico on February 7, 1936 and remained there for nine months, until late October. He first gave three public lectures at *Universidad Nacional Autónoma de México*, in Ciudad del Mexico (Mexico City), looked into traditional and contemporary Mexican cultures and got in touch with Mexican modernists, such as the painter Maria Izquierdo, whom he befriended and considered the greatest Mexican painter of that time, a painter fully capable of overcoming the European influence in order to access her own lost 'racial inconscient' through her paintings (Artaud 1936). Curiously, Diogo

Rivera, on the other hand, was, to Artaud, too Parisian to be a real Mexican painter. Besides such polemics, those months in Mexico City were a very intense and productive time in his life. From May to July, he would publish a series of articles in Mexicans journals (such as *El National* and *La Revista de La Universidad de México*), having written over 25 articles—later also published in France. The last version of some texts from *The Theatre and Its Double* were reviewed and sent from Mexico to Jean Paulhan (Artaud 1988, 364–365). In one of these public lectures, 'What I Came to Mexico to Do', Artaud stated that

> The present civilization of Europe is in a state of Bankruptcy. Dualistic Europe hasn't anything to offer the world. (…) The United States has done nothing but multiply to infinity the decadence and vices of Europe. There remains only Mexico (…). Mexico, that precipitate of innumerable races, appears as the diffuser of history. (1988, 371)

Prior to this, he exposed his vision of a revolution based on a new idea of man, a new form of Humanism (368), as 'the lesson which modern Mexico can teach us'.

> Between the now degenerated vestiges of the "Ancient Red Culture", such one can find them in the last pure indigenous races, and the less degenerate and fragmentary culture of modern Europe, Mexico can find an original form of culture which will constitute its contributions to the civilization of this age. (373)

Yet, racial issues, inside Mexico (and Latin America in general), are a controversial matter. Once the Revolution (1910–1917) was over, a new national unifying identity needed to be created. Indigenous people had their lives improved after the revolution—but were still seen as inferior. Post-revolutionary leaders aimed to assimilate the country's diverse (particularly indigenous) population under the umbrella of official mestizaje alongside an ongoing 'modernisation' project. The indigenous, African and white elements were supposed to mingle and coexist in the new (imagined) national project (Anderson 2006). Artaud went to Mexico by the government's invitation and his discourse, at that very political moment, was very welcome, given the post-revolutionary governments' decision of 'using art' to better communicate such official conceptions. But Mestizaje, as a project, was very problematic, as it brings a false image of racial horizontality, and is not capable of erasing racial differences since, on the contrary, it denies native races any possible political and social representation by themselves, actually reinforcing Mexico's long history of misrepresentation of indigenous people since colonial times. Furthermore, Mestizaje could also be charged for erasing colonial sexual violence and occluding Latin American racism (Hooker 2017). As in most Latin American countries, constructs of race in Mexico are nuanced and contradictory. General common-sense strongly disapproves racial discrimination, while at the same time, marginalizes indigenous peoples and cultures who do not assimilate modern culture (and, overall, modern technologies, see Dalton 2018) in their way of life—there seems to be an invisible but present distinction between indigeneity and mestizaje. In this case, the desired mixing of races in post-revolutionary Mexico was, in fact, aligned with a project aiming at whitewashing the Mexican population (since the 'Indian compounds' were supposed to be absorbed and diluted over time).

However, Artaud would become, in a certain way, aware of this. During one of his lectures in Mexico, Artaud did not spare the Mexican regime of criticism for not valuing the pre-colonial and magic-imbued indigenous past. He realized that the Mexican revolution was nothing like what he had in mind and became afraid that some kind of anti-Indian movement might take place inside such a utopian post-racial future. According to Hertz (2003, 12), Artaud also wrote, a few months after his arrival, an *'Open Letter to the Governors of the States of Mexico*, published in *El Nacional* on May 19, 1936, in which he makes an impassioned plea for the preservation of the Indian way of life'. After that, his stay at Ciudad del Mexico went fast from high expectations to shattered illusions. Yet, Artaud's resolute mind impelled him to go boldly and further on in his search. He began to project his utopia and dream into the far northern mountains of Mexico in the hope that he would find, in the far-distant Sierra Madre, a sacred place of preserved 'ancient solar culture' (as he called the pre-Columbian world-view) still 'untouched' by the colonial invasion.

In fact, during the sixteenth century, Spain focused on conquering densely populated areas, looking for a workforce. The Sierra Madre Occidental (or the Tarahumara Mountains) in the State of Chihuahua, were never fully conquered, neither before, by the Aztec empire, nor after, by the Spaniards. Considered 'the purest and most unmixed of any Indian tribe in Mexico', so little was known about them that their true name 'Rarámuri' (meaning 'nimble feet') was corrupted to 'Tarahumara'—and never corrected. They survived this long because they retreated deep into the highest reaches of the Sierra Madre Occidental, to its high sierras and canyons (Fontana and Schaefer 1997). Their (hard to access) valleys are over 5000 feet above sea level. Such a geography, that the Rarámuri mastered with their long-distance running ability, allowed them to evade conquerors. Likewise, the Rarámuri were not fully converted by the Jesuit missionaries, notwithstanding some influences. *This non-fully assimilated character was what appealed to Artaud the most.*

Artaud, indeed, thinks of pre-Columbian Indians as a 'strangely civilized people'—since we understand here this 'strangely' as surprisingly positive, since it means they are even more civilized than the decadent western civilisation. The Sierra Tarahumara landscape and the perfect equilibrium of the Rarámuri way of life inside it was, to him, unique and marvellous at the same time. Native Mexican people were, of course, influenced by Jesuitical missionaries, yet they assimilated Christianism after their own fashion, to different degrees. We could cautiously use the word Syncretism (which refers to a process of religious blending of faiths and beliefs, a kind of religious interaction over time) in this case. Regarding the Rarámuri, mostly during the late seventeenth and eighteenth centuries, a certain amount of Jesuit mission activity occurred in the Copper Canyon region, but subsequently, the Rarámuri were left free to interpret, modify and maintain (or not) Catholic beliefs, symbols and practices with little outside (or dogmatic) intervention. As Olivia Arrieta (1992, 15–16) explains in detail in her article regarding the maintenance of cultural autonomy through the transformation and resignification of colonizing symbols by Tarahumaras, native and Spanish Catholic religious beliefs were 'in some ways blended and transformed into a new Tarahumara religious phenomenon' in such a level that, given the 'missionization hiatus of over a hundred years between 1767–1900', it is 'difficult to determine which elements are purely of catholic origin' and which are not.

Today, the Rarámuri belief system is a *mélange* (15–16): For instance, most of them believe in a god (*Riosi*) that can be both a mother and father (*Iyeruame*—'Great Mother', and *Onoruame*—'Great Father'), and in their children, 'the Santi', who are beings that are directly linked with the physical world through certain Catholic iconography, such as crosses, but are also linked through natural phenomena, animals and supernatural-shaped animal beings. They also believe in the afterlife, that is a mirror image of the mortal world, in a very shamanistic perspective. Additionally, the Rarámuri share a veneration of Peyote with other Uto-Aztecan tribes, with Peyote ingestion as an important part of their rituals.[4]

4 The Rarámuri and Peyote Through Artaud's Representations

The Rarámuri call the Peyote experience *Ciguri (or Jíkuri)*. Different Ciguri rituals exist, but all involve long periods of singing, dancing and peyote consumption.[5] In Artaud's defence, more than a 'new drug experience',[6] he was really looking for the mystical, healing and transformative powers of peyote.[7] In order to prepare for its ingestion, Artaud had not used narcotics for the first time in seventeen years, a remarkable achievement in his life until then—he discarded the last of his opiates before leaving Mexico City. First, according to Krutak (2014, 32), he travelled by train to Chihuahua, and from there, probably took another train to Boconya, near the Jesuit Mission centre of Sisoguichi, 'the gateway to the heart of the Sierra Tarahumara', where 'he located a "mestizo" guide and translator' and obtained a horse to begin 28 days of an arduous journey, mainly by horse (since no roads were available at the time), presenting drug withdrawal and psychic turbulence symptoms, as well as vast expectations. He accounts that, in the last days, he was so weak he could barely ride. He had to wait for a week, in a cave, before he could take part in a ritual, that only take place because someone from the Rarámuri group had recently passed away.

> The Tutuguri dance is [most times] an invocation intended to raise the soul of a deceased person to heaven. This part is omitted when a funeral celebration is not the purpose. The dances (…) are performed to honour the spirit of Jíkuri and the person named in the homily recited during the ceremony. (Irigoyen-Rascón 2015)

416   L. DA COSTA DIAS

Regarding Rarámuri rituals, Arrieta detailed them as 'central to Tarahumara life'. Their rituals are usually conducted by two people 'the *Oweruame* (shaman) and the *Saweame* (chanter)'. She also explains that 'the major secret activities in these ceremonies are the dancing of the *Yumari* and the *Tutuburi*', another way that the Tutuguri ritual can be graphed. As she states:

> As is common among other Native Americans, offerings are made to the four cardinal directions and the number 4 is a ritual number. Dancing and chanting are part of every ritual, but are especially important in the traditional *Yumari* and *Tutuburi*. (…) Female dancers including women and girls, participate with males in the Tutuburi dance only, moving across the dance pavilion in the opposite direction from the males. The *Oweruame* is the chief ritual specialist and conducts a number of other types of curing ceremonies. (…) Other major responsibilities include the supervision of birth and death rituals. (Arrieta 1992, 15)

Anthropologist Raymonde Carasco (2006) describes the Tutuguri rite as a necessary rite that is also a preparatory ceremony linked to the far more complex Ciguri (or Jíkuri) ritual. Ciguri is not simply the peyote, but 'the god that enters inside' (yet, is not identified as God itself) through different degrees of trances. Based on the Rarámuri myth of creation, the Tutuguri/Tutuburi is a rite where the practitioners symbolically follow the sun in its course through night and until dawn. It is a ritual whose origin goes back to pre-Columbian times and, besides some marginal mythological differences, it is virtually practised by all Tarahumaras.

Artaud describes with extraordinary richness in his writings, how the peyote priestess through elaborate and slow dance gestures traced what he called 'letters' in the earth and with fire in the air during the ritual—something that he would connect with the 'hieroglyphs' from his Theatre of Cruelty. He understands this as the confirmation of his initial vision regarding the extraordinary power of gesture. As Jose Gil explains, it is not a matter of symbols acting from afar. Rather, than gestures and precise actions, forces are set in motion and can be embodied in the ritual. Other (contemporary) 'shamanistic' writers, such as Carlos Castaneda (1998), reinforce the power of certain gestures to encompass forces and emotions into the body, thus affecting the practitioner with a new conscience level. In Artaud's records of the trip and the ritual, which took three entire days of induced trance, he reads signs everywhere, literally inscribed in the Mexican landscape, and at the same time, inside himself. All sorts of metaphysical signs are increasingly described as located in specific parts of the body. He names the liver, for example, as the 'organic filter of the unconscious'. In Artaud's words, his spleen was then transformed into an immense emptiness, an oceanic void where the peyote planted the Ciguri root and then became one within himself and the world. After the three-day ritual, Artaud didn't know whether it was himself or the world that had fainted.

Artaud reports he had a vision of Ciguri that was judged 'authentic' by the Tarahumara high-priest. He describes the realm of Ciguri in this vision as an extraordinary, dramatic reversal—he visited what he described as 'the other side of reality'. He never truly or completely shared his vision during the peyote ritual. In 'The Peyote Ritual of the Tarahumaras' (see Artaud 1984), one of his later written accounts (1947) of his experiences, Artaud wrote that the little bit of peyote that he took 'opened his conscience for ever'. And after that, his own body and mind began to collapse.

5   Mexico's Influence on Artaud's Work

However, trying to lead this chapter to its end, the question (*Why did Artaud go to Mexico?*) can become another one, to be summarized as: *did he find what he was looking for?* His search for a primal theatrical language took him too far and too deep into the Sierras and into the Tarahumaras, turning his fraught and drug-addicted personality into savage combustion (as the incidents during his trip to Ireland, soon after his return to Paris, in 1937,[8] confirm). After his return to France, such an experience would first give form to a psychotic delirium (which brought as a result approximately nine years inside different mental institutions) and, later, would take form into the poetic transformation of his work until its absolute reversal.

Some of his texts on the Mexican experience will be written beginning in 1943, at Rodez. 'For this reason, his experiences inevitably interacted with responses to, and reflections on, cultural and institutional life in France' (Hubert 1998, 184). As stated by Art historian and Artaud biographer Florence Mèredieu (2006) such an 'initiatory voyage' would haunt him throughout the last years of his life. He wrote, as a final movement inside the famous radio transmission *To Have Done with the Judgement of God*, a poem named, precisely, *Tutuguri, The Black Sun Rite* (Sontag 1988). In his last creative piece, he recreated it as a poem for the radio play: 'Artaud was deeply moved by his time with the Tarahumaras (…). He used the Tarahumara ritual cries and gestures as a source for the screams of refusal which he performed (…) for his recording *To Have Done with the Judgment of God*' (Barber 2003, 106–107). Mèredieu (2006, 574–575) argues that certain peyote sensory modifications, notably the loss of usual space and time coordinates, are reproduced in Artaud's asylum experience, especially magnified during the episodes of electroshock coma, so he merges and combines such perceptions [in his later works]. As she notes, the most inspired, and most flamboyant of Artaud's Tarahumara accounts are those written at Rodez.

If Artaud's journey had stopped at the *Theatre of Cruelty Manifestoes*, he would still be one of the great modernist thinkers, a 'trend setter' for certain seminal developments in avant-garde theatre and performance (Cardullo and Knopf 2001). This was not in discussion. What we intended to highlight in the scope of this chapter is what would later be, curiously, named after his work, as 'ethnographic surrealism' (Clifford 1981)—a proof of how deep racial and ethnic issues interpenetrates Artaud's work. For Melanie Nicholson (2013), this was something first registered in the paradigmatic book, *Voyage au pays des*

Tarahumaras (see Artaud 1976), which includes two narratives of his Mexican journey: *The Mountain of Signs (1936)* and *The Peyote Dance* (1937)—with the second being the most popular in the 1960s between the Beat Generation.

Antonin Artaud's geographical and inner-side displacements give us a glimpse of an ethos of insurgency—against European values, against the colonial past, against his own fractured mind and, even, against Modern Rationalism and the Christian god. Thus, despite limited value as an anthropological report, to a certain extent, his venture to Mexico was also 'his personal diaspora' (Su 2012, 2). Maybe, as Su significantly observes, Artaud's travels in Mexico truly concerns only his own diasporic life—his efforts to flee from European civilisation and its violent colonial/rationalist culture, and not, I could add, a racial account of colonisation in Mexico. However, his travelling had also unexpected (ethnic/racial) consequences. Regarding the Artaud after his Mexican experience, such a shift, into the concept of 'Body-without-organs', as we intend to argue now, was deeply influenced by his immersion inside the world-view and culture of a different ethnic group, the Rarámuri. Additionally, two remarks can emphasize such a transformation.

The first remark: there was, as discussed, a confirmation (perhaps a 'reaffirmation') of that early vision, present in early texts, concerning theatrical language as an 'embodied hieroglyphic'. After his own personal experiences, Artaud confirmed that the theatre lost its ritualistic character—as a spiritual and healing practice for both the performer and the audience, while creating a shift in consciousness. He identified the same 'hieroglyphic character' in the Tutuguri ritual—the peyote dance—that is, the subtle integration between gesture and significance from the shaman's movements. It was in the ritualist character of the dance that he found the key to what he expected to be a new theatre language, pure presence, something that he—and others—would pursue in the years to come. Antonin Artaud is one of the most challenging and provocative figures in the twentieth century—somehow still an enigma to be deciphered. Yes, he can be seen as a forerunner to numberless countercultural artists. The use of peyote also played a huge influence on pop culture—from Aldous Huxley to the American rock band The Doors. However, there is more in all this: one of the most relevant aspects of Theatre and Performance Studies on contemporaneity, the ethno-anthropological turn, begins there, in the crossroad of anthropology and theatre, an approach further fully developed by Victor Turner and Richard Schechner, as well as by practitioners such as Jerzy Grotowski and Eugene Barba, and many others.

As Allain and Harvie explain (2006, 14), the field of Theatre Studies underwent a paradigm shift when Performance Studies became an interdisciplinary field, mingling Theatre studies with fine art and various other critical fields, such as anthropology, philosophy and sociology. Performance studies introduced new critical concerns that were shared by new forms of performance, as well as by more traditional theatre forms. In this sense, to Schechner, the founder of Performance Studies, Performance, this theatrical/ritualized approach can be understood as comprising 'restored behaviour', the organized re-enactment of mythic or actual events, as well as the role-playing of religious, political, professional, familial and social life. In his third public lecture at *Universidad Nacional Autónoma del México*, Artaud affirmed that theatre was not born from religion and myth, as commonly believed—but the opposite: the world religions were born of ancient rituals. In other words, even religion could be a kind of performance. As Schechner states regarding Artaud's influence on the field:

> Artaud has muddied the waters by introducing in such a powerful way his notion of ritual. But by "ritual", I understand him to mean nothing other than the transcendence of the actor's personality by outside forces—codified systems of performance such as those used by the Balinese, or trance possession. Artaud does not say that theatre *comes from* this or that ritual. He argues that theatre *is*—or ought to be—ritual. The ritual process—as worked out by Victor Turner and others—applies more to the workshop-rehearsal process than to dramatic literature. (Schechner 2003, 21)

On the other hand, *as* a second remark, a profound break also takes place inside Artaudian work that corroborates the aforementioned shift. The most important concept from his later work—'Body Without Organs'—a 'new body' that Artaud seeks to create at the end of his life could also be, as Raymonde Carasco (1998) suggests, a legacy from the reversal experience to 'the other side of reality' that Artaud went through in his xamanistic experience with the Tutuguri, the Peyote dance. That is a question to be fully developed somewhere, in future research. Nevertheless, some general lines can be traced. For instance, it seems that Artaud was so deeply impacted by such an experience that it would take years to truly elaborate and that such an elaboration was performed (1) through almost nine years in insane asylums, deliberately starved by Nazi occupiers, and (2) later in Rodez (under the endurance of a forced regime of electroshock treatments), making it even more stunning. But, somehow, these experiences lead his work into another level of ferocity and creativity—as the radio play '*To Have Gone with The Judgment of God*' demonstrates.

In this sense, we can say that, in *To Have Done with the Judgment of God* (1947), Artaud performs his sonorous poetry as a ritual, in which language expands, through the destratified voice[9] into a performative and enchanting character. In Nicolas's analysis (2012), Artaud 'performs' words in a ritual manner. In other words, he uses language not with rational purposes but in a performative way presenting, through sounds, a state of flux that is also a kind of liminal experience (or 'liminality', see Turner 1995). She also suggests that the human identity is defined by its mobility and circularity, that is, it is performative and ritualized, or in Schechner's aforementioned quote, ritual as 'nothing other than the transcendence of the actor's personality by outside forces' (Schechner 2003, 21).

Through his diaries and drawings from Rodez, it is possible to realize how he was constantly attempting to recreate the kind of experience he had among

420   L. DA COSTA DIAS

the Rarámuri and how 'the red Indians' (a constant racial feature that he positively highlights) are somehow present in this (re-)conception of his 'true body'—the body to come, the *Body Without Organs*—a central concept in his later work. Particularly, I highlight one of his drawings from Rodez in order to exemplify such an affirmation, entitled *The Projections of the True Body*.[10] Despite the date being unsure (sometimes attributed to between November 1946 and January 1948), this is a drawing that pictures him and what appears to be a Rarámuri. However, as Barbara Sontag states in her preface, Artaud failed,

> both in his work and in his life, he failed (…). That difficulties that Artaud laments persists because he is thinking the unthinkable—about how body is mind and how mind is also body. This inexhaustible paradox is mirrored in Artaud's wish to produce art that is, at the same time, anti-art. (1988, xix)

6   Conclusions

As we intended to highlight, racial issues emerge throughout his work, as it polarizes and tensions categories such as Western/Non-western, colonialism/post-colonialism, white/'red Indian'. And, overall, such polarisations began by the introduction of a racial criticism within his work, revealing a precursory, non-Eurocentric perspective that will resonates throughout Theatre (and Performance) Studies. To Adrian Morfee (2005, 177), what Artaud really looked for with all of this was not feel a stranger to his own body anymore, a kind of 'observational consciousness that treats his life as something distinct from what he is', but quite the opposite: 'to feel life itself, to be aware of himself existing', the simple kind of existence that he attributed to indigenous people—more connected with their own bodies and with nature in general. The concept of *Body Without Organs* would become a key concept later in the twentieth century: an epistemological tool to overcome the dualistic modern view on body/mind,[11] once Artaud's thought also presents great influence on post-structuralist thinkers and philosophers, such as Deleuze and Derrida—which demonstrates a fierce force within his work of unpredictable consequences, capable of conducting western thinking into unmapped territories.

Notes

1. *Tate's online glossary*, 'Primitivism', https://www.tate.org.uk/art/art-terms/p/primitivism. Accessed 29 October 2018.
2. Curiously, in 1938 Mexico would be declared by Andre Breton as 'the surrealist place par excellence'. Breton would also visit the country only two years after Artaud, but for a shorter stay, without leaving Mexico City and only looking to 'meet' the 'ancient cultures' of Mexico… inside Mexican Museum walls. See Nicholson (2013).
3. Artaud's life, one could also say, takes the form of journeys and voids—long periods of institutionalisation, since he remained in different asylums since youth. The nature of his disorder received many different diagnostics through-

out his life, from meningitis, to hereditary syphilis and even schizophrenia, which also resulted in a lifelong addiction to prescribed (and unprescribed) drugs. However, he also displayed intense periods of significant creativity and working, and his total nine-month stay in Mexico can be accounted as one of those.

4. In his description of the Peyote rite, Artaud was sometimes accused of 'Christianising' the ritual by different scholars, but, as Su observes, the Peyote rite by the Rarámuri had already absorbed a certain amount of Christian symbolism. See Su (2012, 2).

5. Peyote (or San Pedro cacti) have a long history of use in Native American religious ceremonies, from Peru to Mexico. It has been used for at least 5000 years by different indigenous tribes (not only by the Rarámuri). They refer to peyote as 'the sacred medicine' whose benefits depends on the inner force of practitioner and they use it in prophecy, healing, and inner strength gain rituals. See Irigoyen-Rascón (2015).

6. As one could suppose, given his personal history of substance abuse—that was not the case. Actually, the use of drugs as a tool is a very sensitive topic—nevertheless, with a long use in human history. We could quote Aldous Huxley and his *The Doors of Perception*, a 1954 book that details his experiences when taking mescaline (the very active principle from peyote): Huxley recalls the visions induced by the drug as going from the 'purely aesthetic' to the 'sacramental vision'. Huxley's book title came from a William Blake's quote, from his 1790 poem *The Marriage of Heaven and Hell*. See Huxley (1954).

7. According to Krutak (2014, 32), Artaud had first learned about the ritual use of the peyote in the Sierra Madre from an Alfonso Reyes' poem, named *Yerbas del Tarahumara (Tarahumara herbs)*. Reyes was a writer and a Mexican ambassador in France and he and Artaud became friends in early 1930s and exchanged several letters: 'In an obscure and posthumous article, Reyes states that this poem, widely regarded as one of his finest, was first published in France in the summer of 1929. It most likely motivated Artaud's curiosity. In his work, Reyes speaks about the Tarahumara coming down from the mountains during a bad Harvest year to sell their medicinal plants in the Streets of Chihuahua.'

8. After returning to France, Artaud takes refuge in Ireland to 'witness the end of the world'. When the war breaks loose, he is deported to France and then institutionalized. See Mèredieu (2008).

9. See Cull (2009, 243–255), as well as Deleuze and Guattari (2004).

10. This one can be seen in the MOMA catalogue. See Rowell (1996, 129).

11. And not only this. I cannot avoid mentioning that when, for instance, Arun Saldanha discusses race in Deleuze's philosophy, he considers Artaud as one of the major influences in order to promote the deterritorialisation of whiteness in flows capable of 'hallucinating history' in Deleuzian work. Especially Artaud's body-without-organs would be paradigmatic for his comprehension of race as one among other strata, that persists as a biocultural and biopolitical historical force amid other forces. For Deleuze, after Artaud's influence, the Body-without-Organs concept is an unmapped potentiality of becomings, in which race is just a construct, another 'organ' from social tissue—See Saldanha and Adams (2013). We can also quote Deleuze and Guattari themselves, who conclude that 'All delirium is racial' (1983, 84).

REFERENCES

Allain, Paul, and Jen Harvie. 2006. *The Routledge Companion to Theatre and Performance*. London: Routledge.

Anderson, Benedict. 2006. *Imagined Communities: Reflections on the Origin and Spread of Nationalism*. London: Verso.

Araeen, Rasheed. 2005. From Primitivism to Ethnic Arts. In *The Myth of Primitivism*, ed. Susan Hiller, 132–150. London: Routledge.

Arrieta, Olivia. 1992. Religion and Ritual among the Tarahumara Indians of Northern Mexico: Maintenance of Cultural Autonomy Through Resistance and Transformation of Colonizing Symbols. *Wicazo Sa Review* 8 (2): 11–23.

Artaud, Antonin. 1936. La pintura de María Izquierdo [María Izquierdo's Artworks]. *Revista El semanario nacional*, no. 1370: 22–23.

———. 1958. *The Theater and Its Double*. New York: Grove Press.

———. 1976. *The Peyote Dance*. Translated by Helen Weaver. New York: Farrar, Straus and Giroux.

———. 1984. *Mexico: Viaje Al Pais De Los Tarahumaras* [Mexico: A Travel to the Country of the Tarahumaras]. Ciudad del Mexico: Fondo de Cultura Economica.

———. 1988. To have Done with the Judgement of God. In *Antonin Artaud: Selected Writings*, ed. Susan Sontag, 555–569. Berkeley: University of California Press.

Ashcroft, Bill, Griffiths Gareth, and Helen Tiffin. 2000. *Post-Colonial Studies: The Key Concepts*. London: Routledge.

Barber, Stephen. 2003. *Artaud: Blows and Bombs*. London: Creation Books.

Bush, Christopher. 1994. Theory and Its Double: Ideology and Ideograph in Orientalist Theory. *Paroles gelées Journal* 1 (12): 5–25.

Carasco, Raymonde. 1998. Ciguri. Voyage(s) au pays des Tarahumaras [Ciguri: Travel(s) to the Country of Tarahumaras]. *Revista de Dialectología y Tradiciones Populares* 53 (2): 241–249.

———. 2006. Approche de la pensee Tarahumara [Approach to Tarahumara Thought]. In *Antonin Artaud*—Catalogue Exposition BNF. Paris, ed. Guillaume Fau. Paris: Bibliothèque National de France/Gallimard.

Cardullo, Bert, and Robert Knopf. 2001. *Theater of the Avant-Garde: 1890–1950 a Critical Anthology*. London: Yale University Press.

Castaneda, Carlos. 1998. *Magical Passes: The Practical Wisdom of the Shamans of Ancient Mexico*. New York: Harper Perennial.

Clifford, James. 1981. On Ethnographic Surrealism. *Comparative Studies in Society and History* 23 (4, Oct.): 539–564.

Cull, Laura. 2009. How do You make Yourself a Theatre without Organs?: Deleuze, Artaud and the Concept of Differential Presence. *Theatre Research International* 34 (3): 243–255.

Dalton, David. 2018. *Mestizo Modernity: Race, Technology, and the Body in Post-Revolutionary Mexico*. Gainesville: University of Florida Press.

Deleuze, Gilles, and Felix Guattari. 1983. *Anti-Oedipus: Capitalism and Schizophrenia*. Minneapolis: University of Minnesota Press.

———. 2004. November 28, 1947: How do You make Yourself a *Body Without Organs?* In *A Thousand Plateaus: Capitalism and Schizophrenia*. New York: Continuum.

Fontana, Bernard, and John Schaefer. 1997. *Tarahumara: Where Night is the Day of the Moon*. Tucson: University of Arizona Press.

Goodall, Jane. 1994. *Artaud and the Gnostic Drama*. Oxford: Oxford University Press.

Hale, Dana S. 2008. *Races on Display: French Representations of Colonized Peoples, 1886–1940*. Bloomington: Indiana University Press.

Hertz, Uri. 2003. Artaud in Mexico. *Fragmentos* 25: 11–17.

Hooker, Juliet. 2017. *Theorizing Race in the Americas: Douglass, Sarmiento, Du Bois, and Vasconcelos*. Oxford: Oxford University Press.

Hubert, Renée Riese. 1998. Antonin Artaud's Itinerary through Exile and Insanity. In *Borders, Exiles, Diasporas*, ed. Elazar Barkan and Marie-Denise Shelton. Stanford: Stanford UP.

Huxley, Aldous. 1954. *The Doors of Perception*. London and New York: Chatto & Windus.

Irigoyen-Rascón, Fructuoso. 2015. *Tarahumara Medicine: Ethnobotany and Healing among the Rarámuri of Mexico*. Norman: University of Oklahoma Press.

Krutak, Lars. 2014. (Sur)real or Unreal? Antonin Artaud in the Sierra Tarahumara of Mexico. *Journal of Surrealism and the Americas* 8 (1): 28–55.

Mèredieu, Florence de. 2006. *C'etait Antonin Artaud* [This was Antonin Artaud]. Paris: Fayard.

———. 2008. *Antonin Artaud: Portraits et gris-gris* [Antonin Artaud: Portraits and talismans]. Paris: Augmentée.

Morfee, Adrian. 2005. *Antonin Artaud's Writing Bodies*. Oxford: Clarendon Press Publication.

Murphy, Jay. 2017. *Artaud's Metamorphosis: From hieroglyphs to Bodies without Organs*. London: Pavement Books.

Nicholson, Melanie. 2013. Surrealism's 'found object': The Enigmatic Mexico of Artaud and Breton. *Journal of European Studies* 43 (1): 27–43.

Rowell, Margit. 1996. *Antonin Artaud: Works on Paper—Exposition Catalogue*. New York: The Museum of Modern Art/H.N. Abrams.

Saldanha, Arun, and Jason Michael Adams. 2013. *Deleuze and Race*. Edinburgh: Edinburgh University Press.

Savarese, Nicola. 2001. 1931: Antonin Artaud Sees Balinese Theatre at the Paris Colonial Exposition. *TDR* 45 (3): 51–77.

Schechner, Richard. 2003. *Performance Theory*. London: Routledge.

Sontag, Susan. 1988. *Antonin Artaud: Selected Writings*. Berkeley: University of California Press.

Stone Peters, Julie. 2002. Artaud in the Sierra Madre: Theatrical Bodies, Primitive Signs, Ritual Landscapes. In *Land/Scape/Theatre*, ed. Elinor Fuchs and Una Chaudhuri, 228–251. Ann Arbor: University of Michigan Press.

Su, Tsu-Chung. 2012. Artaud's Journey to Mexico. *CLCWeb: Comparative Literature and Culture* 14 (5): 1–9.

Thompson, Ayanna. 2008. *Performing Race and Torture on the Early Modern Stage*. London: Routledge.

Torgovnick, Marianna. 1990. *Gone Primitive: Savage Intellects, Modern Lives*. Chicago: University of Chicago Press.

Turner, Victor. 1995. *The Ritual Process: Structure and Anti-Structure*. New York: Aldine.

CHAPTER 23

Representing and Re-presenting Others in Yorùbá Performance

Ṣọlá Adéyẹmí

1 Introduction

The Yorùbá performance culture has always been eclectic and modern in its engagement with other cultures and racial representation, in both social and religious contexts. The performing arts articulate understandings of race, and how the culture intervenes in how this is presented (or represented) both at a community and cultural levels from precolonial periods to the present, but especially during the colonial period when the contacts between the Yorùbá people and the Europeans were most marked and disruptive. This chapter introduces how the Yorùbá represent these encounters with the 'other' in their indigenous performances. The representation can be bold, as in outright depiction of other people for parody or serious exploration of differences and similarities; it can also be subtle. Representation of others is a common way of fostering understanding and investigating points of tension and variances in the culture, customs and traditions. Among the Yorùbá people, representation is coded into the way of life and daily expressions. This can be through the myths, tales and songs, in visual arts, and in the performance arts, including egúngún, which is the focus of this chapter. Some of these representations are stereotypical whilst others are conceived as tangible pieces of ideas and feelings evoked during encounters, cross-culturally revealing Yorùbá worldview and its perception of others as stocks of humanity. The impact of these representations is dynamic, serving as stimulus that is not only important to the understanding of

Ṣ. Adéyẹmí (✉)
Goldsmiths, University of London, London, UK
e-mail: s.adeyemi@gold.ac.uk

© The Author(s), under exclusive license to Springer Nature
Switzerland AG 2021
T. Morosetti, O. Okagbue (eds.), *The Palgrave Handbook of Theatre and Race*, https://doi.org/10.1007/978-3-030-43957-6_23

425

the 'other', but is also enriching and crucial to the development of the performing arts among the Yorùbá. In addition to introducing how the Yorùbá represent others, this chapter will further explore this concept, using egúngún performance culture.

2   THE YORÙBÁ PEOPLE

The Yorùbá are a nation of people who are mainly located in the south-west part of Nigeria and who share the same language, traditions and customs, religions and performance cultures. They are also indigenous to the neighbouring republics of Benin, Togo and Sierra Leone and, resulting from the trans-Atlantic slavery, South America, the Caribbean Islands and the USA.

3   REPRESENTATION OF OTHERS

The Yorùbá people represent others in three basic forms. The first of this is in the myths and tales that serve as the context of the storytelling tradition. Storytelling provides entertainment and relaxation as well as teaching aids about living and maintaining relationships. More significantly, it is used to emphasise interests, outlooks and worldview. Usually staged in the evenings, storytelling uses imagery, allusion and symbolism from real experience and historiography, from abstract concepts, or from imaginative folktales to present ideas that appeal to feelings and the intellect. Often, these concepts involve the invocation of others as characters to critically probe their behaviours or suggest a collective sense of the people's identity by defining and highlighting familiar and positive aspects as well as critical and negative characteristics. Often times, it is to explain the origin of an alien concept. An example of this type of narrative is the tale of how white people emerged among the Yoruba and became objects of representation. Tales are fictitious narratives drawn from imagination though they may sometimes contain allusions to historical events. I first heard this tale from my grandmother when I was growing up.

Once, there lived a woman named Òyì, a worshipper of the god of Wind. Òyì was not married because she was not yet of age. However, she grew impatient and wanted to have a child. She therefore went to the babaláwo, the priest-diviner, who divined that Òyì would have the child she wanted but, since she was in a hurry and did not wait for the right time, after getting married, to have a child, the child would be different from that of other women. When it was time for her to give birth, Òyì gave birth to a child with white skin. Because Òyì was impatient, her child had not gone through the full process of creation by Obatala, the Yorùbá god of creation, and was not ready to be born. People started broadcasting the news that 'Òyì bí omo tí gbogbo ara rè bó' (Òyì birthed a son with peeled skin). This was later shortened to Òyìbó (which is the Yorùbá tag for a white person). However, because the child was not able to cope with the sun, in spite of the shea butter oil and raw eggs that the mother was rubbing on the skin for protection, Òyì consulted the babaláwo again on her next course of action. The diviner, this time, interceded in behalf of Òyì with Olokun, the sea god, who agreed to take the child to a more temperate region of the world. Occasionally, Olokun would bring Òyìbó back home to visit his mother, until gradually, Òyìbó and his descendants were able to live among Òyì's people.

The story uses repetition, parallelism, piling and association, in addition to imagery and allusions—all features of the storytelling tradition—to create a narrative about Europeans, one of whose major differences was the lack of eumelanin which causes the differently pigmented skin colour. The narrative is used to explain the presence of white people among the Yorùbá people. This idea of mythmaking and tales creation would generate different other stories designed to clarify or frame any other perception of the white people. Similar to storytelling is the carnivalesque performance of the Mami-Water mask among the Anago, a subdivision of the Yorùbá people in Benin Republic. This is performed as a rite of passage during funeral ceremonies or other events of personal or communal importance, in particular by families where the Olokun or Yemoja (goddess of the ocean and rivers; mother of fishes) is worshipped. Being a fishing community, there are many myths surrounding the existence of Mami-Water among the people. Olokun or Yemoja in areas of the southern coastal regions of West Africa are depicted as Mami-Water. The relevant excerpt of this performance to this chapter is the mimicry and representation aspects, where performers, including acrobats and mime artists, wear facial masks representing white couples, fishermen, Christian priests, sailors and servants, all disembarking from boats and canoes to perform for the community. The main mask is the huge feminine representation of Mami-Water. The dramatisations mimic the characters represented. For instance, the white couple is always dressed in black dinner jackets (male) and wide-brimmed pleated twentieth century gowns (for the female). They dance European dances, parodies of Twist or Tango, and exhibit behaviours and acts similar to Victorian court attendants, curtsying for every passer-by. The Christian priest declaims loudly and occasionally read from a black book representing the Bible. The sailor is costumed wearing doublet or short coat, wide hat and carrying an imitation sword. The images presented range from that of the eighteenth-century seafarer to a Victorian gentleman, the characters almost always emerge from the direction of the ocean. The performers wear masks that are either painted white, or bright colours, but which are recognisably European, with long noses and thin lips.

Another form of representation common among the Yorùbá is found in visual arts, in wood carvings, sculptures and wall-paintings. These forms and other artefacts 'illustrate dress, ornament, material culture and, sometimes, the custom of the people' (Adedeji 1969, 25) but they are also used to memorialise significant events, especially the type that celebrate important figures and aliens. Some particularly remarkable representations of Queen Victoria, for instance, and lawyers and Christian missionaries—who were mostly white men—are reproduced by William Bascom in his book, *A Handbook of West*

African Art (1953). So, in these artistic forms, and in performing arts, including egúngún, which is the focus of this chapter, the Yorùbá people have always represented others who are not familiar to them. The most popular methods of exhibiting the representation is in performances, which are the foundation of all festivals and ceremonies.

The socio-cultural community of the Yorùbá is filled with festivals and ceremonies all geared towards oneness with nature and the unity of all human beings (Daramola and Jeje 1975), with careful engagement with social, political and cultural manifestations, either as a presentation in sculptures and paintings, or represented in theatres and performances. It is almost impossible to discuss Yorùbá traditional performance culture without reference to the religion, myths and rituals of the people. The beliefs of the Yorùbá people vary significantly across Yorubaland. These variations inevitably arose as myths were orally transmitted between generations and become influenced or modified by doctrinal values from other cultures and religions such as Islam or Christianity. In practice, however, the myths and rituals share the same conventions, including the belief in orí (destiny) and the ancestors, represented by egúngún.[1] Egúngún is a masque or masquerade referring both to a performance given by masked characters as well as to the masked performer. The term 'masquerade' denotes the performance and 'masker' refers to the performer. Egúngún is important among the Yorùbá because of its use in the representation of nature, encounters and issues of modernity. The Yorùbá refer to egúngún as the inhabitants of heaven who are still very close to the world of the living, particularly to their relatives whom they protect from evil and other vicissitudes of life, and who regularly visit the world of the living during festivals, funeral or other ritual ceremonies. Special days are reserved for the veneration of these ancestors who are represented by masques in the form of egúngún. It is from these acts that the Yorùbá performance culture emerged, and consequently, that serves as the premise for investigating the representation of race among the Yorùbá in this chapter.

4   The Concept of Egúngún

The concept of egúngún—also eégún—refers to the practice of ancestor worship. It primarily defines and describes that practice and other varied masked manifestations that are the physical expression of the inseparability of the world of the living and that of the dead, the space of the familiar and the strange. The Yorùbá belief system does not recognise death as the end of life; rather, it is a stage in the cycle of life and, for a while, the departed become denizens of the other world, ará òrun (òrun—space of reflection), where they possess 'limitless potentialities which [... they] can exploit for the benefit or detriment of those who still live on earth' (Idowu 1962, 192). Making use of these 'potentialities', the ará òrun materialise as masquerade, the sacred mask of the ancestors.

The origin of egúngún as a cult and as a belief is coded in Ifá[2] verses. In *Ifa Divination: Communication between Gods and Man in West Africa*, William

Bascom (1969, 208) extensively recites an Ifá verse, the Ogbè-Ìrosùn, to frame the particular reasons for the appearance of egúngún among the Yorùbá and encode the origin of the cult within the primordial belief and philosophy of the people. This is a view supported by S. O. Babayemi (1980), who states, inter alia, that

> One of the principal Odù (verse) which shows how egúngún was originated is Otúrúpòn Méjì. It claims that when a man dies the corpse is buried but the spirit joins the ancestors to become egúngún. As the corpse of the deceased is covered head and feet so as the egúngún in heaven. That is why every egúngún is fully costumed, no part of the masquerade must be revealed to the public. The Odù explains the Yoruba belief in life after death, how the dead joined the ancestors to become dwellers of heaven (Ará Òrun).

Gradually, over time, egúngún came to acquire new contexts and functions of both edifying and entertaining character. Thus, besides the egúngún of the departed, other egúngún, with their varied costumes, began to emerge as figures of ritual and entertainment. Rather than representing a single ancestor, egúngún became a collective entity, a generalised embodiment of the spirit of the ancestors in a particular lineage; others transcend the borders of the family unit and, having materialised as a guild—such as hunters' guild—or town egúngún, they protect the community, give advice or serve as judges and executioners. Other groups, after a merger of guilds,[3] are exclusively entertainers.

Incontrovertibly, in line with the cultural beliefs, egúngún combine two things—(i) a spiritual or ethereal being with human features and definite control over human affairs on this plane; and (ii) the presumed form of that being worn over an ordinary human body for the performances of the egúngún. The Yorùbá accept egúngún as spiritual beings. Egúngún performance share the same origin with the Yorùbá Alárìnjó performance,[4] the first written account of which are found in the travel journals of Hugh Clapperton and Richard Lander who stayed seven weeks at Katunga (Old Ọyọ́; Ọyọ́ Ilé), the capital of Ọyọ́ kingdom in 1826. The king of Ọyọ́ invited his guests to watch a rehearsal of an itinerant troupe whose traditions dated back to the late sixteenth century.[5]

5   The Yorùbá and the Imagination of Other Races

Imagination and ultimately the conception of other people in Yorùbá performance culture were premised on a Cartesian logic which foregrounded the fantasy of an autonomous subject with a privileged view casting his eye over a transparent space which can be ruptured, disrupted, filtered, interpreted or filled with caricatures of that race or representation that are adopted to reflect the value system or the merging of cultural values. This 'Master-Subject-Yorùbá-Others' relationship supposedly inhabiting an Archimedean position outside of discourse with a supposedly unmediated access to transparent space presented in the discourse of encounter or value of contact, created what Mary

430   Ṣ. ADÉYẸMÍ

Louise Pratt (1992, 201) describes as the 'monarch-of-all-I-survey' mode of representation. This process of filtering or engagement happens at both individual and societal levels, between the Yorùbá people and the others—and vice versa—in a process of differentiated hybridity that is presented through translation, reduction or domestication.

The positional authority of this Yorùbá-Others relationship has always been constituted, first, by a division into subject and object with all the dualism involved in this process, and then by a configuration of space to consolidate the resultant visual authority. In *Discipline and Punish: The Birth of the Prison*, Michel Foucault (1977) uses Jeremy Bentham's eighteenth-century design of a prison—the Panopticon—to discuss issues of power and surveillance. Bentham's architectural design for a circular prison with individual cells which can be seen and monitored from a single vantage point consolidates containment and control by a spatial arrangement in which the observed is firmly placed within the visual power of the observer. From this image of a space with a central tower from which everything can be observed, we can define the nature of representation in Yorùbá theatre and performance, in the traverse negotiations that exist between the people and their various others.

Several scholars, among whom are William Bascom (1953), Ulli Beier (1964), Esiaba Irobi (2006) and Osita Okagbue (2007), have looked at the processes of expansion and adaptability which the structures and iconographies of indigenous, pre-colonial African performance cultures had to undergo to accommodate the presences and anxieties of specifically European cultures.

To relate this concept to the Yorùbá performance culture, the rehearsed performance by the nineteenth century Aláriìnjó troupe is instructive.

6   Hugh Clapperton and Richard Lander

In the early 1800s, British exploration was interested in the area of the world now known as West Africa. One of the more famous explorers was Captain Hugh Clapperton (18 May 1788–13 April 1827), a Scottish naval officer who was engaged by the British Secretary of State for War and the Colonies, Lord Bathurst, in 1825 to lead an exploration from the western coast of Africa, by the Bight of Benin, to Sokoto, the capital of the Fulani country. He took with him, along with other assistants, Richard Lander who later compiled his diaries after Clapperton's death in Sokoto in 1827.

A few miles into Yorubaland, the explorers spent some weeks at Ọyọ́, the then capital of the Yorùbá Kingdom, where they watched an open rehearsal of a play on 22 February 1826. Clapperton describes the performance, which he referred to as 'pantomimes, or whatever they may be called' (1829, 54), in three acts, introduced by 'musicians… with drums, horns and whistles', and with interludes of choral songs by the king's women and the assembled crowd. The first act consisted of performers dancing and tumbling in 'sacks'; the second act consisted in catching the boa-constrictor. The third act is particularly important, for this chapter.

23 REPRESENTING AND RE-PRESENTING OTHERS IN YORÙBÁ PERFORMANCE   431

The third act, according to Clapperton, consisted of the white devil.

The actors having retired to some distance in the back ground, one of them was left in the centre, whose sack falling gradually down, exposed *a white head*, at which all the crowd gave a shout, that rent the air; they appeared indeed to enjoy this sight, as the perfection of the actor's art. The whole body was at last cleared of the incumbrance of the sack, when it exhibited *the appearance of a human fig-ure cast in white wax, of the middle size, miserably thin, and starved with cold*. It frequently went through the motion of taking snuff, and rubbing its hands; when it walked, it was with the most awkward gait, treading as the most tender-footed white man would do in walking bare-footed, for the first time, over new frozen ground. The spectators often appealed to us, as to the excellence of the perfor-mance, and entreated I would look and be attentive to what was going on. I pretended to be fully as much pleased with this caricature of a white man as they could be, and certainly the actor burlesqued the part to admiration (*italics mine*; pp. 55–56)

The Alarinjo performer of 1826, in order to demystify the Scottish explorer, created a stylistic performance to domesticate, and therefore to 'manage' the presence of this 'other' in a discursive manner. This form is revealed in stages. There was first the exposure of the 'white head', followed by the entire body of the actor which had '*the appearance of a human figure cast in white wax, of the middle size, miserably thin, and starved with cold*'. Whilst depicting Clapperton (or his assistants) as human figures whitened by wax, the per-former astutely presented a negotiated appearance, between that of a privi-leged white man in Africa and that of a reduced, helpless figure lost so far from his home. This is further accentuated by representing the white man as 'unsure' of his surroundings—'awkward', 'tender-footed' and 'walking bare-footed'. The picture that is presented in neither that of the 'white devil', nor that of Pratt's 'monarch-of-all-I-survey', but that of a 'discursive contain-ment' (Okagbue 2007, 10), rendering the presence of the white man harm-less in this 'contact zone'[6] (Pratt 1992, 7) and in the process unveiling the nature of future encounters.

This performance is all too familiar to observers of Yorùbá performance culture, for it is a version of the Agbégijó performances, a version of the ubiq-uitous Yorùbá travelling theatre. The Agbégijó, or Alárìnjó, performance uti-lised and still utilises dialogue, masks, costumes, music, mime and singing to satirise, comment upon and interact with different social and political encoun-ters. There is no doubt that what Clapperton witnessed was a culture in transi-tion, employing the weapons of syncretism. But, in transitioning, this culture transcended into a selective mode for the rhetoric of performance, as we are going to establish with the description of egúngún in Ìmèsí-Ilé below.

The performance form described by Clapperton existed in the 1826 encoun-ter, but the performers infused their imagination on the performance, giving an interpretation of what they saw in a representation that bordered on a

432   Ş. ADÉYẸMÍ

caricature. As Joel Adeyinka Adedeji has stated, a remark which applies also to performance,

> Yorùbá artists indulge in caricaturing. Whether in reference to an imitation or a representation of a person or thing, in sculpting, chanting or performance, an element of ludicrous exaggeration is introduced as part of the total artistic picture. This art of deliberately distorted picturing relates to mythological characters and important social figures, as well as general types in the society (1969, 25–26).

To the Yorùbá, performance must among other uses provide a means to domesticate that which is wild and strange. It must act like the funnel which arrests the rainwater and directs the torrent into a receptacle. The Yorùbá insist that any presence, which is denied acknowledgement and approval, can become a focus for disruption. So, when an 'other' makes its appearance, especially the European figure in the explorers, the artists promptly *invite* him to the pantheon of stock characters and ciphers, with his idiosyncrasies and identifiable attributes. In colonial Yorùbá performance, the District Officer is even embellished with his helmet and bicycle as has been presented by Ndukaku Amankulor (1981) and William Bascom (1953). Okagbue (2007) is even more forthcoming on this process of domestication, underlining that indigenous forms become resilient because of their ability to dialectically negotiate with the 'other'.

> The indigenous forms are constantly reviewing and revising themselves in response to their ever-changing historical and cultural contexts. They withstood the concerted assaults of colonial politics and those of Christian and Islamic religions by engaging with, adapting and incorporating these intruding elements into their universe as a means of domesticating and coping with them (2007, 10).

Commenting further, Okagbue states, in relation to the *Ijele* masquerade of the Igbo, that

> [it] exhibits an almost irreverent postmodernist appropriation of alien materials and threats in a process of discursive containment. *Ijele* successfully absorbed the colonial experience and presence of late nineteenth and mid-twentieth centuries (2007, 10).

The representation of the 'white devil' is an example of this kind of negotiation and the converse roles of representation by the Yorùbá people. The performances strategically devise means to accommodate and adapt both the Yorùbá cultures and the 'foreign' one in an inscription of the 'white devil'. The presentation of this imagery in performance is an example of the culture's enduring method of translation, contestation, and engagement with the idea of the other and the inscription of that other, and in many instances a re-inscription to query and challenge familiar concepts, where the performance transcends the identity of the original by embedding or releasing several flavours whilst at the same time acknowledging its debt to the antiquated work.

Since Europe's presence among the Yorùbá people produced complex discourses about representation and creative imagination of culture; and whereas the 'encounter' became syncretically embedded through a 'mixed set of literacies' (Irobi 2006, 268) such as conventional forms of literature, iconographs, sonic and other forms of literacies, and performances in the indigenous festivals and rituals; it is important to re-image or re-imagine the concept of Yorùbá performance culture in Alárìnjó and egúngún performances, either in whole or as 'cultural fragments' (Brandon 1990, 92).

7   REPRESENTATION OF OTHERS IN EGÚNGÚN PERFORMANCE

There are various types of egúngún in Yorubaland, including satirical masks, elegant masks that exhibit the beauty and elegance of costumes and dance, and masks that dramatise strength, but the most significant among Yorùbá egúngún are the ancestral masks. Much as these egúngún are performed for ancestral veneration and ritual purposes, the entertainment function is also highlighted, evident in choice of maskers. A performer has to be a good poet or orator and attuned to different styles of music and if, in the course of a performance, a performer 'cannot improve his performance, he may be asked to terminate the performance or to let another masker take over' (Enekwe 1987, 84), presuming that the replacement is a better performer. Although, Enekwe is referring to the performance of Igbo masquerade here, the practice is similar is some performances among the Yorùbá people. The difference is that, among the Yorùbá, the masker would probably be taken back to the grove for the switch, as the shrouding secrecy must be maintained. Amankulor pushes this point further when he asserts that 'among the Igbo of Nigeria, for example, the *Okonko* or *Mmonwu* performances, given by initiation associations with those names, are freely described as *egwu* (play)' (1989, 45). Ancestral masks are recognised by their moral and mystical authority, and attributes which serve as embodiments of the ritual importance of the ancestors. These ancestral egúngún perform various functions, from officiating during burial ceremonies where they are assumed to take the soul of the departed to the land of the ancestors, to performing at night as bull-roarers in a bid to maintain societal equilibrium. Some egúngún use songs and proverbs to ridicule people whose habits or behaviour are considered undesirable in the community. Yet, others adjudicate difficult cases or perform oracular roles.

In a typical Yorùbá town, each household has its own egúngún and a household may have more than one egúngún or even different kinds of egúngún. Usually, the spirit of the most powerful or the most benevolent individual in the household is invoked into the mask of the more representative egúngún. Most communal rites are performed by this egúngún. There are also the dancers, the poets, the acrobats, the satirists, the praise-singers and the *Láyèwú*, the hunter-masques famous for their imitations of wild animals and 'foreigners' in mime and dance.

The many functions of the egúngún make it a valuable source material for dramatic performances; consequently, every aspect of egúngún festival is a performance. The rituals involved in the festival also provide a rich plot for drama. The focus of the rituals is the elaborate process of chanting, dancing and sacrifices which are dramatic performances in themselves.

Egúngún festival is a major cultural event. The staging of the festival in different Yorùbá towns is not consistent as each town has its special festival days and method of organising the festival. However, one thing is common: the festival usually falls during the harvest season as this is the period when majority of the people are free from their agrarian activities. It is also the period when there is abundant food and ritual materials. The mode of worship and duration of the festival vary from place to place, but the general sense behind it is the same and that is seeking communion with the supreme God through the ancestors who have, by the incidence of death, acquired more powers in the world beyond. Generally, the festival lasts between seven and ninety days. The festival has acquired a status of the major festival in some of the towns, especially in Ìmèsí-Ilé where the biennial version has acquired a special status because of its syncretism and representation of the 'other'. To fully understand and contextualise how egúngún is used in depicting and representing other races in performance, we will now focus on the particular circumstances of egúngún in the community.

8 ÌMÈSÍ-ILÉ: A SETTLEMENT THAT BECAME A WAR CAMP

Ìmèsí-Ilé is located in the north-eastern part of Yorùbáland. The first settlers occupied the present location of the town several centuries ago. Situated on a range of hills, Ìmèsí-Ilé is a cosmopolitan community where seventeen dialects of Yorùbá language are spoken primarily due to its importance as the Èkìtìparapò was headquarters during the last major war[7] among the Yorùbá people. Several Èkìtì kings came to reside in Ìmèsí-Ilé during the war, because of the uncertainty surrounding the Peace Agreement signed in 1886. Each of the campaigners occupied particular spaces in and around the town and retained their dialects, customs and ways of life. This heterogenous communal arrangement is unified in the annual egúngún festival.

While the New Yam festival or observance ceremonies for other divinities serve as the beginning of a new year in most other towns, egúngún festival marks the beginning of a new year in Ìmèsí-Ilé. Egúngún is however recent to the community and was introduced by the Òtu-Ókó family of Òyó, who migrated to the town after conquest by the Nupe in 1535.[8] As Babayemi (1980) concludes, the origin of egúngún as both a cult and entertainment is in Òyó. Therefore, upon departing Òyó, the Òtu-Ókó left with their egúngún cult which they introduced to Ìmèsí-Ilé, and which was later accepted by the

23 REPRESENTING AND RE-PRESENTING OTHERS IN YORÙBÁ PERFORMANCE

town as a replacement for the Ìgunnukó mask that the Nupe people had earlier introduced.

The festival period in Ìmèṣí-Ilé extends between twenty-eight and thirty-five days. On a market day, the eve of the commencement of the festival, an elder eguńgún, the *Alágbáàrárá* is led by the chiefs and priests of eguńgún cult to the market to officially broadcast the dates to the community. The initiates however would have known ahead of this date and would have started preparing for the festival. The *Alágbáàrárá* collects the ritual materials like salt, dry fish, shea-butter cream, palm oil and roasted bean powder from the market women. The women regard this contribution as their offering to the ancestors for granting life and sustenance during the past year, as well as prayer offering for a more favourable new year. The materials collected are mixed with giant land snails earlier contributed by each household in the town and taken to the Ìgbàlè, the grove where the shrine of eguńgún is situated.

The ritual for the commencement of eguńgún is usually performed by the cult chiefs and representatives of other important egúngún in the town. The ritual would be performed to invoke the spirits of the ancestors to grant understanding, peace, love and goodwill during the festival period and through the coming year. Prayers are said by the priests for each and every household and for the good administration of the town by the king and his chiefs. Sacrifices are then made at the shrine, at the royal tombs in the king's palace, at the tombs of important individuals and warriors, and at the town square to propitiate Èsù whose main image is at the town centre, where all roads meet. The snails' shells are cracked over the shrine in the Ìgbàlè and also over the shrine of Èsù. The rest of the ritual materials are then taken to the shrine of Òtu-Ókó, the man who brought egúngún to Ìmèṣí-Ilé.

After the sacrifices, another eguńgún called *Àgan* declares the festival open by greeting and praying for all the chiefs and all the households individually. Then the ritual performers proceed to the king's palace where they are joined by the rest of the community to sing songs and dance round the town in a ceremony called *Yèúke*.

The importance of this ritual opening is on the symbolism represented in the main eguńgún who presides over the performance. Like the *Ijele* of the Igbo, *Alágbáàrárá* absorbs elements of foreignness introduced to the community by strangers, or more appropriately, the 'other', to interrogate, domesticate, and more relevant to its performance, to deploy in its annual incarnation. Its economic and ritual roles as the collector of all ritual items from the market stemmed from the colonial practice of tax collectors coming to the community of market days to exact rates and dues from the people. Unlike the tax collector . who forcibly collected his dues from the market women, *Alágbáàrárá* has however modified the practice—in a negotiation with the people—to accept the willing contributions as a gift to the ancestors rather than acts to economically deprive the women of their earnings. Yet, the representation even in its modernity, is that of; its costume is made of white calico but more representatively, his skin, which he reveals to the crowd after collecting the ritual

436   Ṣ. ADÉYẸMÍ

materials, is white. This exposure of white skin is a narrative that runs through the entire egúngún festival, and it is linked to the colonial experience of encounters with the British officers who established a base and a local office in the town, including an experimental research station on measles in the years before and immediately after Nigeria's independence from the British in 1960. More crucially, it takes its antecedents from the practice of the Alárìnjó performers whose constant engagements with the 'others' have led to a series of performance and performative experiences involving representation of negotiated images and forms over the years. The Èmùilè of Ìmẹ̀sí-Ilé in 1988 was insistent though that Alágbáàrárá functions to collect tributes as established in the town's charter for the communal ritual and his white skin symbolises the pallor of the dead, marking the egúngún as an ancestral figure, and deflected the suggestion of a negotiation between the egúngún cult and the British guests.

At night, after the rituals at the Ìgbàlè, all the egúngún from different households and groups parade through the town and end up at the ancestral stream on the outskirts of the town for the ritual purification of their costume prior to emerging the following day. Only the initiates of the egúngún cult could participate in this ritual procession. No woman or non-initiates into the egúngún cult must view the procession or be privy to the secret, except Alápínni, the only woman among the egúngún priests.

Throughout the festival period, the egúngún perform round the town but not in as large a number as the opening and the closing days. The climax of the festival is the dance and prayer for the people by the most significant egúngún of the Òtu-Ókó family, Eyẹkéye.[9] Eyẹkéye represents the diversity of people that constitute the town's population, including 'foreigners' who attend the festival.

On the evening before the final day, a group of elder egúngún expose their legs which are symbolically white, while dancing before the king. Though the legs are white, this is a different 'whiteness' from that of Alágbáàrárá. While the latter depicts a colonial representation, the former, of all the egúngún, symbolises the shrouded imagery of the ancestors. This explanation is closer to the position of Èmùilè Alonge in 1988. The act of exposing the legs is also a reminder of the transition to the world of the ancestors. The egúngún then move to the sloping flat rock in front of the Ìgbàlè where they dance and expose their legs again for the people. At night, all the egúngún proceed through the town singing their valedictory songs. As in the beginning of the festival, they end up at the ancestral stream to purify their costumes for the ceremony of the final day.

On the final day of egúngún festival in Ìmẹ̀sí-Ilé, the egúngún start to emerge from the early morning hours. The herald egúngún are the praise-singers, the poets and the dancers, followed by the jàndùkú, then the comedians and finally, the senior ones with their drummers and retinue of smaller egúngún, praise-singers, men and singing women.

9 LÁDÚNÙNWÒ: A PERFORMATIVE RITUAL

Ládúnùnwò, the two egúngún masked as male and female, come out very late in the afternoon to close the biennial festival. The maskers of *Ládúnùnwò* are usually selected from the Òtu-Ókó family and the selection and masking are kept secret even from many initiates of the cult. The outing of *Ládúnùnwò* is most colourful. The preparation for this outing starts at dawn on the day. This early preparation consists mainly of rituals and prayers for an auspicious outing of the *Ládúnùnwò*. Elaborate rituals are performed with snails and palm oil for peace at the major egúngún shrines in the town, at the tombs of great warriors, and finally at the Ìgbàlè where the *Ládúnùnwò* is finally masked.

In the late afternoon, when the people and the egúngún are all assembled at the market square, in front of the king's palace, with the king seated on his throne, all the egúngún parade along the route the *Ládúnùnwò* would take from the Ìgbàlè to the market square, twitching their whips high above their heads and shaking their gongs and rattles. This procession is executed seven times, with songs and dances, before the *Ládúnùnwò* appear before the throne, totally covered in a rich *Àgan* voluminous garb. At this stage, the *Èmìilè*, the chief priest of the egúngún cult, asks the king whether he should remove the *Àgan* apparel covering the *Ládúnùnwò*. He poses the question three times. This is to give the king the chance to leave the arena because, as the earthly representative of the gods and ancestors, the king must not witness the naked *Ládúnùnwò* perform the ancestral dance.[10]

The action of the *Èmìilè* also signals the womenfolk to loosen whatever style they have plaited their hair, if they have not already done so, as it is a taboo for any woman to have a similar hairstyle to the female *Ládúnùnwò*. Also, as a mark of respect, everybody removes any head cover they might have on.

Immediately after the action of the king and the womenfolk, the *Àgan* apparel is removed in stages, first exposing two raised silvers swords and two black horsetails, then the head before the *Ládúnùnwò* are revealed before the people. The *Ládúnùnwò* are figures of human beings in closely sewn white costume to reveal the entire body shape, with wooden head masks. Every part of the figure is white except the top of the head, which is black, signifying eternal youth. The male figure is in *ìbàntè*, a short groin protector made of black velvet while the female figure is in a *yèrì*, a skirt also made of the same material as the *ìbàntè*. The male holds two silver swords and has beads on his neck, signifying both a warrior and a king while the beads-bedecked female holds two black horsetail emblems, symbolising royalty and at the same time, because of the black colour, an identification with the common people. The beads on the female figure are crossed over the shoulders and extend to the waist where they complement the *lágìdìgbà*, the female waist beads that are worn over and above the *yèrì*. The drummers then start beating their set rhythms for the *Ládúnùnwò* dance.

The *Ládúnùnwò* dance to three ritual rhythms in front of the throne. The dance is to the ancient Gbèdu[11] and Gàngànún[12] drums. The first dance steps

438   Ṣ. ADÉYẸMÍ

are regal steps danced to the rhythm of Gbẹ̀du drums and akin to the royal dance at installation, except that it is more spiritual, and the meaning of the drum rhythms connotes blessing for the towns people rather than a series of advices and warnings, if it is beaten for an installation. The two other dances are more intricate and faster in rhythm. But the performance is the same—a depiction of ancestors who are above all human beings reliving their lives to nurture the well-being of the living. Then, in a dramatic manner, the female *Ládúnùnwò* kneels before the male and the male pats her head and supports her up. After this, the *Ládúnùnwò* pray for the present occupant of the throne and the inhabitants of the town, as well as the visitors.

Then, they move, with the senior egúngún clearing the way, along the set route, praying at five points on the way, to the flat rock in front of the Ìgbàlè. The five points are the ancestral tombs of the first three settlers in the town, the ritual seat[13] of the *Alápínni*, the only woman initiate of egúngún cult and the political head, and the seat of *Ỳèyé Orò* (Festival Mother), a woman chief who acts as the link between all the priests of the different deities and the women of the town. The title is usually given to a woman who has been very active politically and culturally in the town, and who is an initiate of the *Ògbóni*[14] secret society.

Before the Ìgbàlè, the *Ládúnùnwò* have their last performance for the people. The *Ládúnùnwò* dance to seven different ritual rhythms, starting from the slow and sedate to the fast and energetic, all to different beats from the Gàngànún drums. The dances are unique and vary every year. Whilst the three dances in front of the palace are ritual dances, with movements coded in the culture of the people, the dances before the Ìgbàlè are more syncretic, with versions and variations of modern and popular dances. Throughout the dances, the people participate as audience, collaborators and participants. There is another brief drumming after which the *Ládúnùnwò* disappear into the Ìgbàlè, until the next time.

10   CONCLUSIONS: *LÁDÚNÙNWÒ* PERFORMANCE AS REPRESENTATION OF THE OTHER

The performance of *Ládúnùnwò* culturally is quintessentially Yorùbá, with all the elements of the performance culture, including drumming, music, dance. Its performative essence is in the dramatic enactments and re-enactments of the traditions and customs of the people. The purpose is to bring the community together, collectively, to celebrate and perform their culture, and renew the cultural pact with the ancestral codes of living and unifying an amorphous community in search of a definition between that of a war camp, an experimental research station, a border town, a gateway to the Èkìtì region of Yorùbáland, and a modern settlement. In that, egúngún serves as a unifying factor. *Ládúnùnwò* also has a great entertainment value, in particular the seven different performances before the Ìgbàlè and the several encores before disappearing

23 REPRESENTING AND RE-PRESENTING OTHERS IN YORÙBÁ PERFORMANCE 439

into the grove. Not only does the performance represents life and nature of the people, and restores their tradition, it re-presents these annually with modifications, modernisation and re-interpretation of styles. The annual performance further determines the elements of previous performances and engagements to retain and which to reform, in addition to incorporating or assimilating other attributes from 'foreign' incursions into the community.

More importantly, *Ládúnùnwò*'s form is one that has survived from the first encounter of the Alárìnjó with the white man and can be accepted as a homage to Clapperton's 'white devil'. As the explorer describes, the 'white devil' is entirely covered in a concealing sack, gradual unveiling of which finally reveals or exposes a figure strange to the people in its 'whiteness' and actions, or activities. The audience in 1826 expressed surprise and excitement at the revelation of the result of the domestication that the travelling actors had achieved to an exaggerated effect. The similarity with *Ládúnùnwò* is marked, to the stages of exposure. Instead of waxing, the body is tightly wrapped in pure white silk material. The dances, though accomplished, are executed carefully, with *Ládúnùnwò* gingerly demonstrating both traditional and modern dance movements. The final dance is often a version of the one or more of popular dances in vogue. This continual renewal or performances and performance forms, and the engagement with the idea of the 'other', ensures the representation of 'others' in this form of Yorùbá performance.

NOTES

1. See Francis Harding, "Masquerades in Africa" in Martin Banham et al (eds), *The Cambridge Guide to African and Caribbean Theatre*, Cambridge: CUP, 1997: 4. *Egúngún* is used throughout to denote both the singular and plural forms.
2. The Ifá divination system is important in the life of the Yoruba people. All ceremonies and ritual performances involve the consultation of Ifá. The Yoruba people believe that Orunmila, the divinity held as the one sent by the Almighty to guide human beings, established the system of divination. The Ifa system of divination is a corpus with sixteen main chapters. These are *Èjì Ogbè, Oyèkú Méjì, Iwòrì Méjì, Edí Méjì, Obàrà Méjì, Okònròn Méjì, Iròsùn Méjì, Iwònrin Méjì, Ogúndá Méjì, Osá Méjì, Ologbón Méjì, Orètè Méjì, Otúrá Méjì, Osé Méjì, Oràngún Méjì*, and *Eká Méjì*. The different patterns these chapters form on a divination plate dictate the type of divination cast for the person seeking the assistance of Ifá. A *babaláwo* is a person who is responsible for Ifá divination and rituals. For more information, see Daramola and Jeje (1975); and Adeoye (1979).
3. See Adedeji (1969).
4. See Adedeji (1969).
5. For the detailed account of this rehearsed performance, see Hugh Clapperton, *Journal of a Second Expedition into the Interior of Africa*, London, 1829, pp. 53–56; and Richard Lander, *Records of Clapperton's Last Expedition to Africa*, London, 1830, vol. 1, pp. 115–121.
6. Mary Louise Pratt: social spaces where disparate cultures meet, clash and grapple with each other (1992, 7).

440   Ṣ. ADÉYẸMÍ

7. The war was between the combined forces of towns and cities in northern Yorùbáland and the army of Ìbàdàn from 1877 to 1886, For more on the war, also known as Kiriji War, see S. A. Akintoye (1971), *Revolution and Power Politics in Yorubaland*, 1840–1893; *Ibadan Expansion and the Rise of Ekitiparapo*, New York: Humanities Press.
8. For more on this, see Roland Oliver and Anthony Atmore (2001). *Medieval Africa 1250–1800*. Cambridge: Cambridge University Press.
9. *Eyẹkẹyẹ* is so called because the costume is made from feathers of different birds.
10. There is another explanation that the Èmìilè provides for the king not being on the throne and witnessing the performance of Ládúnùnwò, that two rulers cannot be presented before the people at the same time. However, an anti-colonial or postcolonial perspective could suggest a hierarchical conflict between the Yorùbá king and a 'white' colonial 'foreign' authority.
11. Drum usually reserved for royalty in Yorubaland.
12. Gàngànún is a drum set unique to Imesi-Ile and the Ọbalùfọ̀n compound in Ile-Ife. The set is reserved for the rituals of Ọbàtálá, but in Imesi-Ile, it has become a hybrid of other drums, most especially Bata and Gbẹ̀du, and used for eguńgún and other social performances.
13. The ritual seat of the *Alápínni* as well as that of the *Yèyé Orò* (Festival Mother) are spots where rituals were performed to *Alápínni* (as deity) and where all the gods assemble symbolically, respectively.
14. *Ògbóni* is a secret judicial society that recognises the earth as the 'mother' of all human beings. The members pledge solidarity to one another and the spirit of the earth and support one another under *all* circumstances.

REFERENCES

Adedeji, J.A. 1969. *The Alárìnjó Theatre: A Study of Yorùbá Theatrical Art from its Earliest Beginnings to the Present Times*. Unpublished doctoral dissertation, University of Ibadan.

Adeoye, C.L. 1979. *Asà àti Ise Yorùbá*. Oxford University Press.

Alonge (Chief), the Emiile of Imesi-Ile. 1988. Interview with Author, Imesi-Ile, Nigeria.

Amankulor, J. Ndukaku. 1981. Ekpe Festival as Religious Ritual and Dance Drama. In *Drama and Theatre in Nigeria: A Critical Sourcebook*, ed. Yemi Ogunbiyi, 113–128. Lagos: Nigeria Magazine.

Amankulor, J. Ndukaku. 1989. The Condition of Ritual in Theatre: An Intercultural Perspective. *Performing Arts Journal, 11(3), 12*(1), 45–58 (The Interculturalism Issue (1989).

Babayemi, S.O. 1980. *Egúngún Among the Ọyọ́ Yorùbá*. Ibadan: Board Publications Ltd.

Bascom, William Russell. 1953. *Handbook of West African Art*. Milwaukee, Wisc.: Bruce Pub. Co.

———. 1969. *Ifa Divination: Communication between Gods and Man in West Africa*. Bloomington, IN: Indiana University Press.

Beier, Ulli. 1964. The Agbegijo masquerades. *Nigeria Magazine*. No. 82, September, pp. 188–199.

Brandon, James. 1990. Contemporary Japanese Theatre: Interculturalism and Intraculturalism. In *The Dramatic Touch of Difference: Theatre, Own and Foreign*, ed. Erika Fischer-Lichte, Michael Gissenwehrer, and Josephine Riley, 89–97. Tubingen: Narr.

Clapperton, Hugh, and Richard Lander. 1829. *Journal of a Second Expedition into the Interior of Africa, from The Bight of Benin to Soccatoo etc.* London: John Murray.

Daramola, Olu, and Adebayo Jeje. 1975. *Awon Asa ati Orisa Ile Yoruba.* Ibadan: Onibonoje Press and Book Industries Ltd.

Enekwe, Onuora Ossie. 1987. *Igbo Masks: The Oneness of Ritual and Theatre.* Lagos: Nigeria Magazine.

Foucault, Michel. 1977. *Discipline and Punish: The Birth of the Prison.* Translated by Alan Sheridan. New York: Vintage.

Harding, Frances. 1997. Masquerades in Africa. In *The Cambridge Guide to African and Caribbean Theatre*, ed. Martin Banham, Errol Hill, and George Woodyard. Cambridge: Cambridge University Press.

Idowu, Bolaji. 1962. *Olodumare: God in Yoruba Belief.* London: Longmans.

Irobi, Esiaba. 2006. A Theatre for Cannibals: Images of Europe in Indigenous African Theatre of the Colonial Period. *New Theatre Quarterly* 22 (3, Aug.): 268–282.

Lander, Richard. 1830. *Records of Clapperton's Last Expedition to Africa.* London: np.

Okagbue, Osita. 2007. *African Theatres and Performances.* London and New York: Routledge.

Pratt, Mary Louise. 1992. *Imperial Eyes: Travel Writing and Transculturation.* London: Routledge.

CHAPTER 24

Pigs and Dogs and *The Bogus Woman*: Racialised Performance in Anglo-British Women Playwrights

Serena Guarracino

1 Introduction

Caryl Churchill's much acclaimed 1979 play *Cloud Nine* includes one black character, but no black performing body: Joshua, the African servant of the English family from Victorian times featured in Act I, must by the dramatist's own directions be played 'by a white' (1985, 248). This choice is consistent with the use of cross-casting throughout the play, which features two characters in Act I and one in Act II played by a performing body of the opposite gender; in Churchill's vision, the use of cross-racial alongside cross-gender casting explicitly aims at exposing the parallel between sexual and racial repression. Hence Betty, the colonial administrator's angel-of-the-earth-like wife (to be played by a male actor), states in the opening scene that 'the whole aim of my life/Is to be what he looks for in a wife' (251); similarly Joshua proclaims: 'My skin is black but oh my soul is white [...] What white men want is what I want to be' (251–252).

However, while Betty's character returns in the second act, this time played by a woman, and the play shows her somewhat tentative road to emancipation, Joshua's character is granted no such possibility. The two acts of the play are set in 1879 and 1979, respectively; yet for the characters only twenty-five years have passed. Typical doubling between the first and second act of *Cloud Nine*

S. Guarracino (✉)
Università dell'Aquila, L'Aquila, Italy
e-mail: serena.guarracino@univaq.it

© The Author(s), under exclusive license to Springer Nature
Switzerland AG 2021
T. Morosetti, O. Okagbue (eds.), *The Palgrave Handbook of Theatre and Race*, https://doi.org/10.1007/978-3-030-43957-6_24

443

see the actor previously playing Joshua in the role of Gerry, an openly promiscuous homosexual man—this was the choice in the first staging of the play, where both characters were played by Tony Rohr (see Churchill 1985, 248); another common choice is to double Joshua with Cathy, a four-year-old girl and the only character in the second act to be played in cross-casting by an adult actor. No actor (or actress) plays Joshua in act two: not only he, in a twist that may remind one of Shakespeare's Caliban, is apparently left stranded on the African colony while the white family goes back to the motherland; but in the 1970s London park where the second part of the play is set there is no black character to take up his legacy and explore the way gender and race work in what, for the audience of *Cloud Nine*, were contemporary times.

This significant omission has recently brought to a reassessment of the play, and especially of its racial politics: as Mary Luckhurst has recently written, 'Churchill's "Africa" is a literary construct designed to expose sexual stereotypes, but it is also a blunt instrument that totally erases questions of ethnicity' (2014, 81). While such criticism may come across as ungenerous and rather oblivious of the anti-naturalistic approach to character building which is a trademark of Churchill's production, it does spotlight an issue in radical feminist theatre of which the writer herself has shown to be aware. While writing the preface to the American edition, Churchill discusses the lack of black characters in the second act of the play: 'there were no black members of the company and this led to the idea of Joshua being so alienated from himself and so much aspiring to be what white men want him to be that he is played by a white' (Churchill 1984, viii). The fact that in 1979 Joint Stock, the company Churchill was working with for the writing and production of *Cloud Nine*, did not include any black performer is not surprising per se: the first generation of Black British theatre practitioners, fostered by the founding of companies such as Temba (1972) and especially Talawa Theatre Company (1985), was still much in the making at the time (see King-Dorset 2014, 6). Yet, Luckhurst's complaint that '*Cloud Nine* is long overdue for creative reinvention by directors who want to experiment with cross-racial casting' (2014, 81) points to a still fraught relationship between *Cloud Nine*—and feminist British theatre more generally—and the black performing body.

Starting from this insight, the following pages explore a number of plays featuring black characters by British women playwrights who do not align with a Black British identity positioning. While this choice does not assume a homogeneous cultural background for the writers discussed here, it does consider race and the colour line as active signifiers both on and off stage, and the featuring of racially marked characters as a complex and fraught practice in feminist writing for the stage. It must be noted that not all writers included here position themselves as feminists in the same way Churchill does: quite notoriously, for example, Sarah Kane stated that 'I have no responsibility as a woman writer because I don't believe there's such a thing' (Kane qtd. in Aston 2010, 576). Yet her work has been subject to incisive feminist readings (see e.g. Aston 2010), as have the other plays discussed here; as a consequence, this chapter takes the definition 'feminist theatre' to include texts and writers widely received and discussed as such, to some extent independently from the playwrights themselves.

By featuring a black character performed by a white body, *Cloud Nine* highlights race on stage as a performance, and it is significant that there are no directions in the play to indicate how Joshua's blackness should be signified. Yet this feature is regularly referred to, by himself and other characters: in the very first scene Clive, the English patriarch, introduces Joshua noting that 'My boy's a jewel. Really has the knack./ You'd hardly notice the fellow's black' (Churchill 1985, 251). How is blackness represented on stage, however, is a relevant question for all plays discussed, and more generally for every character devised as being ethnically marked as non-white in a context (such as Great Britain, and Europe more generally) where race is a pivotal player in the definition of power relations and imbalances. While this may be considered an issue worth examining independently from the writer's own identity positioning, I have purposefully excluded from the scope of this chapter works by writers who are associated with Black British theatre, and more generally by Afro-descendant writers. This somewhat counterintuitive choice allows to unhinge the agency of writing from that of performing, and to foreground the fraught power relationships at work between a white writing body and a black performing body: in some cases, it also allows to expose whiteness as a performance in its own right, to be elaborated along the line of difference separating it from blackness. Moreover, all plays included here present an explicit concern with the gendered body on stage: my intention is to investigate how the representation of race on stage intersects with the way these plays address sexual politics. Thus, without any pretence of completion—and aware of the fact that the choice of plays here is necessarily shaped by my own experience—the following pages offer an overview of individual plays by white women writers including main or supporting roles to be performed by a black actor or actress, to explore what function the representation of racial difference plays in the elaboration of gender politics—and vice versa.

2   Performing Race

Theatre has traditionally explored and exploited the representation of 'othered' bodies which counter or defy what Nirmal Puwar has termed the 'somatic norm', the set of rules which allows identification—and the subsequent enjoying of social and symbolic privilege—with the 'disembodied abstract universal individual' (2001, 653). Institutional contexts have historically submitted to a racial contract, which in colonial times excluded black bodies altogether while today, with the end of direct colonial rule, has apparently erased the issue of race from public discourse altogether. As a consequence, 'white supremacy is no longer constitutionally and juridicially enshrined, but is rather a matter of social, political, cultural and economic privilege' (656).

446   S. GUARRACINO

Nevertheless, as Judith Butler noted in one of her early conceptualisations of gender as performative, theatre and other performing spaces represent a regulated exception to the norm (somatic and otherwise), which allows interpreters and audiences to experiment in a context that is explicitly distinct from everyday practices: 'the various conventions which announce that "this is only a play" allows strict lines to be drawn between the performance and life' (1990, 278). In this space, racial difference (as well as, in different forms and to a different extent, sexual difference in contexts where female roles were or are performed by men) has traditionally worked as a set of props and performing practices together with all the paraphernalia that identified the spectacular and in particular the 'exotic' on display; however, as Tiziana Morosetti notes in her introduction to *Staging the Other in Nineteenth-Century British Drama*, the necessary focus on the visual elements that mark the body as 'other' in performance must not downplay the fact that 'it is still *texts* that we are confronted by' (2016, 3). This is especially true for the time-span Morosetti writes about, where information about staging practices often comes in the form of reviews and other textual testimonies from times where technology still did not allow for other forms of recording.

However, this remark may be considered technically pertinent to some of the texts discussed here, especially earlier ones: more importantly, it is assumed to be relevant to all the playtexts analysed here, inasmuch performing bodies are racially marked first and foremost on the page when directions include a definition of the characters in racial terms. This definition may emerge explicitly in some instances: for example, Marcia and Neville in Sarah Kane's *Skin* are defined as 'an old black man' and 'a black woman' (Kane 2001, 250); similarly the unnamed protagonist of *The Bogus Woman* is a 'young black woman' (Adshead 2009, 13) in the opening directions. In other works racial characterisation is to be gathered from other elements (such as characters' names), as in a play which will not be discussed here, *Credible Witness* (2001) by Timberlake Wertenbaker: here the main character, a Macedonian woman trying to enter England illegally in search for her son, is detained in a centre with other illegal immigrants named Ali, Aziz, Ameena and Shivan (Wertenbaker 2014, 2) representing refugees from different areas of the world and 'all played by actors of the same ethnic backgrounds', as one reviewer notes (Watkins 2001, 483).

Wertenbaker's play, together with the others discussed here, marks a specific time in the representation of the racialized body on stage: on the one hand, racial impersonation is less and less admissible;[1] on the other, the rise of generation after generation of black performers (in Great Britain and elsewhere) allows for a significant—and signifying—diversity on stage. This has led not only to a practice of racially consistent casting (pioneered by Ira Aldridge's *Othello* in 1833) but to a wider experimentation with racial cross-casting, as emerges from the early all-black Shakespeare plays staged by Talawa Theatre in the 1980s. It is significant, though, that about these productions Talawa founder Yvonne Brewster stated: 'black actors were not being cast in these classical English roles [...] most of the casting directors [...] paid more attention to what the black actors would *look like* on stage rather than their ability to act the part' (cit. in King-Dorset 2014, 16; my emphasis). Hence, while the rise of Black British theatre allowed a higher presence of black performers, the 'visibility' of race on stage remains a vexed question.

Today, black performance continues to be burdened by the interruption created by the irruption of blackness within the field of vision. Consequently, each text that intends to use racial difference as part of its signifying practice is confronted with 'the desire to have the cultural product solve the very problem that it represents: that *seeing black is always a problem in a visual field that structures the troubling presence of blackness*' (Fleetwood 2011, 3, emphasis in original). In this sense, racial difference on stage appears to work in a double capacity: on the one hand, the materiality of performing bodies heightens the significance of what Harvey Young defines 'phenomenal blackness' (2010) ingrained in corporeal features—those 'grosser physical differences of color, hair and bone' that DuBois wrote about in *The Conservation of Races* (1897, 4). On the other, as theatre puts these bodily traits 'to work' in performance, race operates on stage as the 'floating signifier' elaborated by Stuart Hall: 'race works like a language. And signifiers refer to [their] systems and concepts of the classification of a culture to its making meaning practices. And those things gain their meaning, not because of what they contain in their essence, but in the shifting relations of difference' (Hall 1996, n.p.).

My contention here is that in the following plays racially marked characters allow to explore these very 'shifting relations of difference', in particular at the intersection with the relations structured by gender difference. I intend to look at how each playwright writes for a body marked by racial difference, and whether this difference is put 'at work' to engage other binary structures (e.g. sexual difference) or to foreground the possibility of intersection and solidarity. I will also, where possible, investigate the power relationships between writers and performers: while the history of European theatre is founded on the authority of the first over the second—the 'organ' of the author's will in Jacques Derrida's famous comments on Artaud (see Derrida 2001, 233)—both performing practices developed during the 1960s and 1970s (such as workshops and collaborative authorship) and recent scholarship have elaborated a different vision in which the performing body bears an excess in signification which cannot be managed by textual authority. This is especially true for contemporary theatre, which uses the discrepancy between the phenomenal body and the semiotic body to make the performance explicit and self-referential by playing with what Erika Fischer-Lichte terms 'perceptive multistability' (2008, 89).

This will be especially significant for the plays included in the last section, which make explicit use of anti-realist and estrangement techniques; in other plays, racially consistent casting works within a naturalistic framework, thus posing different questions on how the black performing body is put to work. Realism itself is a fraught category in feminist theatre: it played a pivotal role in early productions since the 1920s and 1930s as 'the perfect vehicle with which to place centre stage the issues directly effecting change' (Gale 2000, 23); however, its pre-eminence has been subsequently superseded when feminist criticism started to identify its codes with a conservative view of society and women's role in it. As Dolan has it, 'realism's resolutely domestic locales, with its boxed sets; its middle-class, bourgeois proprieties; its Aristotelian plotlines, which encouraged psychological identification against women's own good; and its rising action, crises, and denouements, was bound to marginalize women' (2012, xiv). For radical feminist theatre as emerges from the work of companies such as The Women's Theatre Group and Monstrous Regiment, whose work was deeply informed by Brechtian epic theatre, realism was non-viable as a political strategy (see Reinelt 1990, 251).

While to trace a clear-cut distinction between naturalistic and non-naturalistic styles is not among the aims of this chapter, it is important to note how different approaches to writing for the stage frame racialized bodies and performances. Indeed, while in the following pages the plays are discussed in a roughly chronological order, this is not to meant to come across as a narrative of progress: the plays are grouped together according to similar themes and techniques, and in no way the later plays are to be considered as more 'progressive' or 'avant-garde' than the earlier ones. However, it is necessary to register the shift between a naturalistic use of racially consistent casting—a character played by a performer of the same ethnic background, as in the case of Wertenbaker's play mentioned earlier—and the use of race as a meaning-laden but shifting category, as in Rebecca Prichard's *Yard Gal* or Adshead's *The Bogus Woman* where (although in very different ways) the black actress on stage is made to play a multiplicity of characters from different backgrounds. On the other hand, all the plays included in the following sections register the black performing body as a signifying presence in the definition of the gendered subject. Some plays feature the black body as pivotal in the redefinition of white femininity and its complicity with post-imperial power relations, while in other works racial and gender oppression are cast as entangled forces against which the black, non-heteronormative body features as a locus of resistance.

3   THE BLACK BODY AS OBJECT OF DESIRE: SHELAGH DELANEY'S *A TASTE OF HONEY*

Racial difference emerges as a crucial element in what is generally deemed one of the founding plays of women's dramaturgy from the second half of the twentieth century, Shelagh Delaney's *A Taste of Honey*. Delaney, 'the only woman from the late 1950s who has received serious and extended critical attention' (Bennett 2000, 40) and consequently considered a precursor of the more explicitly positioned feminist playwriting from later decades, focuses her attention on a troubled mother–daughter relationship in working-class Manchester, spinning out the way class contributes to the making of a gendered subject who does not conform to social expectations on femininity. A social-realist play in the spirit of John Osborne's acclaimed *Look Back in Anger* (1956), *A Taste of Honey* tackles many critical issues of the time, among which Sue-Ellen Case lists 'the moral and legal problems around the legitimate or illegitimate status of the child of a single mother, issues of domestic and child-care labour, the possibility of abortion, and the role or threat of homosexuality to the family unit' (1991, 238).

The man who gets the main character, Jo, pregnant and then disappears leaving her to deal with the issues of single parenting is a 'coloured naval rating' (Delaney 1982, 22) listed in the *dramatis personae* only as 'the boy' (6). While this may stand as shorthand for 'boy friend', which is how the character is defined in the stage direction first introducing him at the beginning of act I, scene ii (22), the racial connotation of the word cannot be overestimated. 'Boy' in Standard English defines 'a male child or youth' (OED 1), but also, in what the Oxford English Dictionary defines a 'dated' and 'offensive' use, 'a black male servant or worker' (OED 2); in this capacity, for example, it is used by the white characters to address Joshua in *Cloud Nine* (see e.g. Churchill 1985, 251, quoted above). Differently from the other characters, the 'boy' is not identified by an individual name, and this marks the role he plays for the protagonist's character development. From an early dialogue, it emerges how the Boy embodies Jo's desire to flee the household where Helen, her mother, is a transient presence between spells of her own fraught relationship with a younger man, Peter. In Jo's fantasy, the Boy functions as an object of both exotic and erotic interest:

> Jo: Sometimes you look three thousand years old. Did your ancestors come from Africa?
> Boy: No. Cardiff. Disappointed? Were you hoping to marry a man whose father beat the tom-tom all night?
> Jo: I don't care where you were born. There's still a bit of jungle in you some-where. (25)

The Boy's role as exotic commodity is ironically debunked by locating his origin not in a faraway, glamorous place but in Cardiff, home of one of the oldest and largest black communities in Great Britain, whose origins date back to the mid-nineteenth century (see Adi 2007, 36). The discrepancy between the audience's perception of the character as familiar and Jo's fantasy of the African Prince thus explicitly stages how his main function in the play is to stage Jo's sexual desire as an exercise of freedom.[2] Jo is not cast as a passive victim of the Boy's seduction, but as a willing partner in their encounter: 'I may as well be naughty while I've got the chance. I'll probably never see you again. I know it' (38). Although his disappearance at the end of act I results in Jo remaining trapped in the same run-down house (which works as setting for the whole play), it is him who is utterly expendable in her fantasy: as she tells her mother, 'He's gone away. He may be back in six months, but there again, he may...' (41).

In his function of empowering Jo, the Boy represents a break from the heteronormative masculinity that characterizes Peter's, Helen's boyfriend and then husband. In this, the Boy's trajectory anticipates and mirrors the one played out in greater detail by Geoffrey, the homosexual art student that is found sharing the apartment with a clearly pregnant Jo in act II. As Geoffrey and differently from Helen and Peter, the Boy is cast in the typically feminine role of the care-taker, nursing Jo when she falls down with the flu; a male nurse who has entered the service looking for a steady job, he overturns the stereotype of the 'black buck', the physically strong and sexually predatory black man (see Williams 2008, 101), and is never portrayed as threatening—differently from Peter, who is a drunkard and often bosses Helen around (see Delaney 1982, 17–19 and 64–65).

Hence, the Boy's blackness is put at work in the displacement of traditional gender roles, allowed by Jo's ability to claim white privilege against his positionality as a black subject. When the Boy asks her to marry him, he openly voices his preoccupation that Jo's mother might object to her marrying a black man: 'She hasn't seen me. […] She'll see a coloured boy' (23). It is in Jo's power—her poverty and social disadvantage notwithstanding—to retort that her mother 'isn't prejudiced against colour' (23) and thus dismiss the racial issue altogether. Yet Jo's pregnancy brings to the fore the impossibility to elude the social dynamics activated by the introduction of racial difference into the picture, as emerges from Helen's reaction to the news that the child her daughter is carrying may be black: 'You mean to say that … that sailor was a black man? … Oh my God! Nothing else can happen to me now. Can you see me wheeling a pram with a …Oh my God' (86). Helen, a destitute subject who is introduced in the first direction as a 'semi-whore' (7) and whose life includes at least one unwanted pregnancy and an unspecified number of husbands and lovers as means of sustenance, finds in whiteness a social value which can be compromised by her grandchild's mixed origins.

The difference of Jo's trajectory from her mother's does not rest on motherhood—she, like Helen, will be a single mother, and she repeatedly expresses her conflictual feelings towards her child (75–76)—but, one may argue, on her becoming part of the Mancunian multiracial community. While, as discussed earlier, the text tells very little about the Boy's background, in the original production the character was played by Clifton Jones, a Jamaican-born British actor and founder of the New Negro Theatre Company (see Chambers 2011, 111–116; in the 1961 film it was Paul Danquah, a British actor of Ghanaian ancestry, who played the same character, billed as 'Jimmy'). One of the emerging black professionals on the London scene of the time, Clifton Jones was part of the more recent migration from the Caribbean to Great Britain (the Windrush generation), which had a strong impact on industrial cities such as Manchester and its white, poor communities including characters such as Helen and Jo. Although no such background is explicitly mentioned in the play, Jones' performing body fills the empty space opened by the Boy, pointing to a less functional and more relational embedding of the character into the wider framework of the play than the playscript may vouch for.

Thus it may be argued that the closing lines of the play prefigure a multicultural and inclusive Manchester as a network of solidarity supporting Jo's coming of age.[3] While the exotic fantasy as a way to escape the dreariness of life resurfaces in later dialogues between Jo and Geoffrey, where she describes the Boy as 'from darkest Africa [...] a Prince, son of a chieftain' (53), at the end of the play the mother-to-be lets go of this fantasy of blackness to make space for a different notion of racial difference. This moment is marked by the first and only mention of the Boy's name: 'What was his name? [...] it was Jimmie!' (75). Jo's *bildung* hence includes a laying down of the exotic gaze and a recognition (at least in retrospect) of the Boy's individuality. This may also anticipate Jo's inclusion in the black community in Manchester, to be briefly inferred by her mentioning that a black nurse will be delivering her baby (86). Mother of a mixed-race child, Jo hence shifts from elaborating racial difference in terms of fantasy and desire to recognizing its founding role in her community.

4   DISEMPOWERING WHITENESS AND THE FEMALE BLACK BODY: *SKIN* BY SARAH KANE

The disempowering of whiteness through the relationship between a white and a black character is elaborated more virulently in Sarah Kane's short piece *Skin* (1997). This screenplay for 'a ten minute film' (Kane 2001, 247) written for and produced by Channel 4[4] has received close to no critical attention; even the introduction to the playwright's complete plays, by David Greig, does not mention the work at all (see Kane 2001, ix–xviii). Its exceptionality within Kane's corpus is remarked by its positioning at the end of the collection, although she had apparently been working on the concept as early as 1994, before the London premiere of *Blasted*; hence, according to Saunders, *Skin* should be considered the writer's second work (see Saunders 2009, 10 and 25). And indeed the naturalistic approach, especially in the depiction of locales, connects this work to Kane's early writing, where background and stage action are described in detail, and marks its distance from later works such as *Crave* (1998) and *4.48 Psychosis* (2000), where both setting and character dissolve.

This difference must also take the issue of form into account. As a screenplay, *Skin* almost becomes narrative as it describes not only the setting, but also the movement of the camera inside it. The eye of the onlooker is not depersonalized, however, but defined through a collective 'we' which attempts at breaking the fourth wall—in this case, the screen—to place the audience, at the opening of the piece, inside the room of the main character, Billy, who is under 'a floral duvet' as the answerphone goes off a couple of times: 'As *we* listen to the message, *we* pan around the room' (Kane 2001, 251; my emphasis). As Billy emerges from under his duvet, 'we' become aware that 'he is a skinhead', 'painfully thin', and that his body is covered in tattoos, including a skull on his back, a Union Jack on his right arm, and the writing 'Mum' over his heart (251): all elements the audience will find on the skin of Ewen Bremner, the actor who plays Billy in the film. That Billy is white, his being a skinhead, is not worth specifying in the directions, but his pale skin immediately becomes central in the film's imagery, as the camera pans around in close-ups of the character who walks around stark naked and draws a swastika on the back of his left hand.

Two other bodies appear in this very first few shots: an old black man, called Neville in the script and played by Yemi Ajibade, who looks at Billy from the garden plot below, and a still unnamed young black woman (played by Marcia Rose) from a window in the building across the street. At the sight of her, 'Billy grabs his penis and makes wanking gestures at her. She stares and then laughs. Billy laughs too' (250). The economy of the gaze here is elaborated across the four different lines of space, age, gender, and race. While both characters are located outside Billy's personal space, framed by the window, Neville, the old man, is looked at from above. Moreover, we do not see his reaction as Billy makes a gesture as if shooting him: 'Billy and Neville make eye-contact. Neville gives a half-nod of recognition. Billy points at him. *Neville shakes his head and goes back to his plants*' (Kane 2001, 250); yet the emphasized sentence is not shown in the film. The young woman, on the other hand, is roughly at a level with Billy's gaze, and her reaction to his provocation is explicitly shown both in the script and in the film. Racial difference is thus inscribed, in Neville's case, on the axis of age, and posed as unequal in terms of the above/below spatial dichotomy; in the woman's case, on the other hand, race as well as gender locate the two subjects on opposite sides—of the same street, but also of the ideological strife immediately thematized by Billy's skinhead persona—but also at the same level and even, unexpectedly, sharing a laugh.

The film builds up on Billy's investment into whiteness and nationalism as a locus of privilege within a context of urban marginalisation and poverty, a setting resonant of the one portrayed in *A Taste of Honey*. The film is set in South London explicitly through scenes 2 and 3, set in a café and in a churchyard respectively; Brixton, setting of the infamous 1981 Brixton Riots, is the acknowledged setting of scene 3. In the first one Billy is seen with the other members of his gang, who are proud of fattening up on 'two English extra rasher, two English extra sausage, one double English, one banana and ketchup omelette, two English extra toast' (Kane 2001, 251); while the second shows the gang attacking a mixed-race crowd of guests at a wedding. While Saunders notes that in these scenes Billy's behaviour 'suggests an individual who is a recent convert or an outsider to the group' (Saunders 2009, 26)—he refuses to eat the very English fare offered in the café, and is troubled by a black child who is looking at him through the café window—this does not reduce, but on the contrary emphasizes the performativity in Billy's process of identity building as an English white male.

This process is disrupted by Billy's encounter with Marcia, whom he goes to see in her apartment after she beckons to him from the window. Here, the apparent naturalism of the screenplay crumbles down, as the following, fast-paced montage follows Billy and Marcia as they engage in sex, fights, and other practices which always see Billy as the submissive partner. He is tied to the bedstead, slapped hard on the face, and made to eat dog food out of a bowl. Marcia overpowers Billy physically and subjugates him psychologically, quite literally through the power of her black skin. At the beginning of this section of the film, she touches his hand to examine the swastika, and he reacts to the touch with total fascination:

> Billy: 'S funny.
> Marcia: What?
> Billy: Soft skin.
> Marcia: You never touched a black woman before?
> Billy: Only with a baseball bat. (259)

Billy's obsession with Marcia's skin is expressed through worship and identification: in a scene included in the script but not in the film, a blindfolded Billy kisses and licks different parts of Marcia's skin 'as she presents different parts of her body to his face' (261); in another, described in more detail in the script but glimpsed at in the film, he puts on her clothes, 'layer by layer, until he's dressed as a woman' (263). Marcia enacts rituals of subjugation and possession over Billy's white skin: she writes her name on his back with a knife, and scrubs at his tattoos with a rough brush—significantly, in the film she concentrates especially on the Union Jack and the 'Mom' on the chest, while Billy wails in pain.

Marcia and Billy's relationship flips over received hierarchies through an ostensibly S/M ritual. As Anne McClintock argues, 'the economy of S/M is the economy of conversion: slave to master, adult to baby, pain to pleasure, man to woman, and back again' (1993, 87). Billy's attempt at empowering through a skinhead persona is thus overturned by his encounter with both gender and racial difference, by the touch of the black woman's skin. Yet the transformative—and somewhat redeeming—power of this practice is shown mostly through Billy's experience. The script gives the reader glimpses of Marcia's feelings: at times 'she is terrified' (Kane 2001, 261), or she 'cries silently' (262) as she cuts her name into Billy's skin. After Billy leaves, she is seen crying on her bed, comforted by her flatmate Kath and muttering a cryptic 'I'm sorry' (267). Then she fades from view as Billy tries to kill himself and is saved by Neville, the only character who manages to enter the enclosed space of the skinhead's room. As Billy vomits down the toilet, 'picture bleaches, then whites out' (Kane 2001, 268): whiteness thus becomes an overwhelming presence as the final frames fade to white instead of the more traditional black. Both Marcia and Neville, then, function in the framework of Billy's enlightenment and the disempowering of both his maleness and his white skin as marks of privilege; yet as individual characters they remain elusive, just outside the frame of the film's investigation of gender and racial dynamics in 1990s London.

454   S. GUARRACINO

5   SISTERHOOD AND THE COLOUR LINE: REBECCA PRICHARD'S *YARD GAL*

Set in roughly the same years and downtrodden neighbourhoods—though located more distinctly in the Hackney area—is Rebecca Prichard's *Yard Gal* (1998), which stages the relationship between two 'gals', Marie and Bukola. The play originates in a coproduction between Royal Court and Clean Break, a company working with women who are or have spent time in prison (see Aston and Reinelt 2000, 16); a metatheatrical framework shows the two former gang members—or 'yard gals'—telling the audience the story of their friendship, culminating in Marie committing a murder and Bukola—who goes by the nickname Boo—going to jail in her friend's stead. In the interplay between the two characters, and the others they impersonate as they tell the story, the play follows Kane's take on the colour line as the field of struggle in situations of hardship, but the presence of two female characters foregrounds a deeper exploration of gendered subjectivity as well as issues of solidarity and conflict among women.

The colour line is immediately visible in the casting: Marie was originally played by Anglo-British Amelia Lowdell, while Black British Sharon Duncan-Brewster played Boo. Racial difference is also made explicit in the playtext, and it takes only a few lines for Marie to foreground her whiteness: talking about another girl of the gang, Threse, she mentions that 'she was a white gal innit, like me' (Prichard 2001, 6). This may seem like a necessary specification: both girls speak, as Aston notes, a 'Cockney-Caribbean rhyme and slang [...] irrespective of Marie being white and Boo being black' (2003, 73). To this milieu Boo, as Marie, belongs because she is a born and bred Londoner, her Nigerian origin notwithstanding: 'My real names Nigerian—Bukola. But that's what everyone calls me. "Boo"' (Prichard 2001, 7). While Marie lives with her abusive father, Bukola has no ties with her family of origin, lives in a foster home (as do other characters of the play), and her only home is the crime-ridden London neighbourhood which she roams with her 'posse': 'Everybody chats about the violence and the guns and drugs on the East Sides, saying we should get out—but uh uh—no way—I don't leave my roots at all. That's what I was born and brought up wiv—and that's what I stay with. I'm a rude gal. I'm a Hackney gal!' (6).

Being 'Hackney gals' apparently removes the racial issue from Marie and Boo's relationship: in a context of poverty, drug dealing and abuse, being gang members overrides ethnic affiliation in the creation of a network of mutual solidarity. The play mirrors this choice through its structure as a narration shared by the two girls: as Aston notes, 'as a shared, rather than single narration, *Yard Gal* moves away from the idea that this is going to be the story of one, individual young girl' (Aston 2003, 73). This also reverberates on the way race works in the characterisation of the posse: with the exception of Marie, Boo, and Threse, the other members of the gang mentioned by the two main characters are not racially marked, at least not explicitly: Sabrine, for example, is mentioned as doing her 'Jamaica act' while detained at the police station (21); yet, as a Caribbean background is embedded in the language used by all characters, this may not point to a racial characterization as much as to a cultural performance. Of Sabrine and Deanne we also know that they put weaves into their hair, a practice generally but not exclusively associated with black hairdoing (see Prichard 2001, 8). Hair is a widely complex and controversial bodily marker of race, especially for women;[5] however, as the girls get ready for a night out, it is Marie who does Boo's hair. And while during most of the play the two performers move separately around the stage, this moment shows both physical closeness and a symbolic effacing of racial subjectivities, as Marie and Boo stage a dialogue among all members of the gang which they impersonate irrespectively of racial affiliation: '*Marie stand behind Boo and begins doing her hair. They take on the different voices of the posse*' (15).

Marie and Boo's intimacy is weaved through the play: in the opening scene, they proudly declare 'we go everywhere together and we done everything together innit' (9). Nonetheless, their relationship is also conflictual: not only they share a lover—a Jamaican drug-dealer called Nero, who may also be the father of Marie's child—but they share the story, and they often struggle to decide who is going to tell it and how. Hence in the opening Boo retorts to Marie calling her a 'pussy': 'don't start calling me names Marie or I ain't doing this play at all!' (5); whereas Marie objects to Boo telling about her life before the gang: 'This is a play about a Yard Gal innit. Telling them how tings [sic.] run in a yard. You keep going on about before I was even in the story. Do you want me to go home or what' (9).

The characters regularly exchange reciprocal threats to quit, to stop telling the story, but they do stick to the show until the end. This solidarity counters, and in effect effaces, its failure as regards the storyline, which sees Marie and Boo estranged: the first remains in Hackney struggling with the difficulties of raising her child, whom she names Bukola; Boo, on the other hand, decides not to return to the neighbourhood after she is released from jail, in order to start anew. In the metanarrative frame, on the other hand, the end of the play shows the two characters still together, both asking—the audience as well as each other—'Can we go now? Can we go?' (42). In this way, the play shuns to resolve the intimate but conflictual relationship between the two characters, who are shown to exist in each other's narration as necessary counterpoint, each one functional to the other in a reciprocity that works across, but does not efface, the colour line.

6   Voices of Resistance: Kay Adshead's *The Bogus Woman* and Caryl Churchill *Pigs and Dogs*

The black body as fluid signifier, taking on different and not necessarily black *personae* via a distinctly anti-naturalistic approach, is central to the last two plays discussed in this overview. In Kay Adshead's *The Bogus Woman* (2001),

Fischer-Lichte's 'perceptive multistability' is put to work to destabilize the denotative function of the black body on stage and at the same time to heighten its work in the power dynamics that crush the main character; while Caryl Churchill's *Pigs and Dogs* (2016) makes not a racially marked body, but diversity in both racial and gender terms the founding element of this political play on the relationship between colonial history and LGBT rights in the African continent. Both plays interrogate the role of racialized performance on the contemporary stage and its relationship with gender as agents of social and political action.

Both plays respond to humanitarian crises inside and outside Europe. *The Bogus Woman* was spurred by Adshead's research in the 1997 Campsfield riots and subsequent trial, which exposed the reiterated violation of human rights happening in refugee detention facilities on British soil. The writing and staging of *Pigs and Dogs*, on the other hand, was inspired by the wave of anti-homosexual laws introduced in the immediately preceding years in some sub-Saharan countries.[6] Both works redefine the *agitprop* genre, with a clear and outspoken political positioning both on the part of the writer and of all the actors and professionals involved; they also share a strategic use of anti-naturalistic techniques and in particular a denaturalized staging of racial difference. Racially marked bodies here do not feature as bearers of a reified difference, but as exposed to epistemic and material violence. Race hence becomes not a mark of difference but of vulnerability, intensified by its intersection with gender difference: the main character of Adshead's play is a woman (although her sources were male Campsfield inmates), while Churchill's performing bodies undergo a 'queering' process as the narrative proceeds.

The only possibility to resist violence, in both cases, is to endow vulnerable bodies with one or more stories. In the published version of the plays, Adshead and Churchill offer additional information on their source material: the first, by mentioning her colloquiums with one among what became known as the 'Campsfield Nine', the nine men charged with causing the riot in 1997 (see Adshead 2009, 9); the second by referring to the 1998 anthropological study *Boy-Wives and Female Husbands* by Stephen O. Murray and Will Roscoe, which is acknowledged as the main source of the play (Churchill 2016, 5). In this way, both playwrights relinquish the power of total authorship and cast themselves as relays between a wider network of political activism and the performing bodies on stage—and of course their audiences. This process is also relevant for the previously discussed *Yard Gal*, produced by a company working with women inmates; however, here the narrative relationship between source material and the eventual play is more direct and explicitly foregrounded by the writers themselves. Moreover, in Adshead's and Churchill's plays the performing bodies on stage surrender to the stories they tell and let themselves be haunted by many and different voices, some of them explicitly fracturing the tenuous bond between their physical materiality and the transient identity they voice.

This 'haunting' mechanism is the main narrative strategy in *The Bogus Woman*, where an unnamed 'young black woman'—the single character listed in the *dramatis personae*—is the only performer on stage. Noma Dumezweni, a Swaziland-born British actress who came to Britain as a refugee in May 1977,[7] originally performed this long monologue, where the main character plays more than forty roles. All lines not attributed to the main character are marked 'the young woman as', creating a refraction or misalignment between the performer playing a character and the character herself playing other characters. These are generally marked in terms of both gender and racial identity: the woman plays the parts of a fellow detainee called the 'child-man' (26) and of a 'female group 4 guard' (32), but also of a 'solicitor' who is defined as a 'he' (66); in a deeply estranging moment, she even plays the soldiers that raped her and murdered her family while she tells her story to the immigration officer (43). Racial or ethnic affiliation here works a marker of difference and of the subjection of the young woman to other people's storytelling: so the immigration official is explicitly 'English', while a later character called Janice, with a London accent, tries to frame the young woman in an acceptable narrative of loss and destitution: after the young woman sings an 'African song', Janice interjects: 'That was beautiful /I'm sure, like myself, /everyone here /feels / that you were singing /not just for yourself, /but /for dispossessed people / everywhere' (66–67).

The play stages the pervasive need of the main character to make her story real and believable in order not to risk being considered a 'bogus' asylum seeker.[8] This means to 'perform' her political-prisoner and rape-victim persona convincingly for her interlocutors—an impossible task, as she morphs into a different character every few lines. The play walks the fine line between the performer's bodily presence and the growing fragmentation of her identity positioning: a process that reaches its climax in the long exchange between the woman and the 'interrogator' (78–88), the longest section of the play which sees only two characters in dialogue. It is significant that the interrogator's racial and gender identity is left unspoken, counterpointing its indefiniteness with Dumezweni's own female, black body. A short time earlier, while telling the same story in a long monologue, the young woman asks another unmarked character, the 'immigration officer' (who, give the playtext's specificity in character definitions, should be considered a different person from the 'English immigration official' mentioned above): 'Forget I'm black /by the way /I could be pink /or puce /or grey' (40). Yet the sheer materiality of the colour line, and the way it works on the body and the stories it is framed into, shines against the immateriality of these characters, whose non-descript features mark their privilege and their power over the body on stage. As Pietro Deandrea has recently written, 'the imaginative force of *The Bogus Woman* [...] is founded on an expressionistic and lyrical monologue, which reaches way beyond simple denunciation, description and analysis' (2018, 56). This is enabled by the anti-naturalistic framing of the play, which allows to question the interlocutors'— and the audience's—need that the black, female subject conforms to received notions of herself to be recognized as such; on the contrary, it exposes how hegemonic narratives exercise violence over a vulnerable body.

The Bogus Woman does not elaborate an exit strategy for its character, who ends up framed in the solicitor's report of how she was eventually killed after she had been refused asylum and returned to her country: the last part of the play ratifies the fracture between body and character anticipated by the last line attributed to the young woman, 'Am I still me?' (127). *Pigs and Dogs* works in a diametrically opposite way, staging characters who reclaim the power of narration as subjects who are located outside both the gender and the somatic norm. As in other works by Churchill of the same period (e.g. *Seven Jewish Children*, 2009, and *Love and Information*, 2012), *Pigs and Dogs* does not include a list of *dramatis personae*, nor does it constrain the distribution of lines: each production can decide the composition of the cast in terms of gender and other possible characteristics, such as age or the colour line. Compared to previous ones, however, *Pigs and Dogs* shows a specific attention to this last element, since the only direction of the play reads: 'Three actors, any gender or race but *not all the same*. Each can play any character, regardless of the character's race or gender' (Churchill 2016, 5; emphasis mine). The text requires more than one character and consequently compels the staging to question the difference in the text, which is explicitly a difference in body, gender, and race.

A typographic sign, a dash at the beginning of each line, indicates the break in a sequence and the consequent passage from one performer to the other. Through this device, the text is structured in a series of usually tripartite dialogues, in which the first character opens the exchange, the second identifies the speaker, and the third person impersonates him or her, quoting their words; this structure is 'stated' at the beginning of the play, and is subsequently subject to a number of variations, although recurring regularly and creating an almost musical pattern. In the opening exchanges, Churchill borrows the technique of direct quotation from *verbatim* theatre to report homophobic statements from different public authorities, including the one that gives the play its title:

- Somebody says
- President Mugabe
- If dogs and pigs don't do it
  why must human beings? (6)

The characters on stage report and witness the spread of the fundamentalist repression of homosexual movements in the African continent. Together with African leaders such as Mugabe, Zuma, Yoweri Museveni, and Winnie Mandela, *Pigs and Dogs* also confronts others of European origin: E. E. Evans-Pritchard (6), founder of contemporary social anthropology and author of *The Nuer* (1940), one of the most influential twentieth-century texts on East Africa; or the missionary Father Cavazzi (9), author of the *Istorica descrizione de' tre' regni Congo, Matamba et Angola* during his stay on the continent between 1654 and 1677.

As a consequence, while a superficial reading could find in *Pigs and Dogs* the paternalistic gaze of the liberal West towards the more backward 'Third World' nations, the text reveals instead the roots of the superimposition between nationalism and homophobia in European rhetoric, of which it reproduces the definition of the 'other' as an abject element that contaminates the 'healthy' body of the nation. If anthropologists and missionaries impose normative heterosexuality as a necessary step towards civilisation, Museveni and Mugabe use the same rhetoric to state the autonomy of post-colonial states against Western interference:

- Museveni says
- President of Uganda
- Ugandan independence in the face of western pressure.
- Mugabe says
- President of Zimbabwe
- We have our own culture. (6)

Nationalist leaders define non-heteronormative sexual behaviour a result of colonialism and contamination of a supposedly untainted (and exclusively heterosexual) African sexuality. However, the cultural work staged by Churchill tells a very different story, where it is not sexual practices which are exported along the routes of colonisation, but the laws that repress them. To do this, the text includes narratives from the aforementioned *Boy-Wives and Female Husbands* by Murray and Roscoe: published in 1998, the volume was positively received by the scientific community not only for the breadth and accuracy of the data, but also for the effort not to impose Western sexual categories on the stories collected and often reported in first person (see Phillips 2001, 196). *Pigs and Dogs* echoes this choice in keeping the terms that describe different identities and relationships in the original African languages, and consequently engaging its audience (which may be imagined to be predominantly European) in understanding the meaning of these words through the stories of the characters embodied by the three performers on stage:

If I had been a man
I could have taken a wife and begat children.
If I had been a woman
I could have taken a husband and borne children.
But I am neither. I am wobo. (6)

Through whom this 'I', and the others who take the floor, becomes embodied rests in the hands of the production. The first staging of the play, at the Royal Court, saw Alex Hassell, Fisayo Akinade, and Sharon D. Clarke sharing the stage; a dramatic reading of the Italian translation held in Bologna in October 2018 featured Tezeta Abraham, Federica Santoro, and Aron Tewelde, a young African-Italian actor who assumed the identity both of the English legislator

460 S. GUARRACINO

condemning homosexuality in 1533, of the 'wobo' quoted earlier, and of Nzinga of Ndongo, the queen who dressed as a man and fought the Portuguese army in the seventeenth-century Angola.

7 CONCLUSION

As clearly emerges from these examples, it is impossible to offer an analysis of how racial and gender performances work in *Pigs and Dogs* without referring to individual stagings, and this is what makes this play so crucial at the conclusion of this (partial) excursion on gender and race as signifiers on the contemporary feminist stage. A fit counterpoint to Churchill's own *Cloud Nine* (discussed at the beginning), it uses race as well as gender as signifiers through performing bodies which are characterized not as black or white, male or female, but different from each other. As previous examples, this play stages racialized as well as gendered bodies as telling, or tolling, the difference among voices, characters, and subject positionings. However, the fluidity of the text makes it impossible to reify the role of difference in the political statement *Pigs and Dogs* puts forward; moreover, the use of stated sources opens to a shared authorship where the playwright is only one element in a network. And indeed the rhythmic passing of voices from one performing body to the other points to the centrality of networks, and the pivotal role of difference in creating relationships of solidarity and shared political action. In this way, it offers race as a crucial language in theatre practices, whose ever-changing role on the feminist scene maps the fraught but fertile intersection of gender and race as necessary, fluid signifiers on stage.

NOTES

1. Fundamental in this respect, although not immediately relevant for the British context, is Eric Lott's work on black minstrelsy in the USA (see Lott 1993).
2. This pattern may be traced in other plays which are not included in this overview, in particular in Pam Gems' *Go West, Young Woman* (1974) and *Deborah's Daughter* (1994) (see Gems 1974 and 1995): in both plays, the coming of age of the white female protagonist happens through a sexual relationship with an exoticized male character. However, as these characters are Native American and Middle Eastern respectively, hence necessitating a different theorisation of racial difference as the one framing this chapter, analysis of these plays has not been included here.
3. Although it is beyond the scope of this contribution, it may be noted that the inclusivity of the Mancunian community is represented even more explicitly by Geoffrey: his berating by Peter and Helen, who calls him 'a pansified little freak' (68), strongly contrasts with his mutual affection for Jo. The play's open ending—with both Geoffrey and Helen walking out on Jo—still foreshadows a lasting relationship between the two: Jo is left 'smiling a little to herself. She remembers Geof' (87), the last direction reads.

4. The film is available on YouTube at https://www.youtube.com/watch?v=G2ZjplLullc (Last access: November 5, 2018).
5. Scholarship about the politics of hair in race studies is ample and far beyond the scope of this chapter: for a preliminary analysis, see Thompson 2009.
6. Although it is far beyond the scope of this contribution, it is worth noticing that the two issues are strictly related, as many refugees and asylum seekers belong to LGBT communities and are persecuted as such in their country of origin (see Amnesty International 2018).
7. As she mentioned in her acceptance speech at the 2017 Olivier Awards; see https://www.youtube.com/watch?v=FpW4tGNJPOE (accessed November 12, 2018).
8. Although the UNHCR clearly states that 'there is no such thing as a bogus asylum seeker', this discourse has been pervasive in European press, supporting stricter measures against migration and causing human rights violations such as witnessed in the Campsfield case (see the UNHCR website at http://www.unhcr.org/asylum-in-the-uk.html, accessed November 12, 2018).

References

Adi, Hakim. 2007. *The History of African and Caribbean Communities in Britain*. London: Wayland.

Adshead, Kay. 2009. *The Bogus Woman*. London: Oberon Books.

Amnesty International. 2018. Suffering in Silence: The Invisibility of LGBTI Refugees. Accessed November 12, 2018. https://www.amnesty.org.uk/blogs/lgbti-network/suffering-silence-invisibility-lgbti-refugees.

Aston, Elaine, and Janelle Reinelt. 2000. A Century in View: From Suffrage to the 1990s. In *The Cambridge Companion to Modern British Women Playwrights*, ed. Elaine Aston and Janelle Reinelt, 1–18. Cambridge: Cambridge University Press.

Aston, Elaine. 2003. *Feminist Views on the English Stage: Women Playwrights, 1990–2000*. Cambridge: Cambridge University Press.

———. 2010. Feeling the Loss of Feminism: Sarah Kane's *Blasted* and an Experiential Genealogy of Contemporary Women's Playwriting. *Theatre Journal* 62 (4): 575–591.

Bennett, Susan. 2000. New Plays and Women's Voices in the 1950s. In *The Cambridge Companion to Modern British Women Playwrights*, ed. Elaine Aston and Janelle Reinelt, 38–52. Cambridge: Cambridge University Press.

Butler, Judith. 1990. Performative Acts and Gender Constitution: An Essay in Phenomenology and Feminist Theory. In *Performing Feminisms: Feminist Critical Theory and Theatre*, ed. Sue-Ellen Case, 270–282. Baltimore: Johns Hopkins Press.

Case, Sue-Ellen. 1991. The Power of Sex: English Plays by Women, 1958–1988. *New Theatre Quarterly* 7 (27): 238–245.

Chambers, Colin. 2011. *Black and Asian Theatre in Britain: A History*. London: Routledge.

Churchill, Caryl. 1984. Introduction. In *Cloud 9. Revised American Edition*, vii–ix. New York: Methuen.

———. 1985. Cloud Nine. In *Plays I. Owners; Traps; Vinegar Tom; Light Shining in Buckinghamshire; Cloud Nine*, 250–320. London: Methuen.

———. 2016. *Pigs and Dogs*. London: Nick Hern Books.

Deandrea, Pietro. 2018. In Every Holt and Heath: Spatial Counter-Actions in Contemporary British Literature on Migrants. *Le Simplegadi* 16 (18): 50–62.

Delaney, Shelagh. 1982. *A Taste of Honey*. London: Methuen.

Derrida, Jacques. 2001. La Paroles Soufflee. In *Writing and Difference*, 212–245. London: Routledge.

Dolan, Jill. 2012 [1988]. *The Feminist Spectator as Critic*. Ann Arbor: University of Michigan Press.

DuBois, W.E.B. 1897. *The Conservation of Races*. Washington, DC: The American Negro Academy. Accessed November 12, 2018. www.gutenberg.org/ebooks/5685.

Fischer-Lichte, Erika. 2008. *The Transformative Power of Performance. A New Aesthetics*. London: Routledge.

Fleetwood, Nicole R. 2011. *Troubling Vision: Performance, Visuality, and Blackness*. Chicago: University of Chicago Press.

Gale, Maggie B. 2000. Women Playwrights in the 20s and 30s. In *The Cambridge Companion to Modern British Women Playwrights*, ed. Elaine Aston and Janelle Reinelt, 23–36. Cambridge: Cambridge University Press.

Gems, Pam. 1974. *Go West, Young Woman* (1974). Accessed 13 November 2018. http://www.pamgemsplays.com/Pam_Gems_Plays/Go_West_Young_Woman.html.

———. 1995. *Deborah's Daughter*. London: Nick Hern Books.

Hall, Stuart. 1996. Is Race a Floating Signifier? The Sage Anniversary Lecture and the Hayward Lecture. Accessed November 12, 2018. http://www.mediaed.org/transcripts/Stuart-Hall-Race-the-Floating-Signifier-Transcript.pdf.

Kane, Sarah. 2001. *Complete Plays. Blasted. Phaedra's Love. Cleansed. Crave. 4.48 Psychosis. Skin*. London: Methuen.

King-Dorset, Rodreguez. 2014. *Black British Theatre Pioneers: Yvonne Brewster and the First Generation of Actors, Playwrights and Other Practitioners*. Jefferson, NC: McFarland.

Lott, Eric. 1993. *Love and Theft: Blackface Minstrelsy and the American Working Class*. Oxford: Oxford University Press.

Luckhurst, Mary. 2014. *Caryl Churchill*. London: Routledge.

McClintock, Anne. 1993. Maid to Order: Commercial Fetishism and Gender Power. *Social Text* (37): 87–116.

Morosetti, Tiziana. 2016. Introduction. In *Staging the Other in Nineteenth-Century British Drama*, ed. Tiziana Morosetti, i–viii. Bern: Peter Lang.

Murray, S.O., and W. Roscoe. 1998. *Boy-Wives and Female Husbands. Studies in African Homosexualities*. New York: Palgrave.

Phillips, O. 2001. Myths and Realities of African Sexuality. Review of *Boy-Wives and Female Husbands: Studies of African Homosexualities* by Stephen O. Murray and Will Roscoe. *African Studies Review* 44 (2): 195–201.

Prichard, Rebecca. 2001. *Yard Gal*. New York: Dramatists Play Service Inc.

Puwar, Nirmal. 2001. The Racialised Somatic Norm and the Senior Civil Service. *Sociology* 35 (3): 651–670.

Reinelt, Janelle. 1990. Beyond Brecht: Britain's New Feminist Drama. In *Performing Feminisms: Feminist Critical Theory and Theatre*, ed. Sue-Ellen Case, 150–159. Baltimore: Johns Hopkins Press.

Saunders, Graham. 2009. *About Kane: The Playwright and the Work*. London: Faber & Faber.

Thompson, Cheryl. 2009. Black Women, Beauty, and Hair as a Matter of Being. *Women's Studies* 38: 831–856.

Watkins, Beth. 2001. *Spinning into Butter* by Rebecca Gilman; *Far Away* by Caryl Churchill; *Credible Witness* by Timberlake Wertenbaker; *The Bogus Woman* by Kay Adshead; *The Mother* by Bertolt Brecht (Review). *Theatre Journal* 53 (3): 481–484.

Wertenbaker, Timberlake. 2014 [2001]. *Credible Witness*. London: Faber & Faber.

Williams, Linda. 2008. *Screening Sex*. Durham, NC: Duke University Press.

Young, Harvey. 2010. *Embodying Black Experience: Stillness, Critical Memory, and the Black Body*. Ann Arbor: University of Michigan Press.

CHAPTER 25

Race, Occidentalism/Orientalism and Sino-centrism in Contemporary Chinese Theatre

Mary Mazzilli

1 Introduction

In her 1995 book, *Occidentalism: A Theory of Counter-Discourse in Post-Mao China*, Chen Xiaomei uses the term Occidentalism to define the appropriation of Western discourse by Chinese culture and stresses its political and ideological liberating effect. In 2004, Claire Conceison's *Significant Other: Staging the American in China* revisits the term Occidentalism by considering the representation of white Americans on the Chinese stage. Both studies are important in that they consider the tensions between West and East in Chinese culture but, even if both studies refer indirectly to race, they never deal with it directly. Thus, two important questions need to be asked: How is race performed on the contemporary Chinese stage, especially China's white 'other'? Is Chinese Occidentalism only further perpetuating a discourse of Orientalism by constructing racialist stereotypes of the 'other'?

The contemporary theatre landscape in China has greatly changed since the two books were published, with more white Caucasians living and making theatre in China and with many more global transnational collaborations and cultural artist exchanges becoming the norm. Wang Chong emerging as one of the new faces in Chinese theatre epitomises China's contemporary fluid cross-cultural theatrical landscape. Wang Chong, educated in both China and the USA, has built his career by adapting Western contemporary classics for the Chinese stage and more recently has produced theatre transnationally in the

M. Mazzilli (✉)
Department of Literature, Film and Theatre Studies, University of Essex, Essex, UK
e-mail: m.mazzilli@essex.ac.uk

© The Author(s), under exclusive license to Springer Nature Switzerland AG 2021
T. Morosetti, O. Okagbue (eds.), *The Palgrave Handbook of Theatre and Race*, https://doi.org/10.1007/978-3-030-43957-6_25

465

Asia-pacific region, as well as working internationally in the UK and in the USA with international theatre-makers.

By considering the transnational nature of Wang's work, a third additional question needs to be asked pointing out the Chinese global and transnational presence: Is there a form of cultural Sino-centrism disguised as a deconstructed racial fluidity? One of the first studies to analyse Wang Chong's theatre in some depth and the only one to consider his work within the context of race, this chapter will address these questions, specifically by considering when/how the white 'other' enters China through the vehicle of adaptation and translation of Western contemporary theatre on the Chinese stage and, most importantly, when/how China looks outwards to export its own history abroad.

2 Wang Chong

From the outset, Wang Chong places his work within a cross-cultural and intercultural discourse by giving his theatre company a French name, *Théâtre du Rêve Expérimental*, as well as a Chinese one. Wang Chong has made a career adapting Western work for the Chinese stage, while also reviving Chinese classics. At the beginning of his directing career, he translated and directed Chinese premieres of Western scripts: Roland Schimmelpfennig's *The Arabian Night* (2007), Peter Handke's *Self-Accusation* (2009), Sarah Kane's *Crave* (2009), Eve Ensler's *The Vagina Monologues* (2009), Heiner Müller's *Hamletmachine* (2010) and Woody Allen's *Central Park West* (2011), the latter was a box-office success in fringe venues and toured several cities in China. Later on, Wang produced award-winning shows, which include both original work and adaptations from existing Chinese scripts: *Thunderstorm 2.0* (2012), noted by *The Beijing News* as one of the best ten 'little theater' works in China, 1982–2012; *The Warfare of Landmine 2.0*, which won the 2013 Festival/ Tokyo Award; *Lu Xun* (2016), noted by *The Beijing News* as 'The Best Chinese Production of Year, 2016'.

At a superficial level, Wang's work is not concerned with racial representation; however, there are some aspects to be considered to qualify this claim. Part of Wang's education took place in the USA, possibly making him less likely to nurture anti-Western sentiments. In his early-directed pieces, he did not concern himself with 'occidentalising' the Western characters in the productions. Predominantly, he focused on adapting non-naturalistic plays, which do not require the staging of characters realistically, that is not making them inhabit their 'realistic' racial identities. But as I will demonstrate in this chapter, performing race instead underpins his intercultural discourse. First, Wang collaborated twice with Ibsen International, a multicultural theatre company which 'believes in the creative potential embedded in the encounter with the "other", without restrictions of nationality, race, gender or (political and religious) faith' (*Ibsen International*). Second, it is in the last productions that he clearly shows some interest in the performance of race on stage. In *Revolutionary Model Play 2.0* (2015), which will be discussed in depth later, he uses a multi-ethnic cast and multi-linguistic approach.[1] I would argue that *Revolutionary Model Play 2.0* cannot be seen in isolation and some of the racial issues raised in this production were in the making already in his early works. Among his works of adaptations, I have chosen Wang's adaptation of Heiner Müller's *Hamletmachine* (2010), which contains elements that, then, reappear in *Revolutionary Model Play 2.0*. In looking at his theatrical works, one should not forget that the abundant use of technology—most, if not all of Wang's pieces use video projections screened at the backdrop of the stage, similar to Katie Mitchel, who uses handheld cameras that project on backdrop of the stage—creates a mediated distancing experience and in some cases, also, connects parallel narratives, which, as we will see, can fragment as well as enhance the theatrical experience. This use of projections and handheld cameras is an important component of how race is performed on stage.

3   THEATRE AND RACE

Before going into the details of his abovementioned productions, we need to look at what we mean by the relation between theatre and race and how these are connected to the ideas set out by Chen Xiaomei and Claire Conceison. Race as a concept did not emerge till the late ninetieth century when social and political campaigns denied equal rights to ethnic minority groups by advocating their biological inferiority (Young 2013, 14). On the performativity of race, Harry Elam's definition of the relationship between theatre and race is particularly telling when he writes that

> … discourse on race … [is] intricately linked to issues of theater and performance. Definitions of race, like the processes of theater, fundamentally depend on the relationship between the seen and unseen, between the visibly marked and unmarked, between the "real" and the illusionary. (2001, 4)

The racial discourse parallels the theatrical process in that it develops a visual language defined by the relation between the seen and unseen, the marked and unmarked, between images/signifiers and connotations/signifieds. These translate into images (signifiers) with cultural connotations (signifieds) that are constructed according to a performative process that define groups of people according to a set of signifiers, such as the colour of the skin, for instance, thus categorising them into particular cultural and/or ethnic groups. By referring to a constructed and performative understanding of race, Elam further emphasises the fluidity of racial discourse:

> The inherent "constructedness" of performance and the malleability of the devices of the theater serve to reinforce the theory that …and race, in general, are hybrid, fluid concepts whose meanings depend upon the social, cultural, and historical conditions of their use. (4)

468 M. MAZZILLI

If race is a fluid concept that can change over time, it also can change according to the geography in which it operates. In China, for instance, the idea of race has its own specific meaning. Frank Dikötter states that the Chinese terms for race stress the physical rather the sociocultural aspect (*zu, zulei, mingzu, zhongzu, renzhong*) of the term (Dikötter 2015, xvi). He also states that Western expansion into East Asia was seen in terms of race, and contacts with frontier people generated proto-nationalist feelings.[2] Western expansion into China has dominated the relation between China and the West thereby generating a racial discourse. This will be further explained below in regard to the terms Occidentalism and Orientalism, which, in China, have strong connections to a notion of race.

4 OCCIDENTALISM AND ORIENTALISM

Chen Xiaomei uses the term Occidentalism almost as a counter-discourse to Orientalism.[3] She sees that Occidentalism is conceived exactly through a process whereby Western ideologies enter the Orient through cultural export. She claims that Western thoughts go through modifications once they are exported into the Chinese Orient:

> Orientalism has been accompanied by instances of what might be termed *Occidentalism*, a discursive practice that, by constructing its Western Other, has allowed the Orient to participate actively and with indigenous creativity in the process of self-appropriation, even after being appropriated and constructed by Western Others. As a result of constantly revising and manipulating imposed Western theories and practices, the Chinese Orient has produced a new discourse, marked by a particular combination of the Western construction of China with the Chinese construction of the West, with both of these components interacting and interpenetrating each other. (Chen 2002, 2)

Chen realises that these modifications not only change Western discourses but also allow the Chinese Orient to produce its own in a process of interaction and interchange. Most importantly, Chen recognises that the process of Western ideologies entering the Chinese 'other' does not generate a discourse of oppression, but one of liberation, not only through official structured agencies but also through individual unofficial cultural agencies.

Chen is essentially saying that Occidentalism, in its basic form, functions as a process of China appropriating Western discourses to push its own agenda, which in most cases is aimed at changing the status quo and promoting innovation of their culture. She describes how both May-Forth writers[4] and Mao used Western ideologies to justify the new democratic revolution (137). The important point that Chen makes is that she defines the Orient not as a passive recipient of Western ideologies but as actively generating its own discourses, by borrowing what it needs from the Occident in its own process of change and countering traditional discourses of oppression. She mentions race as being particularly problematic: 'One needs to be especially aware of the critical issues at the intersection of gender, race, nation, and class in the study of Occidentalism in cross-cultural contexts' (21). However, she does not go further than mentioning race among other aspects, such as gender, nation and class, and she does not really develop the role that race can have in defining the relation between West and the East.

Conceison starts from where Chen left off by bringing the discourse of Occidentalism to the late twentieth century and into the twenty-first,[5] analysing productions from the late 1990s to the early 2000s, mainly featuring Western white Caucasian characters and performers. From the outset, Conceison takes her distance from Chen: while she talks about the 'recurrent images of the Other in Chinese Occidentalism', Chen fails in addressing what these images look like and how the foreign 'other' is represented. Conceison adopts indeed a more critical stance towards Occidentalism, which goes beyond Chen's definition of Occidentalism as liberating force (Conceison 2004, 48).

Conceison's emphasis is on the images of the Western 'other', constructed by Occidentalism, and what these say about Chinese perception of the white 'other'. From the outset, Conceison's project is embedded within a racial discourse in which the white race is reversibly the victim of racist sentiments. In the early stages of the book, she outlines how anti-foreign xenophobia has been part of Chinese history in their contact with the white 'other':

> The cultural and material embeddedness of anti-foreign xenophobia (both symbolic and functional) that was played out in the tribute rituals is most persuasively evident in linguistic prevalence—the extensive circulation of ethnocentric expressions in the Chinese language from early imperial times right up till today. [...] numerous objects and descriptive terms connoting negative images of the foreign are employed in contemporary Chinese speech, reinforcing national superiority in their reiteration in both a symbolic and material sense; much like ritual acts also produce power relations in and of themselves. (Conceison, 19–20)

This challenges the recurrent image of China as a victim of Western Imperialism, as she points out that China conversely has a long history of imperialism (21).

Xenophobia and nationalism, in particular anti-Americanism, which, she argues, are not only institutionalised and initiated by the government, but are also spread amongst ordinary citizens, form the backdrop of her project. One could argue there is an intrinsic inevitable bias to her study, which derives from a perspective of an outsider, an American scholar, a Westerner seeing themselves represented on stage. However, as any foreigner that has lived in China, especially in the pre-Beijing 2008 Olympics period, would tell you, life in China for a white Caucasian is not only one of privilege but also one marked by racial incidents (people staring and calling you names, such as *laowai*-old foreigner or *dabizi*-big nose, etc.). In this regard coincidentally, Colin Mackerras' review of this book laments that Conceison uses the term racism too freely without defining it and that her claim of racism is not justifiable, considering the privileges Westerners enjoy in China (2005, 618). Beside Mackerras' debatable comment on the fairness of her racist claims, if indeed Chinese portrayals of the Western 'other' present some racial issues, we should point out that similarly to Chen, the racial discourse is never explicitly debated in Conceison's book, though it is by far more fully explored and more strongly implied.

Beyond the bias of this study, and her claims of racism, Conceison's work is one of the only studies to thoroughly analyse how non-Chinese white characters are represented and what the implications are in terms of performing race on the Chinese stage. Resonance with the 'blackface'[6] on Western stage can be easily found as the Chinese actor becomes foreign through the prosthetic of makeup, body painting and costume, which render the body of the foreigner:

> Up until the period after the Cultural Revolution, the guise of the foreigner was always grafted onto the Chinese actor through costume, makeup, voice, and movement intended to approximate the appearance of the designated Other in as a realistic a manner as possible. There is long tradition of realistic makeup (*xianshi huanzhuang*) in the spoken-drama tradition—including body painting, rubber noses, chin extensions, and other racial simulations [...] Until very recently the Chinese actor always became the American character through these signifiers. (Conceison 2004, 31–32)

In some of the 1990s productions analysed in her book, realistic traditions, those that want to represent characters by 'realistic' traits, 'accentuate the character's distinct Otherness' through physical connotations, thus confirming Dikötter's emphasis of a Chinese understanding of race by physical traits. Conceison concludes that 'when a Chinese actor is costumed and made up to appear foreign, there is always the reminder that China is commenting on and interpreting the foreigner' (33). She talks about a kind of appropriation that Chen had defined as being part of the Occidentalist discourse.

Furthermore, as she analyses productions that see foreign Western performers[7] take on Western roles, she argues that, on one hand, while such 'appropriation does not occur on the physical level but still exists on a textual level, [and that] though partially concealed by the realism of the bodily representation, China still speaks for the Other' (33). On the other, a cross-cultural negotiation takes place. For instance, this is the case of 1995 Yu Luosheng' *Student Wife* (*Peidu furen*).[8] Making Chinese theatre history (139), as alleged by Conceison, two foreign actors were cast in the role of the American couple, Robert Daly, famous in China at the time for the 1993 TV miniseries *A Beijinger in New York* (*Beijingren zai Niuyue*), and Basa Wajs, German-born actress, respectively for the husband, Jordan, and the wife, Lucia. Conceison stresses that there was a real collaboration between Daly and Yu, the director, to the extent that some of the script was changed, thanks to Daly's intervention (142–143). Faithful to the novel, the script showed strong anti-Semitic sentiment in portraying Lucia as a negative Jewish stereotype. Daly convinced the director to remove references to her Jewishness altogether. This production clearly shows, from a positive point of view, the agency of a white Caucasian performer in influencing the performance of race on the Chinese stage. Nevertheless, concurring with Conceison's aforementioned quote, the textual premises still configure old stereotypes and place the white 'other' as the oppressor of the Chinese self. Heightening the representation of a humiliated China in Yu's production is Su Hongjun's definition of a 'feminized and victimized China'[9] as represented in this play and the novel. This is exactly the sense of victimisation lamented by Conceison, the confirmation that reiterates an Orientalist discourse while actually enacting an Occidentalist discourse of appropriation that confirm the binary bad/good, West/East.

At a textual level, as far as a discourse of race is concerned, the anti-Semitism of this production (the potential anti-Semitism—as mentioned above, this was greatly understated in the end), and indeed the original novel, still foregrounds an extremely flawed and prejudiced discourse of race, one that associates ethnicity to moral and psychological traits. In her analysis of the production, while documenting the 'insult to the American womanhood' (Conceison 2004, 154) that the production provoked, Conceison takes a more positive view, concluding that the mere appearance of the 'other' on stage 'uncovered a whole range of possibilities and opportunities for subsequent productions and collaborations' (166). In a way, although striving for a balanced view, I would argue that Conceison misses slightly the opportunity to reiterate her early view that inherently Chinese Occidentalism on stage still speaks for the Western 'other'. Chapter 7, for instance, deals with *Che Guevara* (2000–2001), an experimental play by the Chinese New Left that was unabashedly anti-American and nationalist while also questioning post-communism and globalisation. In a way her analysis brings to fore a quite inherent Chinese nationalism that communicates, above all, an uncomfortable positioning in relation to its Western counterpart. This renders a racial discourse still present in stereotypical portrayals and the representation of China as a victim, through an Occidentalist discourse that contributes to a negatively constructed discourse of race and racial differences.

In the conclusion to her book, in the search for a 'role-model' of a more balanced representation of the foreigner on stage, she calls for a plurality of images and identities (226). In the end, while she admits that in each production there is 'one image' of the Western 'other'—[in her case American other], she believes that the Occidentalist discourse is always changing over time (230–231) depending on the changing relations between countries, between the USA and China, in this case. By reflecting on the US–China connection, one can find a potential limitation to her study, which puts the American experience at the centre of her analysis. By equating Occidentalism with the American experience, it puts all the Western experience under one umbrella.

Besides Conceison's and Chen's limitations, in responding to the questions posed at the beginning of this chapter, one lesson that can be learnt from Conceison—and to some extent Chen—is that Chinese Occidentalism has, in some way, further perpetuated the same discourse of cultural Orientalism, in reverse, by also constructing racialist stereotypes. This has been carried out through a process of appropriation of cultural ideology to push China's own agenda, which has produced on stage racial stereotypes that have seen China speaking for the Western 'other'. These racial stereotypes have originated from a sense of inferiority of China towards the Western 'other', which is concealed beneath a rhetoric of victimisation, of seeing themselves as victims of Western Imperialism and globalisation.

Beyond Occidentalism, however, performing race has also seen China being actively involved in the creation of cultural meanings that define racial discourses, also in the attempt to take part on the global stage. In her important 1995 book, *Primitive Passions*, Rey Chow defines another kind of Orientalism, 'Oriental's Orientalism' defined a tactic of self-subalternising and self-exoticising visual gestures[10] by Fifth Generation filmmakers (Chow 1995, 170) that contributed to the international success of filmmakers, such as Zhang Yimou. Filmmakers resorted to a glossy display of primitive mythical images that stress its ethnic, and I would argue, racial otherness. This occurs also in theatre and can be seen in the display of 'primitive' traditional forms, or their derivatives or what seemingly stands for them (this is the case of traditional Chinese theatre being mainly promoted abroad), with the intent for it to stand out on the global stage and to meet the expectations of what commodified China should look like. Oriental's Orientalism as defined by Chow adds to Chen and Conceison's discussion around the term Occidentalism in that it describes Chinese cultural behaviour in the attempt to take the global stage, which will be useful when thinking about the export of Chinese cultural products abroad. In terms of racial discourse and theatre, for now it suffices to say that both Occidentalism (towards the Western 'other') and Orientalism (towards themselves) contribute to constructing racial stereotypes that are highly performative in their cultural display of specific pre-assigned traits, which in some cases are 'seen' on stage and in some others are 'unseen' and disguised, as we will see in Wang Chong's work.

5   Wang Chong and Contemporary China

Considering that racial discourse is neither fixed nor immutable, we should acknowledge that changes in terms of race can be possible in contemporary China. The contemporary theatrical landscape of the last ten years (post-Beijing Olympics 2008) is marked by collaborations and exchanges. In a recent interview in 2015, Conceison speaks about the normality of cross-cultural collaborations, resulting from the rise in international festivals (Leng 2015). In fact, festivals are proliferating in China—such as the Beijing Fringe Festival and Wuzhen Theatre Festival, just to mention a few. In the last ten years, China has seen non-Chinese Western theatre-makers making their own work in China.[11] It is in this mix that we find Wang Chong who created *Ibsen in One Take* (*Yi jing yisheng yi bo sheng*)[12] in collaboration with other foreign theatre-makers.

So, considering the changed theatrical landscape in China, marked by some openness and international collaborations, the question to be asked is: Are the parameters delineated by Occidentalism/Orientalism in theatre still valid in more recent productions? This question links well to the third question posed at the beginning of this chapter (Can we talk about a form of cultural Sino-centrism disguised under a deconstructed racial fluidity?).[13] To some extent, Wang Chong is exporting Chinese theatre abroad, but what are his values? What is his racial agenda? Is he also perpetuating an Occidetantalist/Orientalist discourse? The analysis of Wang Chong's adaptation of Müller's *Hamletmachine* at the beginning of his career and a more recent production, *Revolutionary Model Play 2.0*, will outline Wang's journey in terms of performing race.

5.1 *Heiner Müller's* Hamletmachine

Written[14] as a retrospective to a moment of crisis,[15] the play has been considered a 'metaphorical examination of the crisis of a Marxist intellectual'.[16] Only a handful of pages, stylistically, it is an open dense text of literary references (without counting Shakespeare's *Hamlet*) to Joseph Conrad's *Heart of Darkness*, Greek tragedies, Walter Benjamin and named references to political figures, such as Marx, Lenin and even Mao. Divided into five sections following the Shakespeare's five-act structure, it deploys long monologues with two identifiable characters, among a chorus of voices, Hamlet that opens and Ophelia that closes the play—Ophelia is mainly present in Part Three and Part Five. The nature of its openness has made it possible for many adaptations to exploit the physicality and the spectacle that Müller's conception lends itself to. Stage directions (Part Three is entirely made of stage directions), such as the famous tearing of the author's photograph, Hamlet actor putting makeup, the presence of a TV set leaking blood, are highly theatrical and symbolic of the philosophical and political nature of the text, almost an end-of-life scenario.

Just over forty minutes long, Wang went for a visual spectacle with non-diegetic videos projected on the backdrop of the stage, with physical movement and miming sequences throughout, whereas most textual elements are an extra-dimension of this production, as background to the action on stage, through the use of voiceover. The show starts with an emotionally infused montage, the view of clouds on mountains followed by sequences of crowds of North Koreans crying for the death of their leader, Kim Il-sung.[17] Clips of monuments, landmarks of North Korean 'superpower', are also part of the montage, which, together with the broadcast in Korean narrating the events playing throughout the video, frame the public display of grief as political. The dramatic and the emphatic tone of the video, created by the mass of people united in this inhibited display, at the beginning of the show, even before the play starts, both puzzle and amuse. The repetitive nature of the clip makes the tragic thrust of this national mourning almost farcical and over-theatrical. Following the script, Wang's adaptation makes references to past events, political events, charging the production with strong symbolic connotations. Once the screening comes to an end, four performers enter the stage with their back to the audience, starting one of many movement-based sequences, with the voiceover of the script and non-diegetic sound as background; this is a much more sombre atmosphere to that of the video footage. The movements start slowly and become gradually more acrobatic and larger on stage till the focus is only on one performer as the other three disappear; he, then, mimes facial and bodily expressions to the text ' I AM GOOD HAMLET GI'ME A CAUSE FOR GRIEF/AH THE WHOLE GLOBE ...' (Müller 1984, 53). The show develops more or less as it opens: we have video projections, sometimes followed by movement sequence, then, followed by voiceovers played over movement sequences; in some other cases, we have only movement sequences with non-diegetic music, followed by voiceovers played over movement sequences or in some cases mimed sequences.

In terms of the video screened footage, in addition to the initial video screening, there are three others, most of them played in the first half of the show. The second and the third videos are still in Part One of the play, 'Family scrapbook', the second displaying black and white images from the German documentary *Triumph of the Will*[18] and the Chinese Culture Revolution, and the third displaying cross-cuts fragmented clips, close-ups of Communist soldiers and Communist monuments. The latter, unlike all the others, is projected as the main performer executes some physical movements on the floor. The last video is in Part Four of the play, 'Pets in Buddha/Battle for Greenland', and is a montage of Chinese TV clips, symbolically standing for the script reference to TV being 'The daily nausea' and standing for the TV sets on stage in the original script (Müller 1984, 56). The video footages add a strong political connotation to the show with the references to war, to China's communist past and capitalist present. The last footage, in particular, shows a fast sequence of contemporary China on the small screen (panel shows, advertising, costume drama, TV series, etc.) and these go hand in hand with the part of the script where criticism is directed towards capitalism and the kind of 'Gemütlichkeit'—a general sense of feeling nice and friendly—(57) that capitalism has created. The last footage, the only one played alongside the voiceover, becomes signifier for a form of superficial capitalism that is now Chinese reality. Essentially, by considering the videos used, one could argue that Wang Chong is passing some sort of judgement on communism as a regime that idolises the cult of its leader, here embodied not by China but by North Korea; he is also critiquing political fanaticism, in general, here symbolised by the German reference and Cultural Revolution reference, but above all post-Mao/post-socialistic capitalist China. This is not new as Wang seems to follow suit from Müller's script, expressing, as mentioned earlier, an intellectual crisis, the crisis of Marxism that denounces both communism and capitalism.

Other important moments charged with political connotations are present in Part Four of the script, when a red star painted over a large banner is displayed on the back of the stage, as the Hamlet performer stands motionless together with other three performers reading a script (the only time, in the whole production, that the text is recited on stage). This scene describes a situation of chaos and revolution. At the end of the scene, a little girl brings in two illuminated tank toys (before she is suddenly taken away by an adult) while the main performer greets the tanks with a military salute. This scene is highly symbolic. The red star and the tank toys fit well with the army motif present in the video footage, but the toy tanks, in particular, are highly evocative of the famous picture of the Tank Man from the 1989 Tiananmen student protests. In terms of political connotations, Wang seems to follow the footsteps of the play, *Che Guevara*, in criticising communism, China's communist past and post-Mao modernity.[19]

As the video projections become more sparse, the symbolic meaning is deployed more on stage by the physical movement sequences, which at the start are seemingly more randomly physicalised, then become more precise miming sequences that serve as prosthetic to the text, played out by the voiceover, and later on only emphasise the text's dramatic moments. In this case, the movement sequences can stand on their own, then, as they become gradually more theatrical in nature.[20] In essence, most of the physical sequences are 'Oriental' and Chinese, with a strong indication that what they enact are martial arts movements and dance sequence that remind one of Peking opera. The movement performed are stylised controlled movements that originate from *wushu* and Peking opera. Ophelia, for instance, wears long sleeves, which are normally used in Peking opera in *dan* (female roles) characters. So what about the discourse of race?

We should not forget that a political judgement is passed on North Korea, by representing North Koreans in their display of blind adoration for their dead leader. As mentioned earlier, their display is well framed within a political discourse, as crosscuts are made to North Korean communist landmarks. We should not forget the almost farcical tone of the sequence, which awakens the audience with a grand opening, and sets the critical tone of the rest of the production, towards a past that once also belonged to China. It is as if post-Mao China is looking at North Korea and what it was like in China under the Mao regime. Besides the intrinsic political message, from a race point of view, it is important to see that Wang utilises someone else's history passing a judgement also on the East Asian race, possibly meaning that East Asians are easily blinded by the adoration for their leader. Images of the white 'other' are almost absent in this play, but not totally. The white 'other' is associated with German Nazism in the second black-and-white video footage, which also shows footage from the Cultural Revolution. Thus, this could signify that it is not only the East Asians that are blinded by strong military regimes.

The white 'other' is also present in the last footage, with a very brief clip of an American series (not clear which one), which just follows the reference to Coca-Cola 'Hail Coca cola' (Müller 1984, 57) in the script. This is then followed by a still, a photograph of Heiner Müller. The white 'other' is thus represented by Coca-Cola, a cultural symbol par excellence of Western, in particular American, globalisation. It is worth noting that following straight after the

Coca-Cola reference, the clip of an American series and the photograph of the author take the place of the famous tearing apart of the Heiner Müller's photograph in the script. By not having the photograph torn on stage, the display of his photo is not merely a homage to the author because the association with the Coca-Cola reference is addressing a subtle denunciation: despite Müller's attempts to criticise capitalism, his picture, similar to the images of Andy Warhol, and Einstein, has become a commodity, part of the simulacra created by the empty world of capitalism. The fact that the picture is not torn is an important change to the meaning of the production: in the original, some have interpreted this as questioning the authorship of this play made of inter-textual references to other sources (Barnett 2016, 266). In this adaptation, however, the sense of questioning is lost and while the sense of authorship is restored, it paradoxically undermines the value of the original, of Müller's critical stand and ultimately of his own creation. In his own words, Wang says that the 'experimental drama is dead, Hamlet is thunder, Shakespeare is dead, and Heiner Müller is strangled' (https://www.mask9.com/node/11024), which emphatically undermines Müller's own artistic endeavour. Possibly, what is left over is the image, represented by the photo of the author as part of the last video footage, a commodity itself in a capitalist society. The video, thus, functions as self-reference to theatre itself, self-critiquing its own performative function.

At a performative level, considering the self-referential nature of this last footage, the racial discourse is seemingly attached to an Occidentalist portrayal of a Western 'other'. Albeit almost absent, and possibly by the force of its partial absence, Wang's adaptation plays out with a white 'other' that is both seen and unseen, visible and invisible, yet it is ultimately associated with war, capitalism and globalisation, all the wrongs that have changed Chinese society. Furthermore, due to the fact that references to the white 'other's presence and to the author of the original play are placed right towards the end of the show, one could argue that through self-referential allusions, Wang is pointing to the Western 'other', also represented by the play-text from which this show originates, as the one that governs and controls the state of events that are happening on stage and outside the stage.

Before coming to a conclusion on the racial discourse of this adaptation, however, there is another element worth noting, the use of traditional Chinese tropes that are part of the actions on stage, the use of *wushu*, Peking Opera tropes, as part of the physical language used in this piece. While there has been some praise about the Chineseness of this production—one critic even says that Wang has improved the original (An 2010)—and the fact that he confronts Chinese reality,[21] the impact of state control, one critic defined the traditional Chinese theatrical language as 'a pantomime of Peking opera', while also criticising the shallow adaptation of the German original (ibid.). The same critic also highlights that Wang's adaptation is very Chinese:

Artistically speaking, this adaptation of *Hamletmachine* is very Chinese: it uses Peking opera and controversial political events for commercial appeal. Wang Chong spins his audience with a shameless cynicism towards the capitalistic system, taking it as a machine manipulating people by brainwashing them with consumerist ideology. (Ibid.)

The above quote accuses Wang's adaption of being a 'fake' in both its attempt to adapt Müller's play and in his use of traditional Chinese language.[22] If the latter is the case, the question is whether we can talk about this adaptation as a form of self-Orientalisation and, as was the case with Fifth Generation filmmakers, of Chinese traditional tropes being re-packaged for the international stage. It is no coincidence that this production went to the Avignon Festival, where it had a warm reception.

This complicates the production's seemingly Occidentalist discourse, but not totally, as Orientalism and Occidentalism do not necessarily exclude each other. Furthermore, another definite answer could be found in the use of the video projections, which, as mentioned earlier, can create a mediated distancing experience and add parallel narratives that can fragment or enhance the theatrical experience on stage. In this case, one could argue that there is a sense of parallel narratives being played out: on one side, there is the Orientalist discourse being played in the actions on stage, and, on the other, the Occidentalist discourse in the video footages. The two run in parallel but with very few connections, with the only moment being the tank toys image (the tank toys and the military salute echo the military motifs played in the videos). However, with respect to the last video projection, the montage of TV clips and the symbolic connotations attached to the photo of Müller, the Occidentalist discourse overtakes the Orientalist one, pointing the finger to the white 'other' as the origin and the end of the production. In a very subtle way, Wang is reiterating an Occidentalist discourse that makes the white 'other' the source of all evils, thus following, possibly unknowingly, the tradition of the theatre described by Conceison.

5.2   *Revolutionary Model Play 2.0*

Also an attempt to critique Chinese past and present, and more clearly addressing the racial discourse is *Revolutionary Model Play 2.0*.[23] The production deals with Madame Mao's Revolutionary Model Plays (*Yangbanxi* or Revolutionary Model Play), which were the only theatre allowed during the Chinese Cultural Revolution and were conceived as a propaganda tool by Jiang Qing, wife of Mao Zedong. Intended as a documentary theatre, it essentially explores and deconstructs the figure of Madame Mao by presenting her character on stage, and people that have been part of her life;[24] for instance, Zhang Chunqiao, one of the Gang of Four, is represented on stage as a scary baby-doll.

The two main characters are a fictional writer, Yu Zhongkai, and American historian, Roxane Witke, who famously interviewed Madame Mao in 1972 and published in the book, *Comrade Chiang Ch'ing* (1977). It is important to note that in both cases, the Chinese writer and the American historian are not cast according to the ethnicity of their characters: the Chinese writer is played by French actor, Raphael Lecat, and the America historian is played by Indian Singaporean actress, Rebekah Sangeetha Sorai. This is an important fact that shows the fluidity of the racial discourse as advocated by this production, which will be discussed later on.

Writer Yu Zhongkai and Roxane Witke are the ones carrying the narrative, mainly handling the handheld cameras in their attempts to tell Madame Mao's story. The production unfolds as they discuss with each other, and at times addressing the audience, while different other narratives on Jiang Qing's life are played out by other characters. For the first thirty minutes of the show, four cameras are on stage, one at each corner of the stage, mainly stationary on tripods. The projections from the four cameras, onto a screen made of tea-stained newspapers, in some moments, split the screen into four sections, of four footages, each for each corner of the stage, which produces a sense of multiple narratives. Most of the time, there is a performer playing, moving, talking at each corner of the stage and there are close-ups of each one of them on the screen. Thirty minutes into the show, three of the cameras are carried out of the stage and Yu Zhongkai takes hold of the only camera on stage to focus on Roxane Witke, who talks straight to the camera, with her back to the audience—we see a close-up of her face projected on the background screen. The handheld camera is then shared between Yu Zhongkai and Roxane Witke (mainly Yu Zhongkai), who follow, while talking, the events that are displayed on stage, mostly connected to the political persona of Madame Mao. Blood balloons burst on stage as most of the events played out by the other performers are of torture and violence. In this regard, the camera, placed in the mix of the actions, is almost complicit with the actions played on stage by focusing the audience's attention on the details of what is happening on stage. To good effect, close-ups of the doll representing Zhang Chunqiao adds a sense of menace and dread. Twenty minutes from the end of the show, there is a brief return to four cameras and four split screens to represent a scene of execution taking place, till there is an intimate account of Jiang Qin's childhood, played by Kathy Han in Korean. The latter is projected in black and white and as she is joined by Witke, the historical reference to Witke's famous interview is quite clear. This is the last moment with the projection and the handheld camera. In the last ten minutes, a euphoric crowd tears apart the screen; Witke talks about her youth experiences of revolts and all ends with a sombre and intimate reflection of Yu and Witke on Jiang Qin's persona, mostly through Witke's words.

Similar to *Hamletmachine*, there are also non-diegetic footages projected onto the screen, mainly filmed clips from the revolutionary operas, and these open the show at the beginning and are shown intermittently throughout. Unlike *Hamletmachine*, these are very far in between and most of the time the projected footages are diegetic, from what is happening on stage. I would argue that the latter, and the use of cameras on stage, have an important dramaturgical function as they seem to shape the narrative of the piece. At the start, the use of the four split screens is seemingly intended to give a sense of Jiang Qin's past before she was Madame Mao, through the accounts of her second husband, Chinese writer Tang Na, for instance. The use of the hand-held camera, then, gives an account of Jiang Qin's political career, mostly marked by violence and blood, which also is reflected by those involved in her artistic policies as represented through the testimonials of Yu Huiyong and Bai Shuxiang. Towards the final stages of the production, the return to split images also marks a return to the Jiang Qing's persona, not as a politician but as a woman, as given in her account from her childhood of how she was locked in a Confucius temple by some boys. This confession also marks a change of perspective: during most of the show the handheld camera is moved around by Yu, the Chinese writer, as main viewer leading the narrative in a dialogue with Witke. At the end, it is Witke that takes over but she does not need the camera; she talks straight to the audience and to Yu. By giving Witke the lead at the end of the show, Wang makes Witke's interview the conclusive frame of the show, by suggesting that all the show was born out of Witke's insight into Madame Mao's life. Furthermore, it is Witke that ends the play, with the statement: 'Jiang Qing didn't fight for power. She was given the power by Mao and the masses. The Cultural Revolution was a stage for her to act on, and she was an actress, and only an actress'. This self-referential statement at the end, echoing the self-referentiality in *Hamletmachine*, seems to define also the show and as such it frames all the blood and violence portrayed on stage as performative events, undermining the historical and political weight of the subject, the Chinese Cultural Revolution, which was one of the bleakest periods of Chinese modern history.

The emphasis on the performative, the illusion that Wang himself talks about in an interview (Xiong 2012), is key to the reading of the racial discourse of this piece. As mentioned earlier, Wang goes for a multi-linguist and multiracial approach. Apart from English, several other languages are used in the performance, French, Tamil, Malay, Mandarin, German, Filipino, Korean and respective ethnicities and nationalities. A review of the show, in an ironic tone, defines it as 'Racial Harmony Day concert' (Ng 2015a). However, the novelty is not the variety of nationalities and ethnicities, and not even the languages used, but it is the casting, the fact that especially the main roles are not cast, naturalistically, according to the ethnicity of their characters. As mentioned earlier at the beginning of this section, the fictional character of Yu Zhongkai is played by a French actor and the more famous character of Roxane Witke is played by an Indian Singaporean actress; Madame Mao herself is played by a Korean actress. There is an underlying intention to represent the fluidity of ethnicity, of a racial discourse that is open and un-fixed.[25]

Starting with the fact that a Korean performer, talking in Korean, gives voice to Madame Mao's intimate story of childhood on stage, one could argue that, like in *Hamletmachine*, there is an intent to distance themselves from their own history—in *Hamletmachine* we have video footage of Korean adoration of their own leader, emulating Chinese Maoist past—the weight of Chinese history is given by proximity to the North Koreans. The moment of her intimate confession gains momentum as it is the only time we see the character speak. In most of the show, Madame Mao is not a speaking subject: at the start with back to the audience, we see her through a close-up of her face and later she is part of the action on stage, with no speaking role. As such, the last parts of this production, in particular Madame Mao's childhood memories and Witke's self-reflexive statement at the end, humanise her persona and undermine the weight of the responsibility on the Madame Mao's historical figure, who historically has been seen as the mastermind behind the Cultural Revolution. These also create a visual distance from the violence shown on stage, during most of the production, which contradicts the allegedly original intent of this production—which through the topic of the Model plays seemingly wanted to present a critique of the Chinese bleak past, more directly than it was in *Hamletmachine*. Furthermore, the use of the screen projections, almost all of them diegetic and talking directly to the action on stage, generates both a sense of distance and closeness, conveyed by the multiple narratives through the use of the split screen, and the focus of the handheld camera, which is participatory of the violent action onstage. At some level, racial fluidity, the interplay between distance and closeness, the self-referential statement at the end, bring attention to both race and history as construct, by, in particular, playing with the signifiers, the images that make race performative.

At risk of whitewash casting (in the case of a Chinese character being played by a white performer), Wang indeed seemingly celebrates racial fluidity, by offering a discourse that transcends the colours of people's skins. However, beyond this naïve and well-intended racial openness, there are other dynamics to be considered. First of all, the fact that a Chinese character is played by a white performer seems to reverse the tradition as described by Conceison of white characters being played by Chinese performers. In this sense, knowingly or not knowingly, Wang is participating in that tradition by reversing it. However, unlike Chinese representations of white characters, Raphael Lecat's characterisation is devoid of connotative prosthesis, like makeup, beards or the like, at all, which would highlight the stereotypical nature of Chineseness. In fact, if it were not for what is written on the programme, and the fact that towards the end of the show, he talks why Chinese people like Model plays, one would not even realise that his character is Chinese at all. In the case of Witke, the fact that a historical figure is played by a non-white character is more telling and cannot be so easily ignored or confused. The same can be said about Madame Mao being played by a Korean performer, even though here we are talking about nationality, not ethnicity. Some light on the racial discourse as indicated by these facts can be shed if we consider the narrative structure of the piece and the aesthetics, the use of projections and handheld cameras that create this narrative.

Going in more depth, the racial discourse loses its fluidity from an Orientalist point of view, by handing the narrative power to a white performer, who even impersonates the director/creator of this piece—it has been alleged that the character is the director Alter ego (Ng 2015a). One could argue that Wang is lending a Chinese subject voice to a talking white subject. Lecat's character speaks for the Chinese subject, as he speaks about how the Chinese like model operas and why these were so popular. However, as we see at the end of the real frame, and how the narrative is played out on stage (Witke is the one that ends the play and the one that takes over the power but she does not need to speak to the cameras), the historic weight of the narrative is held by the character of Witke. History is reverted here by having a non-white performer playing Witke: Witke as a Western historian had given voice to a Chinese subject yet filtered through her own subjectivity, her perspective of a Western intellectual. The opposite can be said in this case: the history/the story written by Witke has been appropriated twice; firstly by the director/creator of this piece and, second, by the non-white performer. In this regard, one could talk about an Occidentalist discourse of appropriation of a Western discourse, Witke's historical persona and her interview being appropriated by a Chinese director and being given voice by a non-Western performer.

Again, as was the case in *Hamletmachine*, the racial discourse is enacted by the playing out of the unseen and the seen, the visible and invisible. Racial fluidity is all about disguise and nothing is exactly what it seems. For instance, a white performer plays the role of a Chinese character even though there are no signifiers that indicate his racial identity. Furthermore, we have an Orientalist discourse parallel to an Occidentalist one: again, respectively, the Chinese character being played by a white performer and Witke being played by a non-western performer. Again, if we consider the narrative turn, also supported at the performative level by the voice being handed over directly at the end to the performer, who does not need to talk through the camera but can talk freely on stage in this game of hide and seek, the Orientalist discourse is subsided by an Occidentalist one.

6 Conclusion

In conclusion, one could argue that disguised as racial fluidity, it is not only the Occidentalist discourse that is embedded in this production, as was the case in *Hamletmachine*, but also a Sino-centric discourse. This is due to the fact that despite all the disguises, the framework in which it is constructed is still embedded in the context of the Model Plays and has been sold to the Singaporean audience as dealing with Chinese history, in particular Madame Mao.[26] In fact, it is no coincidence that most reviews (Ho Ai Li 2015; Lim 2015; Ng 2015a) saw the racial ambiguity as a distraction and what they really were interested in was the history of the model plays. In this regard, it is commendable that Wang Chong has tried to defy expectations but as it was for the reception of *Hamletmachine*, the response to this work has pointed out its Chineseness.[27] Thus, going back to the question about whether a Sino-centrism has been disguised under a deconstructed racial fluidity, the answer is not a straight-forward one. It is one that sees emerging theatre-makers, knowingly or unknowingly, working within racial paradigms (Chinese fear of the other, patriotism and nationalism, Occidentalism/Orientalism), from which it is not easy to disengage. Wang's work is still part of a discourse that promotes a Chineseness which, both self-orientalises itself through performative oriental markers and applies an Occidentalist discourse to the white 'other'. It must be said, however, that Wang has come a long way since the productions described by Conceison and we cannot talk about an explicit and monolithic representation of the white 'other'. Furthermore, while passing a comment on the white 'other', similar to the theatre analysed in Conceison's book, in the case of Wang Chong's work, one cannot talk at all of racism and xenophobia. This form of Sino-centrism is in itself a compromise between Occidentalism and Orientalism and it comes to the fore especially when Chinese theatre-makers are exporting their work internationally.[28] However, in order to define a trend among Wang's contemporaries, more research is still needed. This chapter being the first to engage with the discourse of race by looking at a contemporary Chinese theatre-maker, such as Wang Chong, is making some important steps in the right direction with the hope to inspire further research.

Notes

1. Most recently, *Little Emperors* premiered in 2017 in Melbourne, Australia, as part of AsiaTOPA. This production uses both Chinese and English and deals with Chinese migration and one-child policy, thus being the first production by Wang Chong to clearly deal with Chinese diaspora.
2. One should not forget that there have been many racial tensions among different ethnicities in China versus the predominant Han *mingzu* and in its history of China foreign non-Han populations had ruled this vast country.
3. Refer to Edward Said's *Orientalism*.
4. The May Fourth Movement (1919) was an intellectual reformist movement that condemned Confucianism and sought to introduce Western ideologies and literature to China. The name is after students' protest on 4 May 1919 in response to the Japanese occupation of Shandong.
5. While Chen's project encompasses not only theatre but poetry and literature in general and mainly in the post-Mao period (1976–1989), Conceison's focus is only on theatre in the late twentieth and early twenty-first centuries.
6. Incidentally, China is not innocent of using the 'blackface' as demonstrated by the recent controversy attached to a skit on China's English language TV station CCTV's *Spring Festival Gala* featuring 'blackface' actors (Roberto Castillo 2018).
7. In note 56 to Chap. 1 she says that 'technically the first foreign actor to play the foreign role in a spoken drama was James Adreassi in The Shanghai People's Art Theatre's production of *The Joy Luck Club* codirected by American Arvin Brown and Yu Luosheng' (Conceison 2004, 243).
8. This was an adaption of 1993 Wang Zuosheng's homonymous novel, about Jiang Zhoujun, wife of a Chinese graduate in the USA and her over-bearing employer, Jewish-American Lucia (the Chinese couple are offered lodging at Jordan and Lucy's Beverly Hills house in exchange for Zhoujun's baby-sitting).

9. 'The experiences of Jiang in the US reinforce for the audience what they already know about the humiliating experiences of thousands of Chinese students and immigrants in Western developed countries, arousing resentment of the real and imagined slights that the Chinese nation has suffered in this global immigration' (Su 2005, 236).

10. It is a kind of Orientalism that requires a re-packaging of the 'ethnicity' in glossy images of its own *primitivism*, the resorting to 'mythical pictures' to which the 'convenient label of otherness' can be easily attached (Chow 1995, 170–171).

11. Bill Aitchison, British performance artist, has been based in China producing work for the last five years. *Elephant in the Room,* independent theatre company led by Italian Fabrizio Massini together with Norwegian writer Oda Fiskum was at the forefront of experimental independent theatre in China. The pair, Massini and Fiskum, collaborated, again in 2012 (Massini as artistic director and Fiskum as writer for one of the company productions), with the company Ibsen International, a company that seeks to initiate 'international collaborations in the fields of art and culture through a genuinely intercultural dialogue based on transparency, tolerance and mutual respect' (http://ibseninternational.com/about/).

12. Wang Chong collaborated with Fiskum to create a new piece of theatre, *Ibsen in One Take* (*Yi jing yisheng yi bo sheng*) inspired by Ibsen's oeuvre, which premiered in Beijing in 2012 and toured to Guangzhou and Shanghai, the Netherlands, Australia and Canada in 2013: Wang Chong created the original story-line and Fiskum penned the script. The script was in Chinese and the full cast was, also, all Chinese. Wang Chong also directed another piece for the company, *GHOSTS 2.0* (Qungui 2.0), based on Henrik Ibsen's original play *Ghosts*, which premiered at 6th Beijing International Fringe Festival in 2014 and toured to Shanghai and to Japan in the same year. The cast again was Chinese and the script was also in Chinese.

13. Contradicting Conceison's statement in her interview that no Chinese work is touring outside china, Wang Chong has managed to tour his directed works not only to Asia-pacific countries (Japan, Singapore and Australia) but also to the West (Canada, USA and UK).

14. Written in 1977, Heiner Müller's *Hamletmachine* has been defined as a play that 'explores human agency and the way that decisions are made at critical points at one's life. […] is a mediation in miniature on the difficulty of achieving political ends' (Barnett 2016, 480–495).

15. According to some, this play reflected Müller's 1956 personal crisis and the political crisis in Europe: Khrushchev's revelation of Stalin's terror years; Hungarian revolution; Brecht's death (he was Müller's mentor). The first scenes of the plays were written in 1956 twenty years circa before its publication (Carl Weber 1984, 23).

16. Marxist, Müller had a difficult relation with the communist regime in Eastern Germany (Kalb 2004, 108).

17. His interest with North Korea can be connected to the fact that Wang visited North Korea on a scholarship in 2008 (Lin 2011).

18. This was directed by 'the controversial German film-maker Leni Riefenstahl, whose hypnotic depiction of Hitler's 1934 Nuremberg rally, *Triumph of the Will,* is renowned and reviled as the best propaganda film ever' (Harding 2003).

19. 'We are still living in the "Mao era" to a certain extent', Wang admits in an interview for the *Nanjing Zhuomo Baodao* (Shi 2011).
20. This is particularly the case of when the focus is on the performer that plays the role of Hamlet.
21. In 2013 interview Wang talks about taking a Western text to talk about Chinese reality, thus emphasising his aim to reflect on Chinese reality (Anderson 2013).
22. A similar tone can be found in other reviews that condemn both Wang's adaptation and use of Peking opera tropes (San 2010).
23. This was staged at the Singaporean International Festival of Arts in 2015 in collaboration with Lasalle College of Arts.
24. These were her second husband, Chinese writer Tang Na, Yu Huiyong, former musician from Jiang's home province who became minister of culture and Jiang's left-hand (Terril 1999); Bai Shuxiang, a Chinese ballerina famous for being one of Jiang's victim who sent her to a labour reform camp between 1966 and 1973 (Song 2013).
25. One of the performers, Deonn Yang, acting student from Lasalle, talks about Wang's intentions of a story beyond China: '[Wang] was able to use the different languages available to create a play and use a script to tell a story of more than just China but kind of a universal story that applies to everyone, regardless of where you're from, because it's everyone's story' (Ng 2015b).
26. '*The Revolutionary Model Play* was the propaganda brainchild of Jiang Qing, wife of Mao Zedong. Created under her patronage for the sole purpose of glorifying the Chinese Communist Party, these model plays combine the traditional Peking opera and ballet with patriotic storylines'. Refer to the blurb on Lasalle website presenting the project (http://www.thelasalleshow.com/projects/jamil-schulze/revolutionary-model-play-2-0/).
27. It is a kind of Chineseness and Sino-centrism that does not shy away from appropriating not only the image of the white 'other' but also that of its neighbouring countries, such as North Korea.
28. One should not forget that *Revolutionary Model Play 2.0* was commissioned by Singaporean Arts Festival and they would have been some expectations on what kind of work was to be produced.

References

An, Dongni. 2010. Yiwen shenghuo boke "Hamuleite jiqi" daoyan Wang Chong fangtan (Art Life Podcast 'Hamletmachine' Interview with Wang Chong). *RFI Shijie zhi sheng*. Last modified July 27, 2010. http://cn.rfi.fr/科技与文化/20110723-«-哈姆雷特机器-»-演王翀访谈.

Anderson, Andrew. 2013 Rise of China's Avant-Garde. Last modified October 2, 2013. http://www.internationalartsmanager.com/features/rise-chinas-avant-garde.html.

Barnett, David. 2016. *Heiner Müller's Hamletmachine*. London and New York: Routledge, Kindle.

Castillo, Roberto. 2018. What "blackface" Tells Us About China's Patronising Attitude Towards Africa. *The Conversation*. Last Modified March 6, 2018. http://theconversation.com/what-blackface-tells-us-about-chinas-patronising-attitude-towards-africa-92449.

Chen, Xiaomei. 2002. *Occidentalism: A Theory of Counter-Discourse in Post-Mao China*. Oxford: Rowman & Littlefield.

Chow, Rey. 1995. *Primitive Passions: Visuality, Sexuality, Ethnography and Contemporary Chinese Cinema*. New York: Columbia University Press.

Conceison, Claire. 2004. *Significant Other – Staging the American in China*. Honolulu: University of Hawai'i Press.

Dikötter, Frank. 2015. *The Discourse of Race in Modern China*. Oxford: Oxford University Press.

Elam, J. Harry, Jr. 2001. The Device of Race – An Introduction. In *African American Performance and Theater History: A Critical Reader*, ed. Harry J. Elam and David Krasner. New York: Oxford University Press.

Haoxi Wang. 2010. Wang Chong daoyan "Hamuleite jiqi"-zhongguo dalu shouyan (China's Premiere of Wang Chong's *Hamletmachine*), in *Haoxi Wang*. Last Modified September 14, 2010. https://www.mask9.com/node/11024.

Harding, Luke. 2003. Leni Riefenstahl, Hitler's Favourite Film Propagandist, Dies at 101. *The Guardian*. Last Modified September 10, 2003. https://www.theguardian.com/world/2003/sep/10/film.germany.

Ho, Ai Li. 2015. Multi-faceted Look at Madame Mao. *Straits Times*. Last Modified September 4, 2015. https://www.straitstimes.com/singapore/multi-faceted-look-at-madam-mao.

Ibsen International. n.d. About *Ibsen International*. Last Accessed November 10, 2018. http://ibseninternational.com/about/.

Kalb, Jonathan. 2004. *The Theatre of Heiner Müller*. New York: Limelight Editions.

Lasalle. n.d. *The Lasalle Show*. Accessed November 20, 2015. http://www.thelasalleshow.com/projects/jamil-schulze/revolutionary-model-play-2-0/.

Leng, Rachel. 2015. The Theatre and US-China Relations: An Interview with Claire Conceison. *China Focus*. Last Modified August 13, 2015. https://chinafocus.ucsd.edu/2015/08/13/claire-conceison/.

Lim, Gabriel. 2015. An Important History Lesson. Last Modified 2 September 2015. http://centre42.sg/the-revolutionary-model-play-2-0-by-by-wang-chong-theatre-du-reve-experimental-lasalle-college-of-the-arts.

Lin, Jing. 2011. Wang Chong – Gaoju "shiyan xiju" daqi (Wang Chong Holding High the Banner for Experimental Theatre). *Basha nanshi baodao*, May 2011.

Mackerras, Colin. 2005. Significant Other: Staging the American in China (Review). *Modern Drama* 48 (3, Fall): 617–619.

Müller, Heiner, 1984. *Hamletmachine and other texts for the stage*. edited and translated by Carl Weber. Imprint New York: Performing Arts Journal Publications.

Ng, Yi-Sheng. 2015a. The Revolutionary Model Play 2.0. *Sifa The Open*. Last Modified September 3, 2015. https://sifa.sg/archive-blog/the-revolutionary-model-play-2-0-2-0.

———. 2015b. Interview with Deonn Yang. *Sifa*. Last Modified September 1, 2015. https://sifa.sg/archive-blog/interview-with-deonn-yang.

San, Ba'er. 2010. Pincou chulai de "Hamuleite jiqi" (The Hamletmachine Patchwork). *Waitan huabao*. Last Modified October 24, 2010. http://yule.sohu.com/20101024/n276342085.shtml.

Shi, Yan. 2011. Hao xuesheng huanshi xiaoxuesheng – yige nianqing xijuren de "yiyiguxing" (Good Students Are Also Good Primary School Students – A Young Theatre-Maker Goes His Own Way). *Nanjing Zhuomo Baodao*, July 7, 2011.

Song, Yuwu, ed. 2013. *Biographical Dictionary of the People's Republic of China*. Jefferson, North Caroline and London: McFarland.

Su, Hongjun. 2005. Reinserting Woman into Contemporary Chinese National Identity: A Comparative Reading of Three "New Immigrant" Plays from 1990s Shanghai. *Theatre Journal* 57 (2): 229–246.

Terril, Ross. 1999. *Madame Mao: The White Boned Demon*. Stanford: Stanford University Press.

Weber, Carl. 1984. Introduction: The Pressure of Experience. In *Hamletmachine and Other Texts for the Stage*, Heiner Müller, ed. and trans. Carl Weber. New York: Performing Art Journal Publications.

Xiong, Siqi. 2012. Wang Chong – Chinese Avant-Garde Director. 35:20, *Cri English*. Last Modified November 1, 2012. http://english.cri.cn/8706/2012/11/01/3181s730350.htm.

Young, Harvey. 2013. *Theatre and Race*. London and New York: Palgrave.

INDEX[1]

NUMBERS AND SYMBOLS

9/11, 27, 333
1800s, 430
1820s, 90, 352, 363
1830s, 221
1840s, 366
1850s, 359, 370, 387n10
1860s, 370, 387
1920s, 126, 129, 447
1930s, 33, 124, 126, 133, 180, 421n7, 447
1948 elections, 221
1950s, 26, 42, 46, 47, 70, 178, 334, 407, 448
1960s, 12, 34, 41, 42, 46, 49, 61, 152, 159, 178, 196, 199, 240, 257, 258, 260, 265, 269, 270n8, 334, 407, 418, 447
1970s, 26, 47, 49, 53, 70, 89, 146, 147, 156n8, 178, 182, 183, 185, 188, 199, 260, 261, 275, 318, 334, 345n3, 393, 444, 447
1980s, 26, 29, 41, 49, 77n14, 83, 146, 147, 160, 163, 178, 182, 185, 188, 191, 261–262, 275, 279, 308, 309, 312, 318, 331, 334, 446
1990s, 11, 29, 49, 83, 147, 154, 159, 170, 178, 183, 188, 200, 205, 206, 211n3, 211n12, 213n27, 260–262, 264, 309, 312, 313, 321, 331, 453, 469, 470

2000s, 41, 49, 51, 53, 197, 262, 269
2010s, 50, 205, 211n3, 212n18
2012 Summer Olympics, 30

A

Abir, 179
Ableism, 318
Abolitionism, 372, 380, 381, 383
Abraham, 188
Abraham, Tezeta, 459
Academics for Peace, 200, 212n13
Accent, 25, 296, 357, 381, 457
Ach, Kamerun! Unsere alte deutsche Kolonie., 53
Acropolis, 202
Act For Change Project, 23, 30
Acting, 45, 47, 49, 51, 53–55, 65, 74, 147, 208, 243, 295, 296, 301, 302, 316, 353, 355, 416, 484n25
Action-cinema, 47
Action-theatre, 47
Actors of colour, 26, 28, 41, 50, 51, 54
Adaptations, 13, 14, 29, 57n5, 62, 128, 135, 143, 164, 179, 197, 232, 262, 295, 305n3, 332, 369–372, 374, 375, 382, 385, 466, 467, 473, 476, 477, 484n22

---

[1] Note: Page numbers followed by 'n' refer to notes.

© The Author(s), under exclusive license to Springer Nature Switzerland AG 2021
T. Morosetti, O. Okagbue (eds.), *The Palgrave Handbook of Theatre and Race*, https://doi.org/10.1007/978-3-030-43957-6

487

488 INDEX

Adebayo, Mojisola, 13, 307, 313,
    314, 316–318
Adedeji, Joel Adeyinka, 427, 432
Adelphi theatre, 363
Adhuuraa Sapnaa–Shattered Dreams, 65
Adorno, Theodor W., 313
Adreassi, James, 482n7
Adshead, Kay, 14, 446, 448, 455–460
Afakasi (mixed race), 70
Afghanistan, 27, 52
Africa(s), 5, 6, 8, 9, 14, 206, 221, 222,
    231–233, 242–247, 249, 265, 273,
    274, 280, 282, 307, 316, 333, 334,
    340, 410, 430, 431, 451
African(s)
    characters, 9, 27, 28, 242, 251, 282,
        346n13, 375, 377, 386
    cultures, 245, 276, 282, 375, 430
    diaspora, 9, 321, 340
    gods, 221, 232, 280
    languages, 329, 369–390, 459
    myths, 280–282
    peoples, 24, 241–244, 246, 273, 274,
        288n6, 375, 377, 403n6
    performance, 9, 274, 430
    playwrights, 248, 319
African American(s)
    actors, 27, 28, 44, 45
    characters, 27, 28, 32, 34, 276, 352,
        364, 370, 375
    population, 366
    practitioners, 44, 57n5
    womanhood, 299
African-American English Vernacular
    (AAVE), 370, 371, 387n7
African and Caribbean theatres, 242
African-Caribbean
    characters, 248, 249
    peoples, 249
African Gothic, 222–236
Afrikaans, 220–223
Afrikaner(s)
    mythology, 221, 230, 231
    myths, 221, 222, 224, 228–231,
        235, 236
Afro-Brazilian cultures, 274, 279, 282
Afro-Brazilian religions, 279
Afro-Cuban artists, 260
Afro-Cubans, 256, 260–262, 266–268
Afrofuturist performance techniques, 41

Afronta, 284
After the Fall, 28, 29
Àgan, 435, 437
Agbégijó, *see* Alárìnjó
Agbégijó performances, 431
Agboluaje, Oladipo, 332
Agit-prop, 164, 165, 169
Aiken, George L., 373, 385
Aïnouz, Karim, 283
Aitchison, Bill, 483n11
Ajibade, Yemi, 452
Akın, Rojin Canan, 205
Akinade, Fisayo, 459
Akko Festival, 182
Akutagawa, Ryunosuke, 108
Alágbáàrárá, 435, 436
Alápínni, 436, 438, 440n13
Alárìnjó
    performance, 429–431, 433, 436
    performers, 431
Alawis, 198, 213n29
Albanians, 169, 174n3
Albany, 354
Aldridge, Ira, 446
Aleksandra Zec, 169
Alexandra Theatre Liverpool, 384
Alfred the Great, 382
Algonquin, 94, 96
Ali, Muhammad, 13, 67, 179, 180,
    307, 308, 310, 313–319,
    323n9, 323n11
Alison's House, 393
Aljarrah, Mohammad, 30, 31
Alla Karim, 179, 185
Allen, Chadwick, 83, 96
Allen, Debbie, 21–23, 26, 28, 32, 33
Allen, Woody, 466
All My Sons, 32, 33
All Wish to Live, 187
A Love Supreme, 320
Almeida Theatre, 32, 33
Al Qaeda, 27
Alternative theatre, 11, 195–197, 206,
    210, 211n2, 212n18, 213n28
*Amakosa; or, Scenes of Kaffir
    Warfare*, 377
Amankulor, Ndukaku, 432, 433
America, 2, 3, 6, 21, 22, 27, 29, 31, 44,
    315, 317, 319, 351–367, 370,
    382, 478

INDEX

American(s)
  black, 2, 74, 297, 303, 313, 353, 363, 369, 377, 386
  characters, 313, 351, 354
  drama, 21, 22, 24, 26–37
  literature, 358, 359
  people, 4, 274, 305, 353, 366n1
  population, 376
  stage, 21, 26, 33, 369–390, 465
American Indians, *see* Native American
American Theater Wing, 21
Amid, Shmuel, 181
A Midsummer Night's Dream, 156n8
AMOK Teatro, 13, 281
Anago people, 427
Anatolia, 206
Ancestors, 67, 68, 114, 115, 142, 143, 148, 152, 156n13, 228, 246, 265, 267, 333, 340, 346n13, 378, 428, 429, 433–438
Ancient Greece, 62
Anđelić, Jadranka, 168
Anglo-Boer war, 221, 226, 229, 232
Anglo-Zulu war, 377
Angola, 460
Ankara, 206, 212n14, 213n28
Annaberg, 129
The Anniversary Present, 66
Anthropological Society of London, 386n5
An Octoroon, 292, 294–296, 298, 303
Anti-Americanism, 469
Antigone, 47, 206, 213n27
Antigone2012, 205
Antigone2013, 206
Anti-Semitism, 43, 471
Antonescu, Ion, 113
Antony and Cleopatra, 32
Aotearoa, *see* New Zealand
Apartheid, 11, 154, 221, 222, 225, 228, 236, 312, 313
The Arabian Night, 466
Arabic, 53, 198
Arab question, 191
Arabs, 179–184
Ararat Republic, 198
Ará òrun, 428, 429
Araújo, Joel Zito, 276
Araújo, Taís, 283
Arcia, Alberto Abreu, 271

Arendt, Hannah, 219, 221, 222, 227, 228, 232
Argentina, 85, 112
Arieli-Orloff, L.A., 179
Aristotle, 321
Armenians, 198
Arndt, Ernst Moritz, 124
Artaud, Antonin, 13, 14, 407–421, 447
Arts Council England, 331
Aryans, 124, 125, 127, 131, 132
Asia, 162, 186, 307
Asian
  artists, 26, 143
  performers, 24, 36
Aspden, Kester, 332
Assimilation, 89, 180, 199, 339, 395
Assyrians, 198
Astley's, 377
Asylum seekers, 397, 457, 461n6, 461n8
As You Like It, 127, 133
Atamira Dance Collective, 156n17
A Taste of Honey, 448–452
Atatürk, Mustafa Kemal, 198
Atelier 212, 164
'At Homes,' 351, 354, 356, 363, 365
Atlanta, 299
Atlantic slave trade, 333, 383
At the Wake, 70
Atwood, Margaret, 94
Auckland, 70, 73–75
Auckland Theatre Company, 77n13, 156n8
Audiences, 34, 41, 45, 65, 75, 76, 84, 88, 90, 102, 126, 130, 131, 142, 145, 146, 149, 151, 164, 177, 182, 185–192, 196, 213n27, 222, 247, 260, 265, 267, 279, 291, 315, 327, 341, 343, 357, 358, 369, 376, 378, 402n3, 431
Australia, 62, 64, 70, 146, 397, 482n1, 483n12, 483n13
Australian Immigration Restriction Act, 397
Austria, 103, 131
Austrian female playwrights, 57
Authenticity, 50, 304, 322, 354
Authorship, 14, 298, 360, 447, 456, 460, 476

490 INDEX

Autobiography, 295, 297–299, 304, 307, 313
Avignon Festival, 477
Ayamba, Maxwell, 346n10
Ayivi, Simone Dede, 54, 55
  War of the Squirrels, 55
Aztec empire, 414

B

Baartman, Sara, 375
Babaláwo, 426, 439n2
Bad Axe Massacre, 394
Bahia, 12, 279, 283
Bai Bai Pelô, 279, 283
Bainimarama, Josaia Voreqe (Frank), 64, 65, 77n9
Baldwin, James, 284, 286, 288n9, 323n12, 323n13, 374
Balinese Dance Company, 408
Balkans, 11, 161, 162, 166, 199
Ballet, 184, 484n26
Ballhaus Naunynstraße theatre, 41, 52, 54, 57n2
Baltic Sea, 125
Baltimore, 357, 394
Bamboozled, 276
BAME, 15n3, 336, 338, 345n9
Bancel, Nicolas, 308, 309
Bando de Teatro Olodum, 12
Bando, um filme de, 283
Barba, Eugenio, 168, 418
Bartholomew Fair, 360
Bascom, William, 427, 429, 430, 432
The Basement Theatre, Auckland, 75
Bathurst, Henryrd Earl Bathurst, 430
Bavadra, Timoci, 64
BBC Radio 4, 336
Beat Generation, 408, 418
The Beatles, 152
Beaton, Norman, 29
Beattie, Maureen, 33
Beckett, Samuel, 179, 188, 203, 204
Becoming a Man Through Crawling, 202, 203, 205, 212n19
Beier, Ulli, 430
Beijing, 483n12
Beijing Fringe Festival, 472

Belgium, 313
Belgrade, 160, 163–165, 168, 169, 171–173, 174n10, 175n10
Belgrade Dramatic Theatre, 164, 167
Belgrade theatres, 164, 172
Belo Horizonte, 283
Belz, Albert, 143, 154, 155, 156n18
Bença, 279, 280
Benin, 426, 427
Benjamin, Walter, 43, 473
Bentham, Jeremy, 430
Berceanu, Alexandru
  Privind prin piele (2016), 103
Berlin, 11, 41, 54, 103, 105, 131, 133–135, 136n4, 297, 310
Berlin Conference, 377
Berlin Grunewald stadium, 130
Berlin Theater des Volkes, 133
Berlin Wall, 46
Bhabha, Homi, 161, 166, 219, 220, 222, 224, 225, 227, 228, 232, 236
Bight of Benin, 430
Biko, Steve, 219
Bildungsroman, 292
Binto, 321
Biography, 295, 297–299, 304, 307, 313, 314, 316, 317, 360, 393, 395
Birmingham, 345n3
Bittersweet Hope (2005), 77n6
Black(s), 81, 228, 250, 252, 253, 262, 265, 271n13, 275, 276, 278, 279, 281, 286, 288n9, 297, 321, 340, 370
  body, 14, 264, 274, 286, 329, 341, 383, 445, 448–453, 455–457
  characters, 13, 50, 246, 249, 250, 253, 256, 261, 270n2, 275–277, 284, 333, 341, 343, 344, 351, 352, 370–373, 375, 376, 381, 383, 443–445, 451
  community, 1–3, 9, 285, 449, 451
  cultures, 32, 280, 296, 302, 315
  female bodies, 256
  female characters, 268, 327
  identity, 3, 246, 257, 279, 287, 292, 293, 300
  interpreters, 277
  minstrelsy, 460n1

INDEX 491

people, 1, 3, 6, 21, 242, 244, 247–253, 269, 274–278, 280, 282, 284, 286, 315, 321, 329, 330, 332–343, 381, 383, 386, 394
performance, 12, 273–288, 293, 447
performers, 27, 276, 278, 282, 298, 387n10, 444, 446, 447
playwrights, 295, 298, 322, 328, 329, 335
power, 260
Black American culture, 74
Black Americans, 74, 309, 353, 363, 369
Black Angel, 277
Black British, 2, 13, 14n1, 21, 23, 24, 27, 28, 32, 34–36, 307, 313, 328, 340, 345n2, 345n6, 444, 445, 447, 454
playwrights, 307, 313, 328
theatre, 444, 445, 447
writers, 345n2
Black diaspora, 274, 276, 278, 287
Black Experimental Theatre (TEN), 276–279, 282, 287
Blackface
characters, 295, 304, 387n11
impersonation, 375
impersonators, 378
mask, 12, 292, 297
minstrelsy, 12, 13, 293, 362, 370, 372, 374, 375, 378, 384, 402n3
Black Faggot, 71
Black Front, 277
Black German(s)
actors, 48, 51, 53, 54
artists, 54, 55
directors, 54
theatre, 53–56, 57n10, 57n13
Black Hawk (Makataimeshekiakiak), 392–395, 401, 402n2
Black Hawk Purchase, 13, 392, 394, 401, 402n4
Black Hawk War, 394
Black Lives Matter, 1–3
Black Man Walking, 334
Black Muslims, 314
'Blackness,' 7–10, 12, 13, 57n7, 244, 247, 248, 251, 253, 258, 269, 287, 288n9, 292–294, 297, 300–304, 333, 336, 337, 341, 342, 369–387, 445, 447, 450, 451

Black Queer Studies, 318
Black women, 12, 251, 255–271, 286, 287n3, 312, 446, 452, 453, 457
characters, 256, 264, 265
Blair, Tony, 30
Blake, William, 340, 421n6
Blakemore, Michael, 28, 29
Blanchard, Pascal, 308, 309
Blanco, Roberto, 260
Blasted, 451
Blige, Mary J., 301
The Blind Child of Africa; or, the Last Prince of Abyssinia and the True British Seaman, 377
Blood and Gifts, 27
Boal, Augusto, 54, 202
Boán, Marianela, 261
Bochum, 133
Boconya, 415
Bodies, 14, 24, 39, 42, 51, 65, 68, 72, 91, 102–104, 107, 109–112, 115, 116, 131, 190, 228, 234, 255, 256, 261, 264, 267, 269, 274, 281, 282, 285–287, 303, 307, 310–312, 320, 322, 329, 330, 335, 337, 341, 342, 344, 376, 383, 384, 398, 403n6, 408, 409, 416, 417, 419, 420, 429, 431, 437, 439, 443–453, 455–460, 470
Boers, 221, 222, 225, 229, 232
The Bogus Woman, 443–460
Bologna, 459
Booth, William, 381
Borders, 40, 45, 46, 55, 115, 124, 172, 195, 198, 203, 204, 245, 248, 298, 303, 308, 314, 366, 408, 429, 438
Bosnia-Hercegovina, 161, 162
Bosnian genocide, 159
Bosnians, 162, 163, 170, 171, 174n6
Bosnian Serb Army, 170
Bossa nova, 85
Boston, 391, 401n1
Boston Tea Party museum, 392
Boucicault, Dion, 292, 295, 296, 303, 305n3, 376
Bow Street, 357
Boxing, 13, 307, 314–322, 323n14, 323n16
The Boy and the Old Man, 283
Bradshaw, Thomas, 293

492 INDEX

Brazil, 12, 85, 273–287
Brazilian people, 287n1
Bread and Iron, 130
Breathing In, 229, 232, 235
Brecht, Bertolt, 40–49, 52, 54, 56,
    57n4, 168, 204, 483n15
Bremner, Ewen, 452
Brewster, Yvonne, 446
Brexit, 8
Brighton, 175n10
Brisbane, 66
Bristol, 1
Britannia, 25, 382
British
    colonisers, 63
    settlers, 144, 156n3
    stage, 13, 21, 27, 33, 36, 328,
        331, 369–386
    theatre, 13, 21–37, 345n5, 444,
        445, 447
    women playwrights, 444
British Black and Asian Shakespeare
    Performance Database, 28
British Empire, 377, 386
British Film Institute, 23
British Isles, 352
Brixton, 452
Brixton Riots, 452
Broadway, 21, 22
Brodt, Stephane, 281
Bronislawa Wajs (Papusza), 113
Brooks, Andy, 331
Brooks, Rayshard, 1
Brother Jonathan, 358, 360
Brough, William, 370–372, 379–383
Broughton, Jim, 146
Broughton, John, 143
Brown, Arvin, 482n7
Brown's Bay, 73, 74
Brownface, 144
Budapest, 103, 105
Buffong, Michael, 28, 32, 33
Bug (river), 113
Bug colony, 114
Bühnenwatch, Bündnis, 54
Bujanovac, 175n10
Bull, John, 361
Burlesque, 363, 364, 384
Burnand, J.C., 383
Burning Vision, 89

Burns, Tony, 147
Burri, Emil, 43
Burton, E.G., 377
Butler, Judith, 446
Butoh, 279
Byrd, Stephen, 21
Byron, Henry, 384
Byzantium, 162

C

Cabaré da Rrrrrraça, 279, 283
Cabaret, 86, 188
Cabildo Teatral Santiago, 261
Calderón, Xiomara, 271n18
Caliban, 444
California, 89, 297
Calvinism, 221, 222, 224–226, 228, 231
Camargo, Aguinaldo, 276
Cameri theatre, 181, 189
Cameron, David, 31
Campsfield, 461n8
Campsfield riots, 456
Canada, 10, 64, 81–97, 307, 355, 376,
    387n12, 392, 397, 398,
    483n12, 483n13
Canadian Indigenous drama, 96
Canan, 205
Candomblé, 280–282
Capitalism, 43, 133, 159, 167, 259, 363,
    474, 476
Cardiff, 449
The Caretaker, 29
Caribbean
    characters, 248
    dramatists, 249
    mythology, 247
    peoples, 240, 241, 249
    plays, 240, 242, 243, 246, 250
    theatre, 12, 239–253
Caricature, 62, 276, 281, 351, 354, 358,
    360, 371, 372, 381, 429, 431, 432
Caroline, Or Change, 33
Carousel, 29
Carvalho, Wagner, 54, 55
Casa de las Américas, 257
Cast, 21–23, 26, 27, 29, 30, 32, 33, 36,
    50, 57n5, 65, 75, 103, 127, 131,
    153, 155, 156n8, 157, 171, 233,
    281, 283, 295, 296, 298, 318, 373,

431, 439n2, 446, 448–450, 456, 458, 470, 478, 479, 483n12
Castaneda, Carlos, 416
Casting, 10, 22–36, 40, 41, 44, 50, 51, 114, 165, 179, 189, 426, 429, 443–448, 454, 479, 480
Castro, Pedro, 271n11
Cat, 21–23, 26–28, 32, 33, 370
The Cataract of the Ganges, 387n9
Cat on a Hot Tin Roof, 21, 23, 26, 27, 32, 33
Catholicism, 131, 162
Caucasian, 93, 95, 96, 465, 469, 471
Cavazzi, Father, 458
Cavendish, Dominic, 29, 30
Cecilia Valdés, 257, 270n9
Celali Uprisings, 213n29
Çelik, Neco, 55, 212n22, 213n25
Celkan, Ebru Nihan, 204
Censorship, 134, 260, 271n13, 395
Central America, 14, 409
Central and Eastern Europe, 105
Central Park West, 466
Cette vieille magie noire, 312, 313, 319, 321, 323n14
Chaikin, Joseph, 181
Chamberlain, Houston Steward, 125, 126, 367n4
  Die Grundlagen des 20. Jahrhunderts, 125
Channel 4, 451
Characters, 9, 27, 51, 169, 178, 195, 225, 240, 256, 275, 295, 333, 351, 370, 396, 443, 466
Chaudhry, Mahendra, 64
Chekhov, Anton, 156n8, 179
Chen, Xiaomei, 465, 467, 468
The Cherry Orchard, 156n8
Chicago Blackhawks, 402n2
Chichester Festival Theatre, 33
Chihuahua, 414, 415, 421n7
A Child for Iva, 65
Chimerica, 36
China, 8, 13, 45, 46, 282, 465, 466, 468–481, 482n2, 482n4, 484n6, 483n11, 483n13, 484n25
Chinese
  actor, 45, 470
  character, 45, 480, 481

culture, 46, 465, 474
diaspora, 482n1
performers, 45, 480
stage, 465, 466, 471
theatre, 14, 465–484
Chinese Communist Party, 45, 484n26
Chineseness, 476, 480–482, 484n27
Chinese New Left, 471
Chita no come maní, 260, 263, 264
Chong, Wang, 14, 465, 466, 472–482, 482n1, 483n12, 483n13
Christian and Islamic religions, 432
Christianity, 87, 374, 428
Christy's Minstrels, 373, 374
Chunqiao, Zhang, 477, 478
Churchill, Caryl, 14, 443, 455, 456
Ciguri (or Jíkuri) ritual, 415, 416
Cine a omorât-o pe Szomna Grancsa?, 104, 108–109
Citizenship, 102, 112, 277, 279
City of York, 340
Ciudad del Mexico, 409, 412, 414
Civil rights, 21, 288n9
Cizre, 200
Clapperton, Hugh (Captain), 429–433, 439, 439n5
Clark, Helen, 72
Clarke, Sharon D., 33, 34, 36, 459
Classes, 106, 129, 208, 227, 352, 353, 356, 363, 375
Clean Break, 454
Clegg, Nick, 31
Clements, Marie, 82, 89–93, 97n10, 97n12
Clinton, Bill, 4, 6, 239
Cloud Nine, 443–445, 449, 460
Clybourne Park, 27, 28, 32
Coast Salish, 398, 399, 403n7
Cobras & Lagartos, 283
Cockney, 359, 360
Cockney-Caribbean, 454
Cofradía de la Negritud, 271n19
Cold War, 199
Collins, Fiona, 77n12
Colman, George, 374
Colman, George (the younger), 367n4
Colonial Exhibition, 409
Colonial Exposition of 1931, 408

494 INDEX

Colonialism, 1, 5, 10, 69, 74, 93, 221, 224, 228, 240, 245, 252, 253, 255, 274, 275, 308, 322n6, 403n6, 403n10, 411, 420, 459
Colonies, 46, 241, 308, 430
Colonisation, 75, 76, 142, 144, 148, 149, 151, 153–155, 245, 246, 274, 310, 311, 333, 403n6, 412, 418, 459
Colour coding, 315
Colston, Edward, 1
Coltrane, John, 320
Commission for Racial Equality, 336
Commission on Race and Ethnic Disparities, 2
Communism, 159, 162, 168, 172, 199, 474, 475
Communist Party, 45, 159, 162–164, 484n26
Compañía Rita Montaner, 271n18
Compassionate Exile (1999), 77n6
Concentration camp, 174n4, 189, 226, 229
Concert party, 145
Confucianism, 482n4
Congadas, 282, 288n7
Congado dos Arturos, 282
Congo, 13, 288n7
Conjunto Dramático de Camagüey, 271n11
Connecticut, 28
Connor, Edric, 403n7
The Conquest of Mexico, 408, 412
Conrad, Joseph, 473
The Conservation of Races, 447
Conservative party, 31
Consumerism, 66
Convention, 61, 68, 77n15, 143, 173, 295, 331, 343, 344, 372, 379–383, 386, 387n8, 428, 446
Conway, H.J., 373
Cook, James, 144
Cook Islands Māori, 70
Cooper, Gary, 70
Copenhagen, 40
Copper Canyon, 415
Copper Thunderbird, 89, 97n9
Corp urban, 104, 109–112, 117n6, 118n7
Cosme, 280

Cotterill, James, 31
Cottesloe, 26
Counter Revolutionary Warfare Unit, 64
Cousins, Frank, 25, 345n5
Covent Garden, 383
COVID-19, 1
Crave, 451, 466
Credible Witness, 446
Cree, 83–85, 88, 96
Creolisation, 7, 82, 84, 85, 87, 89–93, 95, 96
Cricket, 25
Critical Race Theory (CRT), 6, 75, 104, 160, 161, 165
Croatia, 161, 162, 167–170
Croatian(s)
   authors, 167, 169
   directors, 170
Croats, 161–164, 166, 170, 174n9
Croll, Doña, 32
Crossing, 232, 233, 235
Crossing the Line, 160, 171
The Crucible, 27, 34
Crucible Theatre, Sheffield, 34
Cu moartea'n ochi, 113
Cuba, 255, 257–266, 269, 271n13
Cuban(s)
   female playwrights, 256
   independence, 266, 269
   literature, 257
   playwrights, 257, 260, 261
   Revolution, 12, 256–261
   theatre, 12, 255–272
Cultural Revolution, 116, 470, 474, 475, 477, 479, 480
Culture, 10, 11, 13, 14, 24, 32, 46, 48, 49, 52, 55, 62, 63, 68, 69, 71, 73–76, 77n1, 83, 84, 90, 91, 96, 101, 105, 106, 125, 129, 133, 142–146, 148, 149, 155, 159–161, 165, 166, 168, 178, 184, 186, 198, 199, 203, 205, 220, 225, 235, 243–245, 251, 255–257, 261, 273–277, 279–283, 285, 292, 293, 296, 299, 302, 303, 305, 308, 312, 315, 331, 335, 339, 361, 363, 370, 375, 395, 396, 403n6, 408–414, 418, 420n2, 425–433, 438, 439n6, 447, 465, 468, 474, 483n11, 484n24

Cushman, Asa, 373
Cyrillic, 162
Czech Republic, 110

D

Daf, 203, 204, 337
DAH Theatre, 160, 168–171, 173, 174n1
Dakota, 400, 401
Daly, Robert, 470
Damian, 280
Danışman, Funda, 205
Danjé, Michaëla, 309, 322, 322n3, 323n8
Danquah, Paul, 450
Dao, Salim, 189, 191
Daramola, Olu, 428, 439n2
Darby, William (later Pablo Fanque), 340
Dark and Light theatre company, 345n5
Darwin, Charles Robert, 378
Das Fest der Liebe—Die Chance der Jugend, 53
Davenport, 396
Dayan, Moshe, 187
de Souza, Ruth, 276, 282
De Wet, Reeza, 11, 220, 222–236
Dea Loher's Unschuld (Innocence), 50
Death of a Salesman, 22, 27, 29, 33–36
Deborah's Daughter, 460n2
Decolonisation, 74
Deeter, Jasper, 402n5
Defoe, Daniel, 383
Del Duma/Vorbește-le despre mine!, 104–107
Delaney, Shelagh, 14, 448–451
Deleuze, Gilles, 82, 420, 421n11
Democracy, 12, 52, 172, 273, 278, 362, 364
Denazification process, 41
Dengbej, 201, 204, 205, 211n9, 212n16
Denmark, 168, 172, 175n10
Deportation, 113–115
Der Deutsche Bühnenverein, 42
Der gute Mensch von Sezuan, 45
Der kleine Bruder des Ruderers, 54
Derrida, Jacques, 116, 187, 420, 447
Dersim rebellion, 198
Desaparecidos, 112

Desire Under the Elms, 34
Destar Theatre, 201, 203–206, 211n1, 211n6, 212n15, 212n24
Deutsches Theater, 127
Devon, 29
Dialect, 101, 162, 174n9, 358, 360, 362, 370–373, 376–378, 382–384, 387n8, 434
Diaspora, 12, 255, 275–279, 282, 284, 285, 287, 321, 340, 418, 482n1
Diasporic drama, 346
Dibdin, Charles, 374, 386n1
Dick Whittington and His Cat, 370, 386n2
Dickens, Charles, 366n1
Die Massnahme, 45
Dink, Hrant, 206
Dinur, Eran, 188
Diorama, 90–93
Diouf, Penda, 312, 313, 316, 321, 322n4, 323n7, 323n8
Disability, 196
Disco No 5, 201, 202, 212n18
Discrimination, 6, 11, 23, 43, 44, 48, 53, 54, 70, 101, 105, 115, 116, 160, 232, 236, 259, 262, 269, 312, 314, 318, 321, 330, 335, 338, 345, 413
District Officer, 432
"Dixie," 291, 292
Diyarbakır, 197, 199, 202, 211n8
Diyarbakır City Theatre, 197, 211n8
Djukić, Željko, 165
Dniester (river), 113, 114
Dó, 279, 413
Documentary theatre, 117, 205, 477
Documentary, 53, 103, 113, 117, 205, 212n25, 276, 288n9, 297, 474, 477
Domestic drama, 148, 296, 303
Domestication, 430, 432, 439
Don't Cry Mama (1977), 65
The Doors, 116, 230, 311, 418
The Doors of Perception, 421n6
Dot Theatre, 211n3
Doumbia, Eva, 310–312, 321, 322n4, 322n6
Drăgan, Mihaela, 101–107, 110, 112, 113, 117n3, 117n5
Drăgănescu, Catinca, 110

496   INDEX

The Dragon, 281
Dream of a Summer Night, 279
Dream on Monkey Mountain, 240, 243, 246, 249–251, 253
Drew Hayden Taylor's God and the Indian, 82
Driskill, Qwo-Li, 403n6
Drury, Jackie Sibbles, 293, 386n1
Dryden, John, 412
Du Bois, W.E.B., 330, 341
Duany, Monse, 264, 271n12, 271n16
The Duchess of Malfi, 44
Duke of Wellington, 133
Dumezweni, Noma, 457
Duminică, Elena, 103
Duncan-Brewster, Sharon, 30, 33, 454
DuPois, Starletta, 32

E
Earthmen, 375
East Africa, 458
East and West Germany, 39
East Asia, 468
East Coast, 142, 149
Eastern Bloc, 10, 260, 262
Eastern Europe, 10, 11, 124, 168
An Echo in the Bone, 240, 243, 245, 246, 248, 249, 253
Eclipse Theatre Company, 331, 332, 345n4
Eddo-Lodge, Reni, 42
Education, 1, 2, 52, 66, 67, 107, 109, 196, 199, 209, 250–252, 271n13, 377, 381, 395, 466
The Edward Curtis Project: A Modern Picture Story, 89
Effingham Saloon, 382
Eggers, Kurt, 130
    Das Spiel von Job dem Deutschen, 130
Egúngún (Eégún), 14, 425, 426, 428–429, 431, 433–438, 439n1, 440n12
    festival, 434, 436
    masquerade, 14
Egwu, 433
Eighteenth century, 24, 143, 210, 383, 415, 427, 430
Ein Dokumentarstück, 53

Einstein, Albert, 476
Eisler, Hanns, 43
Èkìtì, 438
Èkìtì kings, 434
Elba, Idris, 24
Elban, Rojbin, 212n24
Elephant in the Room, 483n11
Eleventh century, 125
Eljanabi, Abas, 30
Ellis, Maurice, 44
El socialismo y el hombre en Cuba, 258
Emancipation, 117n4, 246, 269, 385, 443
Emelina Cundiamor, 260
Èmìilè, 436, 437, 440n10
Emmel, Felix, 129
Emmet, Dan, 370, 371
Emperor Jones, 276, 277
Empire, 25, 199, 299, 312, 364, 409, 411
Empire Windrush, 2, 15n6
Endo, Tadashi, 279
Enekwe, Onuora Ossie, 433
England, 84, 103, 172, 332–335, 338–340, 345n8, 345n9, 351, 352, 356, 358, 360, 363, 379, 446
English, 8, 22, 25, 52–55, 65, 66, 74, 84–87, 90, 96n2, 136n6, 144, 148, 150, 153, 156n7, 197, 232, 307, 314, 319, 333–336, 338–340, 353, 356, 359, 361, 363–366, 375, 377, 379, 383, 443, 445, 447, 452, 457, 459, 479, 482n1, 482n6
English Opera House, 353, 356, 360, 363, 364
Englishmen, 354, 366
Englishness, 335, 338–340, 342
Enlightenment, 52, 81, 453
Ensler, Eve, 466
Epic theatre, 448
Erê para toda vida-Xirê, 279, 280
Erfurt, 128
Erken Kaybedenler, 213n31
Erlangen, 49
Erpulat, Nurkan, 41, 52, 55
Escuela Nacional de Arte (ENA), 257
Espanca!, 283
Essa é nossa praia, 279
Èsù, 435
Ete, Moana, 77n12

INDEX 497

Ethiopian Serenaders, 370, 373, 374, 382, 386n3
Ethnic drag, 39
Ethnicity, 5, 22, 25, 27, 31, 51, 62, 69, 76, 82, 93, 107, 112, 124, 161, 201, 240, 280, 335, 444, 471, 478–480, 482n2, 483n10
Ethnological Society of London, 386n5
Euringer, Richard, 11, 129–131, 133
  Deutsche Passion 1933, 131
  German Passion 1933, 130, 131, 133
Eurocentrism, 285, 287
Europe, 4, 6, 47, 51, 56n1, 101, 103, 127, 162, 249, 264, 288n9, 297, 307, 314, 409, 411–413, 433, 445, 456, 483n15
European(s)
  art, 410, 411
  canon, 284
  drama, 148
  enslavers, 244
  'Other,' 5
  settlers, 63
  slave traders, 242
  theatre, 13, 49, 102, 149, 154, 408, 447
European Cultural Foundation, 169, 171
European Union (EU), 51, 110, 172, 173, 175n11, 335
Evans-Pritchard, E. E., 458
Evaristo, Conceição, 286, 287n3
The Execution, 187
The Executioner, 281
Exil Ensemble, 52
Expos, 145
Extermination, 114, 115, 280, 333
Extravaganzas, 385
Ẹyẹkẹyẹ, 436, 440n9

F
Faenza, 175n10
Falcão, João, 283
Family Stories, 281
Fanon, Frantz, 341
Farabi Stage, 213n28
Farce, 259, 352, 356–358, 360, 367n4, 370, 371, 379–381, 385, 386n2
Farquhar, George, 29

Fascism, 42, 43
Fasıls, 203
Fassbinder, Rainer Werner, 46–48, 53, 57n7
Fatherland, 124, 224, 229–231
Fauré, Gabriel Urbain, 320
Faust, 319
FBI, 314
Fear and Misery of the Third Reich, 43
Fearon, Ray, 32, 33
Femininity, 91, 224, 269, 372, 448
Feminism, 104, 109
Feminist, 55, 57n13, 101–118, 165, 202, 392, 393, 395, 397, 398, 401, 444, 445, 447, 448, 460
  theatre, 101–118, 401, 444, 445, 447, 448
Fences, 27, 34
Ferringhi, 65
Festival/festivals, 30, 49, 52, 62, 66, 69, 71, 73, 74, 104, 105, 129, 130, 145–147, 172, 261, 282, 314, 316, 428, 433–437, 472, 477, 483n12, 484n23, 484n28
Festival/Tokyo Award, 466
Fifea, Alexandru, 103
  Voi n-aţi văzut nimic, 103
Fifteenth century, 4
Fifth Generation filmmakers, 472, 477
Fiji, 63–65, 67–70, 76, 77n1
Fijian, 63–66, 69, 70, 76, 77n1
Fijian theatre, 65
Fiji-English, 65, 66
Fiji Labour Party (FLP), 64
Filipino, 479
Finsbury Park, 36
Fires in the Mirror, 109
First Black Woman in Space, 54, 55
First Nations, 10, 81, 82, 96
  playwrights, 82, 96
The First Stone, 179, 183
First World War, 124, 131, 132, 136n5, 149, 151, 410
Fiskum, Oda, 483n11, 483n12
Five-Star Dumpster, 169
Flatmates, 181
Floyd, George, 1, 3, 309
Foreman, George, 314, 315
Foucault, Michel, 288n16, 395, 430

498 INDEX

4.48 Psychosis, 451
Fourth century, 340
Fox (Meskwaki) peoples, 392, 393
Fraga, Ardeja, 110
France, 13, 46, 117n3, 308–313, 321,
    322, 322n1, 322n5, 322n6, 352,
    360, 413, 417, 421n7, 421n8
Frankcom, Sarah, 29–34
Frankfurt theatre, 136
Fraser, Toa, 77n12
Frazier, Joe, 314, 318
Fredericks, Franckie, 312, 313
Freitas, Régia Mabel da Silva, 279,
    280, 288n4
French, 14, 52, 84–86, 281, 307–315,
    319, 322n2, 323n12, 323n16, 361,
    365, 366, 379, 392, 407, 409, 466,
    478, 479
French settlers, 392
Friday (character), 198, 371,
    374, 383–385
Fridl-Leonhard acting school, 47
Fringe theatre, 167
Frljić, Oskar, 169
Frumoasa, 108
Fuemana, Dianna, 77n12
Fugard, Athol, 50, 54, 179
Fulani, 430
Funding, 39, 41, 49, 57n2, 70, 117n5,
    167, 168, 173, 196, 211n6, 316,
    331, 369
Furcht und Elend, 43
Furtună, Adrian, 118n8

G
Gabrielino Indian, 91
Gabrielino language, 90
Gabrielino-Tongva, 89
GalataPerform, 209
Gàngànún drums, 437, 438, 440n12
Garajİstanbul theatre, 211n3
Gardenberg, Monique, 283
Gardner, Herb, 54
    Ich bin nicht Rappaport, 54
Gargantua (character), 299
Gaskell, Ian, 63, 66, 69
Gates, Henry Louis, 161
Gaudé, Laurent, 282
Gauguin, Paul, 410

Gay culture, 71
Gay, P., 135
Gbèdu drums, 437, 438, 440n12
Gems, Pam, 460n2
Gender, 7, 8, 13, 51, 74, 87–89, 93, 96,
    102, 105, 107, 112, 116, 131, 222,
    227–231, 255, 286, 295, 298, 309,
    314, 318, 394, 403n6, 443–448,
    450, 452, 453, 456–458, 460,
    466, 469
Genet, Jean, 222
Genocide, 115, 159, 161, 170, 198,
    274, 276, 312, 403n6
Geopathology, 393, 396–398, 401
George, Miria, 77n12, 143, 155
German(s)
    empire, 312
    people, 124, 125
    theatres, 10, 39–60, 123–139
German Enlightenment, 41
German language, 42, 124
German-language theatre, 49, 136n2
German Passion 1933, 130, 131, 133
German Reich, 124
Germany, 40–43, 46–56, 57n2, 103,
    123–129, 131, 134, 135
Germon, G.C., 373
Gerst, Wilhelm Karl, 129
Gezi Park Resistance, 206
Gezi Park Uprising, 211n6
Ghetto, 108, 110, 111, 274
Ghosts, 86–89, 112, 116, 148, 233
GHOSTS 2.0, 483n12
The Gift, 345n6
Gilroy, Paul, 24, 25, 27, 32, 329, 334,
    340, 346n12
Giovani's Room, 288n9
Giuvlipen, 11, 101–120
Glaspell, Susan, 11, 13, 391–405
The Glass Menagerie (Danny Lee
    Wynter), 27, 33
Glissant, Édouard, 82
Gobineau, Joseph Arthur, 125
    *Essai sur l'inégalité des races
    humaines*, 125
God and the Indian, 82, 87–89
Goebbels, Joseph, 130, 132
Goethe, Johann Wolfgang von, 232, 319
Gold rush, 221, 398
Goliath, 224

Gone with the Wind, 299
Gonçalves, Marina, 276
González, Nelson, 271n12, 271n16
González, Tomás, 257
Goodall, Jane, 378, 407, 408
The Good Soldier Švejk, 203
Gor ("Tomb"), 204
Gordon, Natasha, 34
Gorki, Maxim, 41, 53, 55
Gorki Theatre, 52
Gothic drama, 224, 233
Gothic literature, 231
The Governor of Jericho, 181
Go West, Young Woman, 460n2
Grajales, Mariana, 266, 267
Grand Prix Tchicaya U Tam'si, 319
Great Trek, 221
Greece, 4, 47, 48, 199
Greek tragedies, 205, 282, 473
Greeks, 4, 47, 48, 135, 198, 205, 282, 473
Green, debbie tucker, 345n2
Green, Frank W., 384
Greenwood, T. L., 370, 383
Greisil, Marite, 47
Griot, 280
Grotowski, Jerzy, 201, 418
Gründgens, Gustaf, 42
Grupo Espacio Abierto, 271n18
Guangzhou, 483n12
The Guardian, 15n3, 23, 24, 30, 33, 41
Guare, John, 27
Guattari, Felix, 82
Guevara, Che (Ernesto), 258
Guillaume, Robert, 22
Guingané, Jean-Pierre, 310, 323n14
Günther, Hans F.K., 125–127, 136n3
    Rassenkunde, 125, 136n3
Gusmão, Mário, 283
Guys and Dolls, 22, 26, 33

H
Hackett, James, 362
Hackney, 454, 455
Hadrian's wall, 340
Hague, 170, 171
Haifa, 179
Haifa Municipal Theatre, 179
Haifa Theatre, 182, 186

Haka, 142, 143, 145–149, 151–154, 156n16
Hall, Stuart, 447
Halle, 129
Hamlet, 22, 28, 128, 473
Hamlet (Character), 28, 128, 164, 197, 318, 352, 473, 474, 476, 484n20
Hamletmachine, 466, 467, 473–481, 483n14
Hammerstein, Oscar, 29
Hammond, Mona, 32
Han, Kathy, 478, 482n2
Handke, Peter, 466
Han *mingzu*, 482n2
Hansberry, Lorraine, 27, 28, 32, 332
Hanseatic League, 125
Harlem, 33
Harlequin, 382
Harlequin Alfred the Great; or, the Magic Banjo and the Mystic Raven, 382
Harlequin Robinson Crusoe and His Man Friday, 384
Harlequin Uncle Tom, 382, 386n2
Hasse, Ernst, 124, 459
Hassell, Alex, 459
Hate crimes, 335, 345
Hatzor, Ilan, 183
Hau'ofa, Epeli, 76
Hauptmann, Elisabeth, 43
Hauptmann, Gerhart, 127
Havana's International Theater festival, 261
Hawaiki, 143
Haymarket, Leicester, 22, 384
"Headcloth," 211n5
Heart of Darkness, 473
Hebrew, 178, 181
Hebrew theatre, 178, 185, 189
Hedgerow Theatre, 395, 402n5
Hefetz, 186
Heimat bittersüsse Heimat, 55, 57n13
Hənq̓əmínəm̓, 398, 399
Henry, Lenny, 23, 30
Henry V, 22
Hereniko, Rotuman Vilsoni, 65
Herero, 312, 321
Hernández Espinosa, Eugenio, 12, 257, 260, 263–265, 271n12, 271n13, 273n16

500 INDEX

Herrera, Georgina, 12, 256, 257, 266, 271n18
Hewlett, James, 351
Hey Rimona, 183
Heynicke, Kurt, 131
   Neurode: Ein Spiel von deutscher Arbeit, 131
Hickling, Alfred, 32, 33
Highway, Tomson, 10, 82–84, 86, 87, 89, 93, 97n4
Hillje, Jens, 41, 52
Hilpert, Heinz, 127, 128
Hindu culture, 68
Hinkel, Hans, 134
Historical characters, 266
Historiography, 205, 212n18, 266, 267, 269, 426
Hitler, A., 123–126, 132, 136n5, 483n18
Holdbrook-Smith, Kobna, 23
Hollywood, 70, 74, 92, 93, 204, 320
Holocaust, 101, 112, 113, 117n1, 125, 126, 135, 136, 182, 202
Homophobia, 459
Homosexuality, 265, 449, 460
Hone Kouka, 11, 141, 142, 147–149, 155
   Mauri Tu, 147
Horowitz, Anthony, 24
The Hounding of David Oluwale, 332
Hourmazdi, Banafshe, 55
House of Games, 32
Howard, Cordelia, 373
Howard, George, 373
Huang, Hieu, 55
Hughes, Bethany, 391, 401n1, 402n1
Hui, 146
Huiyong, Yu, 479, 484n24
Human Genome Project, 4, 239
Human rights, 163, 169, 211n12, 363, 456, 461n8
Human Rights Watch, 211n12
Humber, 335
Humphreys, David, 356
Hungarian revolution, 486n15
Hungary, 117n3
Hunger (white settler), 13, 391–401
Hunt, James, 375, 386n5
Hutchinson, Mark, 346n10
Huxley, Aldous, 3, 5, 6, 239, 418, 421n6

Hwang, David Henry, 26, 35
Hybridisation, 197, 255, 385
Hytner, Nicholas, 29

I

Ìbàdàn, 440n7
Ìbànté, 437
Ibejis, 280
Ibsen, Henrik, 135, 143, 147, 483n12
Ibsen in One Take (Yi jing yisheng yi bo sheng), 472, 483n12
Ibsen International, 466, 483n11
Idowu, Bolaji, 428
Ifopo, Erolia, 77n12
Ìgbàlè, 435–438
Igbo, 432, 433, 435
Ìgunnukó mask, 435
İhsan Gümüşten, 212n24
Ijele masquerade, 432, 435
İkincikat company, 207, 211n6
Illinois, 393, 394
Ilunga, David-Minor, 310
Im Dickicht der Städte, 45
Imesi-Ile, 14, 431, 434–436, 440n12
Immigrant/immigrants, 25, 27, 30, 31, 51, 52, 94, 95, 151, 199, 200, 322n5, 327, 328, 333–336, 339, 345, 397, 446, 483n9
Immigration, 25, 30, 31, 40, 52, 397, 457, 483n9
Imperial German army, 136n5
Imperial Germany, 129
Imperialism, 3–5, 10, 69, 469
Impersonation, 13, 50, 270n2, 302, 303, 320, 352–362, 364, 370, 375, 387n6, 446
The Importance of Being Earnest, 32
In Darkest England and the Way Out, 381
Indentured labourers, 63, 67, 68, 241–243
Independent Theatre Hungary in Budapest, 103
The Indian Emperor or the Conquest of Mexico by the Spaniards, 412
Indian/Indians, 16n11, 63, 64, 67–69, 77n1, 91, 92, 95, 242, 243, 334, 384, 393–396, 409, 414, 478
Indian labourers, 67, 77n1

INDEX 501

Indian Relocation Act, 89
Indian War, 394
Indigeneity, 7, 10, 82, 89, 90, 93, 392, 414
Indigenous
  and Black people, 275, 394
  characters, 87, 395
  and English languages, 86
  land, 90, 391–393, 397, 400, 401, 401n1
  languages, 85, 400
  people, 81, 88, 89, 92, 94, 143, 275, 392, 393, 395, 397, 398, 401, 402n1, 403n7, 413, 420
  performance, 9, 398, 425
  theatre, 61
Indija, 174–175n10
Indo-Fijian, 77n1
Indonesia, 410
Inheritors, 13, 391–403
Iniciación en blanco y negro para mujeres sin color, 267, 269
Instituto Superior de Arte (ISA), 261
Integration, 3, 37, 42, 101, 105, 109, 261, 264, 270n6, 273, 308, 312, 418
International Commission on the Holocaust in Romania, 113
Intersectional, 101–118, 318, 397, 403n6
In the Heart of the World, 284
In the Heat of the Night, 74
Intifada, 182–185, 189
Invented tradition, 143, 145
In/Visible City, 160, 171–173, 174n10
Iowa, 393, 394, 396, 402n4
Ipeafro, 287n2
Ireland, 95, 387n5, 417, 421n8
Irish, 94, 103, 353, 359, 361, 365, 366
Irobi, Esiaba, 430, 433
Isaac, 188, 189
Ishmael, 188, 189
Iska, 208
Islam, 314, 428
Israel, 178, 180, 184, 187
Israeli/Israelis
  Jews, 181, 183, 185, 191
  playwrights, 180, 181, 190
  theatre, 11, 177–192

Israeli Palestinian/Israeli Palestinians, 179, 181, 183, 191
Israel-Palestine conflict, 52
Issa, Norman, 188, 189
İstanbul, 11
Italy, 47, 172, 175n10, 260, 263
iTaukei, 63–69
iTaukei language, 66
Ivory Bangle Lady, 340
Ivory Coast, 13
Izetbegović, Alia, 167
Izquierdo, Maria, 412

J

Jack Robinson and His Monkey, 384
Jackson, Andrew, 394
Jackson, Glenda, 24
Jackson-Bourke, Leki, 77n12
Jacobs-Jenkins, Branden, 12, 291, 292, 295, 298–300, 303, 304
Jamaica, 12, 240, 241, 266
James, Oscar, 32
James Bond (character), 24
Jandarma İstihbarat ve Terörle Mücadele, 213n30
Jàndùkú, 436
Jankowski, Rahel, 55
Japan, 483n12, 483n13
Jarry, Alfred, 164, 187, 411
Jasenovac, 174n4
Jaz, 321
Jazz, 55, 319, 322
Jeffries, James, 323n16
Jerusalem, 340
The Jerusalem Syndrome, 179, 182
Jesuit missionaries, 414
Jesus Christ, 132
Jew/Jews, 43, 128, 133, 135, 174n4, 178–187, 189–191, 228
Jewish
  actors, 136
  Indigenous, 91
  performers, 133–135
  playwrights, 124, 183
  settlement, 180, 181
  settlers, 191
  theatre, 135
Jewish Israeli theatre, 178, 191

502   INDEX

Jewishness, 43, 124, 470
Jim Crow (character), 299, 300, 304,
    333, 370, 375, 378, 386n3, 386n4,
    394, 402n3
Jim Crow Laws, 402n3
Joan of Arc, 106
Joe Turner's Come and Gone, 28
Johannesburg, 3
Johansson, Michelle, 77n12
Johnson, Boris, 2
Johnson, Jack, 323n16
Joint Stock, 444
Jon, Lil, 300
Jonathan in England, 352, 356, 358,
    359, 362, 363, 365, 367n3, 367n4
Jones, Clifton, 450
Jones, James Earl, 21–23, 136n6
Joseph, Paterson, 29
The Joy Luck Club, 482n7
Jules, Jenny, 32
Juliet (character), 181
Julius Caesar, 30
Júnior, Ricardo Alves, 284
Just Another Day, 66

K
Kabul, 281
*Kafra-Biatanga-Tragödie-Afrikas: ein
    Stück in elf Szenen*, 53
Kailoma, 63, 77n2
Kali Traš/Frica neagră, 104, 112–117,
    117n6, 118n7
Kanat, Helîn Başak, 212n23
Kane, Sarah, 14, 444, 446,
    451–454, 466
Kaney, Miriam, 180, 181
Kapa Haka, 143, 145–146, 148
Kapa Haka festival, 145, 147
Karagöz and Hacivat, 213n26
Katunga, 429
Katzelmacher, 47
Kaufmann, Günter, 48, 53, 57n7
Kaufman, Moisés, 48, 53, 57n7, 109
Keeley, Mary Ann, 379
Kellertheater, 47
Kene, Arinzé, 34
Khan, Ballu, 68, 77n9
Khosa, Collins, 3

Khoun, Ulrich, 57n3
Khouri, Makram, 189
Khrushchev, Nikita Sergeyevich, 483n15
Kightley, Oscar, 70, 77n12
    Dawn Raids, 70
Kim Il-sung, 473
Kindermann, Heinz, 124, 126, 127,
    136n2
King, Martin Luther, 283
King, Martin Luther, Jr, 288n9
Kiriji War, 440n7
Kirkwood, Lucy, 36
Kissoon, Jeffery, 32
Klammer, Michael, 54
Knox, Robert, 375, 386n5
Koblenz, 130
Ko, Dedra, 401n1
Korean, 473, 478–480
Kosovo, 103, 159, 169, 174n3, 175n11
Kouka, Hone, 11, 141–143, 147–149,
    151–155, 155n1, 156n2,
    156n13, 156n16
Kovačević, Dušan, 163–166, 168–170,
    172, 173
Krauß, Werner, 128, 129
Krek, 208
Krleža, Miroslav, 167
Kroepelin, Hermann, 128
Kulturbund theatre(s), 11, 133–135
Kurdish
    female actors, 205
    theatre, 197, 201, 203, 205, 211n9,
        211n10, 212n18, 212n22,
        212n24
Kurdish-Turkish war, 11, 195
Kurds, 196, 198, 200, 201, 208,
    211n12, 212n16
Kushner, Tony, 33
Kusturica, Emir, 164
Kuyu, 206, 212n14
Kwahulé, Koffi, 13, 312–314, 316,
    318–322, 323n14, 323n16

L
Laager, 219, 221–225, 227–230, 232,
    235, 236
Label Noir, 55
Lackface, 12, 291–306

INDEX 503

Ládúnùnwò, 437–439, 440n10
L'Africaine or the Queen of the Cannibal Islands, 382
Lágìdìgbà, 437
Lakovi, 66
Lal, Shailesh, 10, 64, 67, 77n7
Lalonde, Raymond, 84
LAMDA, 23
Lan, David, 28
Land(s), 4, 13, 42, 63, 68, 85, 90, 94, 95, 114, 143, 144, 146, 147, 152, 154, 155, 156n2, 174n3, 180–182, 185, 198, 204, 222, 224, 226, 232, 245, 246, 248, 266, 278, 354–357, 359, 391–403, 410, 433, 435
Lander, Richard, 429–433
Lan-fang, Mei, 45
Langhoff, Shermin, 41, 51, 52, 55
The Laramie Project, 109
Las lágrimas no hacen ruido al caer, 260, 264
Las Ulloa, 257, 258, 270n8
Lasalle, 484n25, 484n26
Lasalle College of Arts, 484n23
The Last Virgin in Paradise, 65
Latin alphabet, 162
Latin script, 198
Lawrence, Stephen, 332, 335
Le Bas, Damien, 103
Le Bas, Delaine, 103
Leading a Dog's Life: Masculinity or Being a Man Through Creeping, 212n19
Lebanon, 178
Lebanon War, 181, 182, 185
Lecat, Raphael, 478, 480, 481
Lee, Harper, 34
Lee, Sandra Soo-Jin, 4, 239, 296
Lee, Spike, 276
Lee, Young Jean, 12, 292, 294, 296, 298, 300–302, 305n1
Leeds, 331, 345n3
Lemon, Mark, 371–379
Lemonade, 207
Lenin, Vladimir Ilyich Ulyanov, 473
León, Gerardo Fulleda, 257
Lersch, Heinrich, 130
    Volk im Werden, 130
Leskovac, 174n10

Lester, Adrian, 21–25, 27, 35
Letters from Rodez, 281
Letts, Quentin, 29
Levin, Hanoch, 183–191
Levi-Strauss, Claude, 184
LGBT, 309, 456, 461n6
LGBTI, 211n4
Liberal Democrats, 31
Lima, Evani Tavares, 277
Liminality, 419
Lispector, Clarice, 283, 284
    Uma aprendizagem ou o livro dos prazeres, 284
Lithuania, 260, 264
The Little Clay Cart, 26
Little Emperors, 482n1
Liverpool, 356, 358
The Living Theatre, 47
Lobato, Monteiro, 275
Lomu, Jonah, 73, 78n18
London, 21, 22, 30, 32–34, 36, 210, 331, 332, 335, 345n3, 345n8, 355, 358, 363, 369, 444, 450–454
London accent, 457
London Stock Exchange, 133
Look Back in Anger, 449
Lorca, Federico García, 222
Los Angeles, 89, 92
Louis, Joe, 315
Louisiana, 292
Love and Information, 458
Love and Intrigue, 52
Lowdell, Amelia, 454
Lower classes, 208, 241, 352
Lu Xun, 466
Lucumí, Fermina, 266, 267
Lugné-Poe, Aurélien, 187
Luhaka, Théo, 309
Lukacs, Mihai, 108
LUME Theatre, 284
Lumuba II, 53
Luosheng, Yu, 470, 482n7
Lyceum Theatre, 371, 386n2

M
Macardle, John Francis, 384
Macbeth, 281

504 INDEX

Macedonia, 161, 162, 167, 172, 175n10
Maceo brothers, 266
The Machine, 283
Macpherson report, 332
Madame Mao, *see* Qing, Jiang
Madame Satã, 283
MaddAddam, 94
Magasiva, Robbie, 72, 77n16
Magic realism, 86, 88, 90, 93, 96, 97n6, 201, 222, 225, 228, 229, 233
Makataimeshekiakiak, 392–394, 402n2, 402n3
Malay, 479
Malcolm X, 288n9
Mamea, David, 77n12
Mamet, David, 32
Mami-Water (mask), 427
Mammy (character), 277, 299, 300, 304
Man Equals Man, 204
Manchester, 29–31, 331, 345n3, 448, 450, 451
Manchester's Royal Exchange Theatre, 29, 30, 331
Mandarin, 479
Mandela, Winnie, 311
Manitoba, 84
Mann, Klaus, 42
Mann, Thomas, 136
Manoljović, Miki, 169
Manusaute, Vela, 75, 77n12
Mao Zedong, 468, 473, 475, 477, 479
Māori
 artists, 144
 characters, 144, 152, 154
 communities, 151
 language, 142, 143, 153
 performers, 144
 playwrights, 142, 143, 147, 154
 theatre, 11, 141–158
Māori TV, 145
M'appelle Mohamed Ali, 313–315, 317
Marae, 143, 145–147, 149–151, 156n4, 156n7
Marae theatre, 143, 146, 147
Maratonce trče počasni krug, 163
Marçalı, Sami Berat, 207
Marcell, Joseph, 22
Mardin, 203
Marea rușine, 103

Marginalisation, 3, 28, 39, 48, 64, 71, 110, 111, 116, 269, 334, 338, 374, 452
María Antonia (Character), 260, 271n13
Marie Clements' Tombs of the Vanishing Indian, 82, 89, 93
Marist Brothers School, Vatuwaqa, 65
The Marriage of Heaven and Hell, 421n6
Marshall Plan, 46
Martello-White, Nathaniel, 23
Martins, Gabriel, 284
Martins, Leda Maria, 274, 284, 285
Martins, Maurílio, 284
Marx, Karl, 473
Marylebone Theatre Royal, 382
Masculinity, 202, 203, 205, 209, 212n19, 221, 224, 229, 328, 403n6, 450
Masked performers, 428
Masks, 4, 12, 50, 126, 226, 239, 247, 253, 256, 292, 293, 296, 297, 303, 316, 333, 382, 410, 411, 427, 428, 431, 433, 435, 437
Mason, Bruce, 144
Masquerade, 13, 14, 42, 50, 305, 359, 428, 429, 432, 433
Masrawa, Riad, 181
Massachusetts, 354, 399
Massini, Fabrizio, 483n11
Matanzas, 266
Mathews, Ann, 360, 361, 365
Mathews, Charles, 13, 351–368, 370, 387n6, 387n8
Matriarchy, 231
Maxim Gorki Theatre, Berlin, 103
May Fourth Movement, 482n4
May, Theresa, 31
Mbembe, Achille, 308–310, 316, 323n12
McColl, Colin, 71, 77n13, 147
Mclean, Donald, 346n10
Measure for Measure, 29
Meddah storytelling, 205
Mediatisation, 299–301
Mediterranean, 6, 313
Mehteran, 203
Meirelles, Marcio, 279, 283
Mek'an, 206, 213n28
Melbourne, 482n1

Melodrama, 292, 295, 372, 374, 384
Memmi, Albert, 244
Men, Women and Insanity, 66
Mephisto (character), 319
Mepistopheles (character), 319
The Merchant of Venice, 11, 128
Meskwaki, 393, 395, 401
Mesopotamian Culture Center, 212n24
Mestizaje, 413, 414
Metatheatricality, 291, 295–298
Mete, Fuat, 208
Metin, Mîrza, 201, 202, 204, 211n1
Métissage, 82
Mexican population, 414
Mexican revolution, 414
Mexico, 13, 14, 407–423
Mexico City, 409, 412, 413, 415, 420n2
Miano, Léonora, 309, 322n3
Michael, Theodor Wonja, 53
Michael James Manaia, 143, 146
Michael X, 332
Middle Ages, 110, 160
Middle classes, 71, 129, 130, 132, 134, 185, 207, 208, 336–338, 342, 344, 448
Middle East, 8, 189, 198
Mideast, 173
Mid-nineteenth century, 7, 8, 398, 449
Midwest, 392, 394, 402n2
Migrants, 40, 49, 57n3, 63, 66, 67, 69, 70, 73, 75, 310, 339
Migration, 4, 40, 46, 48, 52, 57n2, 62, 73, 249, 278, 310, 333, 334, 339, 450, 461n8, 482n1
Milián, José, 12, 257, 259, 265
Miller, Arthur, 22, 26–33, 35, 36
Milošević, Dijana, 162, 167, 168, 171, 173
Milošević, Slobodan, 168–170
Minas Gerais, 282
Miniatures, 203, 205, 302, 483n14
Minorities, 23–27, 29, 31, 33, 36, 40, 49, 135, 196, 252, 263, 297, 308, 334, 335, 338, 339, 467
Minority rights, 162
Minoungou, Etienne, 313–317
Minstrel shows, 12, 276, 298, 300, 303, 304, 370–375, 378, 380, 382–385, 387n11

Minstrelsy, 12, 13, 292–294, 299, 362, 370, 372–375, 378, 383, 384, 402n3, 460n3
Minstrel troupes, 366, 370
Miscegenation, 255
Mishra, Sudesh, 65, 68
Miss Saigon, 35
Mississippi, 394, 402n3
Mississippi (River), 394
Mister Brau, 283
The (Post)Mistress, 82, 84, 87
Misty, 34
Mitchel, Katie, 467
Mittelpunkt, Hillel, 186
Mittelreich, 54
Mixed race (mulattoes), 70, 76, 146, 240, 243, 246, 247, 250, 257, 292, 451, 452
Mixed-race slave, 295
Mmonwu performances, 433
Mnouchkine, Ariane, 281
Moa, Suli, 77n12
Model Plays, 477, 480, 481, 484n26
Modernism, 401, 409–411
Modernity, 101, 114, 166, 403n6, 411, 428, 435, 475
Modest Mouse, 301
Moldovan, Zita, 103, 110
Möller, Eberhard Wolfgang, 131–133
    Das Frankenburger Würfelspiel, 131
    Rothschild siegt bei Waterloo, 132–133
Molnar, Ferenc, 135
MOMA, 421n10
Momeodonu, Ratu Tevita, 64
Monarch-of-all-I-survey, 430, 431
Monarchy, 25, 359, 364
Moncrieff, William T., 387n9
Monodrama, 307, 310, 312, 313, 316, 321
Monogenesis, 375, 377
Monopolylogue, 351, 354
Monroe, Marilyn, 28–29
The Monster, 65
Monstrous Regiment, 448
Montenegro, 161, 162, 167
Moodie, Tanya, 35
Moore, John, 340
Moral drama, 372
Morejón, Nancy, 255, 256

506 INDEX

Moriarty, Jim, 146
Morpurgo, Michael, 29
Moscow, 45
Motherland, 124, 339, 444
Moylan-Rose Valley, 402n5
Mozambique, 40
Muagututi'a, Tanya, 77n12
Much Ado about Nothing, 30
Mugabe, Robert Gabriel, 458, 459
Muhammad Ali and Me, 313, 317
Mujer negra, 255
Mulata (character), 255–257, 260
Mulatto character, 386
Mulatto slaves, 376
Müller, Heiner, 466, 467, 473–477,
    483n14–16
Multiculturalism, 30, 335
Mundi, Joseph, 181, 186
Munich, 47, 133
Munich Kammerspiele, 54
Murat, Lucia, 284
Murder, 183–191
Murray, Stephen O., 456, 459
Muse, Clarence, 57n5
'The Muse of History,' 249
Museveni, Yoweri, 458, 459
Musical, 12, 33, 35, 84, 126, 201, 204,
    267, 292, 297, 300, 319, 458
Muslims, 6, 170, 199, 211n5
Müthel, Lothar, 128, 129
My Name is Gary Cooper, 70
Mythical plays, 184

N
Na iLululu, 66
Nakara-Hadad, Salwah, 183
Nama people, 312
Namib desert, 312
Namibia, 312, 313, 321
Na minha pele, 283, 286, 287
Nanoracism, 309, 310, 312, 314, 317
Napoléon Bonaparte, Emperor of the
    French, 133
Nascimento, Abdias, 12, 273, 276–278,
    282, 287n2
    O Quilombismo, 273
Nation, 2, 4–6, 10–12, 14, 25, 31, 37,
    52, 62, 66, 69, 70, 124–131,
    143–145, 151, 154, 155, 159, 161,

195, 198, 208, 221, 235, 261, 262,
    266, 270n2, 280, 314, 333, 339,
    340, 346n11, 353, 356, 357,
    359–361, 365, 396, 397, 426, 459,
    469, 483n9
National Federation Party (NFP), 64
Nationalism, 69, 70, 102, 161–169, 171,
    172, 204, 270n1, 364, 395, 397,
    452, 459, 469, 471, 482
Nationality, 13, 15n9, 25, 124, 161,
    166, 170, 172, 361, 466, 480
Nationality Acts, 25
National-Kino, 47
National Romanian Television, 112
National Socialism, 42, 56
National Socialist, *see* Nazis
National Theatre (NT), 23, 26, 28, 29,
    34, 117n5, 169, 257, 261, 270n2,
    276, 284, 466
Nationhood, 25, 225, 228, 231,
    364
Native American (s), 4, 5, 16n11, 81, 89,
    97n10, 303, 362, 384, 396–398,
    416, 421n5, 460n2
Native Indians, 243
Native language, 87, 95
Native Mexican people, 414
Naturalism, 50, 149, 453
Nazi Germany, 11, 42
Nazi party, 136n5
Nazi theatre, 123–136
Nazis, 39, 41–43, 56, 117n1, 123, 125,
    129, 130, 134–136, 162, 170,
    174n4, 475
Ndumbe III, Alexandre Kum'a, 53
Neal, John, 358–362, 366
Neal, S., 336, 339
Neale, Frederick, 382, 386n2
The Negation of Brazil, 276
Negro Theatre Workshop, 26
Neighbors, 291, 292, 294, 295,
    298–300, 303–305
Nerde Kalmıştık? ("Where were
    we?"), 204
Netherlands, 483n12
New England, 361, 367n3, 373
New Negro Theatre Company, 450
New Orleans, 85
New World, 12, 31, 132, 241–245, 313,
    321, 363

INDEX 507

New Yam festival, 434
New York, 31, 104–106, 270n1, 305n4, 306n7, 319, 354, 355, 365, 394, 402n3, 440n7
New Zealand, 11, 62, 64, 70–75, 77n14, 141–156, 397
  theatre, 142, 143, 147, 154, 156n6
New Zealand Festival of the Arts, 71
New Zealand International Festival of the Arts in Wellington, 62, 141
Ngā Puhi, 156n18
Nga Tangata Toa, 11, 142, 143, 147–149, 151–153, 155, 156n13
Ngai Tahu 32, 156n17
Ngata, Sir Apirana, 147
Ngāti Awa, 156n20
Ngāti Kahungunu, 147
Ngāti Kuki Airani, 156n20
Ngāti Pōkai, 156n18
Ngati Porou, 147
Ngāti Raukawa, 147
Niangouna, Dieudonné, 13, 307, 313–318, 320
Nigeria, 13, 55, 426, 433, 436
Nine Night, 34, 246, 248
Nine-Night ritual ceremony, 248
Nineteenth century, 8, 12, 49, 81, 124, 144, 198, 221, 256, 257, 266, 207n2, 292, 295, 339, 366, 369, 373, 383, 394, 398, 411, 430, 446
Nineties, 170, 434
Niš, 174n10
Nitzan, Omri, 184, 188, 191
Niueans, 70
Noble savage, 92, 94, 179, 374, 384
Nolan, Yvette, 82, 93–96, 97n12
Norris, Bruce, 26, 27
Norris, Rufus, 23
North America, 10, 81, 82, 359, 364
North Island, 142, 149
North Korea, 474, 475, 483n17, 484n27
North Koreans, 473, 475, 480
Northcott Theatre, Exeter, 345n1, 346n14
Norway, 172, 174–175n10
Nottage, Lynn, 26–28
Nottingham, 327, 331, 332, 345, 346n14

Nottingham Playhouse, 327, 332, 345n1, 346n14
Novi Sad, 174–175n10
N'Sondé, Wilfried, 310
Nü.kolektif, 202, 205, 212n20
Nuffield Theatre, Southampton, 33
Nunes, Antú Romero, 54
Nupe, 434, 435
Nuremberg, 124, 134, 483n18
Nuremberg Laws, 134
Nuremberg Race Laws, 124
Nusaybin, 200, 203

O

Obama, Barack, 2, 293, 305
Obatala, 426, 440n12
Occidentalism, 14, 198, 465–482
Occupied territories, 181, 183, 191
The Octoroon, 292, 303, 376
Odimba, Chinonyerem, 345n6
Odin Theatre, 168
Office of the UN Special Adviser on the Prevention of Genocide (OSAPG), 170
Ògbóni, 440n14
Ògbóni secret society, 438, 440n14
Ogundipe, Theo, 34
O'Hara, Robert, 293
Ohio, 32
Oil, 182
Ojibway, 87, 96
Okagbue, Osita, 9, 12, 242–244, 248–250, 346n13, 430–432
Okoh, Janice, 345n6
Okonko, 433
Old Story Time, 240, 243, 246, 250, 253
Old Testament, 318
Old Vic, 27
Oliveira, André Novais, 284
Olivier Awards, 22, 461n7
Olokun, 427
Olusoga, David, 2, 24
Olympics, 30, 146, 312, 469, 472
O'Neill, Eugene, 22, 26, 34, 36, 276, 277, 393
One-woman monologue, 84
Onovomundo, 279

508 INDEX

Ontario, 87
Ó Paí, Ó!, 279, 283
Ophelia (character), 28, 373, 376–378, 381, 387n12, 473, 475
Orak, Aydin, 203, 204
Orality, 280
Oriel College, Oxford, 1
Oriental Jews/Religious Jews, 185
Orientalism, 14, 45, 465–482
The Origin of Species, 378
Orixá, 280
Orixas, 281
Orizondo, Rogelio, 12, 257, 264, 265
The Orphan of Zhao, 36
Orthodoxy, 162, 206
Osborne, Charles, 29
Osborne, John, 449
Oslo Accords, 184, 186
Othello, 54, 74, 277, 446
Other, 5–10, 13, 14, 46, 56, 63, 82, 123, 161, 179, 185–187, 189, 191, 219, 220, 227, 228, 232, 235, 236, 241, 251, 270n5, 279, 313, 337, 344, 363, 366, 386, 416, 425–439, 468–472, 475–477, 482
Otherness, 9, 45, 71, 179, 297, 341, 383, 395, 470, 472, 483n10
O Topo da Montanha, 283
Ottoman Empire, 198, 206
Òtu-Ókó, 434–437
Ouagadougou, 314, 319
"Our Sea of Islands," 76
Our Town, 33
Outcasts, 66
Oxalá, 280
Oyelowo, David, 23, 30
Òyì, 426, 427
Òyìbó, 426, 427
Ọyọ́, 429, 430, 434
Ọyọ́ kingdom, 429
Özbudak, Ahmet Sami, 209
Öziri, Necat, 52, 53, 56
    Get Deutsch or Die Tryin, 52

P

Pacific, 61–63, 65, 69, 70, 73–76, 77n12, 143
Pacific Arts festival, 62

Pacific drama, 61
Pacific Institute of Performing Arts, 70
Pacific Islands, 62, 70, 71, 73, 77n17
Pacific peoples, 70, 73, 76
Pago Pago, 62, 66, 69
Pākehā, 71–74, 142, 144, 145, 147–155, 156n3
    actors, 71, 144
    artists, 144
    characters, 74, 75, 148, 152, 153
    playwrights, 144, 147
Pakistan, 27
Palestine, 52
Palestine Liberation Organization (PLO), 184
Palestinian characters, 178–180, 183, 185, 186
The Palestinian Girl, 178, 182
Palestinian Israeli actors, 179
Palestinian Question, 178, 183, 186, 191, 192
Palestinians, 11, 16n13, 177–192
Palme D'Or, 164
Panopticon, 430
Pantomimes, 299, 370, 382–385, 430, 476
Paris, 90, 288n9, 309, 408, 409, 417
Paris Square, 284
Park Theatre, 36
Parody, 87, 222, 224, 296, 425
Partiya Karkerên Kurdistanê–Kurdistan Workers' Party (PKK), 195, 197, 199–202, 213n27
Pasifika, 143
Passing Strange, 292, 294, 296–298
Passion plays, 131
Passô, Grace, 283–287
Pastoral novel, 224
Patriarchy, 105, 112, 221, 229, 267, 268
The Patriot, 187, 191
Patterson, Fátima, 12, 256, 257, 267, 268, 346n12
Paulhan, Jean, 413
Pavičević, Borka, 167
Pavilion, 416
Pazarkaya, Yüksel, 49
Peace Agreement, 434
Peak District, 338, 343

INDEX 509

Peak District National Park, 332, 346n9
Peake, Maxine, 352, 354, 356, 357, 360
Peake, R. B., 30
Peasants' War, 131
Pedagogy, 276
Pedro, Alberto, 257, 260, 264
PEN World Voices International Play
  Festival, New York City, 104, 105
Pennington (character), 355
Penúltimo sueño de Mariana, 266, 267
Pere Ubu (character), 164
Período Especial, 262
Perry, Tyler, 299
Persecution, 10, 43, 44, 134, 213n25,
  280, 288n9
Peru, 200, 276, 421n5
Peyote, 14, 407–420
*The Peyote Dance and Other
  Writings*, 409
Philadelphia, 353, 394, 402n3, 402n5
Phillips, Trevor, 336
Picasso, Pablo Ruiz, 410
Pidgin English, 371, 383
Pigs and Dogs, 14, 443–460
Pillai, Raymond, 65
Pinkface, 305n2
Pinter, 29
Pirapora, 283
Pistes, 312, 317
Plato, 230
Playmarket, 70
Playwriting, 10, 62, 83, 136, 257,
  261, 448
Plimoth Plantation, 402n1
Pocock, I., 383
Pogroms, 43, 125, 134
Poitier, Sidney, 27, 74
Police, 1–3, 68, 77n9, 90, 115, 262,
  308–311, 321, 323n18, 332, 334,
  335, 337, 455
Polynesian, 70–74
Polynesian people, 71, 72, 143
Polynesian Performing Arts Festival, 145
Pop culture, 299, 418
Pop music, 300–302
Popoola, Olumide, 53, 55
  Also by Mail, 53
Pop-up Globe, 156n8
Por Elise, 285

Porsgrunn, 174n10, 175n10
Portugal, 47
Portuguese, 288n13, 460
Post-black
  minstrelsy, 299
  plays, 293, 303
  playwrights, 302
  works, 305
Postcolonial drama, 84
Postdramatic practices, 50
Postdramatic theatre, 49, 296
Postmodernism, 411
Post-race, 63
Post-traumatic stress disorder (PTSD),
  196, 204
Potiki, Roma, 152, 153
Powell, Enoch, 25, 334
Powell, Lucy, 22, 23
Pratt, Mary Louise, 429, 431, 439n6
Prichard, Rebecca, 448, 454, 455
Priestley, J.B., 135
Primitivism, 14, 45, 244,
  409–411, 483n10
Princess & the Hustler, 345n6
Priština, 169
Proscenium-arch theatre, 133
Protest theatre, 229
Proto-racism, 4, 15n8
Provincetown Players, 393, 399, 402n5
Pryce, Jonathan, 35
P.T. Barnum's Museum, 373
Pugilists, 385
Pulitzer Prize for Drama, 393

Q

Qarase, Laisenia, 77n9
Qas Hamid, 30, 31
Qing, Jiang, 477–481, 484n26
Queen Elizabeth II, 84
The Queen of the Bathtub, 186–188, 191
Queen Victoria, 427
Queens, 54
Quinquenio gris or Decenio negro, 260

R

Rabelais, François, 299
Raben, Peer, 47

510 INDEX

Rabenhauer, Wilhelm (Peer Raben), 47
Rabin, Yitzhak, 183, 185, 186, 188
Rabuka, Sitiveni, 64
A Race for Rights, 77n6
Race Relations Act, 335
The Races of Men, 386n5
Racial democracy, 12, 273, 278
Racial equality, 10, 21–37, 256, 262, 279
Racial impersonation, 50, 302, 303, 446
Racialisation, 10, 39–57, 108, 112, 115, 116, 159–161, 164–167, 171, 173, 329, 384, 401
Racialism, 163, 352
Racialist thinking, 11, 12, 375
Racial markers, 258, 302
Racial nationalism, 11, 159–175
Racial profiling, 338
Racial projection, 71–74
Racial purity, 7, 220, 226
Racial signifiers, 7, 84
Racial thinking, 5, 8, 9, 61, 62, 69, 72, 76
Racial thought, 41
Racism, 1–10, 12–14, 16n12, 25, 29, 33, 40–42, 44, 47, 48, 53, 55, 56, 61–63, 66, 70, 72, 74, 75, 103, 105, 107, 109, 110, 112, 116, 159, 160, 164, 169, 173, 220–222, 224–226, 228, 230, 232, 236, 245, 250, 251, 253, 256–258, 262, 264, 269, 274, 278, 283, 285, 287, 292, 293, 297, 298, 300, 302–304, 307–326, 328, 330, 332–336, 338, 339, 342, 352, 369, 370, 372–379, 381, 386, 413, 469, 470, 482
RADA, 22
Radmilovic, Zoran, 164
Radovan (character), 165, 166
Radovan III (*Radovan Treći*), 11, 159–175
A Raisin in the Sun, 27, 28, 32, 332
Raiwaqa, 65
Ramos, Lázaro, 279, 283–287
Ranterstantrum, 62, 71–75, 77n16
Ranterstantrum Redux, 75
Rap, 86, 294, 296, 300, 327, 332, 343
Rape, 71, 74, 170, 171, 189, 273, 274, 309, 403n6, 457
Rarámuri, 14, 407–421

Rashad, Phylicia, 21, 22
Rashomon effect, 108
Rationalism, 93
Ravenhill, Mark, 197
Robinson Crusoe RC, 374, 383, 384, 387n9
Realism, 142, 149, 150, 153, 154, 188, 203, 233, 234, 293, 447, 448, 470
Realist drama, 301, 302
The Real Thing, 77n15
Récréâtrales, 314
The Recruiting Officer, 29
Reddy, Jai Ram, 64
Reddy, Michelle, 68
Redface, 303
Refugees, 6, 31, 48, 52, 173, 313, 446, 456, 457, 461n6
Reich Culture Chamber, 124
Reis, João José, 273
Representation, 3, 7, 8, 10–14, 30, 33, 34, 36, 40, 41, 45, 46, 48, 50, 53–55, 61, 62, 74, 81, 82, 87, 93, 102–105, 109, 110, 113, 116, 117n2, 151, 161, 174n7, 184, 187, 189, 195–213, 221, 243, 253, 256, 258, 262, 269, 270n2, 275–277, 286, 294, 301, 303, 328–331, 333–337, 341–344, 351–367, 369–387, 407–421, 425–436, 438–439, 445–446, 465, 466, 470, 471, 480, 482
'Republik Repair,' 55
Republika Srpska, 175n11
Requiem, 320
Restoration, 26, 143, 146, 184
The Return, 180, 181
Return to Paradise, 71
Revolution, 12, 43, 116, 131, 173, 256–262, 265, 268, 269, 413, 414, 468, 475
Revolutionary Model Play 2.0, 14, 466, 467, 473, 477–481, 484n28
Reyes, Alfonso, 421n7
The Rez Sisters, 83
Rhodes, Cecil, 1, 14n2
Rhone, Trevor, 12, 240, 241, 250–252
Ribeiro, Darcy, 287n1, 288n16
Rice, T.D., 374, 402n3
Riefenstahl, Leni, 483n18

INDEX 511

Rimbaud, Jean Nicolas Arthur, 411
Ringebing, 174–175n10
Rio de Janeiro, 12, 172, 276, 281
Ritual, 66, 87, 106, 142, 145–149,
    151–155, 222, 224, 246, 248,
    267–269, 281, 282, 286, 317,
    415–419, 421n4, 421n5, 421n7,
    428, 429, 433–438, 439n2,
    440n12, 440n13, 453, 469
Rivera, Diogo, 413
The Robbers, 52, 54
Robie, David, 65
Robinson, Dylan, 398
Robinson Crusoe (character), 374
*Robinson Crusoe or Friday and His Funny
    Family*, 384
*Robinson Crusoe or Harlequin
    Friday*, 384
*Robinson Crusoe, or the Bold Buccaniers, a
    Romantic Drama*, 383
Robinsonades, 371, 372, 383, 385
Rochdale, 31
Rockefeller Brothers Fund, 169
Rodez, 417, 419, 420
Rodger, Victor, 10, 61, 62,
    70–75, 77n14
Rodrigues, João Jorge, 279
Rodrigues, Nelson, 277
Rogers, J. T., 10, 11, 13, 23, 27, 28
Rohr, Tony, 444
Roma
    actors, 104, 113
    peoples, 10, 101, 104, 106
    theatre, 11, 103, 113, 116,
        117n3, 117n5
    women 102, 104–107, 109–112,
        115, 116
Roma Armee, 103
Roma Heroes International Roma
    Storytelling Festival, 103
Roma Holocaust, 105, 113, 116, 118n8
Roma Kalderash community, 113
Roman Catholicism, 162
Romani, 101–104, 113
Romania, 11, 103, 104, 113–115,
    117n3, 117n5
Romanian(s)
    stages, 10, 101–118
    theatre, 113–116

Romanophobia, 116
Romay, Zuleica, 271n19
Rome, 162
Romeo and Juliet, 154, 169, 181, 258
Romnija, 103
Ronan, Ilan, 179
Ronen, Yael, 52, 53, 103
Roscoe, W., 456, 459
Rose, Marcia, 452
Rosenberg, Alfred, 123, 126
Rothschild, Nathan, 133
The Rothschilds, 133
The Round Heads and Pointed Heads, 43
Rowe, Clive, 29
Royal Anthropological Institute of Great
    Britain and Ireland, 386–387n5
Royal Court Theatre, 454, 459
Royal Exchange Theatre, Manchester,
    29, 30, 331
Royal Shakespeare Company, 30, 36
Royer-Artuso, Nicolas, 202, 205
Rubasingham, Indhu, 28
Ruined, 28
Russia, 264, 265

S
Sadler's Wells, 370, 386n2
Sahia, Alexandru, 113
Said, Edward, 482n3
Sailer, Heinz, 128
Salina-a última vértebra, 281
Salvador, 279, 283
Samaritans, 251
Samba, 85
Sambo (character), 299, 304
Samoa, 62, 71, 72, 77n17
Samoan
    culture, 71
    language, 75
Şan, Cihan, 203
San Nicholas, 89
Santa Barbara Mission, 89
Santería, 260
Santoro, Federica, 459
Santos, Jorge Antônio dos, 282
Santos, Lea Garcia Teodorico dos, 276
Sanyal, Mithu, 41
Sarajevo, 163

512 INDEX

Sardinia, 172, 175n10
Sartre, Jean-Paul, 228
Sassari, 175n10
Satire, 178, 183, 184, 187, 188, 222, 352, 358, 362, 364, 371, 379, 381
Sauk, 392–395, 401, 402n4
Sauk people, 392, 394, 396
Savina, 281
Schechner, Richard, 418, 419
Schiller, Friedrich, 52, 54
Schimmelpfennig, Roland, 51, 466
    Der goldene Drache, 51
Schlösser, Rainer, 127, 134
Schlosspark Theatre, 54
Schnitzler, Arthur, 135
Schramm, Wilhelm von, 131
Scientific racism, 16n12, 370, 375
Scotch, 359, 361, 365
Scott, Dennis, 12, 71, 72, 74, 240, 241, 245, 248
Scott, George C., 29
Scottish, 70, 353, 359, 430, 431
The Scottsboro Boys, 12
Scramble for Africa, 377
Screenplay, 164, 451, 453
Searching for the Smile, 66
Season, 284
Second Intifada, 11, 191
Second World War (WW II), 10, 70, 127, 162, 163, 166, 395
Segregation, 22, 40, 63, 74, 101, 107, 311, 336, 402n3
Seine (River), 312
Selek, Pinar, 202, 212n19, 212n21
Self-Accusation, 466
Seminario de Dramaturgia del Teatro Nacional, 257, 259
Semisonic, 300
Septimius Severus, 340
Şerban, Alina, 103
    Declar pe propria răspundere, 103
Sera's Choice, 65
Şerban, Andrei, 103
    Vi me som rom, 103
Šerbedžija, Rade, 167
Serbes, Emrah, 207, 208, 213n31
Serbia, 11, 103, 159, 161, 162, 167, 169, 170, 172, 173, 174n6, 174n10, 175n10

Serbian(s)
    authors, 169
    theatre, 159–175
Serbs, 162–164, 166, 169, 170, 172, 174n4, 174n9, 175n11
Şermola Performans, 201, 204, 205, 211n1, 211n6, 212n14, 212n15
Settler, 13, 63, 87, 144, 150, 156n3, 188, 189, 191, 391–403, 434, 438
Sevdi, Ülfet, 202, 203
Seven Jewish Children, 458
Seventeenth century, 4, 213n29, 460
Sexism, 116, 318
Sexuality, 8, 102, 105, 107, 110, 255, 256, 265, 292, 294, 309, 314, 318, 403n6, 459
Sexualisation, 268, 269, 300
Seyri Mesel, 212n24
Shadow puppetry, 205, 213n26
Shakespeare, William, 7, 11, 23, 24, 26, 29, 34, 127, 128, 133, 135, 143, 144, 169, 170, 277, 379, 444, 446, 473, 476
Shames, Anton, 179
Shandong, 482n4
Shanghai, 483n12
The Shanghai People's Art Theatre, 482n7
Shaw, George Bernard, 135
Sheikh Said of Palu, 198
Sheinfeld, Ilan, 183
Shen, Kevin, 35, 36
The Shipment, 292, 294, 296, 298–300, 302, 305
Shoot/Get Treasure/Repeat, 197
Shoshner, Avraham, 182
Shuffle Along, 12
Shuxiang, Bai, 479, 484n24
Shylock, Jessica, 128, 129
Sicily, 31
Sierra Leone, 426
Sierra Madre, 414, 421n7
Sierra Tarahumara, 409, 414, 415
Sign language, 317, 318
Silva, Eduardo, 273
Simon, Josette, 28, 29
Sing Yer Heart Out for the Lads, 345n2
Singapore, 483n13
Singaporean Arts Festival, 484n28

INDEX 513

Singaporean International Festival of
Arts, 484n23
Singer, Kurt, 134
Sino-centrism, 14, 465–482, 484n27
Sítio do Picapau Amarelo, 275
The Situation, 52
Six Day War, 185
Six Degrees of Separation, 27, 28, 32
Sixteenth century, 414, 429
6th Beijing International Fringe
Festival, 483n12
Sizwe Bansi is Dead, 54
Skin, 446, 451–453
Skirt, 77n17, 102, 437
Skit, 182, 186, 187, 292, 482n6
Skopje, 175n10
Slave(s)
owners, 241, 242, 245, 248, 360
traders, 1, 242, 244, 308, 311, 333
trope, 376, 386
Slave Life; or, Uncle Tom's Cabin, 371,
376, 379, 386n1
Slaveholder, 363
Slavery, 1, 24, 103, 112, 117n4,
240–245, 249, 252, 253, 265, 274,
276, 278, 294, 295, 315, 322n6,
340, 346n12, 355, 357, 362–364,
367n3, 369, 372, 374, 378, 382,
387n12, 426
Slavs, 125
Slovakia, 110
Slovenia, 161, 162, 167
Smith, Anna Deavere, 109
Smith, James, 353, 354
Soap operas, 275, 276
Sobol, Yehoshua, 179, 182, 186
Sobral, Cristiane, 275, 277, 278, 287
Socialism, 42, 159, 262
Social-realist play, 449
Sodré, Muniz, 288n5
Söhnlein, Horst, 47
Sokoto, 430
Sons, 70
Sophiensälen, 54
Sorai, Rebekah Sangeetha, 478
South Africa, 154, 221, 222, 232, 233, 236
South African National Defence Force
(SANDF), 3

South African theatre, 12, 16n14,
219, 221
South Africans, 3, 12, 16n14, 50, 54, 82,
228, 312
South America, 426
South Asia, 334
Southeast Anatolia, 200, 201, 205,
207
Southern Europe, 16n11, 46
Southern Europeans, 47
South Island, 142
South Pacific, 8, 10, 61, 63, 66, 75–77,
143, 410
Soviet Union, 134, 162, 260, 262
Soy Cuba, 259
Spain, 47, 117n3, 266, 414
Spanish, 90, 103, 263, 415
Spectators, *see* Audiences
'Speculations of a Traveller concerning
the People of North America and
Great Britain,' 359
Speight, George, 64
Spengler, Oswald, 125
Der Untergang des Abendlandes, 125
Sports, 312, 319
Spring into January, 164
Springboks, 154
SS Empire Windrush, 339
Staatstheatre in Stuttgart, 54
Stalin, Joseph, 483n15
Stancu, Zaharia, 113
Standard English (SE), 372, 376, 377,
382, 384, 387n14, 449
Stănescu, Valerică, 113, 114
State Jewish Theatre, Bucharest,
113, 118n8
State of Chihuahua, 414
Steiger, Rod, 74
Steffin, Margarete, 45
Stereotypes, 2, 13, 23–34, 51, 62,
69, 71–74, 89–93, 102, 115, 179,
220, 223, 228, 229, 231, 256, 268,
269, 275–276, 282, 283, 291–295,
298, 299, 303–305, 310, 315,
322n5, 337, 342, 354, 361, 362,
364–366, 369–372, 374–377, 381,
382, 386, 410, 444, 450,
465, 470–472

514 INDEX

Stereotyping, 10, 23, 71, 72, 74, 83, 184, 189, 190, 219, 220, 224, 226–228, 235, 236, 296, 298, 300, 303, 305n2, 329, 351, 361
Sterilisation, 89, 91, 93, 115, 155
St. Lucia, 12, 240
Stock characters, 381, 432
Stoning mary, 345
Stoppard, Tom, 77n15
Storytelling, 76, 84, 103, 201, 204, 205, 222, 317, 321, 426, 427, 457
Stowe, Harriet Beecher, 13, 292, 369, 371–375, 377–379, 381, 382, 387n12
Strand, 363, 370, 382, 386n2
Strätz, Ursula, 47
A Streetcar Named Desire, 29, 33
Strindberg, Johan August, 179
Struggling for a Better Living: Squatters in Fiji, 77n6
Student Wife (Peidu furen), 470
Subalternity, 274, 278
Subotica, 174n10, 175n10
Sunni, 198
Super Bowl, 21
Sun Ra, 55
Surrealism, 411, 417
Surrey Theatres, 363, 364, 374
Suva, 65, 66, 69
Sweden, 103
Swift, Jonathan, 299
Syncretism, 280, 288n5, 414, 434
Syria, 52, 203
Szomna Grancsa, 108, 109

T
Taki Rua Theatre, 147
Talawa Theatre Company, 26, 30, 32, 33, 444, 446
Talbot, Edward Allen, 355
Tamasha, 26
Tamata, Apolonia, 66
Tamil, 479
Tang Na, 479, 484n24
Tango, 427
Tanzania, 40
Tara Arts, 26
Tarahumara Mountains, 414

Tarahumaras, 409, 414–417, 421n7
Tarzan (character), 263
Taş, Özlem, 211n10
Taukei Movement, 64
Taylor, Drew Hayden, 82, 83, 87–89, 93, 97n7
Taylor, Tom, 371–379, 386
Te Arawa, 156n20
Te Auaha, 70
Te Karakia, 143, 153, 154
Te reo, see Māori (language)
Teaiwa, Teresia, 62, 65, 69
Teatra Demsal, 212n24
Teatro Buendía, 261
Teatro bufo, 256, 270n2
Teatro de sala, 261
Teatro Escambray, 261
Teatro Experimental Negro (TEN), 12
Teatro Nacional de Cuba, 257
Teatro negro, 256
Teatrul Rom nu e nomad, 113
The Tectonic Theatre Project, 109
Teixeira, Ana, 281
Temba Theatre Company, 26, 444
Temur, Pelin, 206
10th Pacific Festival of Arts in Pago Pago, 66
Terreiro, 286
Terrell, Ernie, 318
Terrorism, 305, 333
The Terrorist Upstairs, 207, 208
Tesori, Jeanine, 33
Testament, 13, 245, 327–346
Te Ūkaipō, 142
Tewelde, Aron, 459
Thatcher, Margaret Hilda, Baroness Thatcher, 25
Theater Deng u Bej, 197
The Theatre and Its Double, 408, 411, 413
Theatre Avesta, 204, 212n24
Theatre companies, 11, 12, 26, 117n5, 212n15, 275, 331, 345n3, 466, 483n11
Theatre de L'Oeuvre, 187
Théâtre du Rêve Expérimental, 466
Théâtre du Soleil, 281, 282
Theatre of Cruelty, 408, 409, 412, 416, 417

INDEX   515

Theatre of Cruelty Manifestoes, 417
Theatre of the Oppressed, 54, 202
Theatre XIX, 283
They, 181
Thing movement, 129–132
Thing theatre, 129, 130
Third Reich, 11, 42, 44, 46, 123, 136
Thirteenth century, 143
Thomas, Ben, 32
Thomas, Dominic, 308, 309, 311, 312, 332, 337, 340–342
Thomas, Larry, 10, 61–70, 76, 77n6
Thompson, Mervyn, 144
Thompson, Pelham, 384
Those Dear Blacks!, 371, 372, 379–383, 386n2
Three-Mirrored Opera, 279
The Threepenny Opera, 57
Thunderstorm 2.0, 466
Tiananmen student protests, 475
Tibor Galarraga, 260
Tihngang, Buom, 33
Tilbury, 339
Till, Emmett, 307, 309, 317
Till, Louis, 309
The Times, 22, 23, 31
Timor Leste, 62
Tindano, Mahamadou, 319
Tito (Josip Broz), 11, 162–168, 172
To Have Done with the Judgment of God, 417, 419
To Kill A Mockingbird, 34
To Let You Know, 66, 77n5
Togo, 426
Toi Whakaari, 70
Tokelauan, 70
Tombs of the Vanishing Indian, 82, 89, 93
Tongan, 70, 73, 76
Topsy (character), 291, 292, 299, 304, 370, 372–379, 381, 387n12
Totalitarianism, 219
Total theatre, 318
Trace, 209, 213n32
Tradition, 12, 24, 25, 31, 49, 55, 105, 114, 141, 143, 149, 151, 155, 179, 201, 204, 205, 211n9, 212n16, 212n22, 222, 229, 274, 280, 281, 288n6, 329, 330, 335, 340, 346n13, 371, 372, 384, 385,

386n3, 402n3, 425–427, 429, 438, 439, 470, 477, 480
Tragedy, 90, 151, 154, 169, 184, 205, 206, 210, 257, 260, 282, 332, 473
Tragic farce, 259
Traité du Tout-Monde, 82
Transatlantic Slave Trade, 383
Transgender identities, 71
Transnistria, 113, 114
Traoré, Adama, 309, 311
Trauma, 70, 87–89, 93, 195–200, 207, 209, 259, 334
Travellers, 103, 155, 235, 352, 353, 356, 359, 363
Travelogues, 356, 362, 363
Treaty of Waitangi, 144
Trickster, 83–87, 93, 96, 235
Trifles, 13, 354, 391–403
Trip to America, 351–358, 360, 362–365
Triumph of the Will, 474, 483n18
Trump, Donald, 161, 305, 306n7
Tsalagi, 401
Tuđman, Franjo, 167
Turkey, 47–49, 51, 173, 195–213
Turkish, 11, 49, 195, 197–202, 204–209, 211n9, 211n111, 212n21, 213n27
Turkish Armed Forces (TAF), 195, 198–201
Turkish German theatre, 49, 51
Turkish Germans, 49, 51, 53
Turkish theatre, 49, 195, 203
Turner, Victor, 243, 418, 419
Turtle Island, 398
Tutuguri, 415, 416, 418, 419
Tutuguri ritual, 416, 418
Tu'u, Louise, 77n12
Twelfth century, 125
Twentieth century, 4, 7, 13, 24, 39, 53, 81, 125, 136n2, 141, 145, 147, 172, 196, 199, 211n11, 212n22, 212n25, 222, 335, 401, 407, 409–411, 418, 420, 427, 448, 458, 469
Twenty-first century, 7, 11, 12, 24, 26, 28, 29, 33, 35, 39, 63, 82, 83, 154–155, 256, 260, 262–268, 275, 293, 296, 482n5
Twist, 71, 91, 92, 135, 208, 232, 302, 427, 444

516 INDEX

U

Ubu Roi, 164, 187
Uganda, 459
UKIP, 31
Uma aprendizagem ou o livro dos prazeres, 284
Uncle Tom, 277, 370, 371, 373–376, 383, 385, 386n3, 386n4
Uncle Tom mania, 369, 370
Uncle Tom's Cabin, 13, 292, 369–390
Uncle Tom's Cabin: or, Life among the Lowly: A Domestic Drama in Six Acts, 373
Uncle Tom's Crib, 370, 386n2, 386n3
Underground, 164
Unification, 39
Union Jack, 452, 453
United Kingdom (UK), 1, 3, 7, 31, 37, 46, 308, 328, 331, 334–336, 338, 345, 346n11, 407, 466, 483n13
United Nations International Tribunal for the former Yugoslavia (ICTY), 170
United States (USA), 1–4, 6–8, 12, 16n11, 21, 40, 45, 46, 64, 70, 89, 112, 160, 169, 171, 264, 276, 288n9, 291–295, 298, 302, 305, 308, 309, 319, 321, 333, 354, 359, 369, 392, 394–398, 401, 402n4, 403n6, 413, 426, 460n1, 465, 466, 471, 482n8, 483n9, 483n13
Universidad Nacional Autónoma de México, 412
University of Arts (ISA), in Havana, 265
University of Belgrade, 163
University of Brasília, 287n1
University of Surrey, 407
University of the South Pacific, 66
Unknown soldier, 132
The Unplugging, 82, 93, 96, 97n12
Unschuld, 50
Upper classes, 241, 250, 340, 353, 363
Urale, Makerita, 77n12
Urban Body, 105, 109–117
U.S. Family Planning Act, 89
US Naturalization Act, 397
Uto-Aztecan tribes, 415

V

Vacas, 264, 265
Vade Retro, 259, 270n8, 271n11
Vaga Carne, 284, 286
The Vagina Monologues, 466
Vancouver, 398, 399
Varela, Victor, 261
Vera, Maité, 12, 256–259
Verbatim theatre, 458
Verfremdungseffekt, 41, 43, 45
Vermont, 360, 367
Verrücktes Blut, 41, 52
Vicente, Juliana, 284
Victorian, 12, 13, 16n12, 340, 372–379, 381, 383, 386, 427, 443
theatre, 369, 371, 382
Vienna, 128
Vietnam, 40, 47, 204, 313–315, 318
A View From the Bridge, 30–32
Views of Society and Manners in America, 355
The Vikings at Helgeland, 147
Villaverde, Cirilo, 257
Virginia Minstrels, 370
The Visitors, 62, 65–71, 75
Völker Schlöndorff's *Baal*, 53
Völkischer Beobachter, 127
Voyage au pays des Tarahumaras, 417–418
Vranje, 174n10

W

Waiata, 141, 143, 145, 148, 151–153
Waiora, 11, 141–143, 147–149, 151–155, 156n13
Te Ūka-ipō–The Homeland, 11, 142
Waitangi Tribunal, 144
Waiting for Godot, 179, 188, 203
Wajs, Basa, 470
Walcott, Derek, 12, 240, 241, 246–249
Wales, 335, 345n8, 345n9
Walters, Vanessa, 332
Walton, Dawn, 331, 345n4
War, 3, 10, 11, 32, 46, 61, 115, 124, 128, 132, 146, 159, 160, 162, 163, 165–173, 174n1, 174n7, 175n11, 178, 184, 188, 195–210, 230–232,

266, 274, 394, 395, 411, 421n8, 434–436, 438, 440n7, 474, 476
War crimes, 170, 206, 207
The Warfare of Landmine 2.0, 466
War Horse, 29
Warhol, Andy, 476
Warrington, Don, 32, 33
Washington, Irving, 353
We are the Universe, 55
'We are Tomorrow,' 55
Weigel, Helene, 43
Weill, Kurt, 43
Weimar Republic, 123, 129, 131
Well-Intentions, 284
Welsh, 359, 361, 365
Wendt, Albert, 77n12
Wenzel, Olivia, 41, 54, 55
    Mais in Deutschland, 54
Wertenbaker, Timberlake, 446, 448
West, 9, 40, 46, 52, 198, 328, 329, 361, 410, 426, 459, 465, 468, 469, 471, 483n13
West Africa, 280, 427, 430
West End, 21, 26, 33, 34, 36, 364
Western theatre, 61, 62, 396, 408, 412, 472
West Germany, 39, 40, 42, 46–48, 50
West Papua, 62
West Yorkshire, 331
Wharf Theatre in Provincetown, 399
White(s)
    characters, 9, 27, 32, 96, 225, 228, 247, 248, 250, 253, 275, 333, 337, 341–344, 346n14, 373, 449, 470, 480
    colonisers, 88, 283
    devil, 431, 432, 439
    people, 1, 53, 72, 74, 244, 248, 249, 251–253, 294, 315, 328–331, 333, 337, 338, 340–345, 397, 426, 427
    performers, 22, 23, 169, 276, 370, 480, 481
    possession, 393, 397, 401
    settlers, 13, 87, 391–401
    slaves, 248, 372
    supremacy, 333, 334, 344, 445
    women, 36, 253, 267, 268, 337, 341, 445
White Americans, 13, 352, 365, 366, 465

White German, 39, 41, 46, 48, 51, 53, 57n6
Whiteface, 44, 275, 303, 305n2
Whiteness, 7–9, 12–14, 50, 51, 73, 82, 144, 221, 228, 247, 253, 269, 285, 302, 304, 327–345, 345n2, 387n13, 391, 392, 395–398, 401, 421n11, 436, 439, 445, 450–454
Who Killed Szomna Grancsa?, 104, 108–109, 117
The Wild Duck, 151
Wilde, Oscar, 32
Williams, Roy, 345n2
Williams, Tennessee, 21–27, 29, 36
Willing, James, 384
Wilson, August, 26–28, 34
Windrush generation, 450
Winterreise, 52
Wisconsin, 393
Witke, Roxane, 477–481
Wolfgang, Eberhard, 11
Woman's Hour, 24
Womanhood, 299, 471
The Women of Dada, 173
The Women's Side of War, 171
The Women's Theatre Group, 448
Working classes, 43, 352, 363, 402n3, 448
World War I (WWI), *see* First World War
World War II (WWII), *see* Second World War
World Wide Workshop, 31
World's fairs, 145
Woyzeck, 203, 279
Wright, Douglas, 77n14
Wright, Fanny, 355
Wushu, 475, 476
Wuzhen Theatre Festival, 472
Wynter, Danny Lee, 23, 30, 33

X
Xalide, Dengbej, 205
Xenophobia, 48, 102, 469, 482

Y
Ya'ari, Hagit, 179
Yachil-Wax, Miriam, 179, 183
Yang, Deonn, 484n25

518 INDEX

Yankee, 13, 351–367
Yankee impersonation, 13, 352–362, 364
The Yankey in England, 356, 363
Yard Gal, 448, 454–456
Yellow face, 36
Yellow Face, 35, 36
Yemayá, *see* Yemoja
Yemoja, 266, 267, 427
Yèrì, 437
Yèúke, 435
Yèyé Orò (Festival Mother), 438, 440n13
Yıldız, İsmail, 205, 212n24
Yimou, Zhang, 472
Yorkshire, 332, 333, 335, 340
Yorkshireman, 366
Yorùbá
    ceremonies, 267, 428
    culture, 13, 425, 426, 428–434, 438
    Kingdom, 430
    language, 426, 434
    people, 425–430, 432–434, 439n2
    performance, 14, 425–440
    performance culture, 425, 426,
        428–431, 433, 438
    theatre, 9, 430
    travelling theatre, 431
Yorùbá Afro-cuban religion, 266
Yorùbá Alárìnjó, 429
Yorùbáland, 428, 430, 433, 434,
    440n7, 440n11
Yorùbá theatre, 9, 430

You and I and the Next War, 188
Young Germany, 132
Yours Dearly, 66
Yu Zhongkai (character), 477–479
Yüce, Gülistan, 211n10
Yugoslavia, 11, 47, 159–164, 166–168,
    170, 171, 174
Yugoslavian army, 168
Yugoslavian theatre, 169
Yugoslavian war, 170
Yugoslavism, 163, 166
Yugoslavs, 160, 162–165, 168

Z
Zagreb, 169
Zenderlioğlu, Berfin, 201, 205, 211n1
Žene dada, 173
Zhangazha, Ashley, 33–35
Zimbabwe, 328, 459
Zionism, 134
Zip Coon (character), 299, 370,
    375, 382
Zombie, 279
Zoungrana, Paul, 323n14
Zulu people, 377
Zuma, Jacob, 459
Zumbi, 283
Zuosheng, Wang, 482n8
Zurbano, Roberto, 271
Zweig, Stefan, 135

Printed in the United States
by Baker & Taylor Publisher Services